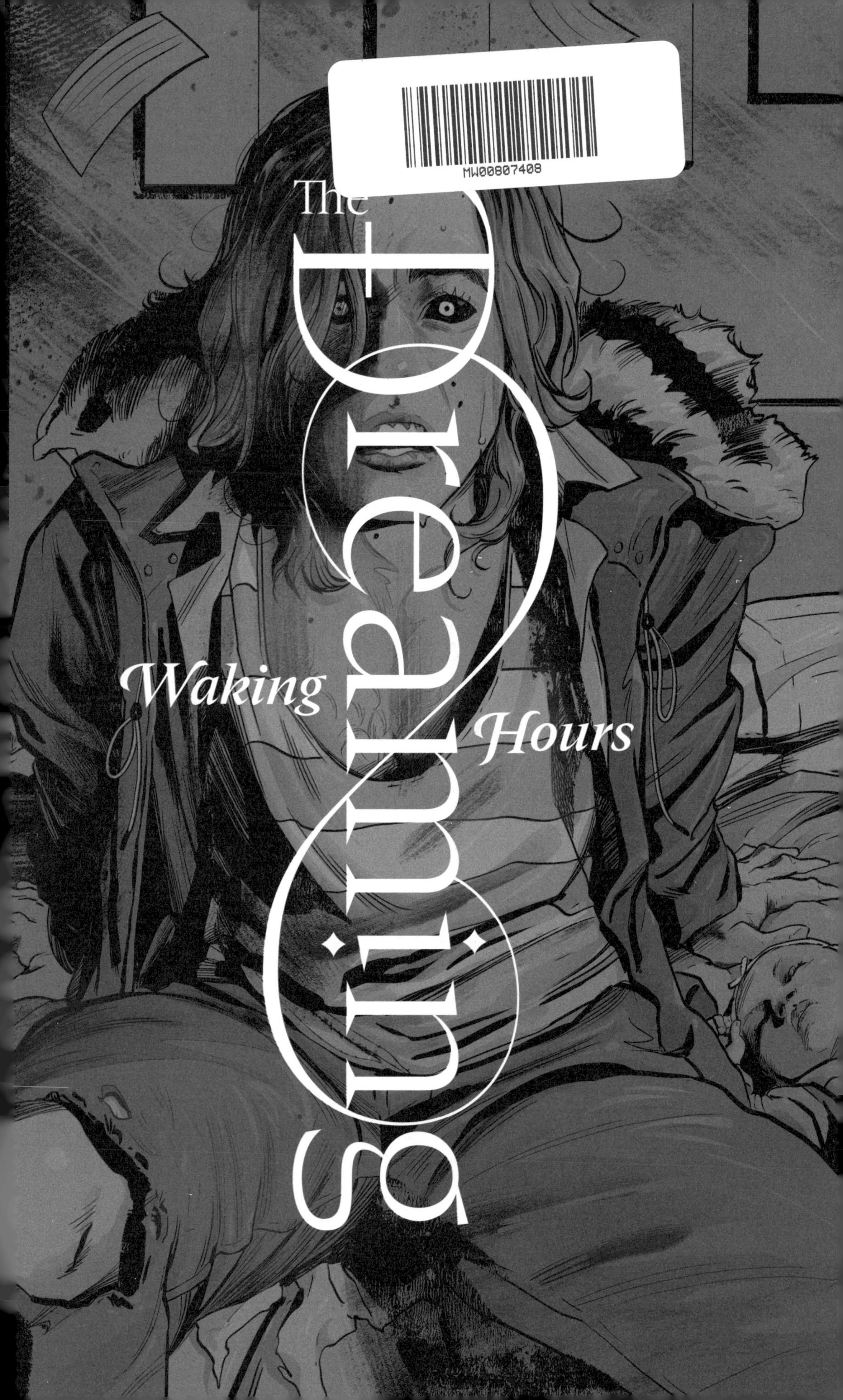
The
Dreaming
Waking
Hours

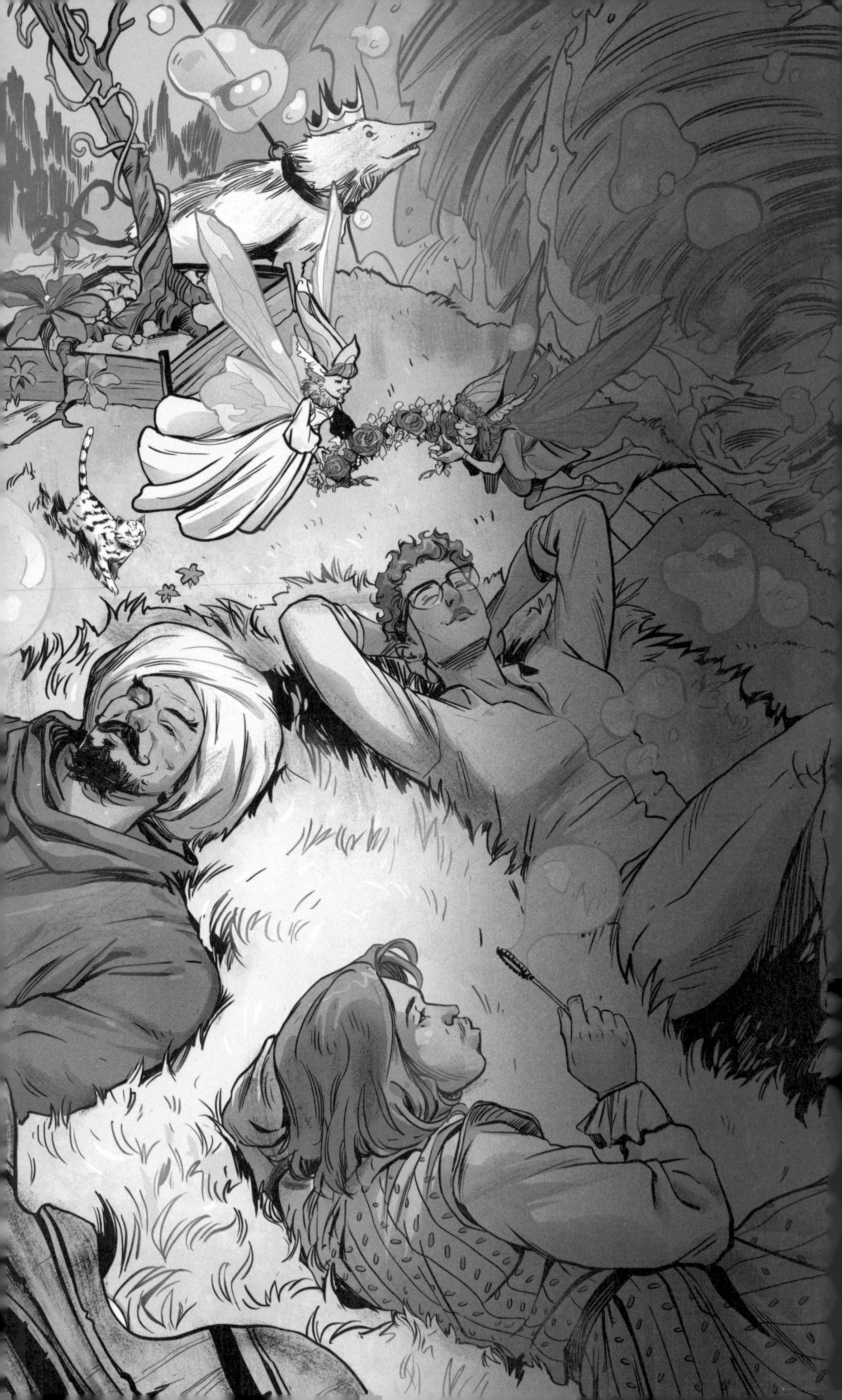

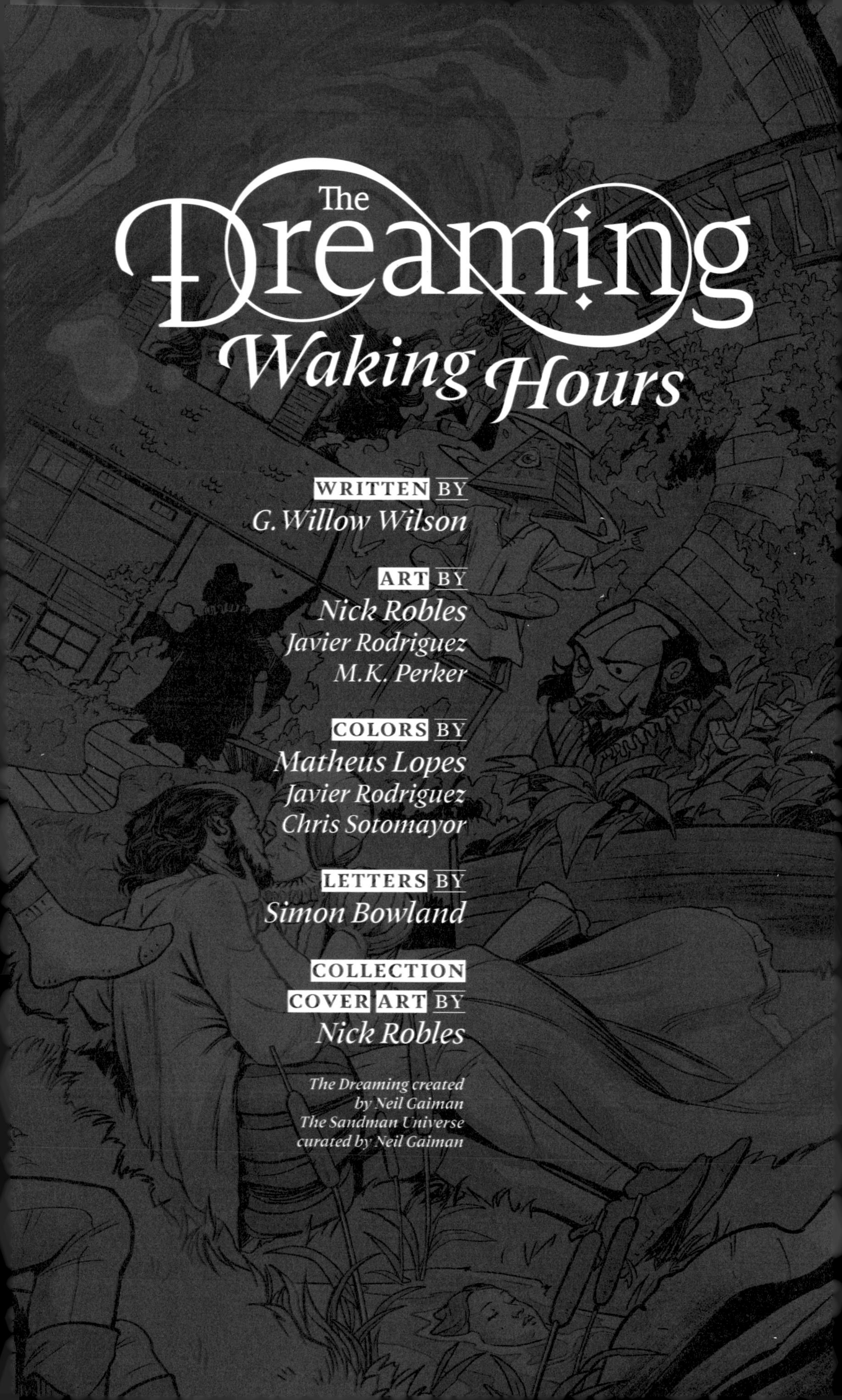

The Dreaming
Waking Hours

WRITTEN BY
G. Willow Wilson

ART BY
Nick Robles
Javier Rodriguez
M.K. Perker

COLORS BY
Matheus Lopes
Javier Rodriguez
Chris Sotomayor

LETTERS BY
Simon Bowland

COLLECTION
COVER ART BY
Nick Robles

The Dreaming created
by Neil Gaiman
The Sandman Universe
curated by Neil Gaiman

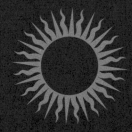

CHRIS CONROY — *Editor – Original Series & Collected Edition*
MAGGIE HOWELL — *Associate Editor – Original Series*
STEVE COOK — *Design Director – Books & Publication Design*
SUZANNAH ROWNTREE — *Publication Production*

MARIE JAVINS — *Editor-in-Chief, DC Comics*

DANIEL CHERRY III — *Senior VP – General Manager*
JIM LEE — *Publisher & Chief Creative Officer*
JOEN CHOE — *VP – Global Brand & Creative Services*
DON FALLETTI — *VP – Manufacturing Operations & Workflow Management*
LAWRENCE GANEM — *VP – Talent Services*
ALISON GILL — *Senior VP – Manufacturing & Operations*
NICK J. NAPOLITANO — *VP – Manufacturing Administration & Design*
NANCY SPEARS — *VP – Revenue*

THE DREAMING: WAKING HOURS

DC Comics, 2900 West Alameda Ave., Burbank, CA 91505
Printed by LSC Communications, Owensville, MO, USA. 10/8/21. First Printing.
ISBN: 978-1-77951-273-4

Library of Congress Cataloging-in-Publication Data is available.

PEFC Certified
This product is from sustainably managed forests and controlled sources
PEFC/29-31-337
www.pefc.org

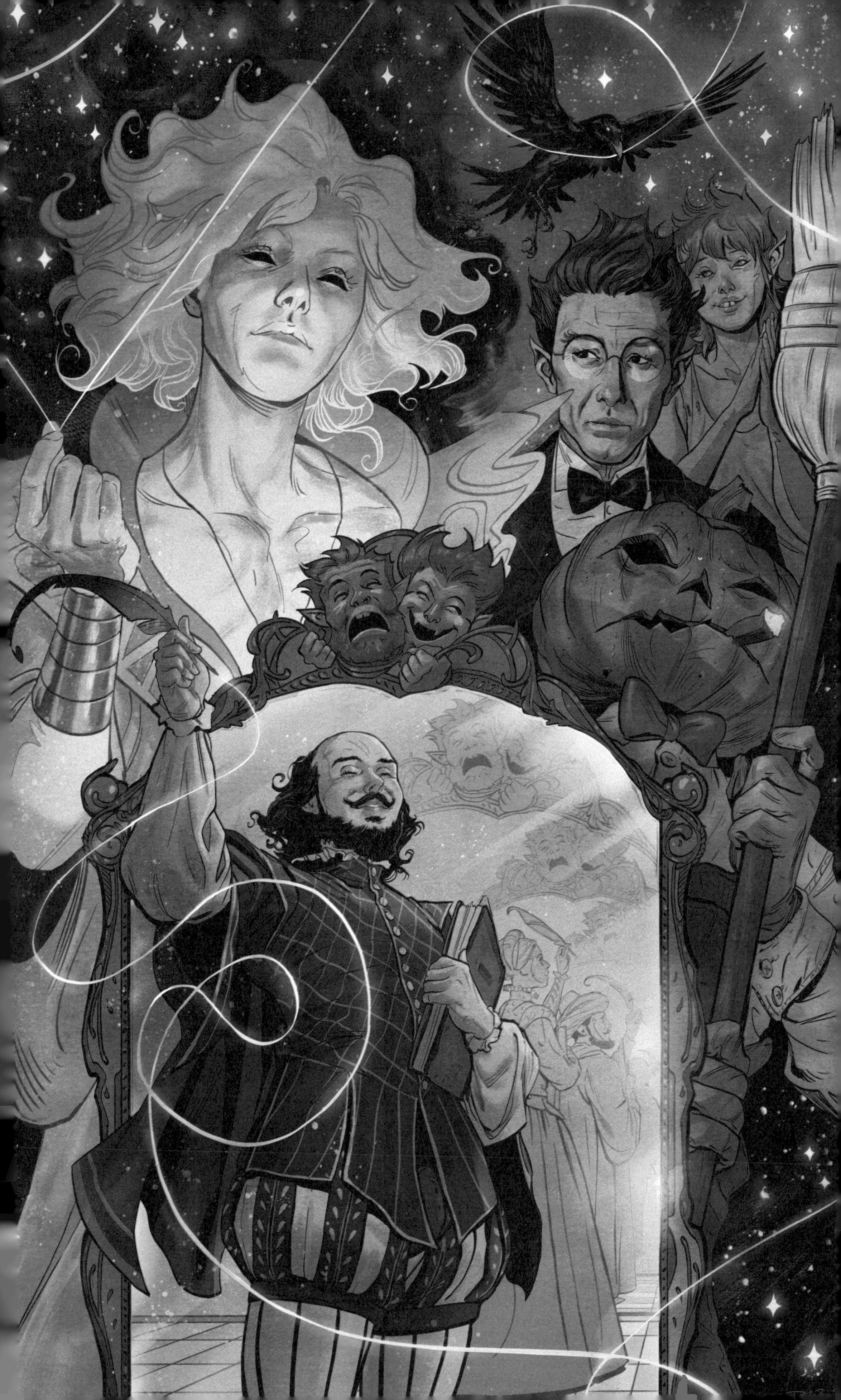

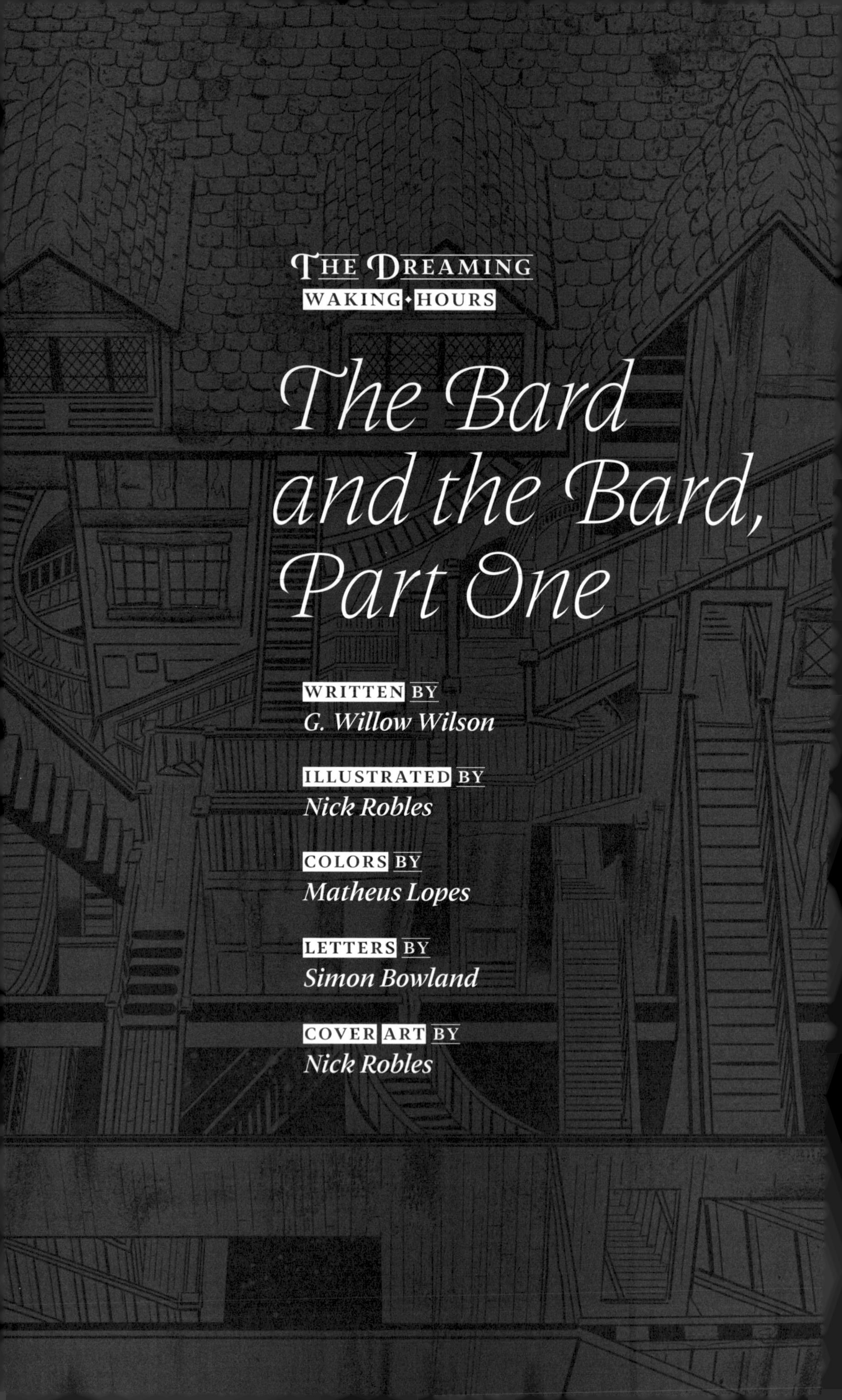

THE DREAMING
WAKING · HOURS

The Bard and the Bard, Part One

WRITTEN BY
G. Willow Wilson

ILLUSTRATED BY
Nick Robles

COLORS BY
Matheus Lopes

LETTERS BY
Simon Bowland

COVER ART BY
Nick Robles

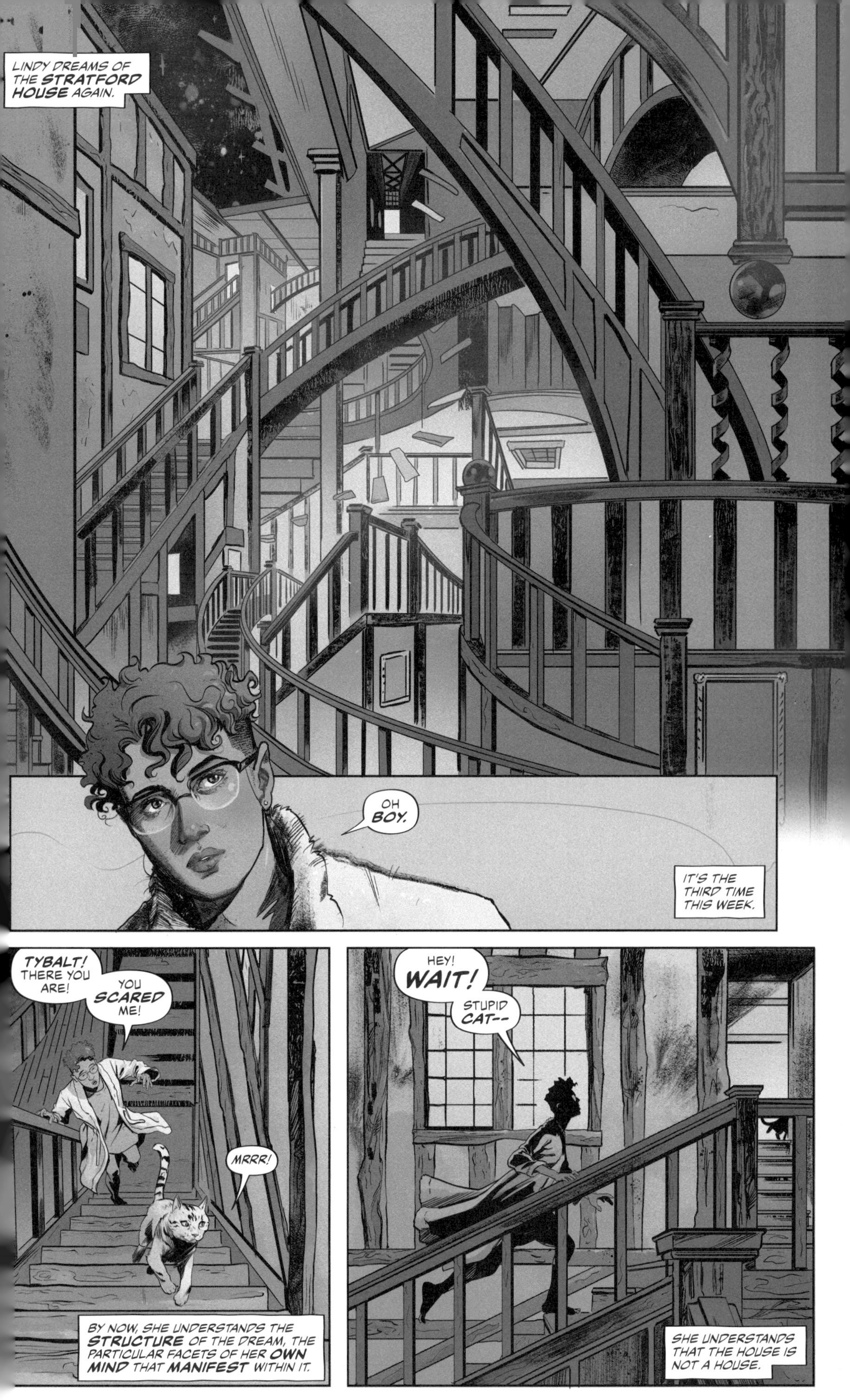
LINDY DREAMS OF THE STRATFORD HOUSE AGAIN.
OH BOY.
IT'S THE THIRD TIME THIS WEEK.
TYBALT! THERE YOU ARE!
YOU SCARED ME!
MRRR!
BY NOW, SHE UNDERSTANDS THE STRUCTURE OF THE DREAM, THE PARTICULAR FACETS OF HER OWN MIND THAT MANIFEST WITHIN IT.
HEY! WAIT!
STUPID CAT--
SHE UNDERSTANDS THAT THE HOUSE IS NOT A HOUSE.

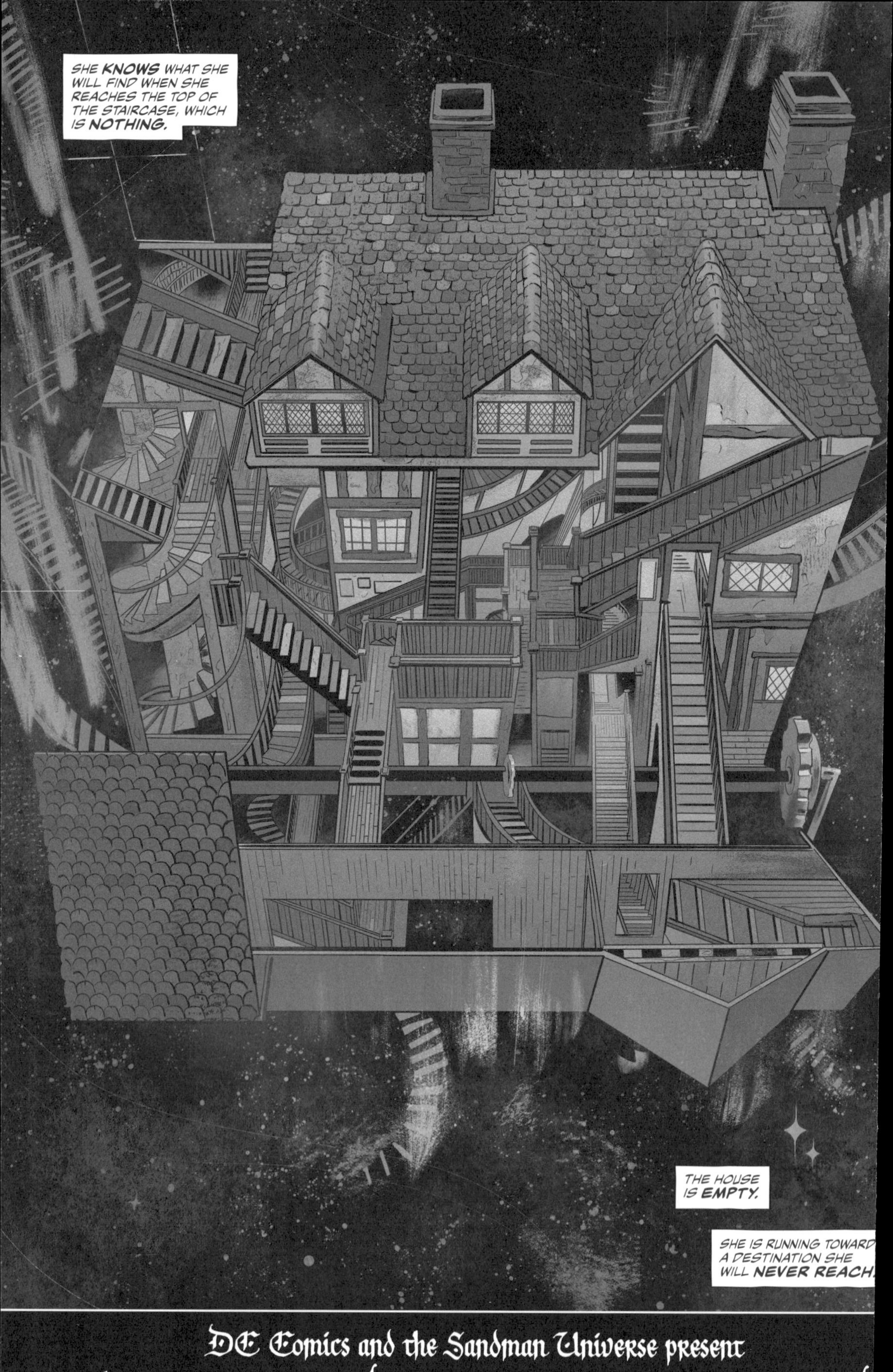
SHE KNOWS WHAT SHE WILL FIND WHEN SHE REACHES THE TOP OF THE STAIRCASE, WHICH IS NOTHING.
THE HOUSE IS EMPTY.
SHE IS RUNNING TOWARD A DESTINATION SHE WILL NEVER REACH.

DC Comics and the Sandman Universe present

THE BARD and THE BAR

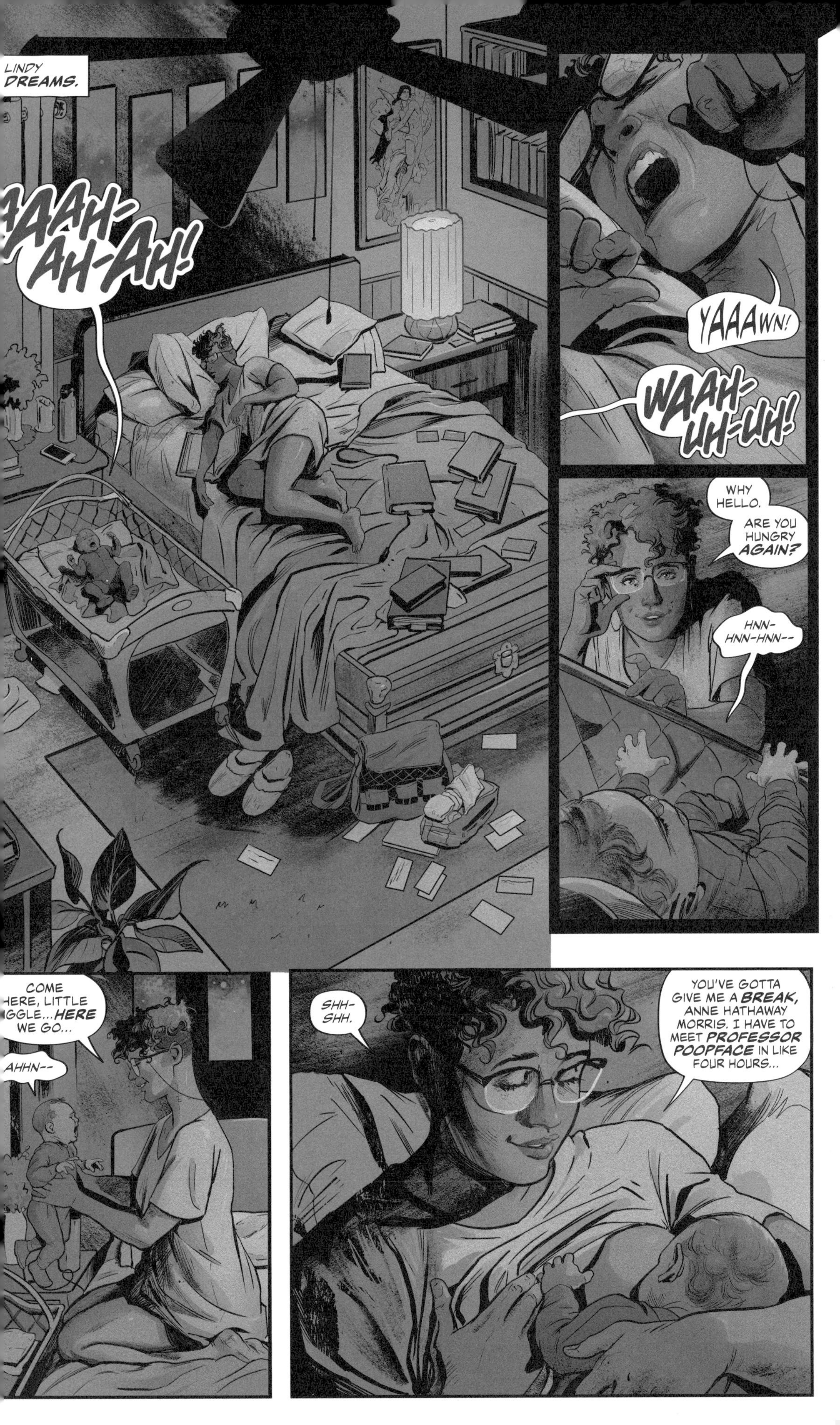
LINDY DREAMS.
WAAAH-AH-AH!
YAAAWN!
WAAH-UH-UH!
WHY HELLO.
ARE YOU HUNGRY AGAIN?
HNN-HNN-HNN--
COME HERE, LITTLE GGLE...HERE WE GO...
AHHN--
SHH-SHH.
YOU'VE GOTTA GIVE ME A BREAK, ANNE HATHAWAY MORRIS. I HAVE TO MEET PROFESSOR POOPFACE IN LIKE FOUR HOURS...

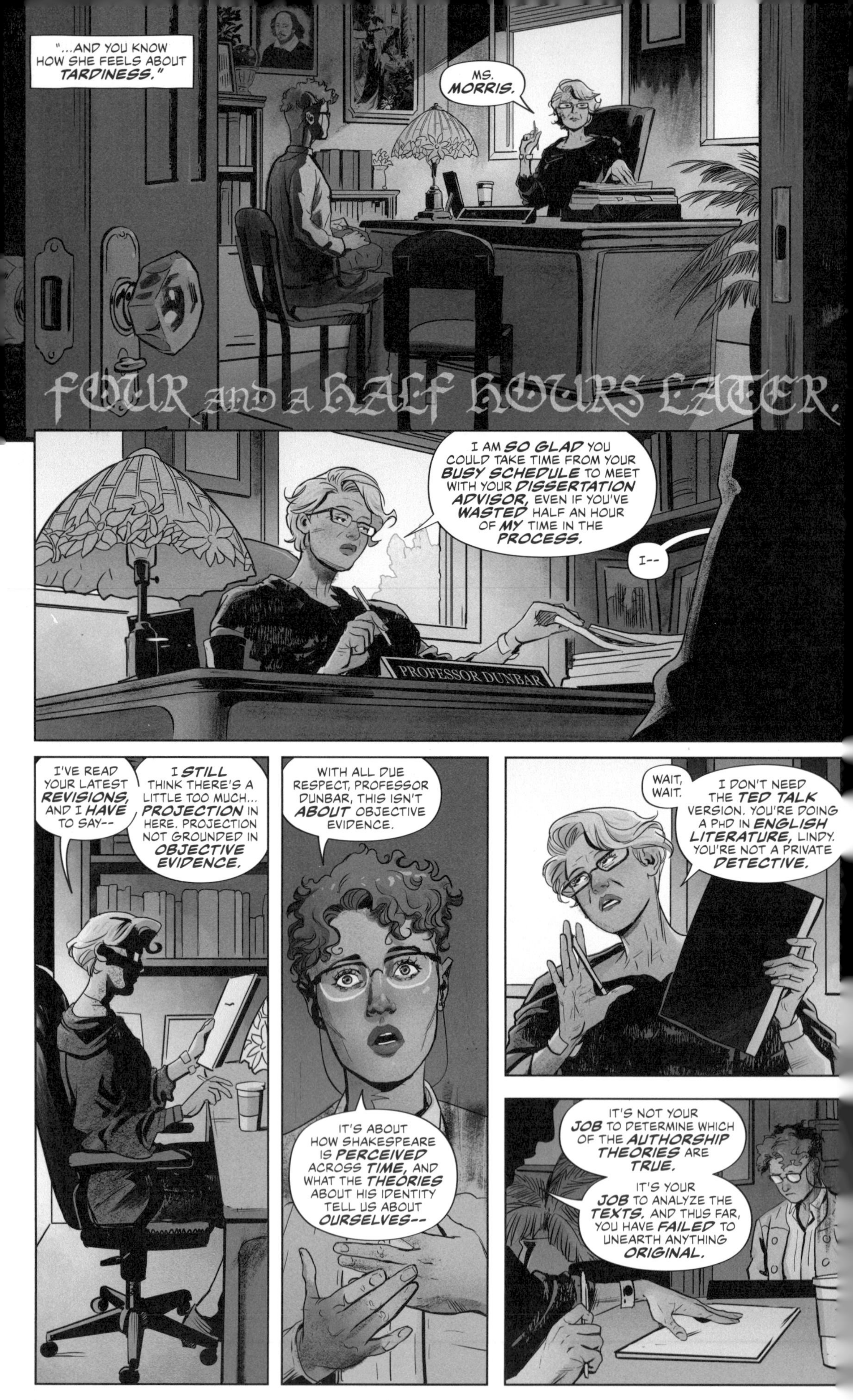
"...AND YOU KNOW HOW SHE FEELS ABOUT TARDINESS."
MS. MORRIS.
FOUR AND A HALF HOURS LATER.
I AM SO GLAD YOU COULD TAKE TIME FROM YOUR BUSY SCHEDULE TO MEET WITH YOUR DISSERTATION ADVISOR, EVEN IF YOU'VE WASTED HALF AN HOUR OF MY TIME IN THE PROCESS.
I--
PROFESSOR DUNBAR
I'VE READ YOUR LATEST REVISIONS, AND I HAVE TO SAY--
I STILL THINK THERE'S A LITTLE TOO MUCH... PROJECTION IN HERE. PROJECTION NOT GROUNDED IN OBJECTIVE EVIDENCE.
WITH ALL DUE RESPECT, PROFESSOR DUNBAR, THIS ISN'T ABOUT OBJECTIVE EVIDENCE.
IT'S ABOUT HOW SHAKESPEARE IS PERCEIVED ACROSS TIME, AND WHAT THE THEORIES ABOUT HIS IDENTITY TELL US ABOUT OURSELVES--
WAIT, WAIT.
I DON'T NEED THE TED TALK VERSION. YOU'RE DOING A PHD IN ENGLISH LITERATURE, LINDY. YOU'RE NOT A PRIVATE DETECTIVE.
IT'S NOT YOUR JOB TO DETERMINE WHICH OF THE AUTHORSHIP THEORIES ARE TRUE.
IT'S YOUR JOB TO ANALYZE THE TEXTS. AND THUS FAR, YOU HAVE FAILED TO UNEARTH ANYTHING ORIGINAL.

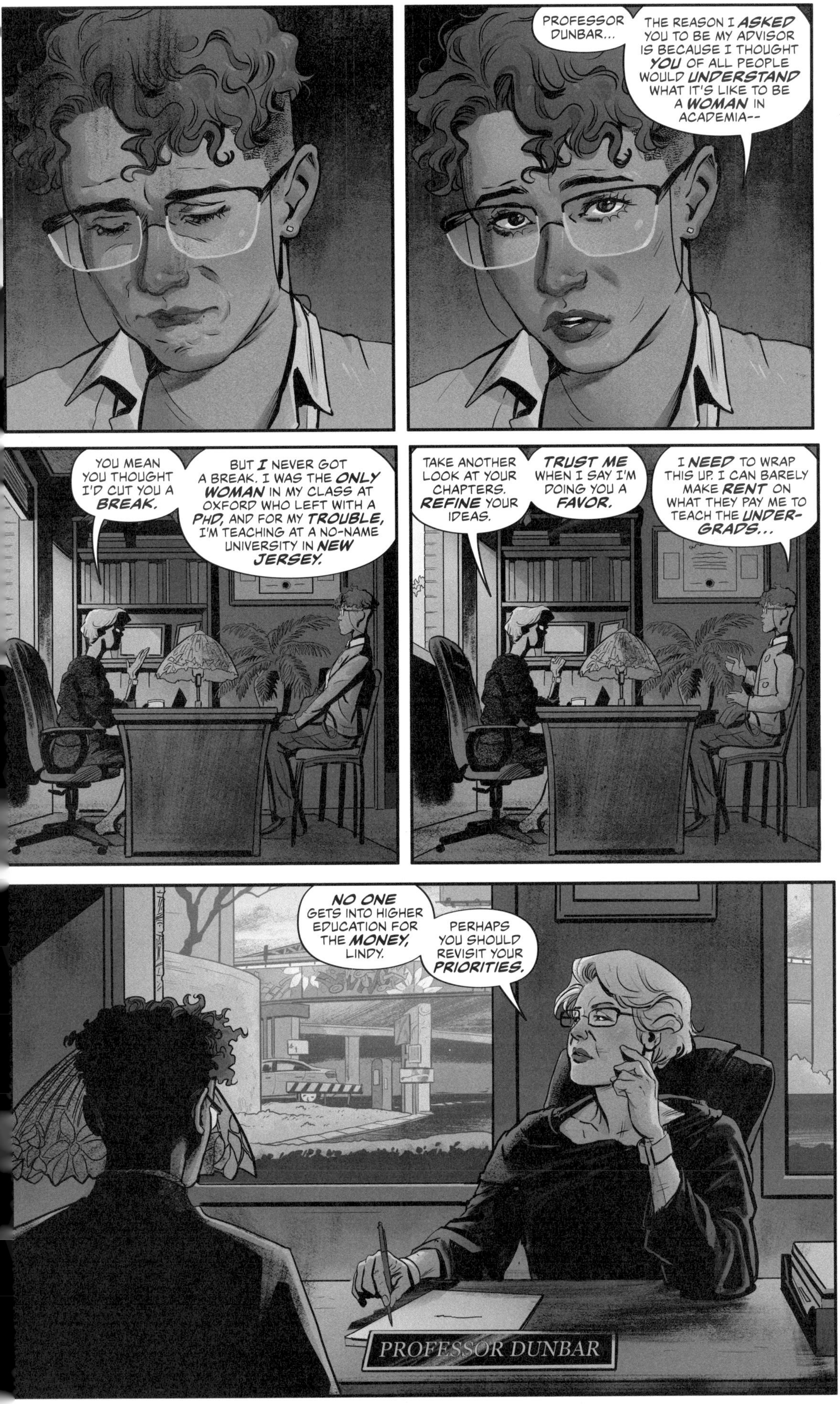

PROFESSOR DUNBAR...
THE REASON I ASKED YOU TO BE MY ADVISOR IS BECAUSE I THOUGHT YOU OF ALL PEOPLE WOULD UNDERSTAND WHAT IT'S LIKE TO BE A WOMAN IN ACADEMIA--
YOU MEAN YOU THOUGHT I'D CUT YOU A BREAK.
BUT I NEVER GOT A BREAK. I WAS THE ONLY WOMAN IN MY CLASS AT OXFORD WHO LEFT WITH A PHD, AND FOR MY TROUBLE, I'M TEACHING AT A NO-NAME UNIVERSITY IN NEW JERSEY.
TAKE ANOTHER LOOK AT YOUR CHAPTERS. REFINE YOUR IDEAS.
TRUST ME WHEN I SAY I'M DOING YOU A FAVOR.
I NEED TO WRAP THIS UP. I CAN BARELY MAKE RENT ON WHAT THEY PAY ME TO TEACH THE UNDER-GRADS...
NO ONE GETS INTO HIGHER EDUCATION FOR THE MONEY, LINDY.
PERHAPS YOU SHOULD REVISIT YOUR PRIORITIES.
PROFESSOR DUNBAR

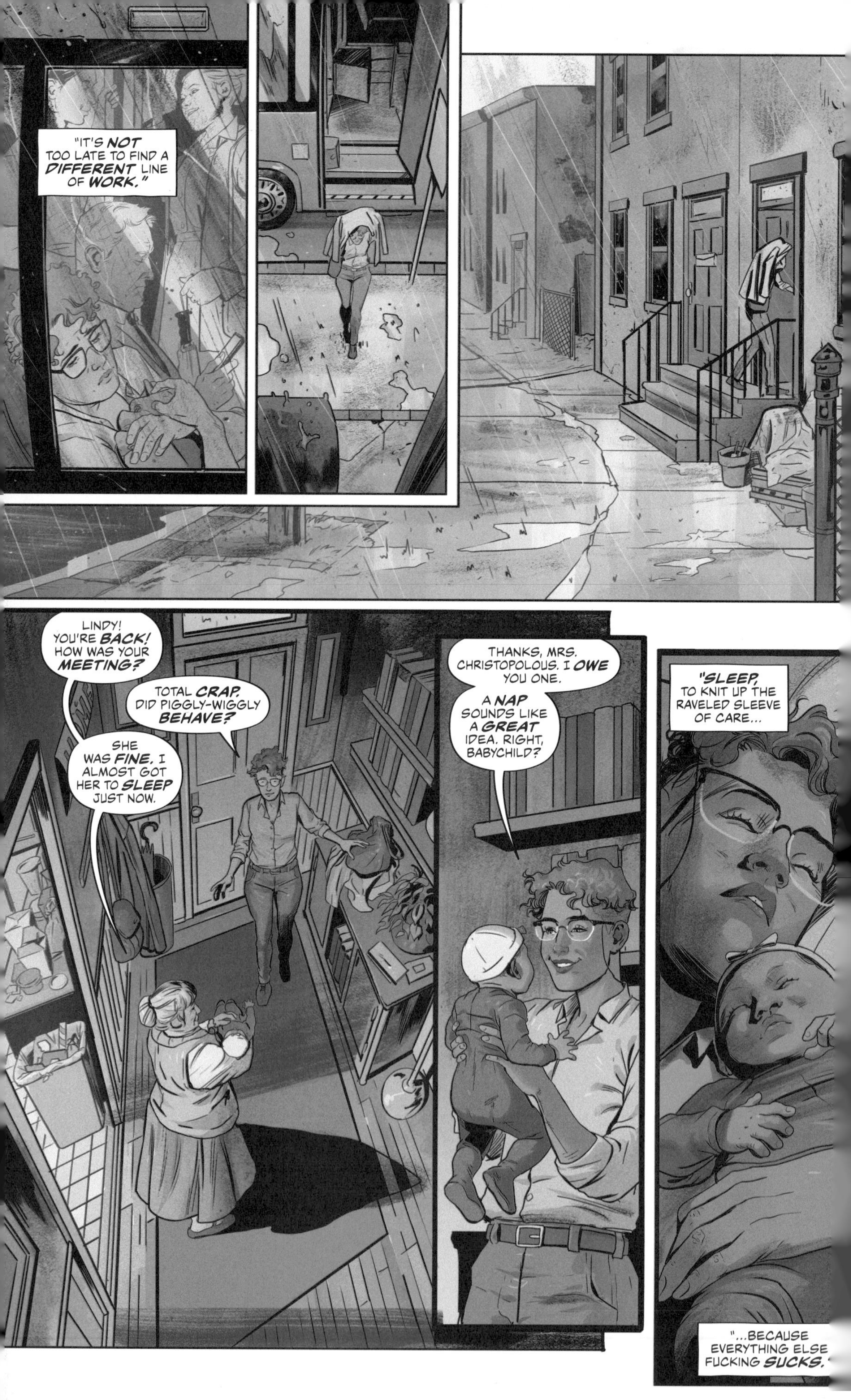
"IT'S NOT TOO LATE TO FIND A DIFFERENT LINE OF WORK."
LINDY! YOU'RE BACK! HOW WAS YOUR MEETING?
TOTAL CRAP. DID PIGGLY-WIGGLY BEHAVE?
SHE WAS FINE. I ALMOST GOT HER TO SLEEP JUST NOW.
THANKS, MRS. CHRISTOPOLOUS. I OWE YOU ONE.
A NAP SOUNDS LIKE A GREAT IDEA. RIGHT, BABYCHILD?
"SLEEP, TO KNIT UP THE RAVELED SLEEVE OF CARE...
"...BECAUSE EVERYTHING ELSE FUCKING SUCKS."

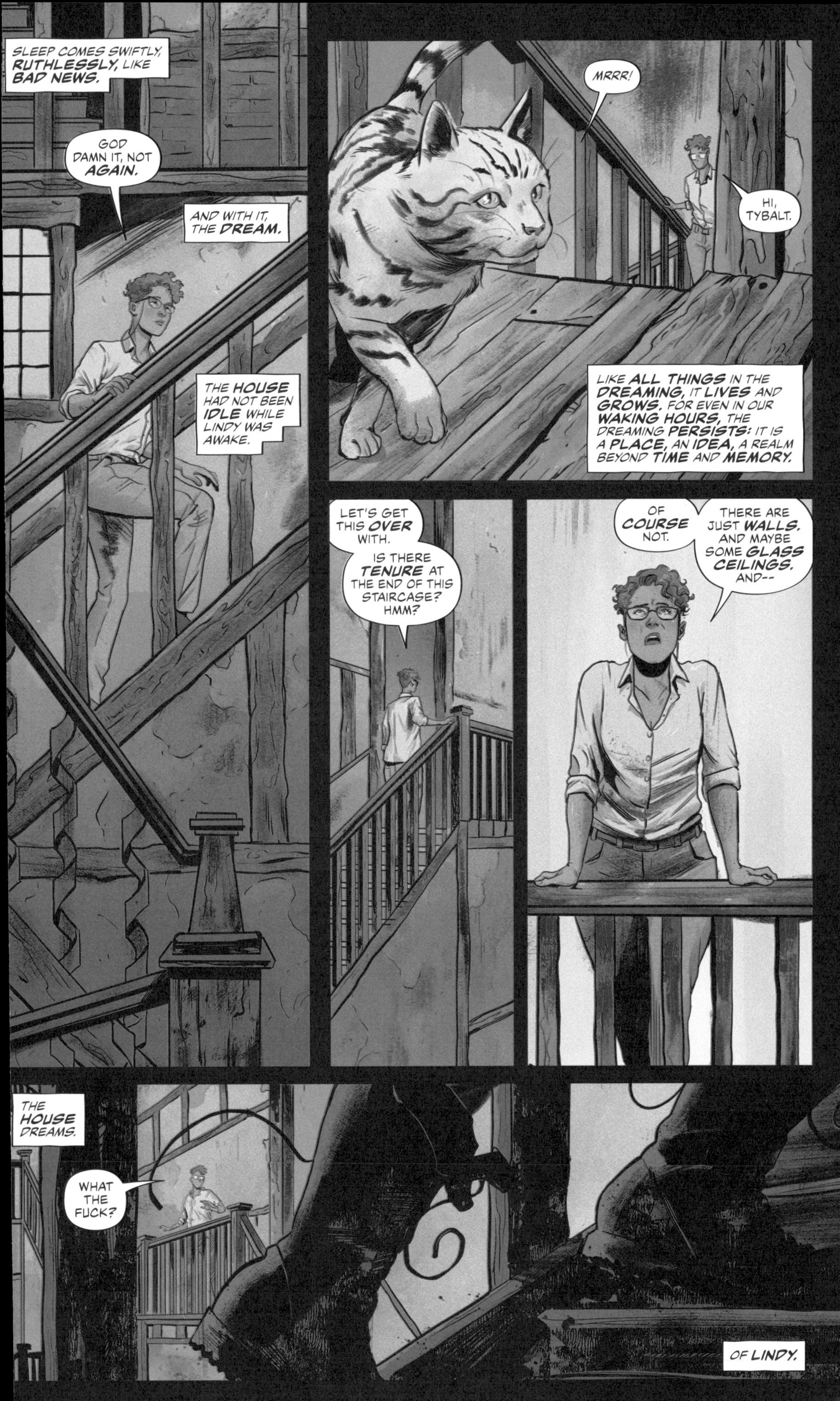
SLEEP COMES SWIFTLY, RUTHLESSLY, LIKE BAD NEWS.
GOD DAMN IT, NOT AGAIN.
AND WITH IT, THE DREAM.
THE HOUSE HAD NOT BEEN IDLE WHILE LINDY WAS AWAKE.
MRRR!
HI, TYBALT.
LIKE ALL THINGS IN THE DREAMING, IT LIVES AND GROWS. FOR EVEN IN OUR WAKING HOURS, THE DREAMING PERSISTS: IT IS A PLACE, AN IDEA, A REALM BEYOND TIME AND MEMORY.
LET'S GET THIS OVER WITH.
IS THERE TENURE AT THE END OF THIS STAIRCASE? HMM?
OF COURSE NOT.
THERE ARE JUST WALLS. AND MAYBE SOME GLASS CEILINGS. AND--
THE HOUSE DREAMS.
WHAT THE FUCK?
OF LINDY.

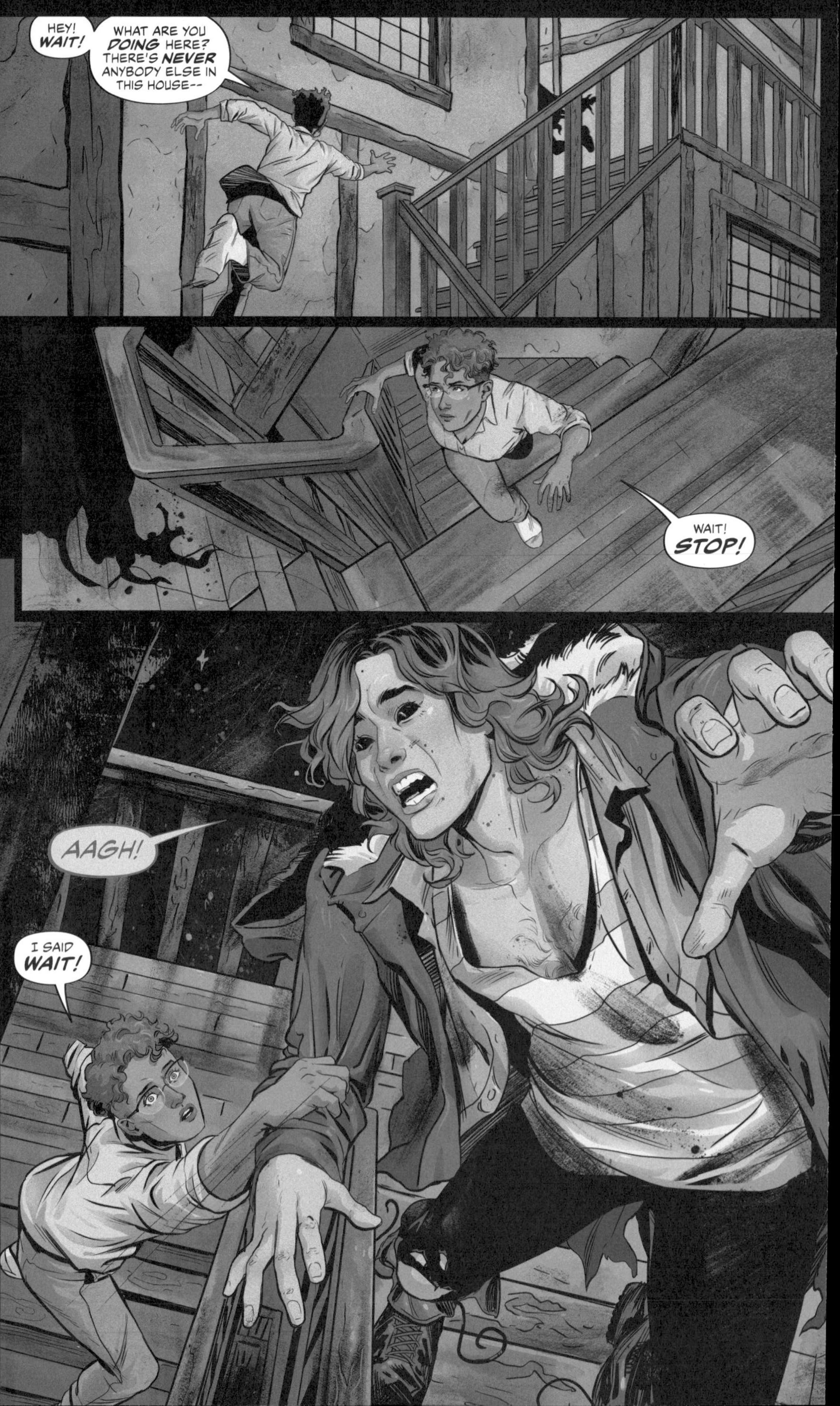
HEY! WAIT!
WHAT ARE YOU DOING HERE? THERE'S NEVER ANYBODY ELSE IN THIS HOUSE--
WAIT! STOP!
AAGH!
I SAID WAIT!

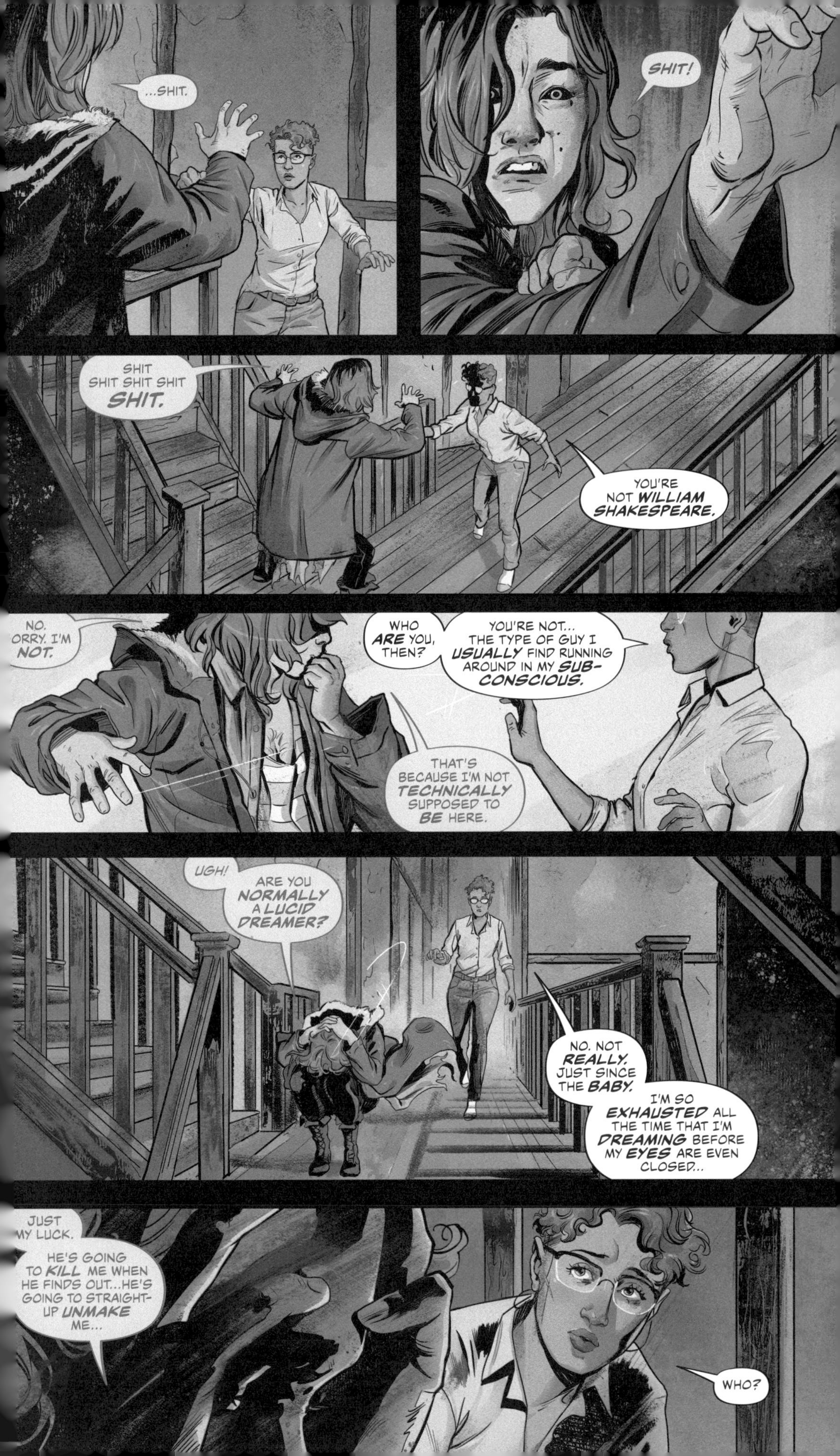
...SHIT.
SHIT!
SHIT SHIT SHIT SHIT SHIT.
YOU'RE NOT WILLIAM SHAKESPEARE.
NO. ORRY. I'M NOT.
WHO ARE YOU, THEN?
YOU'RE NOT... THE TYPE OF GUY I USUALLY FIND RUNNING AROUND IN MY SUB-CONSCIOUS.
THAT'S BECAUSE I'M NOT TECHNICALLY SUPPOSED TO BE HERE.
UGH!
ARE YOU NORMALLY A LUCID DREAMER?
NO. NOT REALLY. JUST SINCE THE BABY.
I'M SO EXHAUSTED ALL THE TIME THAT I'M DREAMING BEFORE MY EYES ARE EVEN CLOSED...
JUST MY LUCK.
HE'S GOING TO KILL ME WHEN HE FINDS OUT...HE'S GOING TO STRAIGHT-UP UNMAKE ME...
WHO?

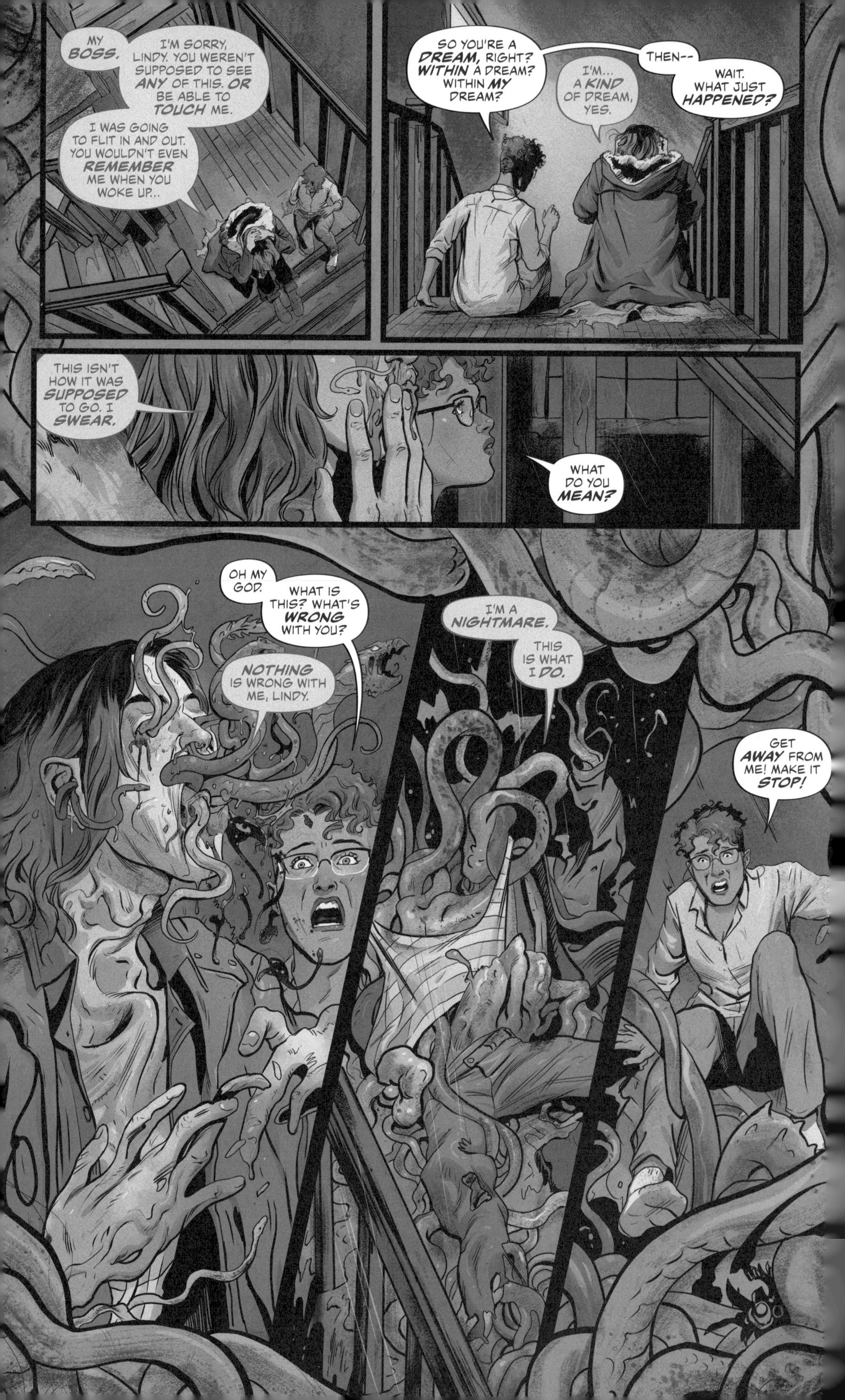
MY BOSS.
I'M SORRY, LINDY. YOU WEREN'T SUPPOSED TO SEE ANY OF THIS. OR BE ABLE TO TOUCH ME.
I WAS GOING TO FLIT IN AND OUT. YOU WOULDN'T EVEN REMEMBER ME WHEN YOU WOKE UP...
SO YOU'RE A DREAM, RIGHT? WITHIN A DREAM? WITHIN MY DREAM?
THEN--
I'M... A KIND OF DREAM, YES.
WAIT. WHAT JUST HAPPENED?
THIS ISN'T HOW IT WAS SUPPOSED TO GO. I SWEAR.
WHAT DO YOU MEAN?
OH MY GOD.
WHAT IS THIS? WHAT'S WRONG WITH YOU?
NOTHING IS WRONG WITH ME, LINDY.
I'M A NIGHTMARE.
THIS IS WHAT I DO.
GET AWAY FROM ME! MAKE IT STOP!

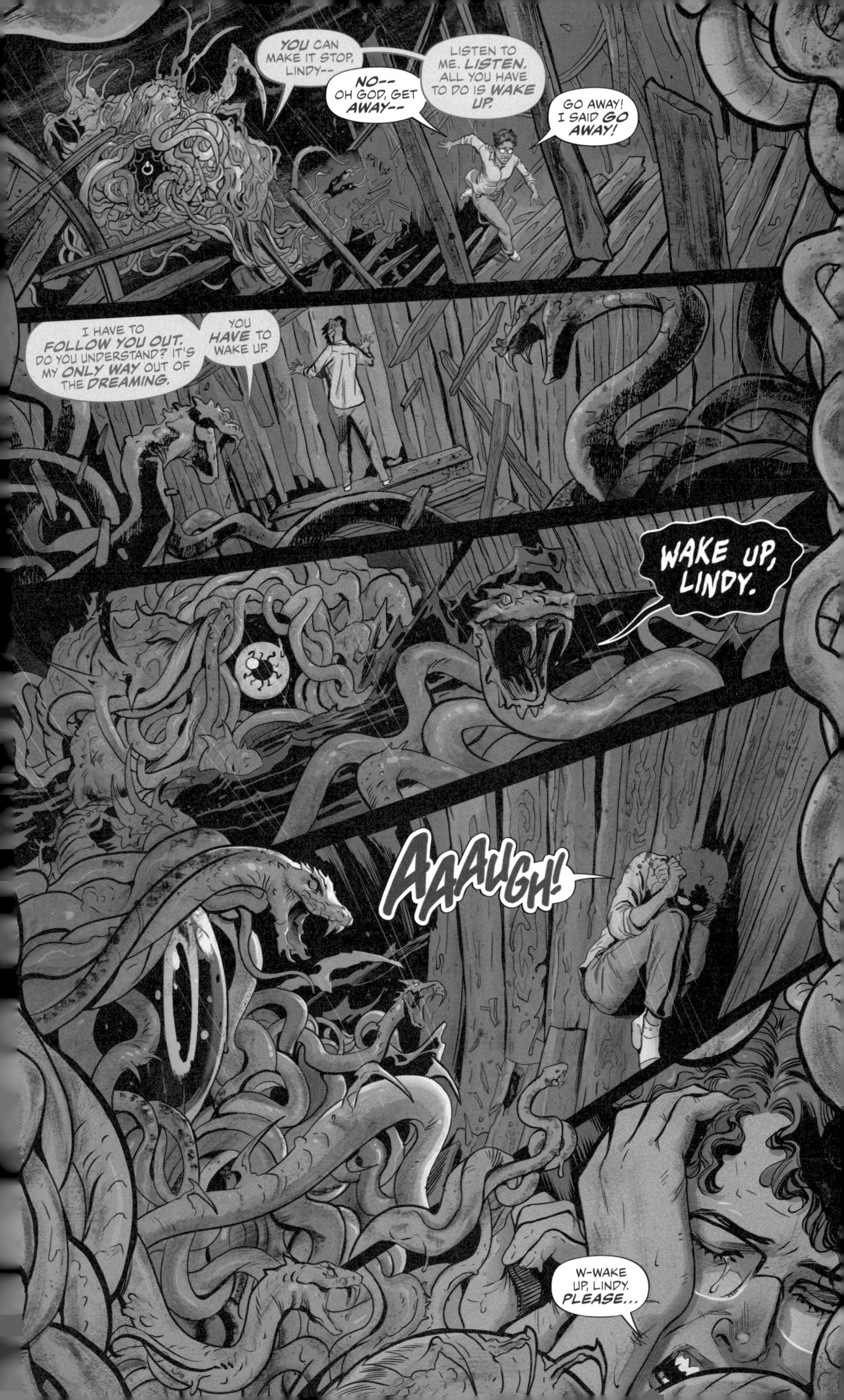
YOU CAN MAKE IT STOP, LINDY--
NO-- OH GOD, GET AWAY--
LISTEN TO ME. LISTEN. ALL YOU HAVE TO DO IS WAKE UP.
GO AWAY! I SAID GO AWAY!
I HAVE TO FOLLOW YOU OUT. DO YOU UNDERSTAND? IT'S MY ONLY WAY OUT OF THE DREAMING.
YOU HAVE TO WAKE UP.
WAKE UP, LINDY.
AAAUGH!
W-WAKE UP, LINDY. PLEASE...

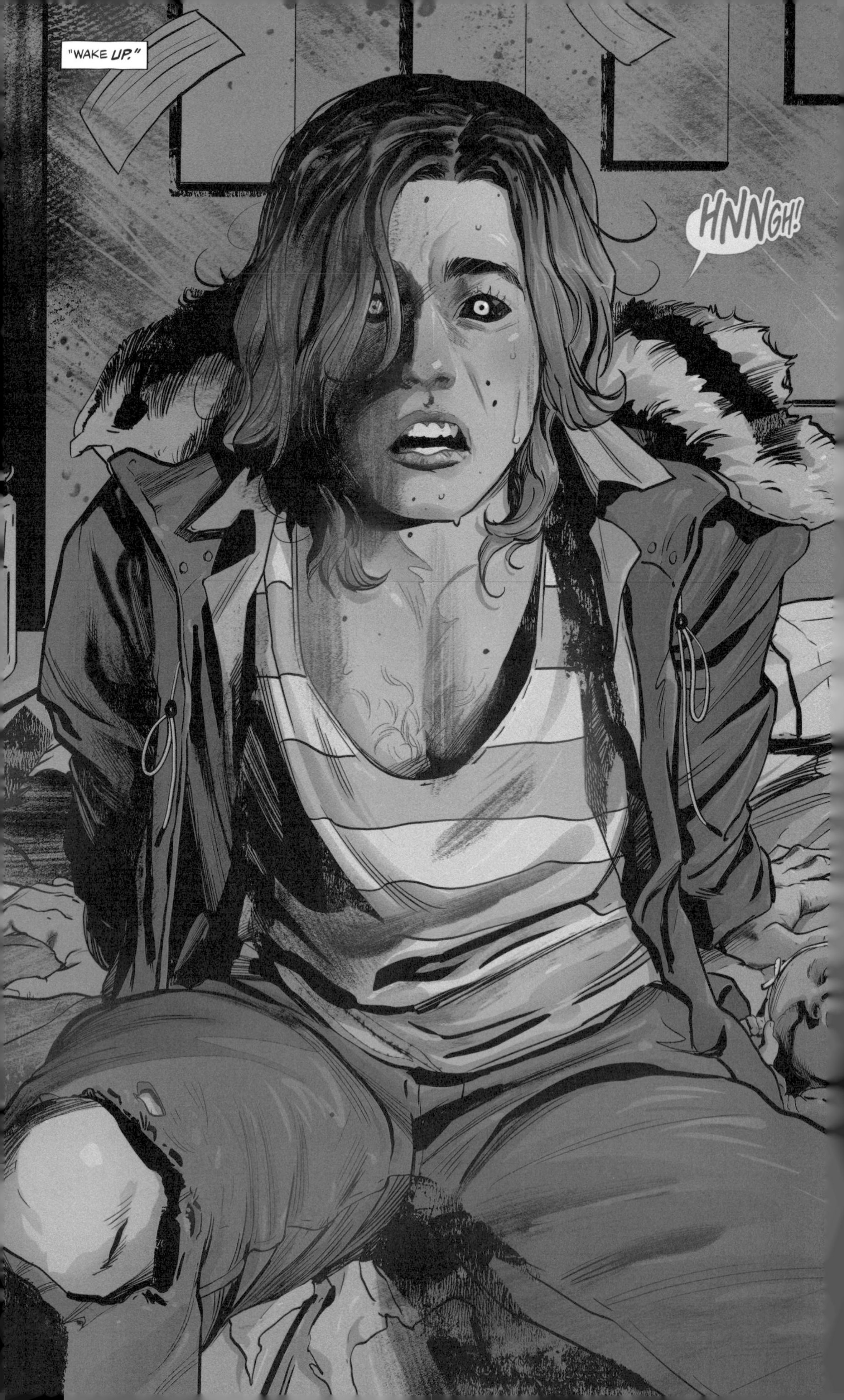
"WAKE UP."
HNNGH!

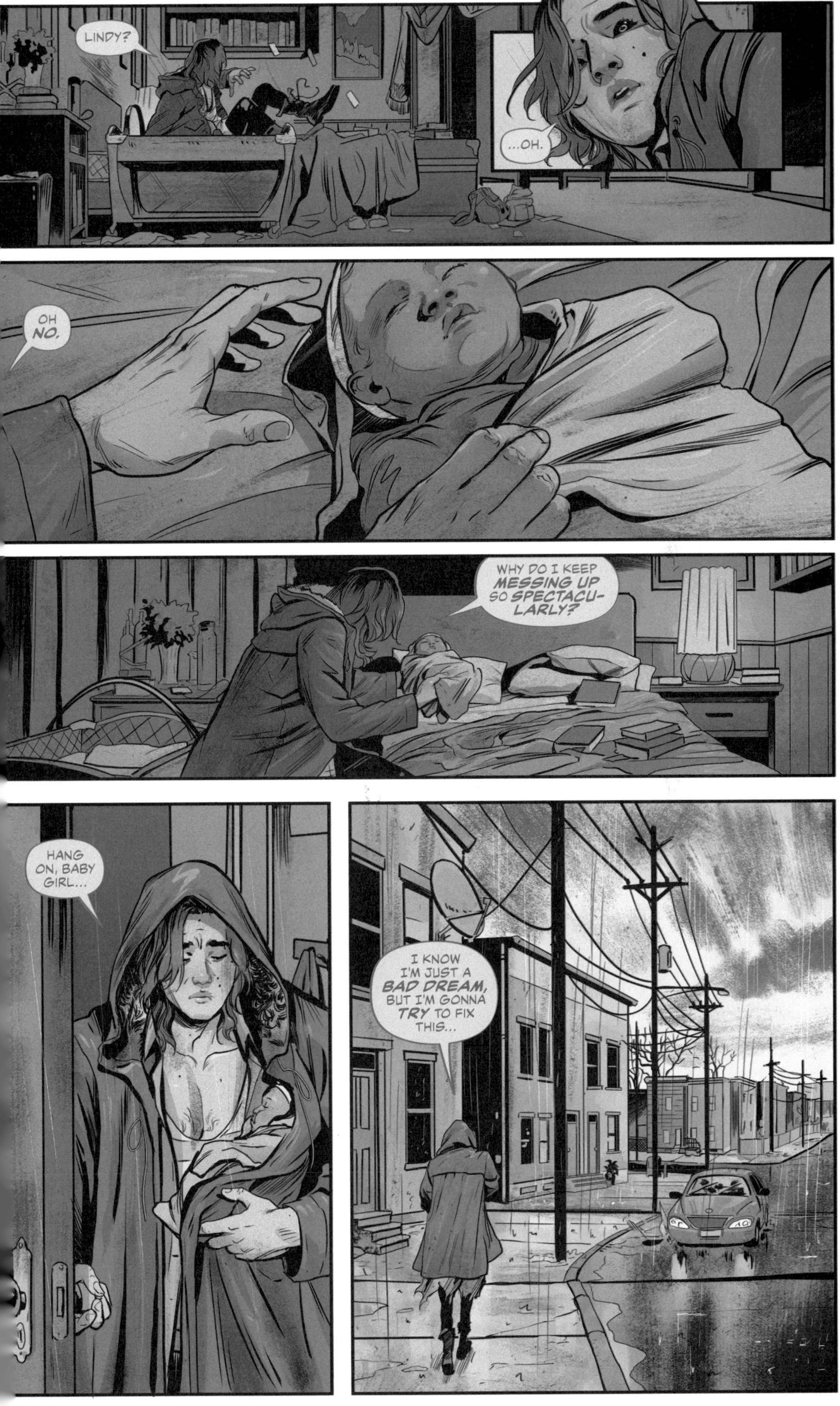
LINDY?
...OH.
OH NO.
WHY DO I KEEP MESSING UP SO SPECTACU-LARLY?
HANG ON, BABY GIRL...
I KNOW I'M JUST A BAD DREAM, BUT I'M GONNA TRY TO FIX THIS...

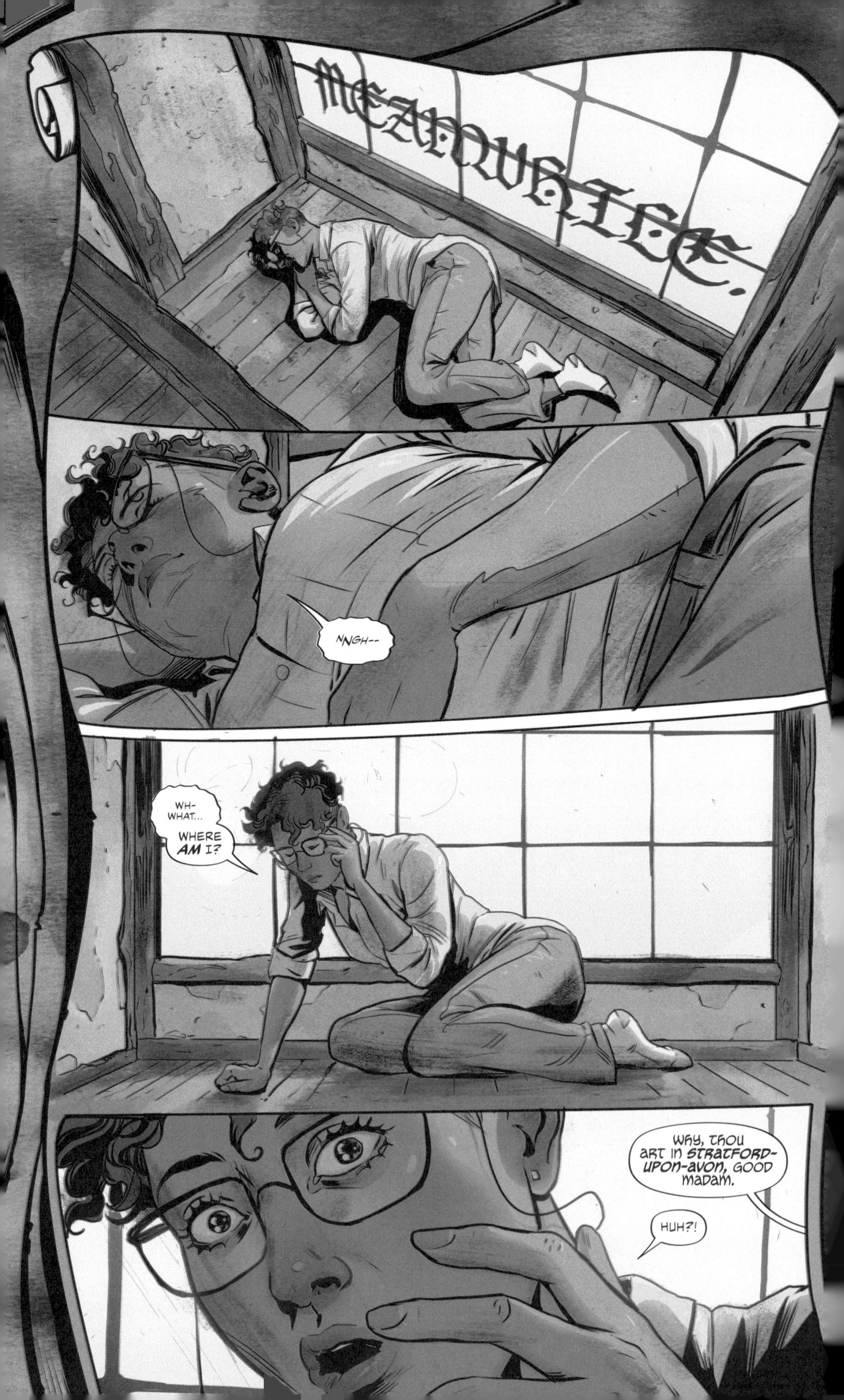
MEANWHILE.
NNGH--
WH-WHAT...
WHERE AM I?
WHY, THOU ART IN STRATFORD-UPON-AVON, GOOD MADAM.
HUH?!

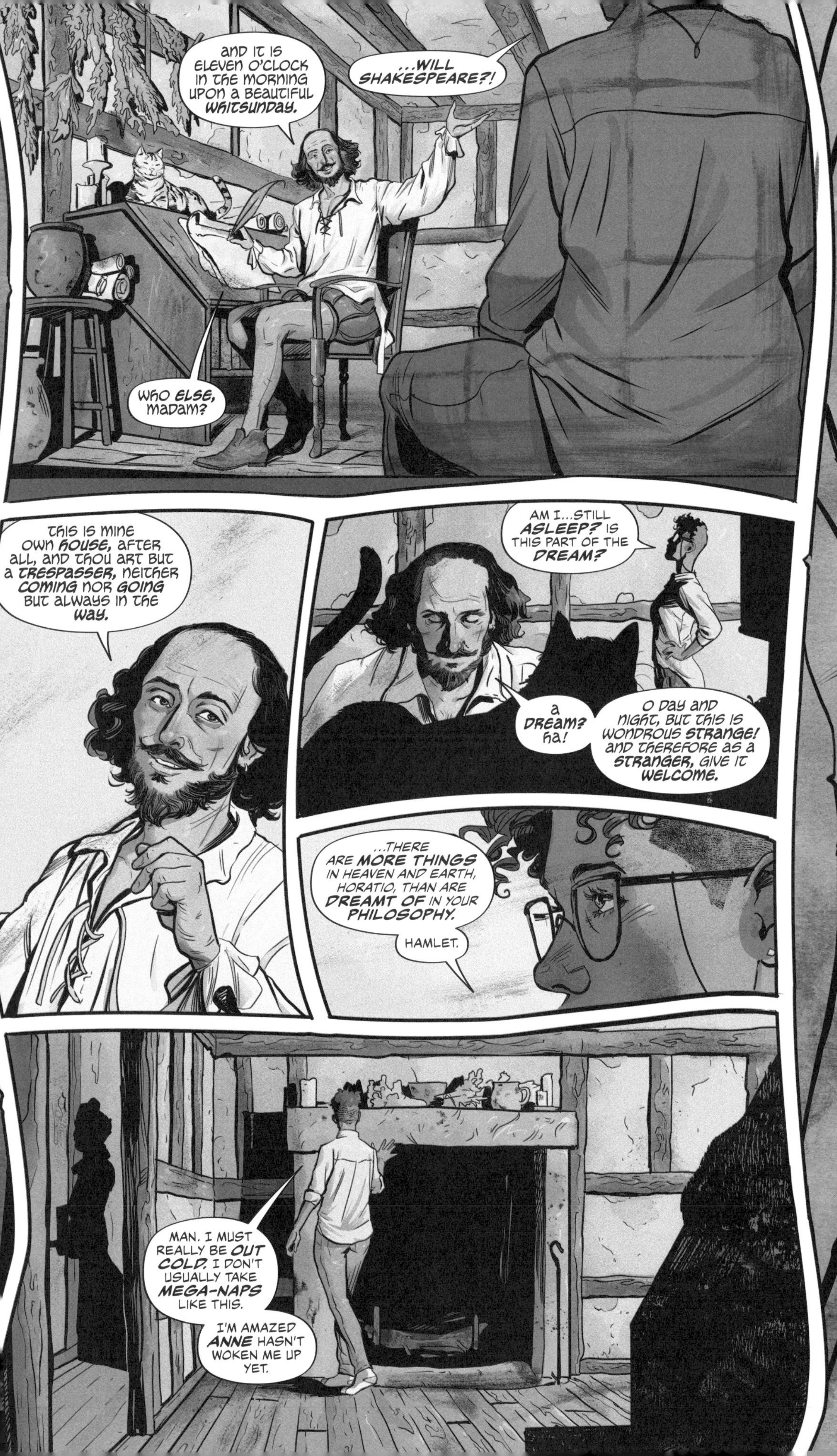

AND IT IS ELEVEN O'CLOCK IN THE MORNING UPON A BEAUTIFUL WHITSUNDAY.
...WILL SHAKESPEARE?!
WHO ELSE, MADAM?
THIS IS MINE OWN HOUSE, AFTER ALL, AND THOU ART BUT A TRESPASSER, NEITHER COMING NOR GOING BUT ALWAYS IN THE WAY.
AM I...STILL ASLEEP? IS THIS PART OF THE DREAM?
A DREAM? HA!
O DAY AND NIGHT, BUT THIS IS WONDROUS STRANGE! AND THEREFORE AS A STRANGER, GIVE IT WELCOME.
...THERE ARE MORE THINGS IN HEAVEN AND EARTH, HORATIO, THAN ARE DREAMT OF IN YOUR PHILOSOPHY.
HAMLET.
MAN. I MUST REALLY BE OUT COLD. I DON'T USUALLY TAKE MEGA-NAPS LIKE THIS.
I'M AMAZED ANNE HASN'T WOKEN ME UP YET.

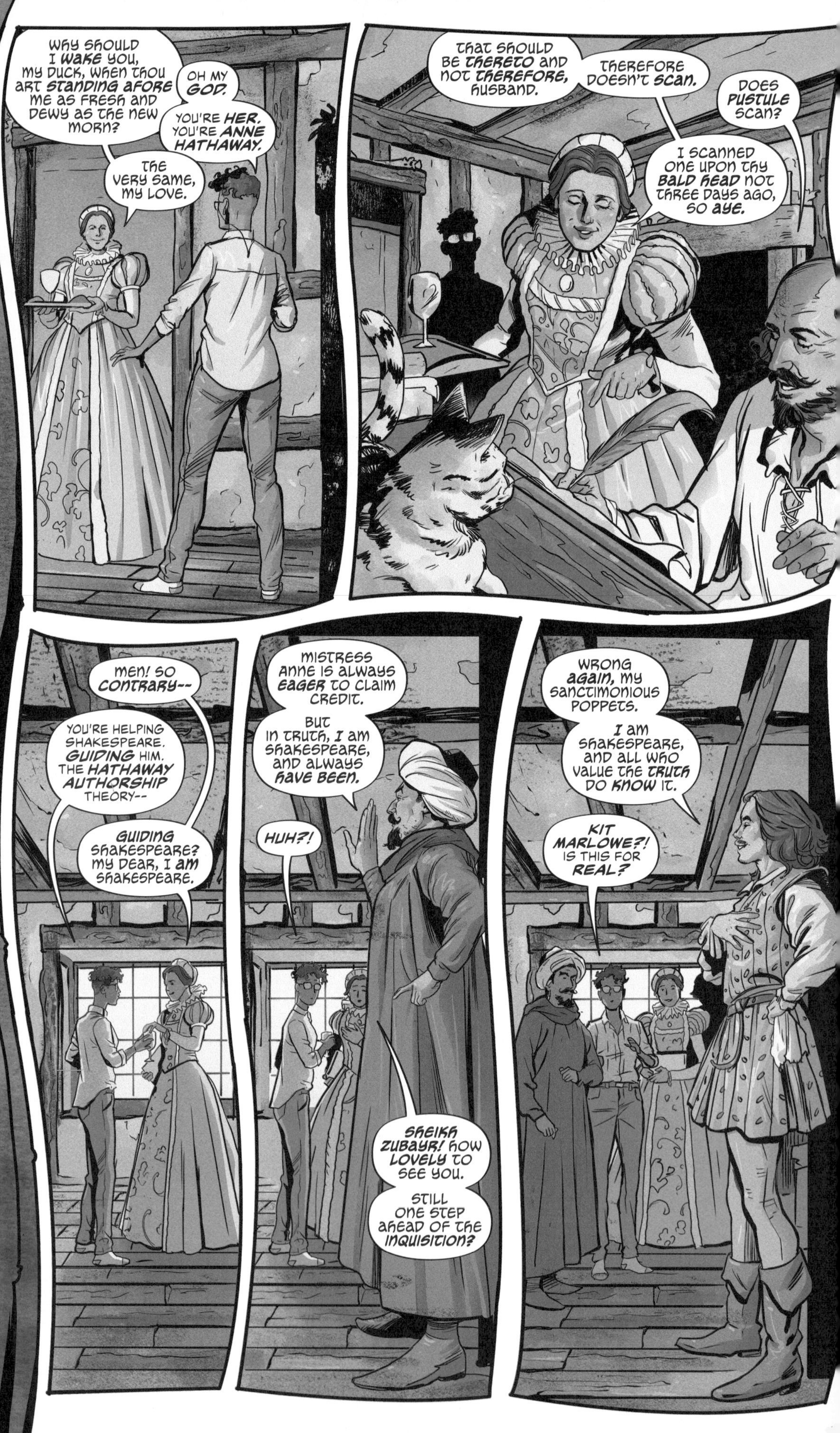
WHY SHOULD I WAKE YOU, MY DUCK, WHEN THOU ART STANDING AFORE ME AS FRESH AND DEWY AS THE NEW MORN?
OH MY GOD.
YOU'RE HER. YOU'RE ANNE HATHAWAY.
THE VERY SAME, MY LOVE.
THAT SHOULD BE THERETO AND NOT THEREFORE, HUSBAND.
THEREFORE DOESN'T SCAN.
DOES PUSTULE SCAN?
I SCANNED ONE UPON THY BALD HEAD NOT THREE DAYS AGO, SO AYE.
MEN! SO CONTRARY--
YOU'RE HELPING SHAKESPEARE. GUIDING HIM. THE HATHAWAY AUTHORSHIP THEORY--
GUIDING SHAKESPEARE? MY DEAR, I AM SHAKESPEARE.
MISTRESS ANNE IS ALWAYS EAGER TO CLAIM CREDIT.
BUT IN TRUTH, I AM SHAKESPEARE, AND ALWAYS HAVE BEEN.
HUH?!
SHEIKH ZUBAYR! HOW LOVELY TO SEE YOU.
STILL ONE STEP AHEAD OF THE INQUISITION?
WRONG AGAIN, MY SANCTIMONIOUS POPPETS.
I AM SHAKESPEARE, AND ALL WHO VALUE THE TRUTH DO KNOW IT.
KIT MARLOWE?! IS THIS FOR REAL?

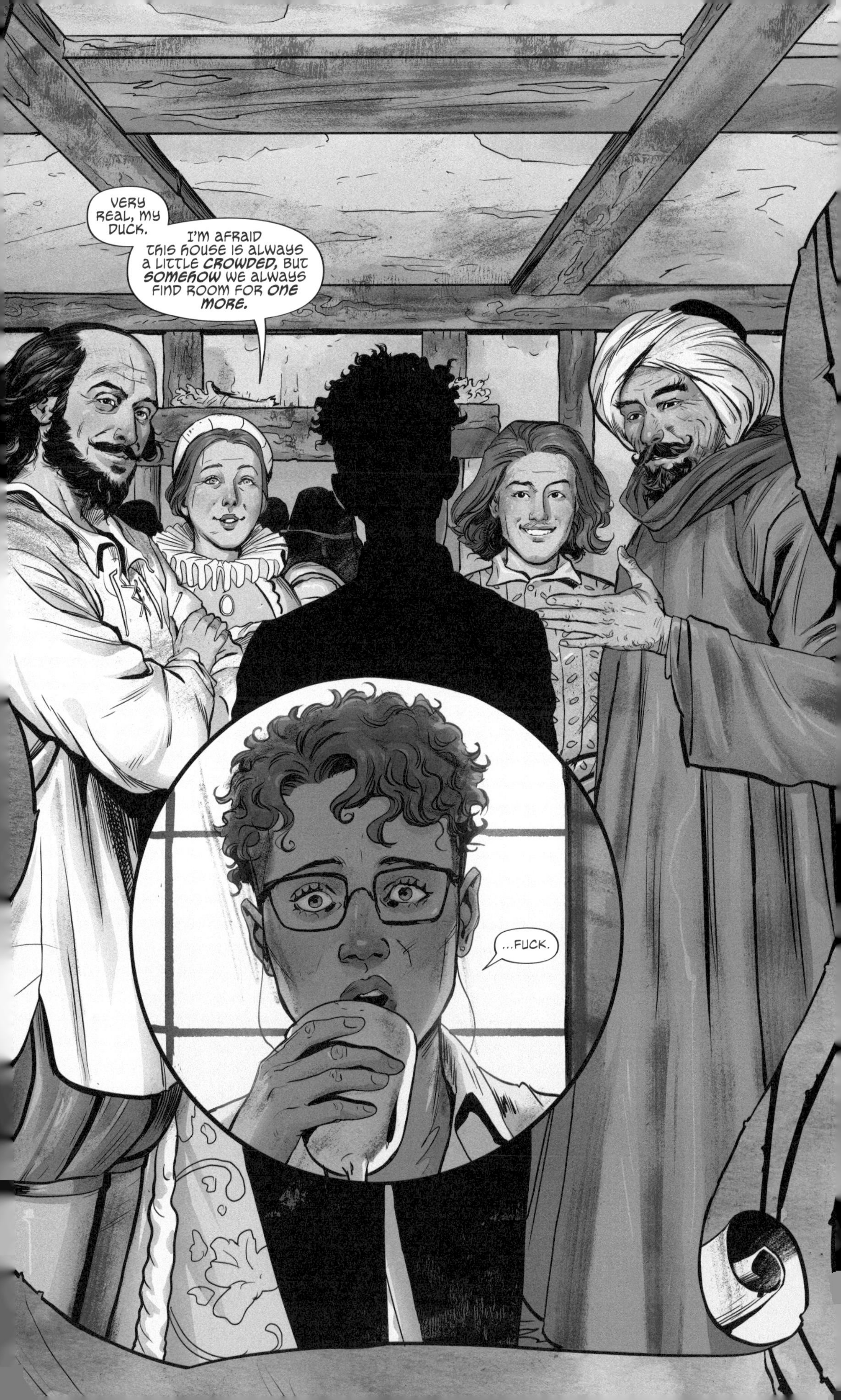
VERY REAL, MY DUCK.
I'M AFRAID THIS HOUSE IS ALWAYS A LITTLE CROWDED, BUT SOMEHOW WE ALWAYS FIND ROOM FOR ONE MORE.
...FUCK.

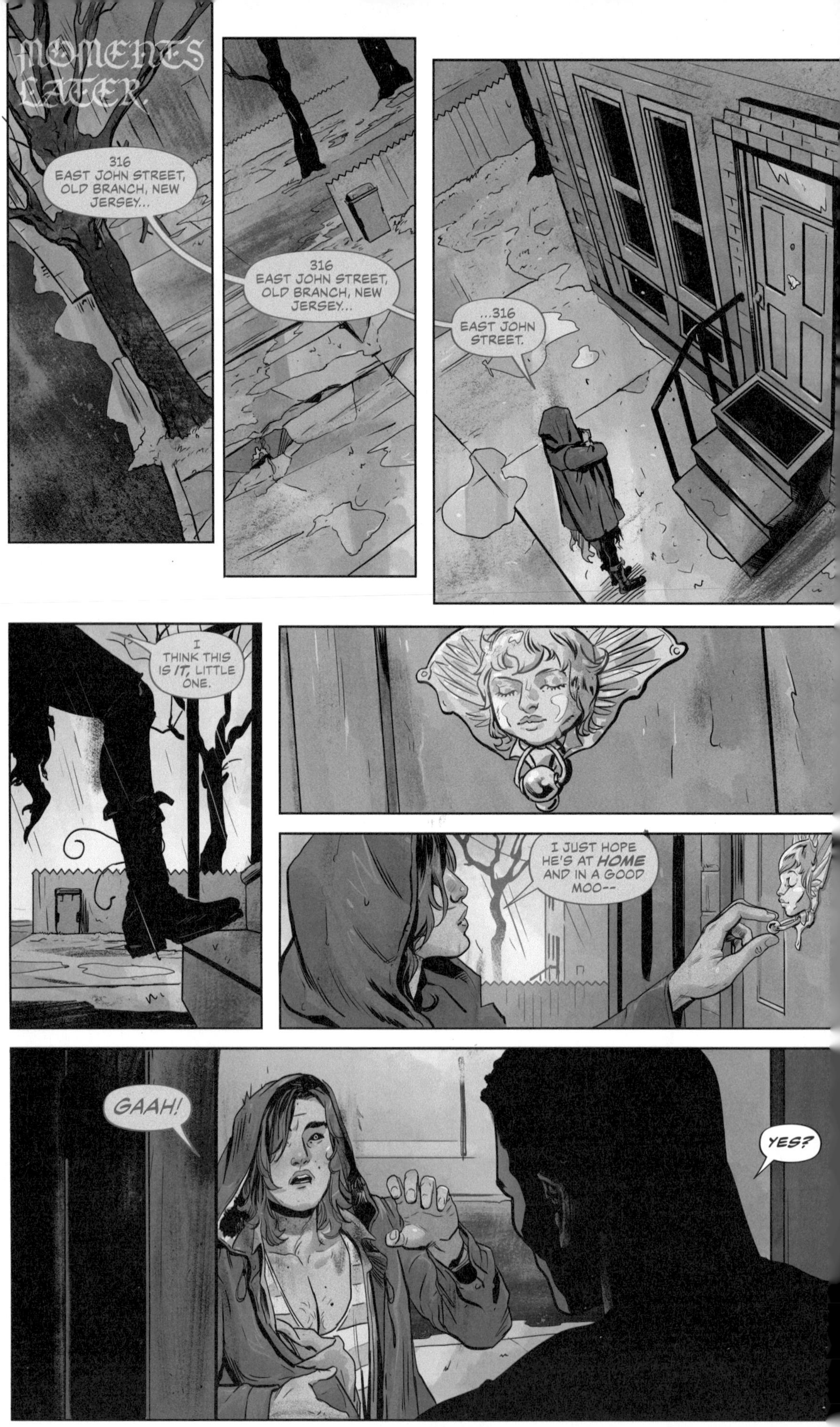
MOMENTS LATER.
316 EAST JOHN STREET, OLD BRANCH, NEW JERSEY...
316 EAST JOHN STREET, OLD BRANCH, NEW JERSEY...
...316 EAST JOHN STREET.
I THINK THIS IS IT, LITTLE ONE.
I JUST HOPE HE'S AT HOME AND IN A GOOD MOO--
GAAH!
YES?

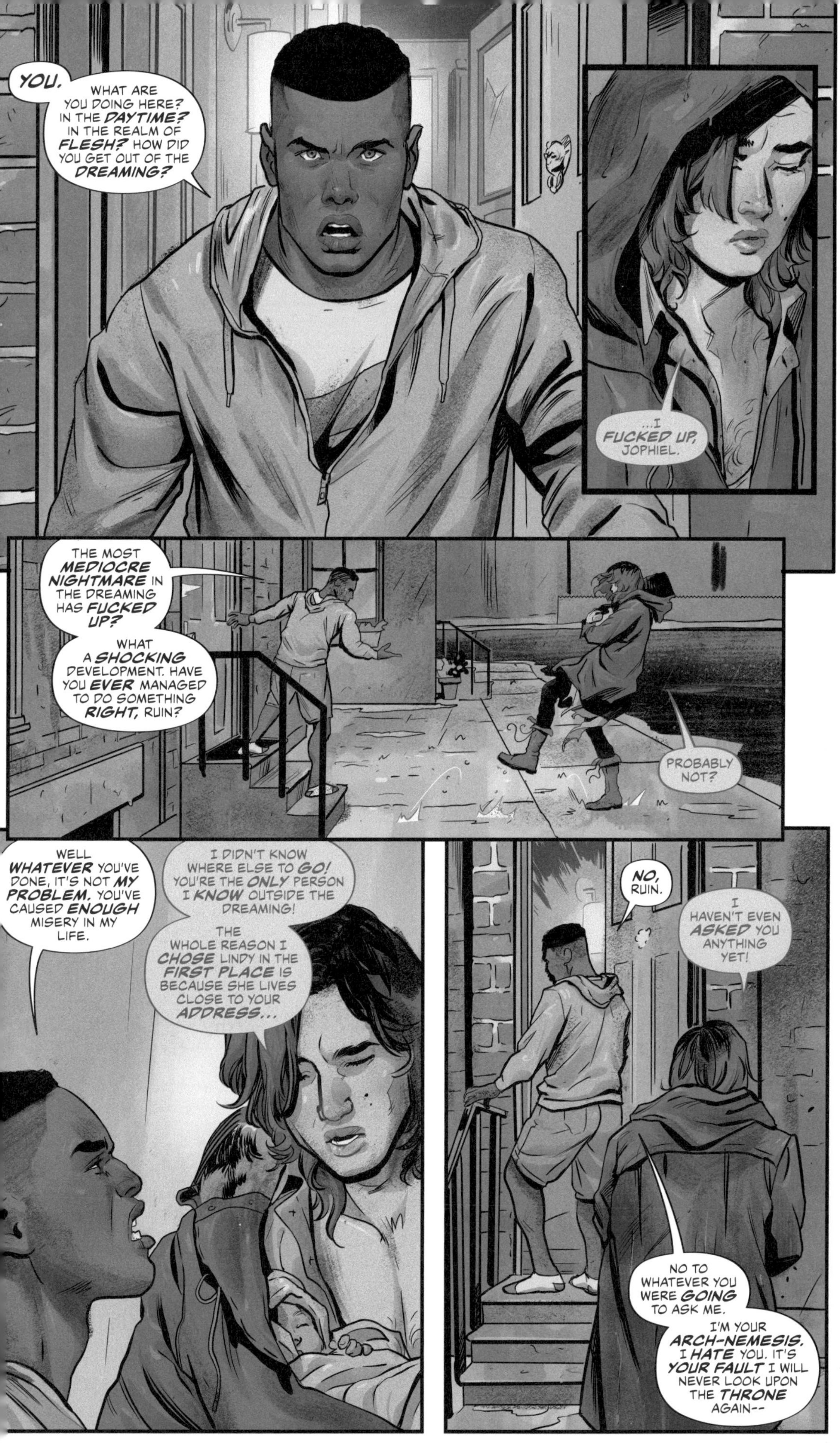
YOU.
WHAT ARE YOU DOING HERE? IN THE DAYTIME? IN THE REALM OF FLESH? HOW DID YOU GET OUT OF THE DREAMING?
...I FUCKED UP, JOPHIEL.
THE MOST MEDIOCRE NIGHTMARE IN THE DREAMING HAS FUCKED UP?
WHAT A SHOCKING DEVELOPMENT. HAVE YOU EVER MANAGED TO DO SOMETHING RIGHT, RUIN?
PROBABLY NOT?
WELL WHATEVER YOU'VE DONE, IT'S NOT MY PROBLEM. YOU'VE CAUSED ENOUGH MISERY IN MY LIFE.
I DIDN'T KNOW WHERE ELSE TO GO! YOU'RE THE ONLY PERSON I KNOW OUTSIDE THE DREAMING!
THE WHOLE REASON I CHOSE LINDY IN THE FIRST PLACE IS BECAUSE SHE LIVES CLOSE TO YOUR ADDRESS...
NO, RUIN.
I HAVEN'T EVEN ASKED YOU ANYTHING YET!
NO TO WHATEVER YOU WERE GOING TO ASK ME.
I'M YOUR ARCH-NEMESIS. I HATE YOU. IT'S YOUR FAULT I WILL NEVER LOOK UPON THE THRONE AGAIN--

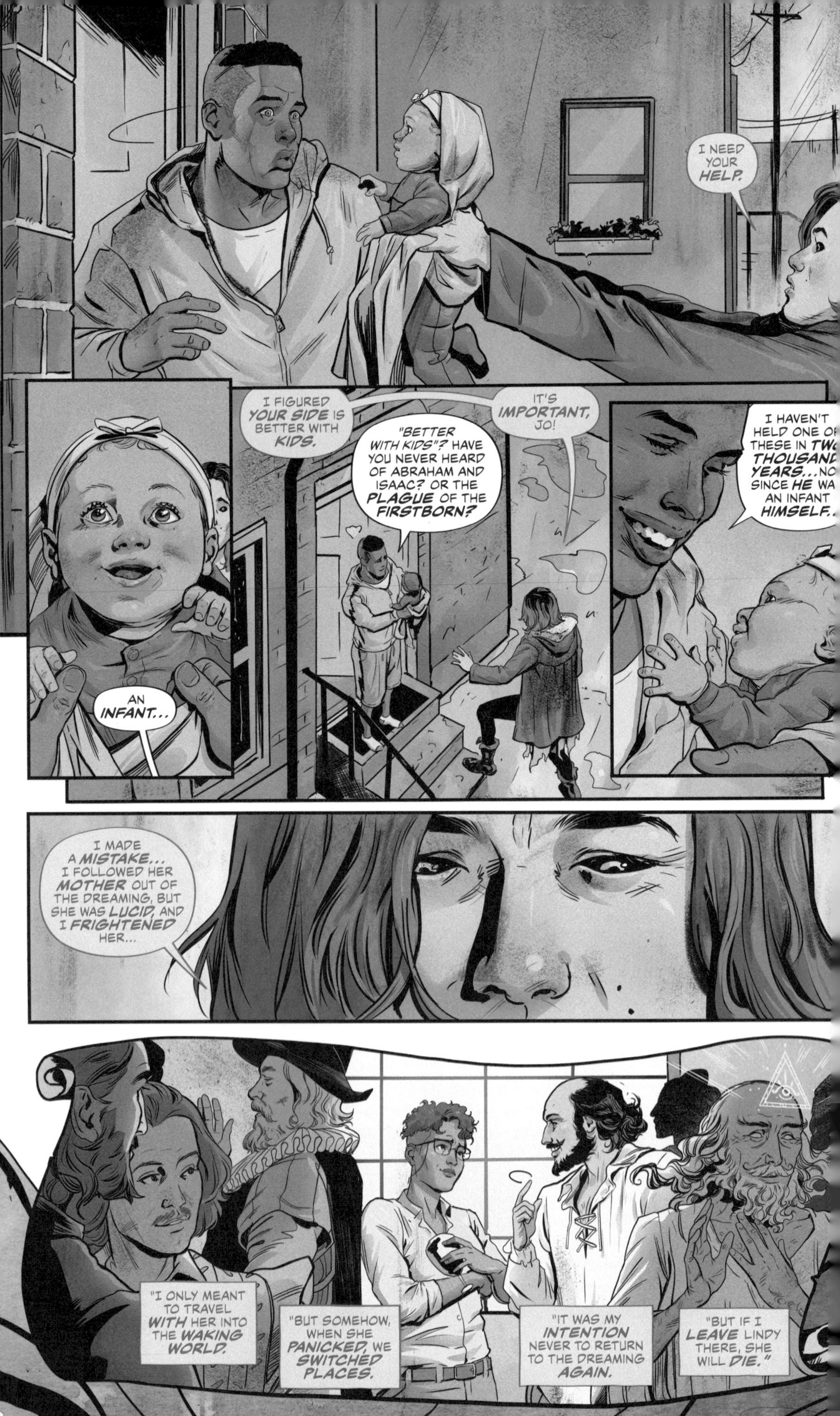
I NEED YOUR HELP.
AN INFANT...
I FIGURED YOUR SIDE IS BETTER WITH KIDS.
"BETTER WITH KIDS"? HAVE YOU NEVER HEARD OF ABRAHAM AND ISAAC? OR THE PLAGUE OF THE FIRSTBORN?
IT'S IMPORTANT, JO!
I HAVEN'T HELD ONE OF THESE IN TWO THOUSAND YEARS...NOT SINCE HE WAS AN INFANT HIMSELF...
I MADE A MISTAKE... I FOLLOWED HER MOTHER OUT OF THE DREAMING, BUT SHE WAS LUCID, AND I FRIGHTENED HER...
"I ONLY MEANT TO TRAVEL WITH HER INTO THE WAKING WORLD.
"BUT SOMEHOW, WHEN SHE PANICKED, WE SWITCHED PLACES.
"IT WAS MY INTENTION NEVER TO RETURN TO THE DREAMING AGAIN.
"BUT IF I LEAVE LINDY THERE, SHE WILL DIE."

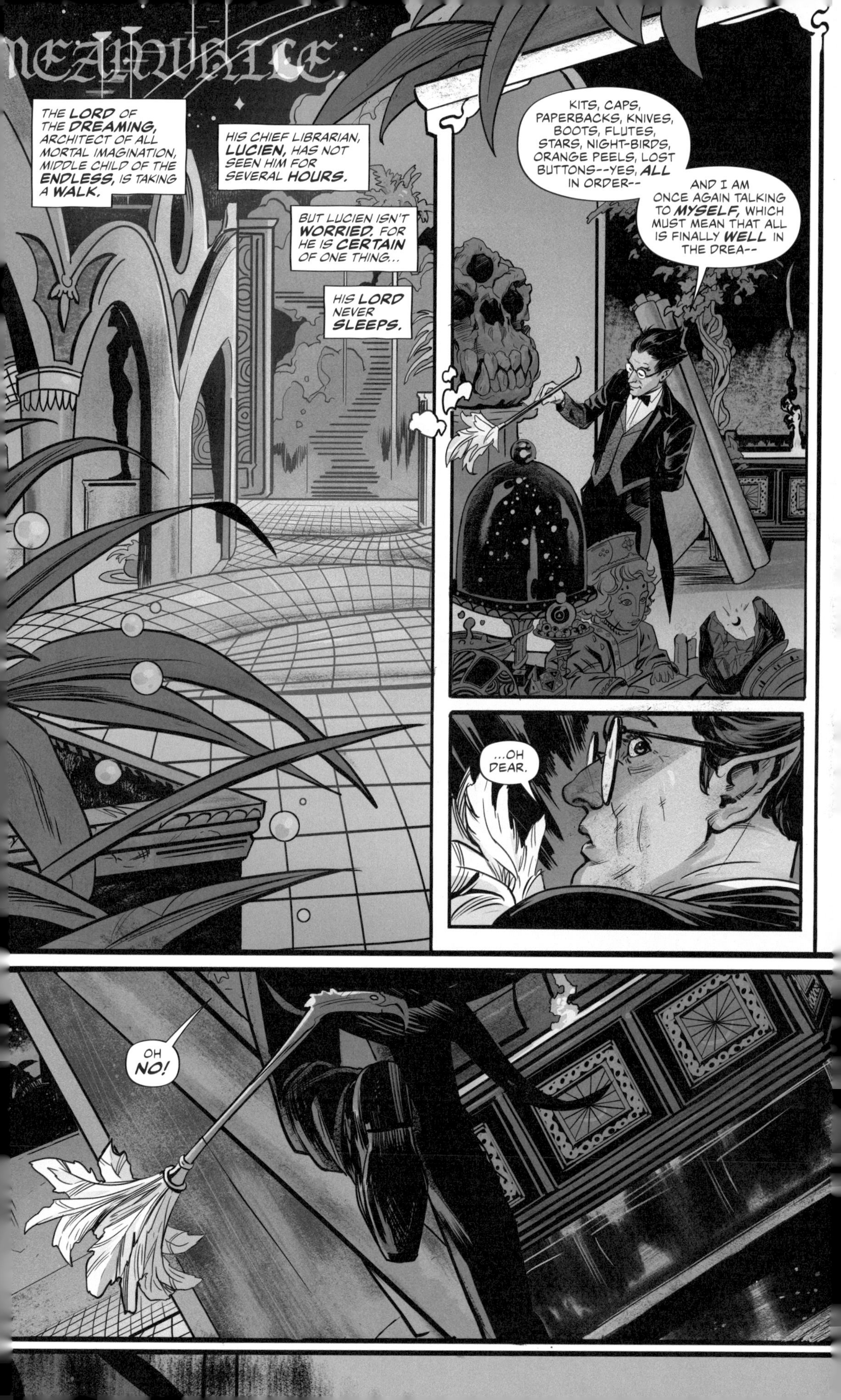
MEANWHILE.
THE LORD OF THE DREAMING, ARCHITECT OF ALL MORTAL IMAGINATION, MIDDLE CHILD OF THE ENDLESS, IS TAKING A WALK.
HIS CHIEF LIBRARIAN, LUCIEN, HAS NOT SEEN HIM FOR SEVERAL HOURS.
BUT LUCIEN ISN'T WORRIED, FOR HE IS CERTAIN OF ONE THING...
HIS LORD NEVER SLEEPS.
KITS, CAPS, PAPERBACKS, KNIVES, BOOTS, FLUTES, STARS, NIGHT-BIRDS, ORANGE PEELS, LOST BUTTONS--YES, ALL IN ORDER--
AND I AM ONCE AGAIN TALKING TO MYSELF, WHICH MUST MEAN THAT ALL IS FINALLY WELL IN THE DREA--
...OH DEAR.
OH NO!

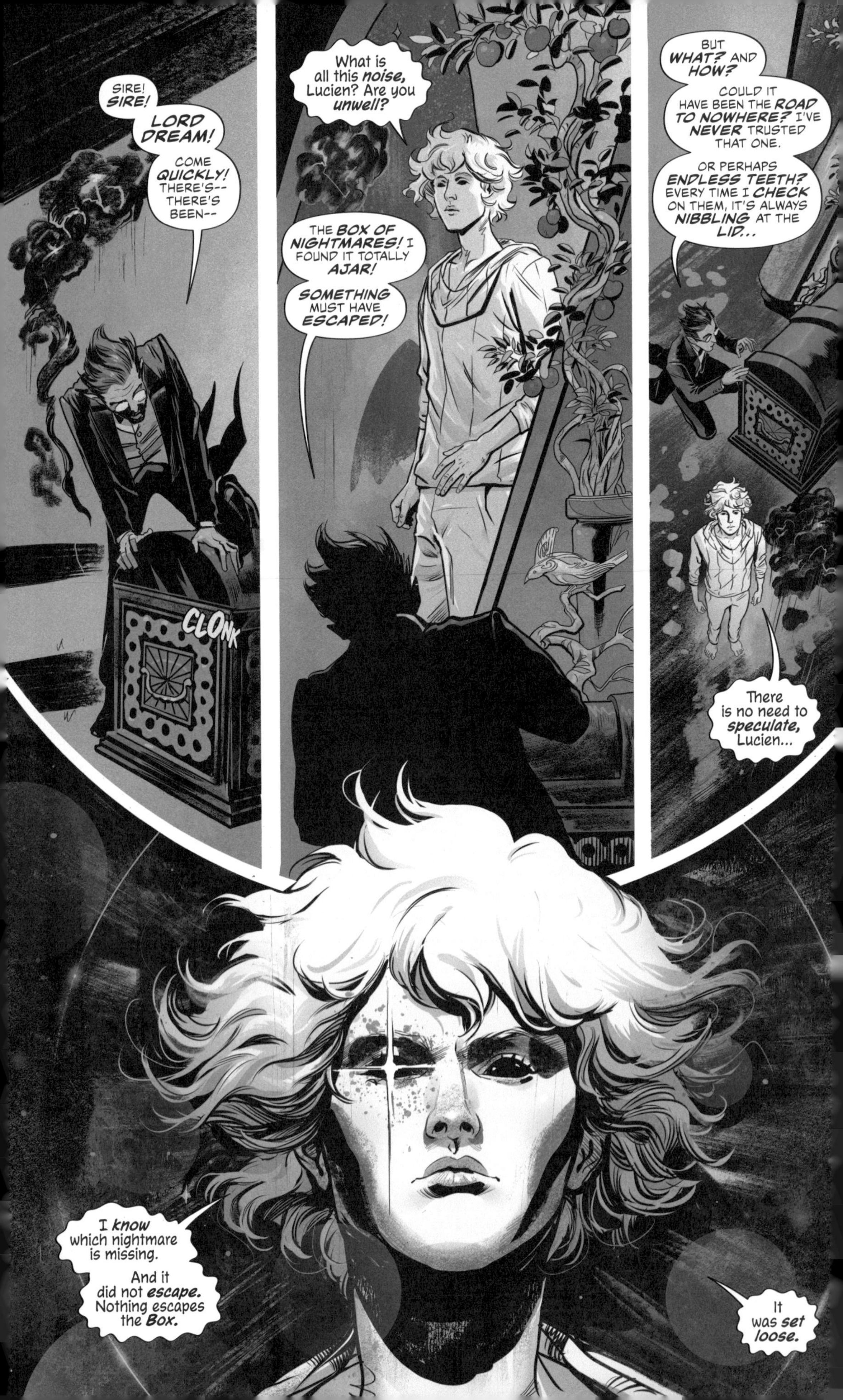
SIRE! SIRE!
LORD DREAM!
COME QUICKLY! THERE'S-- THERE'S BEEN--
CLONK
What is all this noise, Lucien? Are you unwell?
THE BOX OF NIGHTMARES! I FOUND IT TOTALLY AJAR!
SOMETHING MUST HAVE ESCAPED!
BUT WHAT? AND HOW?
COULD IT HAVE BEEN THE ROAD TO NOWHERE? I'VE NEVER TRUSTED THAT ONE.
OR PERHAPS ENDLESS TEETH? EVERY TIME I CHECK ON THEM, IT'S ALWAYS NIBBLING AT THE LID...
There is no need to speculate, Lucien...
I know which nightmare is missing.
And it did not escape. Nothing escapes the Box.
It was set loose.

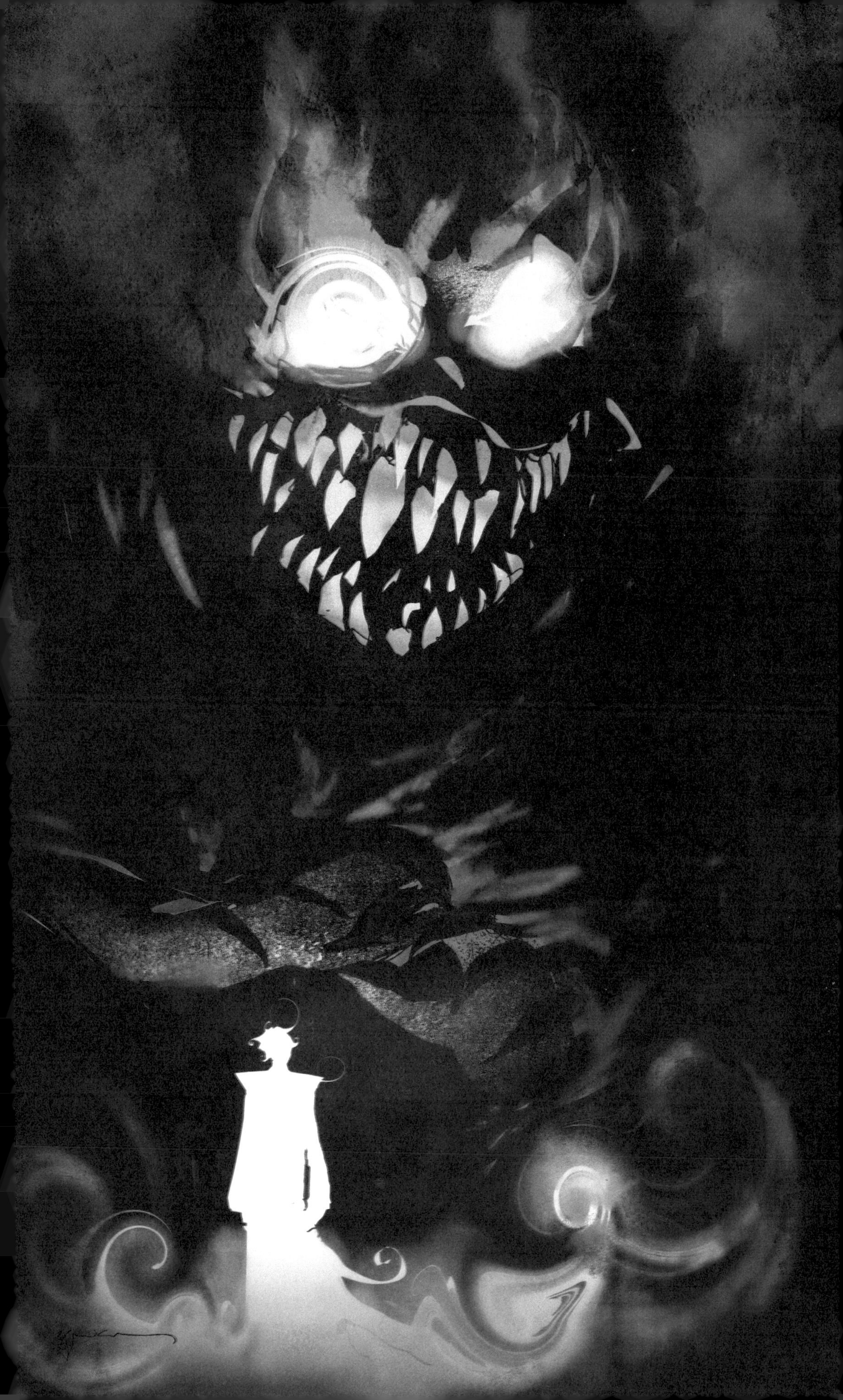

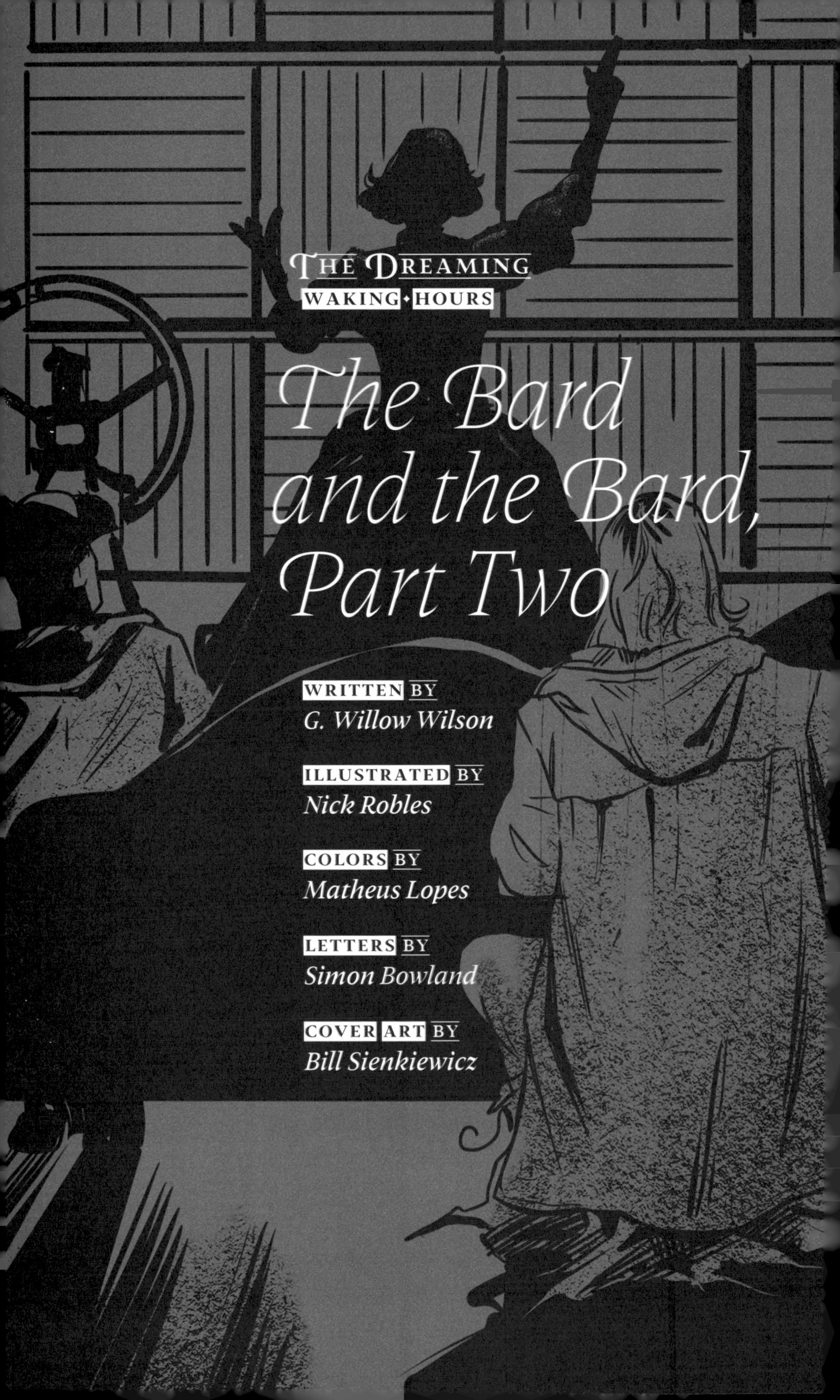

THE DREAMING
WAKING • HOURS

The Bard and the Bard, Part Two

WRITTEN BY
G. Willow Wilson

ILLUSTRATED BY
Nick Robles

COLORS BY
Matheus Lopes

LETTERS BY
Simon Bowland

COVER ART BY
Bill Sienkiewicz

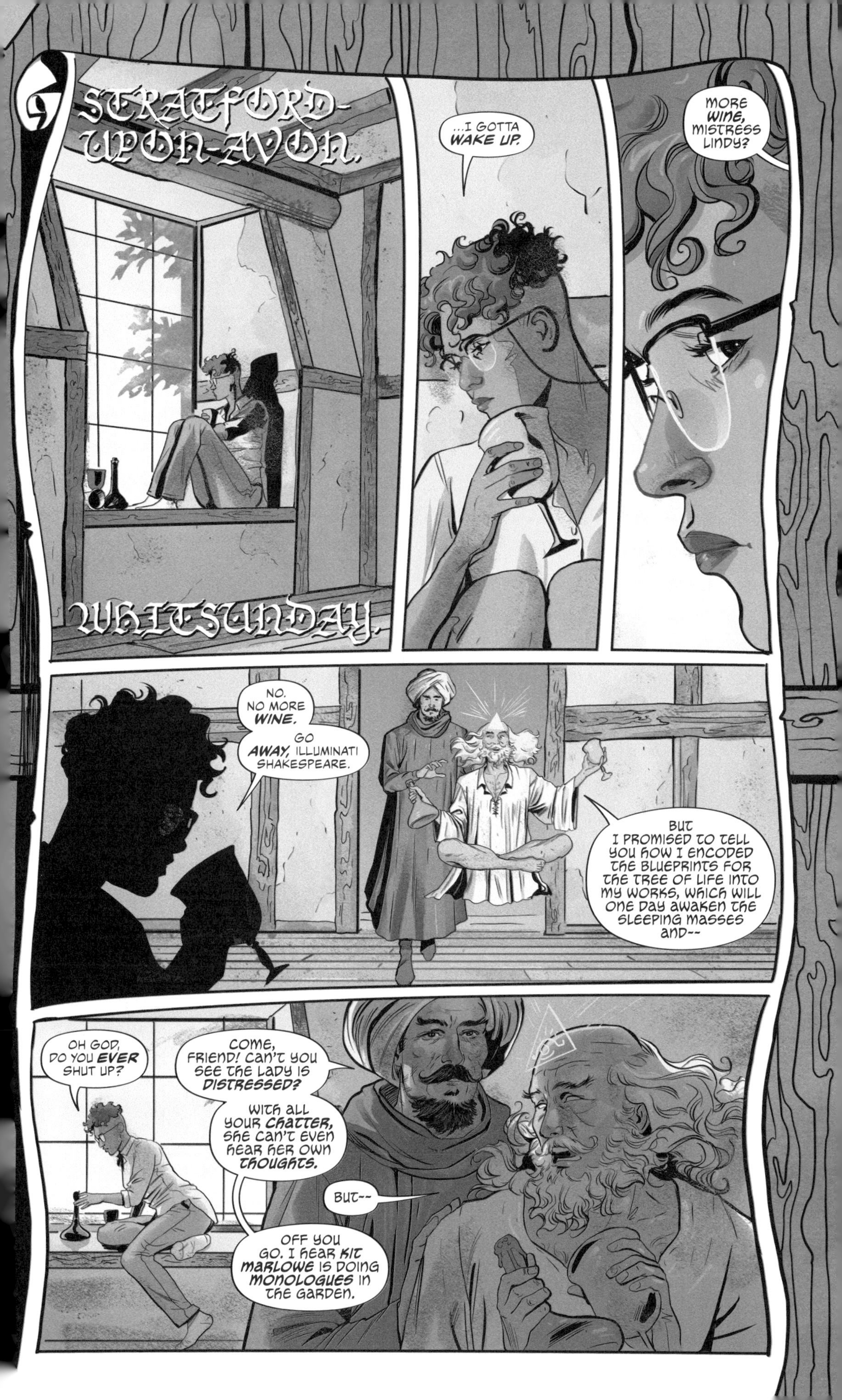
STRATFORD-UPON-AVON.
WHITSUNDAY.
...I GOTTA WAKE UP.
MORE WINE, MISTRESS LINDY?
NO. NO MORE WINE.
GO AWAY, ILLUMINATI SHAKESPEARE.
BUT I PROMISED TO TELL YOU HOW I ENCODED THE BLUEPRINTS FOR THE TREE OF LIFE INTO MY WORKS, WHICH WILL ONE DAY AWAKEN THE SLEEPING MASSES AND--
OH GOD, DO YOU EVER SHUT UP?
COME, FRIEND! CAN'T YOU SEE THE LADY IS DISTRESSED?
WITH ALL YOUR CHATTER, SHE CAN'T EVEN HEAR HER OWN THOUGHTS.
BUT--
OFF YOU GO. I HEAR KIT MARLOWE IS DOING MONOLOGUES IN THE GARDEN.

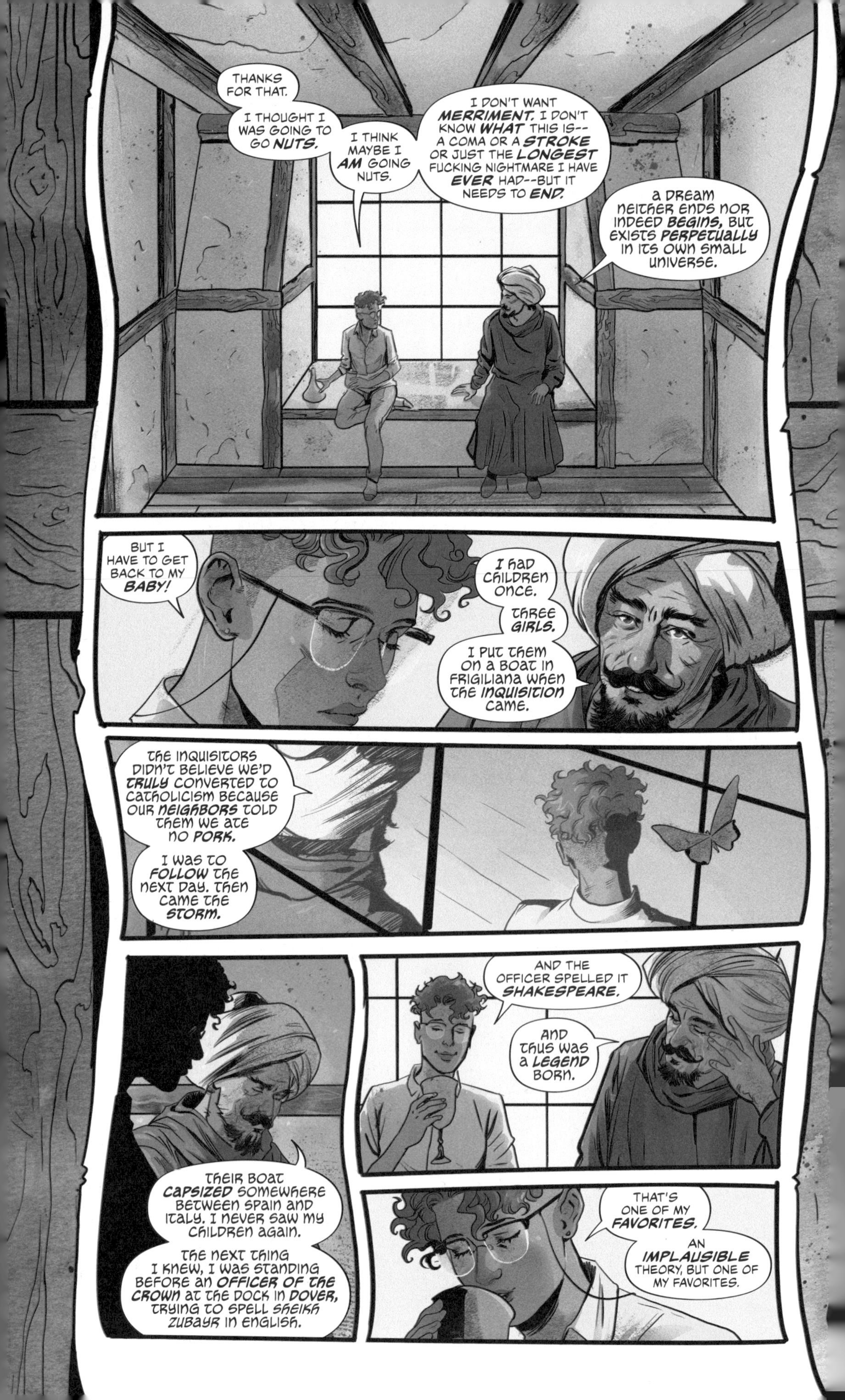
THANKS FOR THAT.
I THOUGHT I WAS GOING TO GO NUTS.
I THINK MAYBE I AM GOING NUTS.
I DON'T WANT MERRIMENT. I DON'T KNOW WHAT THIS IS--A COMA OR A STROKE OR JUST THE LONGEST FUCKING NIGHTMARE I HAVE EVER HAD--BUT IT NEEDS TO END.
A DREAM NEITHER ENDS NOR INDEED BEGINS, BUT EXISTS PERPETUALLY IN ITS OWN SMALL UNIVERSE.
BUT I HAVE TO GET BACK TO MY BABY!
I HAD CHILDREN ONCE.
THREE GIRLS.
I PUT THEM ON A BOAT IN FRIGILIANA WHEN THE INQUISITION CAME.
THE INQUISITORS DIDN'T BELIEVE WE'D TRULY CONVERTED TO CATHOLICISM BECAUSE OUR NEIGHBORS TOLD THEM WE ATE NO PORK.
I WAS TO FOLLOW THE NEXT DAY. THEN CAME THE STORM.
THEIR BOAT CAPSIZED SOMEWHERE BETWEEN SPAIN AND ITALY. I NEVER SAW MY CHILDREN AGAIN.
THE NEXT THING I KNEW, I WAS STANDING BEFORE AN OFFICER OF THE CROWN AT THE DOCK IN DOVER, TRYING TO SPELL SHEIKH ZUBAYR IN ENGLISH.
AND THE OFFICER SPELLED IT SHAKESPEARE.
AND THUS WAS A LEGEND BORN.
THAT'S ONE OF MY FAVORITES.
AN IMPLAUSIBLE THEORY, BUT ONE OF MY FAVORITES.

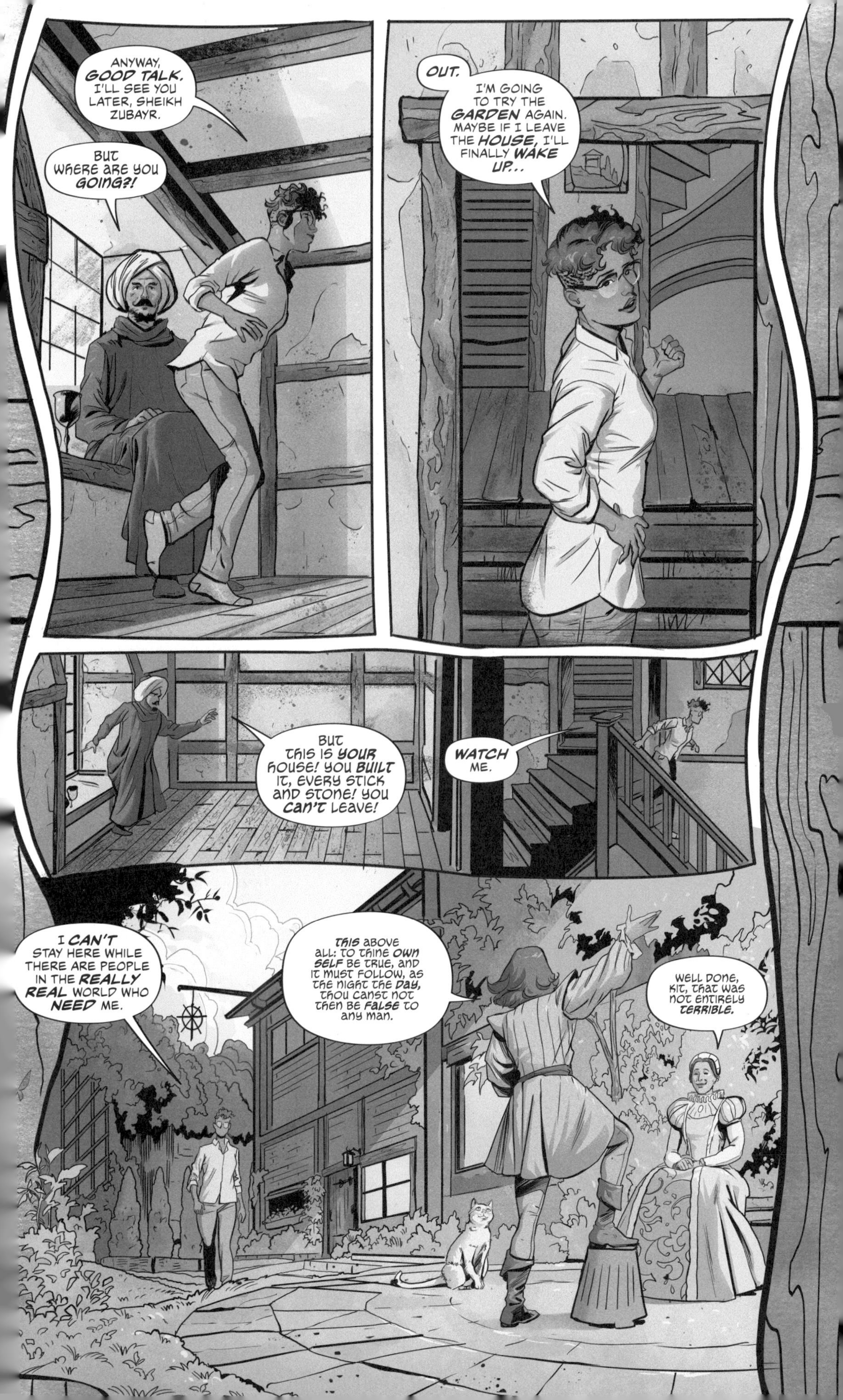
ANYWAY, GOOD TALK. I'LL SEE YOU LATER, SHEIKH ZUBAYR.
BUT WHERE ARE YOU GOING?!
OUT.
I'M GOING TO TRY THE GARDEN AGAIN. MAYBE IF I LEAVE THE HOUSE, I'LL FINALLY WAKE UP...
BUT THIS IS YOUR HOUSE! YOU BUILT IT, EVERY STICK AND STONE! YOU CAN'T LEAVE!
WATCH ME.
I CAN'T STAY HERE WHILE THERE ARE PEOPLE IN THE REALLY REAL WORLD WHO NEED ME.
THIS ABOVE ALL: TO THINE OWN SELF BE TRUE, AND IT MUST FOLLOW, AS THE NIGHT THE DAY, THOU CANST NOT THEN BE FALSE TO ANY MAN.
WELL DONE, KIT, THAT WAS NOT ENTIRELY TERRIBLE.

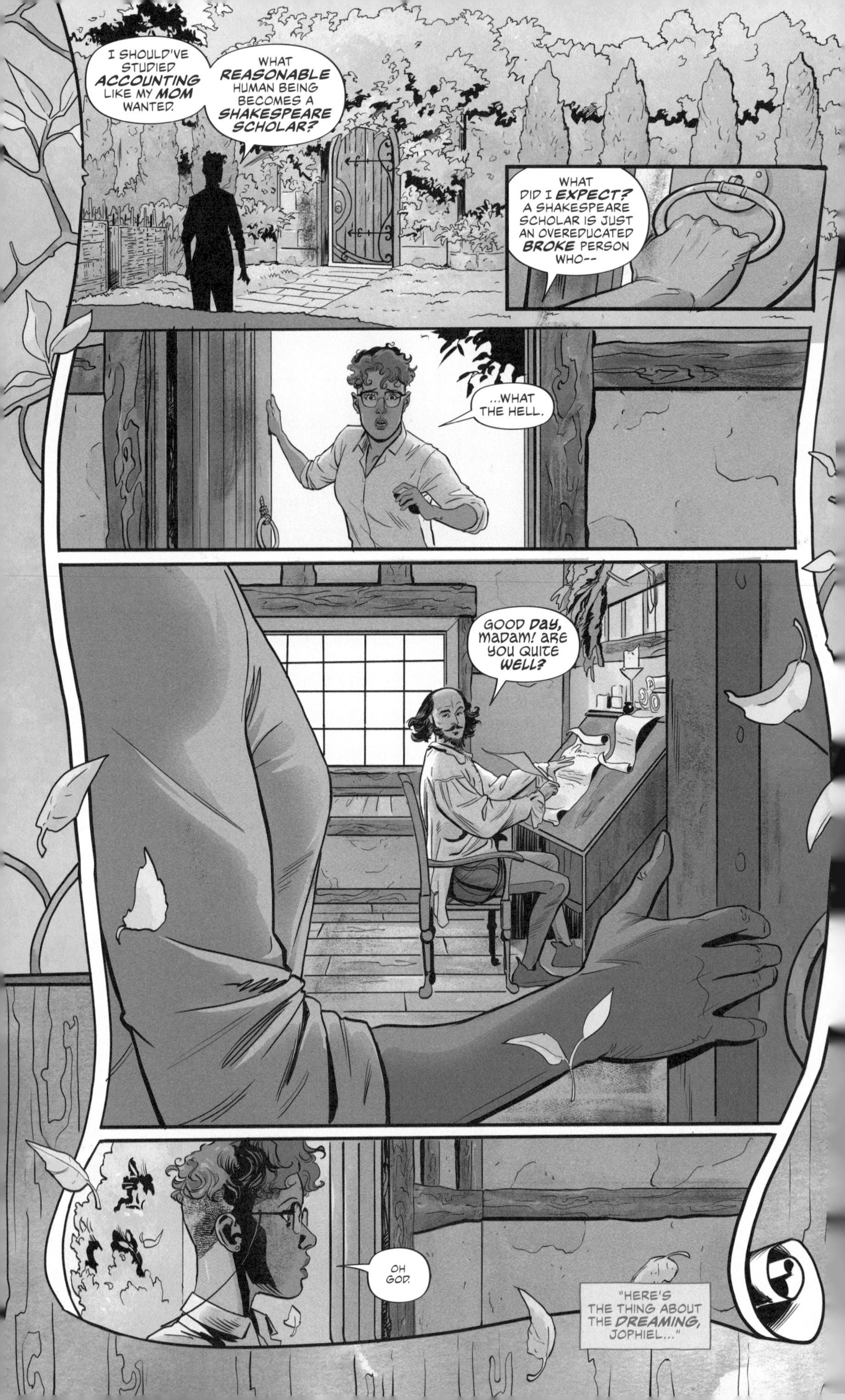
I SHOULD'VE STUDIED ACCOUNTING LIKE MY MOM WANTED.
WHAT REASONABLE HUMAN BEING BECOMES A SHAKESPEARE SCHOLAR?
WHAT DID I EXPECT? A SHAKESPEARE SCHOLAR IS JUST AN OVEREDUCATED BROKE PERSON WHO--
...WHAT THE HELL.
GOOD DAY, MADAM! ARE YOU QUITE WELL?
OH GOD.
"HERE'S THE THING ABOUT THE DREAMING, JOPHIEL..."

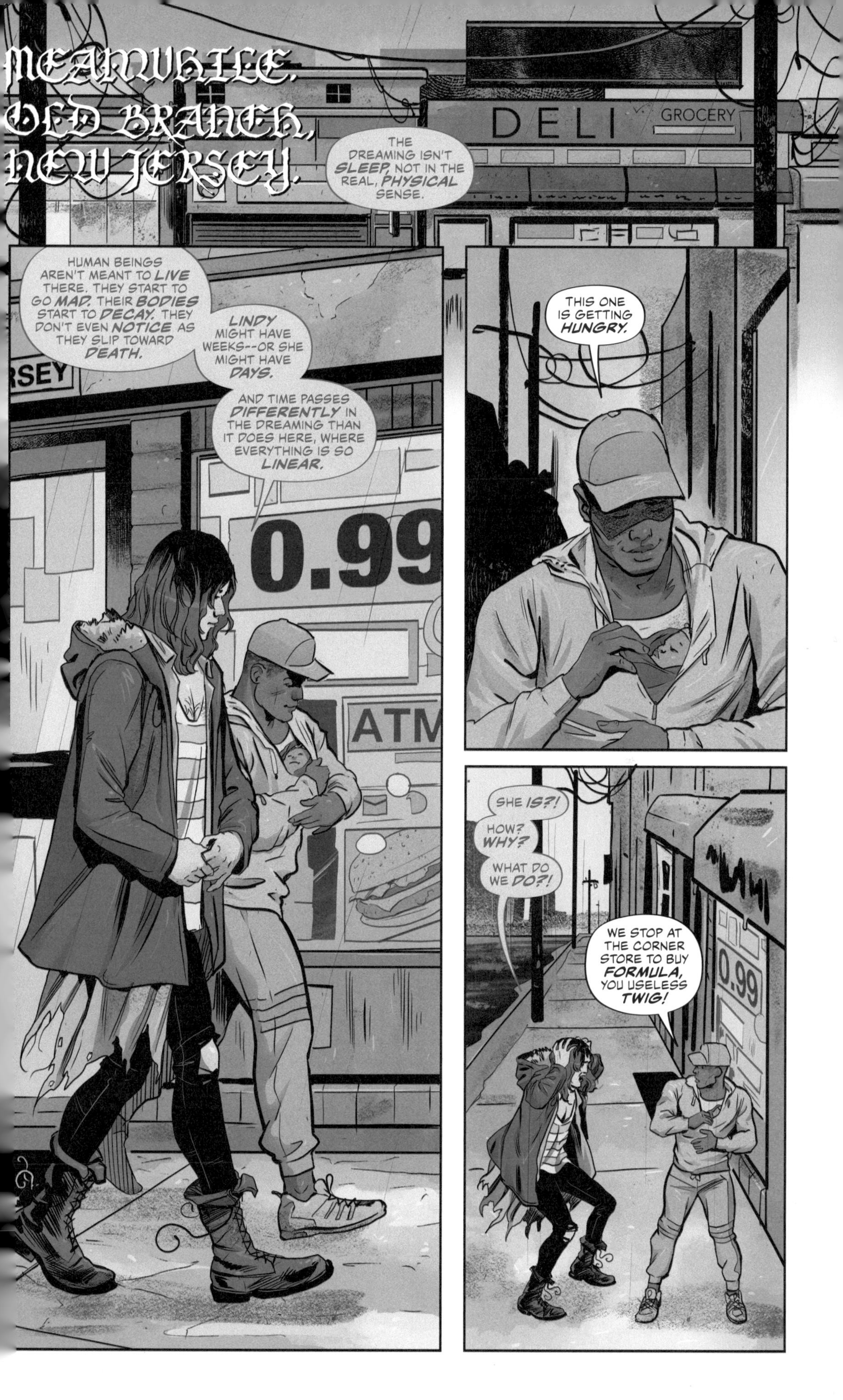
MEANWHILE, OLD BRANCH, NEW JERSEY.
THE DREAMING ISN'T SLEEP, NOT IN THE REAL, PHYSICAL SENSE.
DELI
GROCERY
HUMAN BEINGS AREN'T MEANT TO LIVE THERE. THEY START TO GO MAD. THEIR BODIES START TO DECAY. THEY DON'T EVEN NOTICE AS THEY SLIP TOWARD DEATH.
LINDY MIGHT HAVE WEEKS--OR SHE MIGHT HAVE DAYS.
AND TIME PASSES DIFFERENTLY IN THE DREAMING THAN IT DOES HERE, WHERE EVERYTHING IS SO LINEAR.
0.99
ATM
THIS ONE IS GETTING HUNGRY.
SHE IS?!
HOW? WHY?
WHAT DO WE DO?!
WE STOP AT THE CORNER STORE TO BUY FORMULA, YOU USELESS TWIG!
0.99

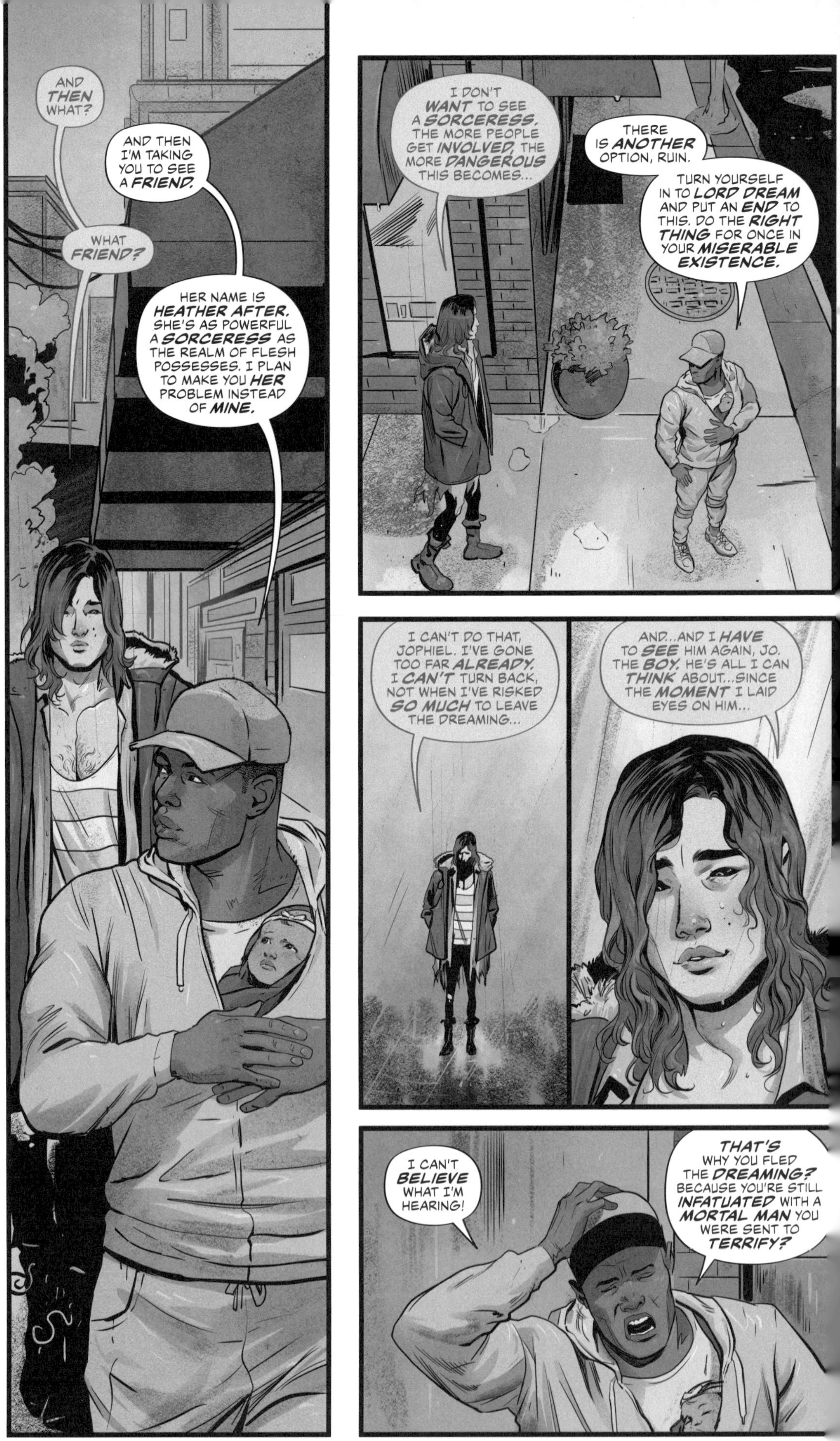
AND THEN WHAT?
AND THEN I'M TAKING YOU TO SEE A FRIEND.
WHAT FRIEND?
HER NAME IS HEATHER AFTER. SHE'S AS POWERFUL A SORCERESS AS THE REALM OF FLESH POSSESSES. I PLAN TO MAKE YOU HER PROBLEM INSTEAD OF MINE.
I DON'T WANT TO SEE A SORCERESS. THE MORE PEOPLE GET INVOLVED, THE MORE DANGEROUS THIS BECOMES...
THERE IS ANOTHER OPTION, RUIN.
TURN YOURSELF IN TO LORD DREAM AND PUT AN END TO THIS. DO THE RIGHT THING FOR ONCE IN YOUR MISERABLE EXISTENCE.
I CAN'T DO THAT, JOPHIEL. I'VE GONE TOO FAR ALREADY. I CAN'T TURN BACK, NOT WHEN I'VE RISKED SO MUCH TO LEAVE THE DREAMING...
AND...AND I HAVE TO SEE HIM AGAIN, JO. THE BOY. HE'S ALL I CAN THINK ABOUT...SINCE THE MOMENT I LAID EYES ON HIM...
I CAN'T BELIEVE WHAT I'M HEARING!
THAT'S WHY YOU FLED THE DREAMING? BECAUSE YOU'RE STILL INFATUATED WITH A MORTAL MAN YOU WERE SENT TO TERRIFY?

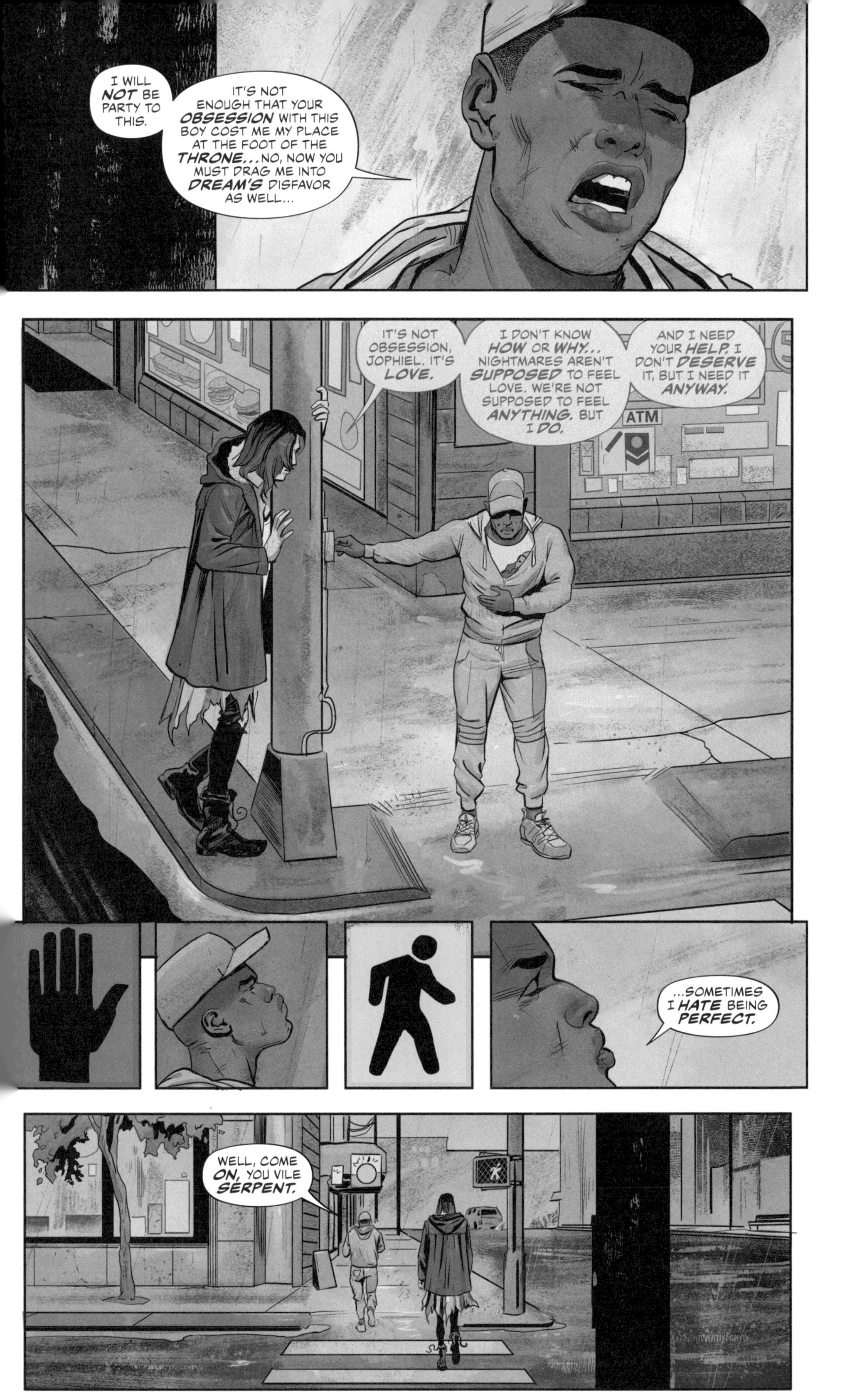
I WILL NOT BE PARTY TO THIS.
IT'S NOT ENOUGH THAT YOUR OBSESSION WITH THIS BOY COST ME MY PLACE AT THE FOOT OF THE THRONE... NO, NOW YOU MUST DRAG ME INTO DREAM'S DISFAVOR AS WELL...
IT'S NOT OBSESSION, JOPHIEL. IT'S LOVE.
I DON'T KNOW HOW OR WHY... NIGHTMARES AREN'T SUPPOSED TO FEEL LOVE. WE'RE NOT SUPPOSED TO FEEL ANYTHING. BUT I DO.
AND I NEED YOUR HELP. I DON'T DESERVE IT, BUT I NEED IT ANYWAY.
ATM
...SOMETIMES I HATE BEING PERFECT.
WELL, COME ON, YOU VILE SERPENT.

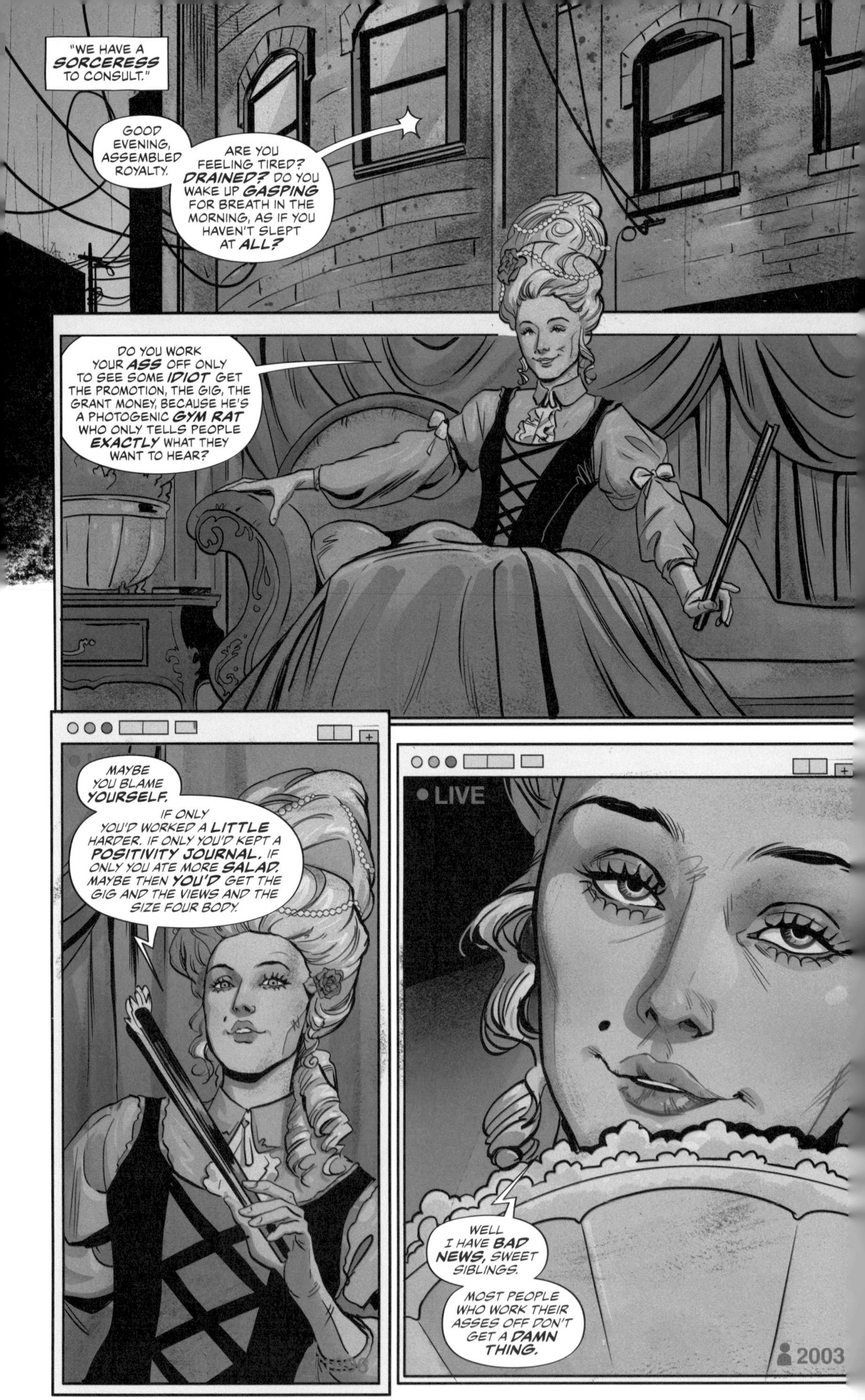
"WE HAVE A SORCERESS TO CONSULT."
GOOD EVENING, ASSEMBLED ROYALTY.
ARE YOU FEELING TIRED? DRAINED? DO YOU WAKE UP GASPING FOR BREATH IN THE MORNING, AS IF YOU HAVEN'T SLEPT AT ALL?
DO YOU WORK YOUR ASS OFF ONLY TO SEE SOME IDIOT GET THE PROMOTION, THE GIG, THE GRANT MONEY, BECAUSE HE'S A PHOTOGENIC GYM RAT WHO ONLY TELLS PEOPLE EXACTLY WHAT THEY WANT TO HEAR?
MAYBE YOU BLAME YOURSELF.
IF ONLY YOU'D WORKED A LITTLE HARDER. IF ONLY YOU'D KEPT A POSITIVITY JOURNAL. IF ONLY YOU ATE MORE SALAD. MAYBE THEN YOU'D GET THE GIG AND THE VIEWS AND THE SIZE FOUR BODY.
LIVE
WELL I HAVE BAD NEWS, SWEET SIBLINGS.
MOST PEOPLE WHO WORK THEIR ASSES OFF DON'T GET A DAMN THING.
2003

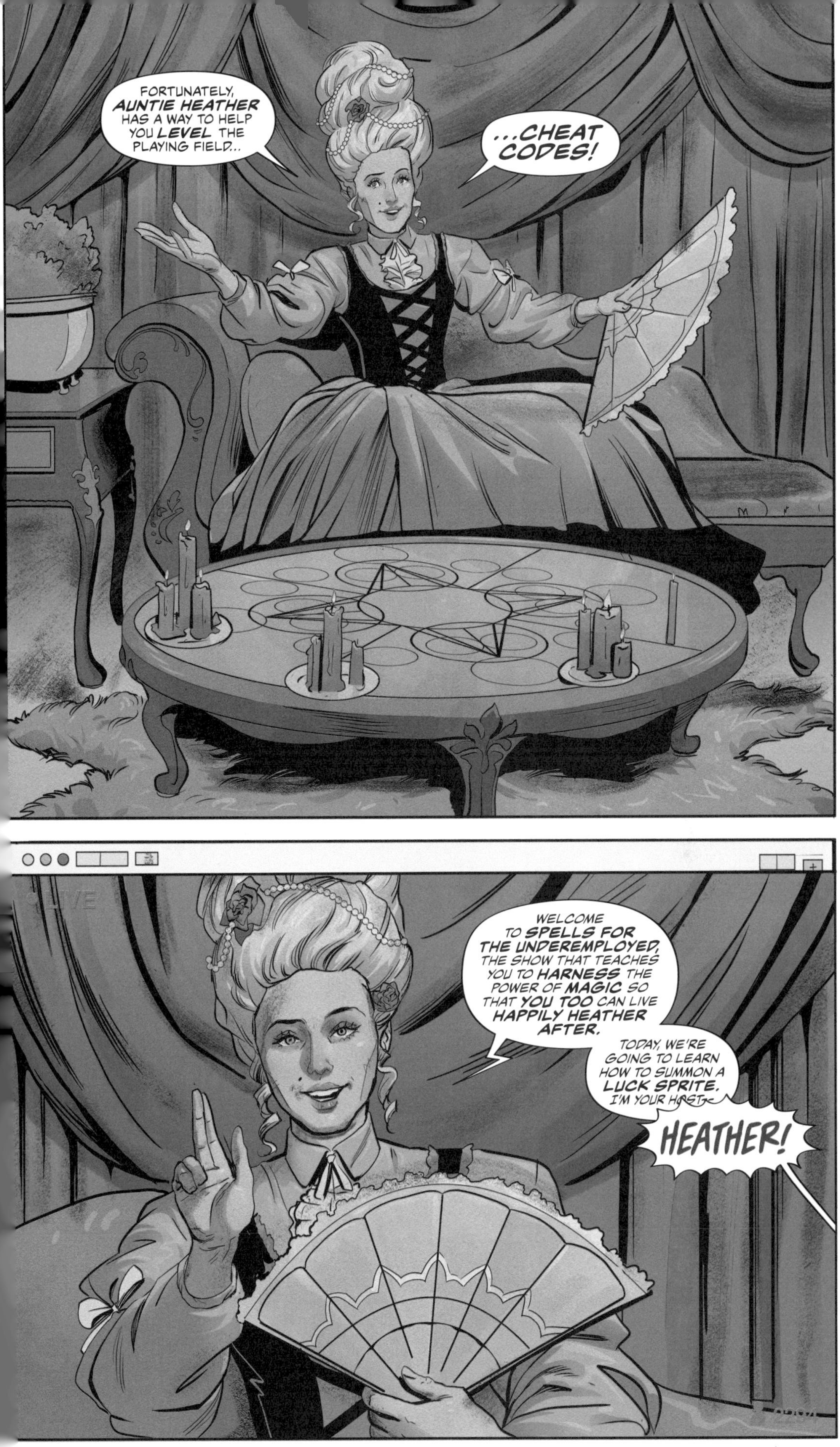
FORTUNATELY, AUNTIE HEATHER HAS A WAY TO HELP YOU LEVEL THE PLAYING FIELD...
...CHEAT CODES!
WELCOME TO SPELLS FOR THE UNDEREMPLOYED, THE SHOW THAT TEACHES YOU TO HARNESS THE POWER OF MAGIC SO THAT YOU TOO CAN LIVE HAPPILY HEATHER AFTER.
TODAY, WE'RE GOING TO LEARN HOW TO SUMMON A LUCK SPRITE. I'M YOUR HOST—
HEATHER!

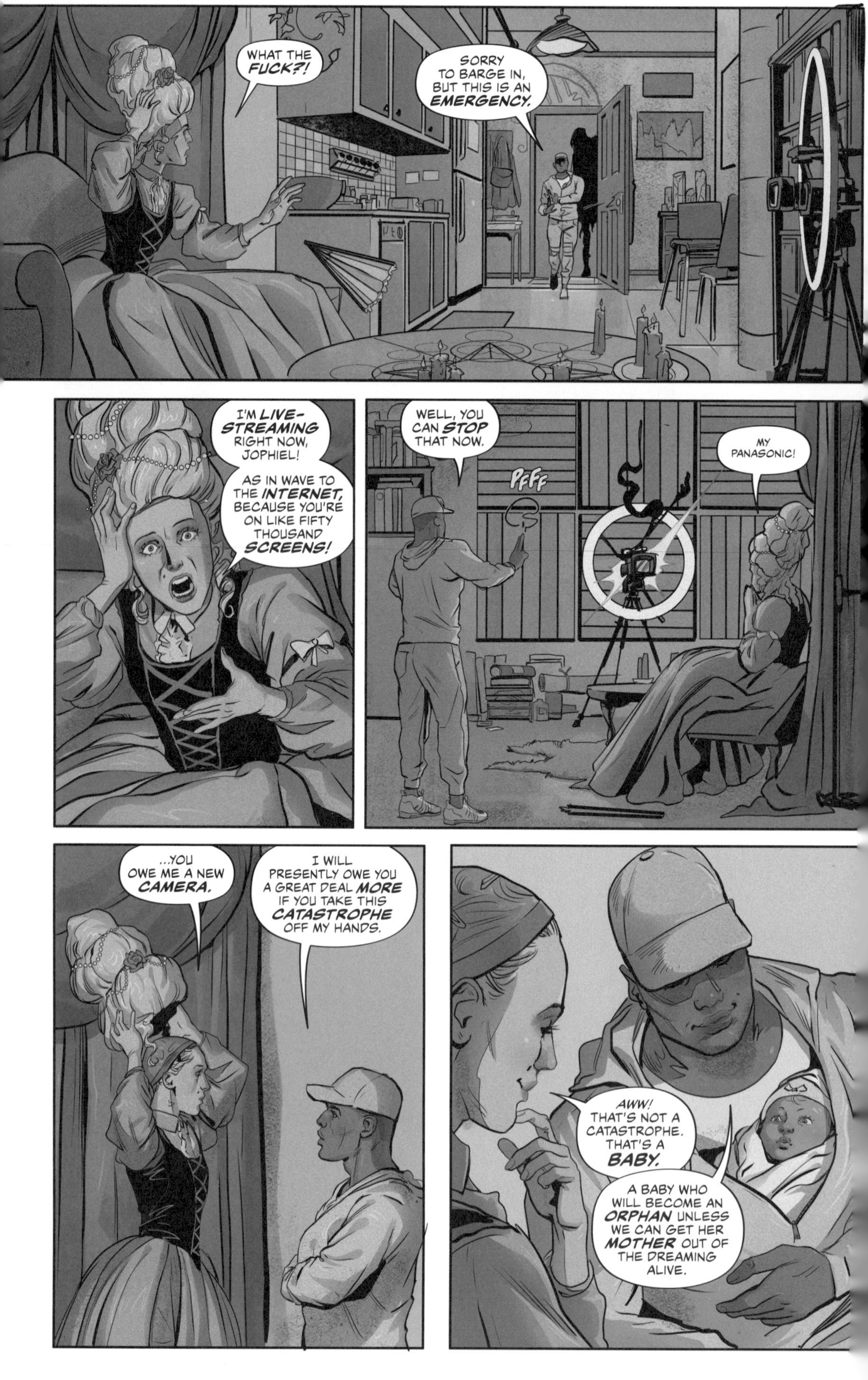
WHAT THE FUCK?!
SORRY TO BARGE IN, BUT THIS IS AN EMERGENCY.
I'M LIVE-STREAMING RIGHT NOW, JOPHIEL!
AS IN WAVE TO THE INTERNET, BECAUSE YOU'RE ON LIKE FIFTY THOUSAND SCREENS!
WELL, YOU CAN STOP THAT NOW.
PFFF
MY PANASONIC!
...YOU OWE ME A NEW CAMERA.
I WILL PRESENTLY OWE YOU A GREAT DEAL MORE IF YOU TAKE THIS CATASTROPHE OFF MY HANDS.
AWW! THAT'S NOT A CATASTROPHE. THAT'S A BABY.
A BABY WHO WILL BECOME AN ORPHAN UNLESS WE CAN GET HER MOTHER OUT OF THE DREAMING ALIVE.

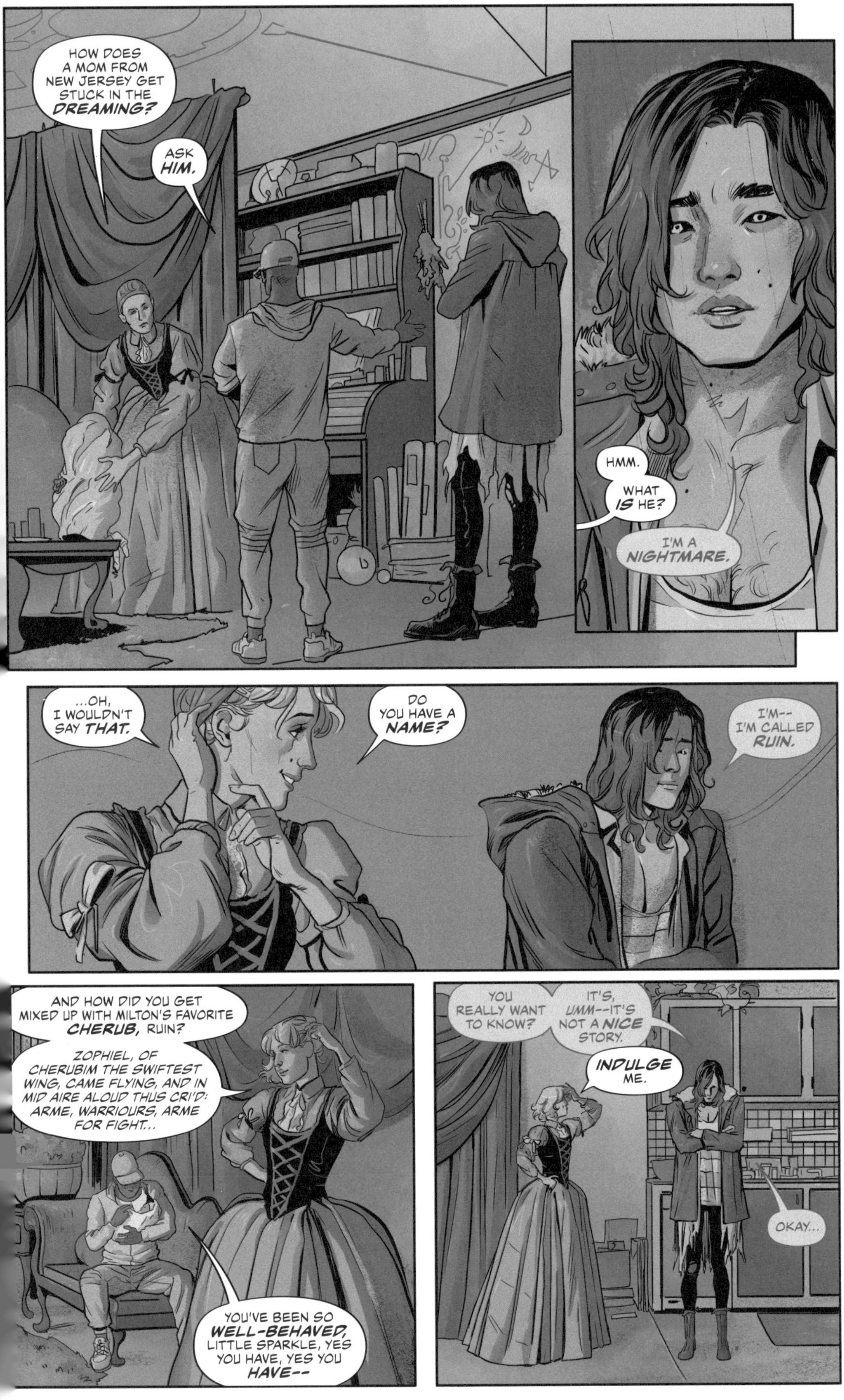
HOW DOES A MOM FROM NEW JERSEY GET STUCK IN THE DREAMING?
ASK HIM.
HMM.
WHAT IS HE?
I'M A NIGHTMARE.
...OH, I WOULDN'T SAY THAT.
DO YOU HAVE A NAME?
I'M-- I'M CALLED RUIN.
AND HOW DID YOU GET MIXED UP WITH MILTON'S FAVORITE CHERUB, RUIN?
ZOPHIEL, OF CHERUBIM THE SWIFTEST WING, CAME FLYING, AND IN MID AIRE ALOUD THUS CRI'D: ARME, WARRIOURS, ARME FOR FIGHT...
YOU'VE BEEN SO WELL-BEHAVED, LITTLE SPARKLE, YES YOU HAVE, YES YOU HAVE--
YOU REALLY WANT TO KNOW?
IT'S, UMM--IT'S NOT A NICE STORY.
INDULGE ME.
OKAY...

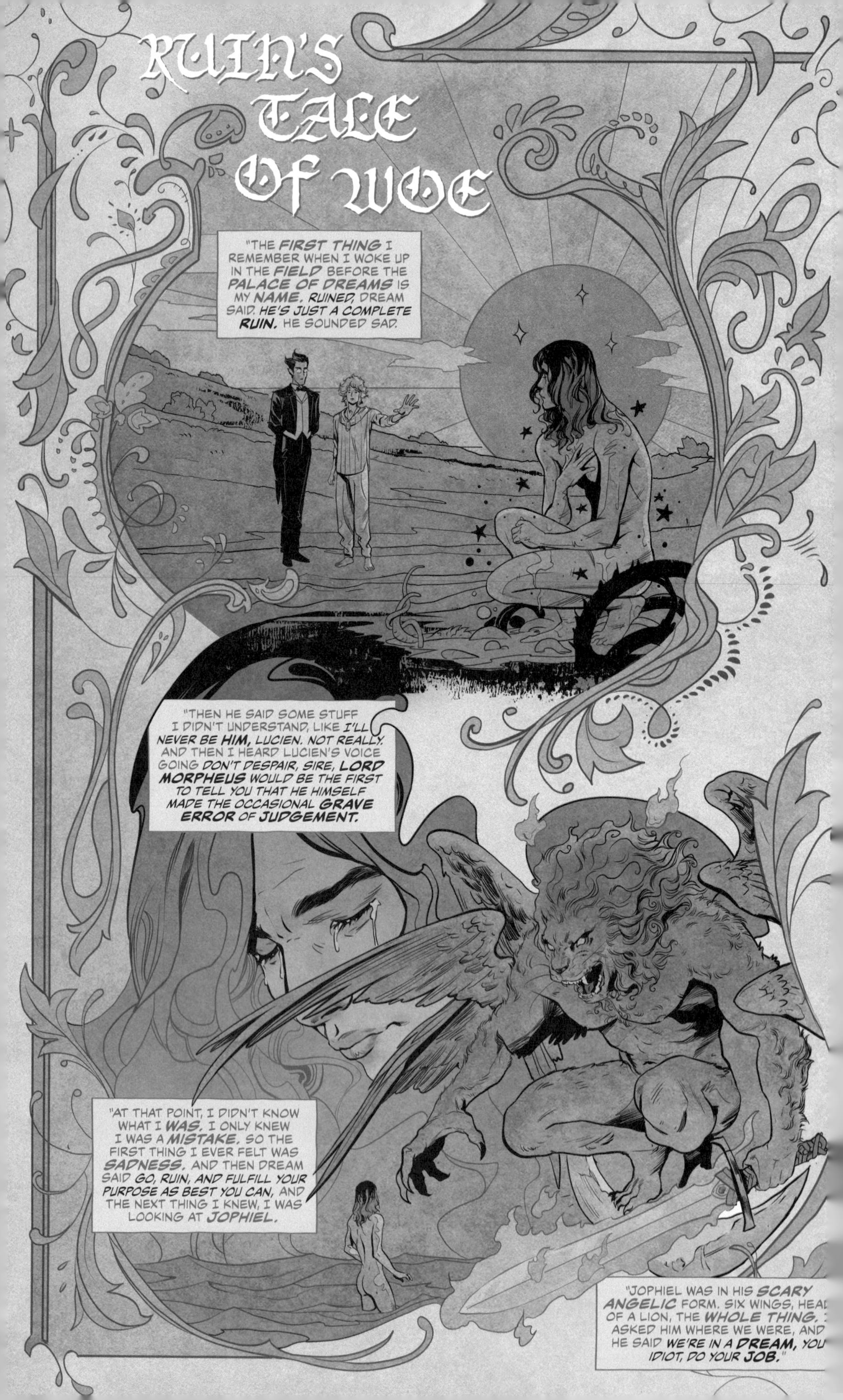
RUIN'S TALE OF WOE
"THE FIRST THING I REMEMBER WHEN I WOKE UP IN THE FIELD BEFORE THE PALACE OF DREAMS IS MY NAME. RUINED, DREAM SAID. HE'S JUST A COMPLETE RUIN. HE SOUNDED SAD.
"THEN HE SAID SOME STUFF I DIDN'T UNDERSTAND, LIKE I'LL NEVER BE HIM, LUCIEN. NOT REALLY. AND THEN I HEARD LUCIEN'S VOICE GOING DON'T DESPAIR, SIRE, LORD MORPHEUS WOULD BE THE FIRST TO TELL YOU THAT HE HIMSELF MADE THE OCCASIONAL GRAVE ERROR OF JUDGEMENT.
"AT THAT POINT, I DIDN'T KNOW WHAT I WAS. I ONLY KNEW I WAS A MISTAKE. SO THE FIRST THING I EVER FELT WAS SADNESS. AND THEN DREAM SAID GO, RUIN, AND FULFILL YOUR PURPOSE AS BEST YOU CAN, AND THE NEXT THING I KNEW, I WAS LOOKING AT JOPHIEL.
"JOPHIEL WAS IN HIS SCARY ANGELIC FORM. SIX WINGS, HEA OF A LION, THE WHOLE THING. ASKED HIM WHERE WE WERE, AND HE SAID WE'RE IN A DREAM, YOU IDIOT, DO YOUR JOB."

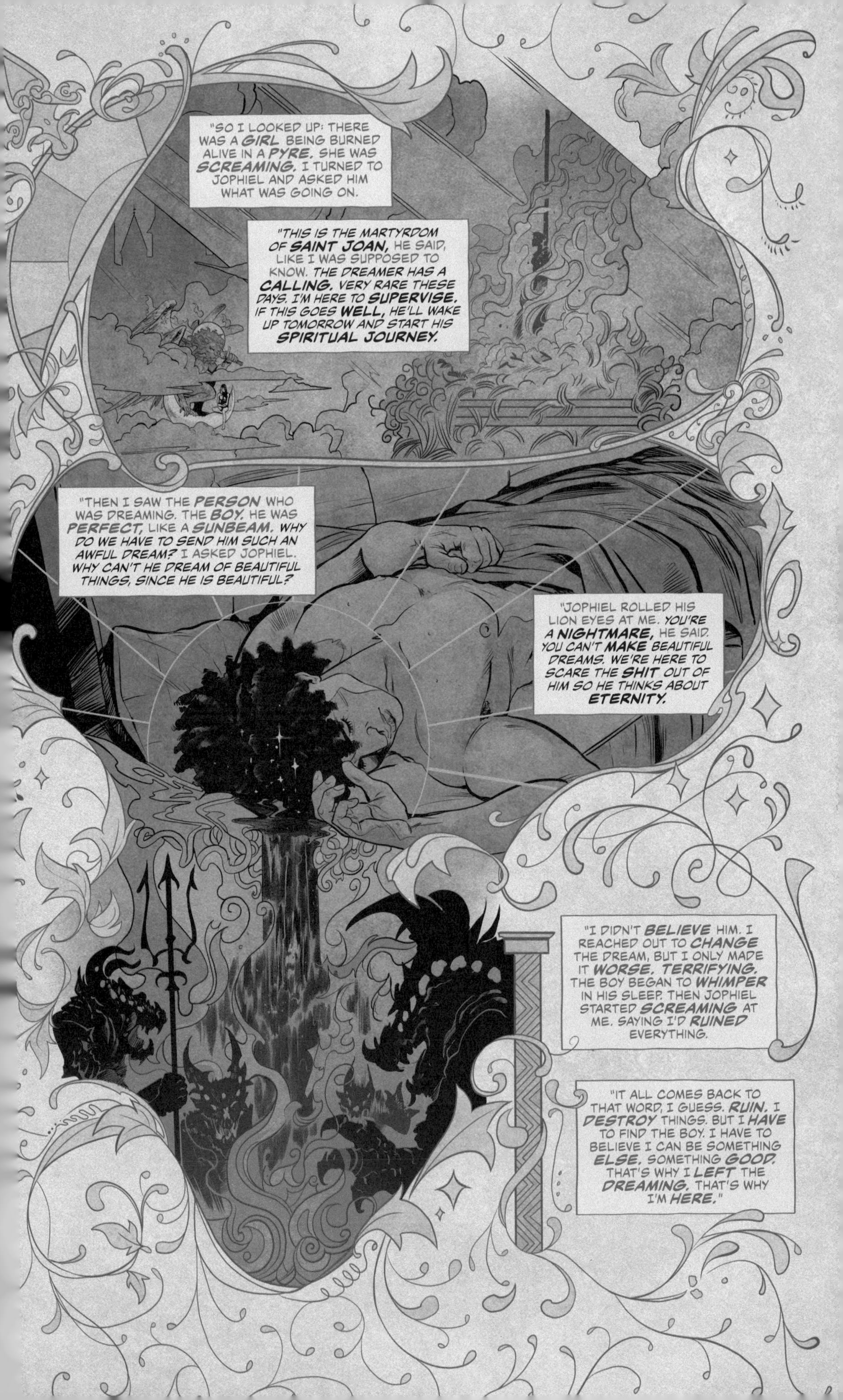
"SO I LOOKED UP: THERE WAS A GIRL BEING BURNED ALIVE IN A PYRE. SHE WAS SCREAMING. I TURNED TO JOPHIEL AND ASKED HIM WHAT WAS GOING ON.
"THIS IS THE MARTYRDOM OF SAINT JOAN, HE SAID, LIKE I WAS SUPPOSED TO KNOW. THE DREAMER HAS A CALLING. VERY RARE THESE DAYS. I'M HERE TO SUPERVISE. IF THIS GOES WELL, HE'LL WAKE UP TOMORROW AND START HIS SPIRITUAL JOURNEY.
"THEN I SAW THE PERSON WHO WAS DREAMING. THE BOY. HE WAS PERFECT, LIKE A SUNBEAM. WHY DO WE HAVE TO SEND HIM SUCH AN AWFUL DREAM? I ASKED JOPHIEL. WHY CAN'T HE DREAM OF BEAUTIFUL THINGS, SINCE HE IS BEAUTIFUL?
"JOPHIEL ROLLED HIS LION EYES AT ME. YOU'RE A NIGHTMARE, HE SAID. YOU CAN'T MAKE BEAUTIFUL DREAMS. WE'RE HERE TO SCARE THE SHIT OUT OF HIM SO HE THINKS ABOUT ETERNITY.
"I DIDN'T BELIEVE HIM. I REACHED OUT TO CHANGE THE DREAM, BUT I ONLY MADE IT WORSE. TERRIFYING. THE BOY BEGAN TO WHIMPER IN HIS SLEEP. THEN JOPHIEL STARTED SCREAMING AT ME. SAYING I'D RUINED EVERYTHING.
"IT ALL COMES BACK TO THAT WORD, I GUESS. RUIN. I DESTROY THINGS. BUT I HAVE TO FIND THE BOY. I HAVE TO BELIEVE I CAN BE SOMETHING ELSE. SOMETHING GOOD. THAT'S WHY I LEFT THE DREAMING. THAT'S WHY I'M HERE."

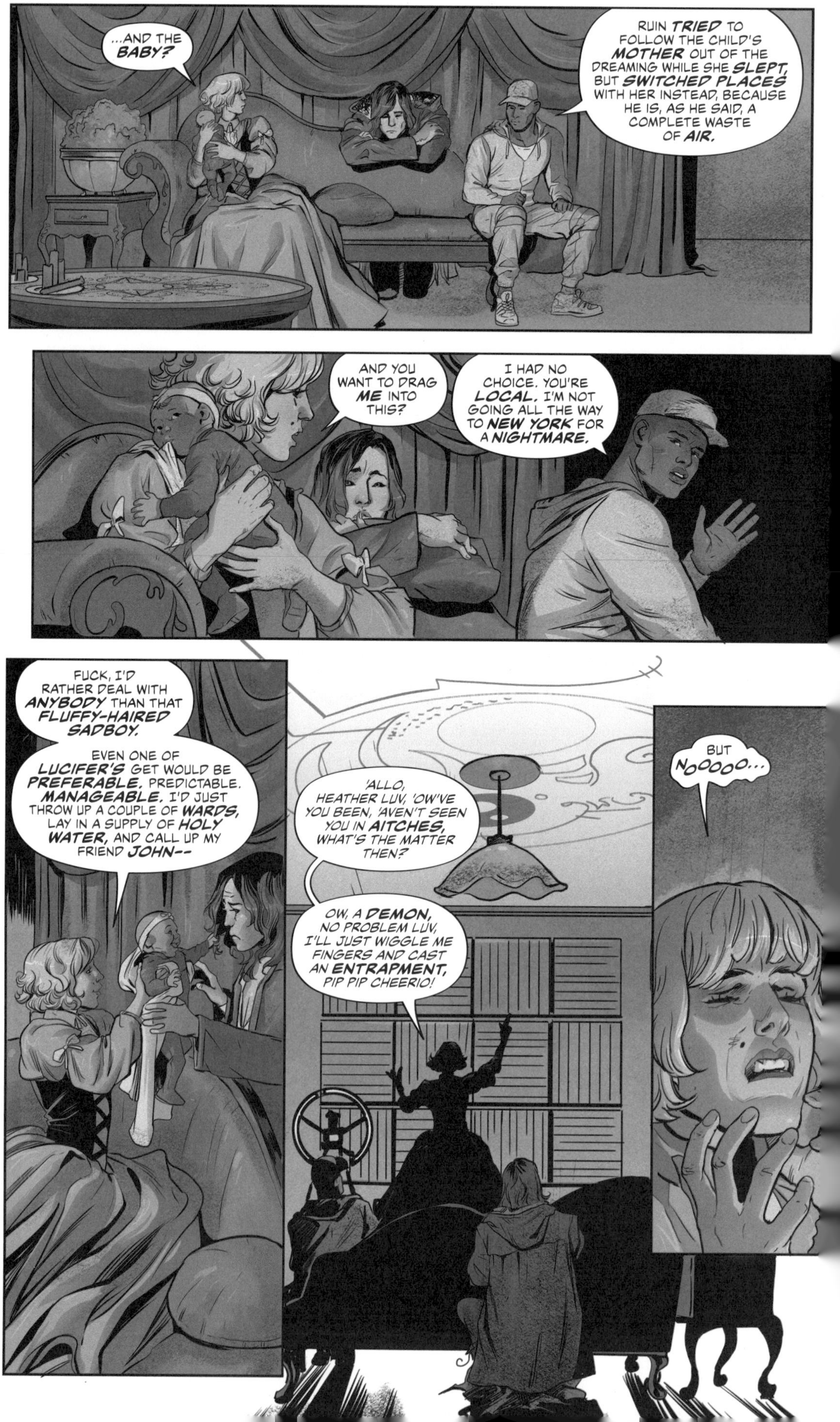
...AND THE BABY?
RUIN TRIED TO FOLLOW THE CHILD'S MOTHER OUT OF THE DREAMING WHILE SHE SLEPT, BUT SWITCHED PLACES WITH HER INSTEAD, BECAUSE HE IS, AS HE SAID, A COMPLETE WASTE OF AIR.
AND YOU WANT TO DRAG ME INTO THIS?
I HAD NO CHOICE. YOU'RE LOCAL. I'M NOT GOING ALL THE WAY TO NEW YORK FOR A NIGHTMARE.
FUCK, I'D RATHER DEAL WITH ANYBODY THAN THAT FLUFFY-HAIRED SADBOY.
EVEN ONE OF LUCIFER'S GET WOULD BE PREFERABLE. PREDICTABLE. MANAGEABLE. I'D JUST THROW UP A COUPLE OF WARDS, LAY IN A SUPPLY OF HOLY WATER, AND CALL UP MY FRIEND JOHN--
'ALLO, HEATHER LUV, 'OW'VE YOU BEEN, 'AVEN'T SEEN YOU IN AITCHES, WHAT'S THE MATTER THEN?
OW, A DEMON, NO PROBLEM LUV, I'LL JUST WIGGLE ME FINGERS AND CAST AN ENTRAPMENT, PIP PIP CHEERIO!
BUT NOOOOO...

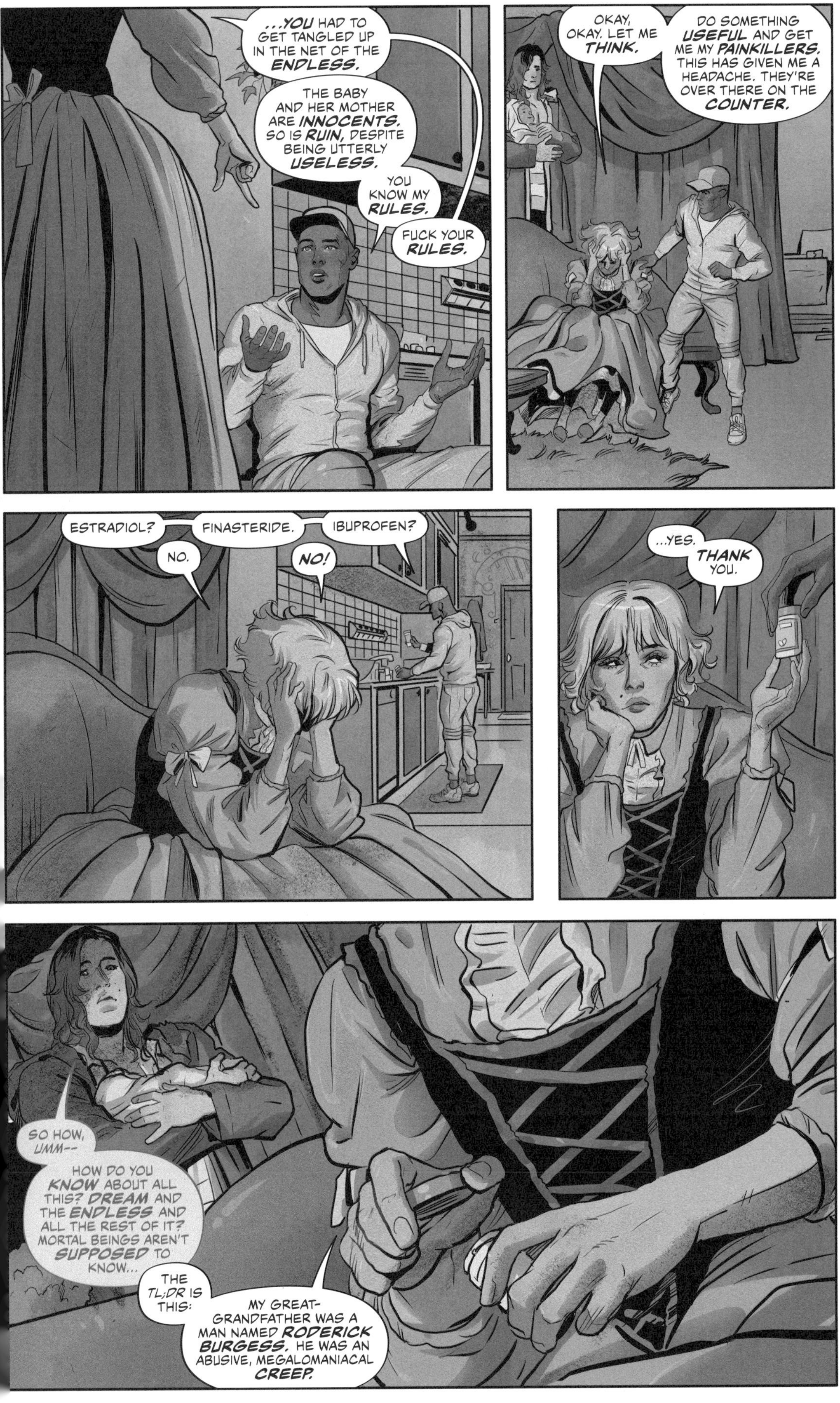
...YOU HAD TO GET TANGLED UP IN THE NET OF THE ENDLESS.
THE BABY AND HER MOTHER ARE INNOCENTS. SO IS RUIN, DESPITE BEING UTTERLY USELESS.
YOU KNOW MY RULES.
FUCK YOUR RULES.
OKAY, OKAY. LET ME THINK.
DO SOMETHING USEFUL AND GET ME MY PAINKILLERS. THIS HAS GIVEN ME A HEADACHE. THEY'RE OVER THERE ON THE COUNTER.
ESTRADIOL?
NO.
FINASTERIDE.
NO!
IBUPROFEN?
...YES. THANK YOU.
SO HOW, UMM--
HOW DO YOU KNOW ABOUT ALL THIS? DREAM AND THE ENDLESS AND ALL THE REST OF IT? MORTAL BEINGS AREN'T SUPPOSED TO KNOW...
THE TL;DR IS THIS:
MY GREAT-GRANDFATHER WAS A MAN NAMED RODERICK BURGESS. HE WAS AN ABUSIVE, MEGALOMANIACAL CREEP.

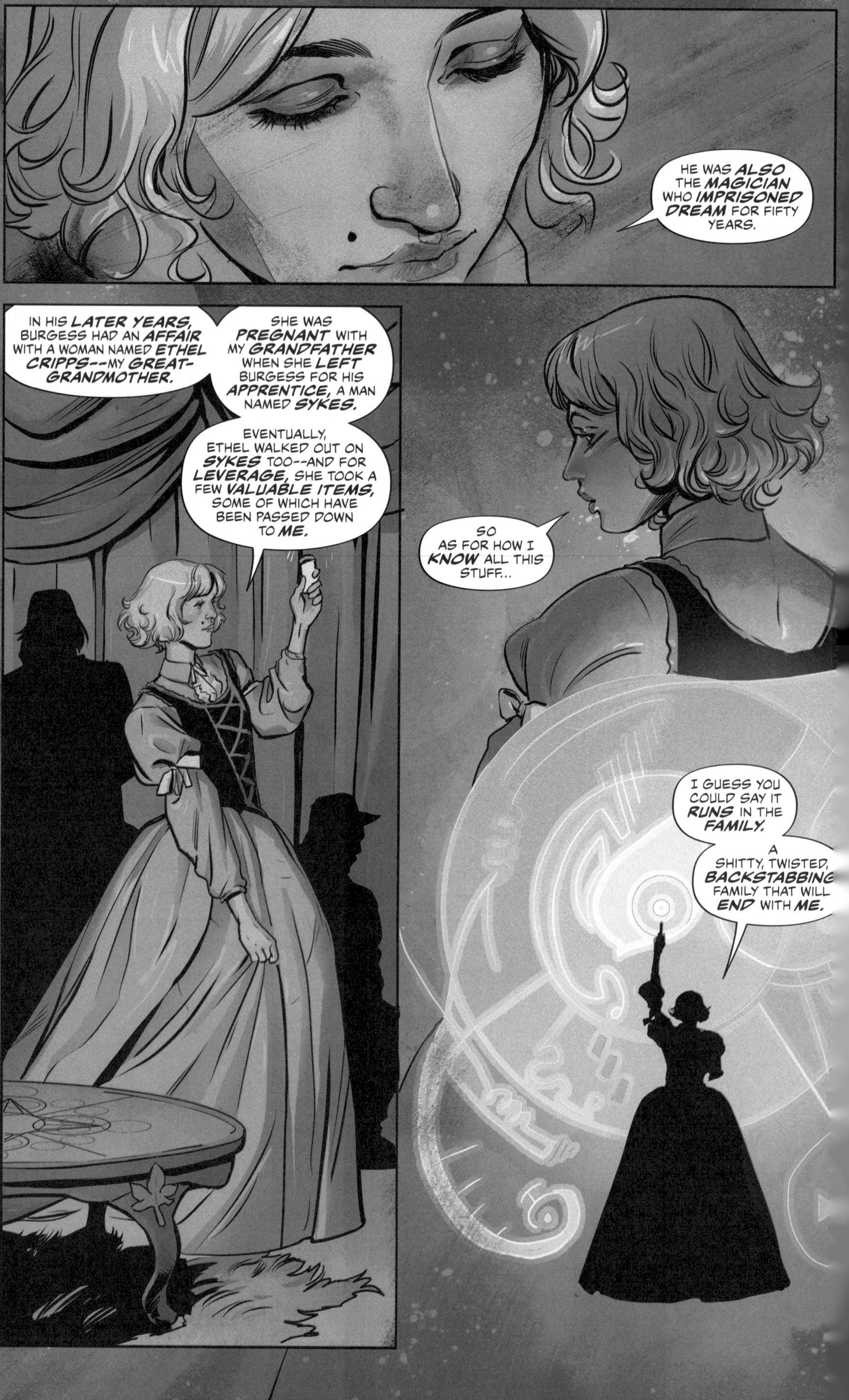
HE WAS ALSO THE MAGICIAN WHO IMPRISONED DREAM FOR FIFTY YEARS.
IN HIS LATER YEARS, BURGESS HAD AN AFFAIR WITH A WOMAN NAMED ETHEL CRIPPS--MY GREAT-GRANDMOTHER.
SHE WAS PREGNANT WITH MY GRANDFATHER WHEN SHE LEFT BURGESS FOR HIS APPRENTICE, A MAN NAMED SYKES.
EVENTUALLY, ETHEL WALKED OUT ON SYKES TOO--AND FOR LEVERAGE, SHE TOOK A FEW VALUABLE ITEMS, SOME OF WHICH HAVE BEEN PASSED DOWN TO ME.
SO AS FOR HOW I KNOW ALL THIS STUFF...
I GUESS YOU COULD SAY IT RUNS IN THE FAMILY.
A SHITTY, TWISTED, BACKSTABBING FAMILY THAT WILL END WITH ME.

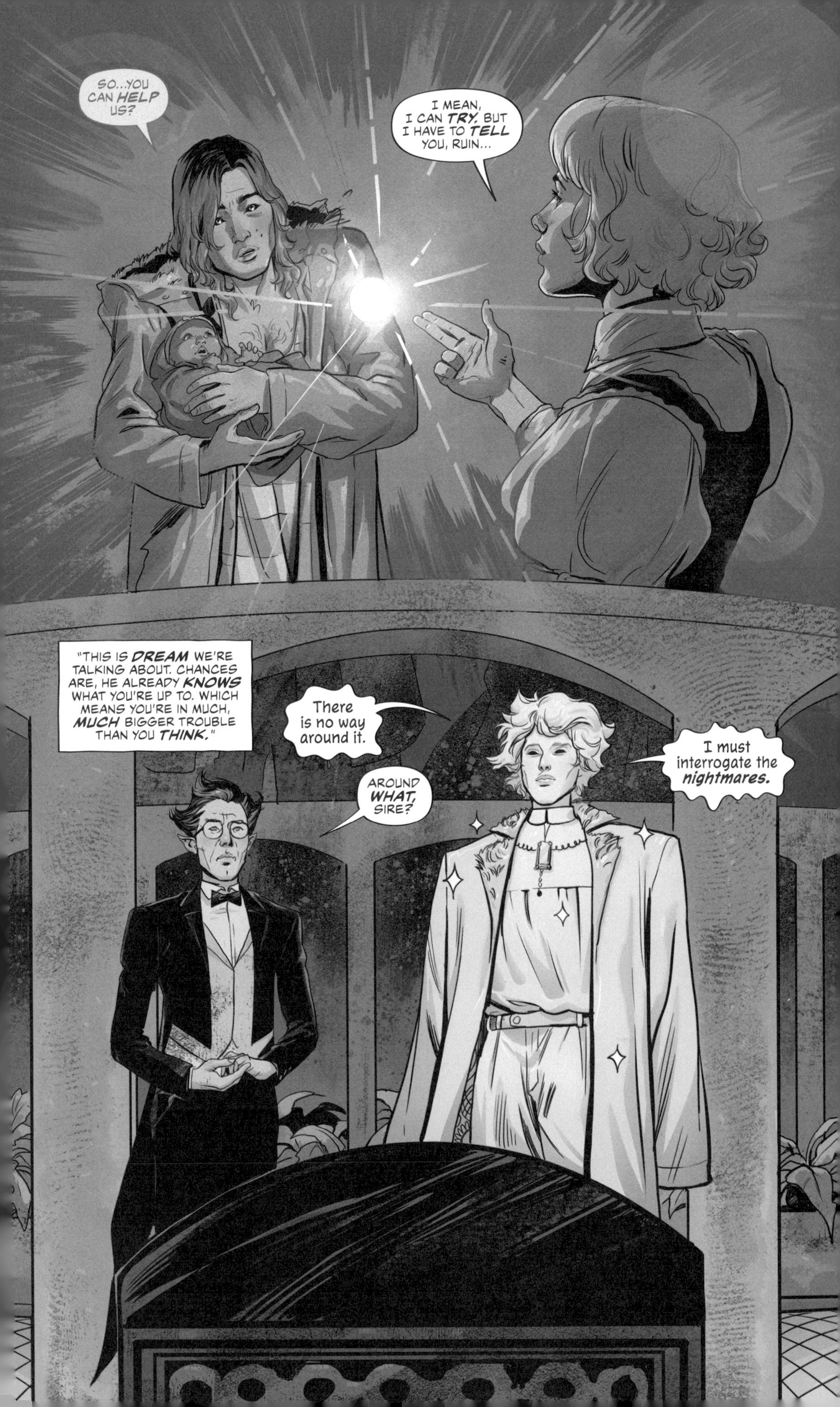
SO...YOU CAN HELP US?
I MEAN, I CAN TRY. BUT I HAVE TO TELL YOU, RUIN...
"THIS IS DREAM WE'RE TALKING ABOUT. CHANCES ARE, HE ALREADY KNOWS WHAT YOU'RE UP TO. WHICH MEANS YOU'RE IN MUCH, MUCH BIGGER TROUBLE THAN YOU THINK."
There is no way around it.
I must interrogate the nightmares.
AROUND WHAT, SIRE?

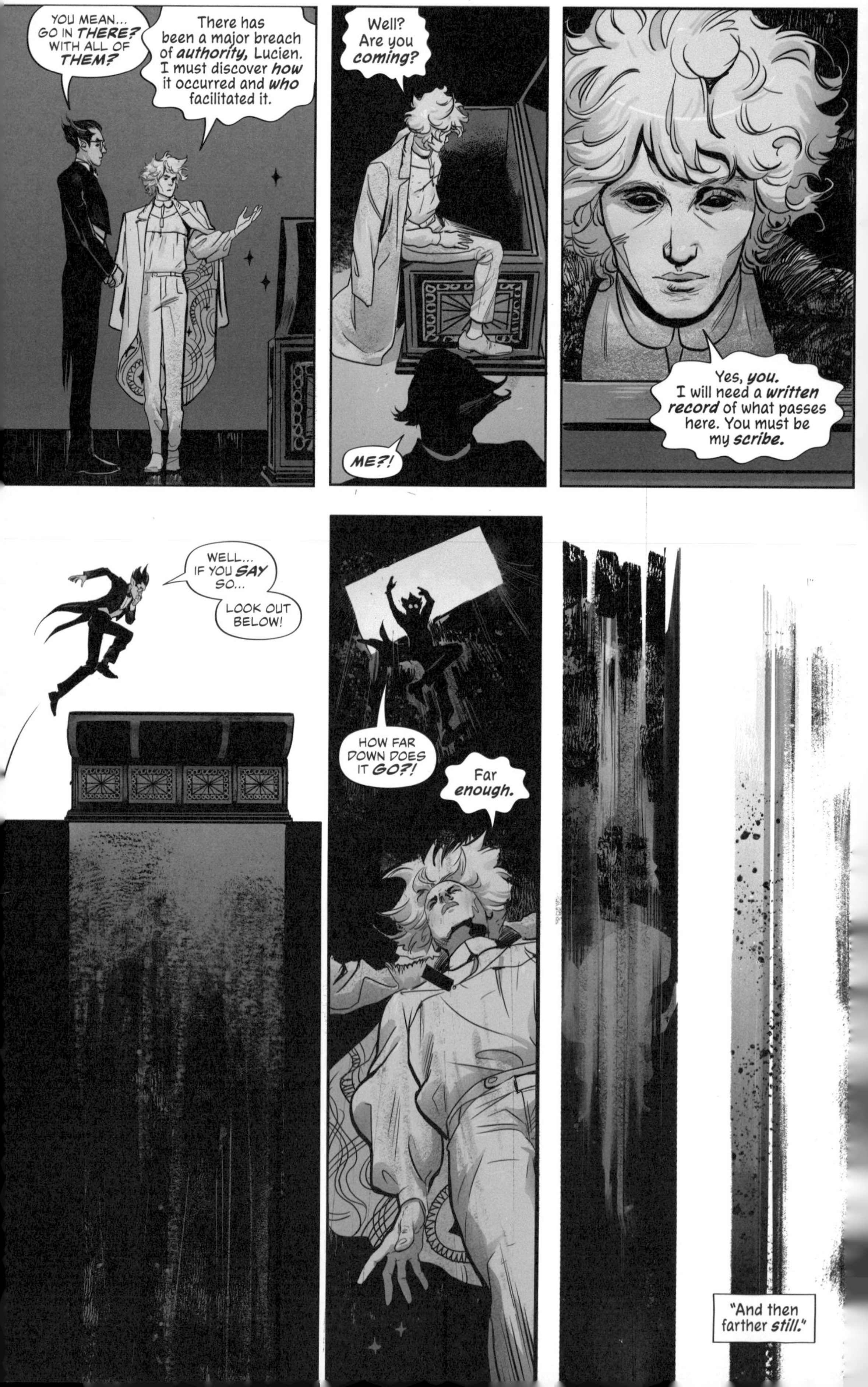
YOU MEAN... GO IN THERE? WITH ALL OF THEM?
There has been a major breach of authority, Lucien. I must discover how it occurred and who facilitated it.
Well? Are you coming?
ME?!
Yes, you. I will need a written record of what passes here. You must be my scribe.
WELL... IF YOU SAY SO...
LOOK OUT BELOW!
HOW FAR DOWN DOES IT GO?!
Far enough.
"And then farther still."

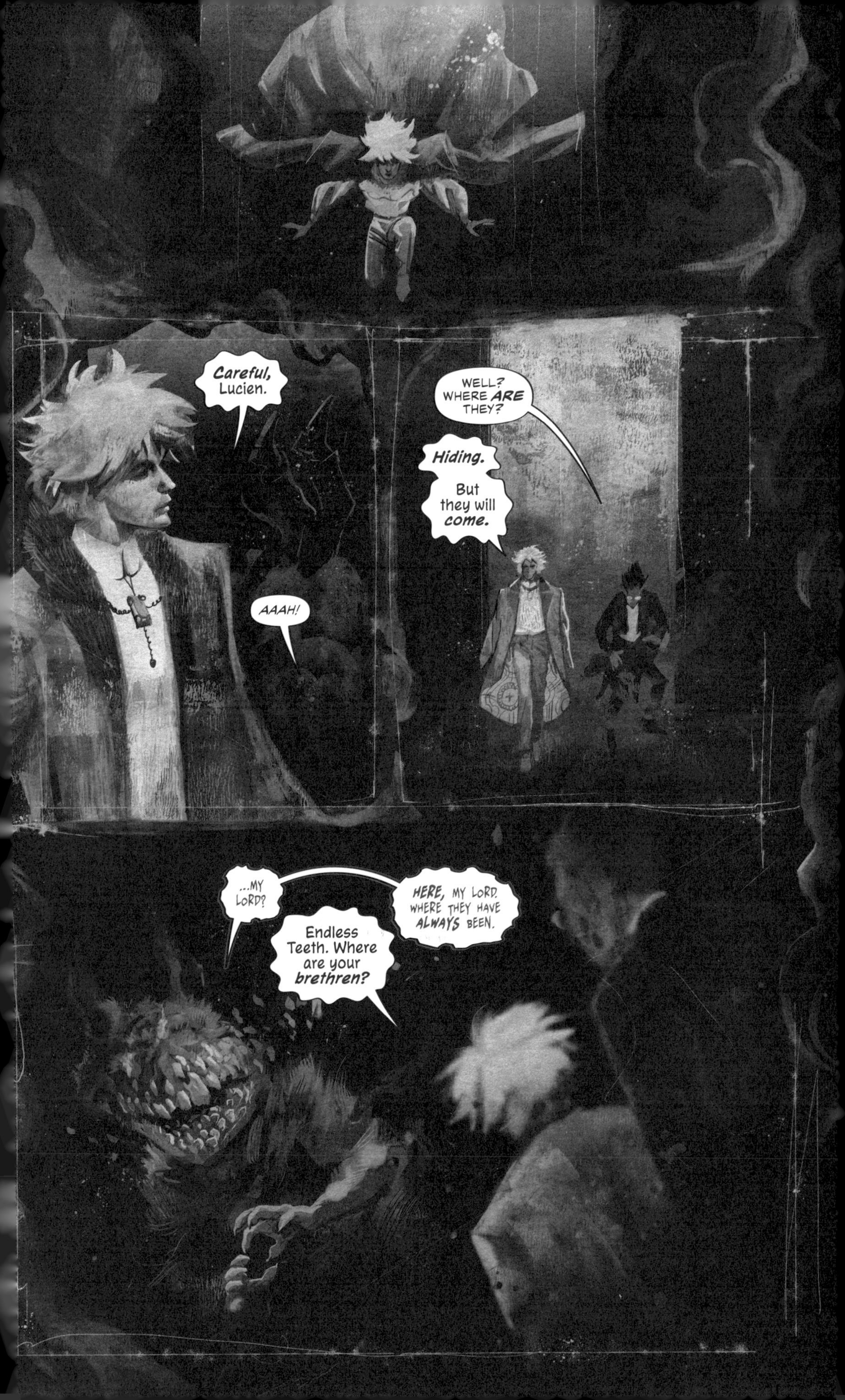

Careful, Lucien.
AAAH!
WELL? WHERE ARE THEY?
Hiding.
But they will come.
...MY LORD?
Endless Teeth. Where are your brethren?
HERE, MY LORD. WHERE THEY HAVE ALWAYS BEEN.

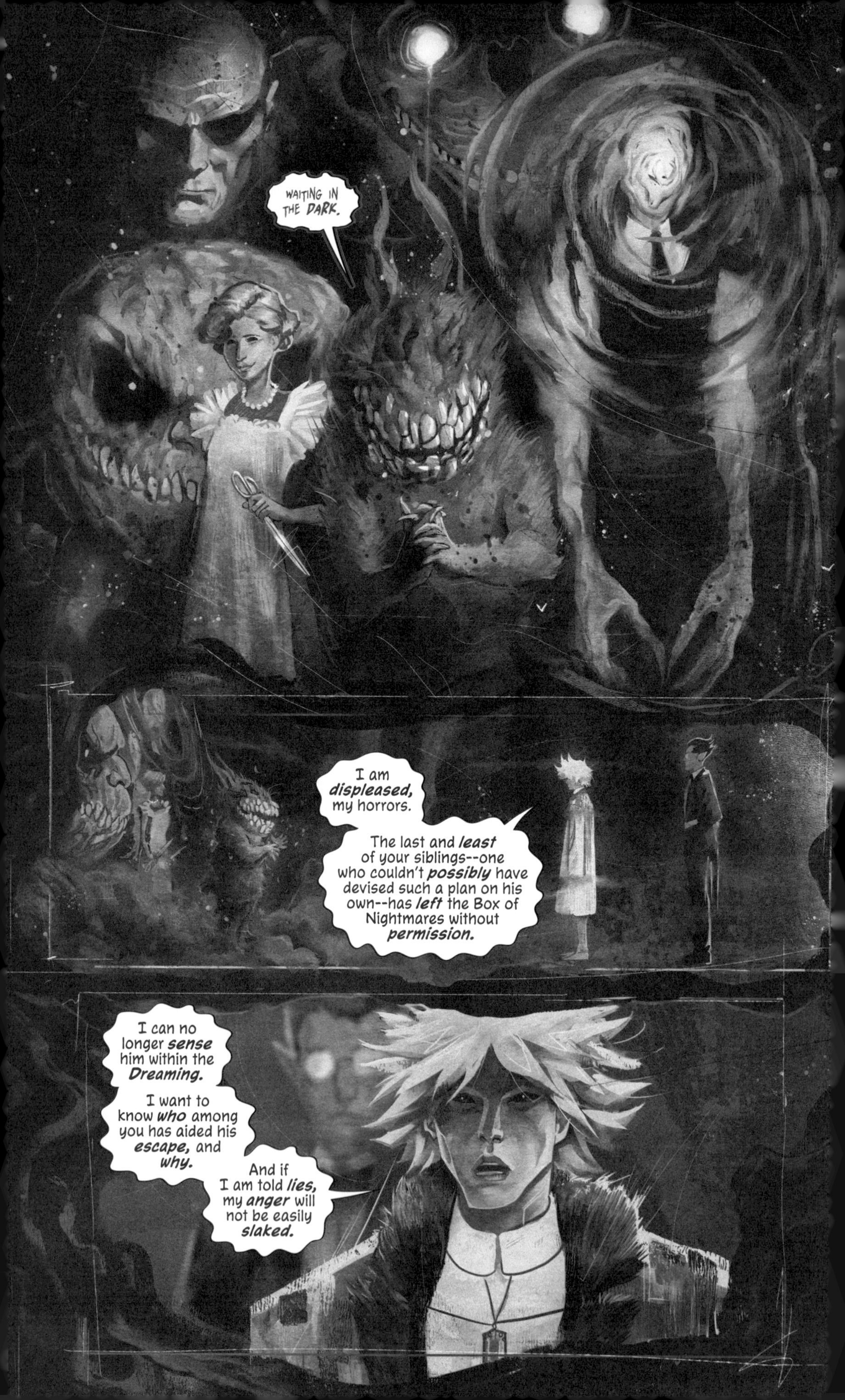
WAITING IN THE DARK.
I am displeased, my horrors.
The last and least of your siblings--one who couldn't possibly have devised such a plan on his own--has left the Box of Nightmares without permission.
I can no longer sense him within the Dreaming.
I want to know who among you has aided his escape, and why.
And if I am told lies, my anger will not be easily slaked.

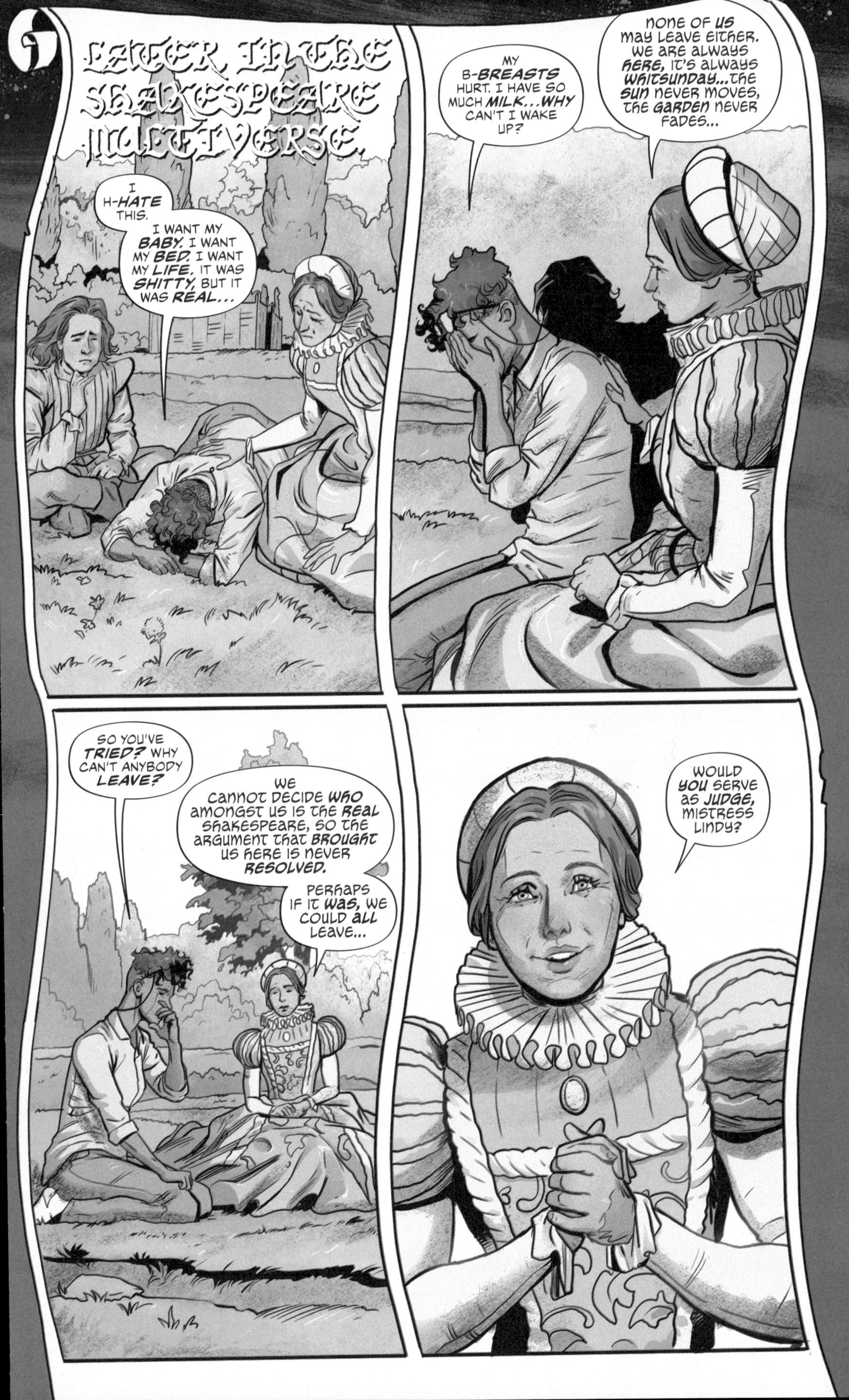
LATER IN THE SHAKESPEARE MULTIVERSE.
I H-HATE THIS.
I WANT MY BABY. I WANT MY BED. I WANT MY LIFE. IT WAS SHITTY, BUT IT WAS REAL...
MY B-BREASTS HURT. I HAVE SO MUCH MILK...WHY CAN'T I WAKE UP?
NONE OF US MAY LEAVE EITHER. WE ARE ALWAYS HERE, IT'S ALWAYS WHITSUNDAY...THE SUN NEVER MOVES, THE GARDEN NEVER FADES...
SO YOU'VE TRIED? WHY CAN'T ANYBODY LEAVE?
WE CANNOT DECIDE WHO AMONGST US IS THE REAL SHAKESPEARE, SO THE ARGUMENT THAT BROUGHT US HERE IS NEVER RESOLVED.
PERHAPS IF IT WAS, WE COULD ALL LEAVE...
WOULD YOU SERVE AS JUDGE, MISTRESS LINDY?

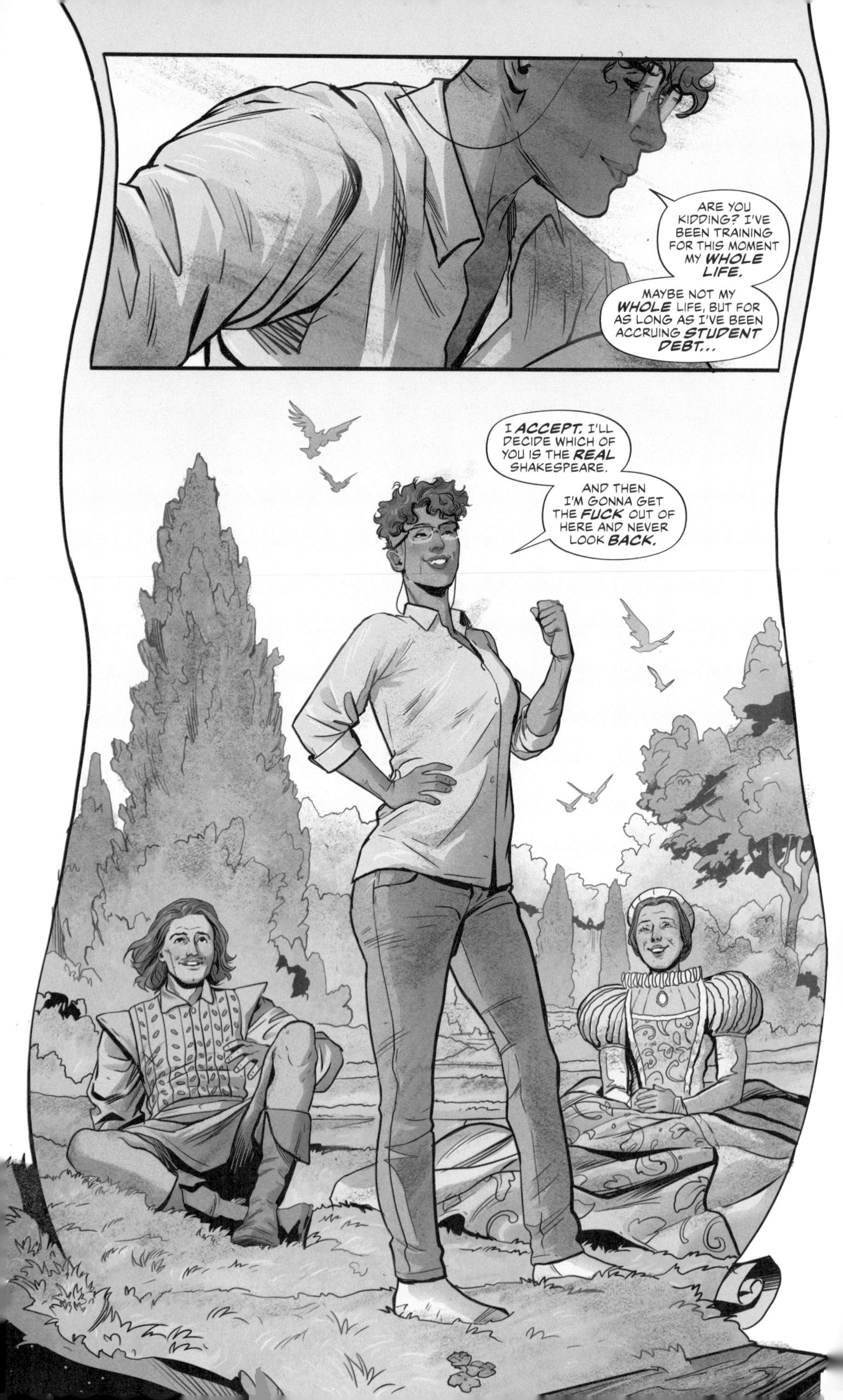
ARE YOU KIDDING? I'VE BEEN TRAINING FOR THIS MOMENT MY WHOLE LIFE.
MAYBE NOT MY WHOLE LIFE, BUT FOR AS LONG AS I'VE BEEN ACCRUING STUDENT DEBT...
I ACCEPT. I'LL DECIDE WHICH OF YOU IS THE REAL SHAKESPEARE.
AND THEN I'M GONNA GET THE FUCK OUT OF HERE AND NEVER LOOK BACK.

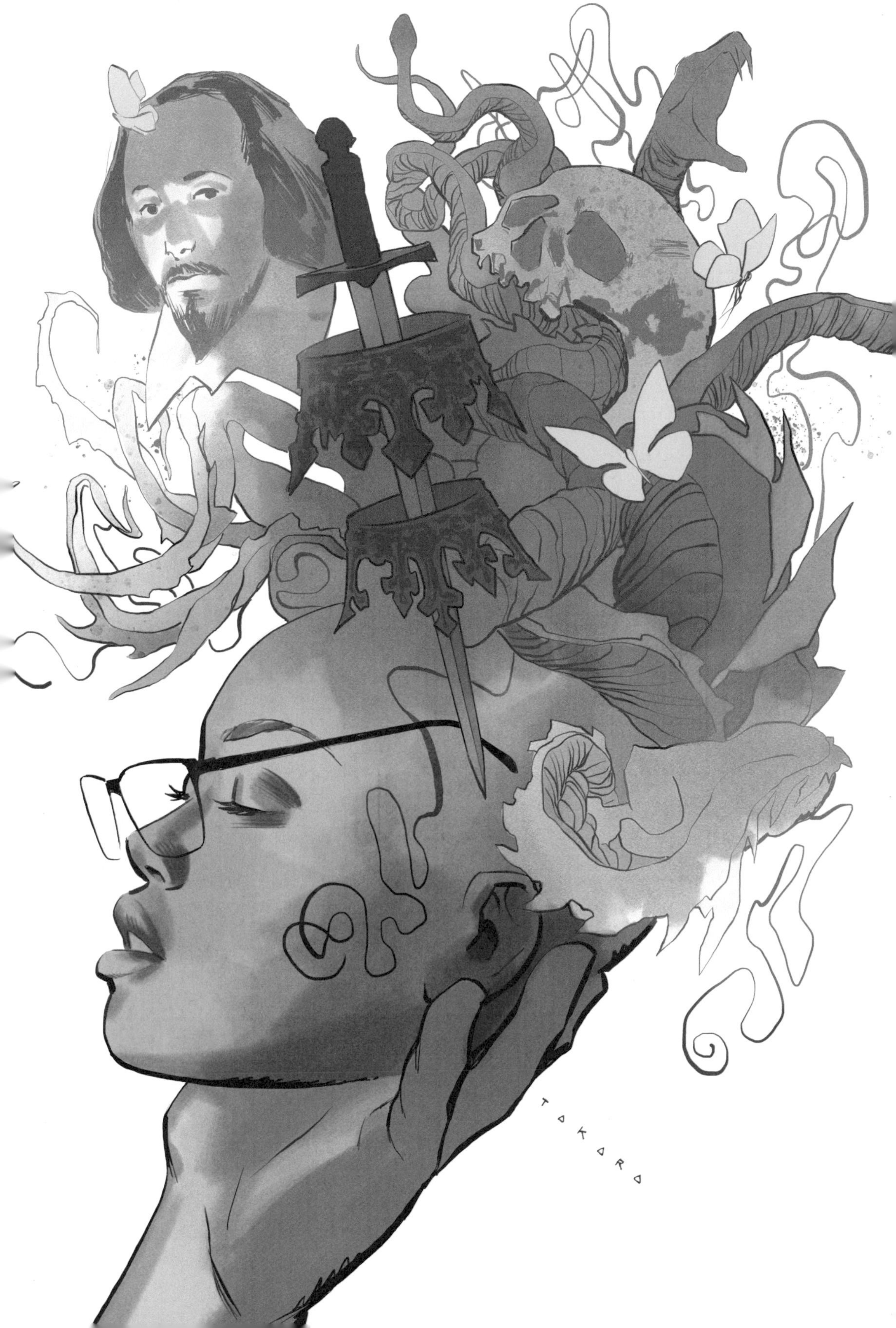
TAKARA

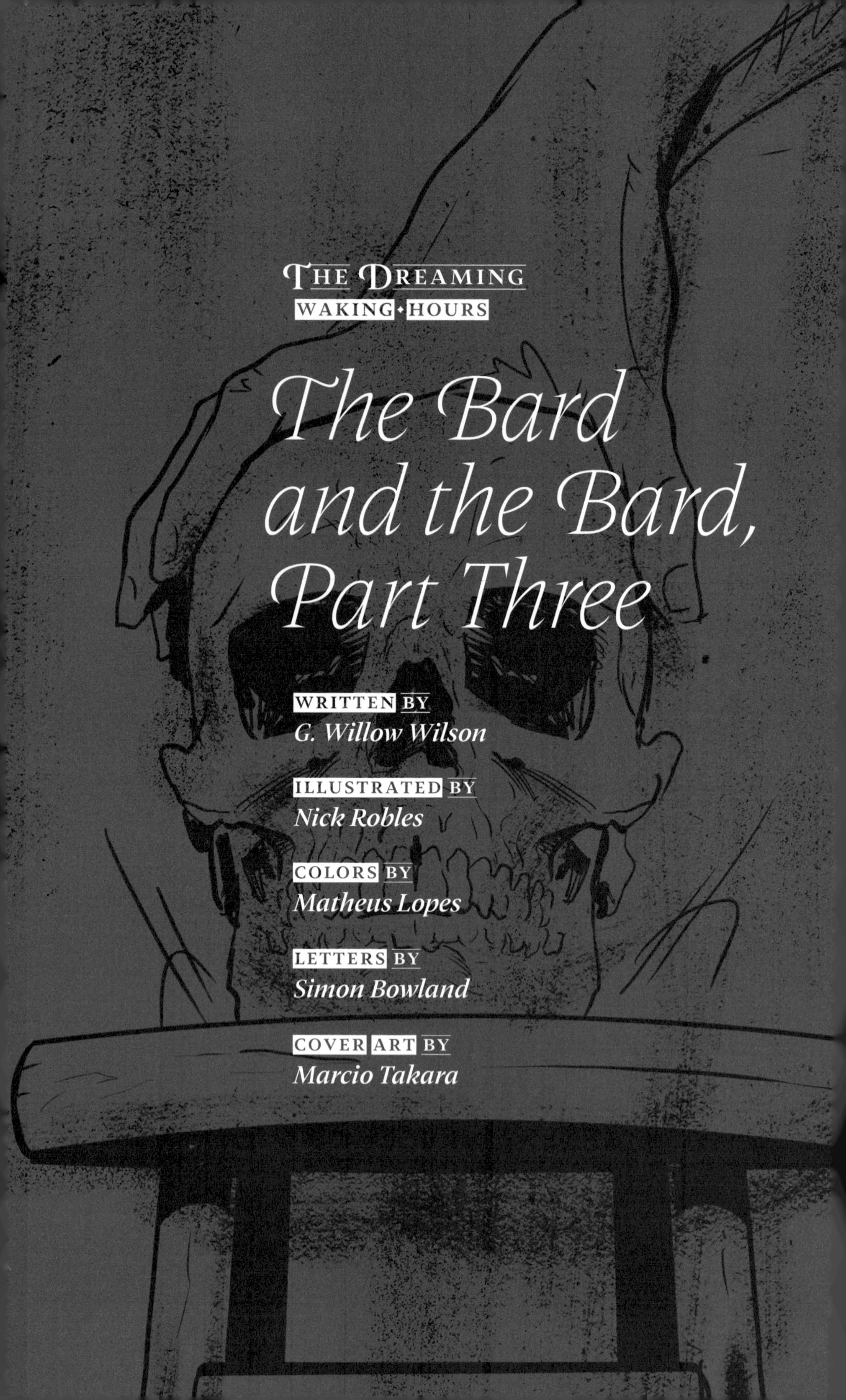

THE DREAMING
WAKING • HOURS

The Bard and the Bard, Part Three

WRITTEN BY
G. Willow Wilson

ILLUSTRATED BY
Nick Robles

COLORS BY
Matheus Lopes

LETTERS BY
Simon Bowland

COVER ART BY
Marcio Takara

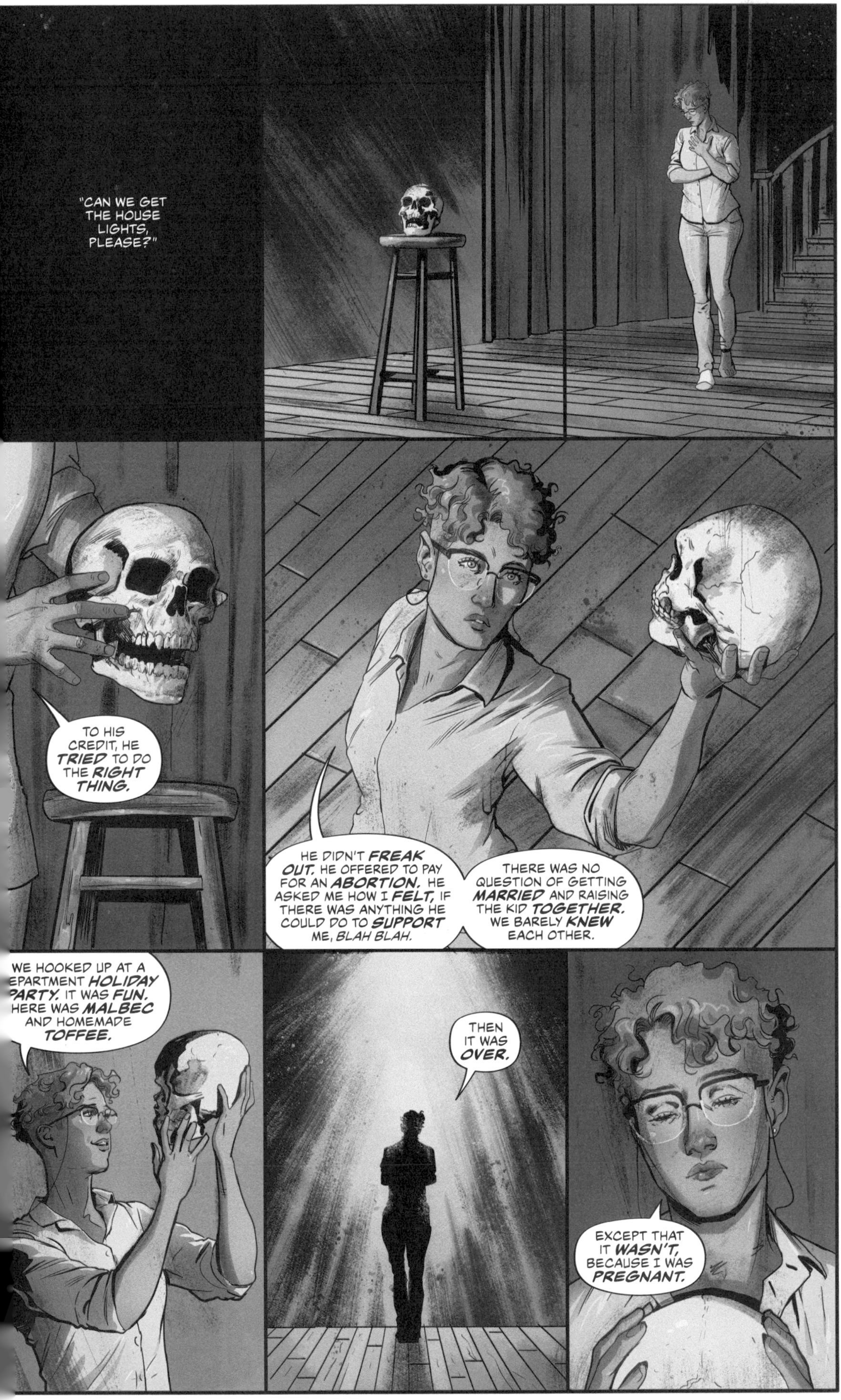
"CAN WE GET THE HOUSE LIGHTS, PLEASE?"
TO HIS CREDIT, HE TRIED TO DO THE RIGHT THING.
HE DIDN'T FREAK OUT. HE OFFERED TO PAY FOR AN ABORTION. HE ASKED ME HOW I FELT, IF THERE WAS ANYTHING HE COULD DO TO SUPPORT ME, BLAH BLAH.
THERE WAS NO QUESTION OF GETTING MARRIED AND RAISING THE KID TOGETHER. WE BARELY KNEW EACH OTHER.
WE HOOKED UP AT A EPARTMENT HOLIDAY ARTY. IT WAS FUN. HERE WAS MALBEC AND HOMEMADE TOFFEE.
THEN IT WAS OVER.
EXCEPT THAT IT WASN'T, BECAUSE I WAS PREGNANT.

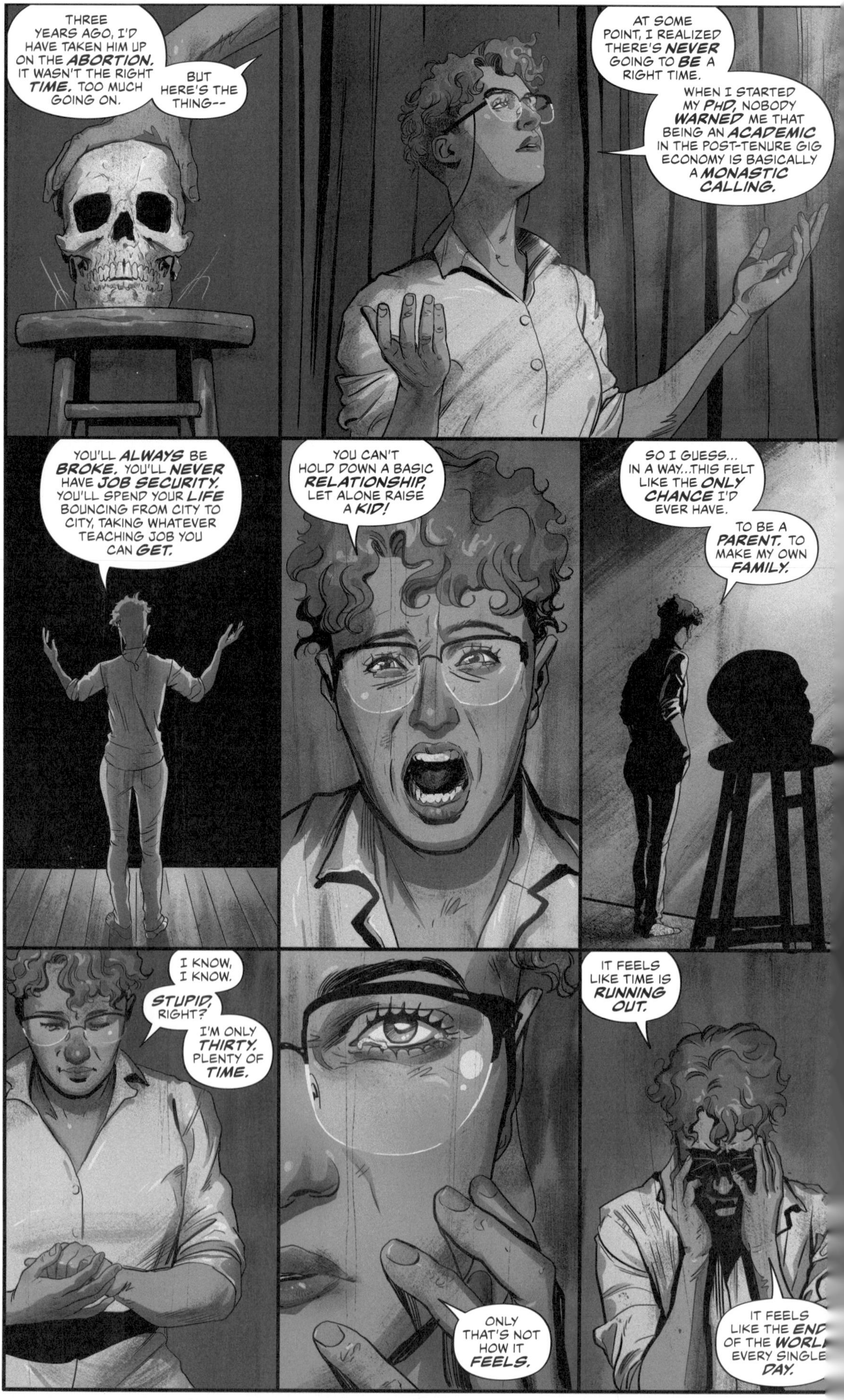
THREE YEARS AGO, I'D HAVE TAKEN HIM UP ON THE ABORTION. IT WASN'T THE RIGHT TIME. TOO MUCH GOING ON.
BUT HERE'S THE THING--
AT SOME POINT, I REALIZED THERE'S NEVER GOING TO BE A RIGHT TIME.
WHEN I STARTED MY PHD, NOBODY WARNED ME THAT BEING AN ACADEMIC IN THE POST-TENURE GIG ECONOMY IS BASICALLY A MONASTIC CALLING.
YOU'LL ALWAYS BE BROKE. YOU'LL NEVER HAVE JOB SECURITY. YOU'LL SPEND YOUR LIFE BOUNCING FROM CITY TO CITY, TAKING WHATEVER TEACHING JOB YOU CAN GET.
YOU CAN'T HOLD DOWN A BASIC RELATIONSHIP, LET ALONE RAISE A KID!
SO I GUESS... IN A WAY...THIS FELT LIKE THE ONLY CHANCE I'D EVER HAVE.
TO BE A PARENT. TO MAKE MY OWN FAMILY.
I KNOW, I KNOW.
STUPID, RIGHT?
I'M ONLY THIRTY. PLENTY OF TIME.
ONLY THAT'S NOT HOW IT FEELS.
IT FEELS LIKE TIME IS RUNNING OUT.
IT FEELS LIKE THE END OF THE WORLD EVERY SINGLE DAY.

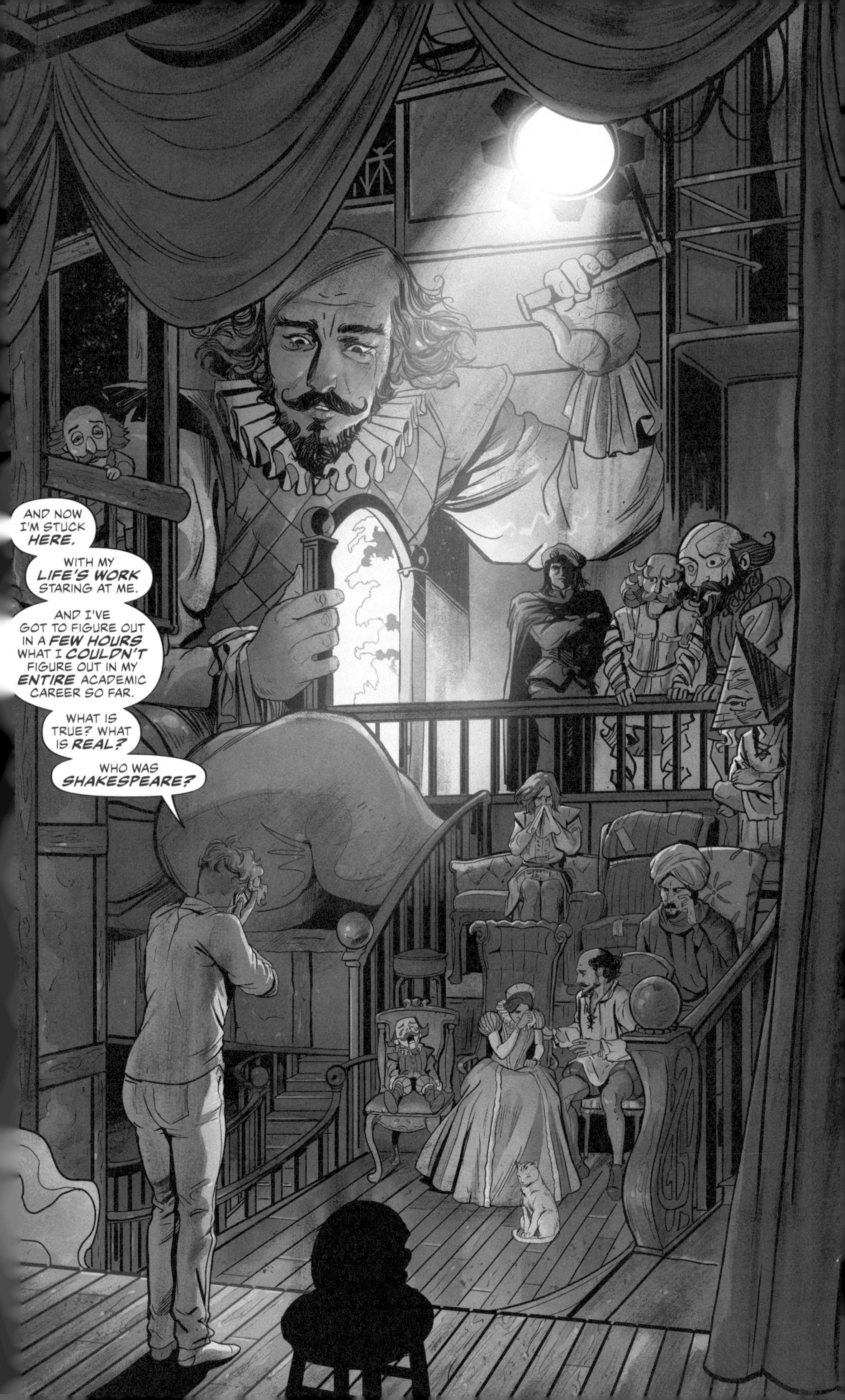
AND NOW I'M STUCK HERE.
WITH MY LIFE'S WORK STARING AT ME.
AND I'VE GOT TO FIGURE OUT IN A FEW HOURS WHAT I COULDN'T FIGURE OUT IN MY ENTIRE ACADEMIC CAREER SO FAR.
WHAT IS TRUE? WHAT IS REAL?
WHO WAS SHAKESPEARE?

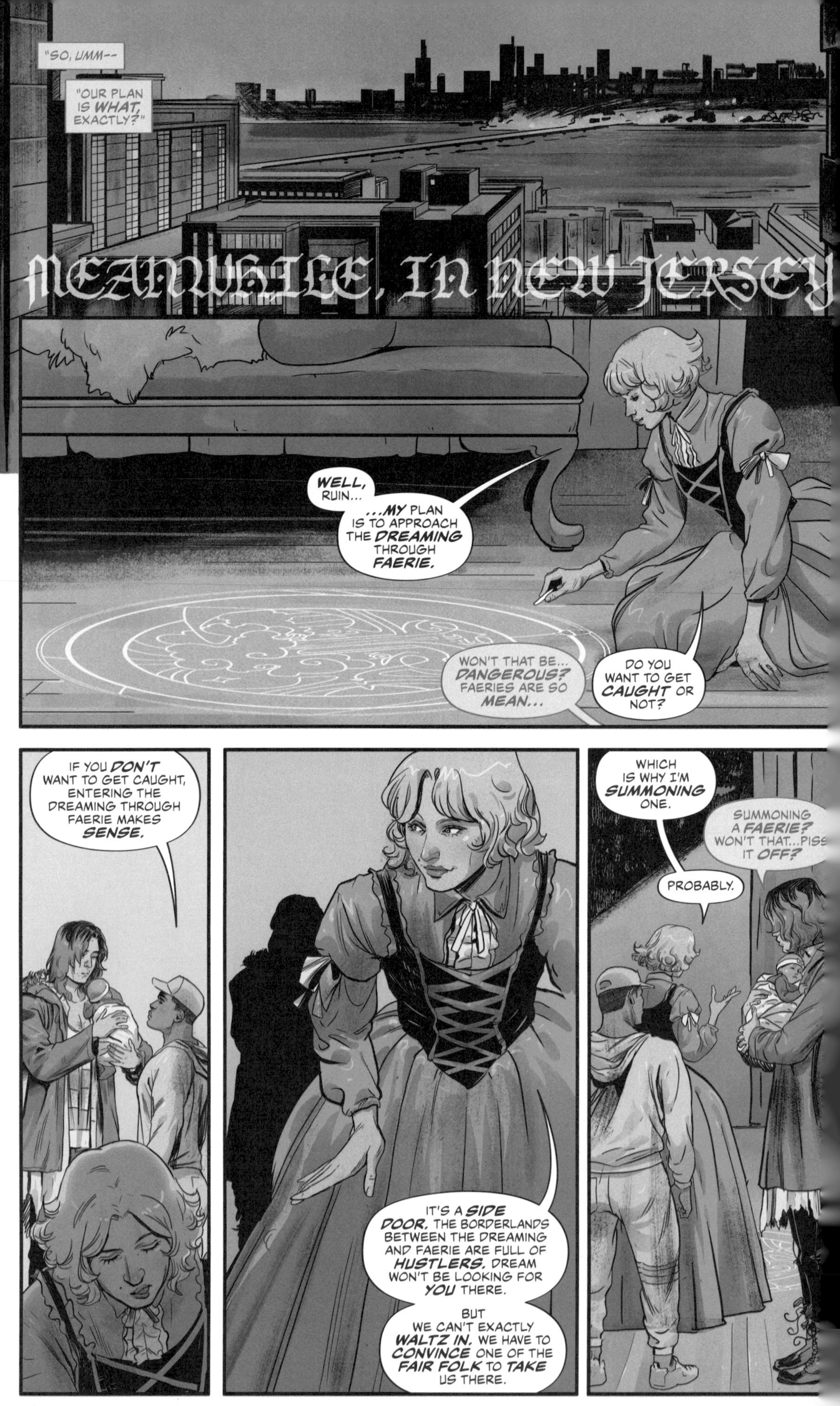
"SO, UMM--
"OUR PLAN IS WHAT, EXACTLY?"
MEANWHILE, IN NEW JERSEY
WELL, RUIN...
...MY PLAN IS TO APPROACH THE DREAMING THROUGH FAERIE.
WON'T THAT BE... DANGEROUS? FAERIES ARE SO MEAN...
DO YOU WANT TO GET CAUGHT OR NOT?
IF YOU DON'T WANT TO GET CAUGHT, ENTERING THE DREAMING THROUGH FAERIE MAKES SENSE.
IT'S A SIDE DOOR. THE BORDERLANDS BETWEEN THE DREAMING AND FAERIE ARE FULL OF HUSTLERS. DREAM WON'T BE LOOKING FOR YOU THERE.
BUT WE CAN'T EXACTLY WALTZ IN. WE HAVE TO CONVINCE ONE OF THE FAIR FOLK TO TAKE US THERE.
WHICH IS WHY I'M SUMMONING ONE.
SUMMONING A FAERIE? WON'T THAT...PISS IT OFF?
PROBABLY.

IF YOU HAVE ANOTHER **BRILLIANT IDEA**, RUIN, PLEASE **SHARE**.

I'VE NEVER HAD A BRILLIANT IDEA IN MY **LIFE**.

FINALLY, SOMETHING UPON WHICH WE CAN **ALL AGREE**.

THE BABY'S GETTING **SLEEPY**.

THAT'S **GOOD**, RIGHT? SHE MUST FEEL **SAFE** WITH YOU.

NO. I MEAN **YES**, BUT--

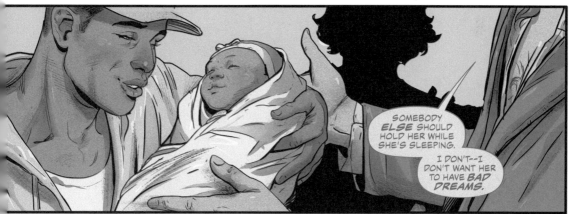

SOMEBODY **ELSE** SHOULD HOLD HER WHILE SHE'S SLEEPING.

I DON'T--I DON'T WANT HER TO HAVE **BAD DREAMS**.

ARE YOU **CERTAIN** THIS CIRCLE WILL SUMMON ONE OF THE **FAIR FOLK**, AND NOT SOMETHING **ELSE?**

IF THIS IS A **POLITE WAY** OF REMINDING ME HOW WE **MET**, TOUCHÉ.

YOU **SUMMONED** JOPHIEL?

NOT ON **PURPOSE**. I WAS **TRYING** TO SUMMON A **FIRE ELEMENTAL**.

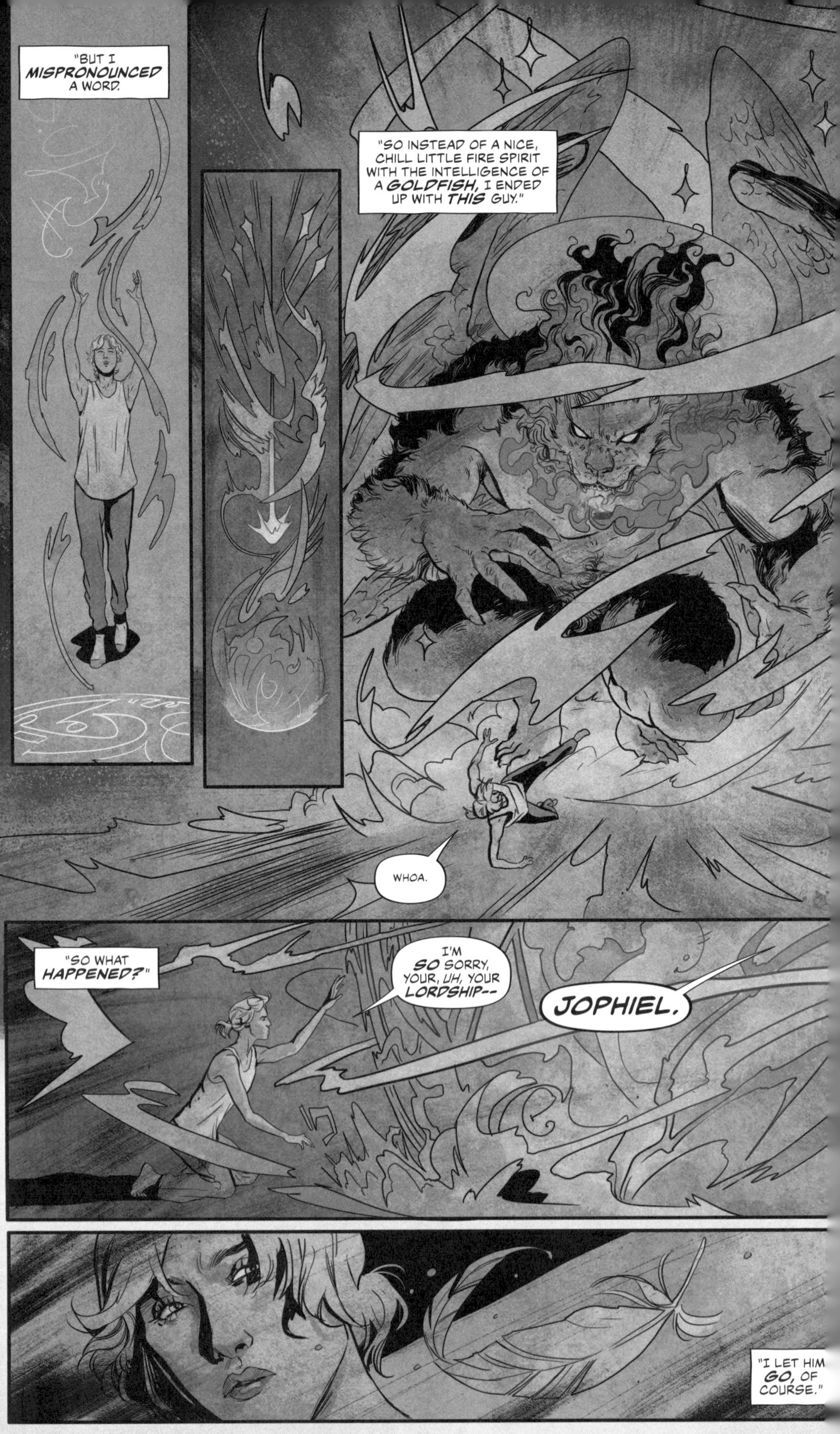
"BUT I MISPRONOUNCED A WORD.
"SO INSTEAD OF A NICE, CHILL LITTLE FIRE SPIRIT WITH THE INTELLIGENCE OF A GOLDFISH, I ENDED UP WITH THIS GUY."
WHOA.
"SO WHAT HAPPENED?"
I'M SO SORRY, YOUR, UH, YOUR LORDSHIP--
JOPHIEL.
"I LET HIM GO, OF COURSE."

JUST LIKE THAT? *WHY?*

BECAUSE I'M NOT AN *ASSHOLE.*

SUMMONING IS LIKE *SPORT FISHING.*

YOU SET YOUR *BAIT* FOR THE FISH YOU *WANT* TO CATCH, BUT IF YOU *ACCIDENTALLY* HOOK A *SHARK,* YOU'RE MORALLY OBLIGATED TO SET IT *FREE,* OTHERWISE THE WHOLE *ECOSYSTEM* SUFFERS.

WHICH MY *ANCESTORS* LEARNED THE *HARD* WAY.

THERE, THAT SHOULD DO IT.

STAND BACK...

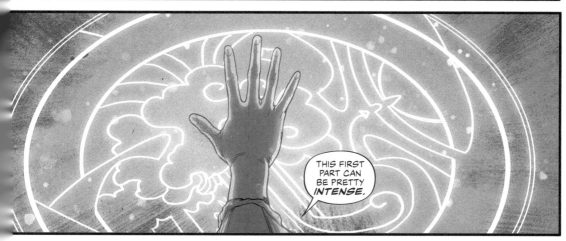

THIS FIRST PART CAN BE PRETTY *INTENSE.*

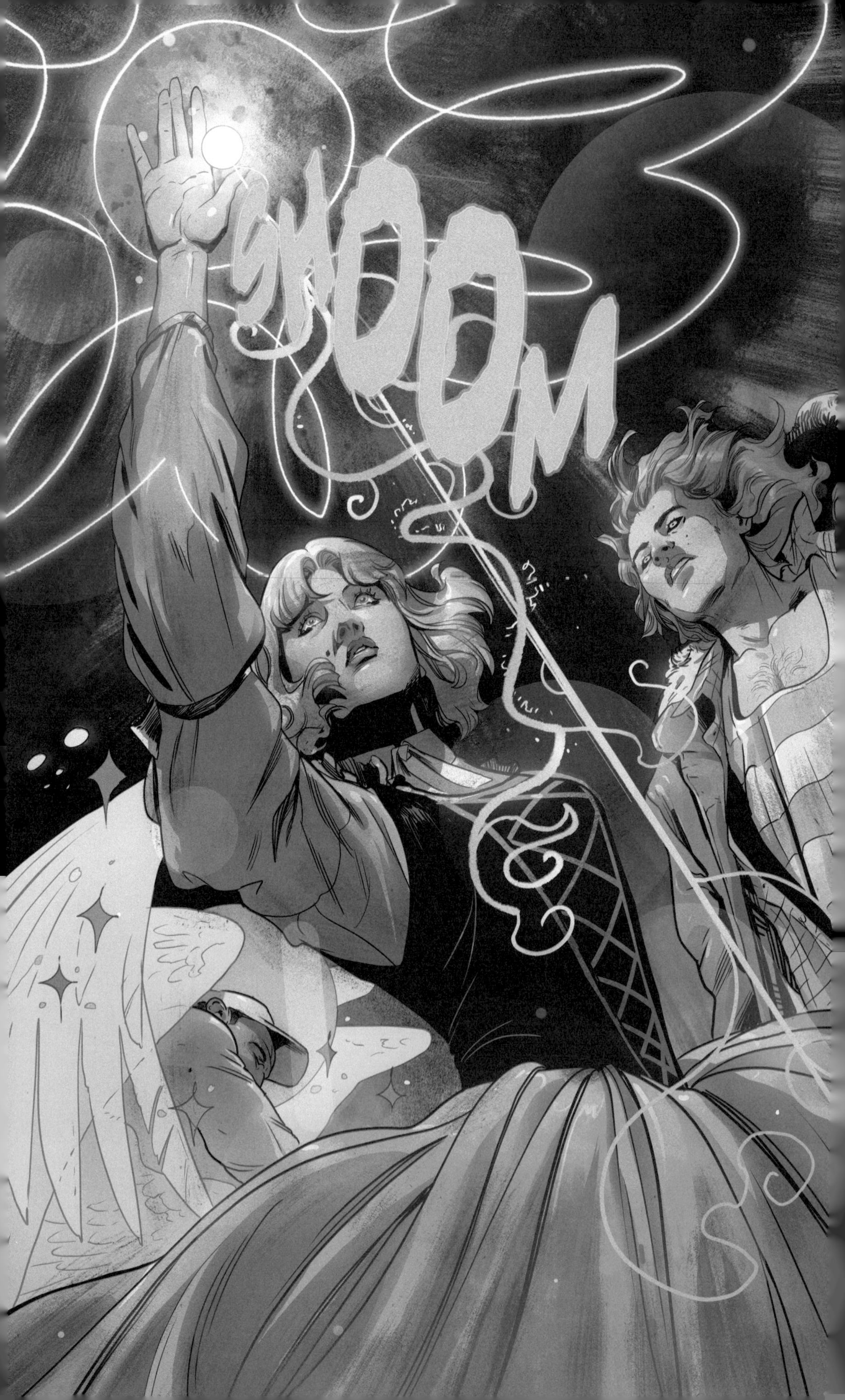
SHOOOM

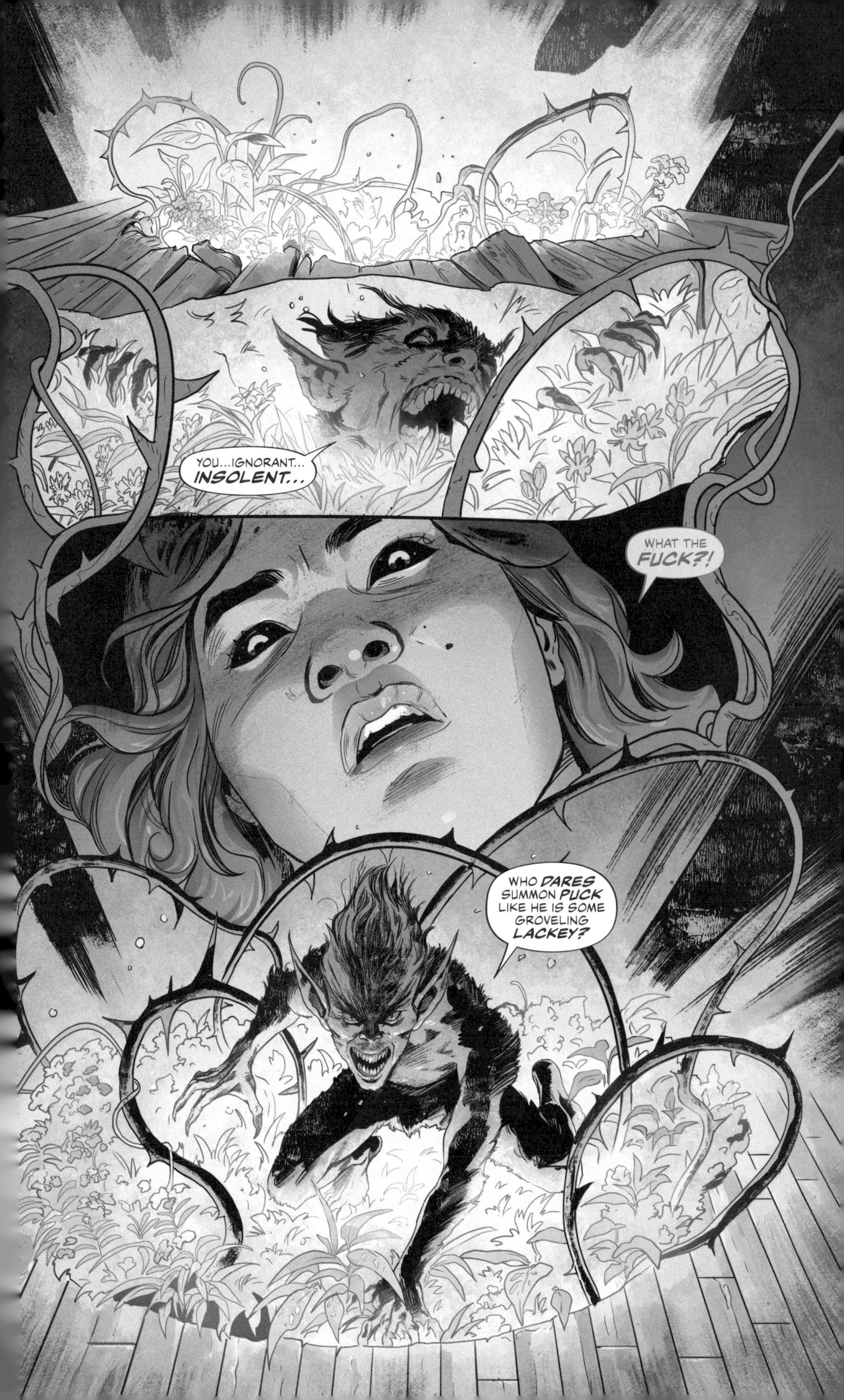
YOU...IGNORANT...
INSOLENT...
WHAT THE FUCK?!
WHO DARES SUMMON PUCK LIKE HE IS SOME GROVELING LACKEY?

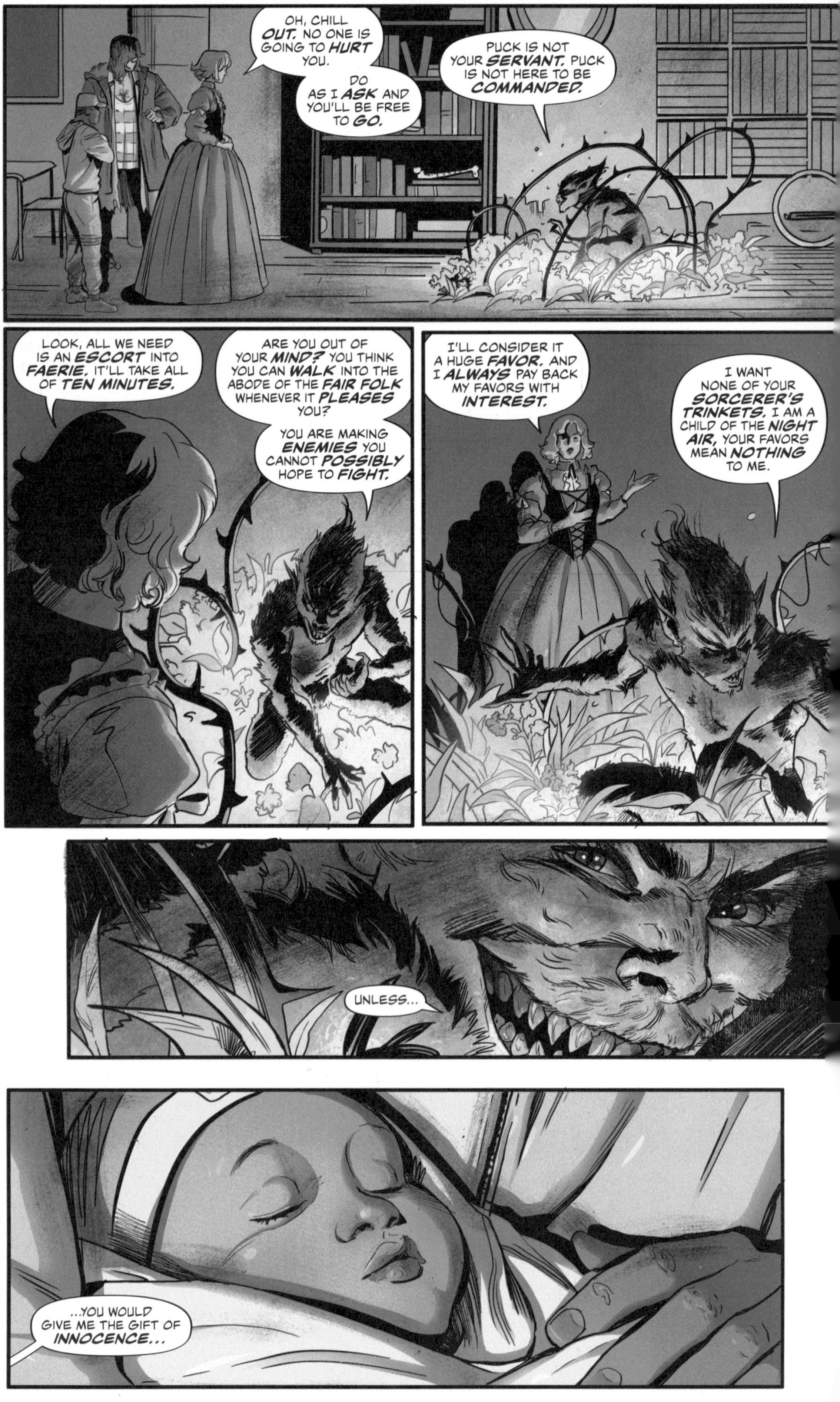

OH, CHILL OUT. NO ONE IS GOING TO HURT YOU.
DO AS I ASK AND YOU'LL BE FREE TO GO.
PUCK IS NOT YOUR SERVANT. PUCK IS NOT HERE TO BE COMMANDED.
LOOK, ALL WE NEED IS AN ESCORT INTO FAERIE. IT'LL TAKE ALL OF TEN MINUTES.
ARE YOU OUT OF YOUR MIND? YOU THINK YOU CAN WALK INTO THE ABODE OF THE FAIR FOLK WHENEVER IT PLEASES YOU?
YOU ARE MAKING ENEMIES YOU CANNOT POSSIBLY HOPE TO FIGHT.
I'LL CONSIDER IT A HUGE FAVOR. AND I ALWAYS PAY BACK MY FAVORS WITH INTEREST.
I WANT NONE OF YOUR SORCERER'S TRINKETS. I AM A CHILD OF THE NIGHT AIR, YOUR FAVORS MEAN NOTHING TO ME.
UNLESS...
...YOU WOULD GIVE ME THE GIFT OF INNOCENCE...

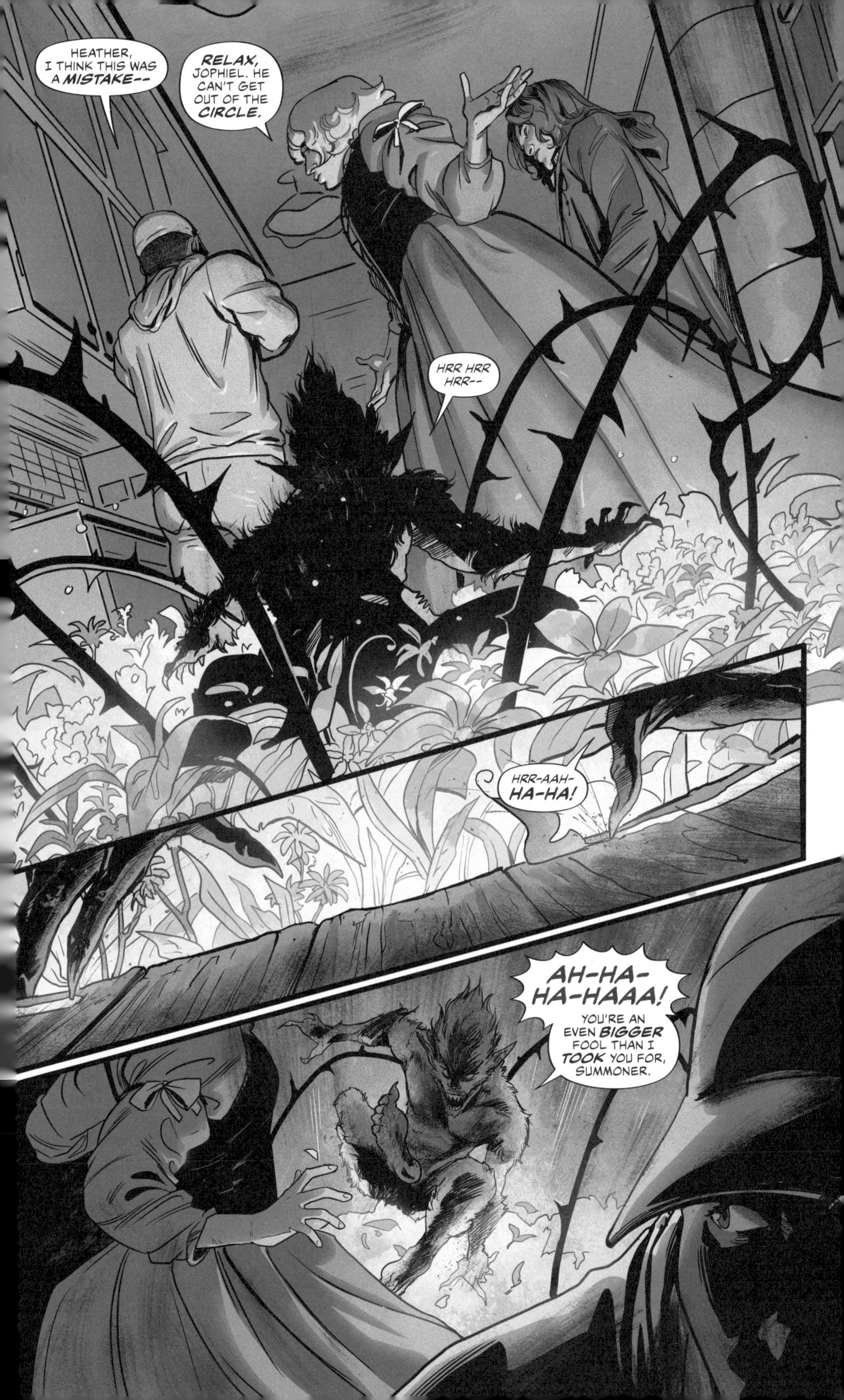
HEATHER, I THINK THIS WAS A MISTAKE--
RELAX, JOPHIEL. HE CAN'T GET OUT OF THE CIRCLE.
HRR HRR HRR--
HRR-AAH-HA-HA!
AH-HA-HA-HAAA!
YOU'RE AN EVEN BIGGER FOOL THAN I TOOK YOU FOR, SUMMONER.

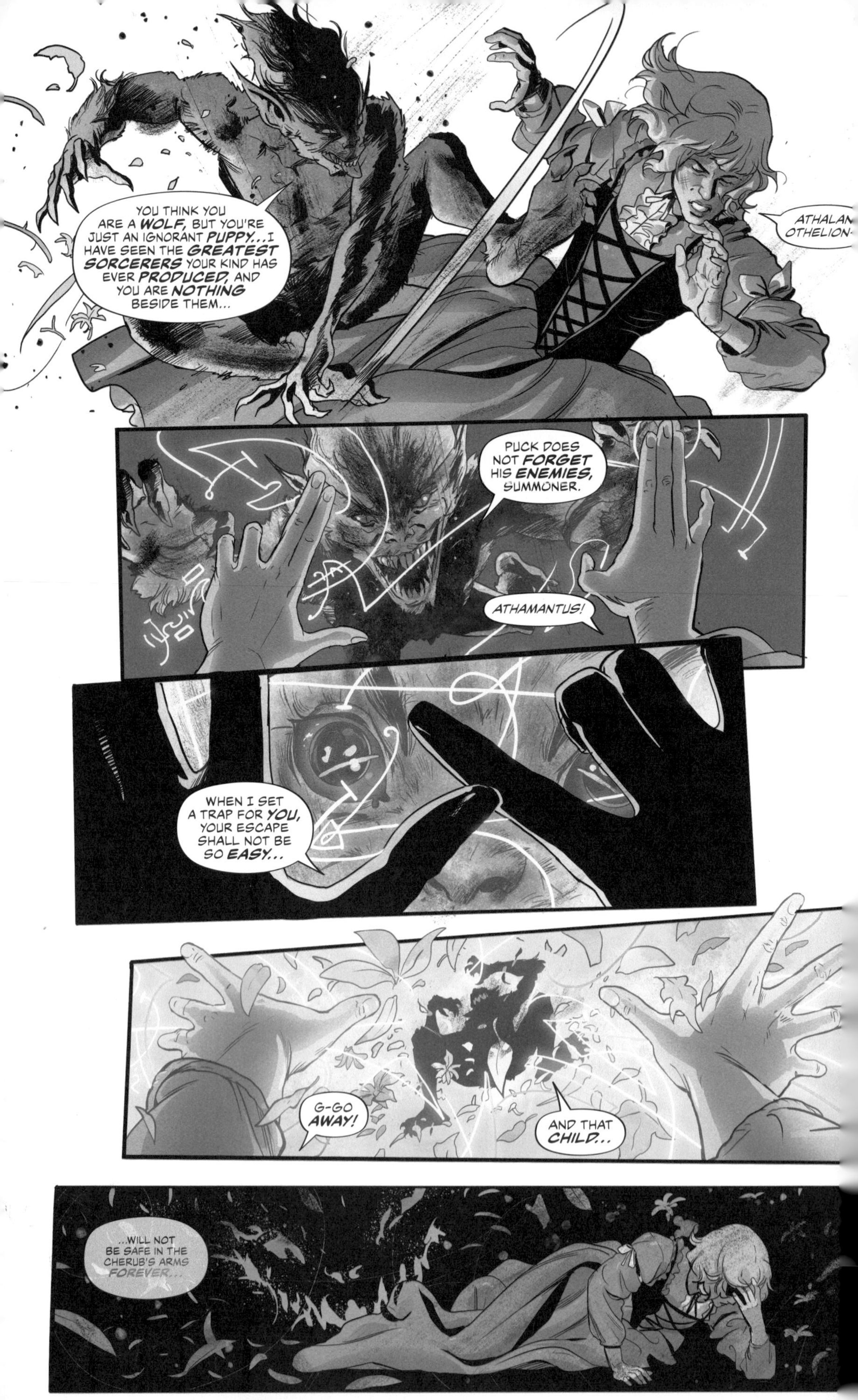
YOU THINK YOU ARE A WOLF, BUT YOU'RE JUST AN IGNORANT PUPPY... I HAVE SEEN THE GREATEST SORCERERS YOUR KIND HAS EVER PRODUCED, AND YOU ARE NOTHING BESIDE THEM...
ATHALAN OTHELION-
PUCK DOES NOT FORGET HIS ENEMIES, SUMMONER.
ATHAMANTUS!
WHEN I SET A TRAP FOR YOU, YOUR ESCAPE SHALL NOT BE SO EASY...
G-GO AWAY!
AND THAT CHILD...
...WILL NOT BE SAFE IN THE CHERUB'S ARMS FOREVER...

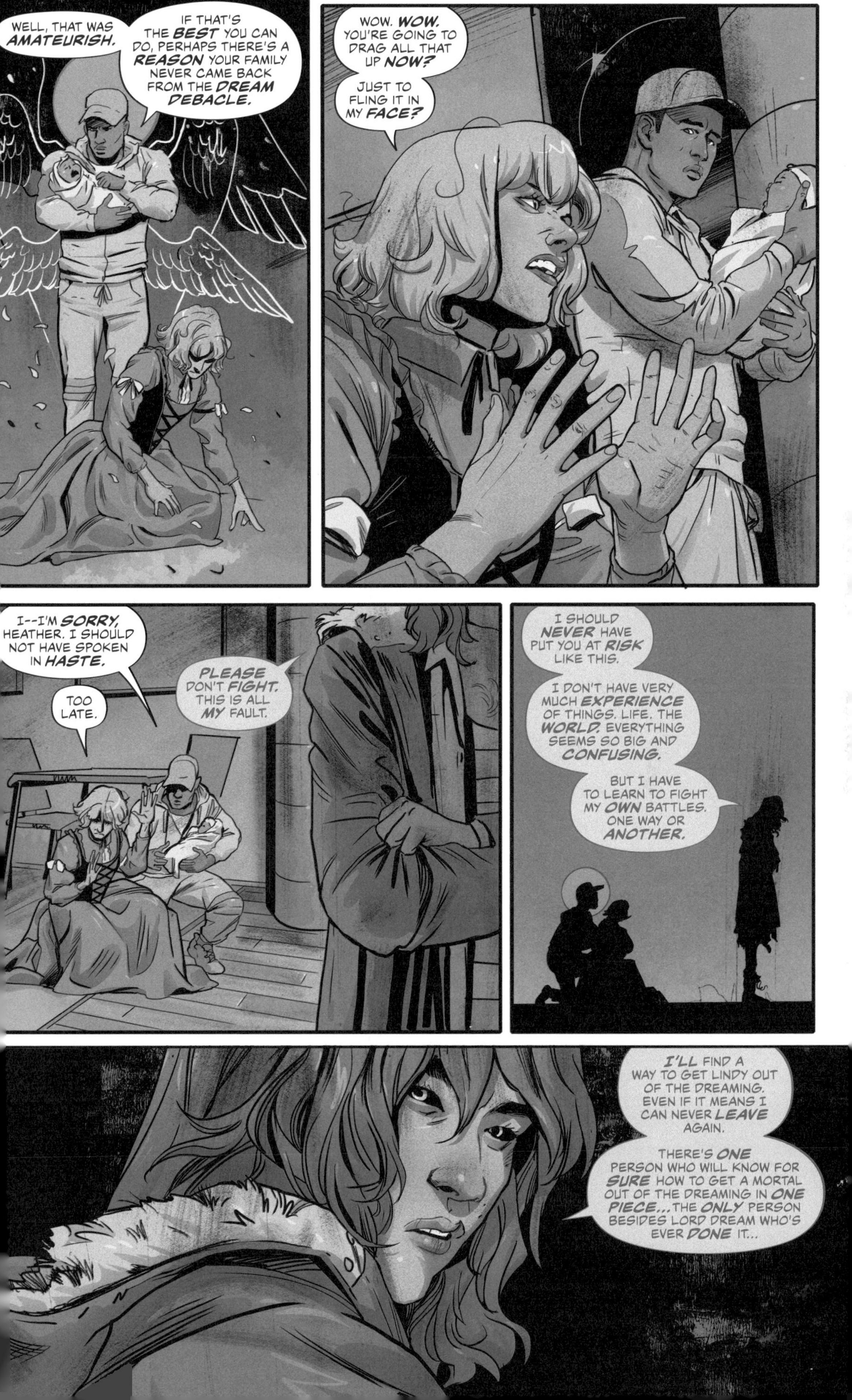
WELL, THAT WAS AMATEURISH.
IF THAT'S THE BEST YOU CAN DO, PERHAPS THERE'S A REASON YOUR FAMILY NEVER CAME BACK FROM THE DREAM DEBACLE.
WOW. WOW. YOU'RE GOING TO DRAG ALL THAT UP NOW?
JUST TO FLING IT IN MY FACE?
I--I'M SORRY, HEATHER. I SHOULD NOT HAVE SPOKEN IN HASTE.
TOO LATE.
PLEASE DON'T FIGHT. THIS IS ALL MY FAULT.
I SHOULD NEVER HAVE PUT YOU AT RISK LIKE THIS.
I DON'T HAVE VERY MUCH EXPERIENCE OF THINGS. LIFE. THE WORLD. EVERYTHING SEEMS SO BIG AND CONFUSING.
BUT I HAVE TO LEARN TO FIGHT MY OWN BATTLES. ONE WAY OR ANOTHER.
I'LL FIND A WAY TO GET LINDY OUT OF THE DREAMING. EVEN IF IT MEANS I CAN NEVER LEAVE AGAIN.
THERE'S ONE PERSON WHO WILL KNOW FOR SURE HOW TO GET A MORTAL OUT OF THE DREAMING IN ONE PIECE... THE ONLY PERSON BESIDES LORD DREAM WHO'S EVER DONE IT...

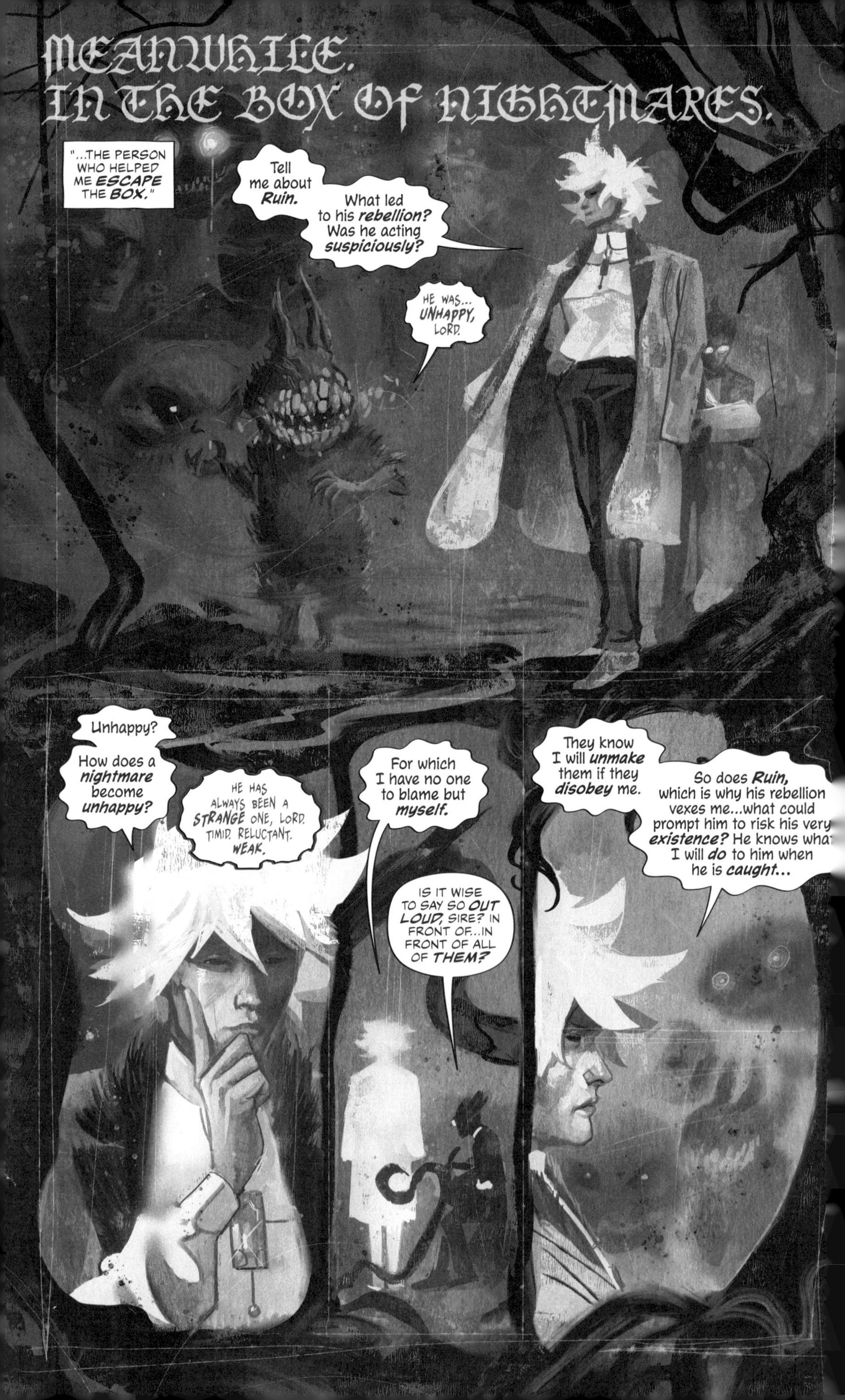

MEANWHILE, IN THE BOX OF NIGHTMARES.
"...THE PERSON WHO HELPED ME ESCAPE THE BOX."
Tell me about Ruin.
What led to his rebellion? Was he acting suspiciously?
HE WAS... UNHAPPY, LORD.
Unhappy?
How does a nightmare become unhappy?
HE HAS ALWAYS BEEN A STRANGE ONE, LORD. TIMID. RELUCTANT. WEAK.
For which I have no one to blame but myself.
IS IT WISE TO SAY SO OUT LOUD, SIRE? IN FRONT OF...IN FRONT OF ALL OF THEM?
They know I will unmake them if they disobey me.
So does Ruin, which is why his rebellion vexes me...what could prompt him to risk his very existence? He knows what I will do to him when he is caught...

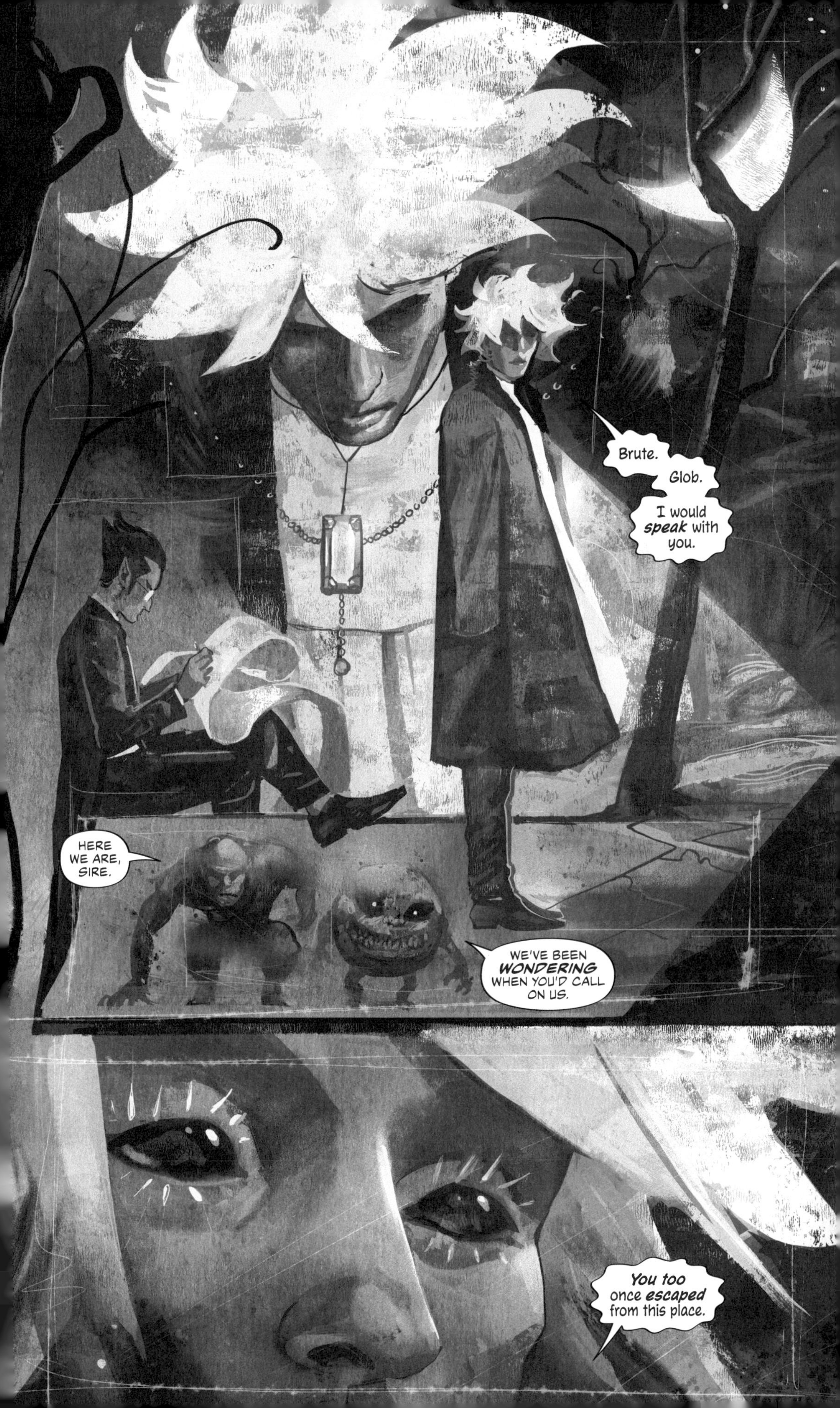
Brute.
Glob.
I would speak with you.
HERE WE ARE, SIRE.
WE'VE BEEN WONDERING WHEN YOU'D CALL ON US.
You too once escaped from this place.

WE SURE DID.
THAT'S HOW WE MET YOU. IN A MANNER OF SPEAKING.
IN YOUR MOTHER'S **WOMB.** BEFORE YOU WERE **BORN.**
And after I ascended to the throne, I brought you back from ***exile.***
WE NEVER REALLY UNDERSTOOD ***WHY,*** LORD. AFTER ALL--
THE ***LAST*** DREAM--THE ***OTHER*** ONE--HE WANTED TO ***PUNISH*** US--
I brought you back so that you would owe ***me*** the ***loyalty*** you ***failed*** to show to ***him.***
Loyalty I wish to call upon ***now.***
So ***tell*** me.
Who let Ruin out of the Box?
Well. Your betrayal ***did*** indirectly result in his ***death.***
And in my ***birth.***

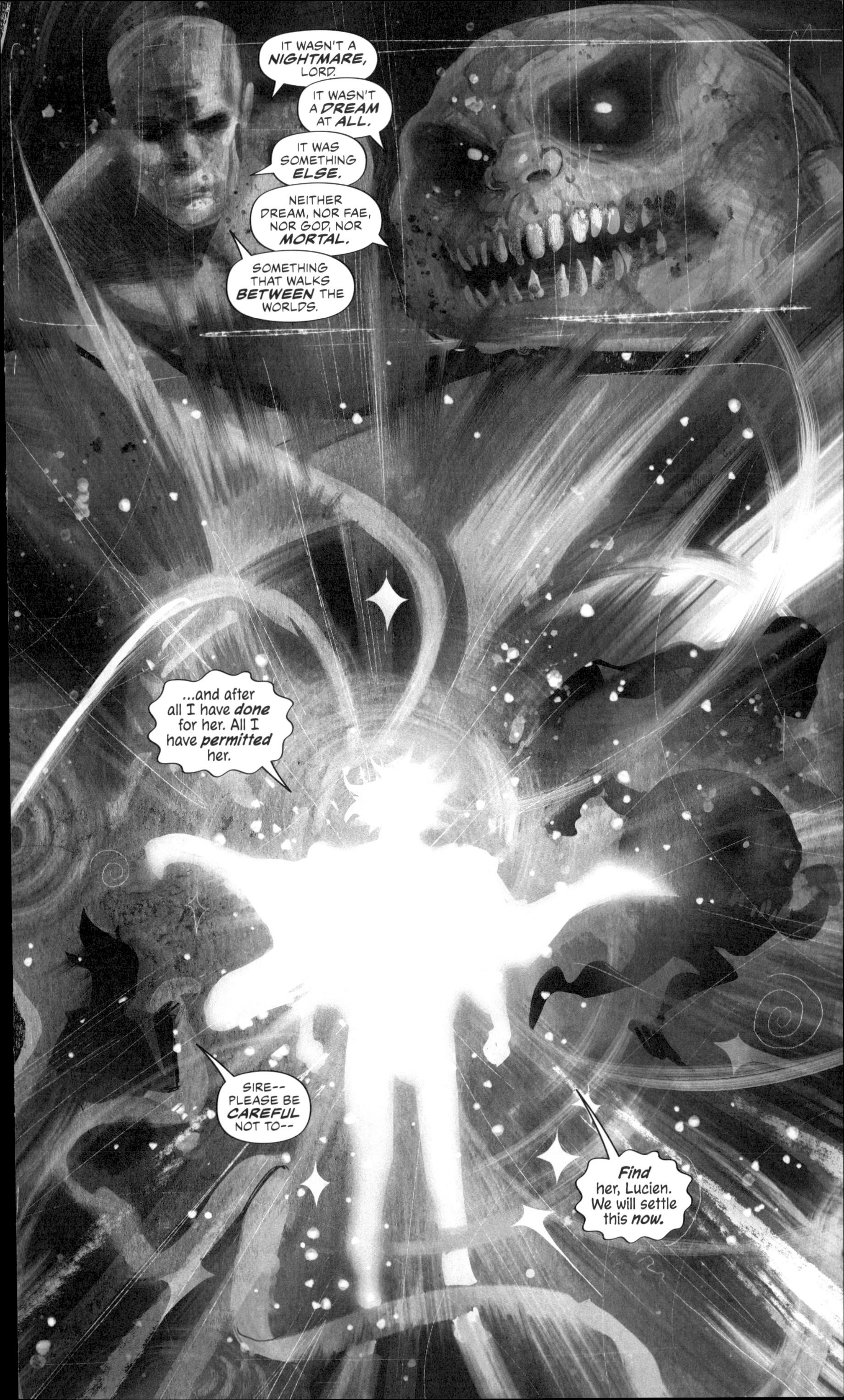
IT WASN'T A NIGHTMARE, LORD.
IT WASN'T A DREAM AT ALL.
IT WAS SOMETHING ELSE.
NEITHER DREAM, NOR FAE, NOR GOD, NOR MORTAL.
SOMETHING THAT WALKS BETWEEN THE WORLDS.
...and after all I have done for her. All I have permitted her.
SIRE-- PLEASE BE CAREFUL NOT TO--
Find her, Lucien. We will settle this now.

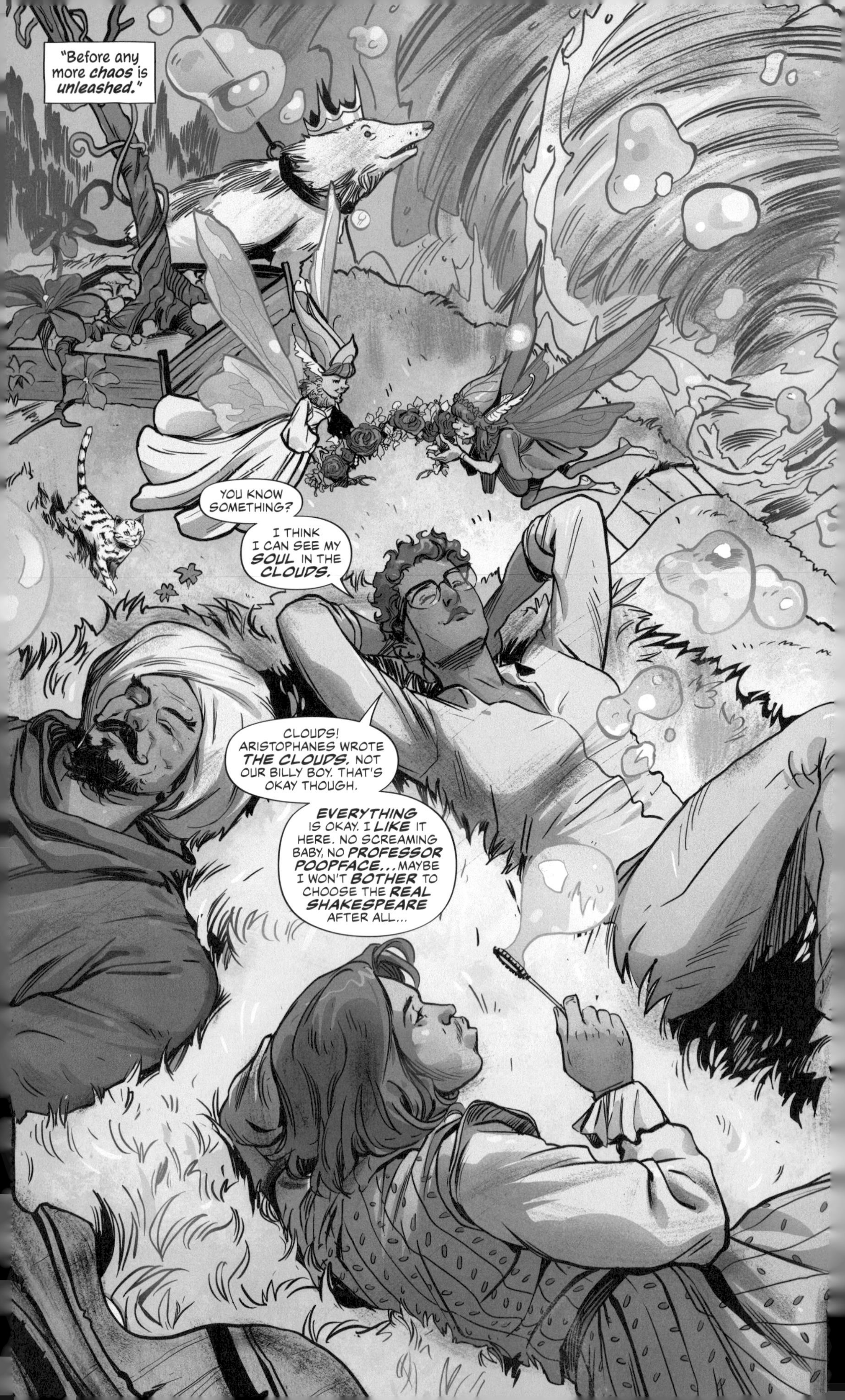
"Before any more *chaos* is *unleashed.*"
YOU KNOW SOMETHING?
I THINK I CAN SEE MY ***SOUL*** IN THE ***CLOUDS.***
CLOUDS! ARISTOPHANES WROTE ***THE CLOUDS***, NOT OUR BILLY BOY. THAT'S OKAY THOUGH.
EVERYTHING IS OKAY. I ***LIKE*** IT HERE. NO SCREAMING BABY, NO ***PROFESSOR POOPFACE...*** MAYBE I WON'T ***BOTHER*** TO CHOOSE THE ***REAL SHAKESPEARE*** AFTER ALL...

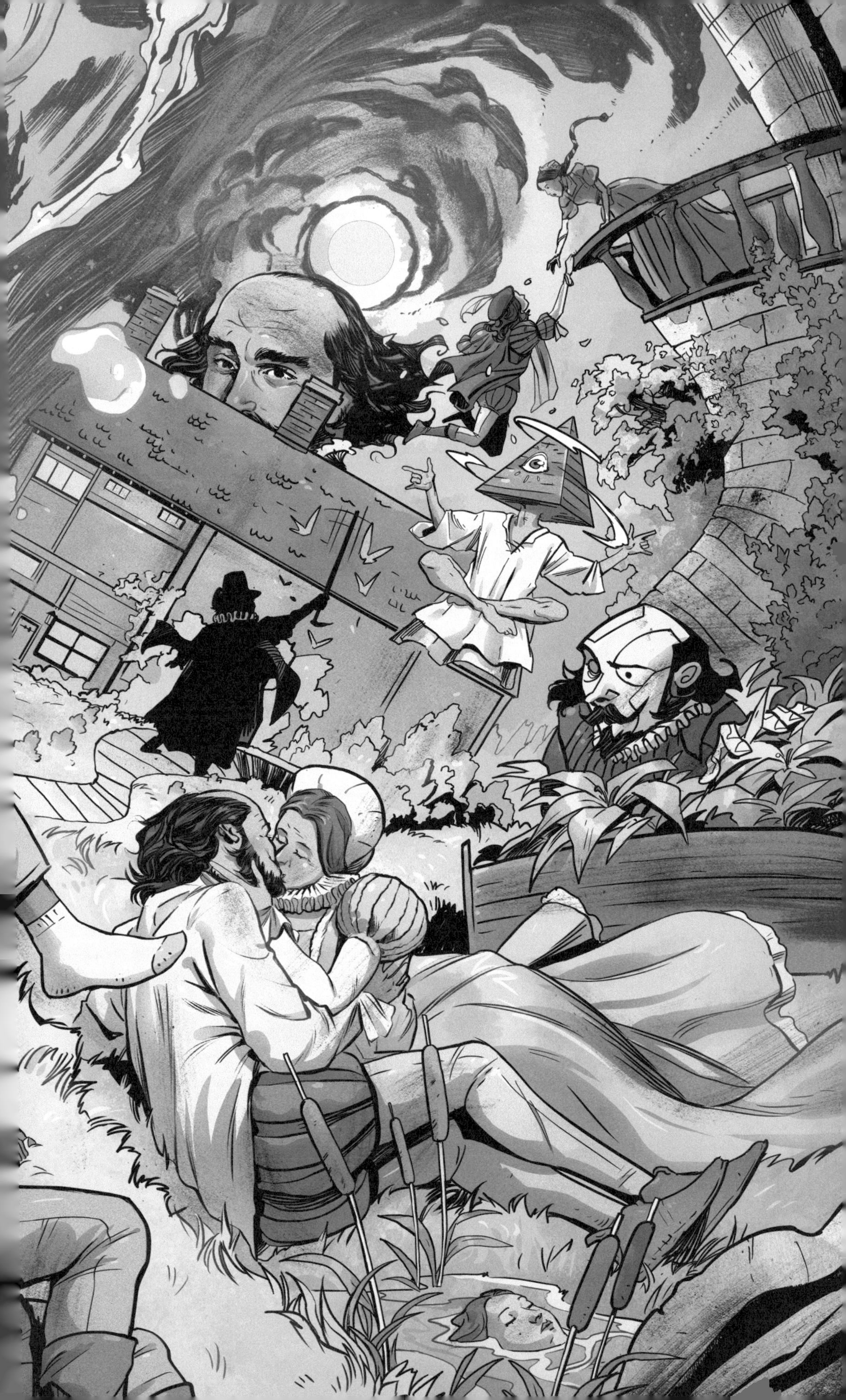

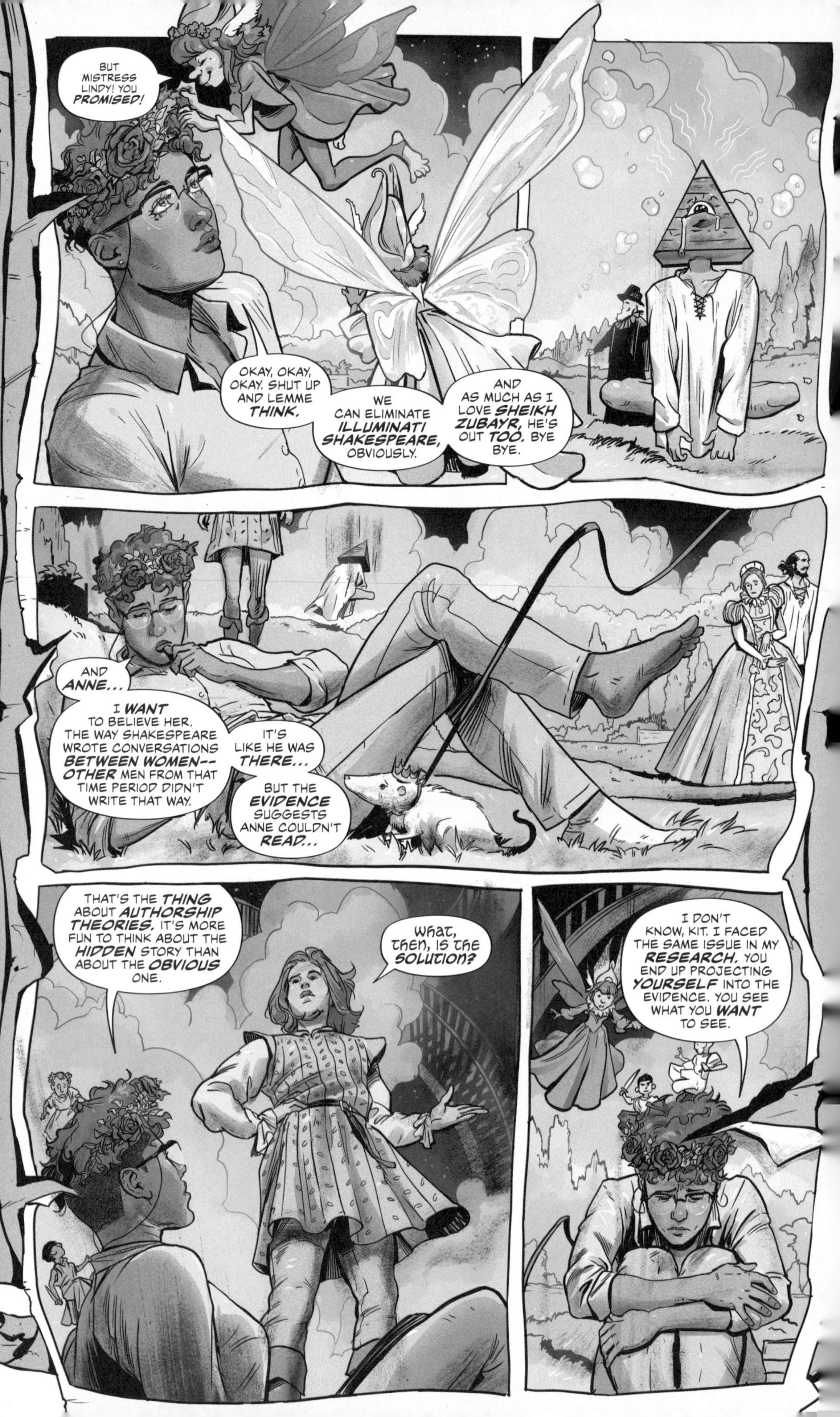

BUT MISTRESS LINDY! YOU PROMISED!
OKAY, OKAY, OKAY. SHUT UP AND LEMME THINK.
WE CAN ELIMINATE ILLUMINATI SHAKESPEARE, OBVIOUSLY.
AND AS MUCH AS I LOVE SHEIKH ZUBAYR, HE'S OUT TOO. BYE BYE.
AND ANNE...
I WANT TO BELIEVE HER. THE WAY SHAKESPEARE WROTE CONVERSATIONS BETWEEN WOMEN--OTHER MEN FROM THAT TIME PERIOD DIDN'T WRITE THAT WAY.
IT'S LIKE HE WAS THERE...
BUT THE EVIDENCE SUGGESTS ANNE COULDN'T READ...
THAT'S THE THING ABOUT AUTHORSHIP THEORIES. IT'S MORE FUN TO THINK ABOUT THE HIDDEN STORY THAN ABOUT THE OBVIOUS ONE.
What, then, is the solution?
I DON'T KNOW, KIT. I FACED THE SAME ISSUE IN MY RESEARCH. YOU END UP PROJECTING YOURSELF INTO THE EVIDENCE. YOU SEE WHAT YOU WANT TO SEE.

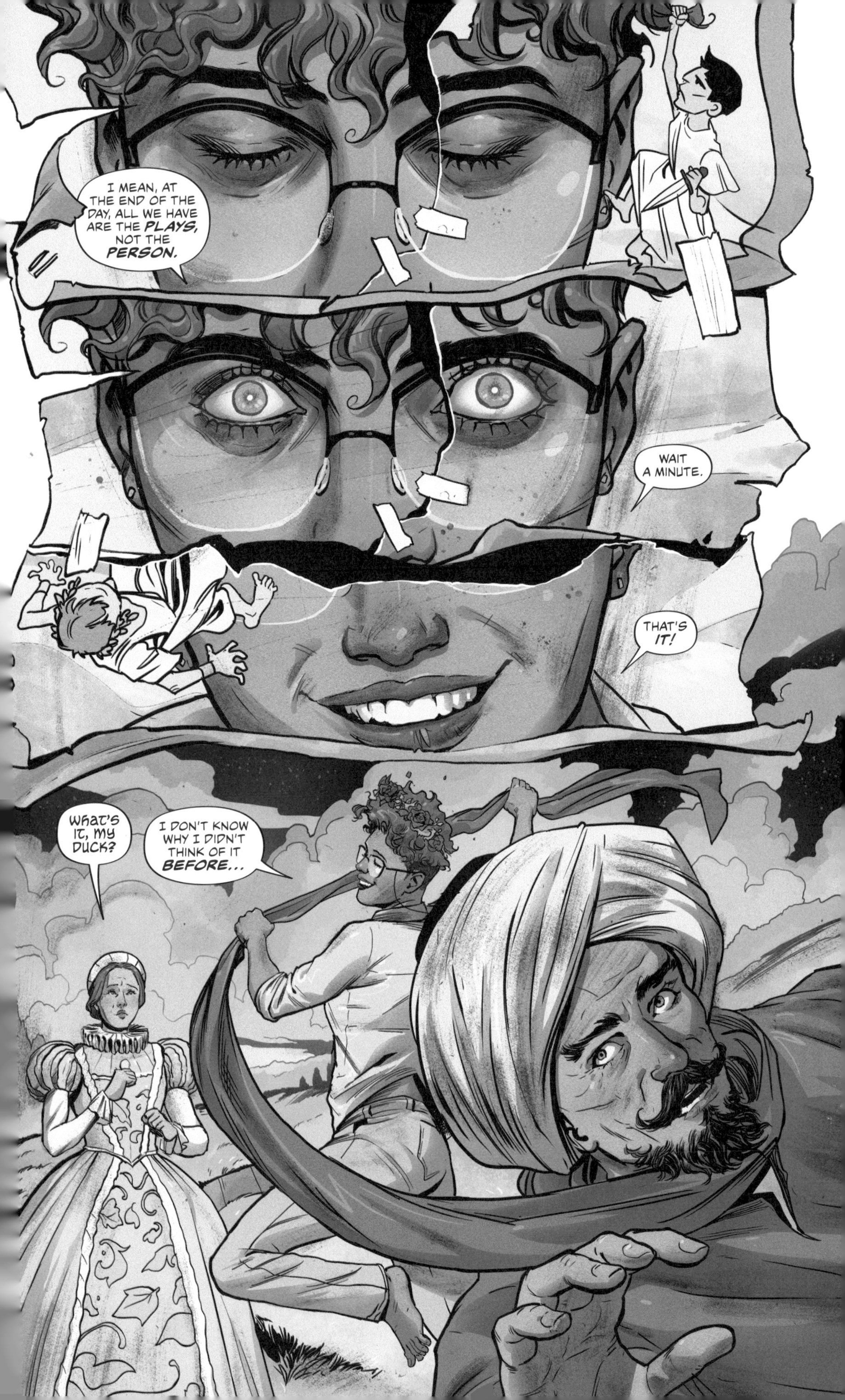
I MEAN, AT THE END OF THE DAY, ALL WE HAVE ARE THE PLAYS, NOT THE PERSON.
WAIT A MINUTE.
THAT'S IT!
WHAT'S IT, MY DUCK?
I DON'T KNOW WHY I DIDN'T THINK OF IT BEFORE...

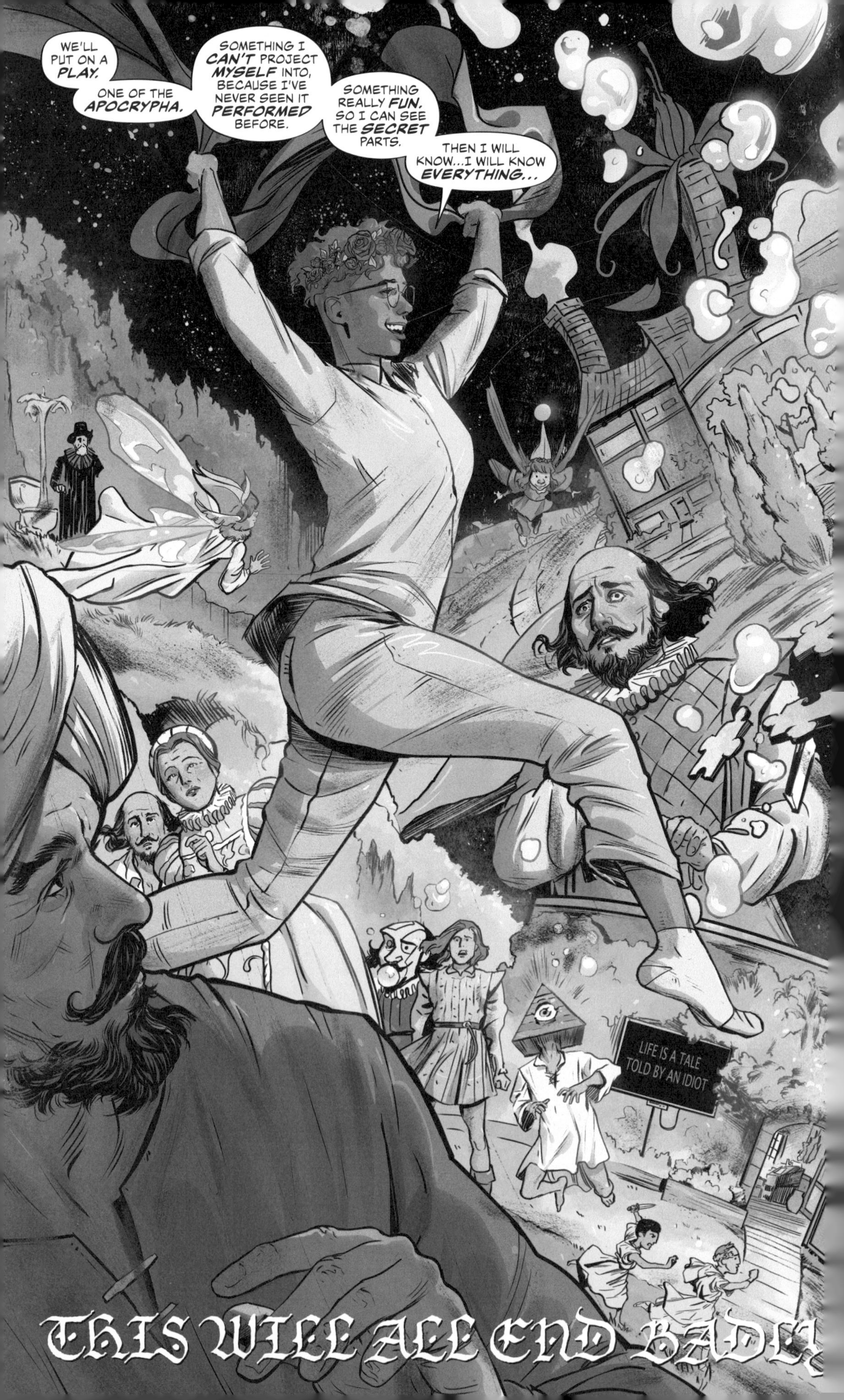
WE'LL PUT ON A PLAY.
ONE OF THE APOCRYPHA.
SOMETHING I CAN'T PROJECT MYSELF INTO, BECAUSE I'VE NEVER SEEN IT PERFORMED BEFORE.
SOMETHING REALLY FUN. SO I CAN SEE THE SECRET PARTS.
THEN I WILL KNOW...I WILL KNOW EVERYTHING...
LIFE IS A TALE TOLD BY AN IDIOT
THIS WILL ALL END BADLY

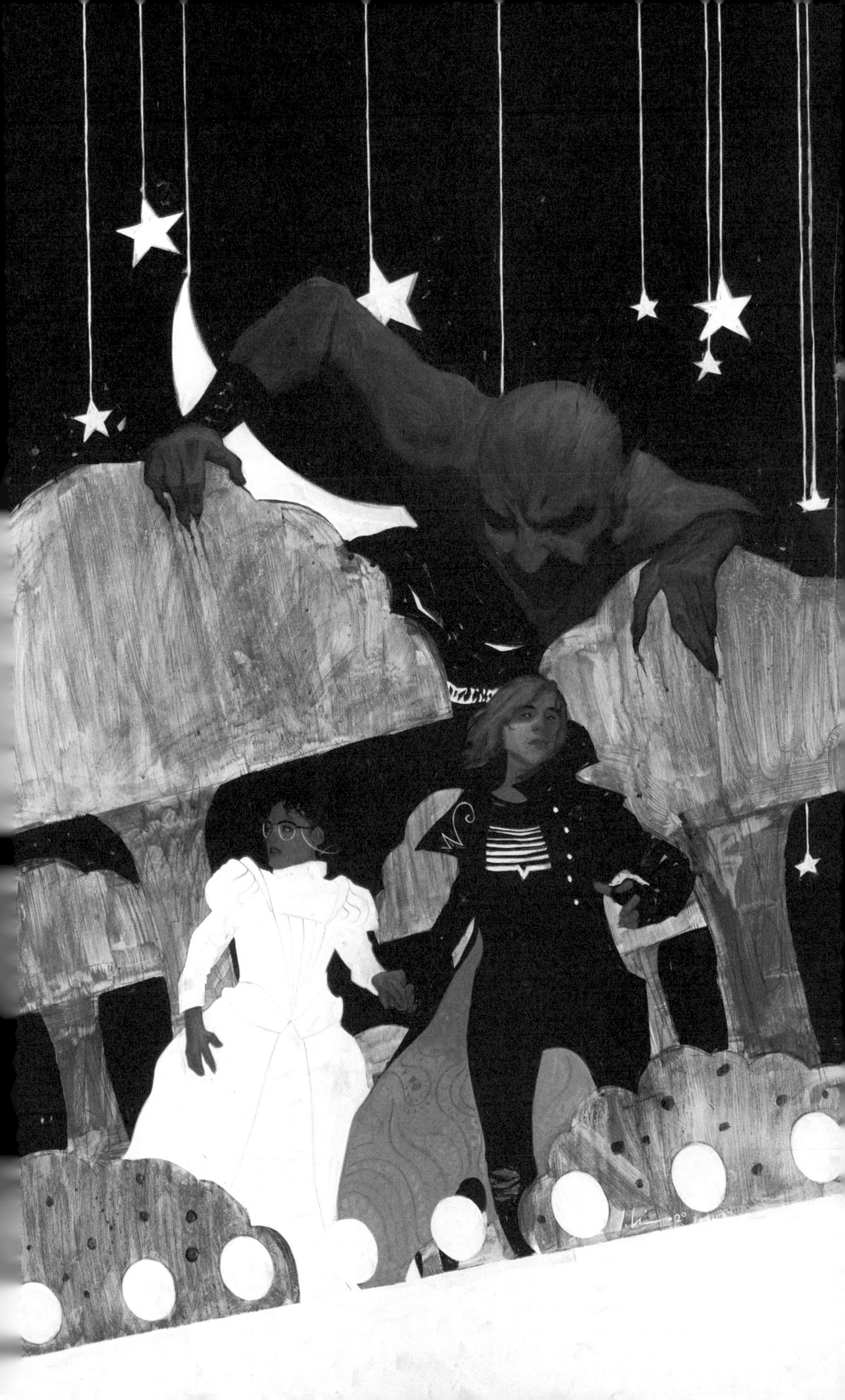

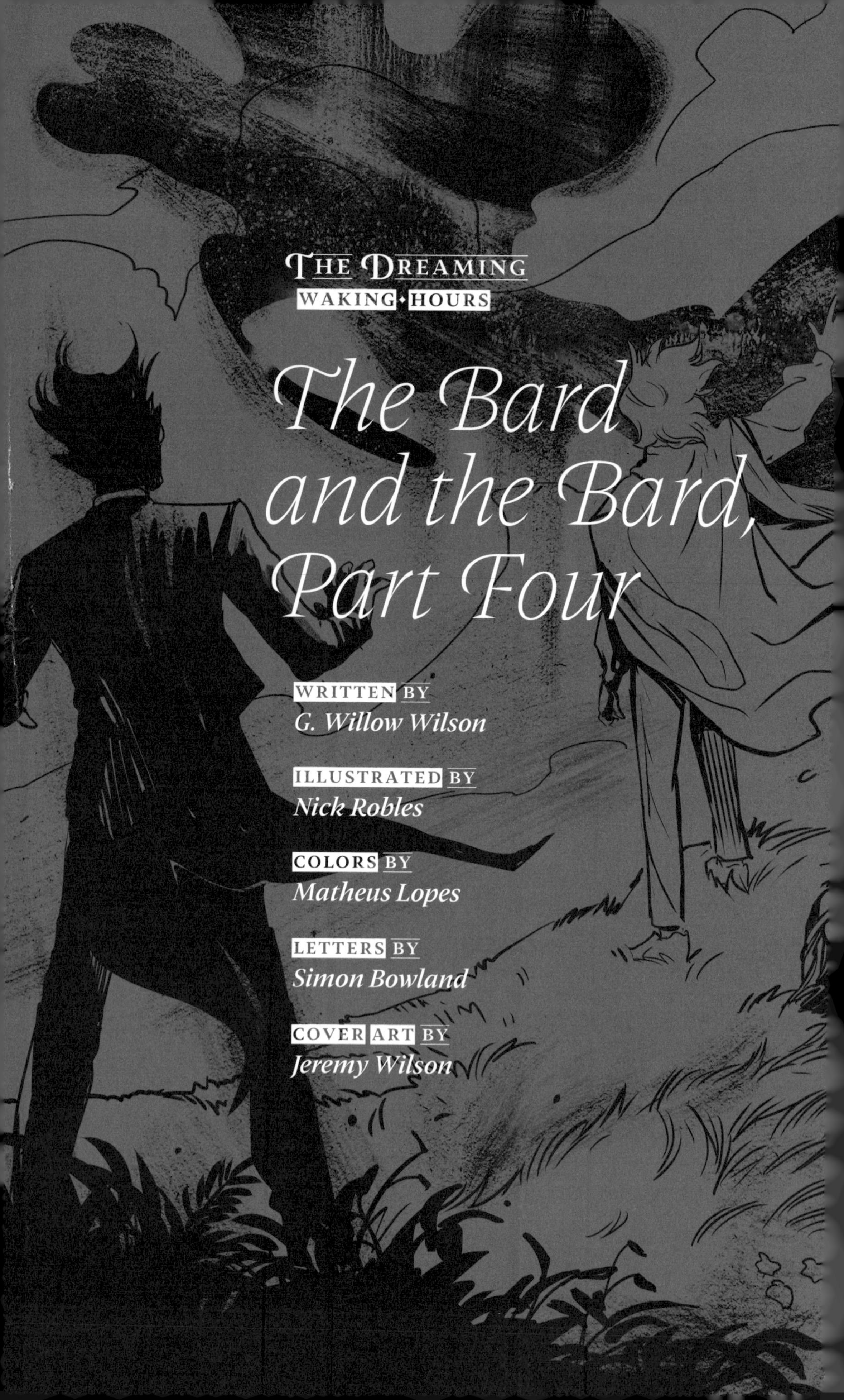

THE DREAMING
WAKING • HOURS

The Bard and the Bard, Part Four

WRITTEN BY
G. Willow Wilson

ILLUSTRATED BY
Nick Robles

COLORS BY
Matheus Lopes

LETTERS BY
Simon Bowland

COVER ART BY
Jeremy Wilson

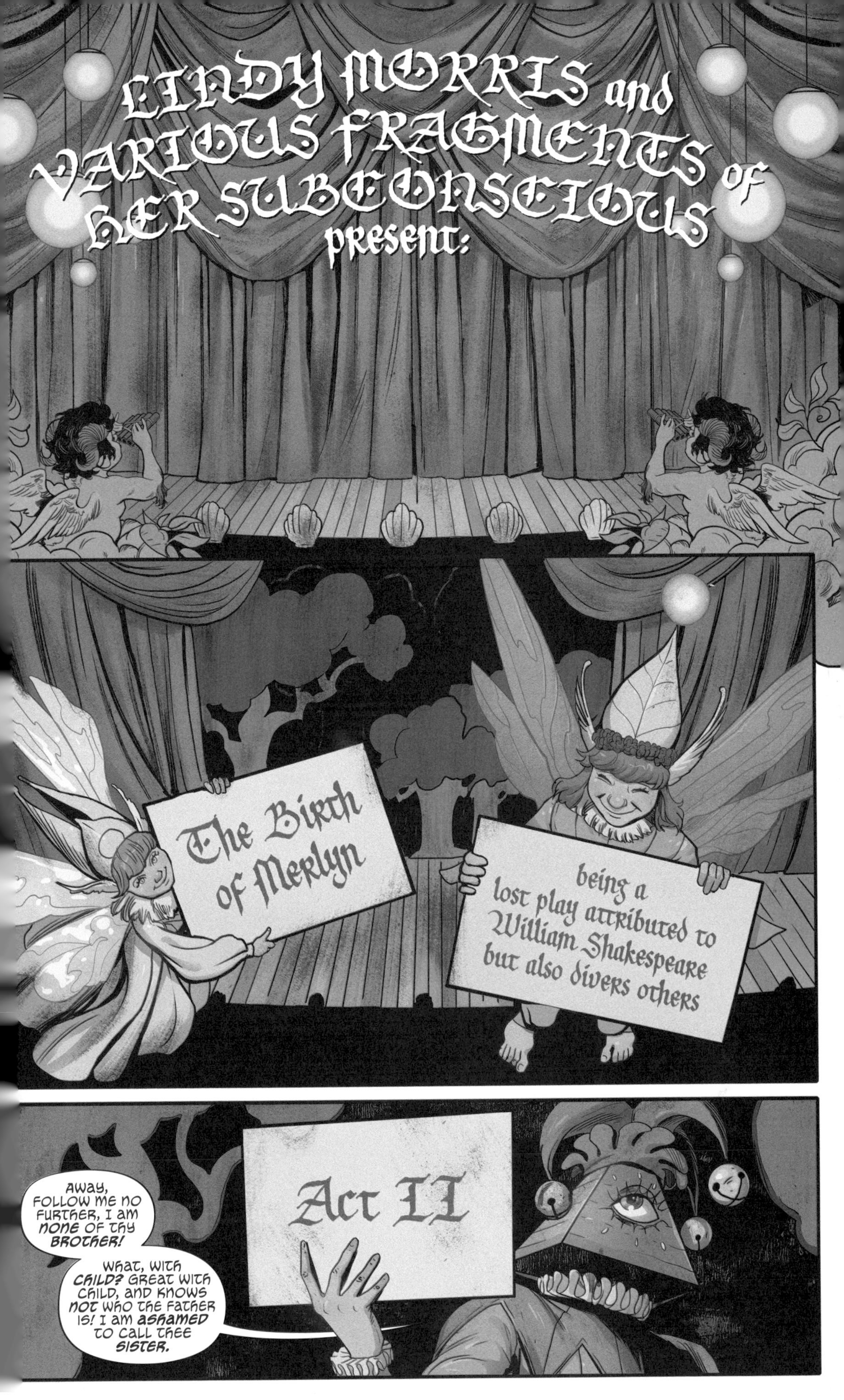
LINDY MORRIS and VARIOUS FRAGMENTS of HER SUBCONSCIOUS present:
The Birth of Merlyn
being a lost play attributed to William Shakespeare but also divers others
Act II
AWAY, FOLLOW ME NO FURTHER, I AM NONE OF THY BROTHER!
WHAT, WITH CHILD? GREAT WITH CHILD, AND KNOWS NOT WHO THE FATHER IS! I AM ASHAMED TO CALL THEE SISTER.

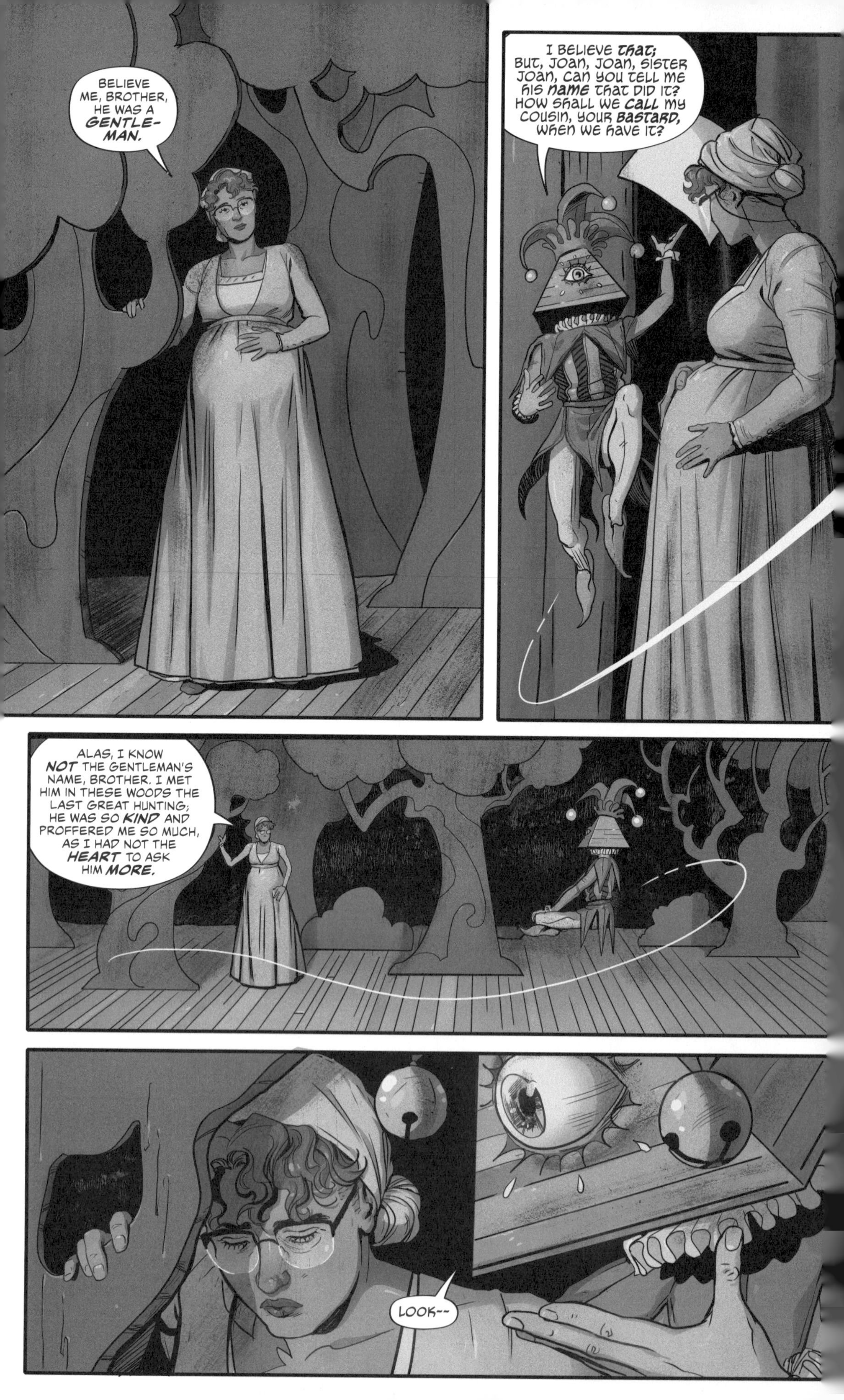
BELIEVE ME, BROTHER, HE WAS A GENTLE-MAN.
I BELIEVE THAT; BUT, JOAN, JOAN, SISTER JOAN, CAN YOU TELL ME HIS NAME THAT DID IT? HOW SHALL WE CALL MY COUSIN, YOUR BASTARD, WHEN WE HAVE IT?
ALAS, I KNOW NOT THE GENTLEMAN'S NAME, BROTHER. I MET HIM IN THESE WOODS THE LAST GREAT HUNTING; HE WAS SO KIND AND PROFFERED ME SO MUCH, AS I HAD NOT THE HEART TO ASK HIM MORE.
LOOK--

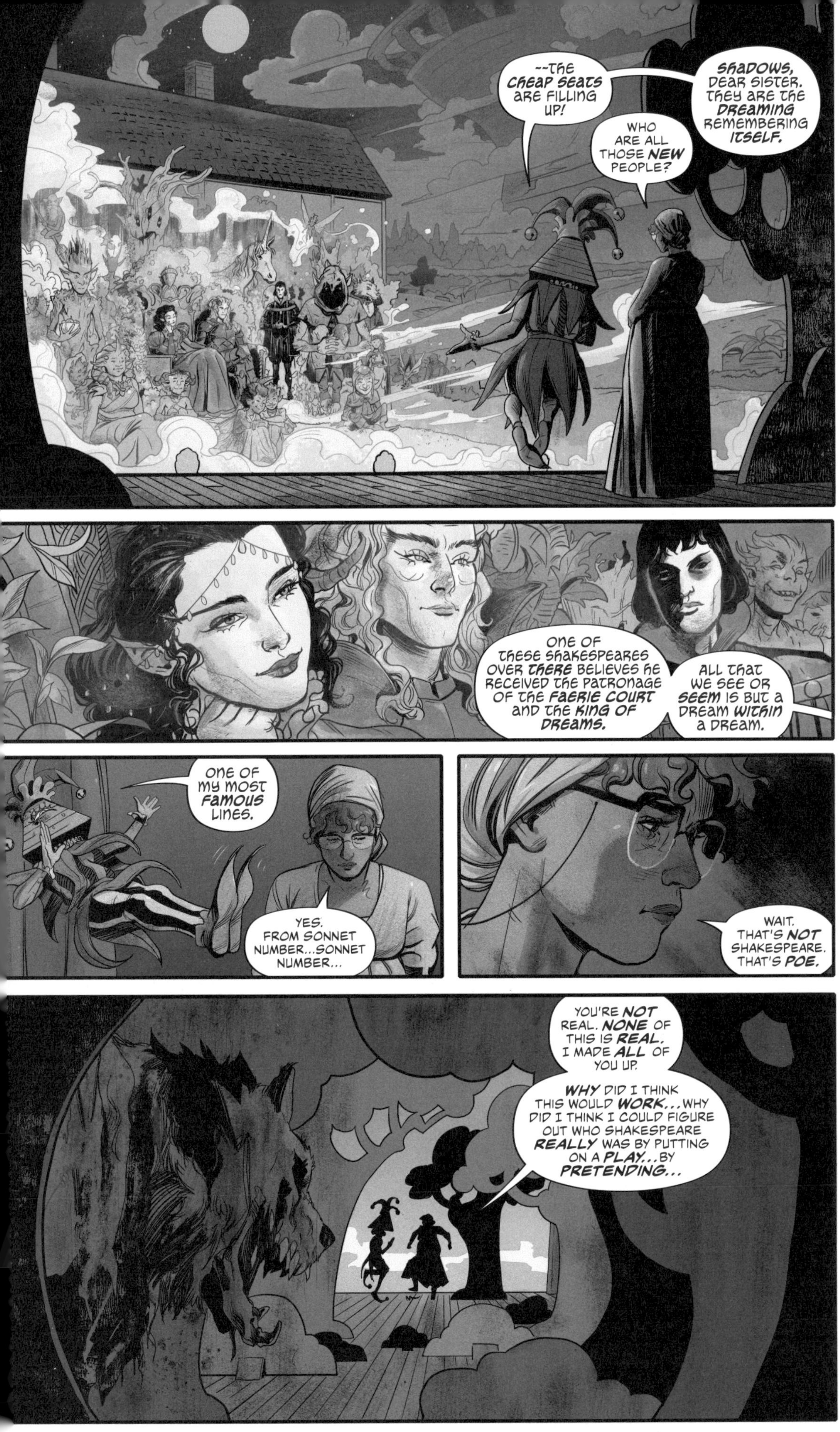
--THE CHEAP SEATS ARE FILLING UP!
SHADOWS, DEAR SISTER. THEY ARE THE DREAMING REMEMBERING ITSELF.
WHO ARE ALL THOSE NEW PEOPLE?
ONE OF THESE SHAKESPEARES OVER THERE BELIEVES HE RECEIVED THE PATRONAGE OF THE FAERIE COURT AND THE KING OF DREAMS.
ALL THAT WE SEE OR SEEM IS BUT A DREAM WITHIN A DREAM.
ONE OF MY MOST FAMOUS LINES.
YES. FROM SONNET NUMBER...SONNET NUMBER...
WAIT. THAT'S NOT SHAKESPEARE. THAT'S POE.
YOU'RE NOT REAL. NONE OF THIS IS REAL. I MADE ALL OF YOU UP.
WHY DID I THINK THIS WOULD WORK...WHY DID I THINK I COULD FIGURE OUT WHO SHAKESPEARE REALLY WAS BY PUTTING ON A PLAY...BY PRETENDING...

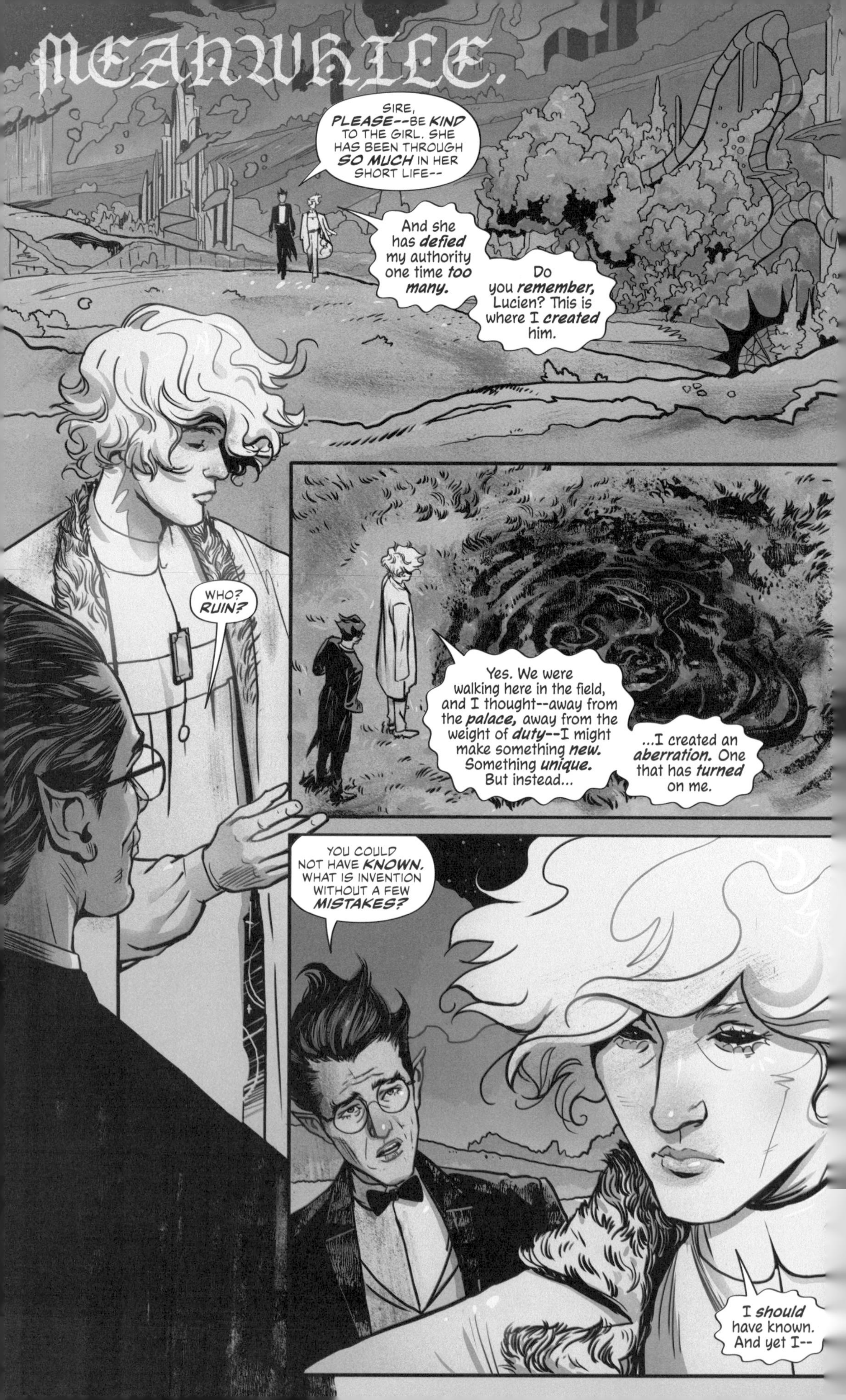
MEANWHILE.
SIRE, PLEASE--BE KIND TO THE GIRL. SHE HAS BEEN THROUGH SO MUCH IN HER SHORT LIFE--
And she has defied my authority one time too many.
Do you remember, Lucien? This is where I created him.
WHO? RUIN?
Yes. We were walking here in the field, and I thought--away from the palace, away from the weight of duty--I might make something new. Something unique. But instead...
...I created an aberration. One that has turned on me.
YOU COULD NOT HAVE KNOWN. WHAT IS INVENTION WITHOUT A FEW MISTAKES?
I should have known. And yet I--

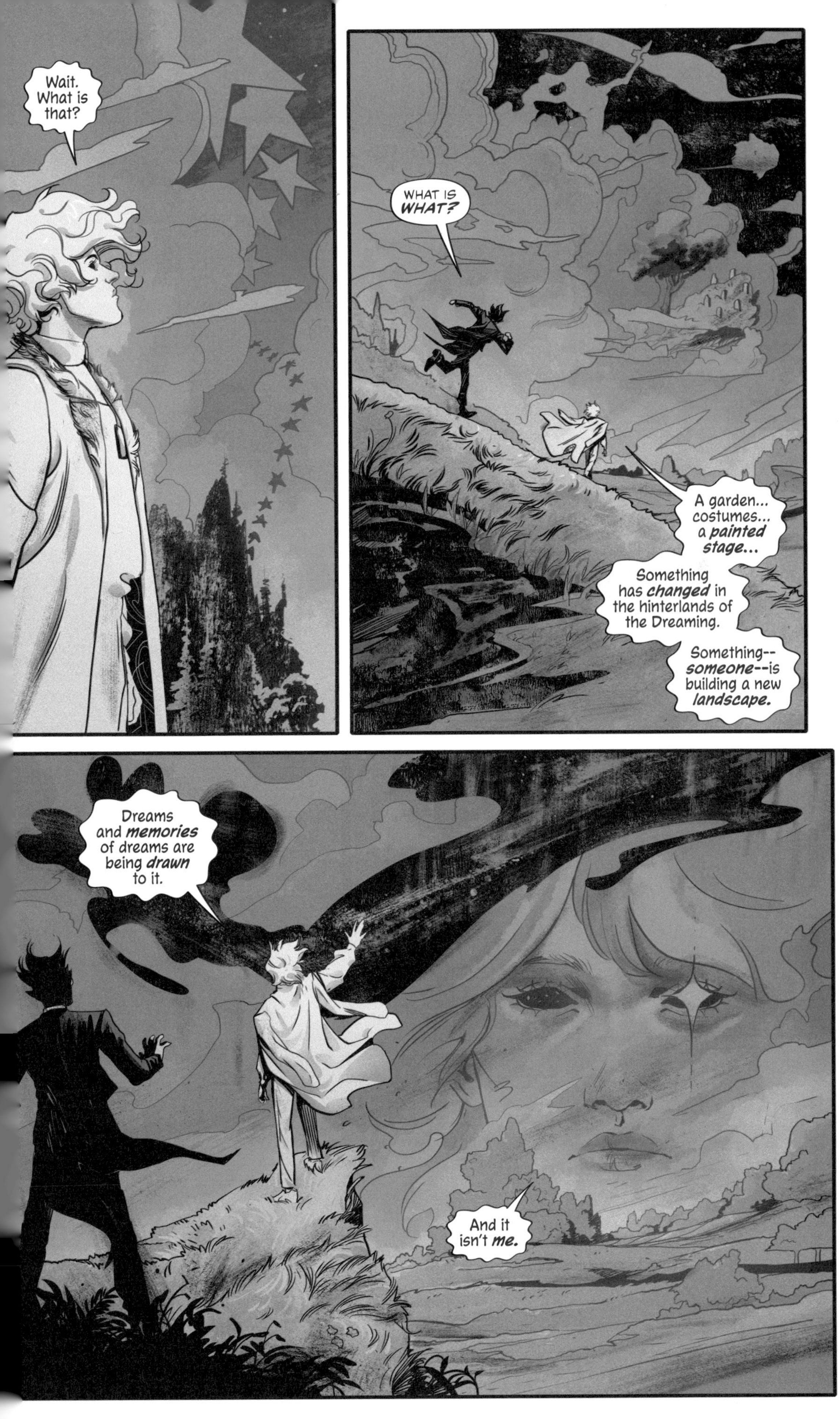
Wait. What is that?
WHAT IS WHAT?
A garden... costumes... a painted stage...
Something has changed in the hinterlands of the Dreaming.
Something--someone--is building a new landscape.
Dreams and memories of dreams are being drawn to it.
And it isn't me.

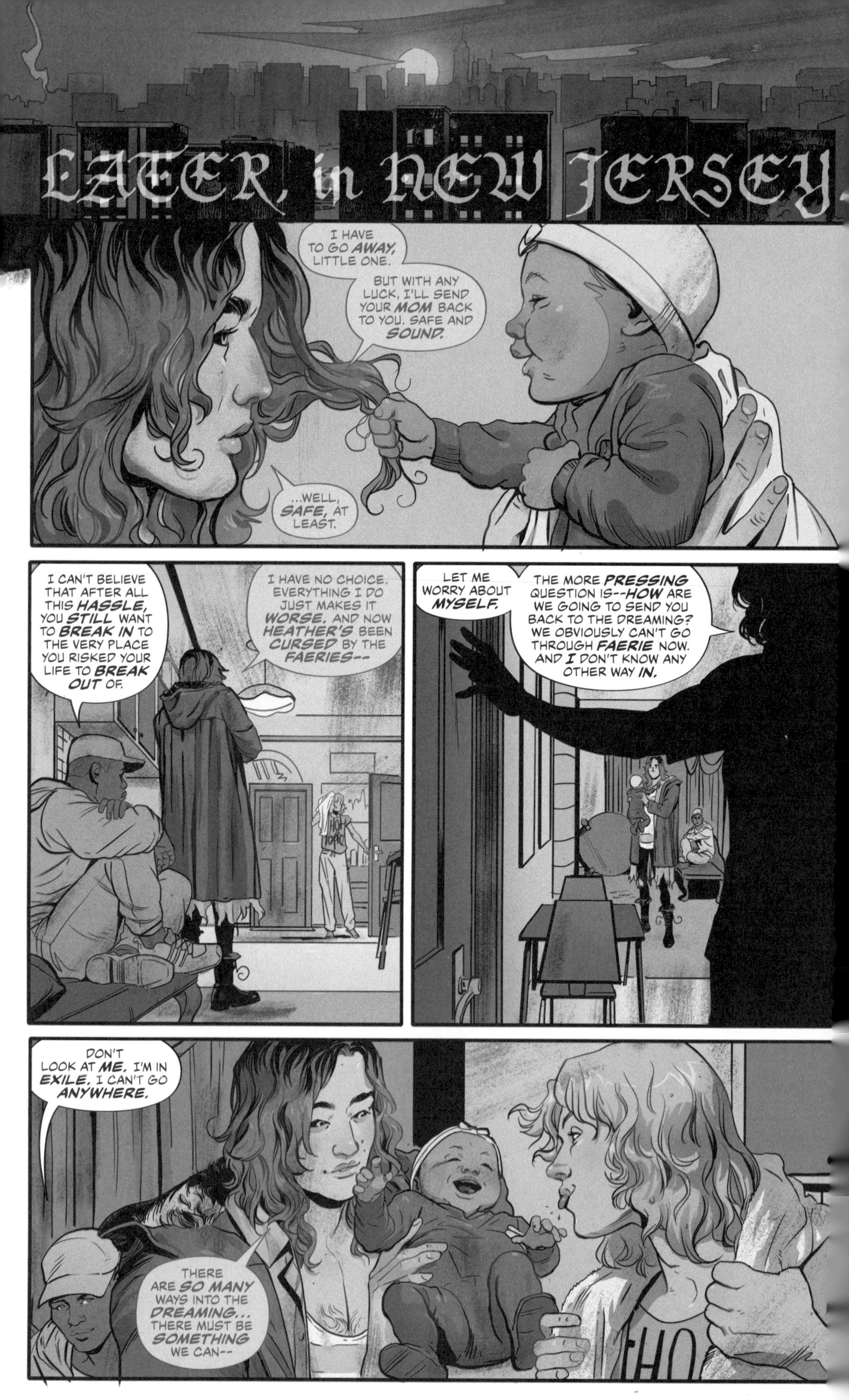
LATER, in NEW JERSEY...
I HAVE TO GO AWAY, LITTLE ONE.
BUT WITH ANY LUCK, I'LL SEND YOUR MOM BACK TO YOU. SAFE AND SOUND.
...WELL, SAFE, AT LEAST.
I CAN'T BELIEVE THAT AFTER ALL THIS HASSLE, YOU STILL WANT TO BREAK IN TO THE VERY PLACE YOU RISKED YOUR LIFE TO BREAK OUT OF.
I HAVE NO CHOICE. EVERYTHING I DO JUST MAKES IT WORSE. AND NOW HEATHER'S BEEN CURSED BY THE FAERIES--
LET ME WORRY ABOUT MYSELF.
THE MORE PRESSING QUESTION IS--HOW ARE WE GOING TO SEND YOU BACK TO THE DREAMING? WE OBVIOUSLY CAN'T GO THROUGH FAERIE NOW. AND I DON'T KNOW ANY OTHER WAY IN.
DON'T LOOK AT ME. I'M IN EXILE. I CAN'T GO ANYWHERE.
THERE ARE SO MANY WAYS INTO THE DREAMING... THERE MUST BE SOMETHING WE CAN--

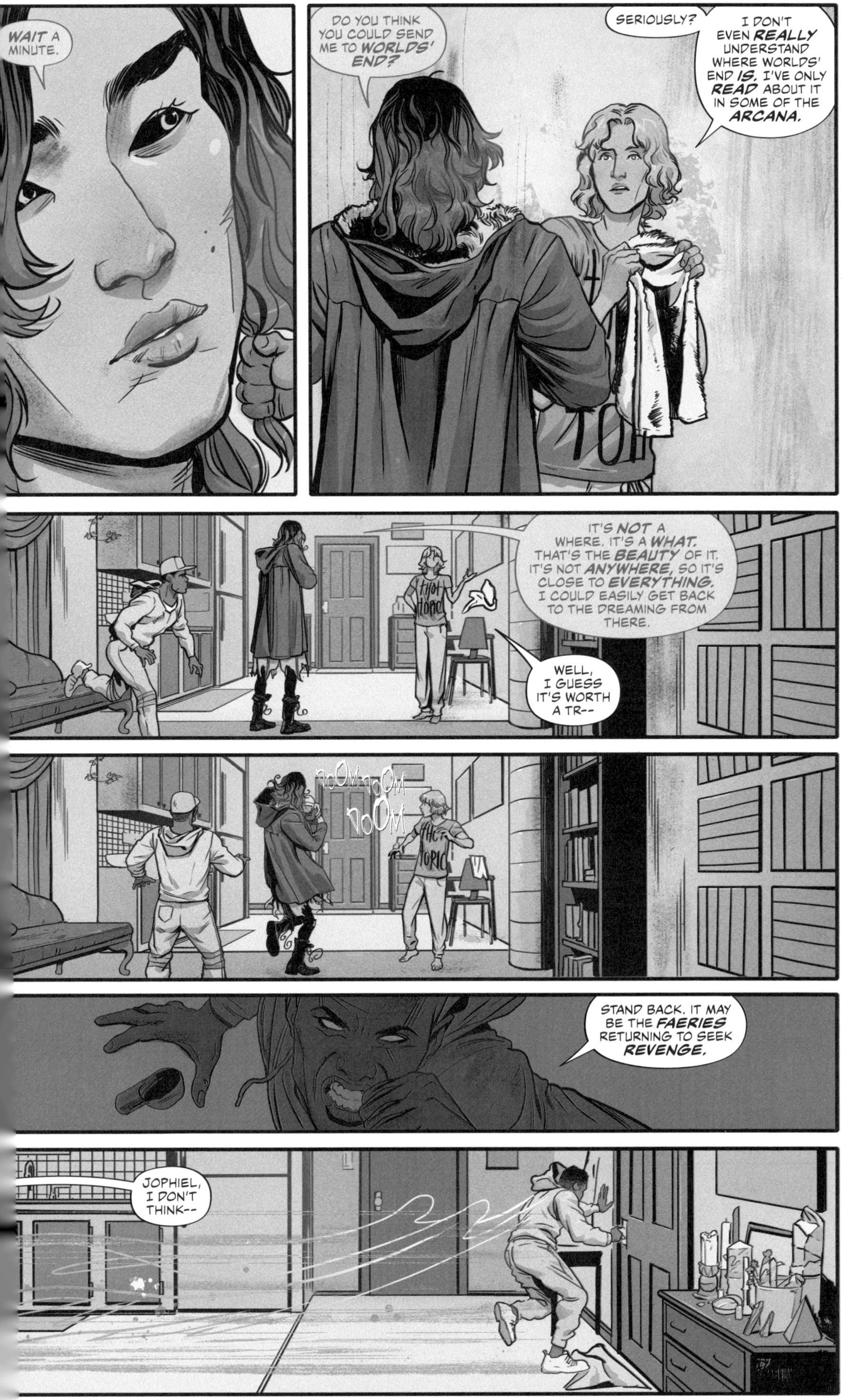
WAIT A MINUTE.
DO YOU THINK YOU COULD SEND ME TO WORLDS' END?
SERIOUSLY?
I DON'T EVEN REALLY UNDERSTAND WHERE WORLDS' END IS. I'VE ONLY READ ABOUT IT IN SOME OF THE ARCANA.
IT'S NOT A WHERE. IT'S A WHAT. THAT'S THE BEAUTY OF IT. IT'S NOT ANYWHERE, SO IT'S CLOSE TO EVERYTHING. I COULD EASILY GET BACK TO THE DREAMING FROM THERE.
WELL, I GUESS IT'S WORTH A TR--
DOOM DOOM DOOM
STAND BACK. IT MAY BE THE FAERIES RETURNING TO SEEK REVENGE.
JOPHIEL, I DON'T THINK--

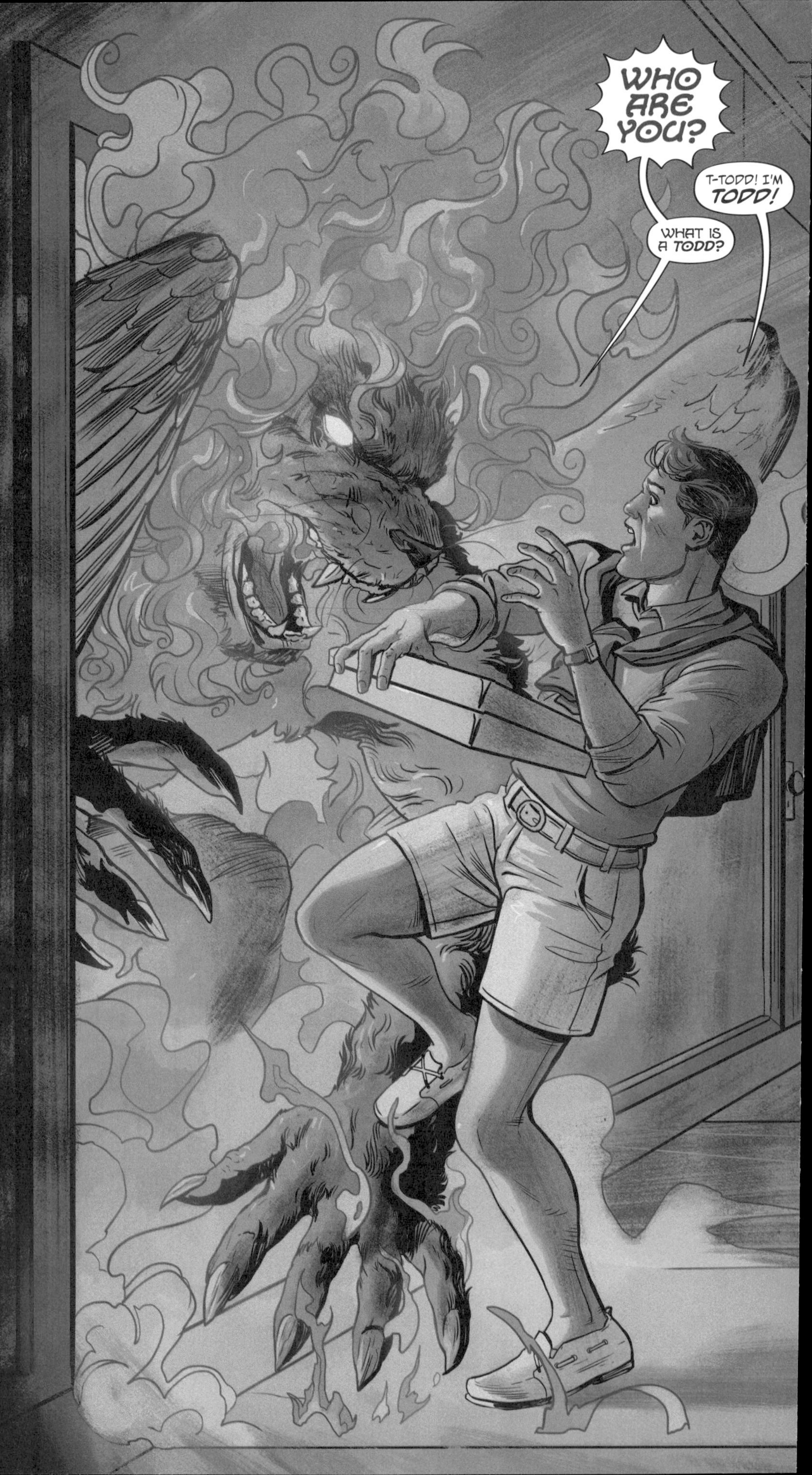
WHO ARE YOU?
T-TODD! I'M TODD!
WHAT IS A TODD?

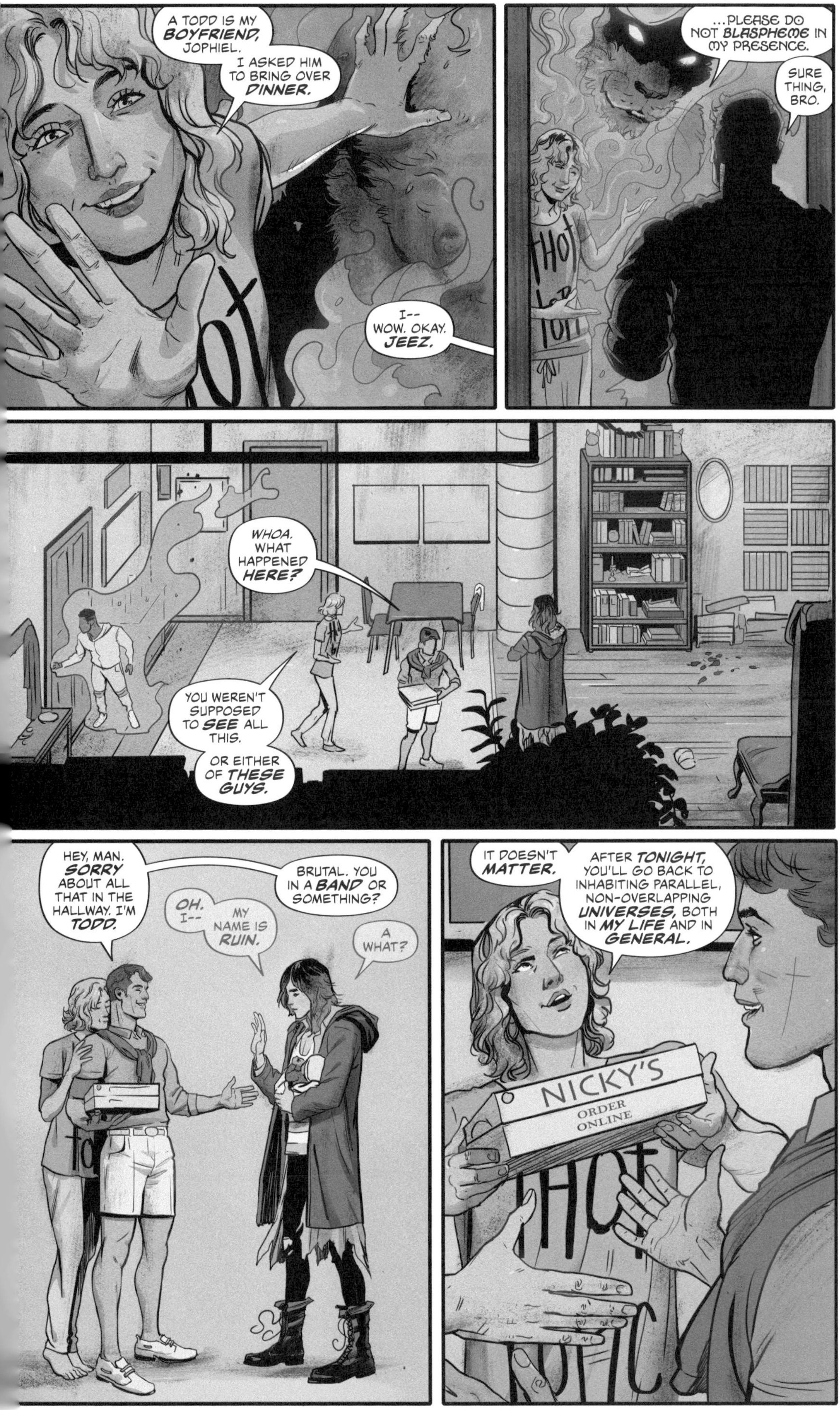
A TODD IS MY BOYFRIEND, JOPHIEL.
I ASKED HIM TO BRING OVER DINNER.
I-- WOW. OKAY. JEEZ.
...PLEASE DO NOT BLASPHEME IN MY PRESENCE.
SURE THING, BRO.
WHOA. WHAT HAPPENED HERE?
YOU WEREN'T SUPPOSED TO SEE ALL THIS.
OR EITHER OF THESE GUYS.
HEY, MAN. SORRY ABOUT ALL THAT IN THE HALLWAY. I'M TODD.
OH. I--
MY NAME IS RUIN.
BRUTAL. YOU IN A BAND OR SOMETHING?
A WHAT?
IT DOESN'T MATTER.
AFTER TONIGHT, YOU'LL GO BACK TO INHABITING PARALLEL, NON-OVERLAPPING UNIVERSES, BOTH IN MY LIFE AND IN GENERAL.
NICKY'S
ORDER ONLINE

THERE'S **NO WAY** I'M GETTING MY **SAFETY DEPOSIT** BACK AFTER ALL THIS...

ORDER ONLIN

NICKY

N

BABE? WHAT ARE, UHH--WHAT ARE YOU **DOING?**

CREATING A **PORTAL** THAT WILL SEND **RUIN** TO A NO-MAN'S-LAND **BETWEEN WORLDS.** OR, IF I FUCK IT U SUSPEND HIM ETERNALLY IN **NOTHINGNESS.**

WAIT, **REALLY?**

THIS NEEDS AN **INSURANCE POLICY**...AN **UNCLOUDED SOUL**...SOMEONE WHO HAS NEVER BEEN **EXPOSED** TO THIS KIND OF **MAGIC** BEFORE...

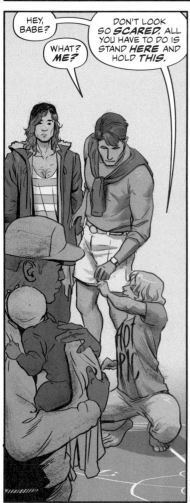

HEY, BABE?

WHAT? **ME?**

DON'T LOOK SO **SCARED.** ALL YOU HAVE TO DO IS STAND **HERE** AND HOLD **THIS.**

LAST TIME SOMEBODY TOLD ME THAT, I WAS RUSHING FOR **PHI DELTA DOUBLE-EPSILON,** AND I WOKE UP IN A **TOPIARY** WEARING SOMEONE ELSE'S **THONG--**

I'M AFRAID THIS IS GOING TO BE **LESS FUN.**

EVERYBODY **BREATHE NORMALLY** AND TRY TO **RELAX.**

THOT TOPIC

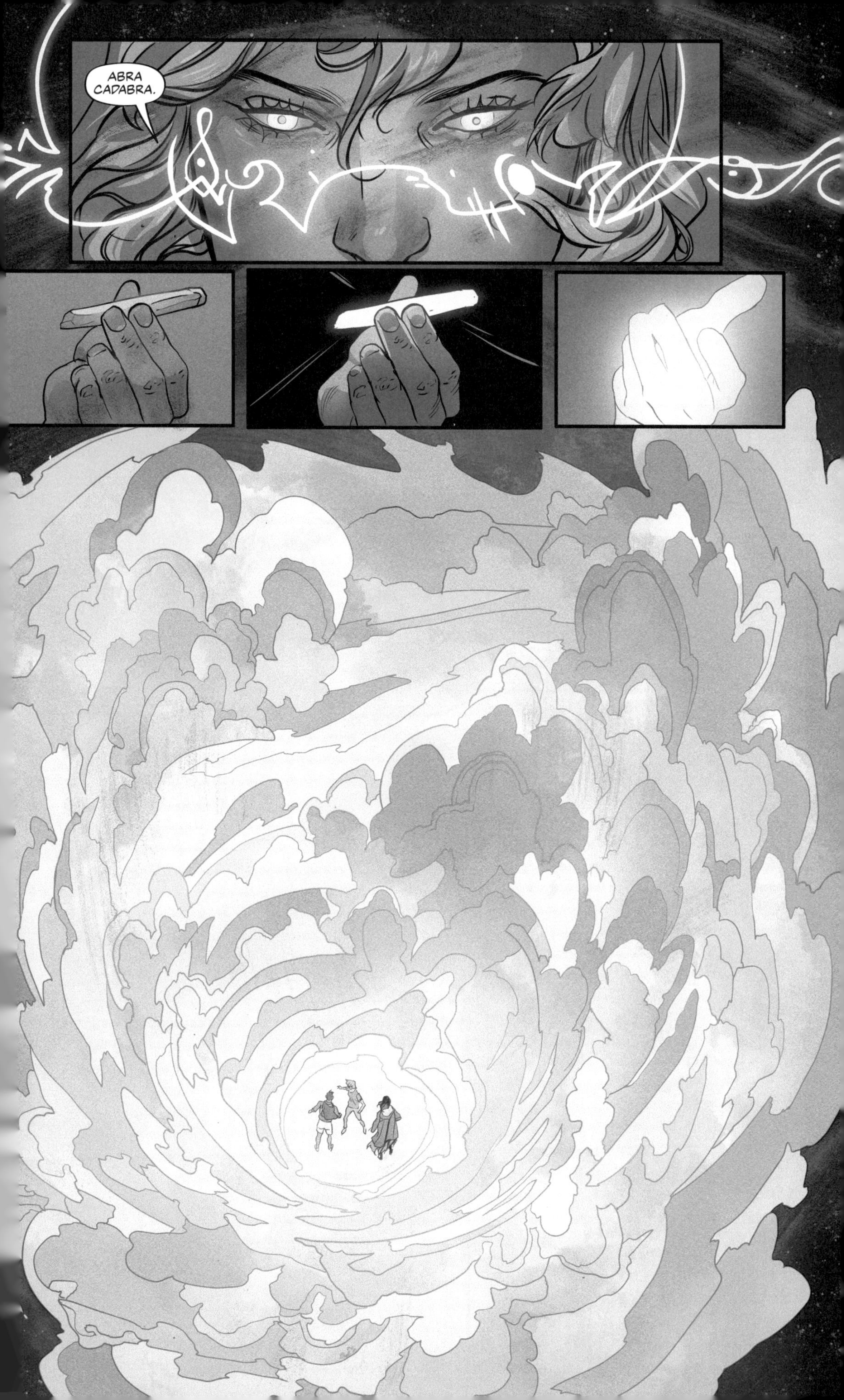
ABRA CADABRA.

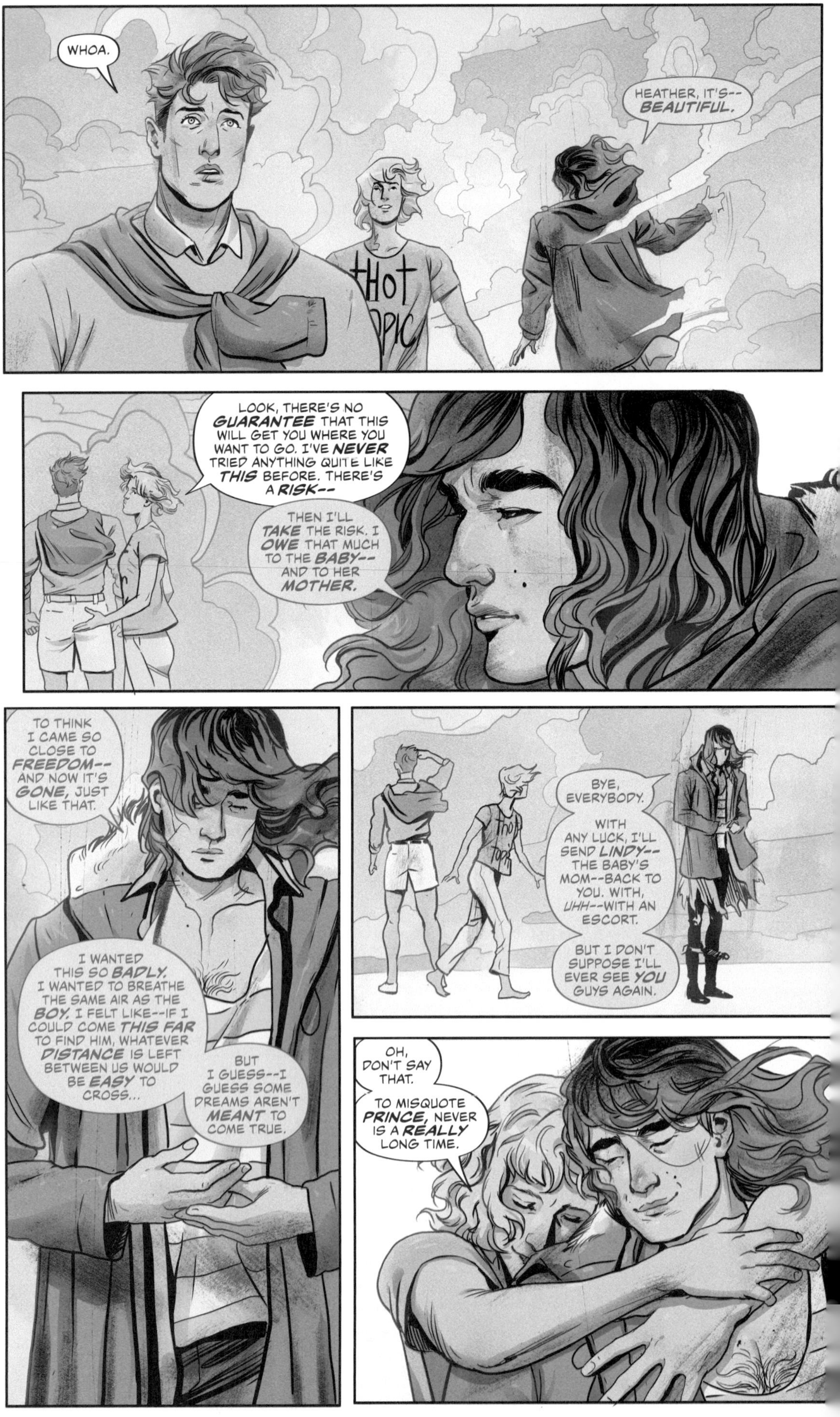
WHOA.
HEATHER, IT'S-- BEAUTIFUL.
tHot TOPIC
LOOK, THERE'S NO GUARANTEE THAT THIS WILL GET YOU WHERE YOU WANT TO GO. I'VE NEVER TRIED ANYTHING QUITE LIKE THIS BEFORE. THERE'S A RISK--
THEN I'LL TAKE THE RISK. I OWE THAT MUCH TO THE BABY-- AND TO HER MOTHER.
TO THINK I CAME SO CLOSE TO FREEDOM-- AND NOW IT'S GONE, JUST LIKE THAT.
I WANTED THIS SO BADLY. I WANTED TO BREATHE THE SAME AIR AS THE BOY. I FELT LIKE--IF I COULD COME THIS FAR TO FIND HIM, WHATEVER DISTANCE IS LEFT BETWEEN US WOULD BE EASY TO CROSS...
BUT I GUESS--I GUESS SOME DREAMS AREN'T MEANT TO COME TRUE.
BYE, EVERYBODY.
WITH ANY LUCK, I'LL SEND LINDY-- THE BABY'S MOM--BACK TO YOU. WITH, UHH--WITH AN ESCORT.
BUT I DON'T SUPPOSE I'LL EVER SEE YOU GUYS AGAIN.
OH, DON'T SAY THAT.
TO MISQUOTE PRINCE, NEVER IS A REALLY LONG TIME.

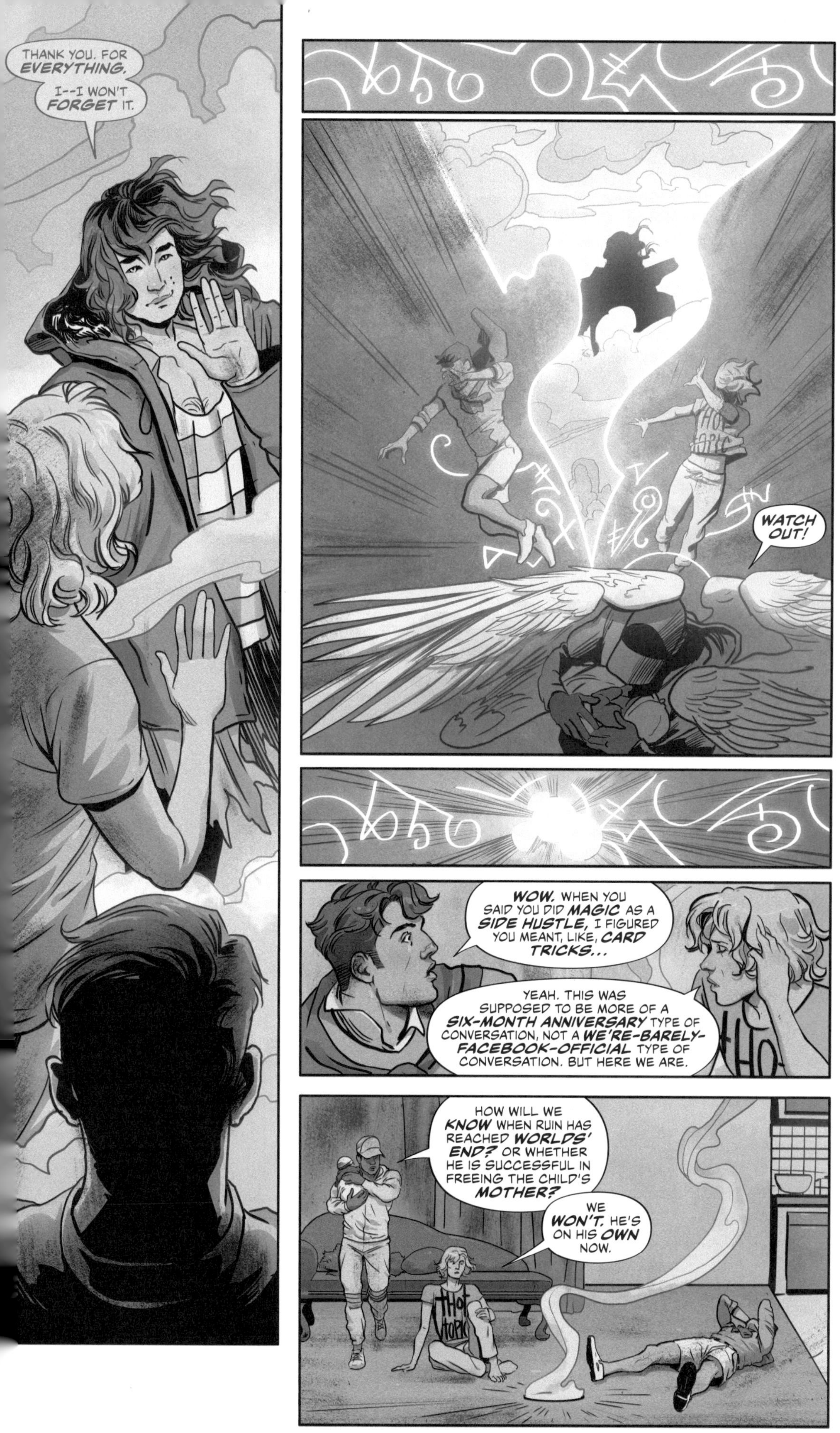

THANK YOU. FOR EVERYTHING. I--I WON'T FORGET IT.
WATCH OUT!
WOW. WHEN YOU SAID YOU DID MAGIC AS A SIDE HUSTLE, I FIGURED YOU MEANT, LIKE, CARD TRICKS...
YEAH. THIS WAS SUPPOSED TO BE MORE OF A SIX-MONTH ANNIVERSARY TYPE OF CONVERSATION, NOT A WE'RE-BARELY-FACEBOOK-OFFICIAL TYPE OF CONVERSATION. BUT HERE WE ARE.
HOW WILL WE KNOW WHEN RUIN HAS REACHED WORLDS' END? OR WHETHER HE IS SUCCESSFUL IN FREEING THE CHILD'S MOTHER?
WE WON'T. HE'S ON HIS OWN NOW.

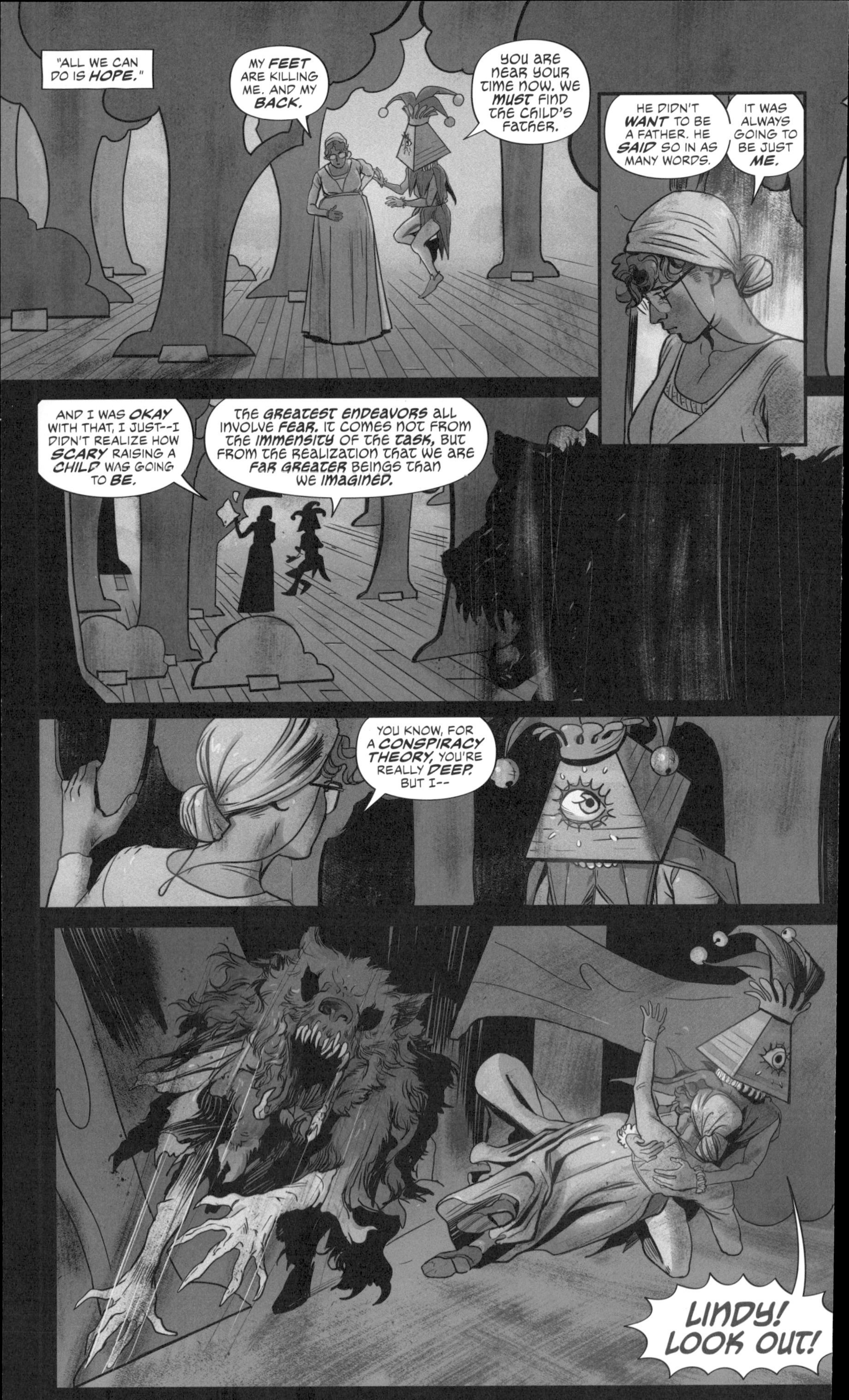
"ALL WE CAN DO IS HOPE."
MY FEET ARE KILLING ME. AND MY BACK.
YOU ARE NEAR YOUR TIME NOW. WE MUST FIND THE CHILD'S FATHER.
HE DIDN'T WANT TO BE A FATHER. HE SAID SO IN AS MANY WORDS.
IT WAS ALWAYS GOING TO BE JUST ME.
AND I WAS OKAY WITH THAT, I JUST--I DIDN'T REALIZE HOW SCARY RAISING A CHILD WAS GOING TO BE.
THE GREATEST ENDEAVORS ALL INVOLVE FEAR. IT COMES NOT FROM THE IMMENSITY OF THE TASK, BUT FROM THE REALIZATION THAT WE ARE FAR GREATER BEINGS THAN WE IMAGINED.
YOU KNOW, FOR A CONSPIRACY THEORY, YOU'RE REALLY DEEP. BUT I--
LINDY! LOOK OUT!

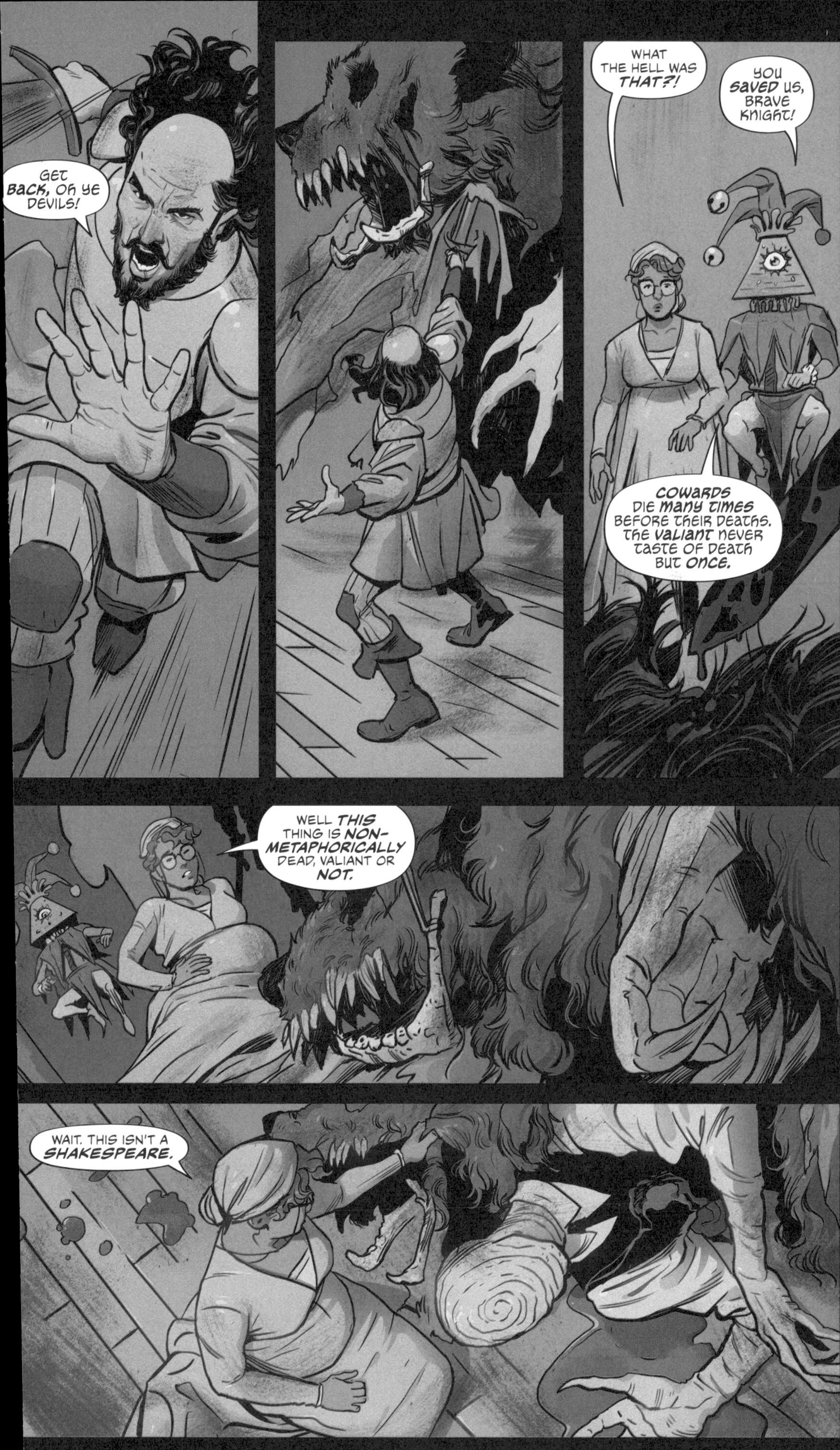
GET BACK, OH YE DEVILS!
WHAT THE HELL WAS THAT?!
YOU SAVED US, BRAVE KNIGHT!
COWARDS DIE MANY TIMES BEFORE THEIR DEATHS. THE VALIANT NEVER TASTE OF DEATH BUT ONCE.
WELL THIS THING IS NON-METAPHORICALLY DEAD, VALIANT OR NOT.
WAIT. THIS ISN'T A SHAKESPEARE.

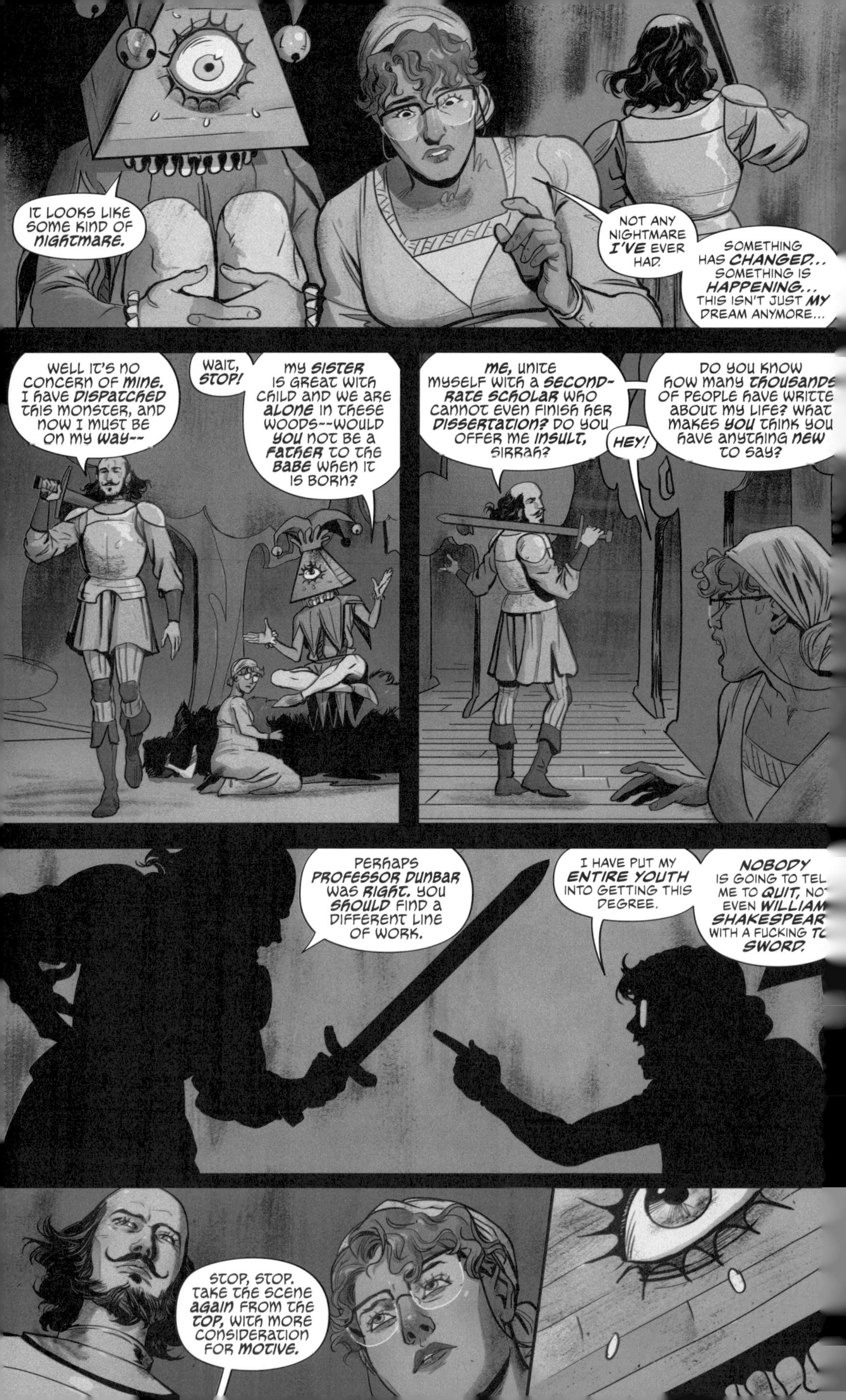
IT LOOKS LIKE SOME KIND OF NIGHTMARE.
NOT ANY NIGHTMARE I'VE EVER HAD.
SOMETHING HAS CHANGED... SOMETHING IS HAPPENING... THIS ISN'T JUST MY DREAM ANYMORE...
WELL IT'S NO CONCERN OF MINE. I HAVE DISPATCHED THIS MONSTER, AND NOW I MUST BE ON MY WAY--
WAIT, STOP!
MY SISTER IS GREAT WITH CHILD AND WE ARE ALONE IN THESE WOODS--WOULD YOU NOT BE A FATHER TO THE BABE WHEN IT IS BORN?
ME, UNITE MYSELF WITH A SECOND-RATE SCHOLAR WHO CANNOT EVEN FINISH HER DISSERTATION? DO YOU OFFER ME INSULT, SIRRAH?
HEY!
DO YOU KNOW HOW MANY THOUSANDS OF PEOPLE HAVE WRITTE ABOUT MY LIFE? WHAT MAKES YOU THINK YOU HAVE ANYTHING NEW TO SAY?
PERHAPS PROFESSOR DUNBAR WAS RIGHT. YOU SHOULD FIND A DIFFERENT LINE OF WORK.
I HAVE PUT MY ENTIRE YOUTH INTO GETTING THIS DEGREE.
NOBODY IS GOING TO TEL ME TO QUIT, NO EVEN WILLIAM SHAKESPEAR WITH A FUCKING TO SWORD.
STOP, STOP. TAKE THE SCENE AGAIN FROM THE TOP, WITH MORE CONSIDERATION FOR MOTIVE.

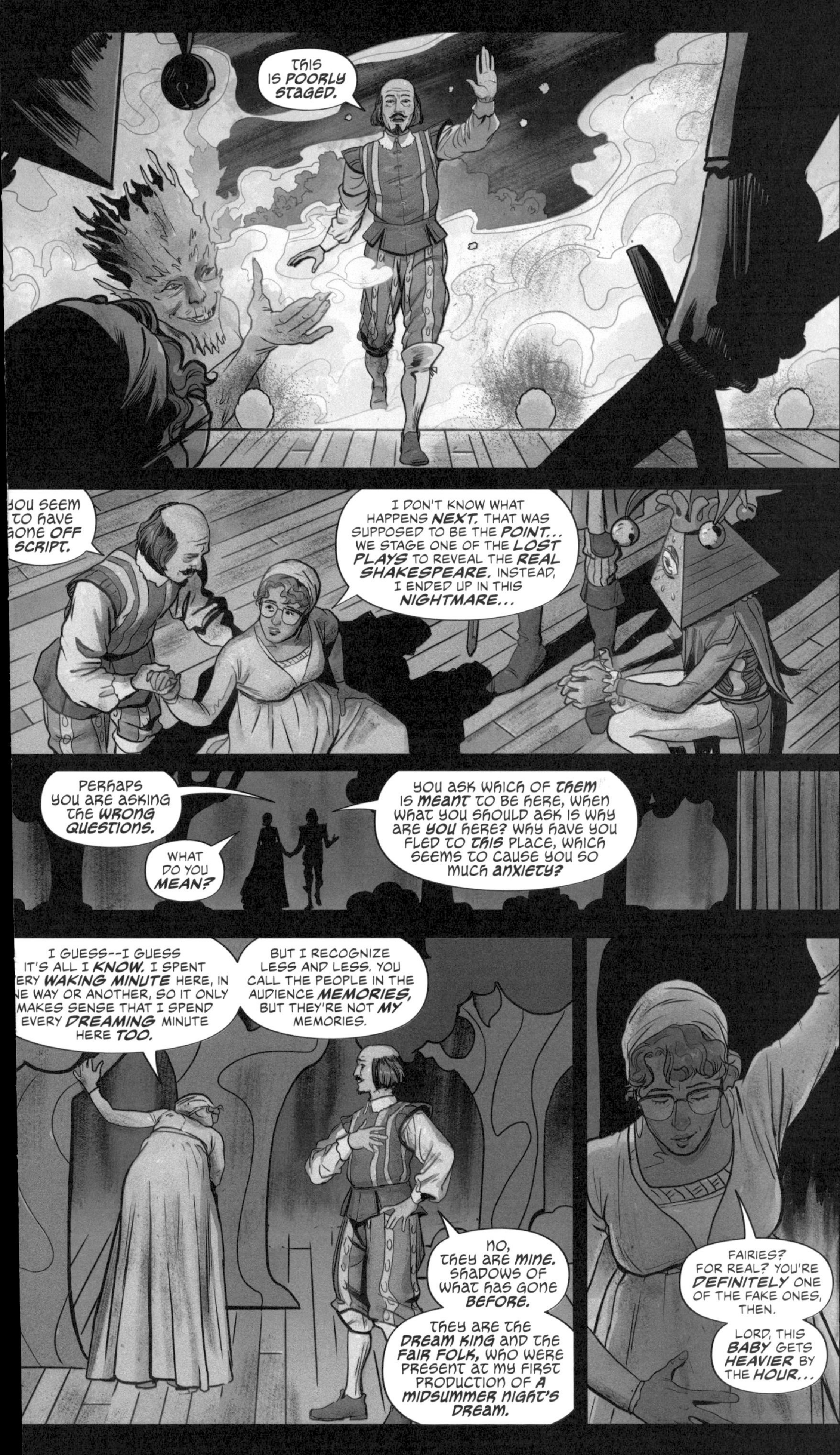
THIS IS POORLY STAGED.
YOU SEEM TO HAVE GONE OFF SCRIPT.
I DON'T KNOW WHAT HAPPENS NEXT. THAT WAS SUPPOSED TO BE THE POINT... WE STAGE ONE OF THE LOST PLAYS TO REVEAL THE REAL SHAKESPEARE. INSTEAD, I ENDED UP IN THIS NIGHTMARE...
PERHAPS YOU ARE ASKING THE WRONG QUESTIONS.
WHAT DO YOU MEAN?
YOU ASK WHICH OF THEM IS MEANT TO BE HERE, WHEN WHAT YOU SHOULD ASK IS WHY ARE YOU HERE? WHY HAVE YOU FLED TO THIS PLACE, WHICH SEEMS TO CAUSE YOU SO MUCH ANXIETY?
I GUESS--I GUESS IT'S ALL I KNOW. I SPENT ERY WAKING MINUTE HERE, IN NE WAY OR ANOTHER, SO IT ONLY MAKES SENSE THAT I SPEND EVERY DREAMING MINUTE HERE TOO.
BUT I RECOGNIZE LESS AND LESS. YOU CALL THE PEOPLE IN THE AUDIENCE MEMORIES, BUT THEY'RE NOT MY MEMORIES.
NO, THEY ARE MINE. SHADOWS OF WHAT HAS GONE BEFORE.
THEY ARE THE DREAM KING AND THE FAIR FOLK, WHO WERE PRESENT AT MY FIRST PRODUCTION OF A MIDSUMMER NIGHT'S DREAM.
FAIRIES? FOR REAL? YOU'RE DEFINITELY ONE OF THE FAKE ONES, THEN.
LORD, THIS BABY GETS HEAVIER BY THE HOUR...

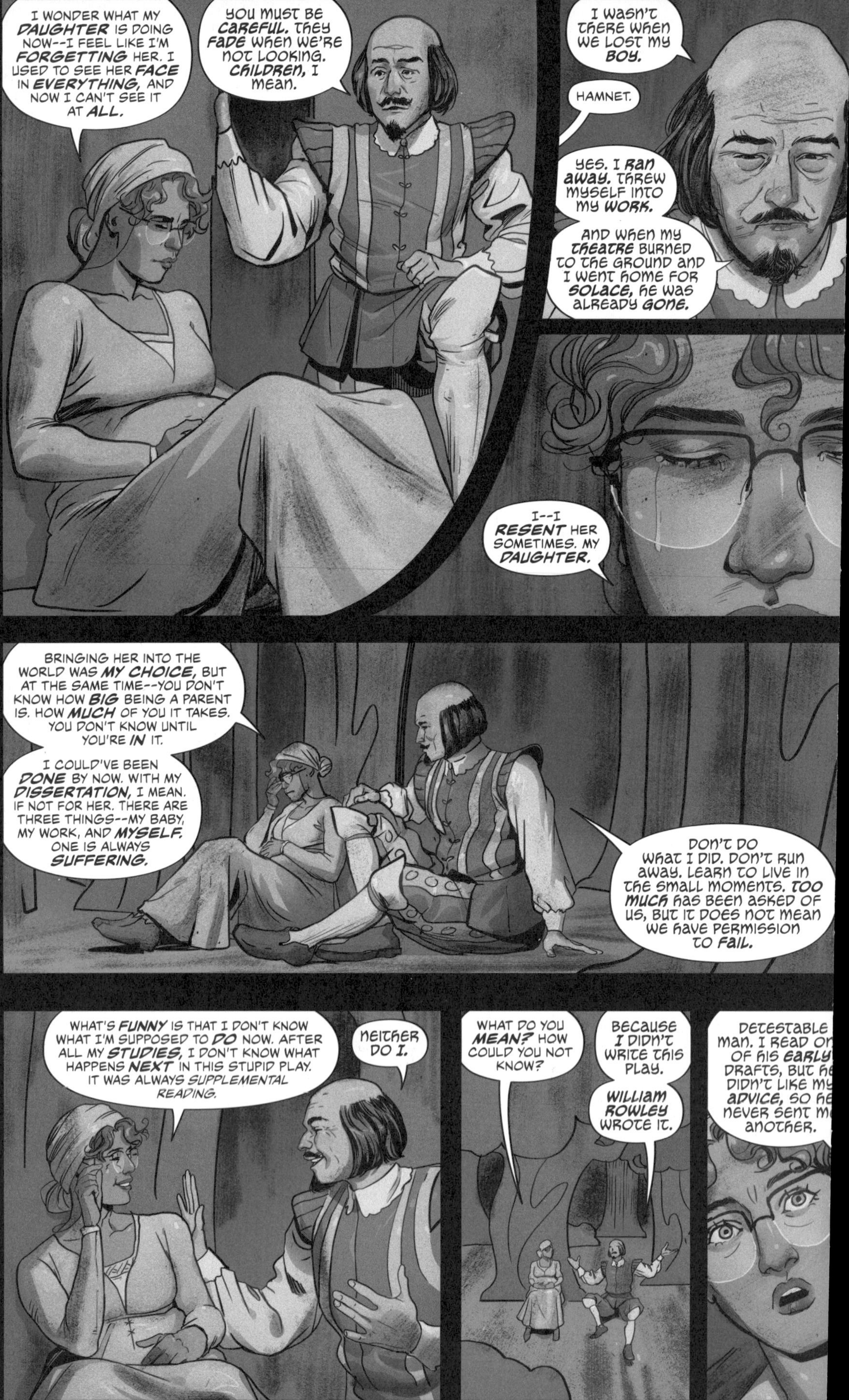
I WONDER WHAT MY DAUGHTER IS DOING NOW--I FEEL LIKE I'M FORGETTING HER. I USED TO SEE HER FACE IN EVERYTHING, AND NOW I CAN'T SEE IT AT ALL.
YOU MUST BE CAREFUL. THEY FADE WHEN WE'RE NOT LOOKING. CHILDREN, I MEAN.
I WASN'T THERE WHEN WE LOST MY BOY.
HAMNET.
YES. I RAN AWAY. THREW MYSELF INTO MY WORK.
AND WHEN MY THEATRE BURNED TO THE GROUND AND I WENT HOME FOR SOLACE, HE WAS ALREADY GONE.
I--I RESENT HER SOMETIMES. MY DAUGHTER.
BRINGING HER INTO THE WORLD WAS MY CHOICE, BUT AT THE SAME TIME--YOU DON'T KNOW HOW BIG BEING A PARENT IS. HOW MUCH OF YOU IT TAKES. YOU DON'T KNOW UNTIL YOU'RE IN IT.
I COULD'VE BEEN DONE BY NOW. WITH MY DISSERTATION, I MEAN. IF NOT FOR HER. THERE ARE THREE THINGS--MY BABY, MY WORK, AND MYSELF. ONE IS ALWAYS SUFFERING.
DON'T DO WHAT I DID. DON'T RUN AWAY. LEARN TO LIVE IN THE SMALL MOMENTS. TOO MUCH HAS BEEN ASKED OF US, BUT IT DOES NOT MEAN WE HAVE PERMISSION TO FAIL.
WHAT'S FUNNY IS THAT I DON'T KNOW WHAT I'M SUPPOSED TO DO NOW. AFTER ALL MY STUDIES, I DON'T KNOW WHAT HAPPENS NEXT IN THIS STUPID PLAY. IT WAS ALWAYS SUPPLEMENTAL READING.
NEITHER DO I.
WHAT DO YOU MEAN? HOW COULD YOU NOT KNOW?
BECAUSE I DIDN'T WRITE THIS PLAY.
WILLIAM ROWLEY WROTE IT.

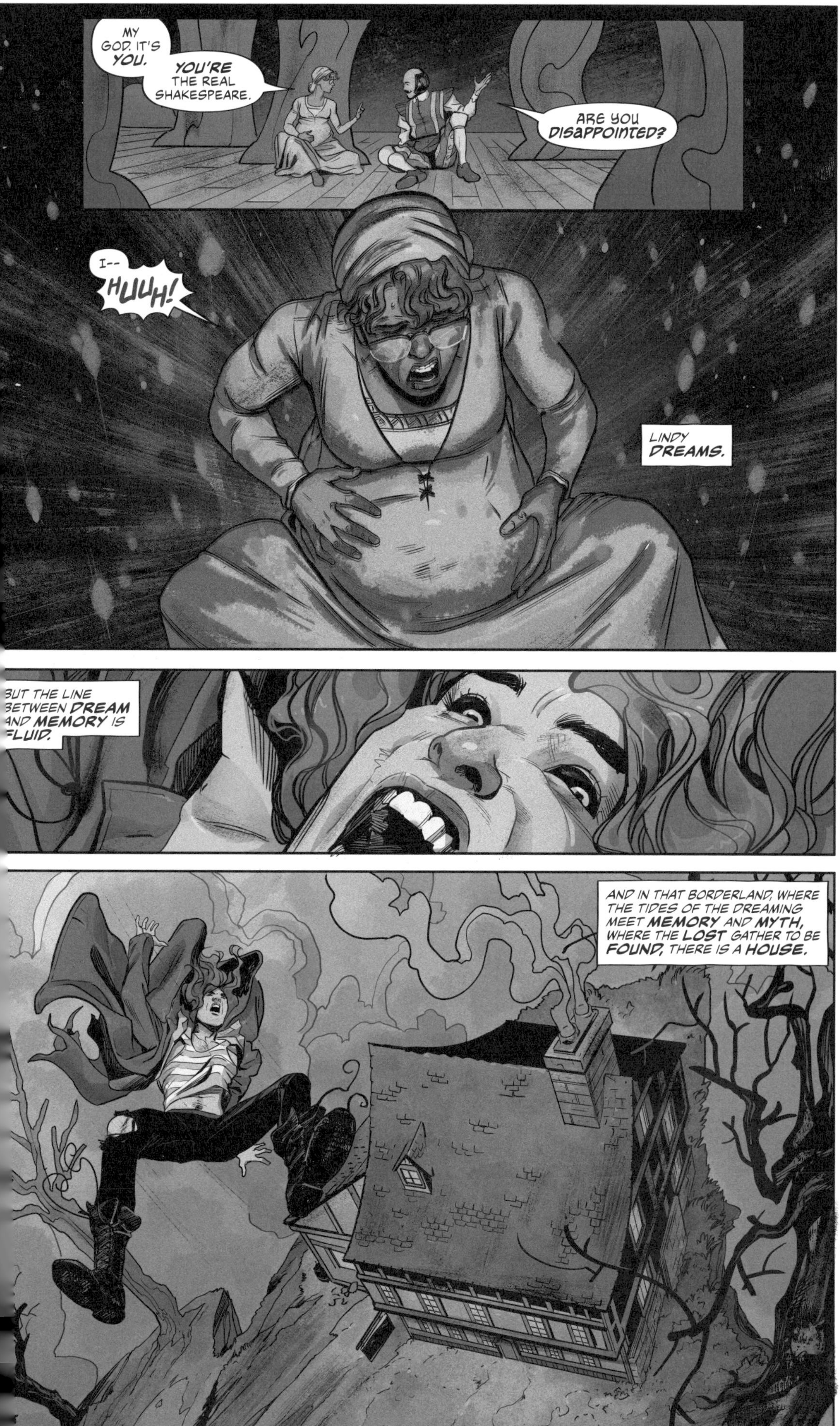
MY GOD. IT'S YOU.
YOU'RE THE REAL SHAKESPEARE.
ARE YOU DISAPPOINTED?
I--
HUUH!
LINDY DREAMS.
BUT THE LINE BETWEEN DREAM AND MEMORY IS FLUID.
AND IN THAT BORDERLAND, WHERE THE TIDES OF THE DREAMING MEET MEMORY AND MYTH, WHERE THE LOST GATHER TO BE FOUND, THERE IS A HOUSE.

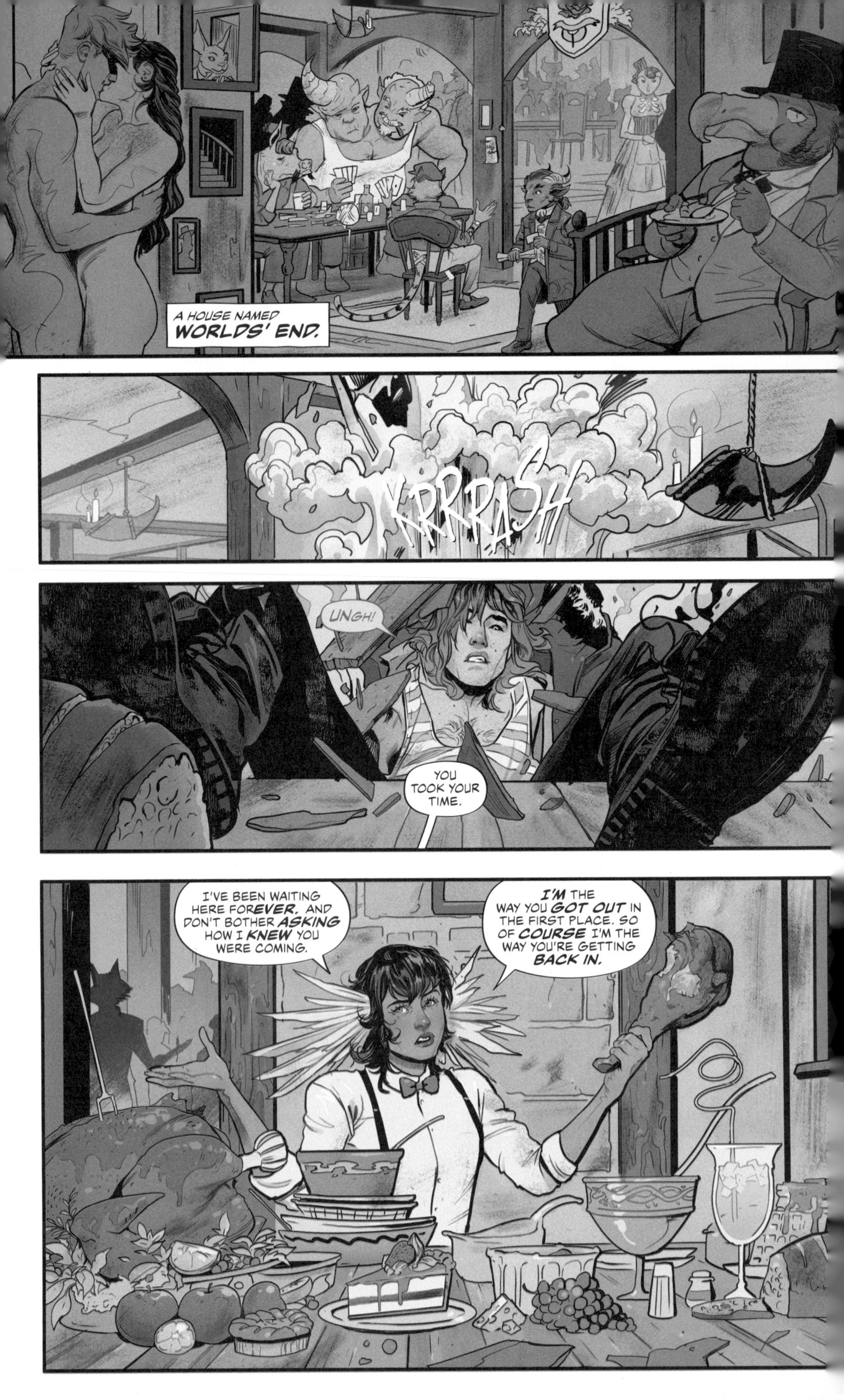

A HOUSE NAMED WORLDS' END.
KRRRRASH
UNGH!
YOU TOOK YOUR TIME.
I'VE BEEN WAITING HERE FOREVER. AND DON'T BOTHER ASKING HOW I KNEW YOU WERE COMING.
I'M THE WAY YOU GOT OUT IN THE FIRST PLACE. SO OF COURSE I'M THE WAY YOU'RE GETTING BACK IN.

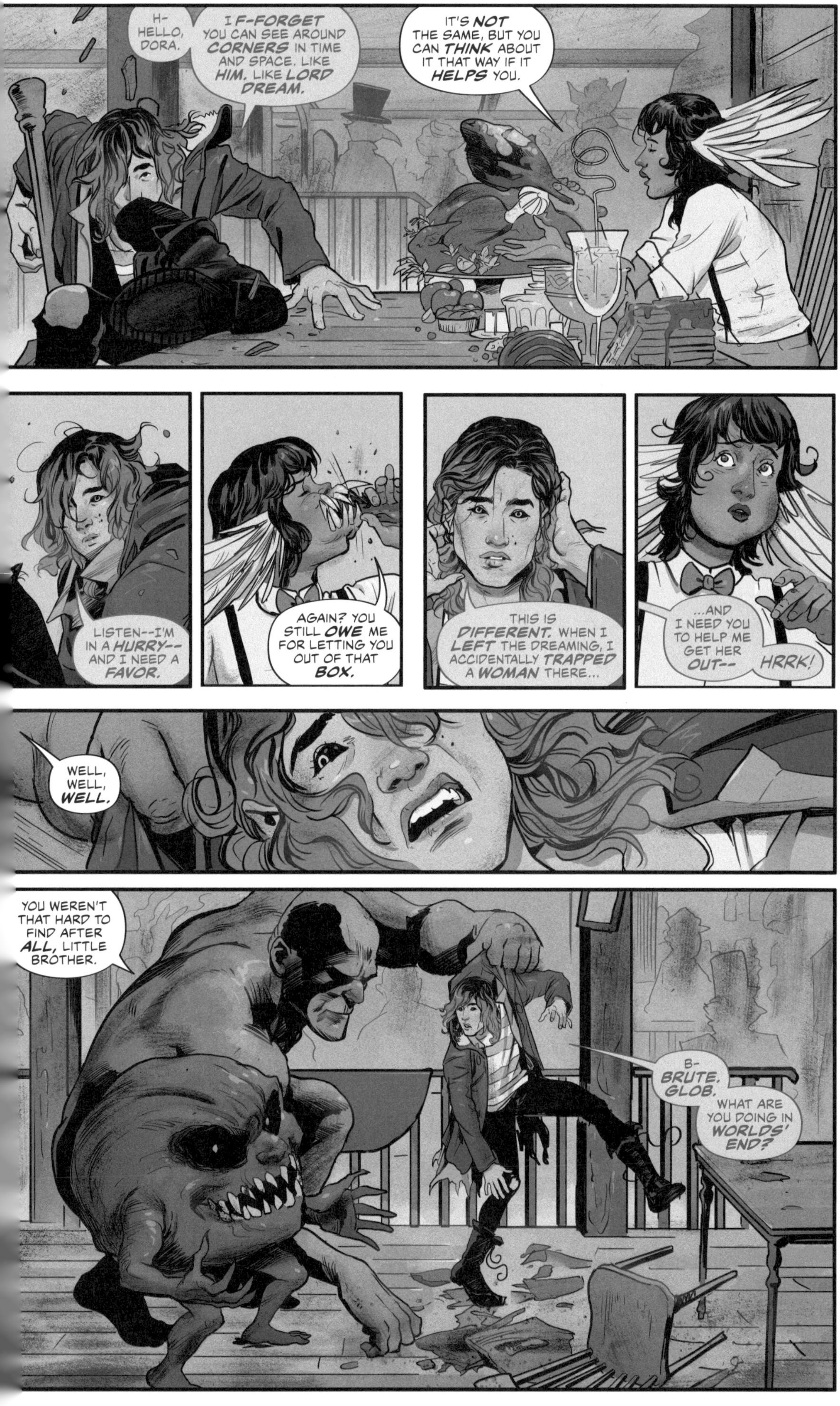
H-HELLO, DORA.
I F-FORGET YOU CAN SEE AROUND CORNERS IN TIME AND SPACE. LIKE HIM. LIKE LORD DREAM.
IT'S NOT THE SAME, BUT YOU CAN THINK ABOUT IT THAT WAY IF IT HELPS YOU.
LISTEN--I'M IN A HURRY--AND I NEED A FAVOR.
AGAIN? YOU STILL OWE ME FOR LETTING YOU OUT OF THAT BOX.
THIS IS DIFFERENT. WHEN I LEFT THE DREAMING, I ACCIDENTALLY TRAPPED A WOMAN THERE...
...AND I NEED YOU TO HELP ME GET HER OUT--
HRRK!
WELL, WELL, WELL.
YOU WEREN'T THAT HARD TO FIND AFTER ALL, LITTLE BROTHER.
B-BRUTE. GLOB. WHAT ARE YOU DOING IN WORLDS' END?

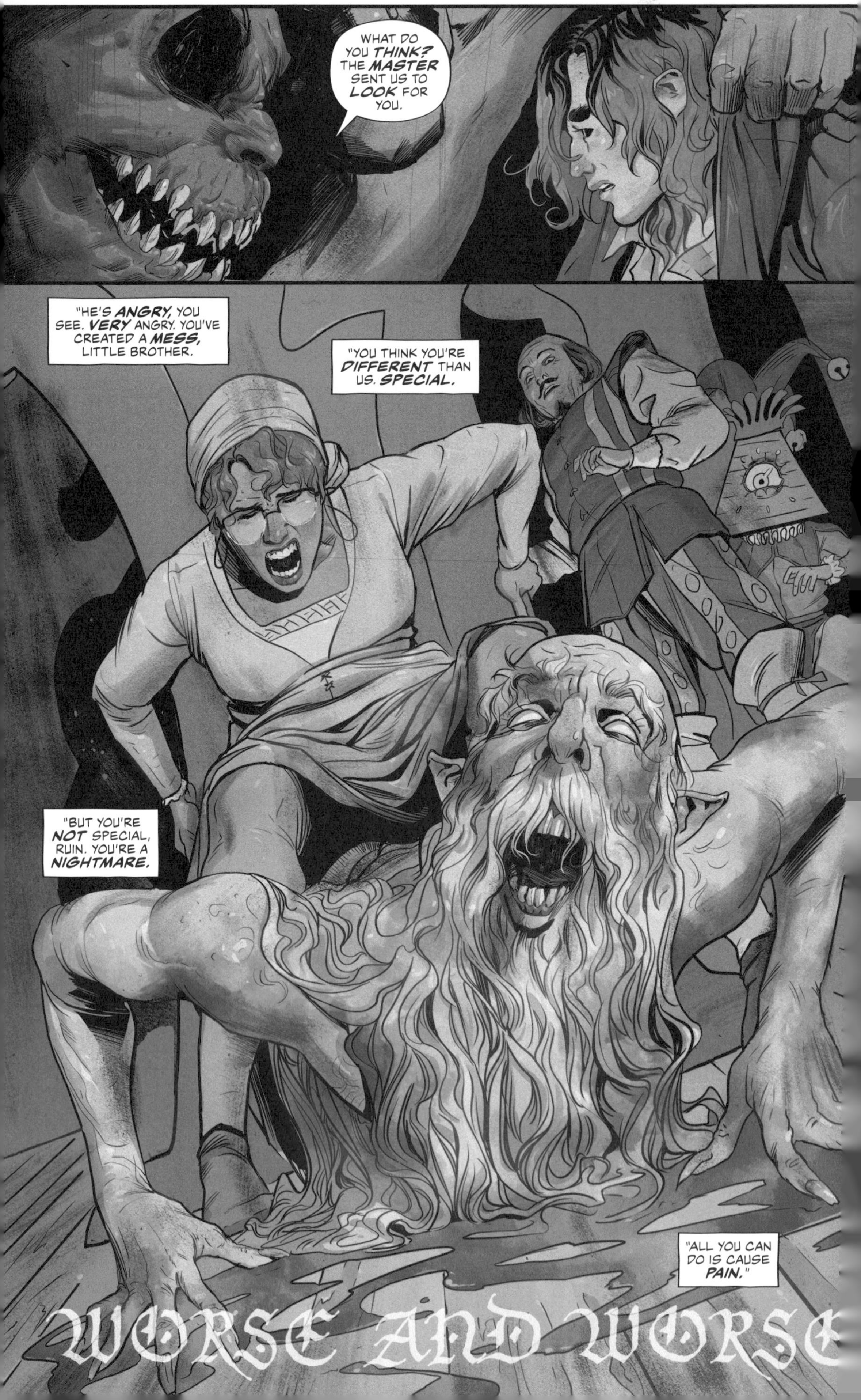
WHAT DO YOU THINK? THE MASTER SENT US TO LOOK FOR YOU.
"HE'S ANGRY, YOU SEE. VERY ANGRY. YOU'VE CREATED A MESS, LITTLE BROTHER.
"YOU THINK YOU'RE DIFFERENT THAN US. SPECIAL.
"BUT YOU'RE NOT SPECIAL, RUIN. YOU'RE A NIGHTMARE.
"ALL YOU CAN DO IS CAUSE PAIN."
WORSE AND WORSE

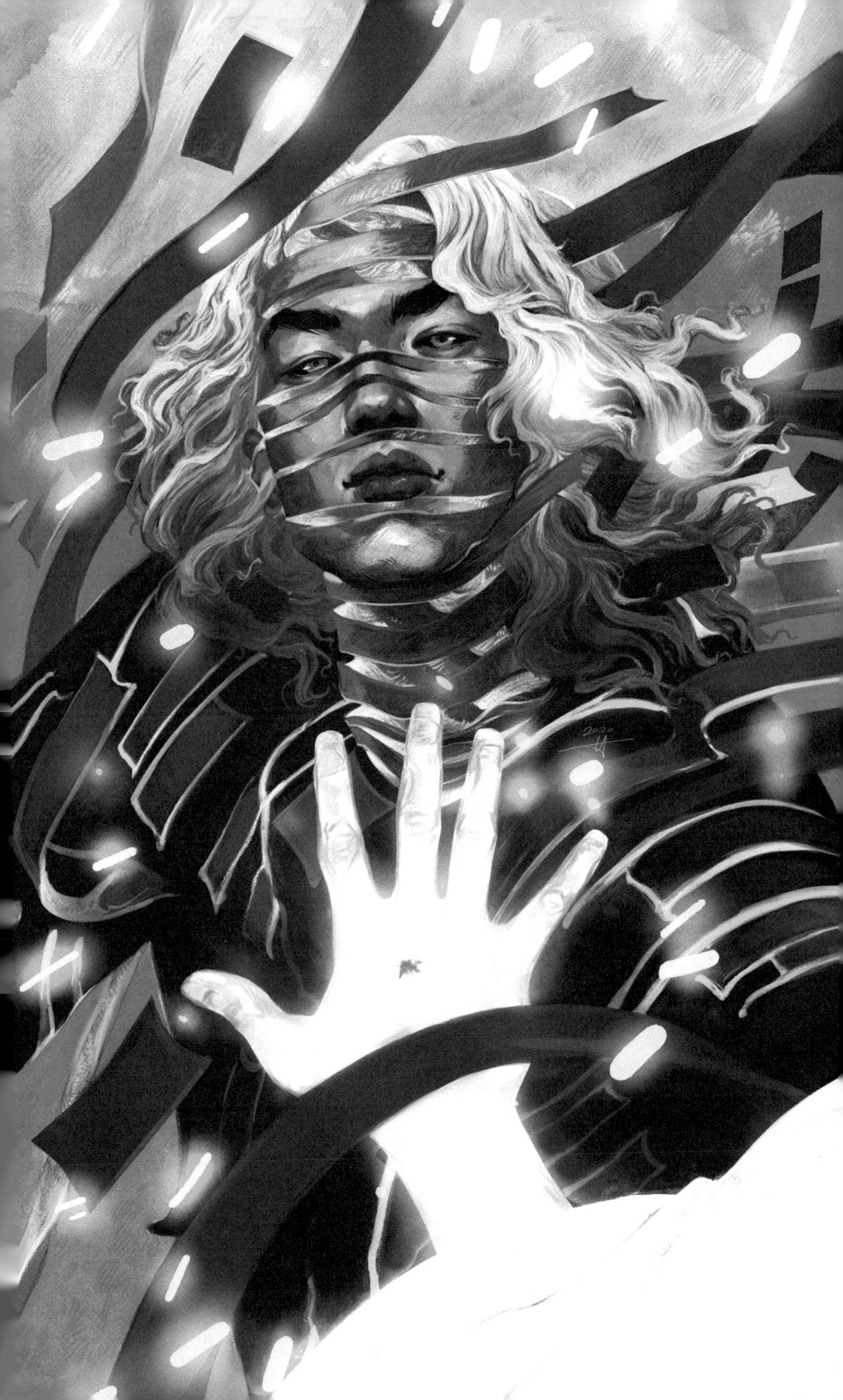

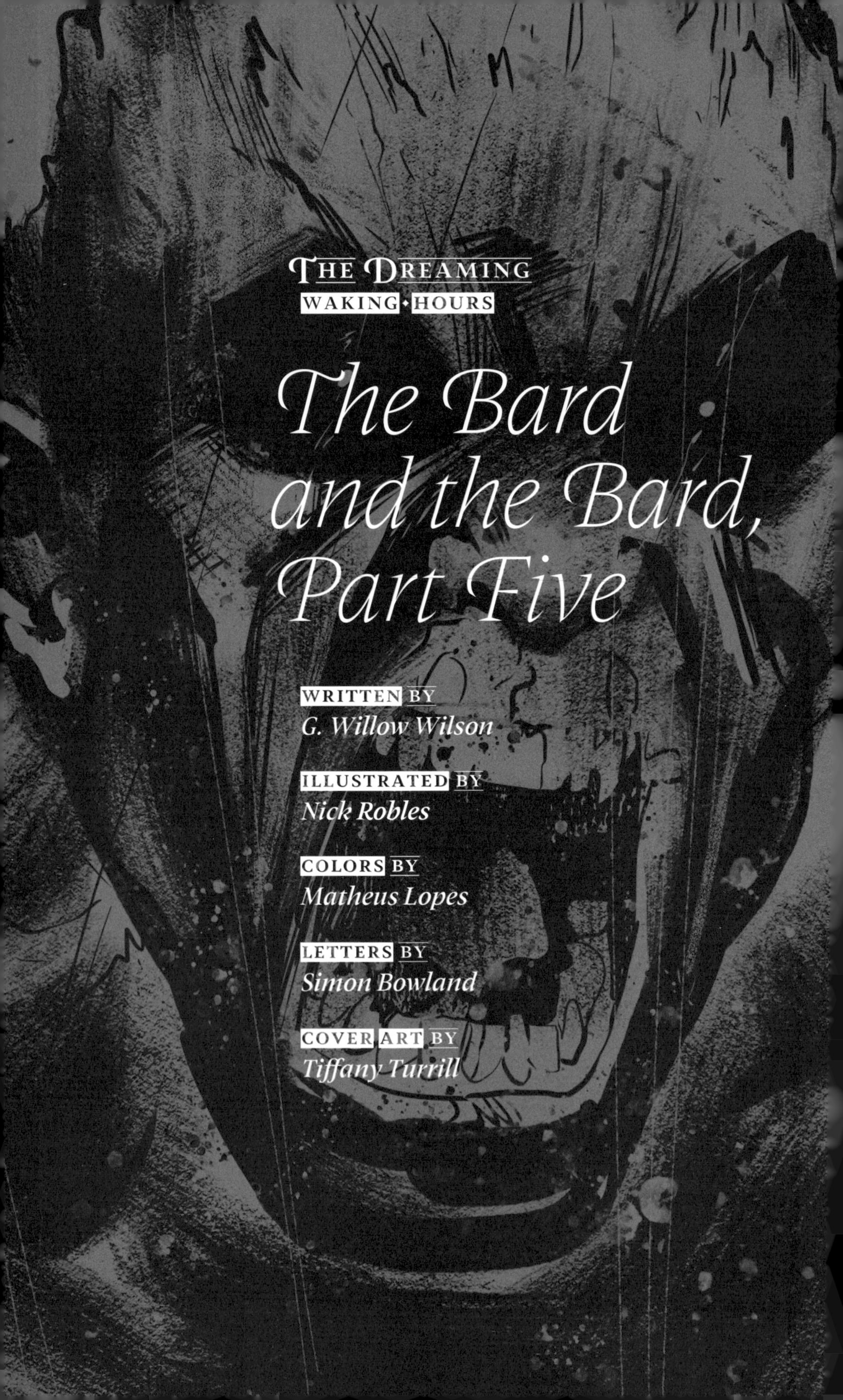

THE DREAMING

WAKING · HOURS

The Bard and the Bard, Part Five

WRITTEN BY
G. Willow Wilson

ILLUSTRATED BY
Nick Robles

COLORS BY
Matheus Lopes

LETTERS BY
Simon Bowland

COVER ART BY
Tiffany Turrill

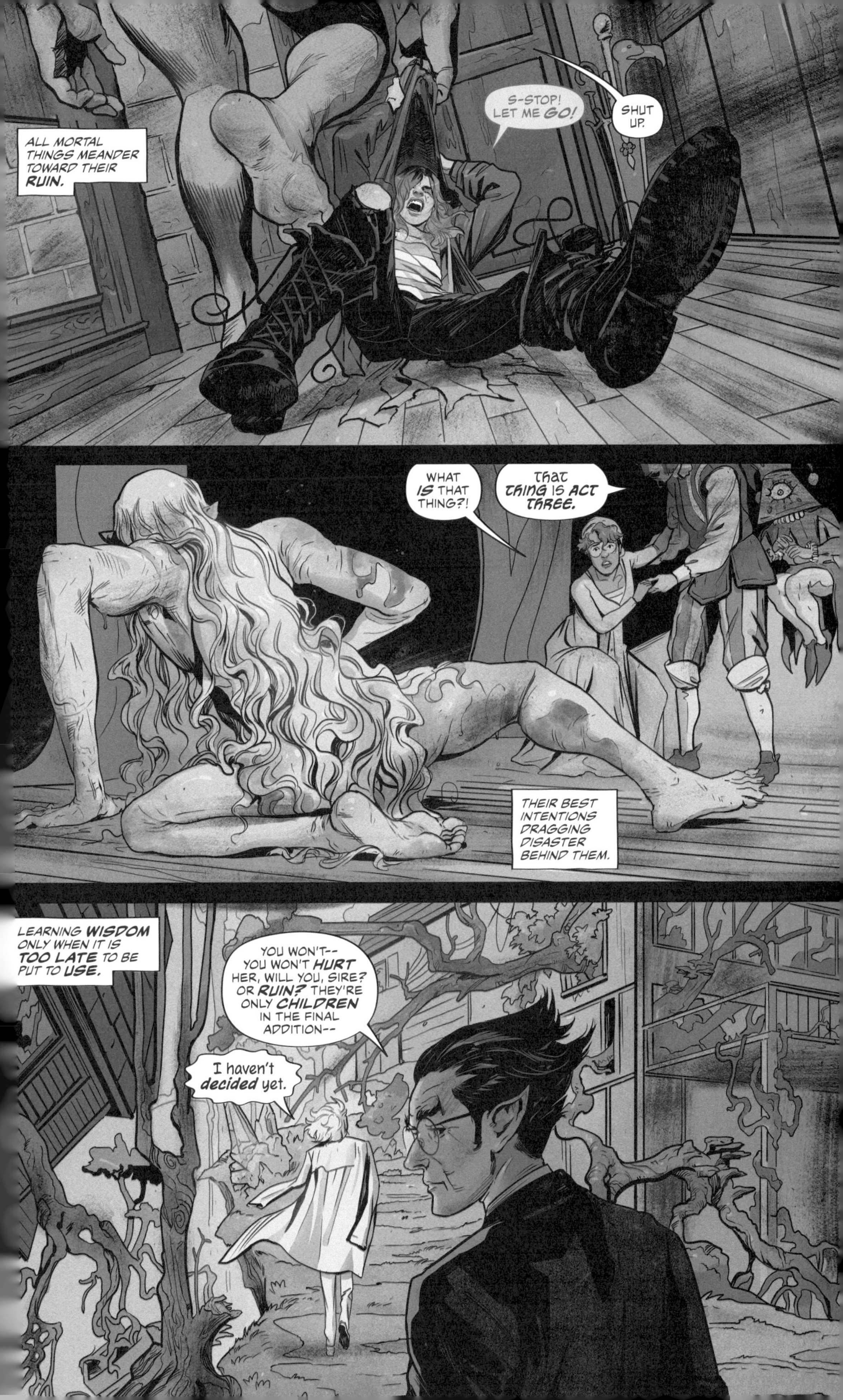
ALL MORTAL THINGS MEANDER TOWARD THEIR RUIN.
S-STOP! LET ME GO!
SHUT UP.
WHAT IS THAT THING?!
THAT THING IS ACT THREE.
THEIR BEST INTENTIONS DRAGGING DISASTER BEHIND THEM.
LEARNING WISDOM ONLY WHEN IT IS TOO LATE TO BE PUT TO USE.
YOU WON'T-- YOU WON'T HURT HER, WILL YOU, SIRE? OR RUIN? THEY'RE ONLY CHILDREN IN THE FINAL ADDITION--
I haven't decided yet.

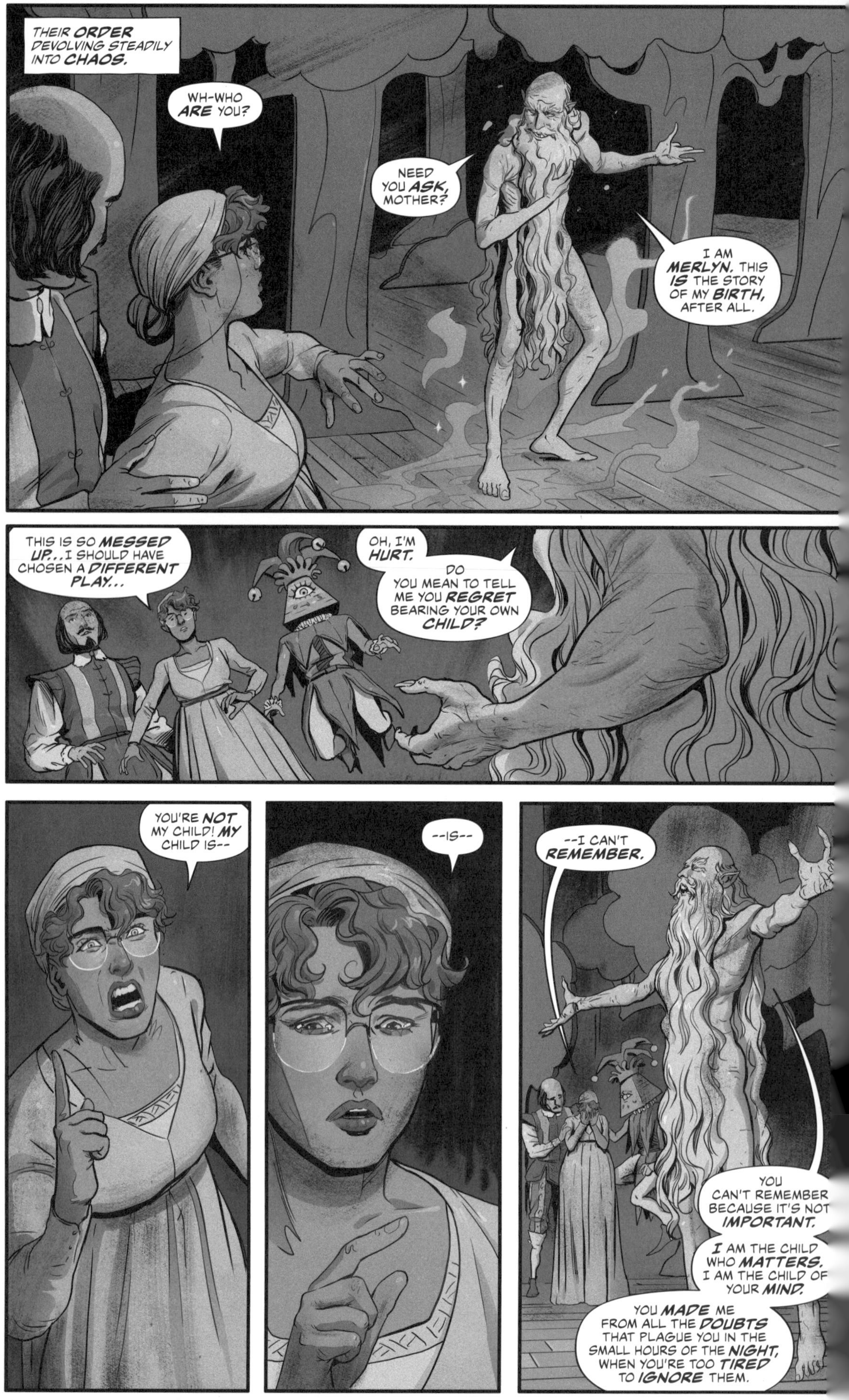
THEIR ORDER DEVOLVING STEADILY INTO CHAOS.
WH-WHO ARE YOU?
NEED YOU ASK, MOTHER?
I AM MERLYN. THIS IS THE STORY OF MY BIRTH, AFTER ALL.
THIS IS SO MESSED UP... I SHOULD HAVE CHOSEN A DIFFERENT PLAY...
OH, I'M HURT.
DO YOU MEAN TO TELL ME YOU REGRET BEARING YOUR OWN CHILD?
YOU'RE NOT MY CHILD! MY CHILD IS--
--IS--
--I CAN'T REMEMBER.
YOU CAN'T REMEMBER BECAUSE IT'S NOT IMPORTANT.
I AM THE CHILD WHO MATTERS. I AM THE CHILD OF YOUR MIND.
YOU MADE ME FROM ALL THE DOUBTS THAT PLAGUE YOU IN THE SMALL HOURS OF THE NIGHT, WHEN YOU'RE TOO TIRED TO IGNORE THEM.

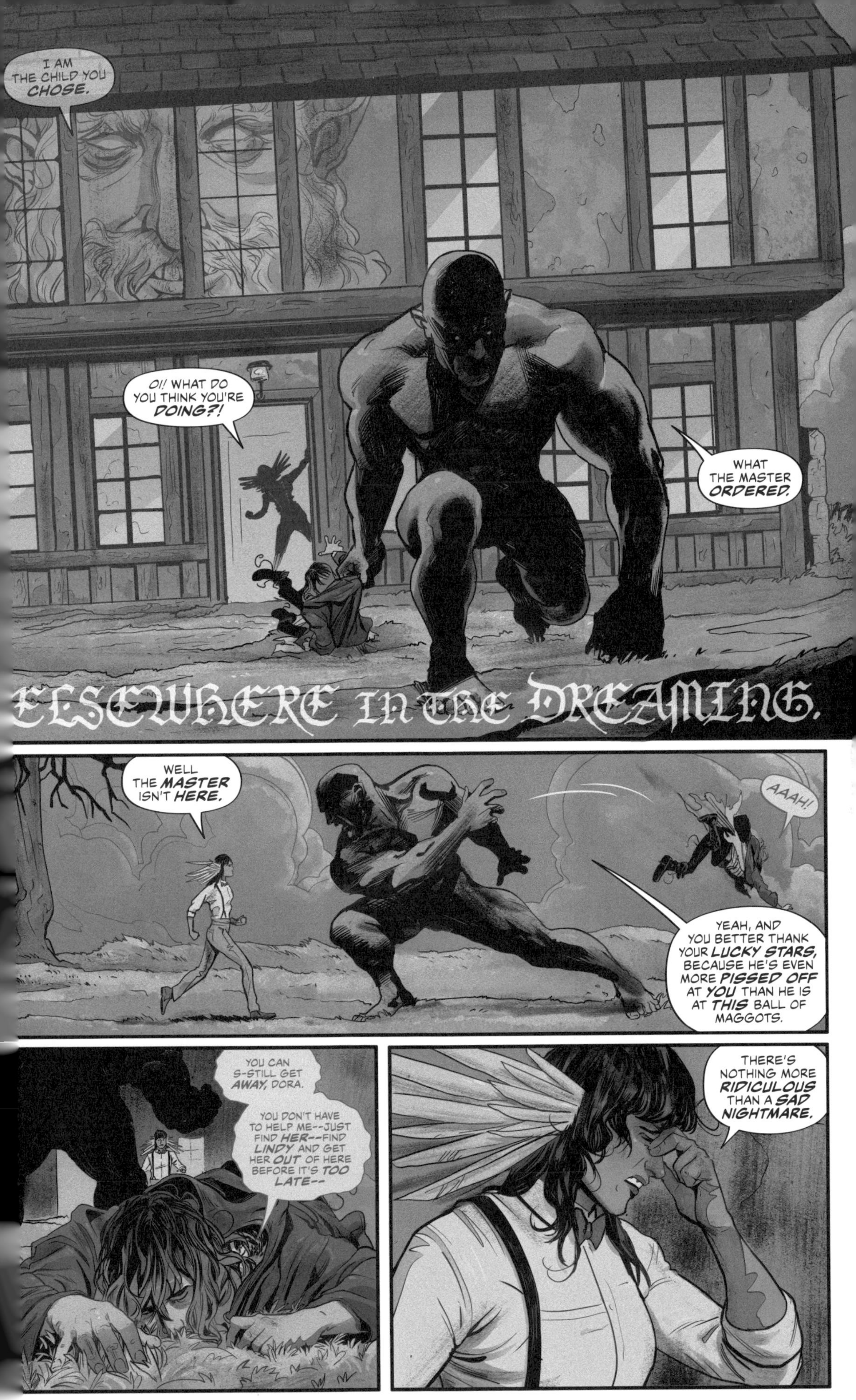
I AM THE CHILD YOU CHOSE.
OI! WHAT DO YOU THINK YOU'RE DOING?!
WHAT THE MASTER ORDERED.
ELSEWHERE IN THE DREAMING.
WELL THE MASTER ISN'T HERE.
AAAH!
YEAH, AND YOU BETTER THANK YOUR LUCKY STARS, BECAUSE HE'S EVEN MORE PISSED OFF AT YOU THAN HE IS AT THIS BALL OF MAGGOTS.
YOU CAN S-STILL GET AWAY, DORA.
YOU DON'T HAVE TO HELP ME--JUST FIND HER--FIND LINDY AND GET HER OUT OF HERE BEFORE IT'S TOO LATE--
THERE'S NOTHING MORE RIDICULOUS THAN A SAD NIGHTMARE.

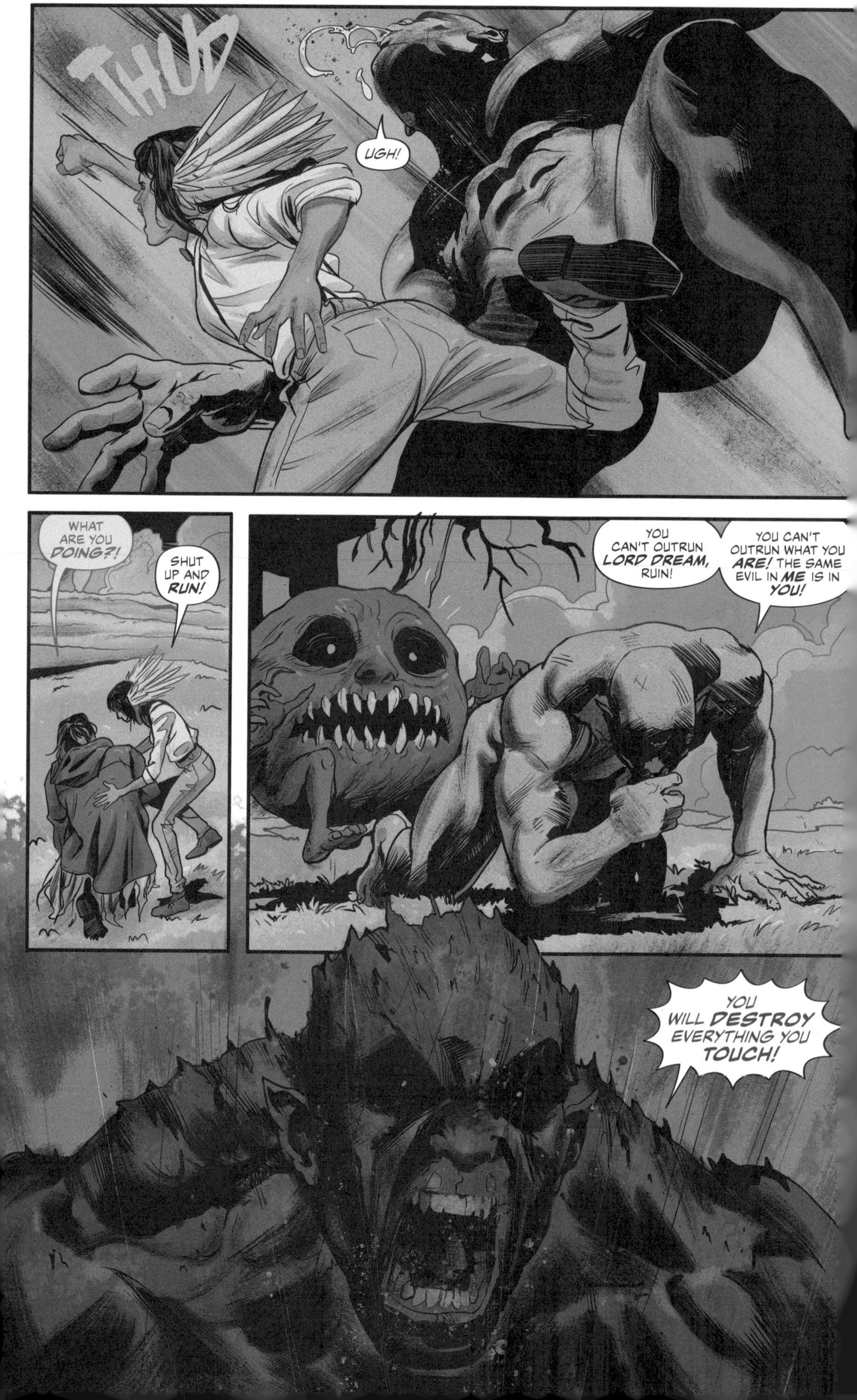
THUD
UGH!
WHAT ARE YOU DOING?!
SHUT UP AND RUN!
YOU CAN'T OUTRUN LORD DREAM, RUIN!
YOU CAN'T OUTRUN WHAT YOU ARE! THE SAME EVIL IN ME IS IN YOU!
YOU WILL DESTROY EVERYTHING YOU TOUCH!

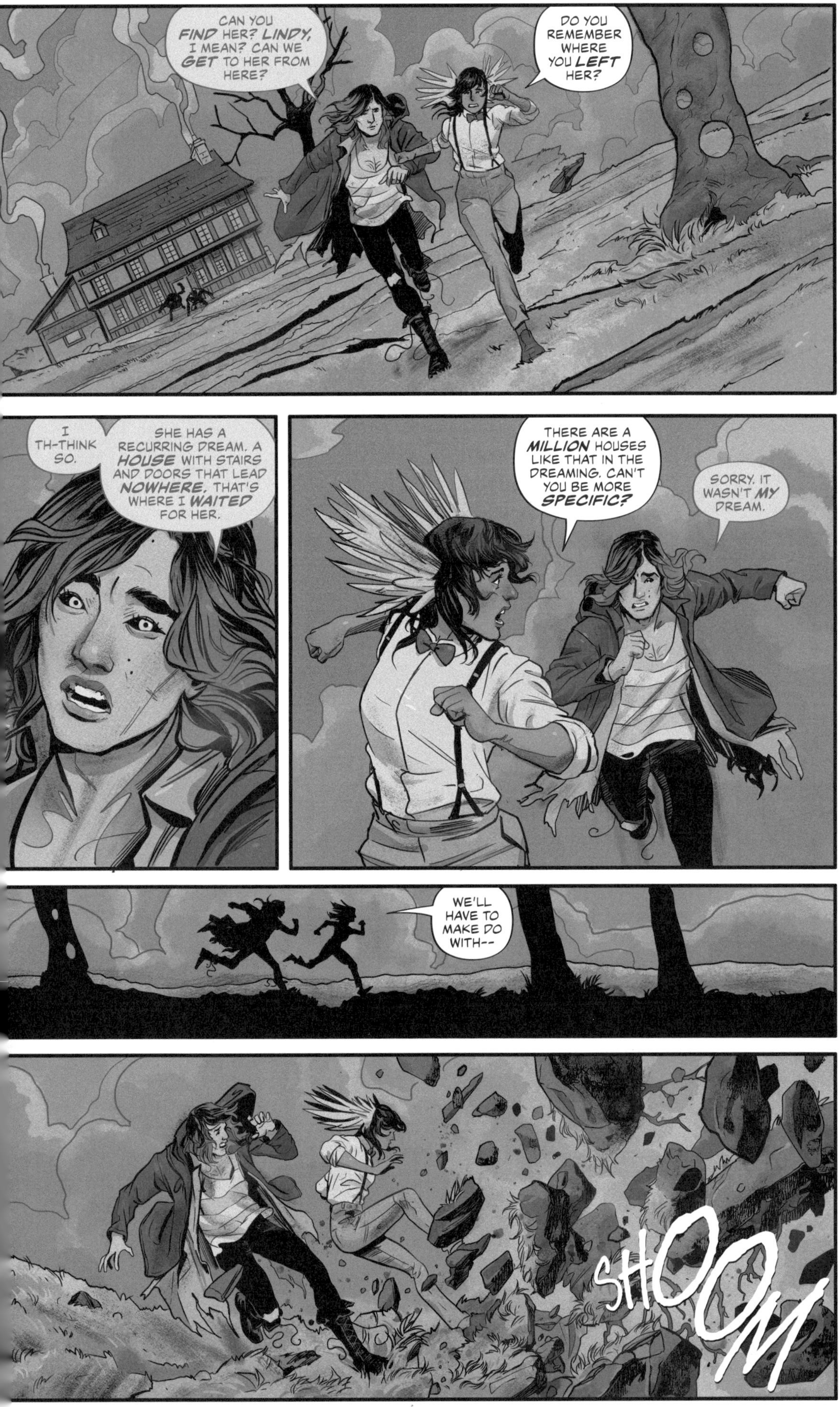
CAN YOU FIND HER? LINDY, I MEAN? CAN WE GET TO HER FROM HERE?
DO YOU REMEMBER WHERE YOU LEFT HER?
I TH-THINK SO.
SHE HAS A RECURRING DREAM. A HOUSE WITH STAIRS AND DOORS THAT LEAD NOWHERE. THAT'S WHERE I WAITED FOR HER.
THERE ARE A MILLION HOUSES LIKE THAT IN THE DREAMING. CAN'T YOU BE MORE SPECIFIC?
SORRY. IT WASN'T MY DREAM.
WE'LL HAVE TO MAKE DO WITH--
SHOOOM

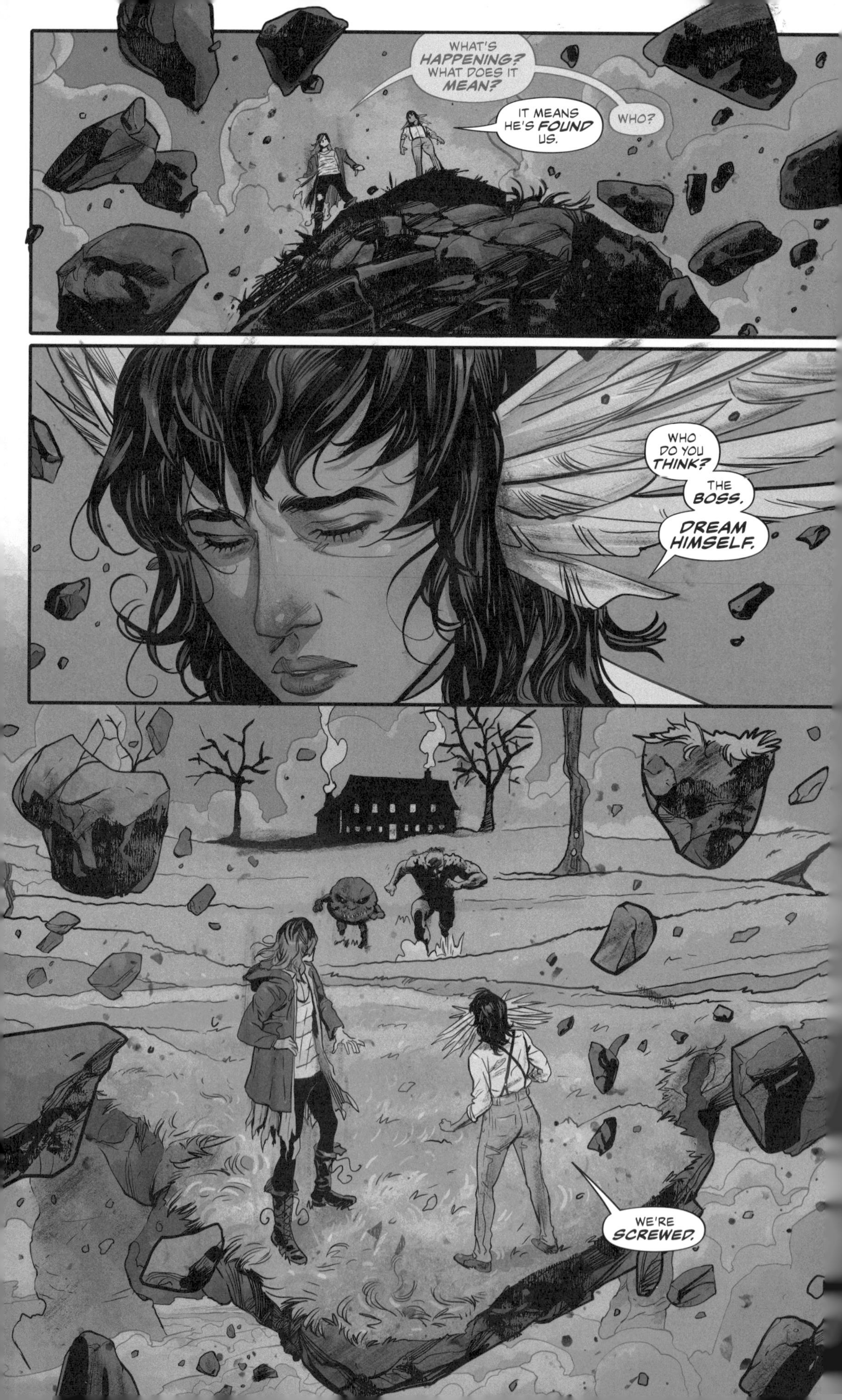
WHAT'S HAPPENING? WHAT DOES IT MEAN?
IT MEANS HE'S FOUND US.
WHO?
WHO DO YOU THINK?
THE BOSS.
DREAM HIMSELF.
WE'RE SCREWED.

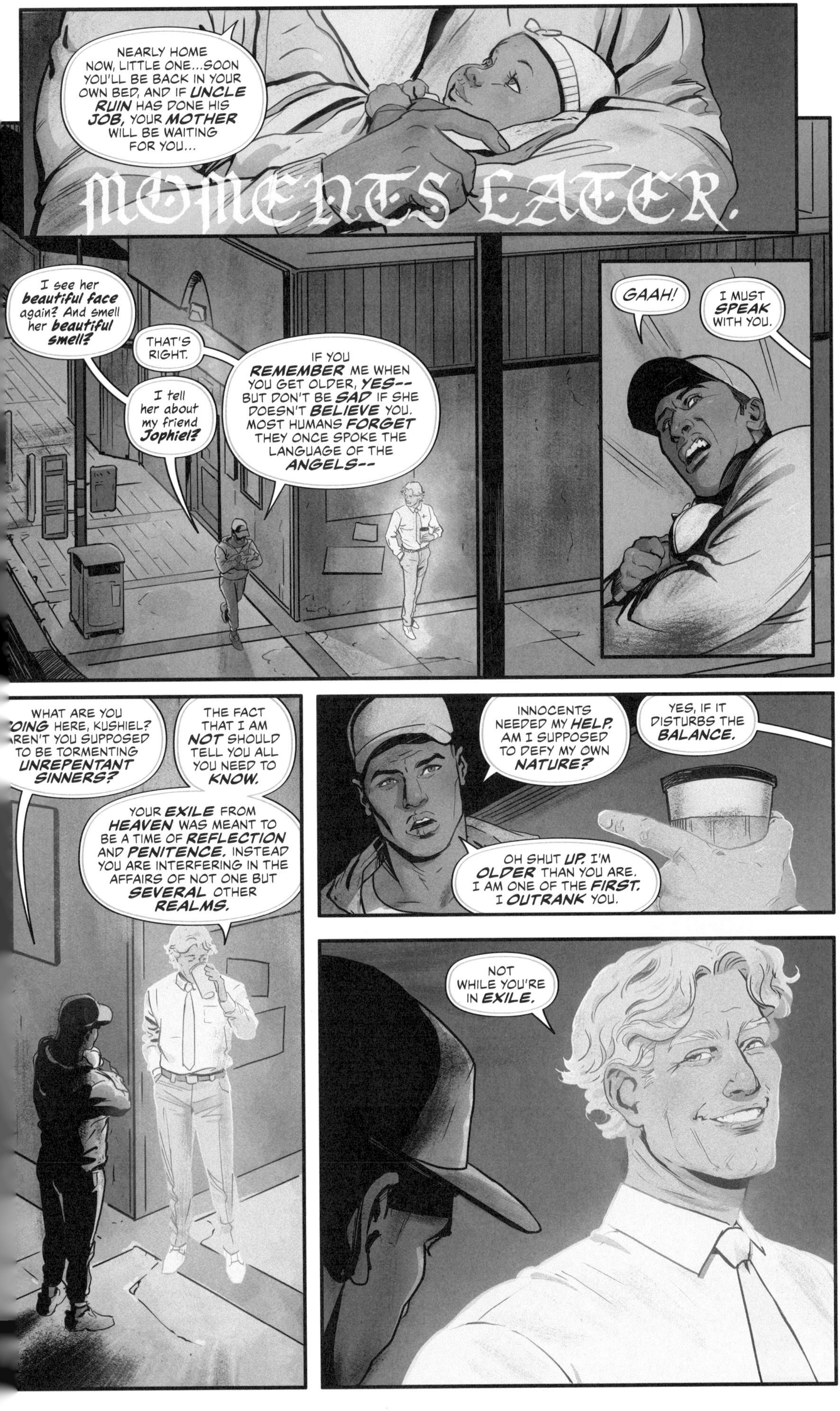
NEARLY HOME NOW, LITTLE ONE...SOON YOU'LL BE BACK IN YOUR OWN BED, AND IF UNCLE RUIN HAS DONE HIS JOB, YOUR MOTHER WILL BE WAITING FOR YOU...
MOMENTS LATER.
I see her beautiful face again? And smell her beautiful smell?
THAT'S RIGHT.
I tell her about my friend Jophiel?
IF YOU REMEMBER ME WHEN YOU GET OLDER, YES--BUT DON'T BE SAD IF SHE DOESN'T BELIEVE YOU. MOST HUMANS FORGET THEY ONCE SPOKE THE LANGUAGE OF THE ANGELS--
GAAH!
I MUST SPEAK WITH YOU.
WHAT ARE YOU DOING HERE, KUSHIEL? AREN'T YOU SUPPOSED TO BE TORMENTING UNREPENTANT SINNERS?
THE FACT THAT I AM NOT SHOULD TELL YOU ALL YOU NEED TO KNOW.
YOUR EXILE FROM HEAVEN WAS MEANT TO BE A TIME OF REFLECTION AND PENITENCE. INSTEAD YOU ARE INTERFERING IN THE AFFAIRS OF NOT ONE BUT SEVERAL OTHER REALMS.
INNOCENTS NEEDED MY HELP. AM I SUPPOSED TO DEFY MY OWN NATURE?
YES, IF IT DISTURBS THE BALANCE.
OH SHUT UP. I'M OLDER THAN YOU ARE. I AM ONE OF THE FIRST. I OUTRANK YOU.
NOT WHILE YOU'RE IN EXILE.

I AM NOT HERE TO **REMONSTRATE.** I COME ONLY AS A **MESSENGER.**

IF YOU CONTINUE TO **MEDDLE** WITH THE MORTAL WORLD, YOU COULD **FORFEIT** ANY CHANCE YOU HAVE OF **RETURNING** TO YOUR PLACE AT THE FOOT OF THE **THRONE.**

JUST... **THINK** ABOUT IT.

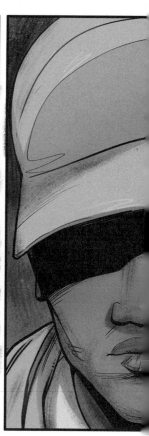

He is too shiny and very **mean.**

IGNORE HIM.

HE WAS **DEMOTED** AFTER BUNGLING HIS **FIRST JOB** AND HE THINKS THIS IS HIS CHANCE TO **DUNK** ON ME.

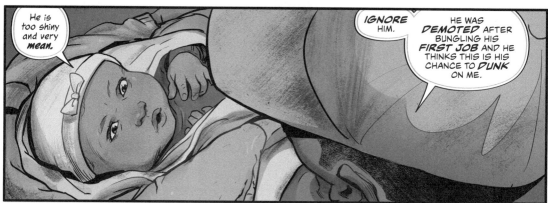

SOMETIMES, TO DO A GREAT RIGHT, YOU HAVE TO DO A LITTLE **WRONG.**

I THINK IT WAS **SHAKESPEARE** WHO SAID THAT...

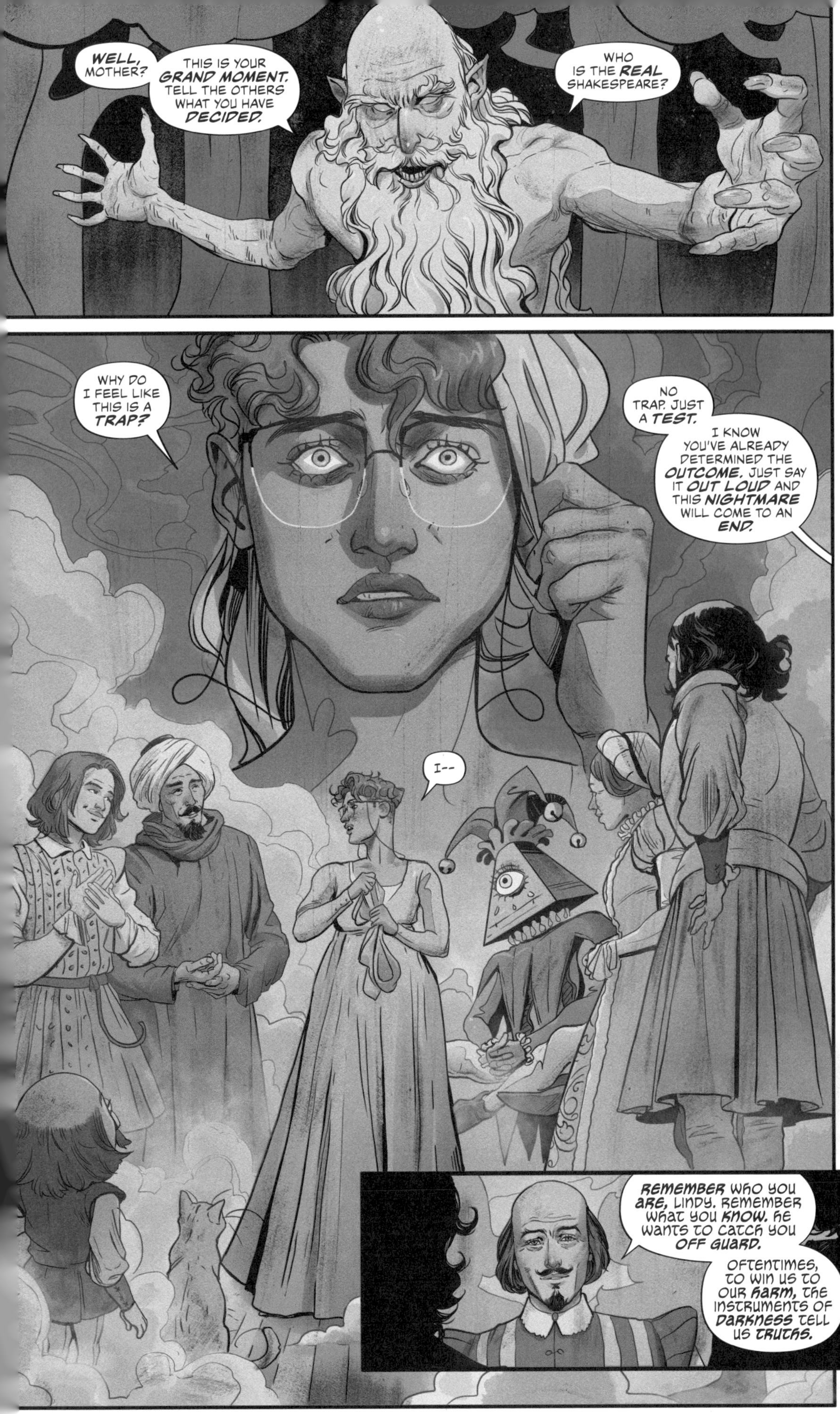
WELL, MOTHER?
THIS IS YOUR GRAND MOMENT. TELL THE OTHERS WHAT YOU HAVE DECIDED.
WHO IS THE REAL SHAKESPEARE?
WHY DO I FEEL LIKE THIS IS A TRAP?
NO TRAP. JUST A TEST.
I KNOW YOU'VE ALREADY DETERMINED THE OUTCOME. JUST SAY IT OUT LOUD AND THIS NIGHTMARE WILL COME TO AN END.
I--
REMEMBER WHO YOU ARE, LINDY. REMEMBER WHAT YOU KNOW. HE WANTS TO CATCH YOU OFF GUARD.
OFTENTIMES, TO WIN US TO OUR HARM, THE INSTRUMENTS OF DARKNESS TELL US TRUTHS.

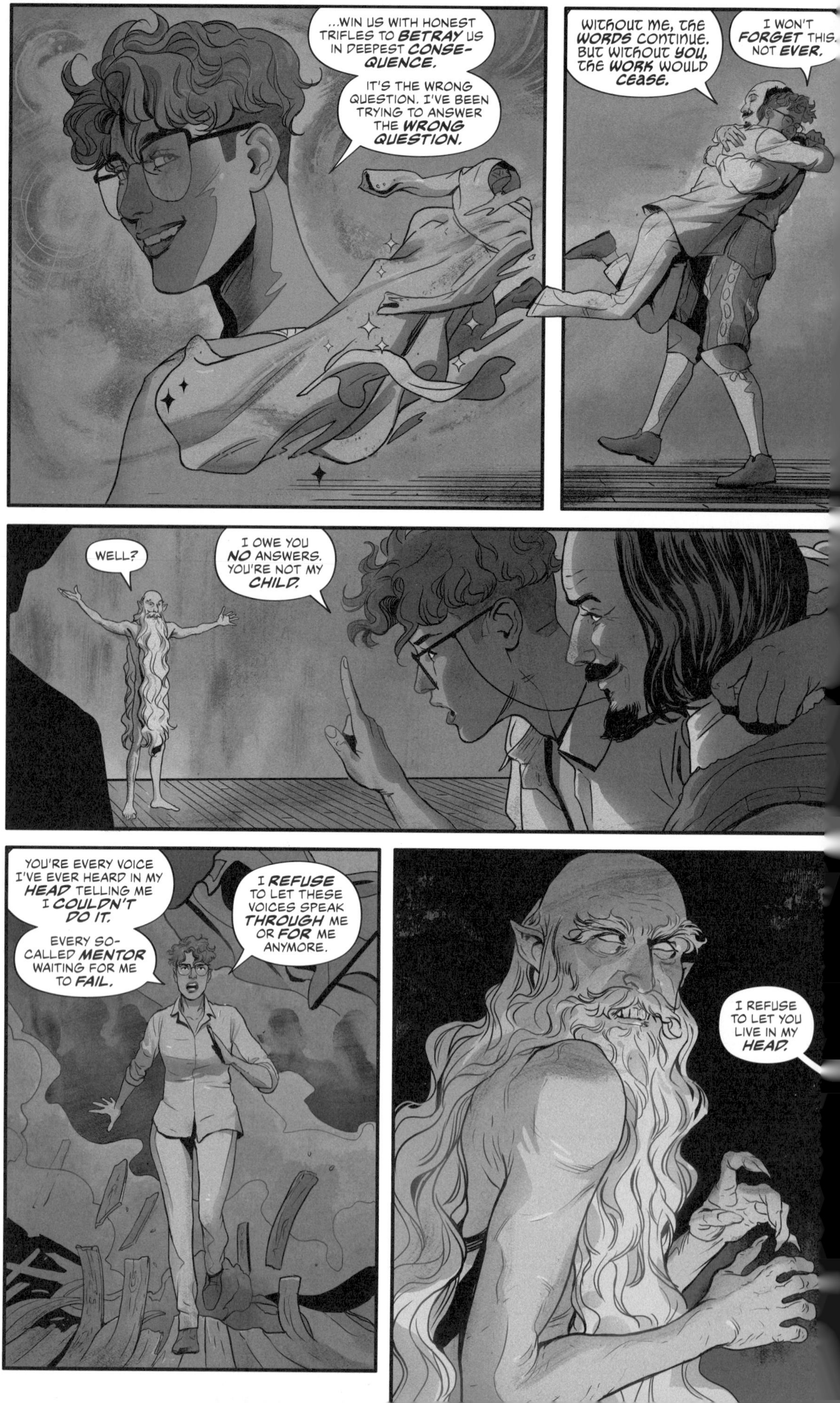

...WIN US WITH HONEST TRIFLES TO BETRAY US IN DEEPEST CONSE- QUENCE.
IT'S THE WRONG QUESTION. I'VE BEEN TRYING TO ANSWER THE WRONG QUESTION.
WITHOUT ME, THE WORDS CONTINUE. BUT WITHOUT YOU, THE WORK WOULD CEASE.
I WON'T FORGET THIS. NOT EVER.
WELL?
I OWE YOU NO ANSWERS. YOU'RE NOT MY CHILD.
YOU'RE EVERY VOICE I'VE EVER HEARD IN MY HEAD TELLING ME I COULDN'T DO IT.
EVERY SO- CALLED MENTOR WAITING FOR ME TO FAIL.
I REFUSE TO LET THESE VOICES SPEAK THROUGH ME OR FOR ME ANYMORE.
I REFUSE TO LET YOU LIVE IN MY HEAD.

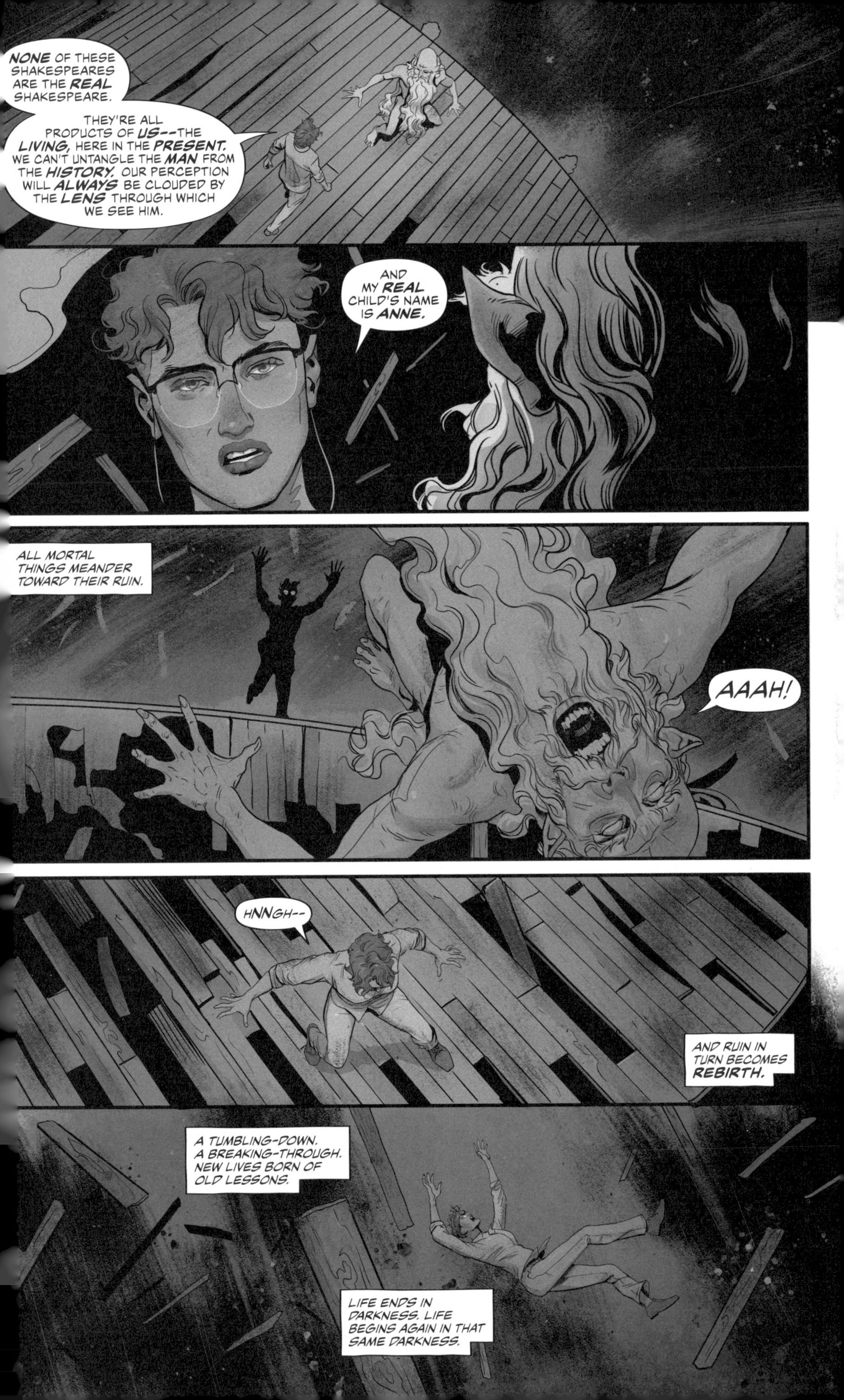
NONE OF THESE SHAKESPEARES ARE THE REAL SHAKESPEARE.
THEY'RE ALL PRODUCTS OF US--THE LIVING, HERE IN THE PRESENT. WE CAN'T UNTANGLE THE MAN FROM THE HISTORY. OUR PERCEPTION WILL ALWAYS BE CLOUDED BY THE LENS THROUGH WHICH WE SEE HIM.
AND MY REAL CHILD'S NAME IS ANNE.
ALL MORTAL THINGS MEANDER TOWARD THEIR RUIN.
AAAH!
HNNGH--
AND RUIN IN TURN BECOMES REBIRTH.
A TUMBLING-DOWN. A BREAKING-THROUGH. NEW LIVES BORN OF OLD LESSONS.
LIFE ENDS IN DARKNESS. LIFE BEGINS AGAIN IN THAT SAME DARKNESS.

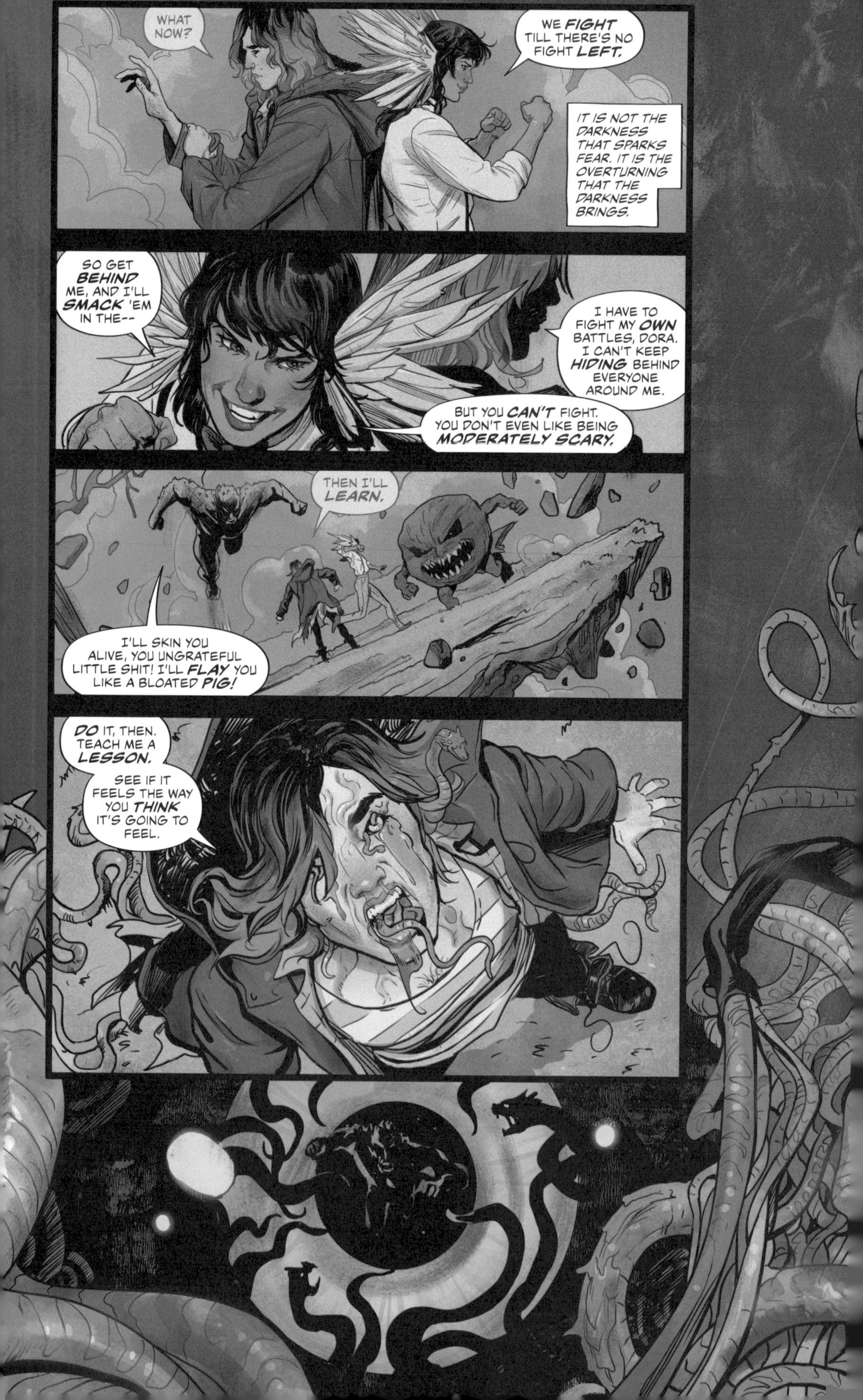
WHAT NOW?
WE FIGHT TILL THERE'S NO FIGHT LEFT.
IT IS NOT THE DARKNESS THAT SPARKS FEAR. IT IS THE OVERTURNING THAT THE DARKNESS BRINGS.
SO GET BEHIND ME, AND I'LL SMACK 'EM IN THE--
I HAVE TO FIGHT MY OWN BATTLES, DORA. I CAN'T KEEP HIDING BEHIND EVERYONE AROUND ME.
BUT YOU CAN'T FIGHT. YOU DON'T EVEN LIKE BEING MODERATELY SCARY.
THEN I'LL LEARN.
I'LL SKIN YOU ALIVE, YOU UNGRATEFUL LITTLE SHIT! I'LL FLAY YOU LIKE A BLOATED PIG!
DO IT, THEN. TEACH ME A LESSON.
SEE IF IT FEELS THE WAY YOU THINK IT'S GOING TO FEEL.

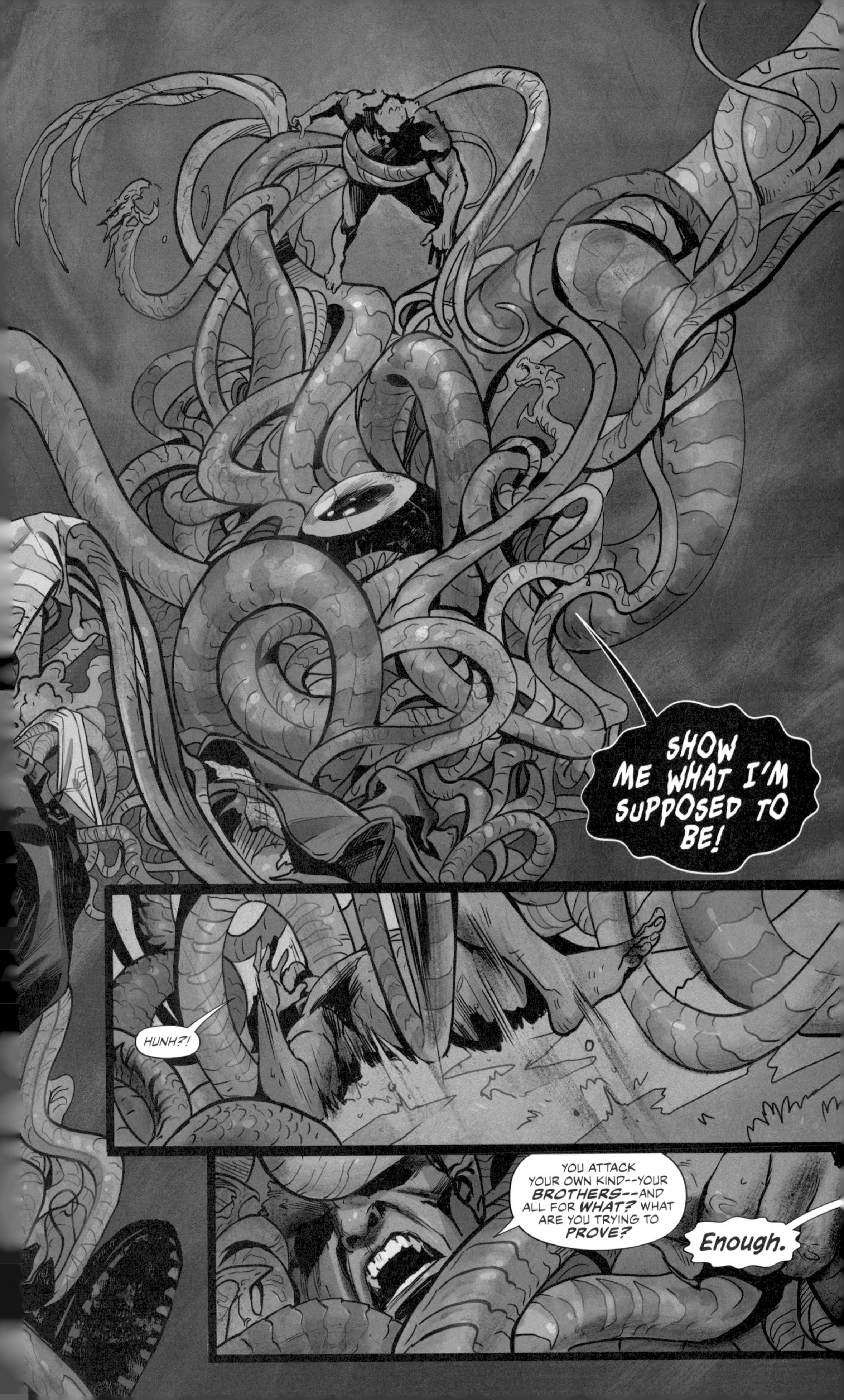
SHOW ME WHAT I'M SUPPOSED TO BE!
HUNH?!
YOU ATTACK YOUR OWN KIND--YOUR BROTHERS--AND ALL FOR WHAT? WHAT ARE YOU TRYING TO PROVE?
Enough.

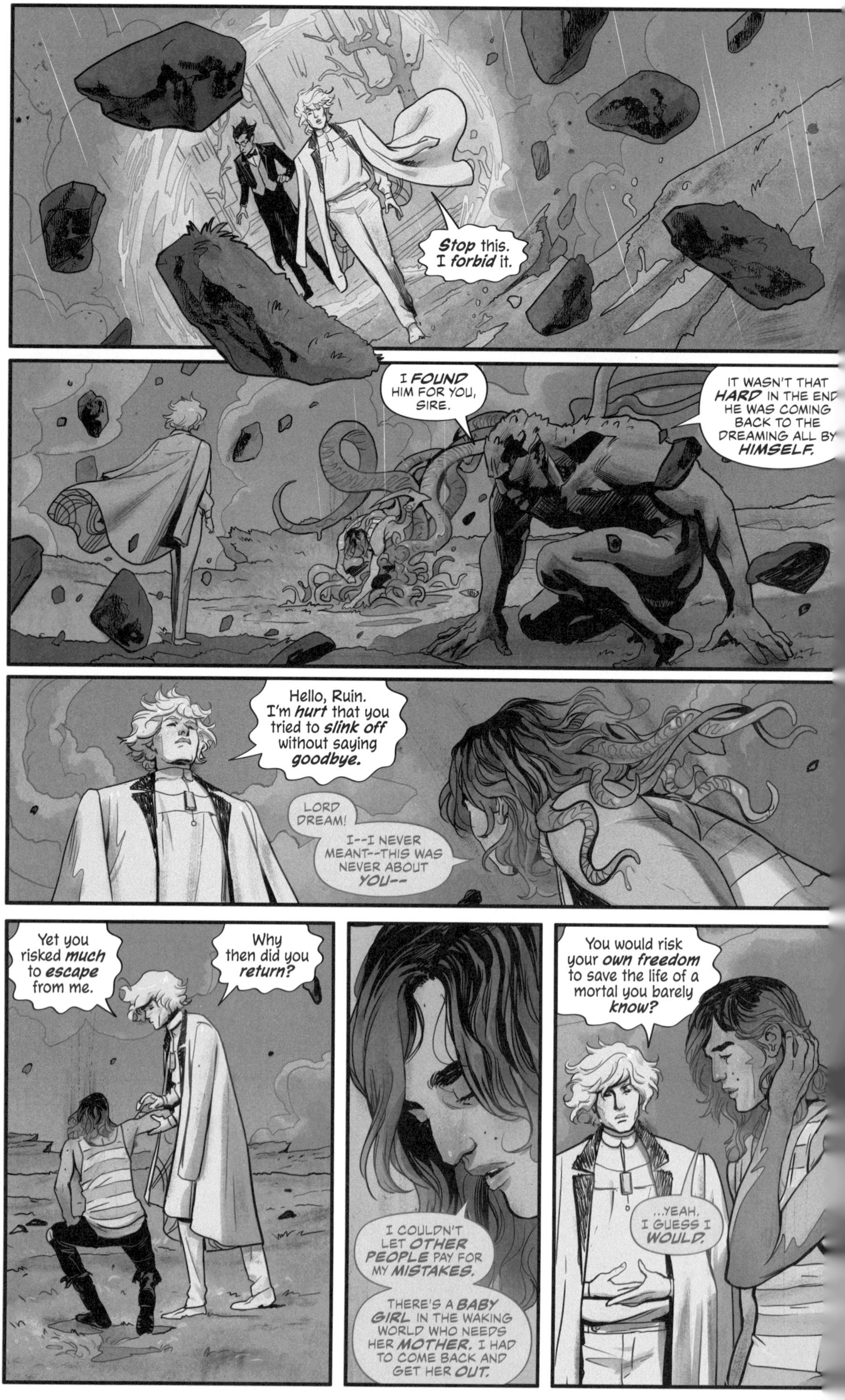
Stop this. I forbid it.
I FOUND HIM FOR YOU, SIRE.
IT WASN'T THAT HARD IN THE END HE WAS COMING BACK TO THE DREAMING ALL BY HIMSELF.
Hello, Ruin. I'm hurt that you tried to slink off without saying goodbye.
LORD DREAM!
I--I NEVER MEANT--THIS WAS NEVER ABOUT YOU--
Yet you risked much to escape from me.
Why then did you return?
I COULDN'T LET OTHER PEOPLE PAY FOR MY MISTAKES.
THERE'S A BABY GIRL IN THE WAKING WORLD WHO NEEDS HER MOTHER. I HAD TO COME BACK AND GET HER OUT.
You would risk your own freedom to save the life of a mortal you barely know?
...YEAH. I GUESS I WOULD.

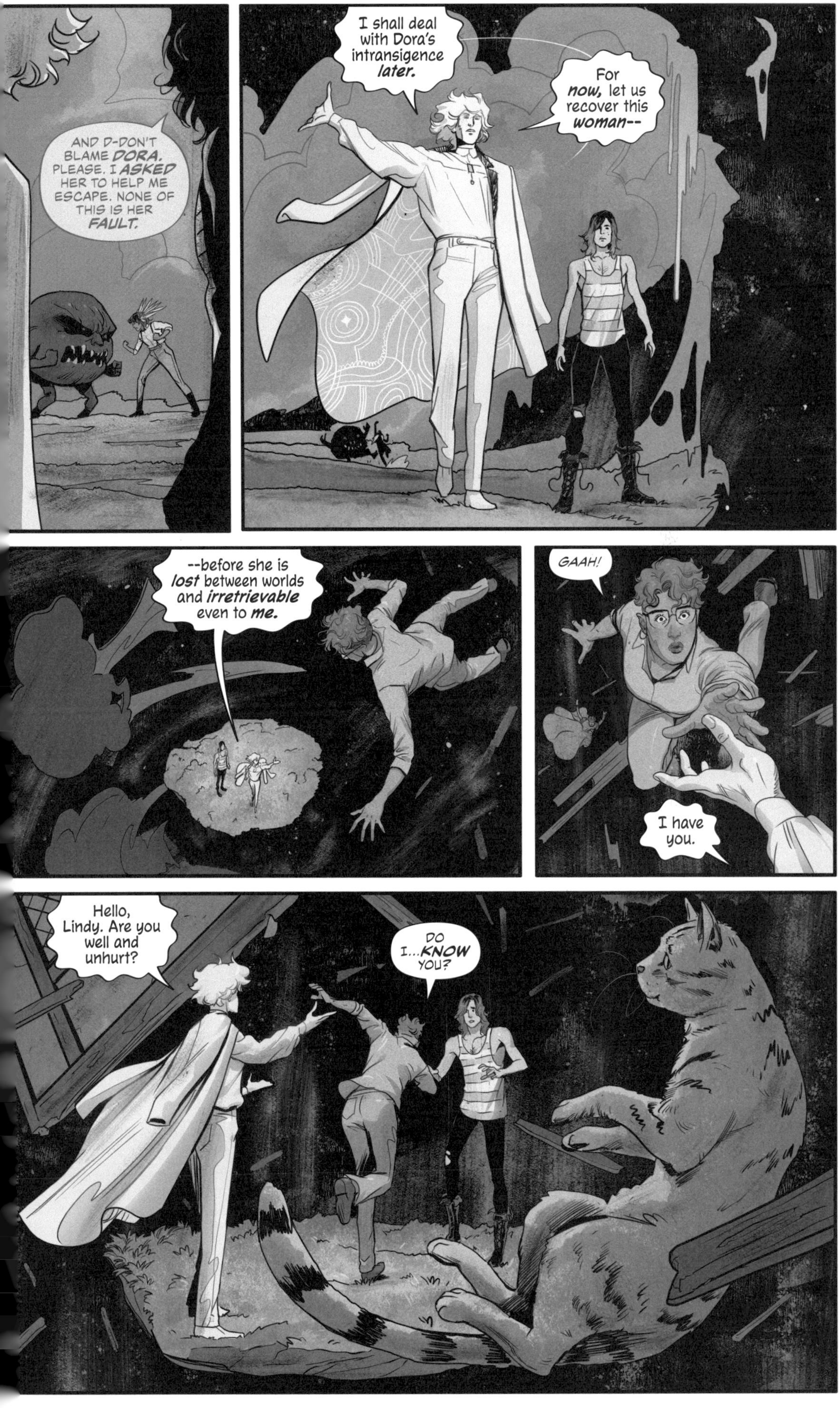
AND D-DON'T BLAME DORA. PLEASE. I ASKED HER TO HELP ME ESCAPE. NONE OF THIS IS HER FAULT.
I shall deal with Dora's intransigence later.
For now, let us recover this woman--
--before she is lost between worlds and irretrievable even to me.
GAAH!
I have you.
Hello, Lindy. Are you well and unhurt?
DO I...KNOW YOU?

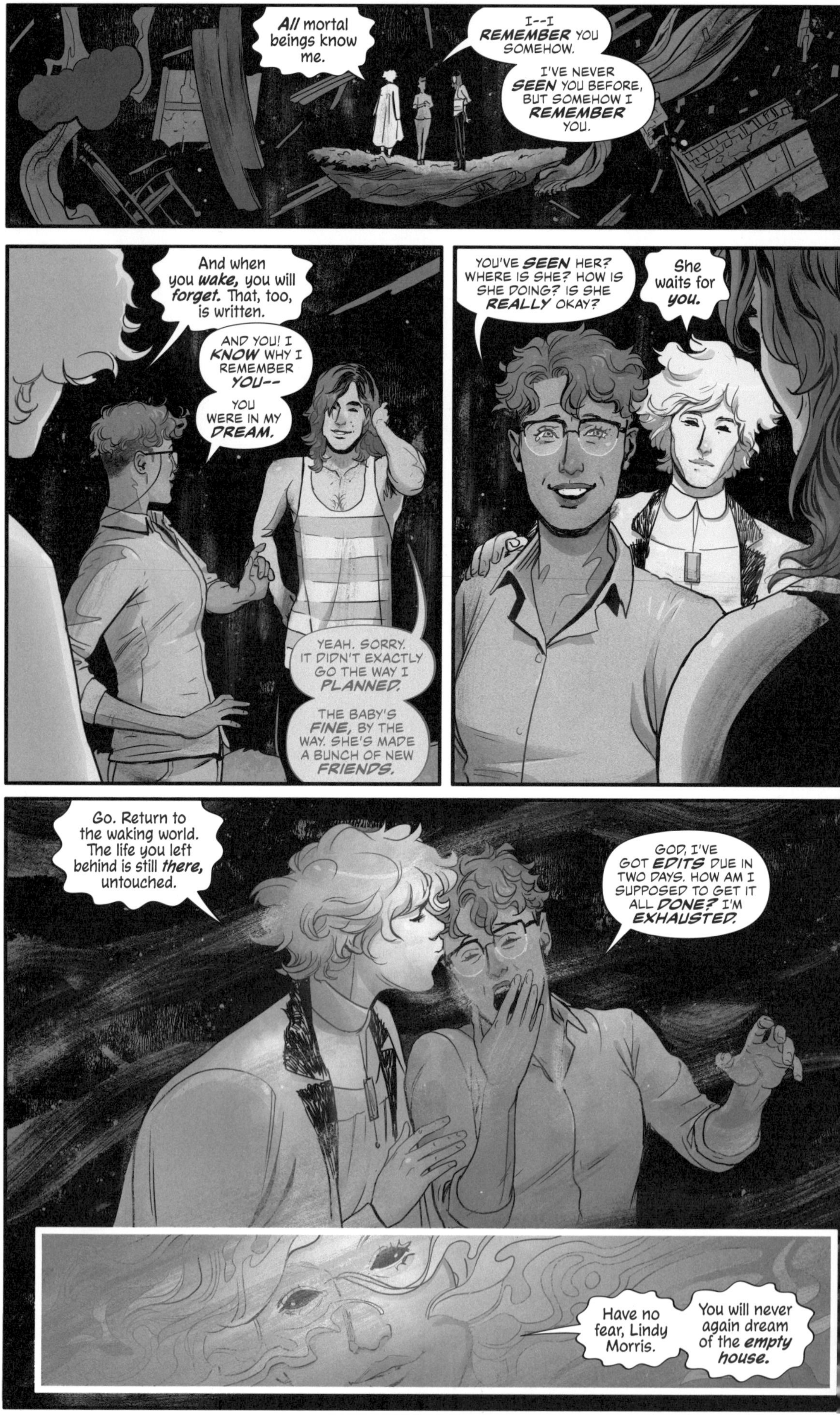

All mortal beings know me.
I--I REMEMBER YOU SOMEHOW.
I'VE NEVER SEEN YOU BEFORE, BUT SOMEHOW I REMEMBER YOU.
And when you wake, you will forget. That, too, is written.
AND YOU! I KNOW WHY I REMEMBER YOU--
YOU WERE IN MY DREAM.
YEAH. SORRY. IT DIDN'T EXACTLY GO THE WAY I PLANNED.
THE BABY'S FINE, BY THE WAY. SHE'S MADE A BUNCH OF NEW FRIENDS.
YOU'VE SEEN HER? WHERE IS SHE? HOW IS SHE DOING? IS SHE REALLY OKAY?
She waits for you.
Go. Return to the waking world. The life you left behind is still there, untouched.
GOD, I'VE GOT EDITS DUE IN TWO DAYS. HOW AM I SUPPOSED TO GET IT ALL DONE? I'M EXHAUSTED.
Have no fear, Lindy Morris.
You will never again dream of the empty house.

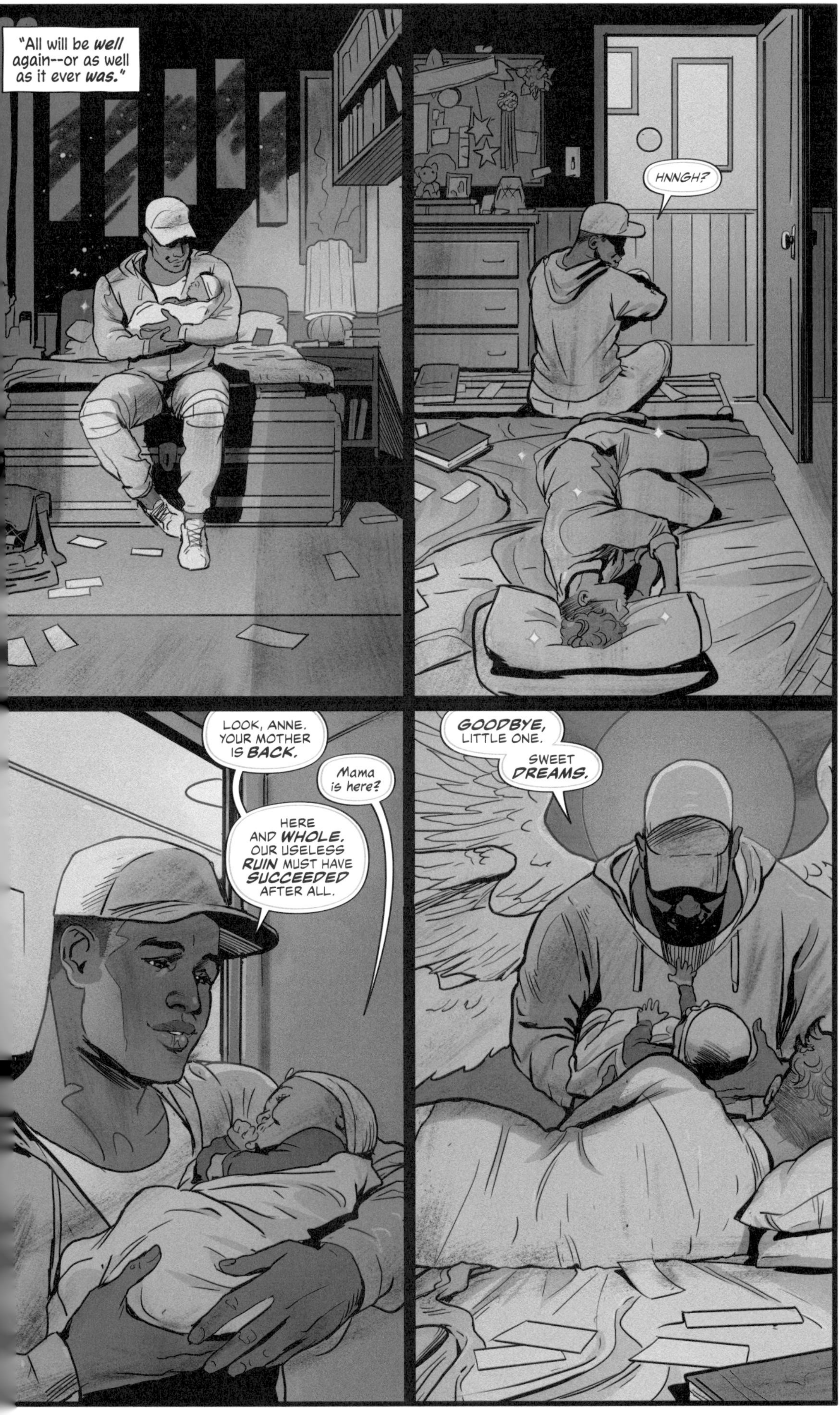
"All will be *well* again--or as well as it ever *was*."
HNNGH?
LOOK, ANNE. YOUR MOTHER IS *BACK*.
Mama is here?
HERE AND *WHOLE*. OUR USELESS *RUIN* MUST HAVE *SUCCEEDED* AFTER ALL.
GOODBYE, LITTLE ONE.
SWEET *DREAMS*.

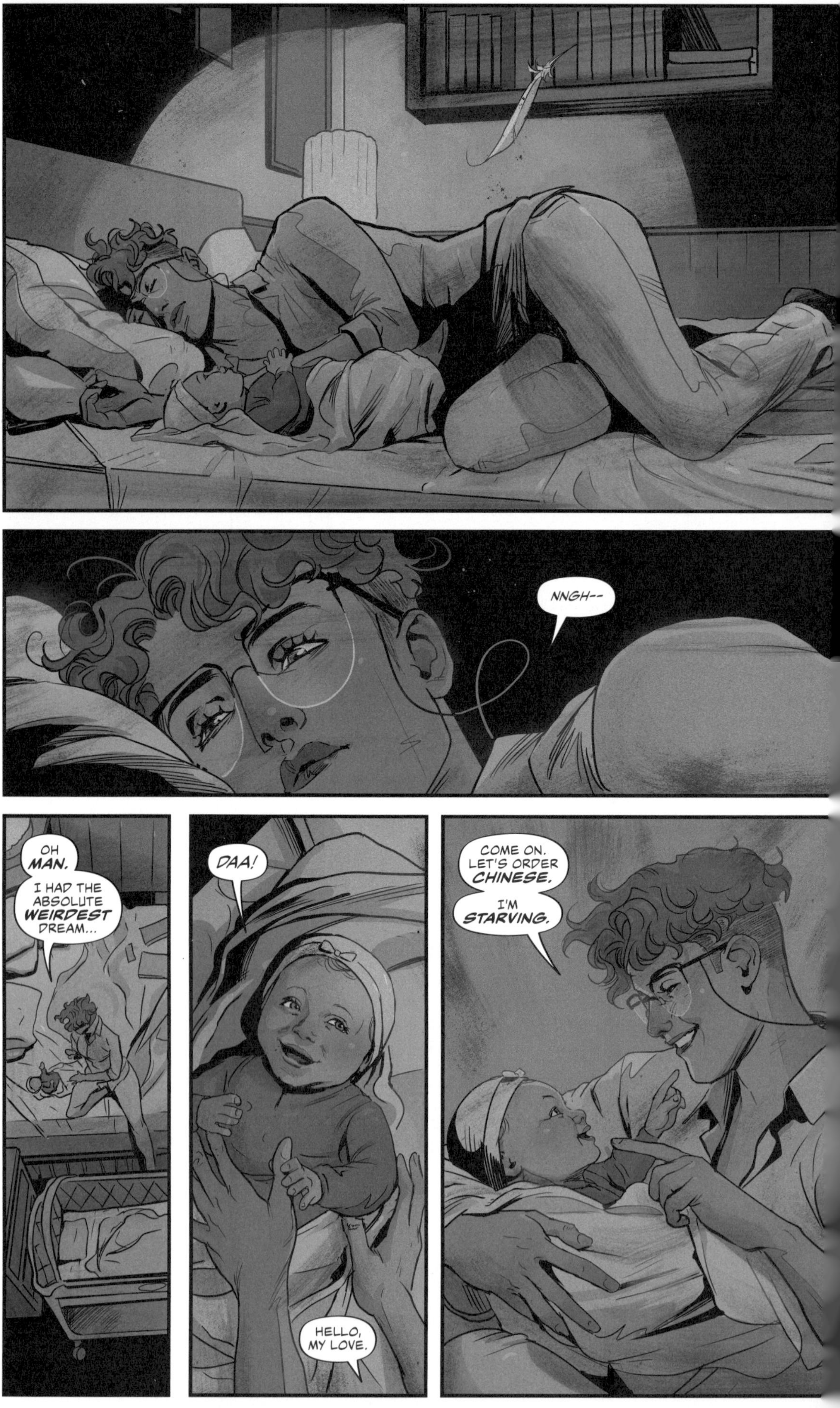
NNGH--
OH MAN.
I HAD THE ABSOLUTE WEIRDEST DREAM...
DAA!
HELLO, MY LOVE.
COME ON. LET'S ORDER CHINESE.
I'M STARVING.

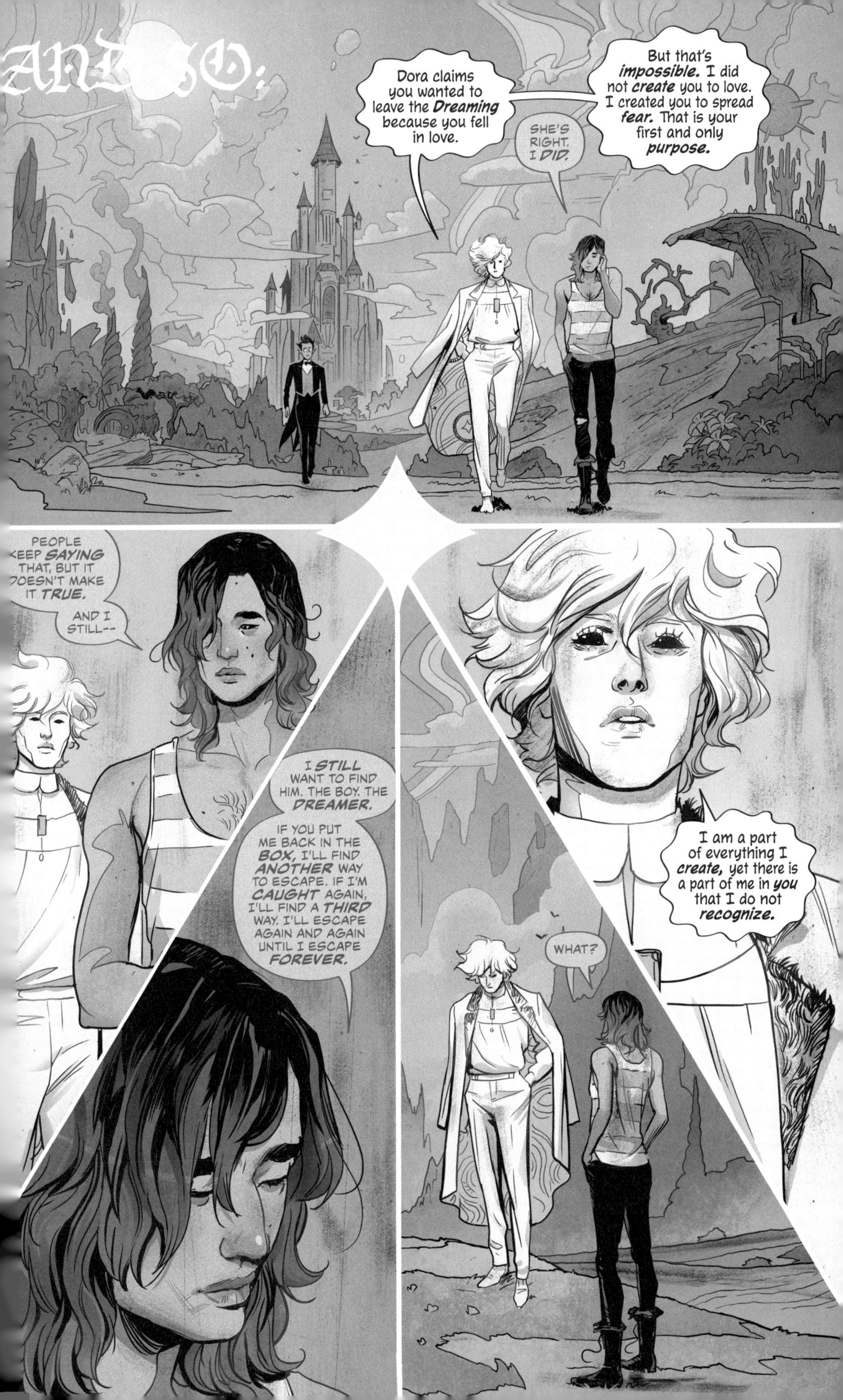
AND SO:
Dora claims you wanted to leave the *Dreaming* because you fell in love.
SHE'S RIGHT. I *DID.*
But that's ***impossible.*** I did not ***create*** you to love. I created you to spread ***fear.*** That is your first and only ***purpose.***
PEOPLE KEEP ***SAYING*** THAT, BUT IT DOESN'T MAKE IT ***TRUE.***
AND I STILL--
I ***STILL*** WANT TO FIND HIM. THE BOY. THE ***DREAMER.***
IF YOU PUT ME BACK IN THE ***BOX,*** I'LL FIND ***ANOTHER*** WAY TO ESCAPE. IF I'M ***CAUGHT*** AGAIN, I'LL FIND A ***THIRD*** WAY. I'LL ESCAPE AGAIN AND AGAIN UNTIL I ESCAPE ***FOREVER.***
I am a part of everything I ***create,*** yet there is a part of me in ***you*** that I do not ***recognize.***
WHAT?

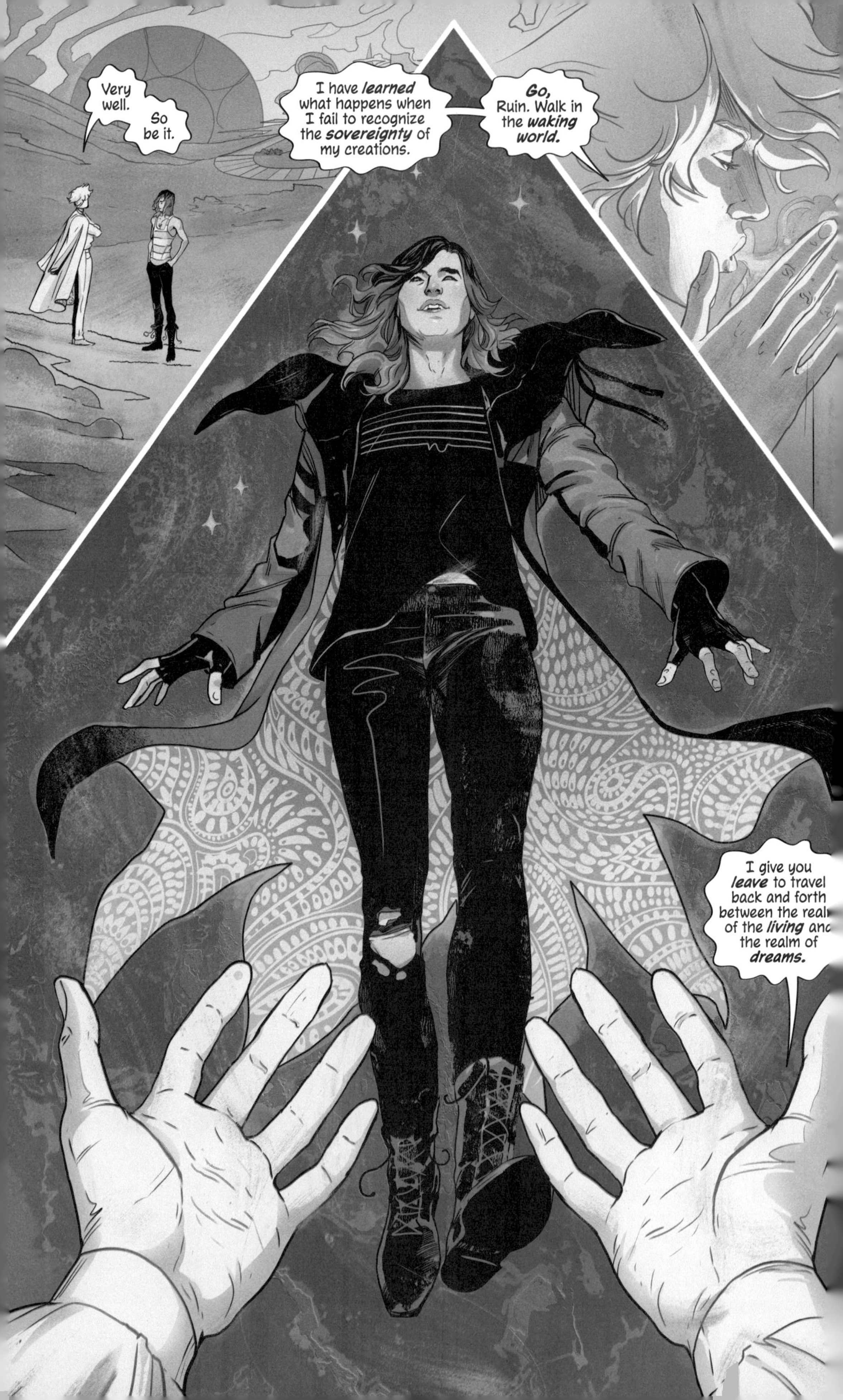

Very well.
So be it.
I have learned what happens when I fail to recognize the sovereignty of my creations.
Go, Ruin. Walk in the waking world.
I give you leave to travel back and forth between the real of the living an the realm of dreams.

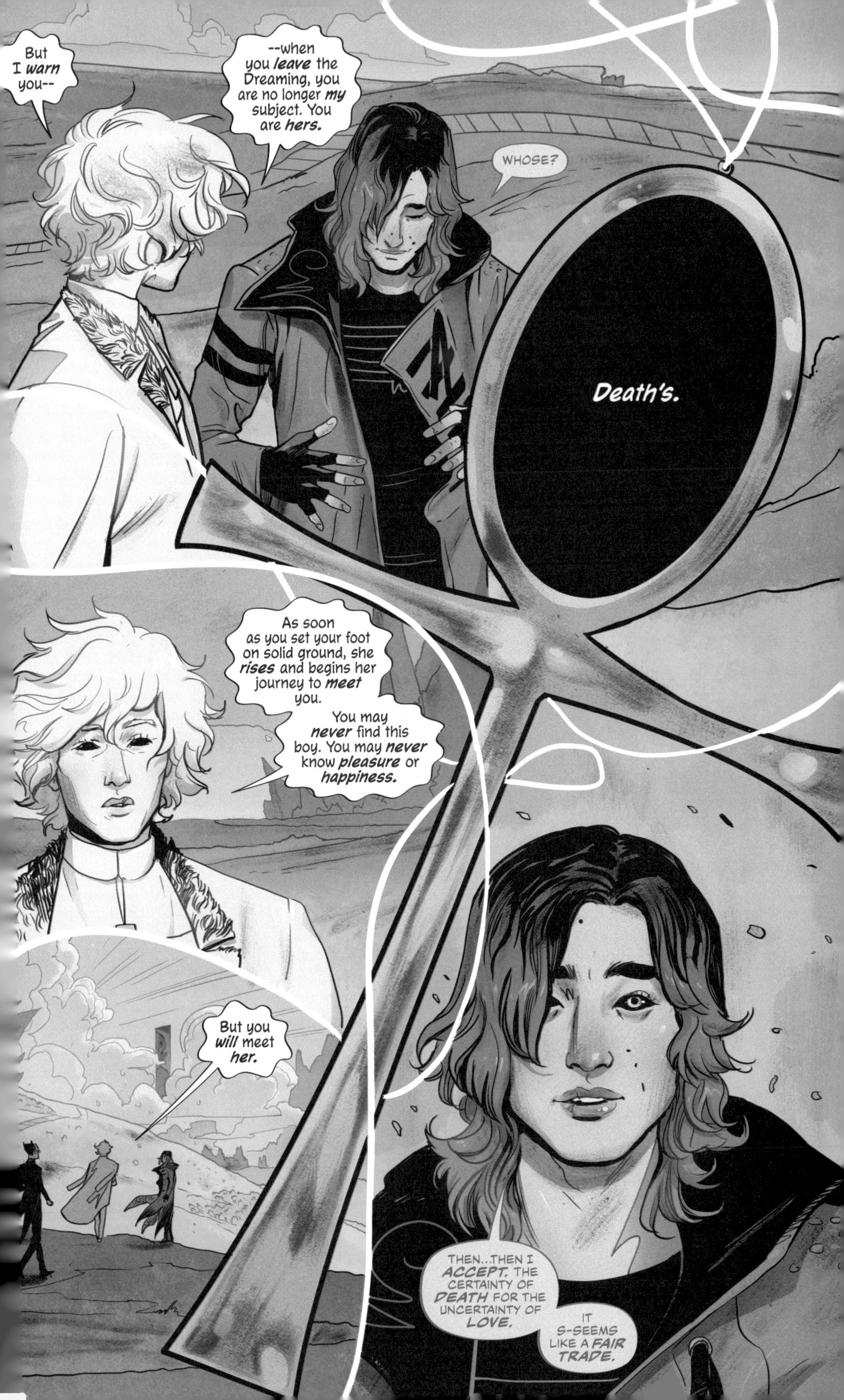
But I warn you--
--when you leave the Dreaming, you are no longer my subject. You are hers.
WHOSE?
Death's.
As soon as you set your foot on solid ground, she rises and begins her journey to meet you.
You may never find this boy. You may never know pleasure or happiness.
But you will meet her.
THEN...THEN I ACCEPT. THE CERTAINTY OF DEATH FOR THE UNCERTAINTY OF LOVE.
IT S-SEEMS LIKE A FAIR TRADE.

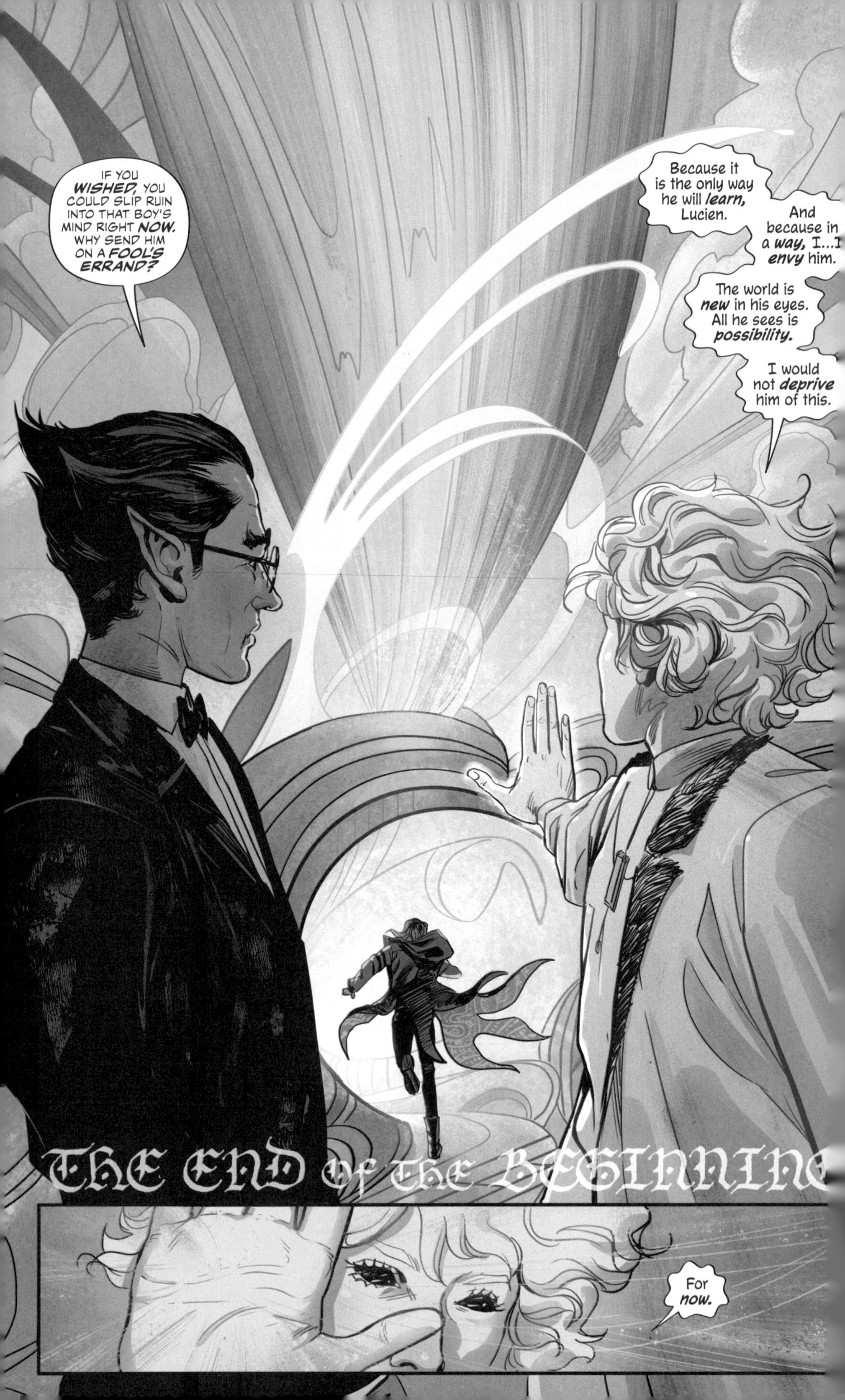
IF YOU WISHED, YOU COULD SLIP RUIN INTO THAT BOY'S MIND RIGHT NOW. WHY SEND HIM ON A FOOL'S ERRAND?
Because it is the only way he will learn, Lucien.
And because in a way, I...I envy him.
The world is new in his eyes. All he sees is possibility.
I would not deprive him of this.
THE END of THE BEGINNING
For now.

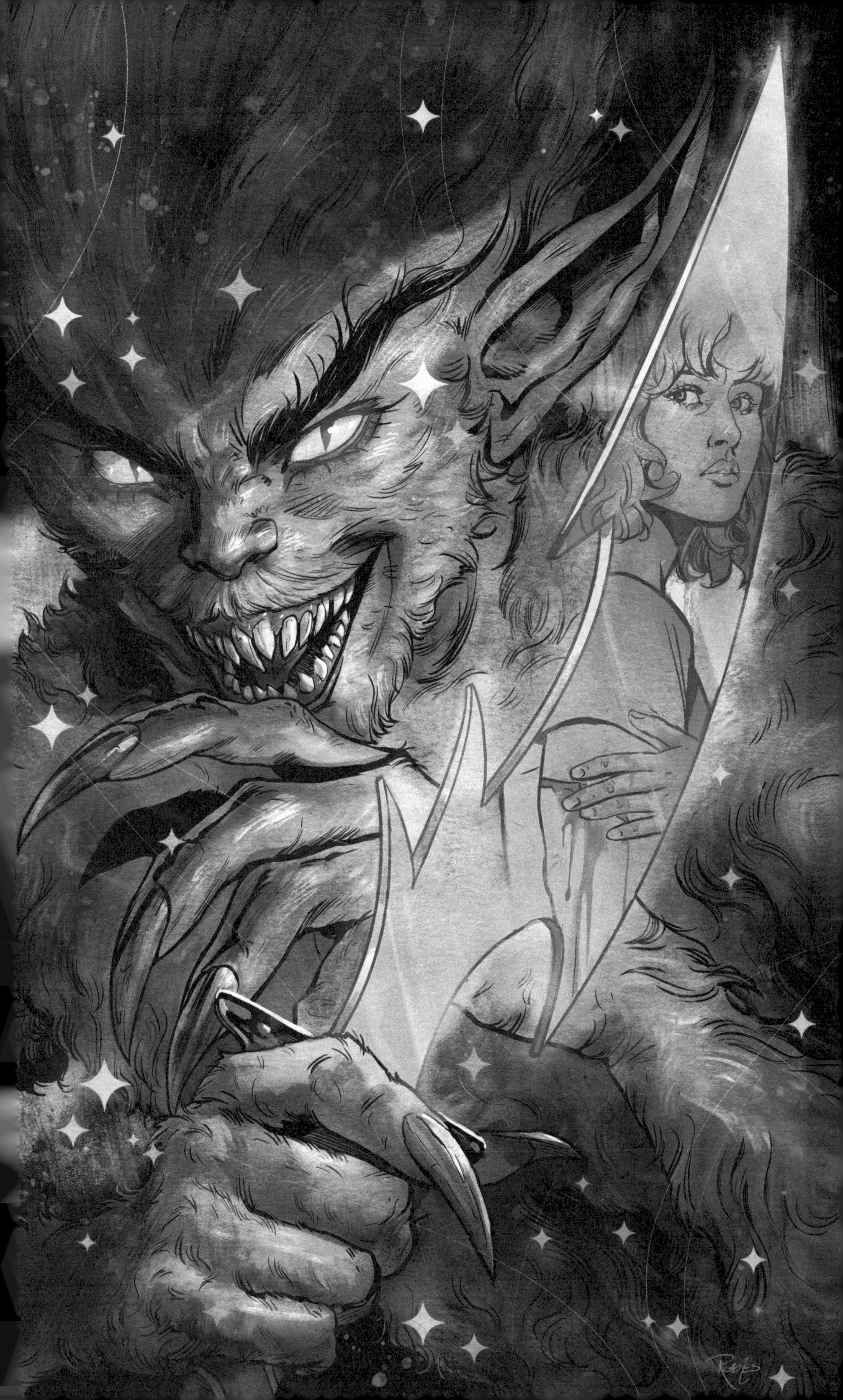

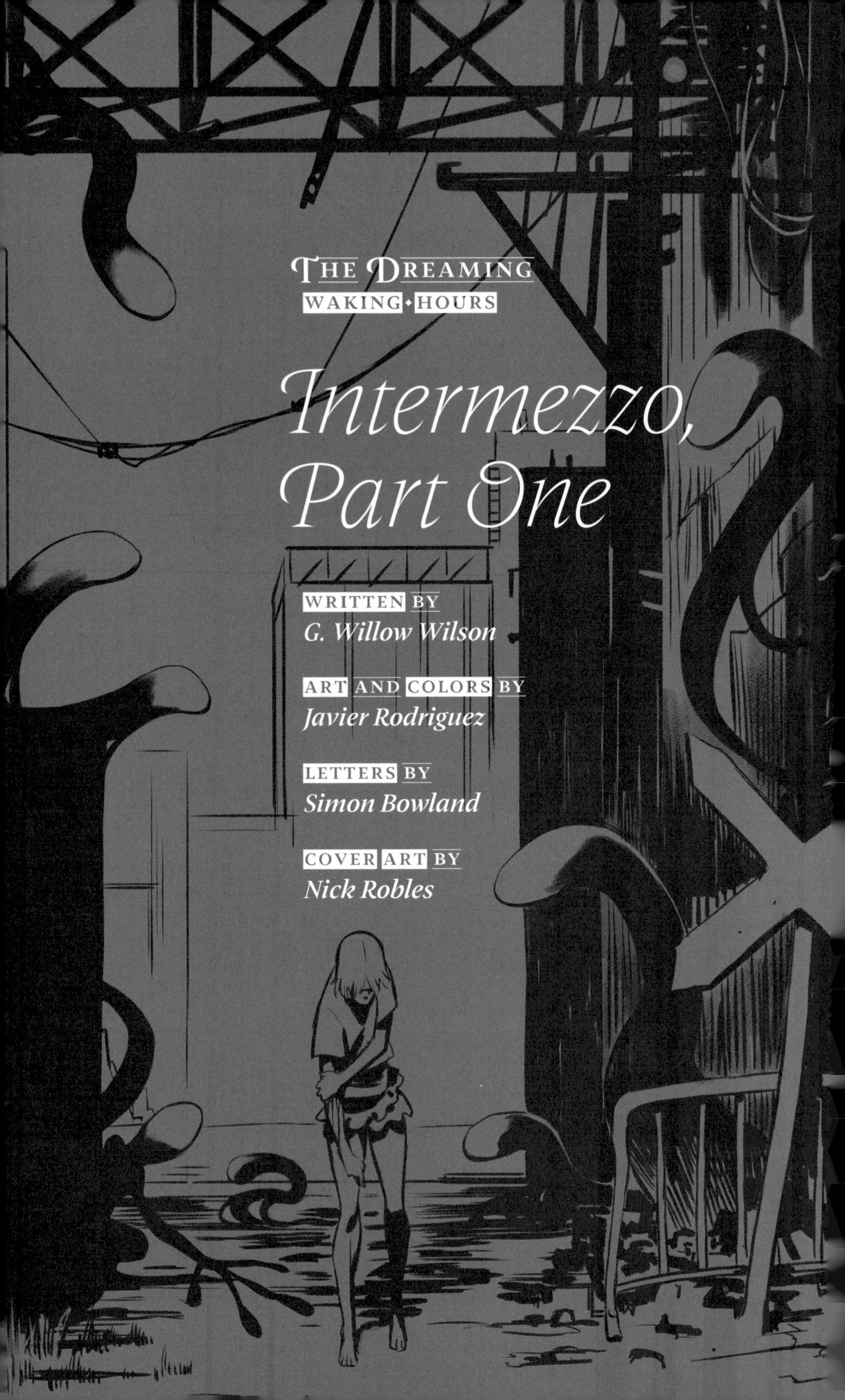
THE DREAMING
WAKING HOURS
Intermezzo, Part One
WRITTEN BY
G. Willow Wilson
ART AND COLORS BY
Javier Rodriguez
LETTERS BY
Simon Bowland
COVER ART BY
Nick Robles

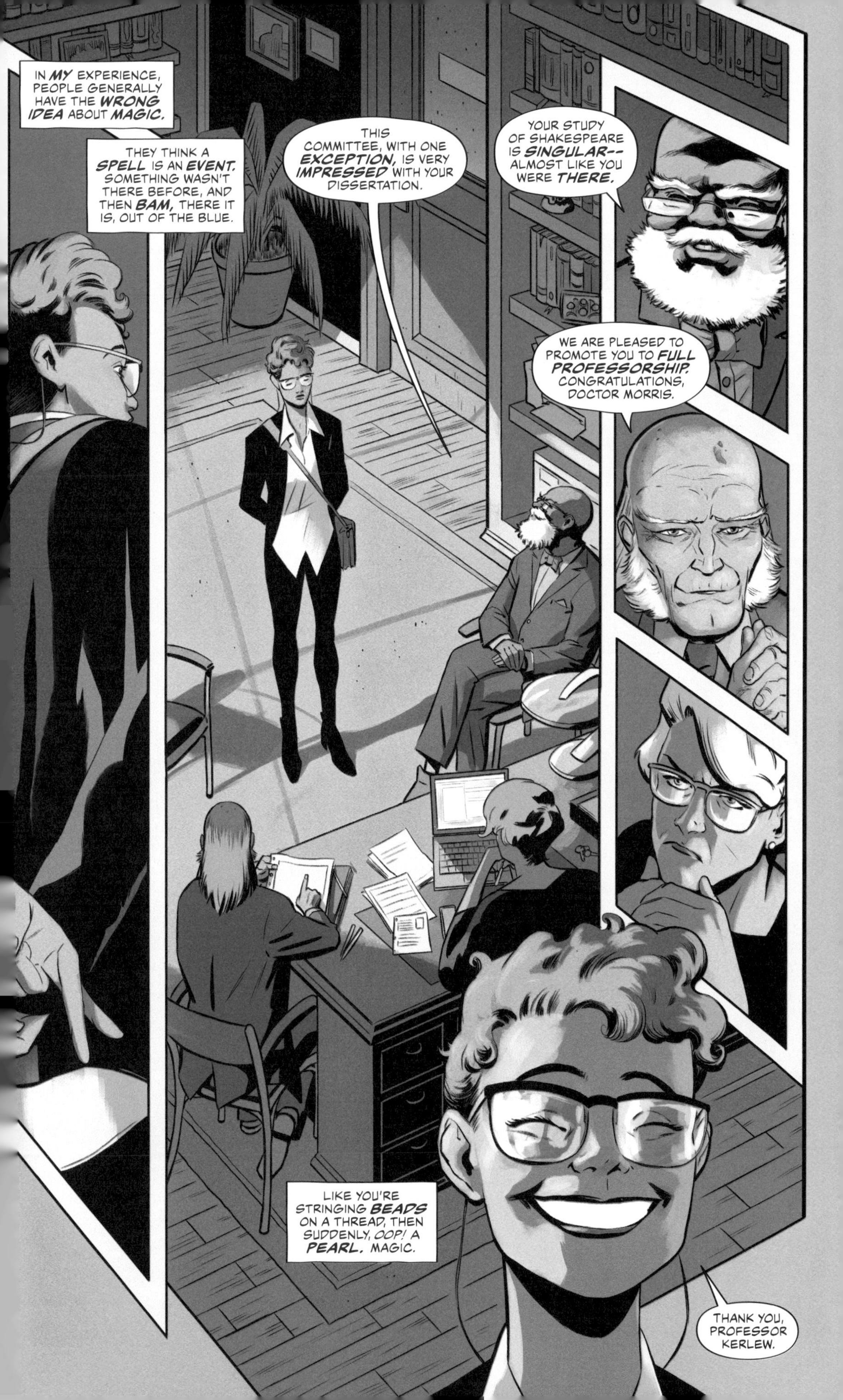
IN MY EXPERIENCE, PEOPLE GENERALLY HAVE THE WRONG IDEA ABOUT MAGIC.
THEY THINK A SPELL IS AN EVENT. SOMETHING WASN'T THERE BEFORE, AND THEN BAM, THERE IT IS, OUT OF THE BLUE.
THIS COMMITTEE, WITH ONE EXCEPTION, IS VERY IMPRESSED WITH YOUR DISSERTATION.
YOUR STUDY OF SHAKESPEARE IS SINGULAR-- ALMOST LIKE YOU WERE THERE.
WE ARE PLEASED TO PROMOTE YOU TO FULL PROFESSORSHIP. CONGRATULATIONS, DOCTOR MORRIS.
LIKE YOU'RE STRINGING BEADS ON A THREAD, THEN SUDDENLY, OOP! A PEARL. MAGIC.
THANK YOU, PROFESSOR KERLEW.

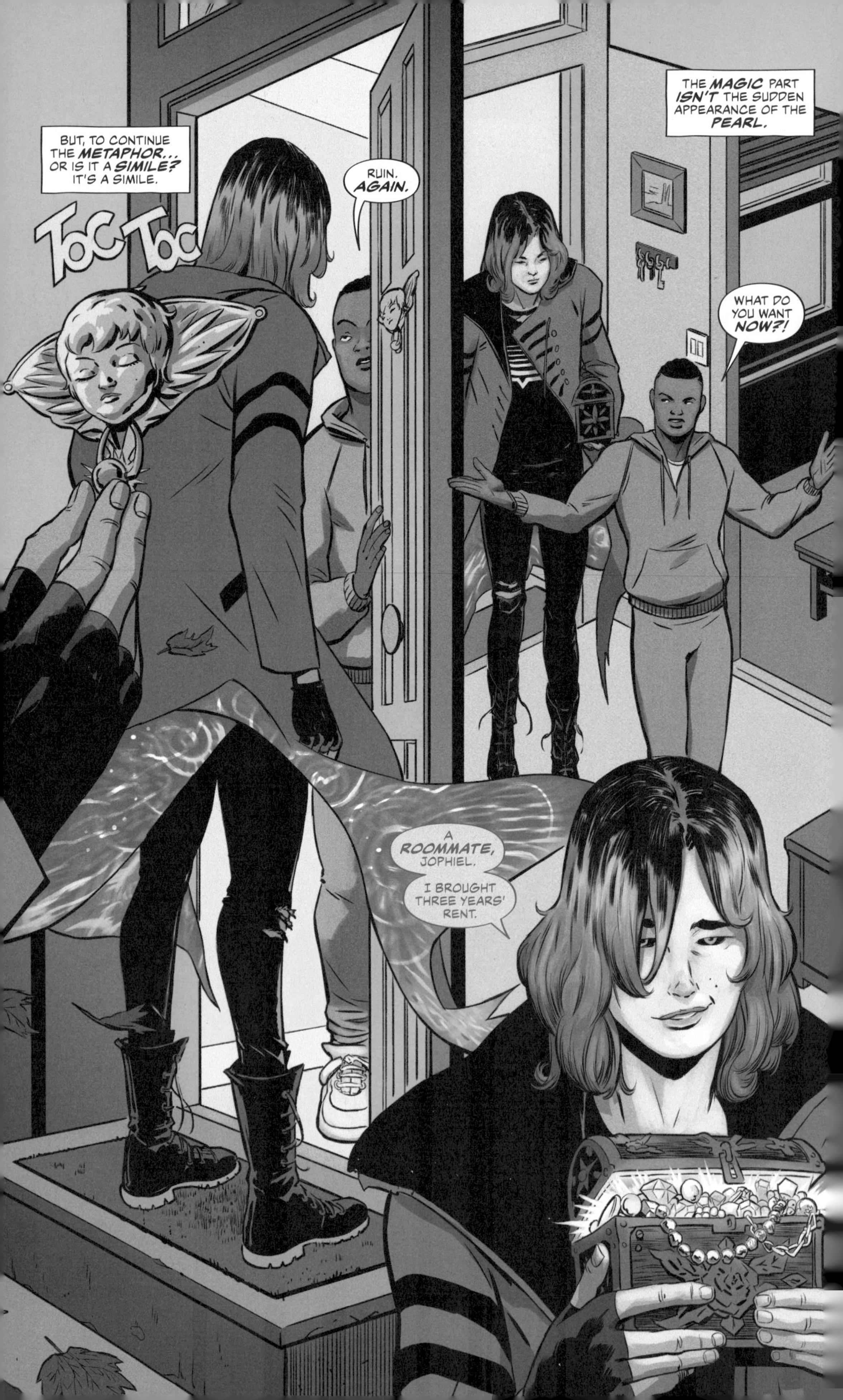
BUT, TO CONTINUE THE METAPHOR... OR IS IT A SIMILE? IT'S A SIMILE.
TOC TOC
RUIN. AGAIN.
THE MAGIC PART ISN'T THE SUDDEN APPEARANCE OF THE PEARL.
WHAT DO YOU WANT NOW?!
A ROOMMATE, JOPHIEL.
I BROUGHT THREE YEARS' RENT.

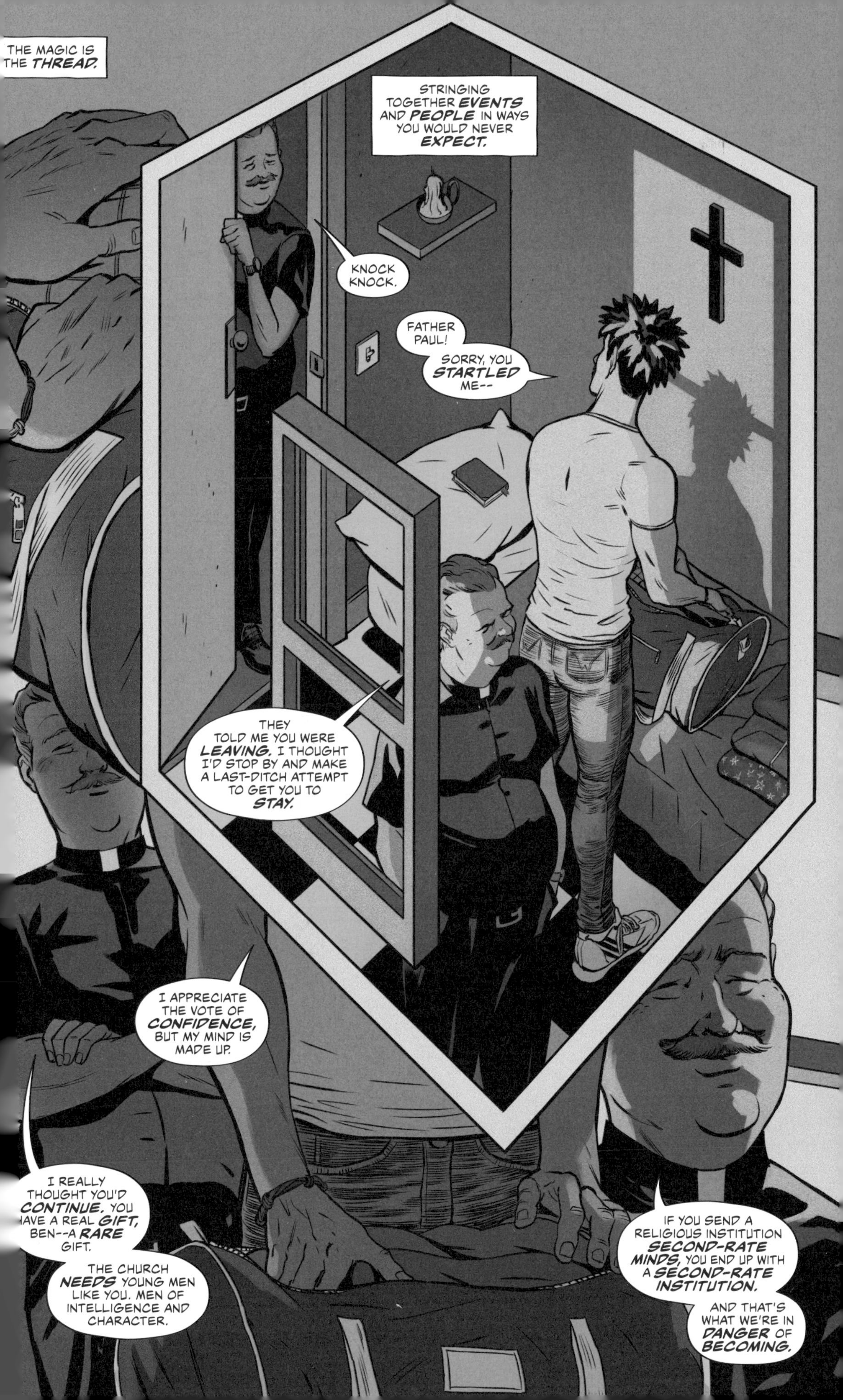

THE MAGIC IS THE THREAD.
STRINGING TOGETHER EVENTS AND PEOPLE IN WAYS YOU WOULD NEVER EXPECT.
KNOCK KNOCK.
FATHER PAUL!
SORRY, YOU STARTLED ME--
THEY TOLD ME YOU WERE LEAVING. I THOUGHT I'D STOP BY AND MAKE A LAST-DITCH ATTEMPT TO GET YOU TO STAY.
I APPRECIATE THE VOTE OF CONFIDENCE, BUT MY MIND IS MADE UP.
I REALLY THOUGHT YOU'D CONTINUE. YOU HAVE A REAL GIFT, BEN--A RARE GIFT.
THE CHURCH NEEDS YOUNG MEN LIKE YOU. MEN OF INTELLIGENCE AND CHARACTER.
IF YOU SEND A RELIGIOUS INSTITUTION SECOND-RATE MINDS, YOU END UP WITH A SECOND-RATE INSTITUTION.
AND THAT'S WHAT WE'RE IN DANGER OF BECOMING.

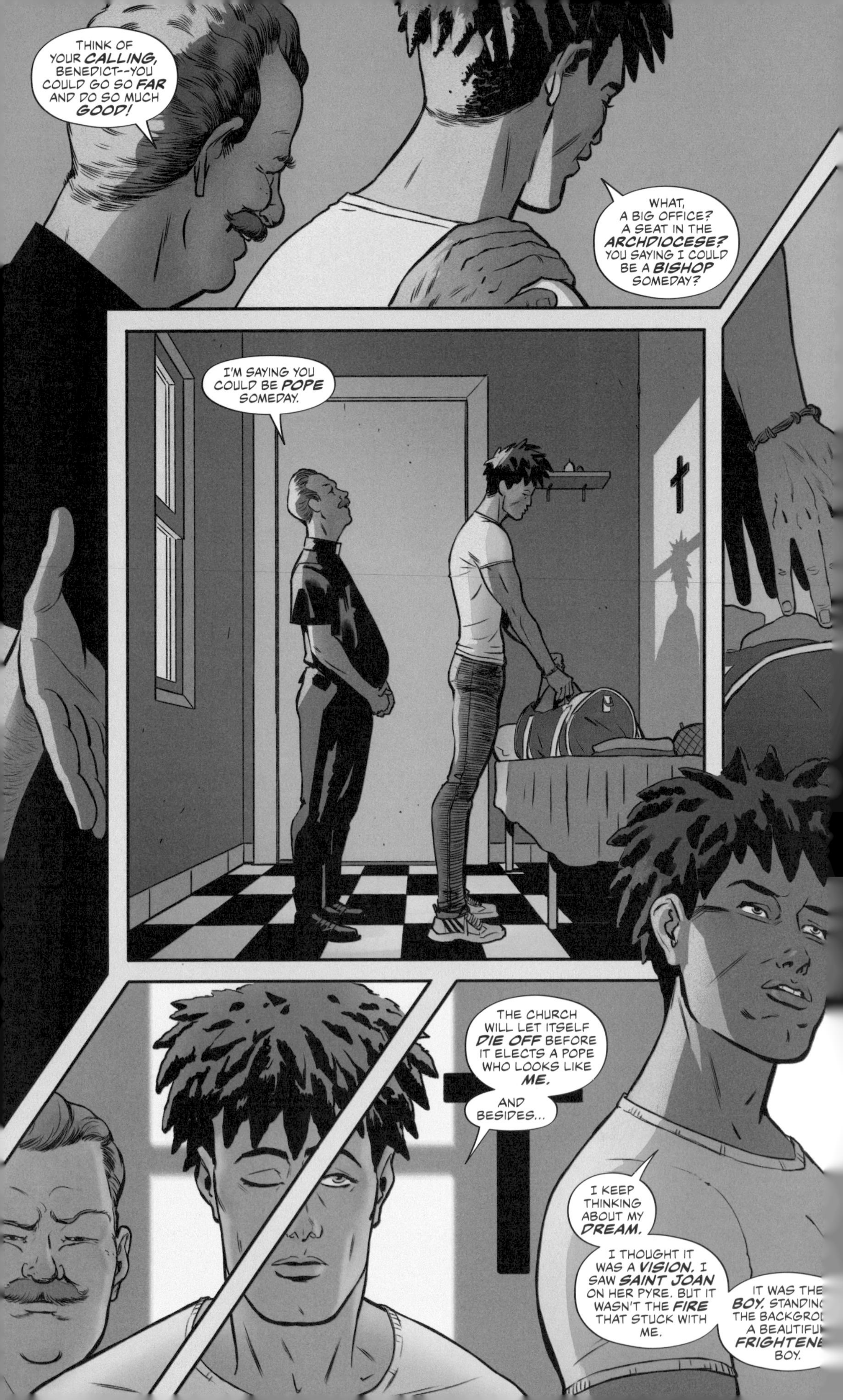
THINK OF YOUR CALLING, BENEDICT--YOU COULD GO SO FAR AND DO SO MUCH GOOD!
WHAT, A BIG OFFICE? A SEAT IN THE ARCHDIOCESE? YOU SAYING I COULD BE A BISHOP SOMEDAY?
I'M SAYING YOU COULD BE POPE SOMEDAY.
THE CHURCH WILL LET ITSELF DIE OFF BEFORE IT ELECTS A POPE WHO LOOKS LIKE ME.
AND BESIDES...
I KEEP THINKING ABOUT MY DREAM.
I THOUGHT IT WAS A VISION. I SAW SAINT JOAN ON HER PYRE. BUT IT WASN'T THE FIRE THAT STUCK WITH ME.

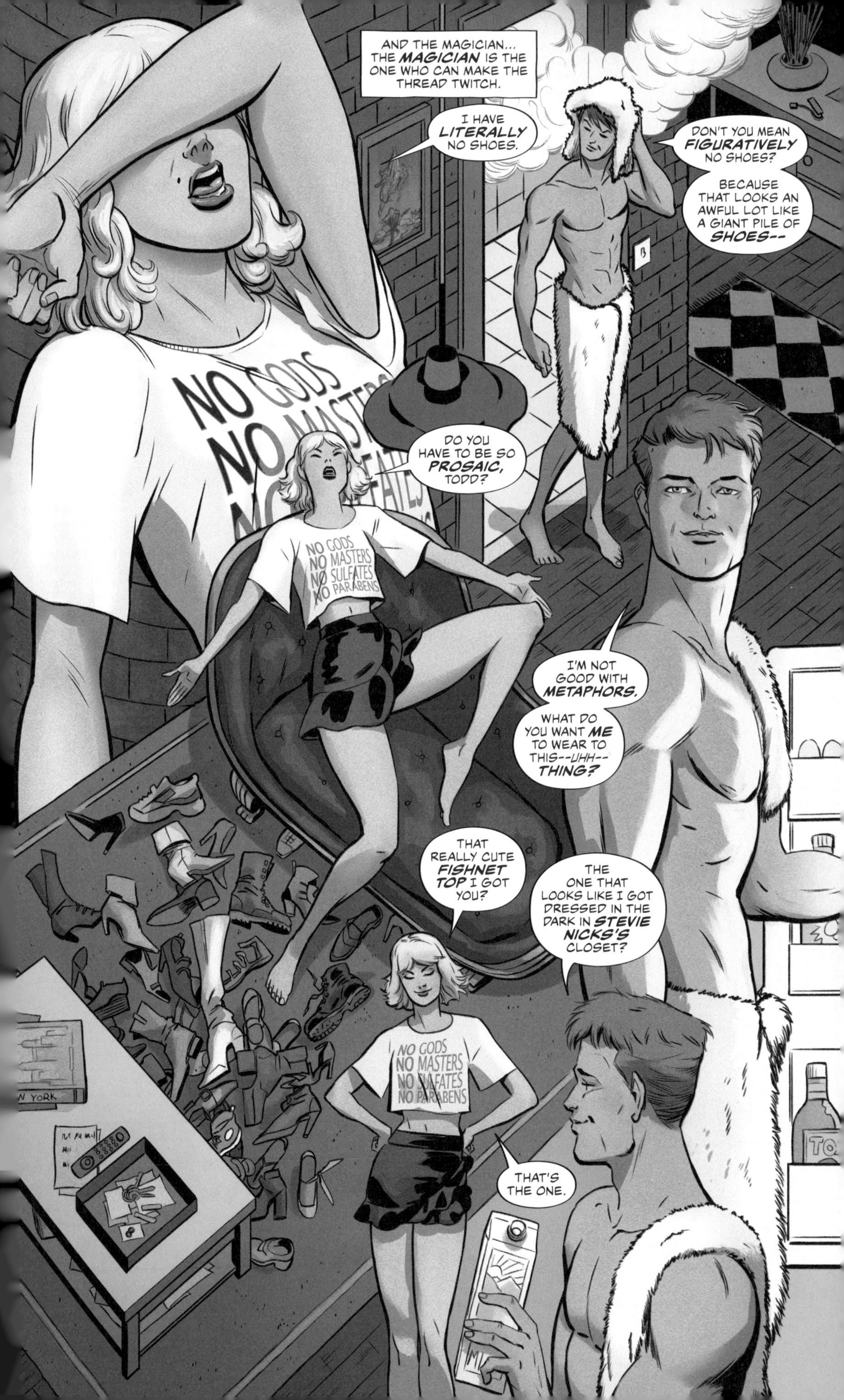

AND THE MAGICIAN... THE MAGICIAN IS THE ONE WHO CAN MAKE THE THREAD TWITCH.
I HAVE LITERALLY NO SHOES.
DON'T YOU MEAN FIGURATIVELY NO SHOES?
BECAUSE THAT LOOKS AN AWFUL LOT LIKE A GIANT PILE OF SHOES--
NO GODS NO MASTERS NO SULFATES NO PARABENS
DO YOU HAVE TO BE SO PROSAIC, TODD?
I'M NOT GOOD WITH METAPHORS.
WHAT DO YOU WANT ME TO WEAR TO THIS--UHH-- THING?
THAT REALLY CUTE FISHNET TOP I GOT YOU?
THE ONE THAT LOOKS LIKE I GOT DRESSED IN THE DARK IN STEVIE NICKS'S CLOSET?
THAT'S THE ONE.

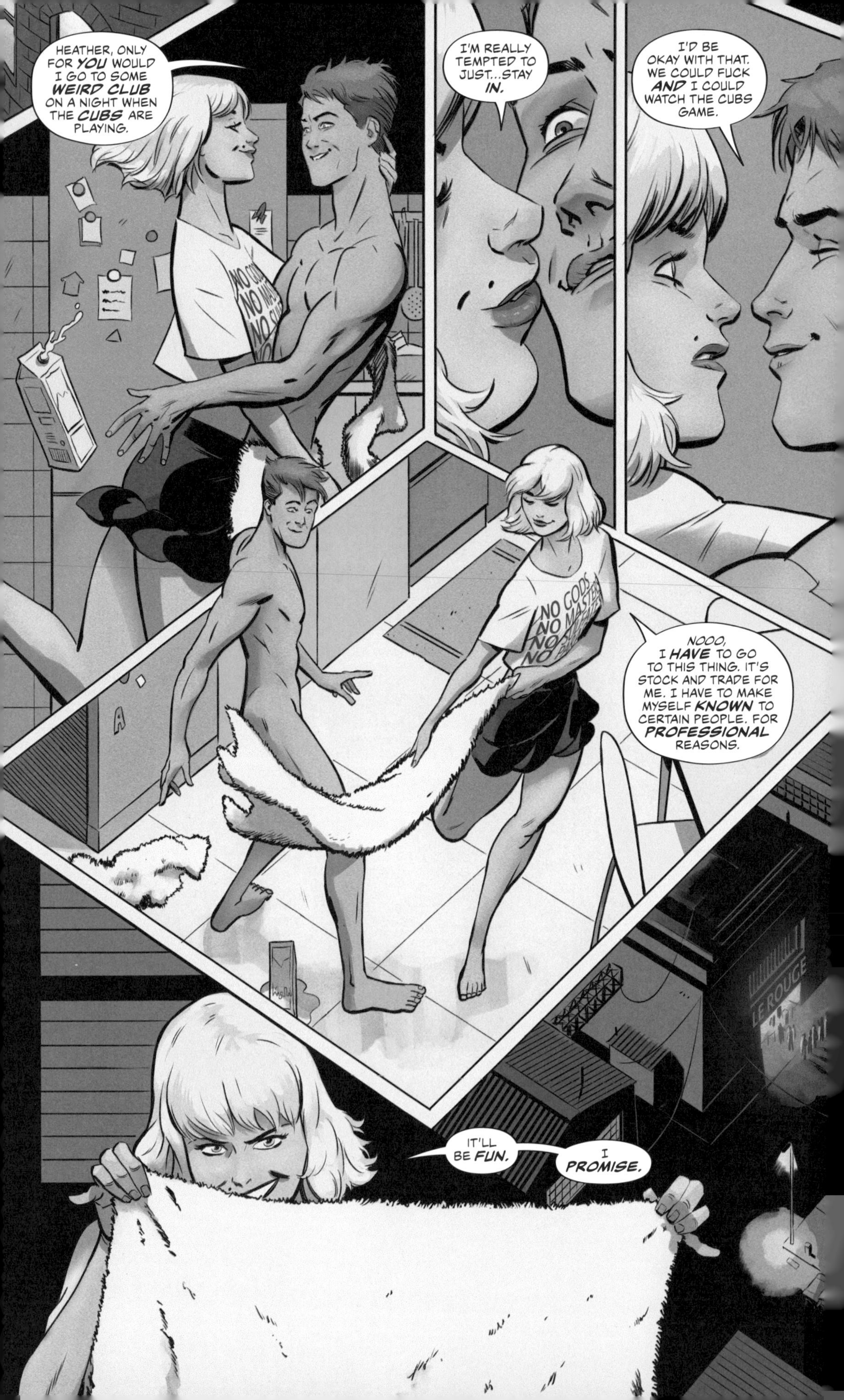
HEATHER, ONLY FOR YOU WOULD I GO TO SOME WEIRD CLUB ON A NIGHT WHEN THE CUBS ARE PLAYING.
I'M REALLY TEMPTED TO JUST...STAY IN.
I'D BE OKAY WITH THAT. WE COULD FUCK AND I COULD WATCH THE CUBS GAME.
NOOO, I HAVE TO GO TO THIS THING. IT'S STOCK AND TRADE FOR ME. I HAVE TO MAKE MYSELF KNOWN TO CERTAIN PEOPLE. FOR PROFESSIONAL REASONS.
LE ROUGE
IT'LL BE FUN.
I PROMISE.

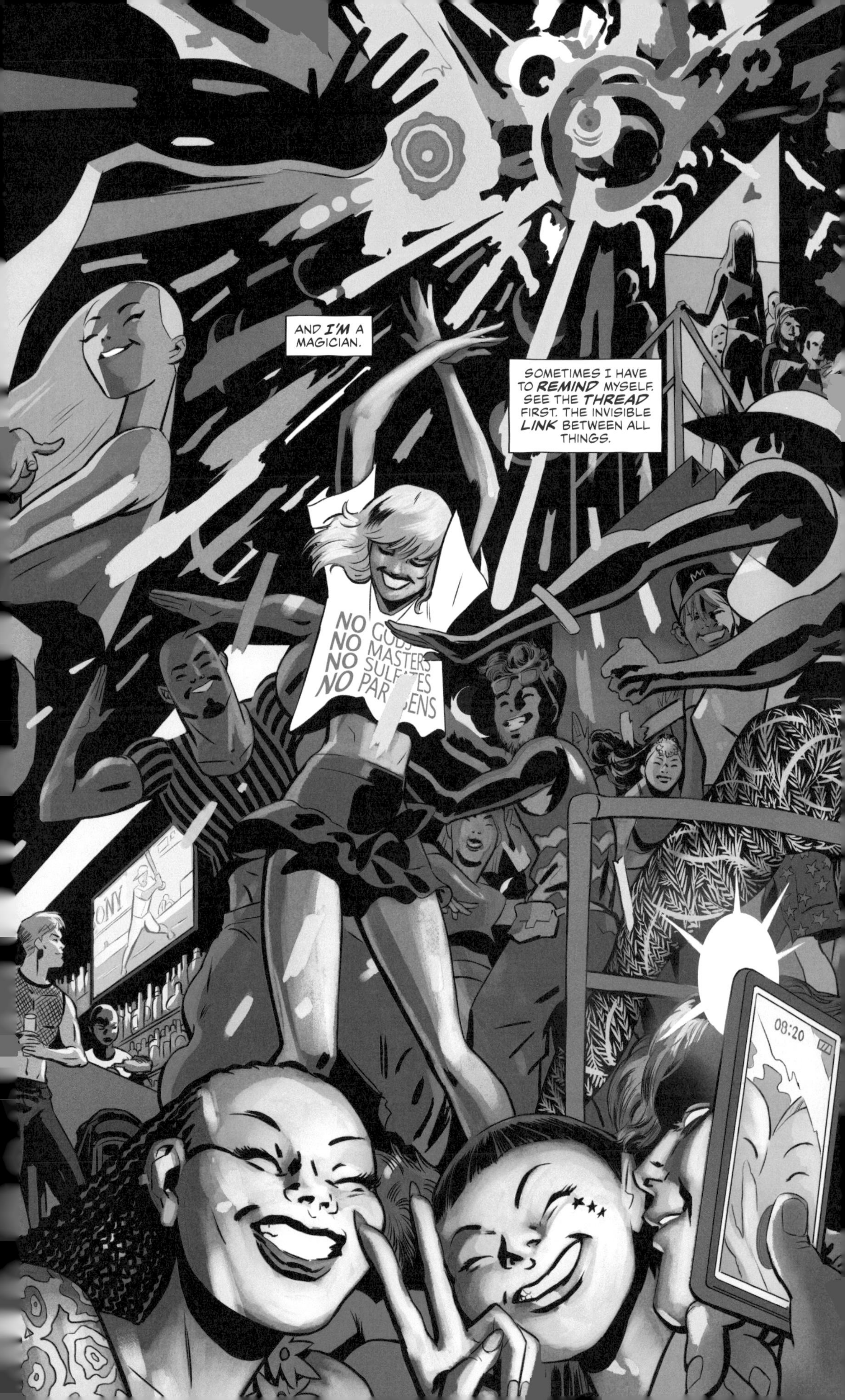
AND I'M A MAGICIAN.
SOMETIMES I HAVE TO REMIND MYSELF. SEE THE THREAD FIRST. THE INVISIBLE LINK BETWEEN ALL THINGS.
NO GODS NO MASTERS NO SULFATES NO PARABENS
08:20

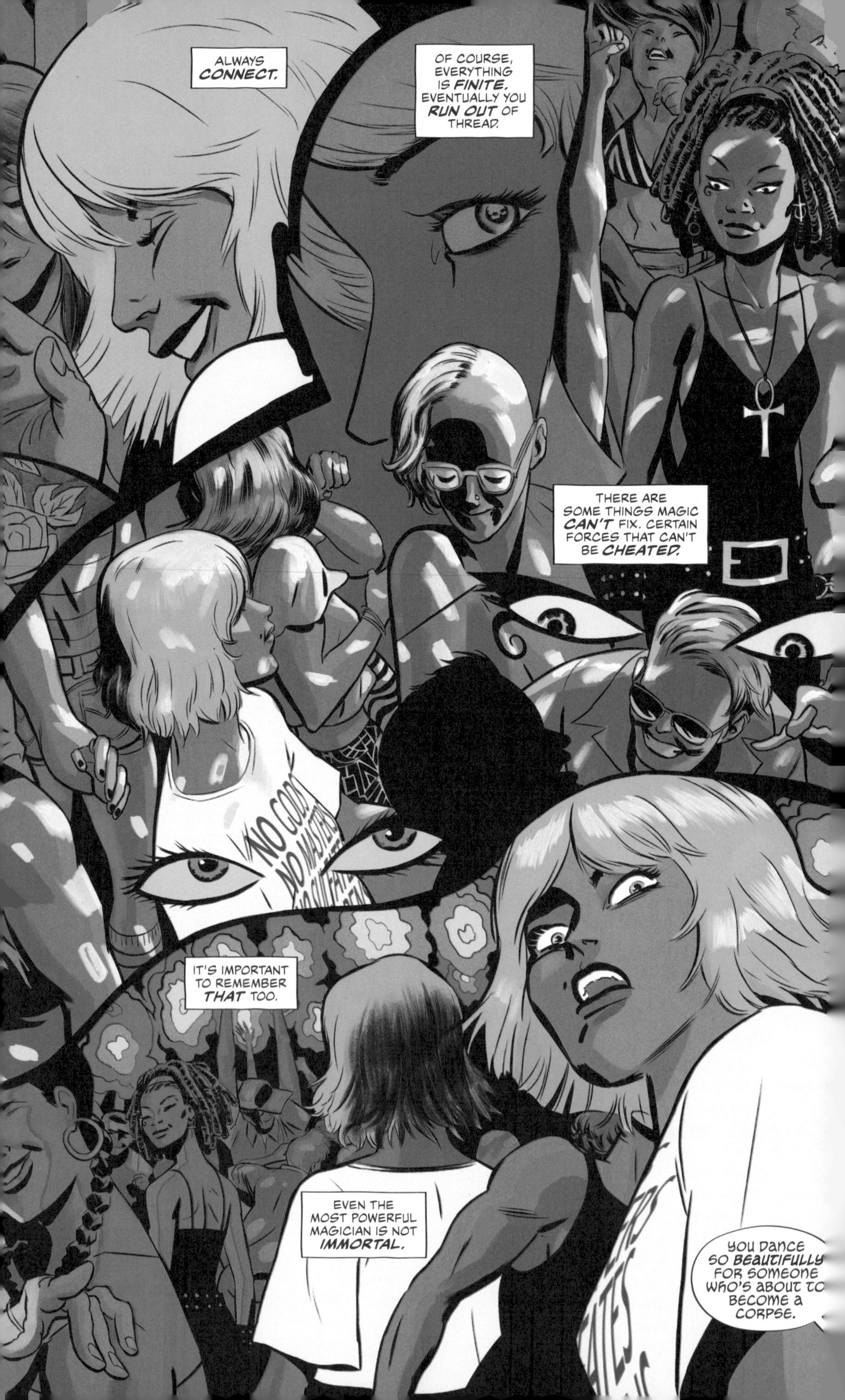
ALWAYS CONNECT.
OF COURSE, EVERYTHING IS FINITE. EVENTUALLY YOU RUN OUT OF THREAD.
THERE ARE SOME THINGS MAGIC CAN'T FIX. CERTAIN FORCES THAT CAN'T BE CHEATED.
NO GODS NO MASTERS
IT'S IMPORTANT TO REMEMBER THAT TOO.
EVEN THE MOST POWERFUL MAGICIAN IS NOT IMMORTAL.
YOU DANCE SO BEAUTIFULLY FOR SOMEONE WHO'S ABOUT TO BECOME A CORPSE.

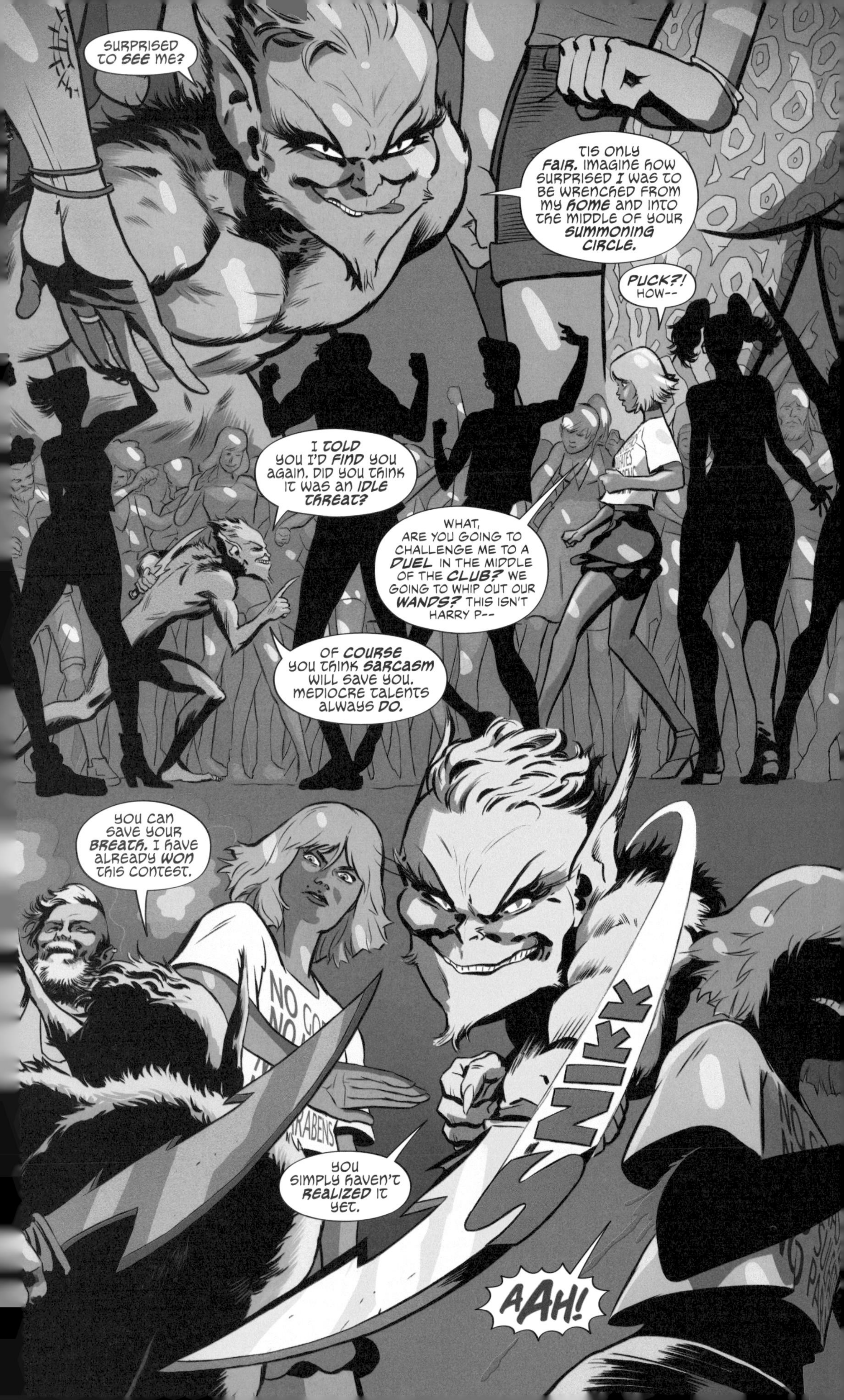
SURPRISED TO SEE ME?
TIS ONLY FAIR. IMAGINE HOW SURPRISED I WAS TO BE WRENCHED FROM MY HOME AND INTO THE MIDDLE OF YOUR SUMMONING CIRCLE.
PUCK?! HOW--
I TOLD YOU I'D FIND YOU AGAIN. DID YOU THINK IT WAS AN IDLE THREAT?
WHAT, ARE YOU GOING TO CHALLENGE ME TO A DUEL IN THE MIDDLE OF THE CLUB? WE GOING TO WHIP OUT OUR WANDS? THIS ISN'T HARRY P--
OF COURSE YOU THINK SARCASM WILL SAVE YOU. MEDIOCRE TALENTS ALWAYS DO.
YOU CAN SAVE YOUR BREATH. I HAVE ALREADY WON THIS CONTEST.
YOU SIMPLY HAVEN'T REALIZED IT YET.
SNIKK
AAH!

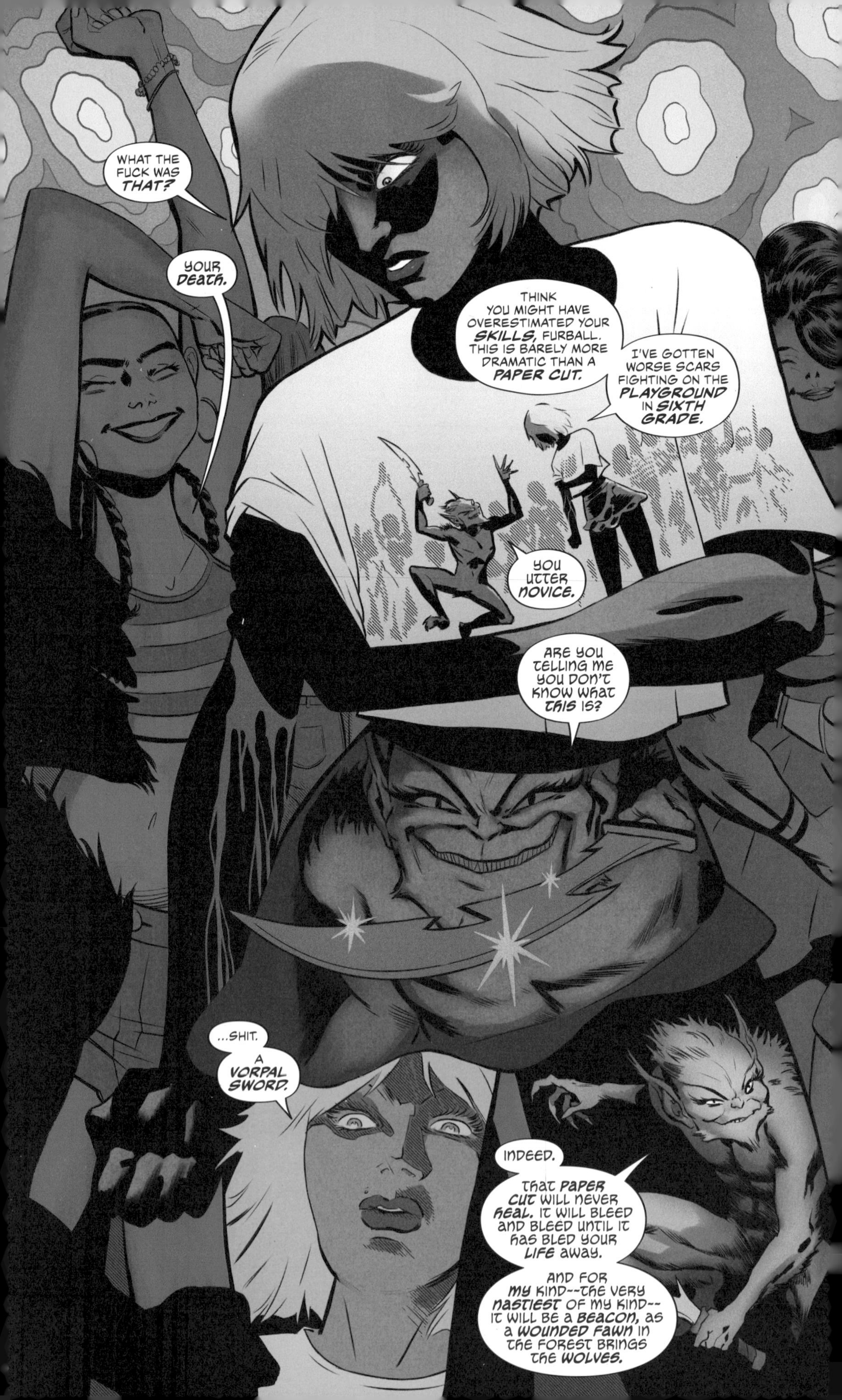
WHAT THE FUCK WAS THAT?
YOUR DEATH.
THINK YOU MIGHT HAVE OVERESTIMATED YOUR SKILLS, FURBALL. THIS IS BARELY MORE DRAMATIC THAN A PAPER CUT.
I'VE GOTTEN WORSE SCARS FIGHTING ON THE PLAYGROUND IN SIXTH GRADE.
YOU UTTER NOVICE.
ARE YOU TELLING ME YOU DON'T KNOW WHAT THIS IS?
...SHIT. A VORPAL SWORD.
INDEED.
THAT PAPER CUT WILL NEVER HEAL. IT WILL BLEED AND BLEED UNTIL IT HAS BLED YOUR LIFE AWAY.
AND FOR MY KIND--THE VERY NASTIEST OF MY KIND--IT WILL BE A BEACON, AS A WOUNDED FAWN IN THE FOREST BRINGS THE WOLVES.

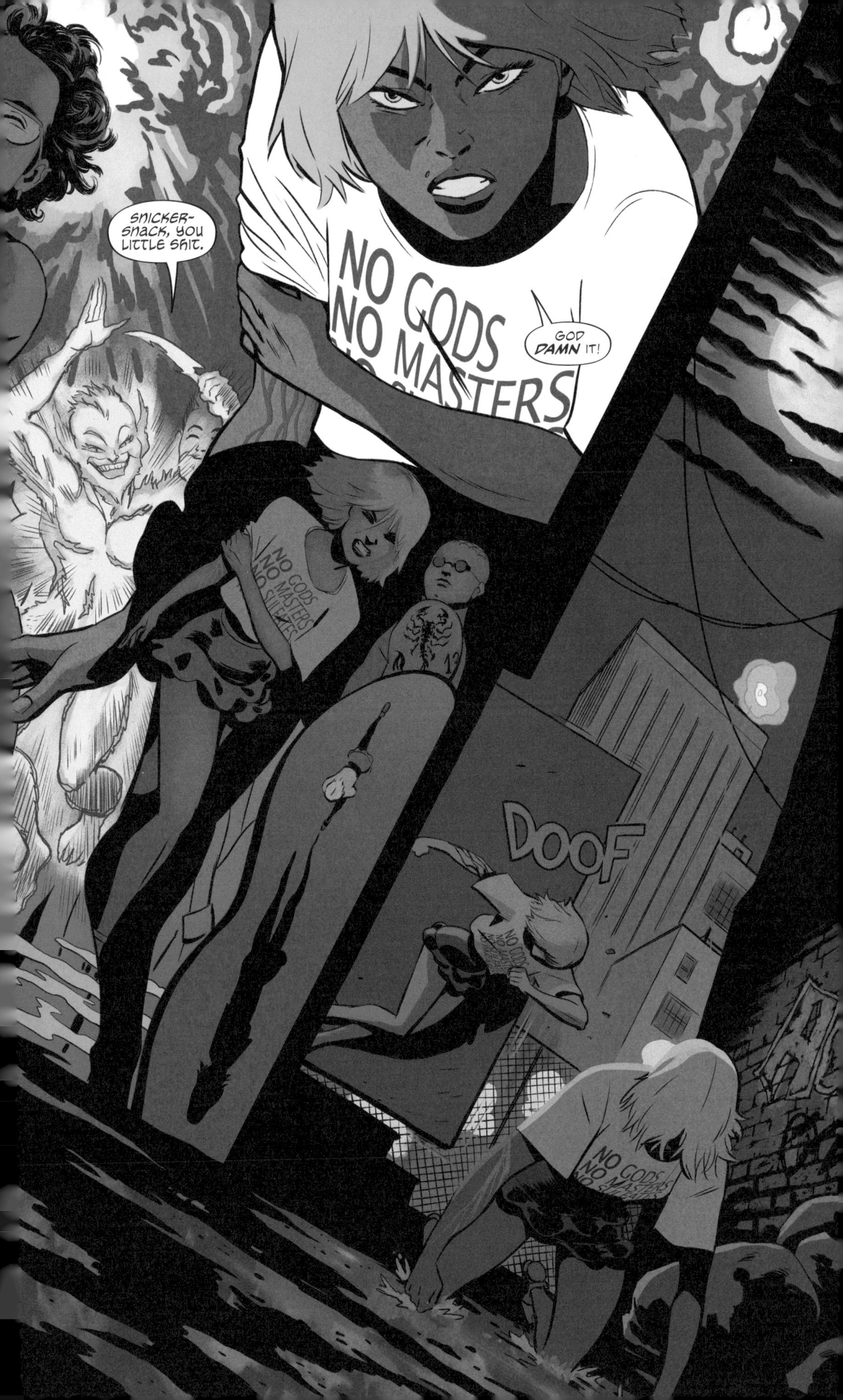
SNICKER-SNACK, YOU LITTLE SHIT.
NO GODS NO MASTERS
GOD DAMN IT!
DOOF

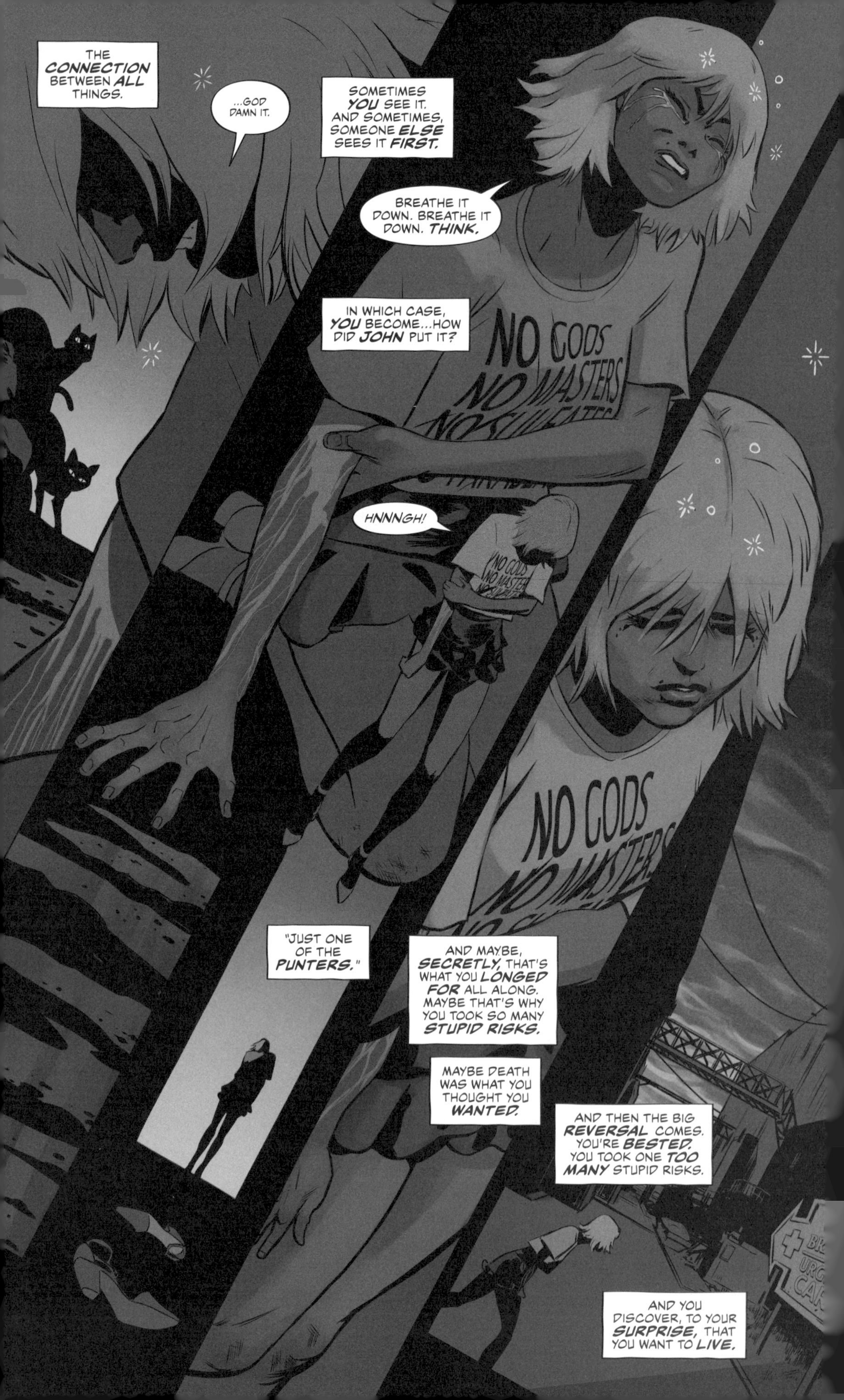
THE CONNECTION BETWEEN ALL THINGS.
...GOD DAMN IT.
SOMETIMES YOU SEE IT. AND SOMETIMES, SOMEONE ELSE SEES IT FIRST.
BREATHE IT DOWN. BREATHE IT DOWN. THINK.
IN WHICH CASE, YOU BECOME...HOW DID JOHN PUT IT?
NO GODS NO MASTERS
HNNNGH!
NO GODS NO MASTERS
"JUST ONE OF THE PUNTERS."
AND MAYBE, SECRETLY, THAT'S WHAT YOU LONGED FOR ALL ALONG. MAYBE THAT'S WHY YOU TOOK SO MANY STUPID RISKS.
MAYBE DEATH WAS WHAT YOU THOUGHT YOU WANTED.
AND THEN THE BIG REVERSAL COMES. YOU'RE BESTED. YOU TOOK ONE TOO MANY STUPID RISKS.
AND YOU DISCOVER, TO YOUR SURPRISE, THAT YOU WANT TO LIVE.

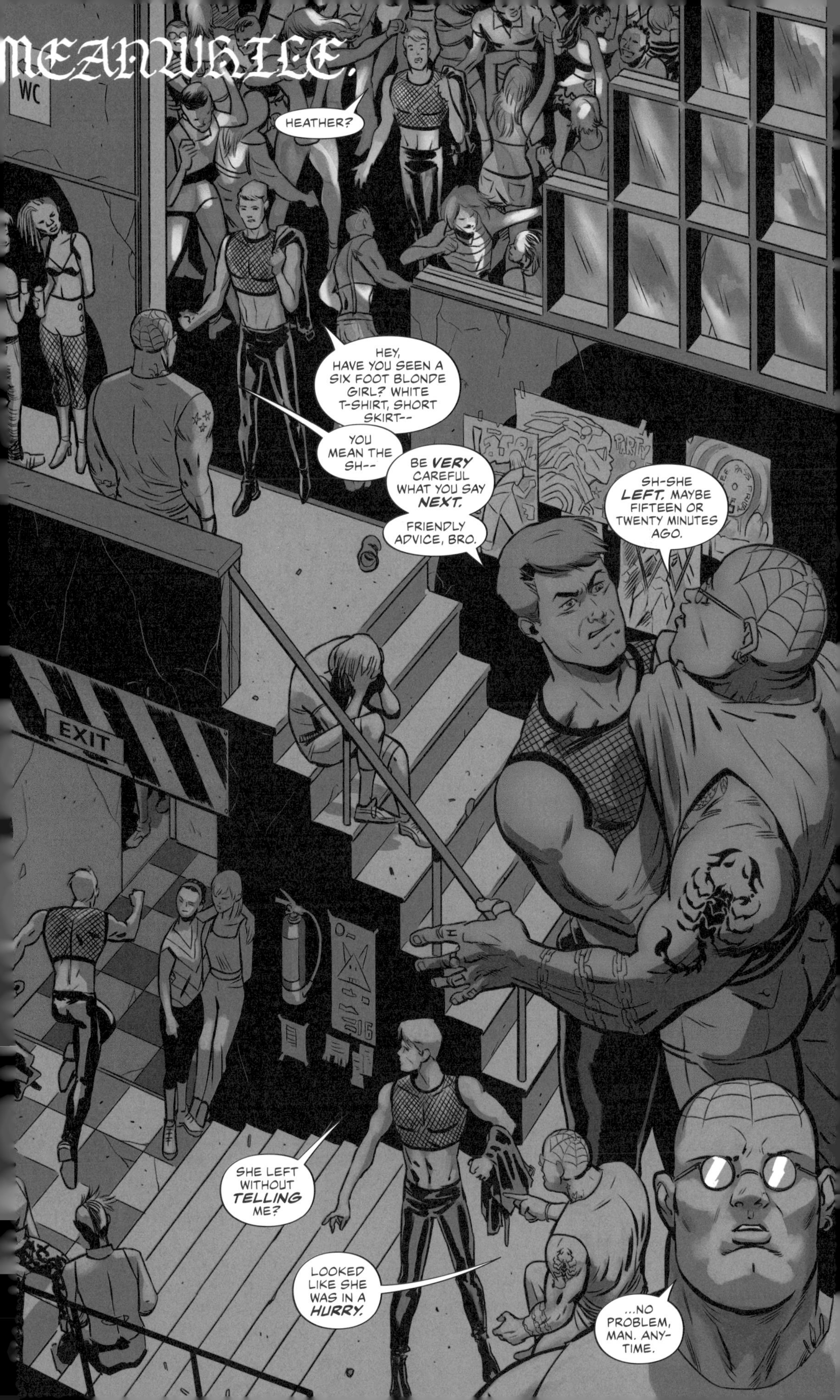
MEANWHILE.
WC
HEATHER?
HEY, HAVE YOU SEEN A SIX FOOT BLONDE GIRL? WHITE T-SHIRT, SHORT SKIRT--
YOU MEAN THE SH--
BE VERY CAREFUL WHAT YOU SAY NEXT.
FRIENDLY ADVICE, BRO.
SH-SHE LEFT. MAYBE FIFTEEN OR TWENTY MINUTES AGO.
EXIT
SHE LEFT WITHOUT TELLING ME?
LOOKED LIKE SHE WAS IN A HURRY.
...NO PROBLEM, MAN. ANY-TIME.

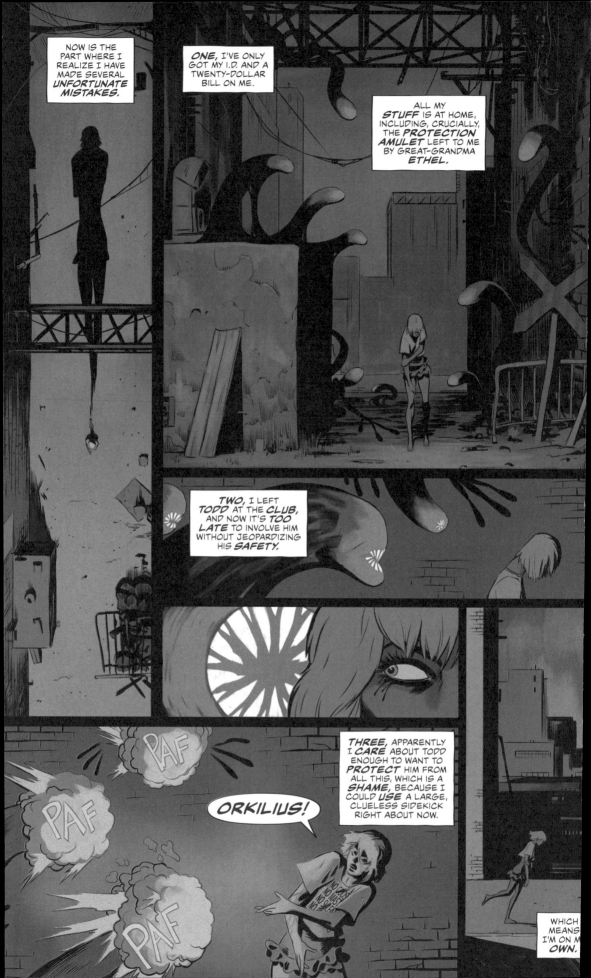

NOW IS THE PART WHERE I REALIZE I HAVE MADE SEVERAL *UNFORTUNATE MISTAKES.*

ONE, I'VE ONLY GOT MY I.D. AND A TWENTY-DOLLAR BILL ON ME.

ALL MY *STUFF* IS AT HOME, INCLUDING, CRUCIALLY, THE *PROTECTION AMULET* LEFT TO ME BY GREAT-GRANDMA *ETHEL.*

TWO, I LEFT *TODD* AT THE *CLUB,* AND NOW IT'S *TOO LATE* TO INVOLVE HIM WITHOUT JEOPARDIZING HIS *SAFETY.*

THREE, APPARENTLY I *CARE* ABOUT TODD ENOUGH TO WANT TO *PROTECT* HIM FROM ALL THIS, WHICH IS A *SHAME,* BECAUSE I COULD *USE* A LARGE, CLUELESS SIDEKICK RIGHT ABOUT NOW.

PAF

PAF

PAF

ORKILIUS!

WHICH MEANS I'M ON MY *OWN.*

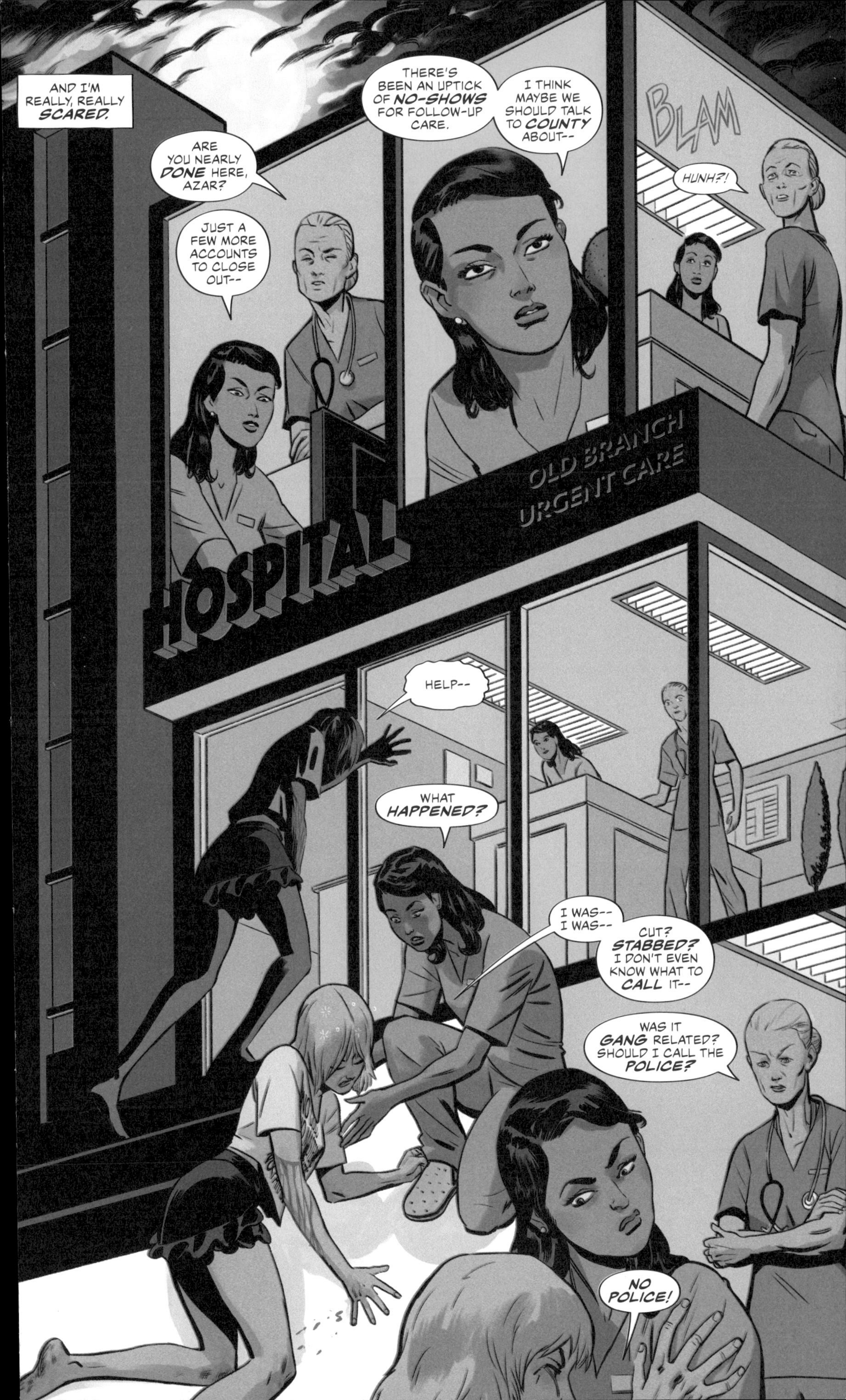
AND I'M REALLY, REALLY SCARED.
ARE YOU NEARLY DONE HERE, AZAR?
JUST A FEW MORE ACCOUNTS TO CLOSE OUT--
THERE'S BEEN AN UPTICK OF NO-SHOWS FOR FOLLOW-UP CARE.
I THINK MAYBE WE SHOULD TALK TO COUNTY ABOUT--
BLAM
HUNH?!
HOSPITAL
OLD BRANCH URGENT CARE
HELP--
WHAT HAPPENED?
I WAS-- I WAS--
CUT? STABBED? I DON'T EVEN KNOW WHAT TO CALL IT--
WAS IT GANG RELATED? SHOULD I CALL THE POLICE?
NO POLICE!

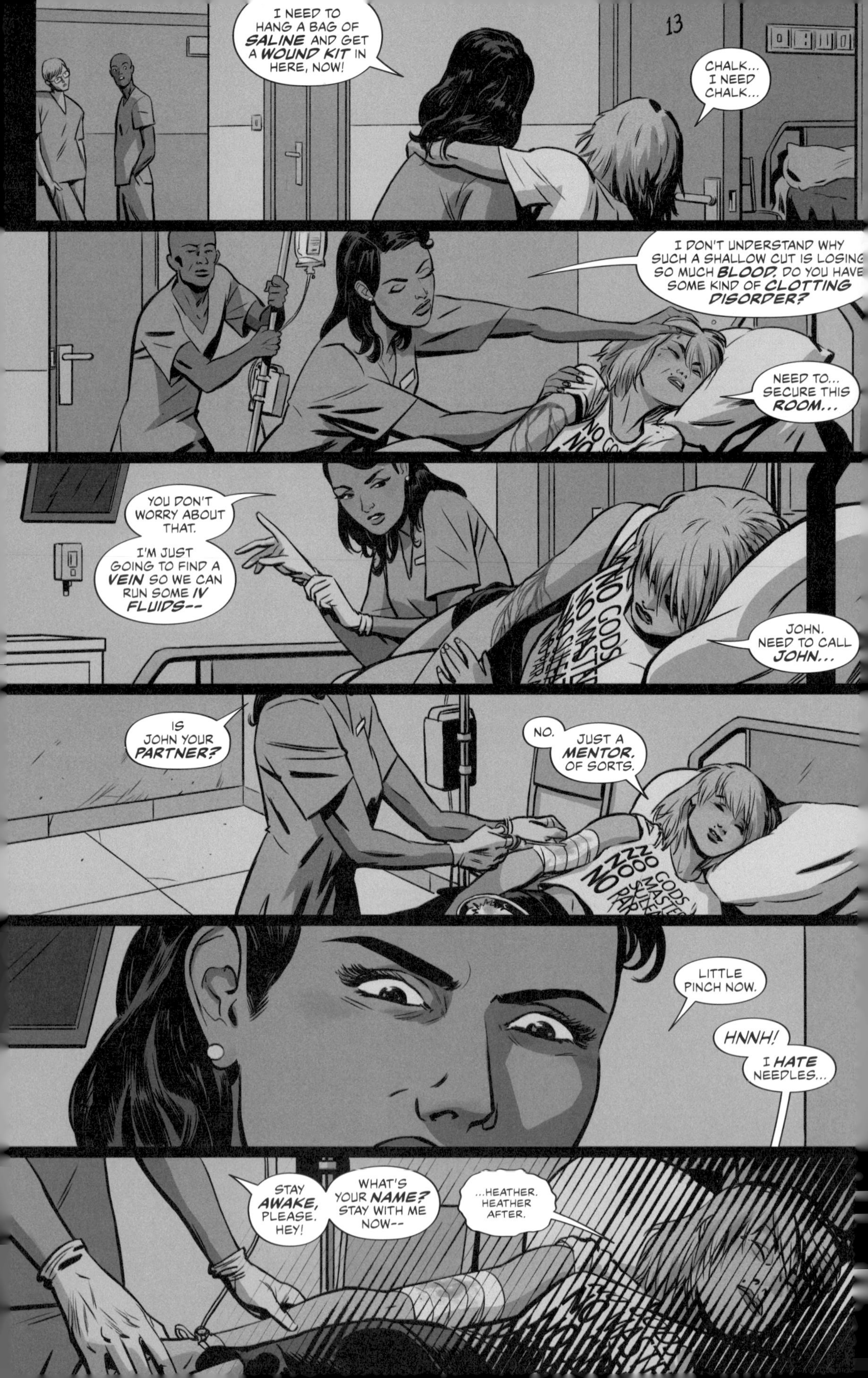
13
I NEED TO HANG A BAG OF SALINE AND GET A WOUND KIT IN HERE, NOW!
CHALK... I NEED CHALK...
I DON'T UNDERSTAND WHY SUCH A SHALLOW CUT IS LOSING SO MUCH BLOOD. DO YOU HAVE SOME KIND OF CLOTTING DISORDER?
NEED TO... SECURE THIS ROOM...
YOU DON'T WORRY ABOUT THAT.
I'M JUST GOING TO FIND A VEIN SO WE CAN RUN SOME IV FLUIDS--
JOHN. NEED TO CALL JOHN...
IS JOHN YOUR PARTNER?
NO.
JUST A MENTOR. OF SORTS.
LITTLE PINCH NOW.
HNNH!
I HATE NEEDLES...
STAY AWAKE, PLEASE. HEY!
WHAT'S YOUR NAME? STAY WITH ME NOW--
...HEATHER. HEATHER AFTER.

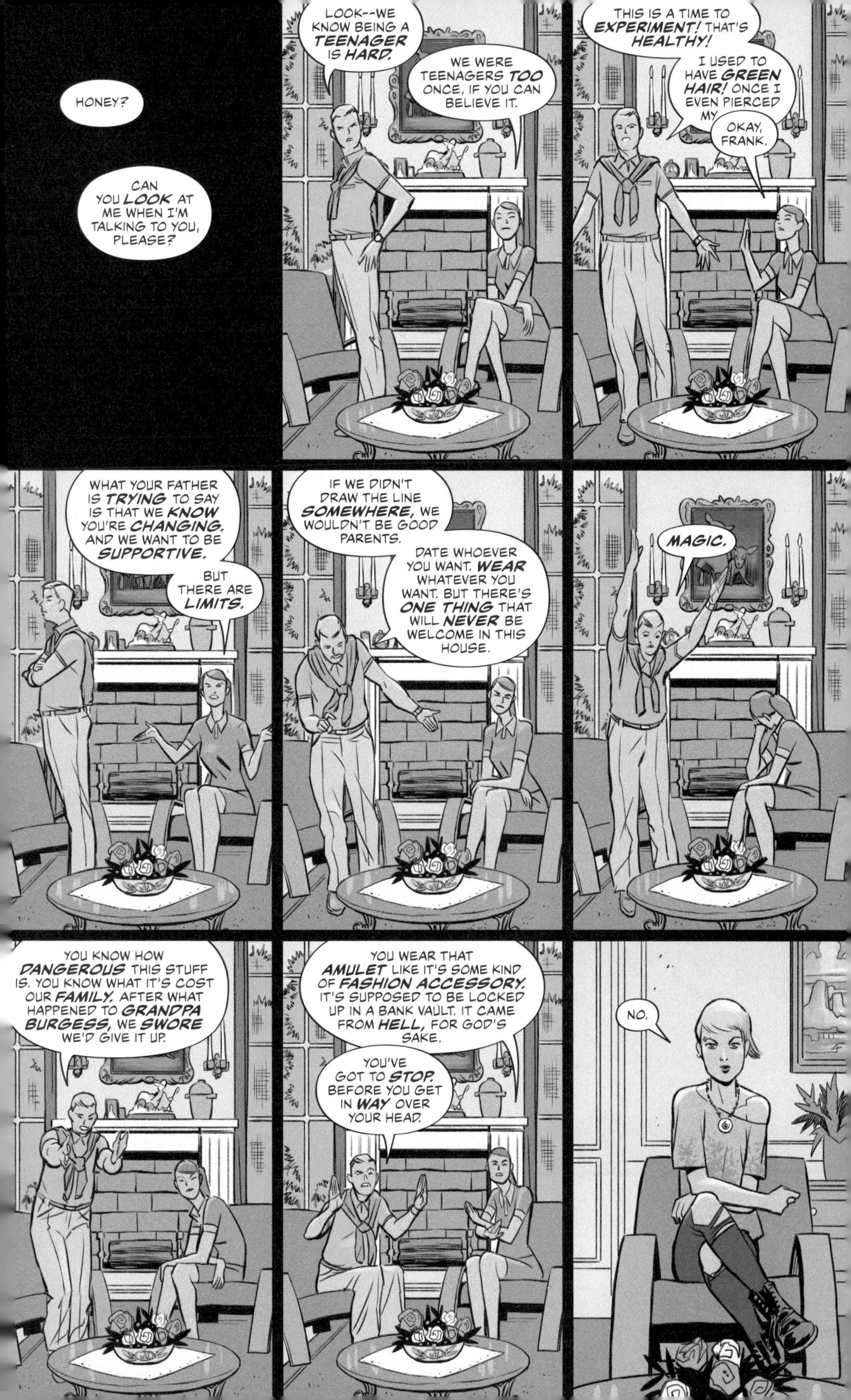
HONEY?
CAN YOU LOOK AT ME WHEN I'M TALKING TO YOU, PLEASE?
LOOK--WE KNOW BEING A TEENAGER IS HARD.
WE WERE TEENAGERS TOO ONCE, IF YOU CAN BELIEVE IT.
THIS IS A TIME TO EXPERIMENT! THAT'S HEALTHY!
I USED TO HAVE GREEN HAIR! ONCE I EVEN PIERCED MY
OKAY, FRANK.
WHAT YOUR FATHER IS TRYING TO SAY IS THAT WE KNOW YOU'RE CHANGING, AND WE WANT TO BE SUPPORTIVE.
BUT THERE ARE LIMITS.
IF WE DIDN'T DRAW THE LINE SOMEWHERE, WE WOULDN'T BE GOOD PARENTS.
DATE WHOEVER YOU WANT. WEAR WHATEVER YOU WANT. BUT THERE'S ONE THING THAT WILL NEVER BE WELCOME IN THIS HOUSE.
MAGIC.
YOU KNOW HOW DANGEROUS THIS STUFF IS. YOU KNOW WHAT IT'S COST OUR FAMILY. AFTER WHAT HAPPENED TO GRANDPA BURGESS, WE SWORE WE'D GIVE IT UP.
YOU WEAR THAT AMULET LIKE IT'S SOME KIND OF FASHION ACCESSORY. IT'S SUPPOSED TO BE LOCKED UP IN A BANK VAULT. IT CAME FROM HELL, FOR GOD'S SAKE.
YOU'VE GOT TO STOP. BEFORE YOU GET IN WAY OVER YOUR HEAD.
NO.

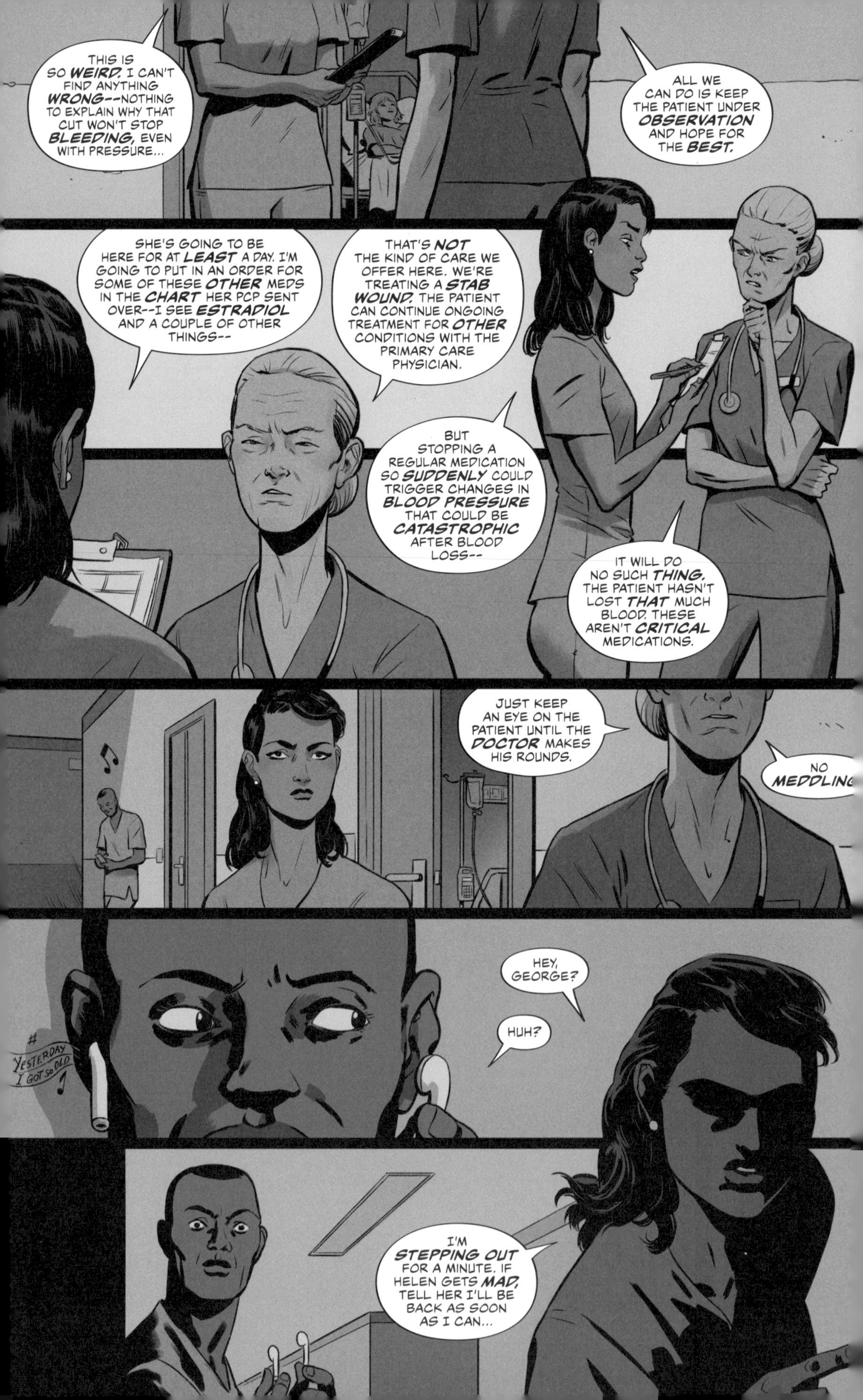
THIS IS SO WEIRD. I CAN'T FIND ANYTHING WRONG--NOTHING TO EXPLAIN WHY THAT CUT WON'T STOP BLEEDING, EVEN WITH PRESSURE...
ALL WE CAN DO IS KEEP THE PATIENT UNDER OBSERVATION AND HOPE FOR THE BEST.
SHE'S GOING TO BE HERE FOR AT LEAST A DAY. I'M GOING TO PUT IN AN ORDER FOR SOME OF THESE OTHER MEDS IN THE CHART HER PCP SENT OVER--I SEE ESTRADIOL AND A COUPLE OF OTHER THINGS--
THAT'S NOT THE KIND OF CARE WE OFFER HERE. WE'RE TREATING A STAB WOUND. THE PATIENT CAN CONTINUE ONGOING TREATMENT FOR OTHER CONDITIONS WITH THE PRIMARY CARE PHYSICIAN.
BUT STOPPING A REGULAR MEDICATION SO SUDDENLY COULD TRIGGER CHANGES IN BLOOD PRESSURE THAT COULD BE CATASTROPHIC AFTER BLOOD LOSS--
IT WILL DO NO SUCH THING. THE PATIENT HASN'T LOST THAT MUCH BLOOD. THESE AREN'T CRITICAL MEDICATIONS.
JUST KEEP AN EYE ON THE PATIENT UNTIL THE DOCTOR MAKES HIS ROUNDS.
NO MEDDLING
YESTERDAY I GOT SO OLD
HEY, GEORGE?
HUH?
I'M STEPPING OUT FOR A MINUTE. IF HELEN GETS MAD, TELL HER I'LL BE BACK AS SOON AS I CAN...

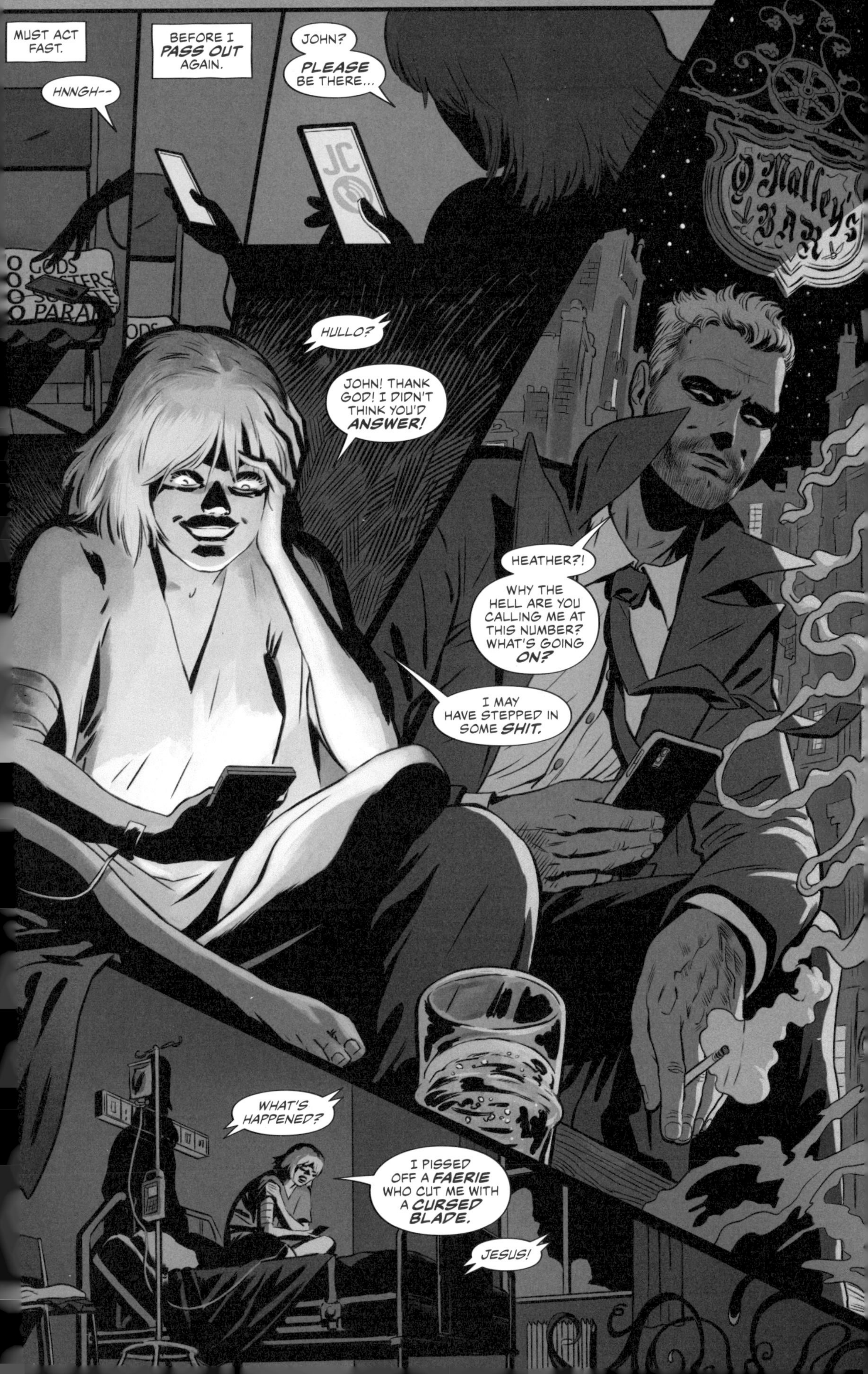

MUST ACT FAST.
HNNGH--
BEFORE I PASS OUT AGAIN.
JOHN? PLEASE BE THERE...
O'Malley's BAR
HULLO?
JOHN! THANK GOD! I DIDN'T THINK YOU'D ANSWER!
HEATHER?!
WHY THE HELL ARE YOU CALLING ME AT THIS NUMBER? WHAT'S GOING ON?
I MAY HAVE STEPPED IN SOME SHIT.
WHAT'S HAPPENED?
I PISSED OFF A FAERIE WHO CUT ME WITH A CURSED BLADE.
JESUS!

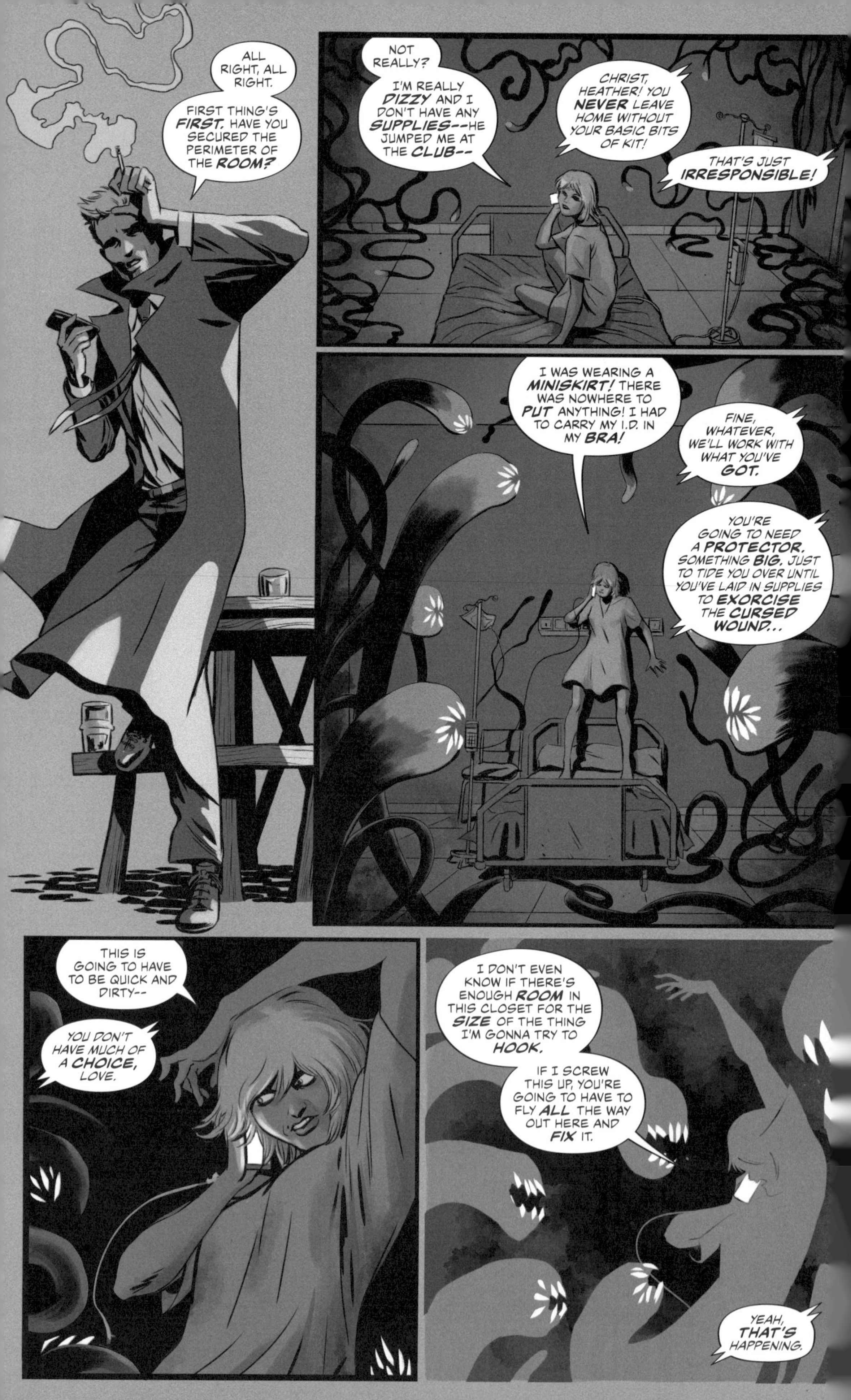
ALL RIGHT, ALL RIGHT.
FIRST THING'S FIRST. HAVE YOU SECURED THE PERIMETER OF THE ROOM?
NOT REALLY?
I'M REALLY DIZZY AND I DON'T HAVE ANY SUPPLIES--HE JUMPED ME AT THE CLUB--
CHRIST, HEATHER! YOU NEVER LEAVE HOME WITHOUT YOUR BASIC BITS OF KIT!
THAT'S JUST IRRESPONSIBLE!
I WAS WEARING A MINISKIRT! THERE WAS NOWHERE TO PUT ANYTHING! I HAD TO CARRY MY I.D. IN MY BRA!
FINE, WHATEVER, WE'LL WORK WITH WHAT YOU'VE GOT.
YOU'RE GOING TO NEED A PROTECTOR. SOMETHING BIG. JUST TO TIDE YOU OVER UNTIL YOU'VE LAID IN SUPPLIES TO EXORCISE THE CURSED WOUND...
THIS IS GOING TO HAVE TO BE QUICK AND DIRTY--
YOU DON'T HAVE MUCH OF A CHOICE, LOVE.
I DON'T EVEN KNOW IF THERE'S ENOUGH ROOM IN THIS CLOSET FOR THE SIZE OF THE THING I'M GONNA TRY TO HOOK.
IF I SCREW THIS UP, YOU'RE GOING TO HAVE TO FLY ALL THE WAY OUT HERE AND FIX IT.
YEAH, THAT'S HAPPENING.

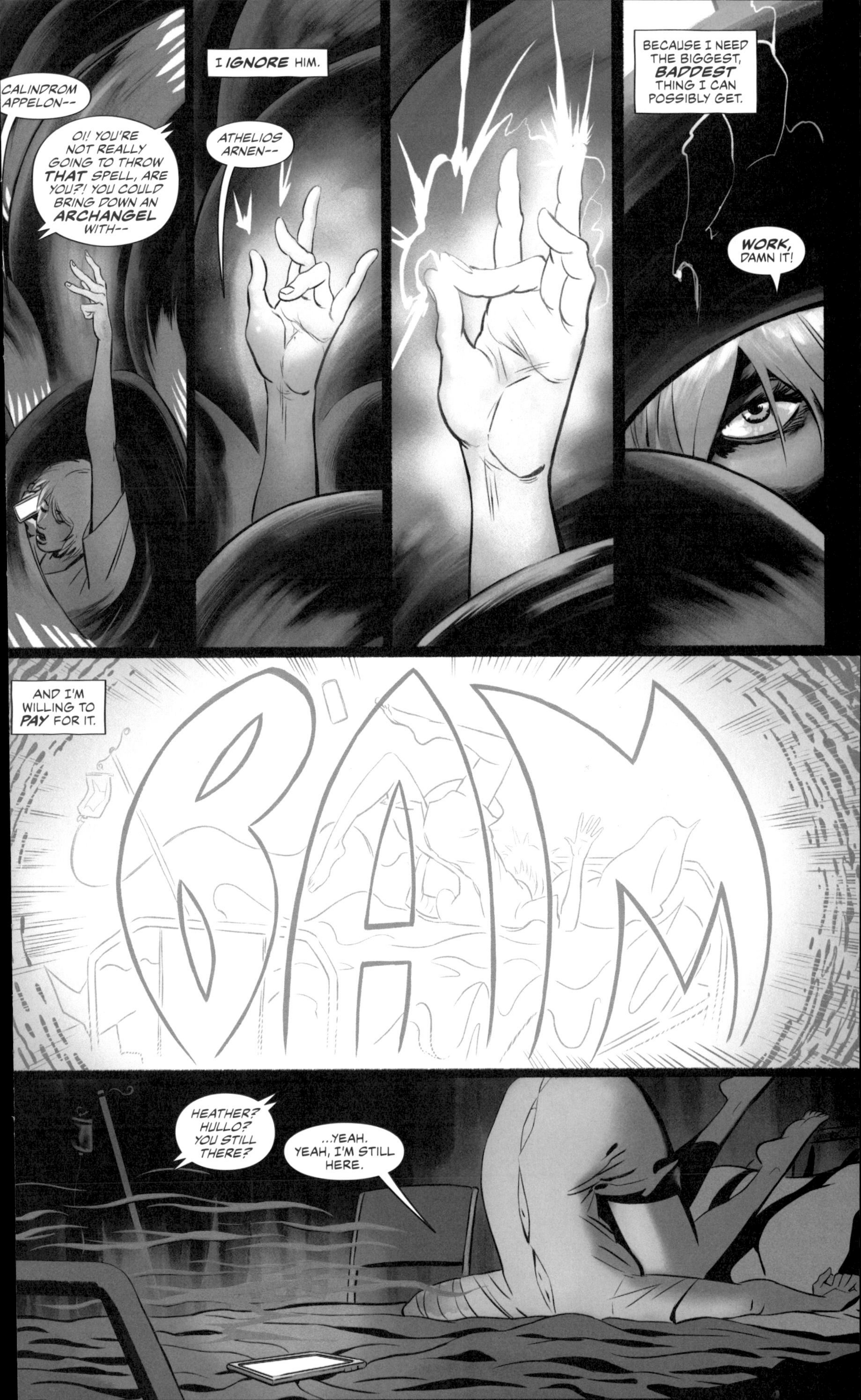

CALINDROM APPELON--
OI! YOU'RE NOT REALLY GOING TO THROW THAT SPELL, ARE YOU?! YOU COULD BRING DOWN AN ARCHANGEL WITH--
I IGNORE HIM.
ATHELIOS ARNEN--
BECAUSE I NEED THE BIGGEST, BADDEST THING I CAN POSSIBLY GET.
WORK, DAMN IT!
AND I'M WILLING TO PAY FOR IT.
B'AM
HEATHER? HULLO? YOU STILL THERE?
...YEAH. YEAH, I'M STILL HERE.

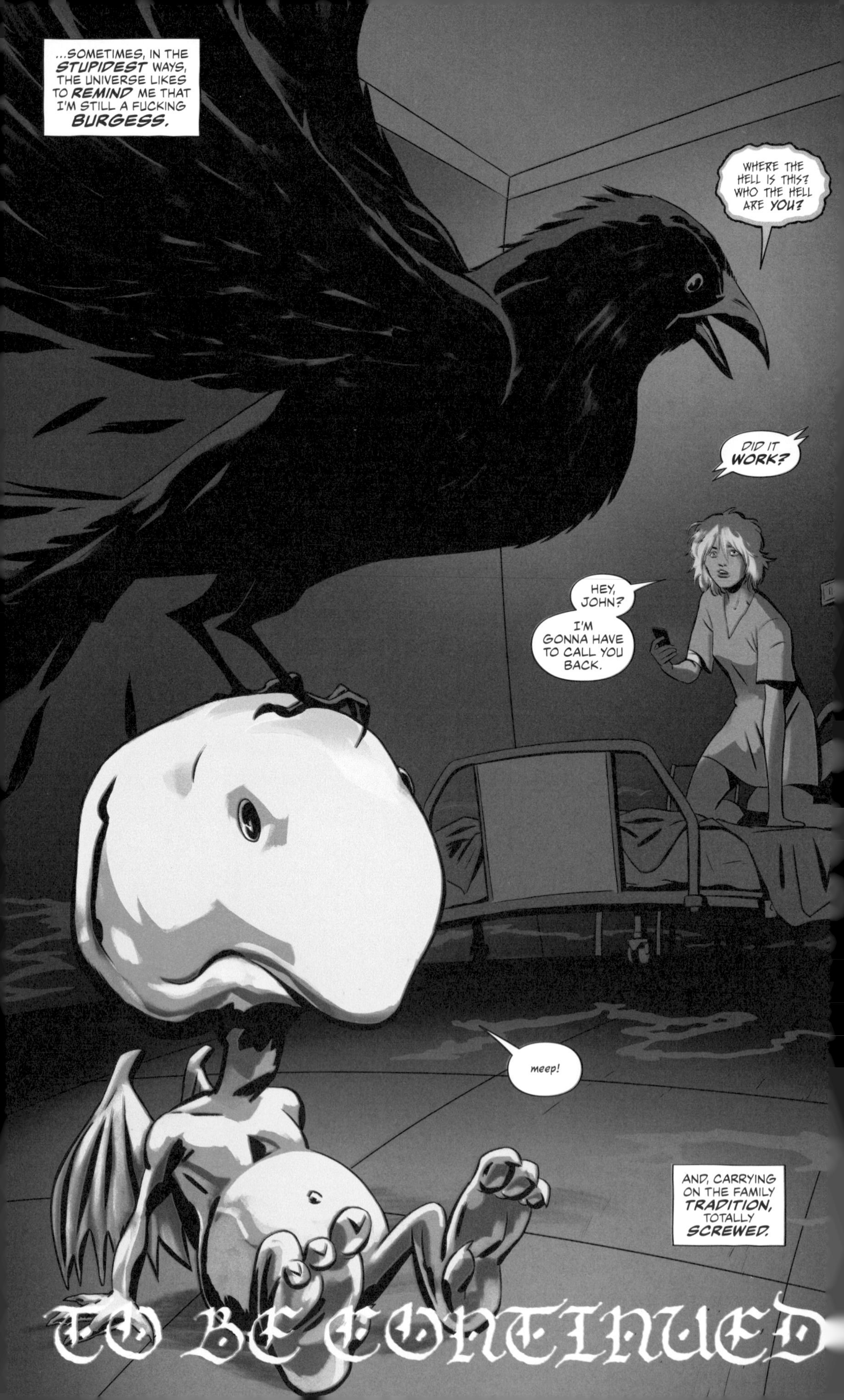
...SOMETIMES, IN THE STUPIDEST WAYS, THE UNIVERSE LIKES TO REMIND ME THAT I'M STILL A FUCKING BURGESS.
WHERE THE HELL IS THIS? WHO THE HELL ARE YOU?
DID IT WORK?
HEY, JOHN?
I'M GONNA HAVE TO CALL YOU BACK.
meep!
AND, CARRYING ON THE FAMILY TRADITION, TOTALLY SCREWED.
TO BE CONTINUED

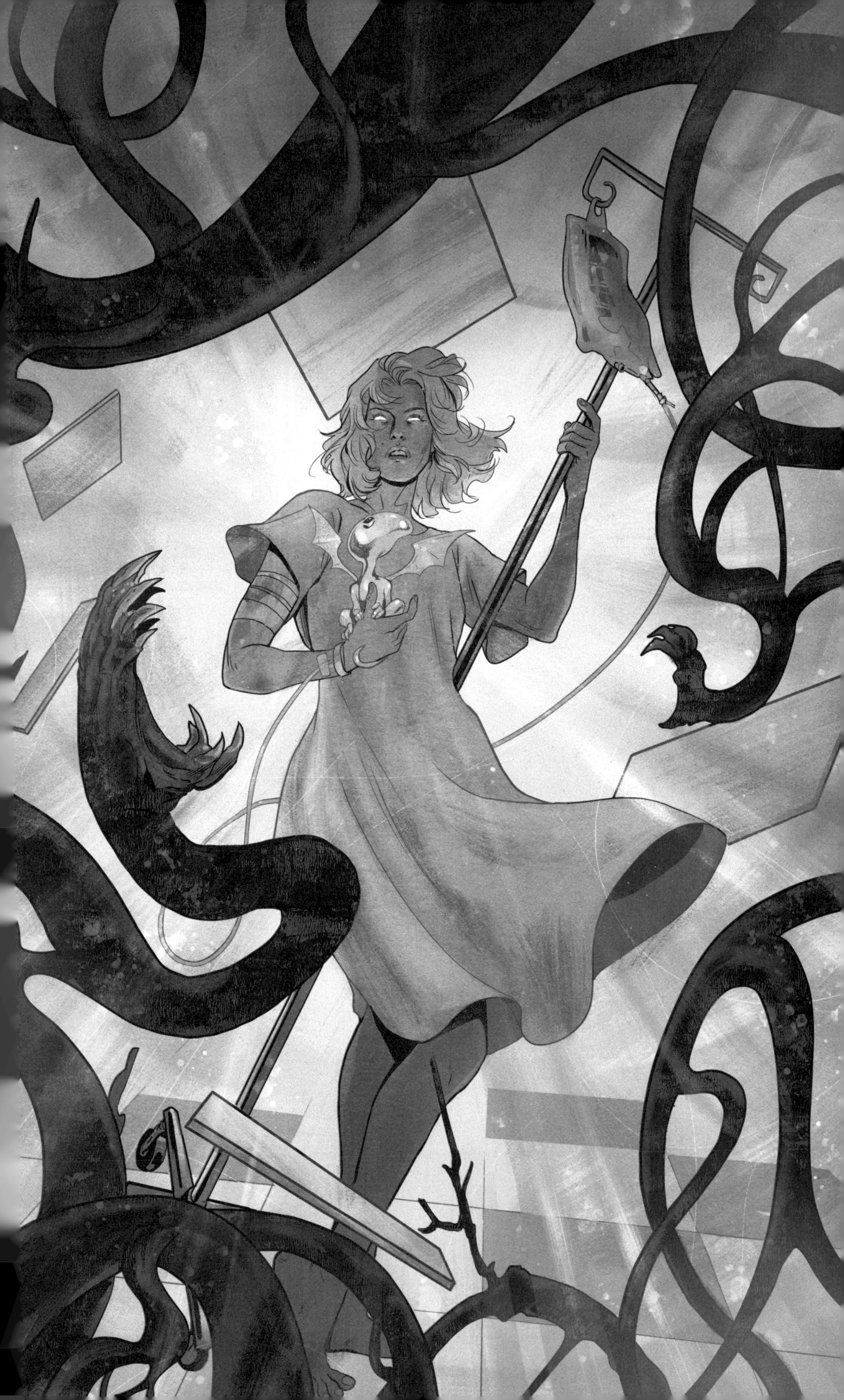

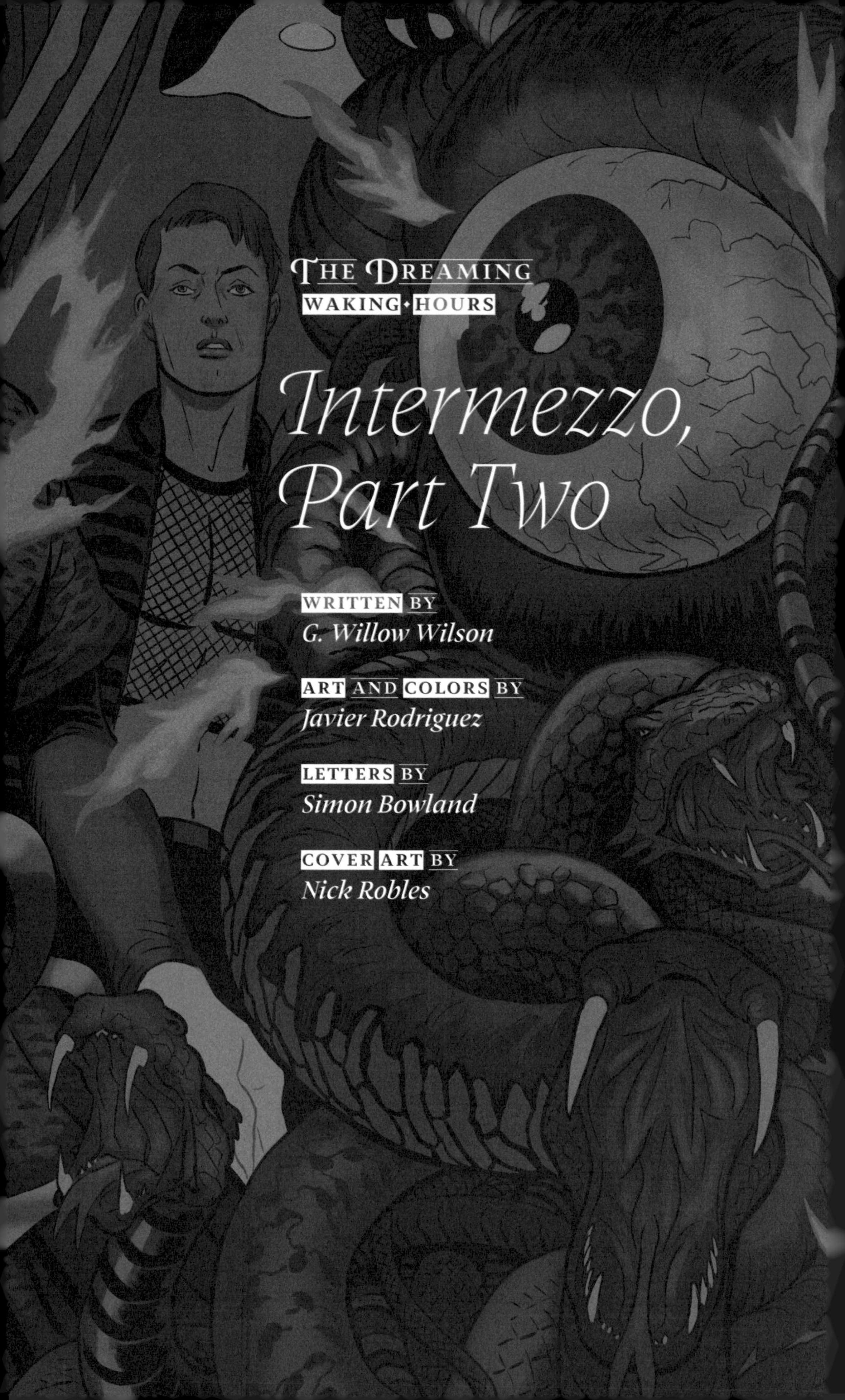

THE DREAMING
WAKING HOURS

Intermezzo, Part Two

WRITTEN BY
G. Willow Wilson

ART AND COLORS BY
Javier Rodriguez

LETTERS BY
Simon Bowland

COVER ART BY
Nick Robles

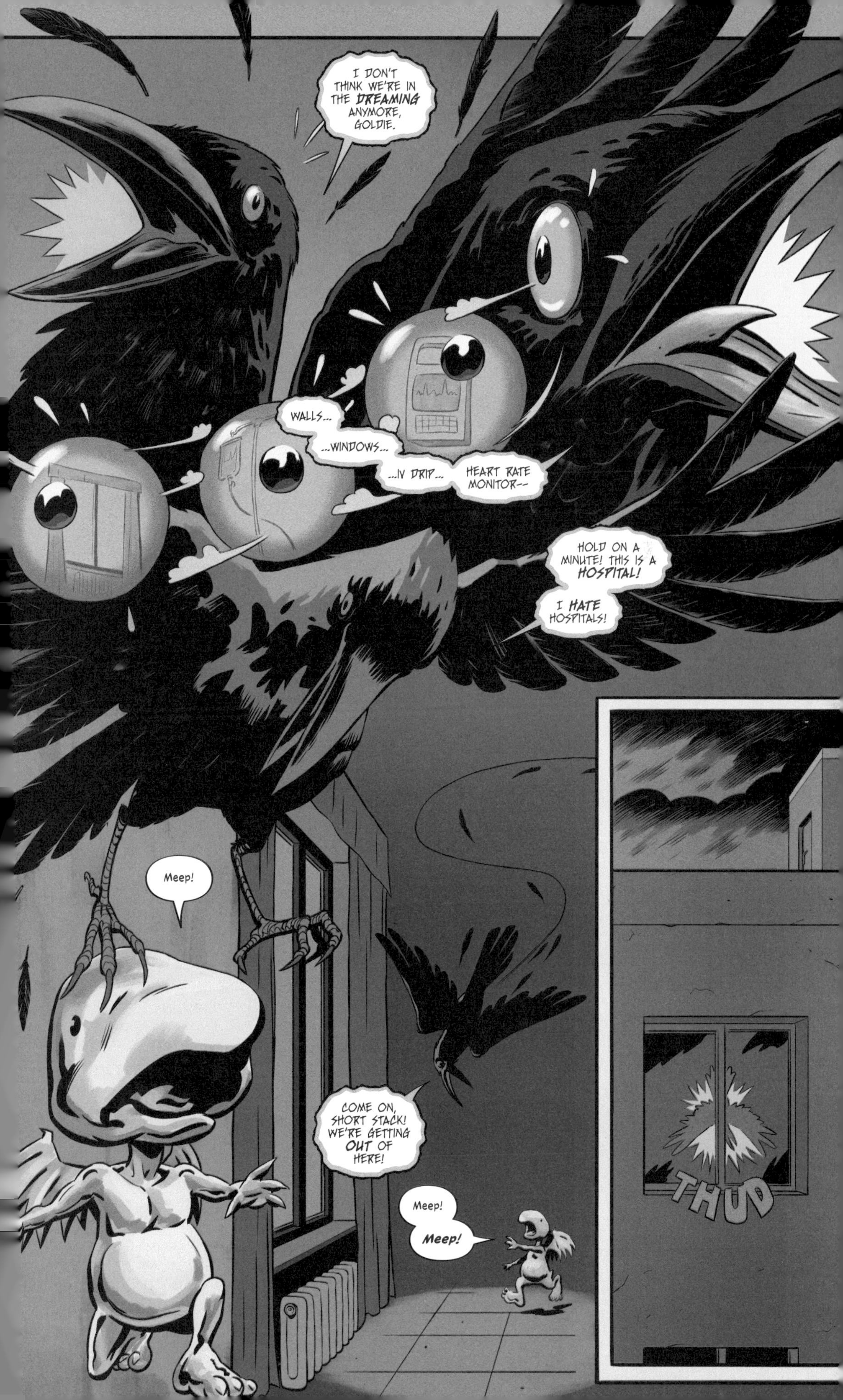
I DON'T THINK WE'RE IN THE DREAMING ANYMORE, GOLDIE.
WALLS...
...WINDOWS...
...IV DRIP...
HEART RATE MONITOR--
HOLD ON A MINUTE! THIS IS A HOSPITAL!
I HATE HOSPITALS!
Meep!
COME ON, SHORT STACK! WE'RE GETTING OUT OF HERE!
Meep!
Meep!
THUD

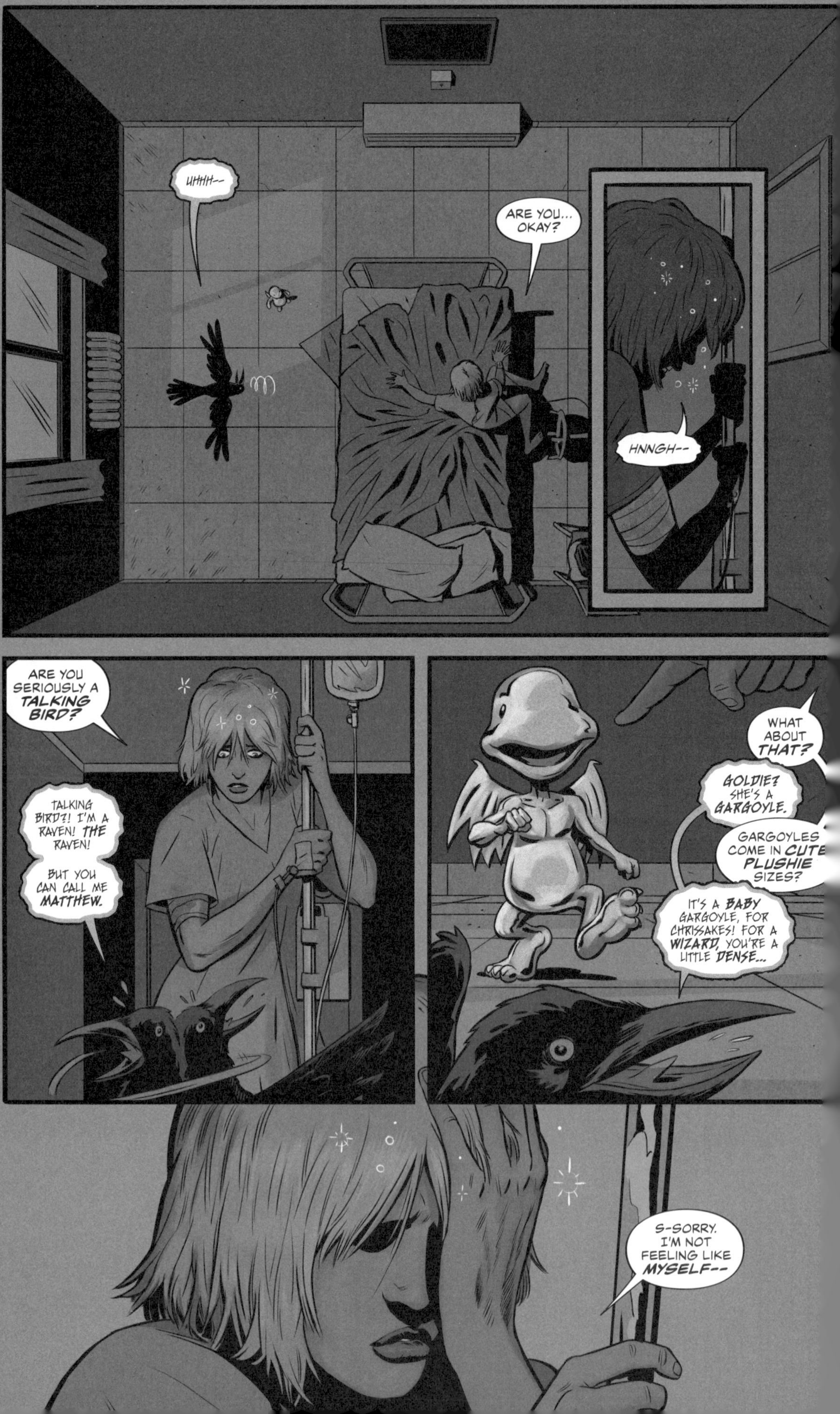
UHHH--
ARE YOU... OKAY?
HNNGH--
ARE YOU SERIOUSLY A TALKING BIRD?
TALKING BIRD?! I'M A RAVEN! THE RAVEN!
BUT YOU CAN CALL ME MATTHEW.
WHAT ABOUT THAT?
GOLDIE? SHE'S A GARGOYLE.
GARGOYLES COME IN CUTE PLUSHIE SIZES?
IT'S A BABY GARGOYLE, FOR CHRISSAKES! FOR A WIZARD, YOU'RE A LITTLE DENSE...
S-SORRY. I'M NOT FEELING LIKE MYSELF--

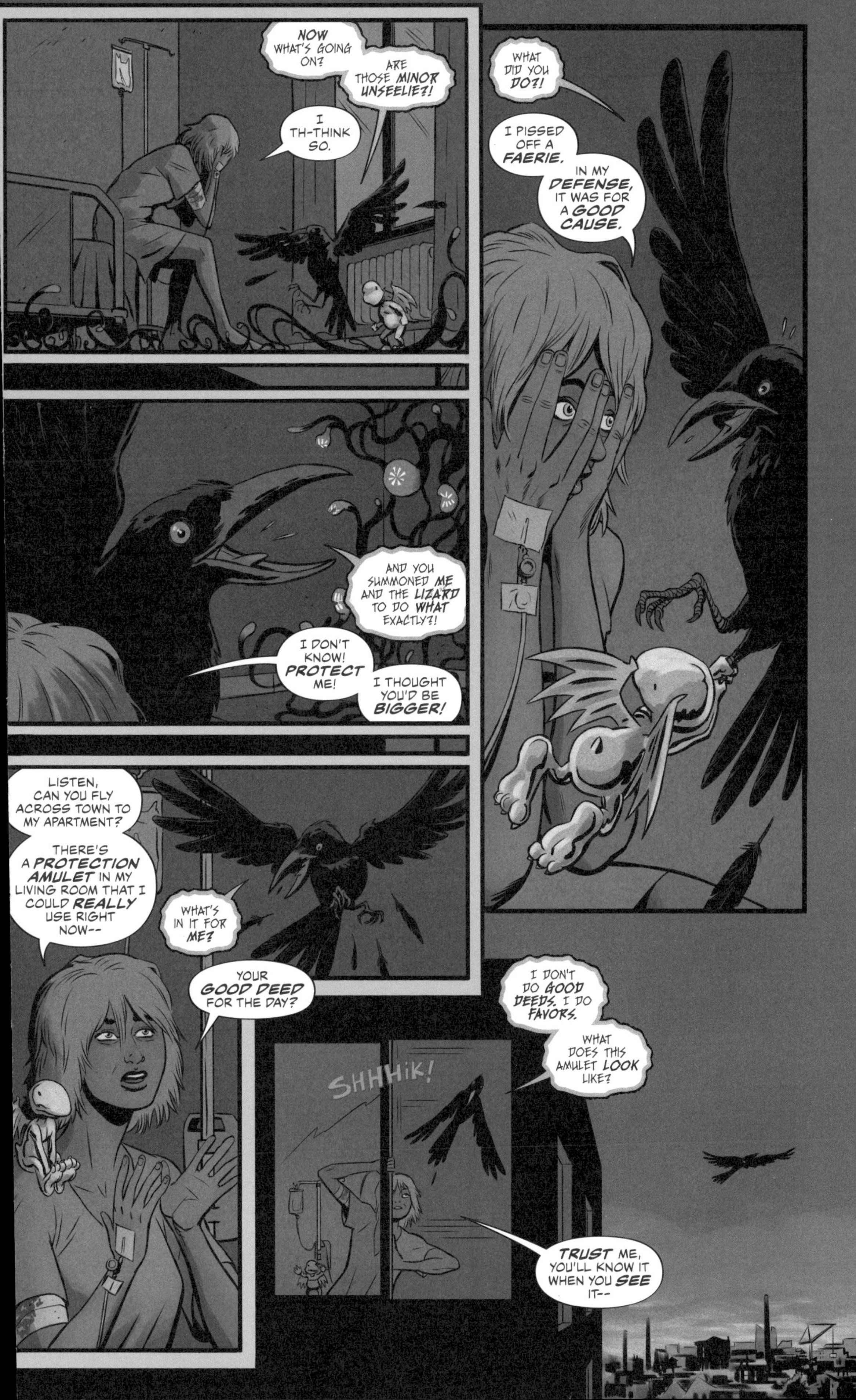
NOW WHAT'S GOING ON?
ARE THOSE MINOR UNSEELIE?!
I TH-THINK SO.
WHAT DID YOU DO?!
I PISSED OFF A FAERIE.
IN MY DEFENSE, IT WAS FOR A GOOD CAUSE.
AND YOU SUMMONED ME AND THE LIZARD TO DO WHAT EXACTLY?!
I DON'T KNOW! PROTECT ME!
I THOUGHT YOU'D BE BIGGER!
LISTEN, CAN YOU FLY ACROSS TOWN TO MY APARTMENT?
THERE'S A PROTECTION AMULET IN MY LIVING ROOM THAT I COULD REALLY USE RIGHT NOW--
WHAT'S IN IT FOR ME?
YOUR GOOD DEED FOR THE DAY?
I DON'T DO GOOD DEEDS. I DO FAVORS.
WHAT DOES THIS AMULET LOOK LIKE?
SHHHiK!
TRUST ME, YOU'LL KNOW IT WHEN YOU SEE IT--

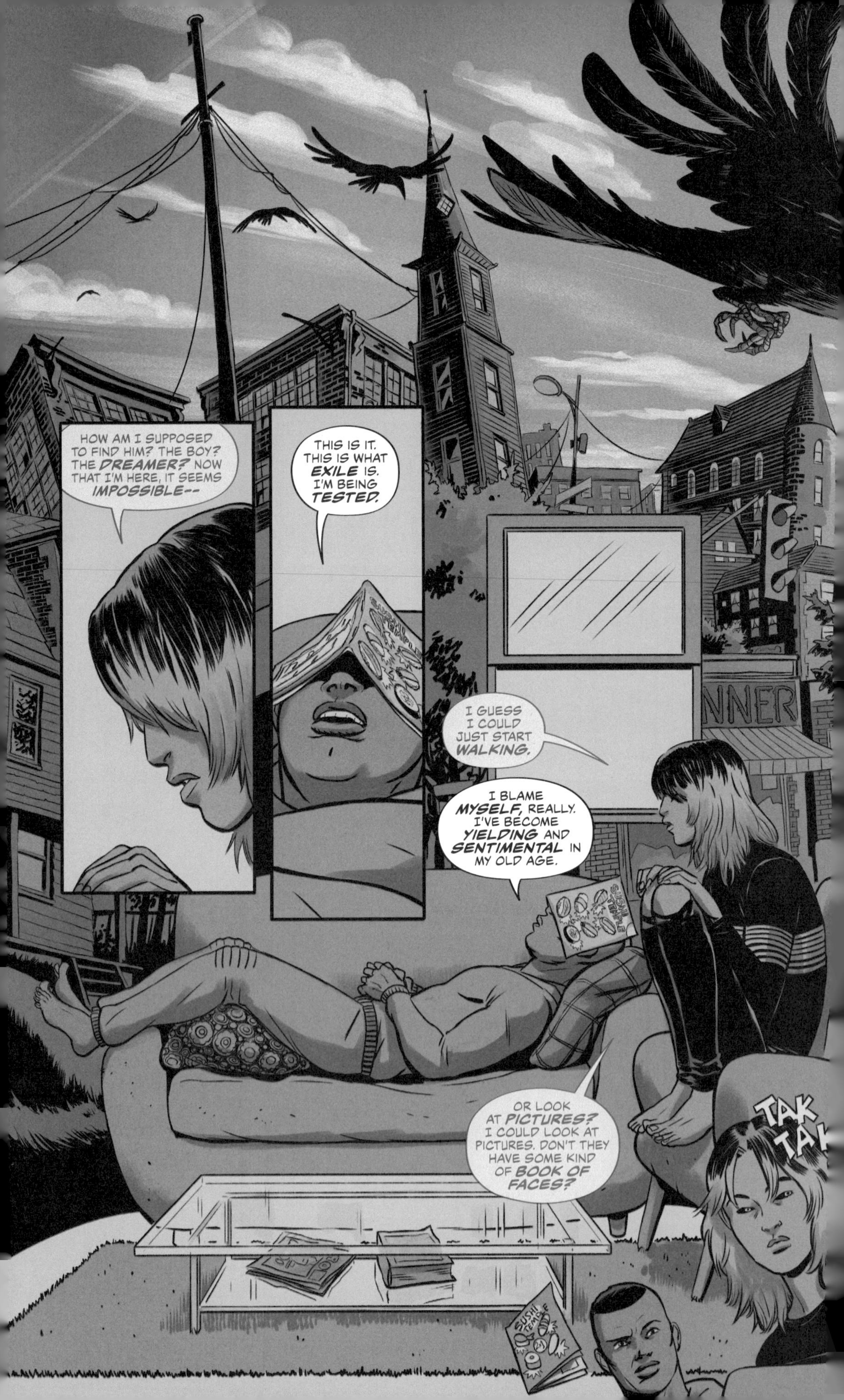
HOW AM I SUPPOSED TO FIND HIM? THE BOY? THE DREAMER? NOW THAT I'M HERE, IT SEEMS IMPOSSIBLE--
THIS IS IT. THIS IS WHAT EXILE IS. I'M BEING TESTED.
SUSHI TEMPLE
I GUESS I COULD JUST START WALKING.
I BLAME MYSELF, REALLY. I'VE BECOME YIELDING AND SENTIMENTAL IN MY OLD AGE.
NNER
SUSHI TEMPLE
OR LOOK AT PICTURES? I COULD LOOK AT PICTURES. DON'T THEY HAVE SOME KIND OF BOOK OF FACES?
TAK TAK
SUSHI TEMPLE

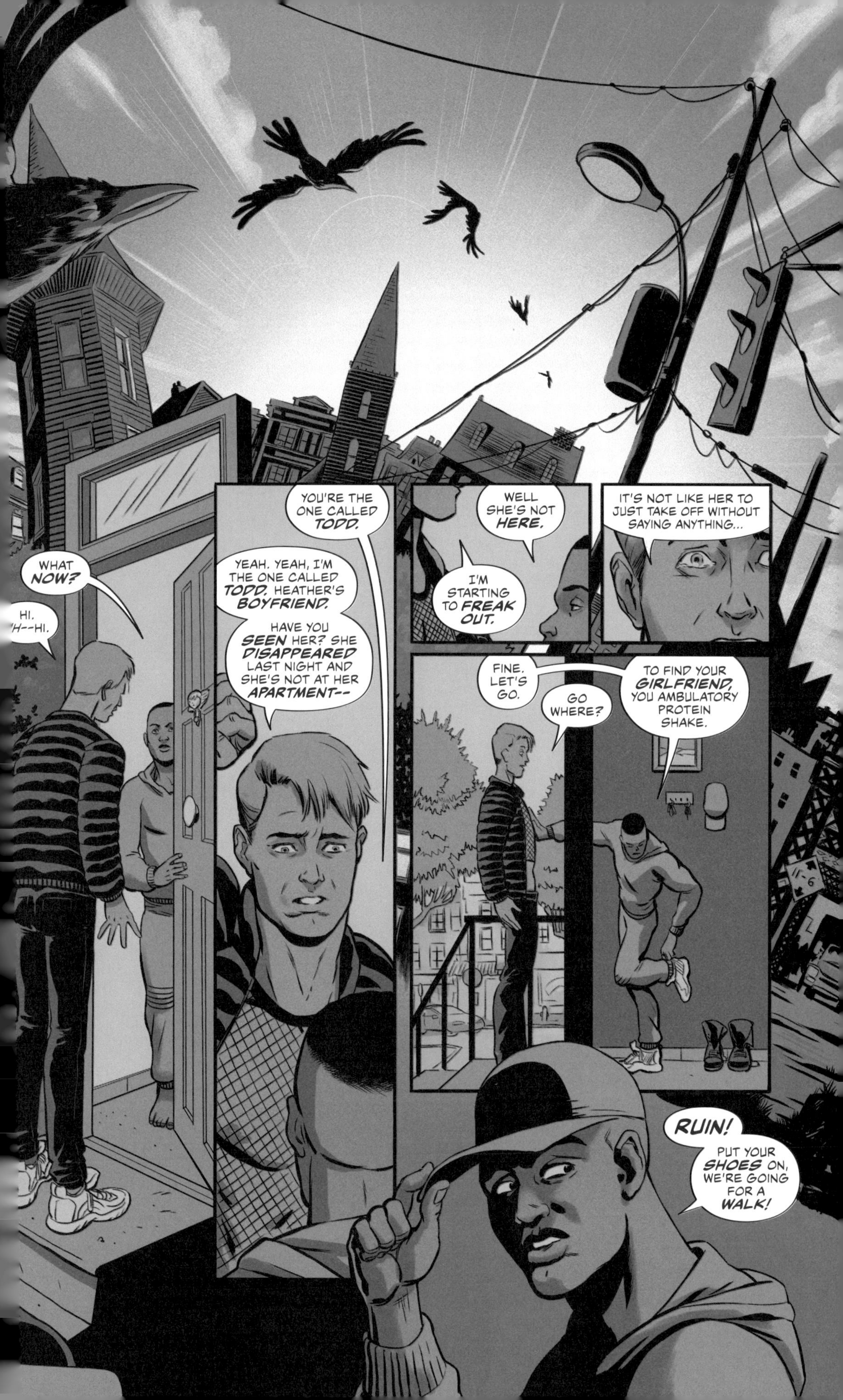
WHAT NOW?
HI. H--HI.
YOU'RE THE ONE CALLED TODD.
YEAH. YEAH, I'M THE ONE CALLED TODD. HEATHER'S BOYFRIEND.
HAVE YOU SEEN HER? SHE DISAPPEARED LAST NIGHT AND SHE'S NOT AT HER APARTMENT--
WELL SHE'S NOT HERE.
I'M STARTING TO FREAK OUT.
IT'S NOT LIKE HER TO JUST TAKE OFF WITHOUT SAYING ANYTHING...
FINE. LET'S GO.
GO WHERE?
TO FIND YOUR GIRLFRIEND, YOU AMBULATORY PROTEIN SHAKE.
RUIN!
PUT YOUR SHOES ON, WE'RE GOING FOR A WALK!

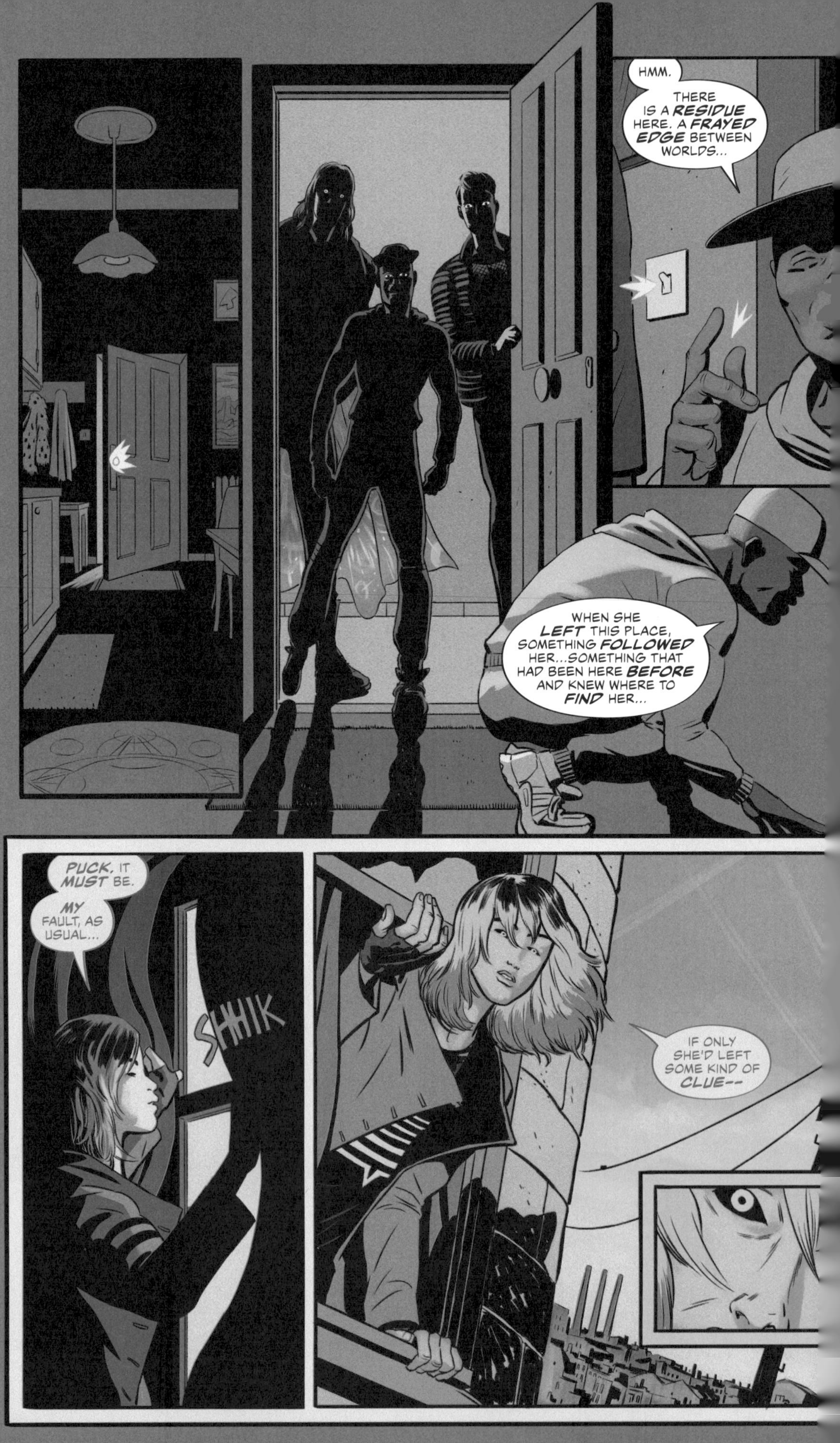
HMM.
THERE IS A RESIDUE HERE. A FRAYED EDGE BETWEEN WORLDS...
WHEN SHE LEFT THIS PLACE, SOMETHING FOLLOWED HER...SOMETHING THAT HAD BEEN HERE BEFORE AND KNEW WHERE TO FIND HER...
PUCK, IT MUST BE.
MY FAULT, AS USUAL...
SHHIK
IF ONLY SHE'D LEFT SOME KIND OF CLUE--

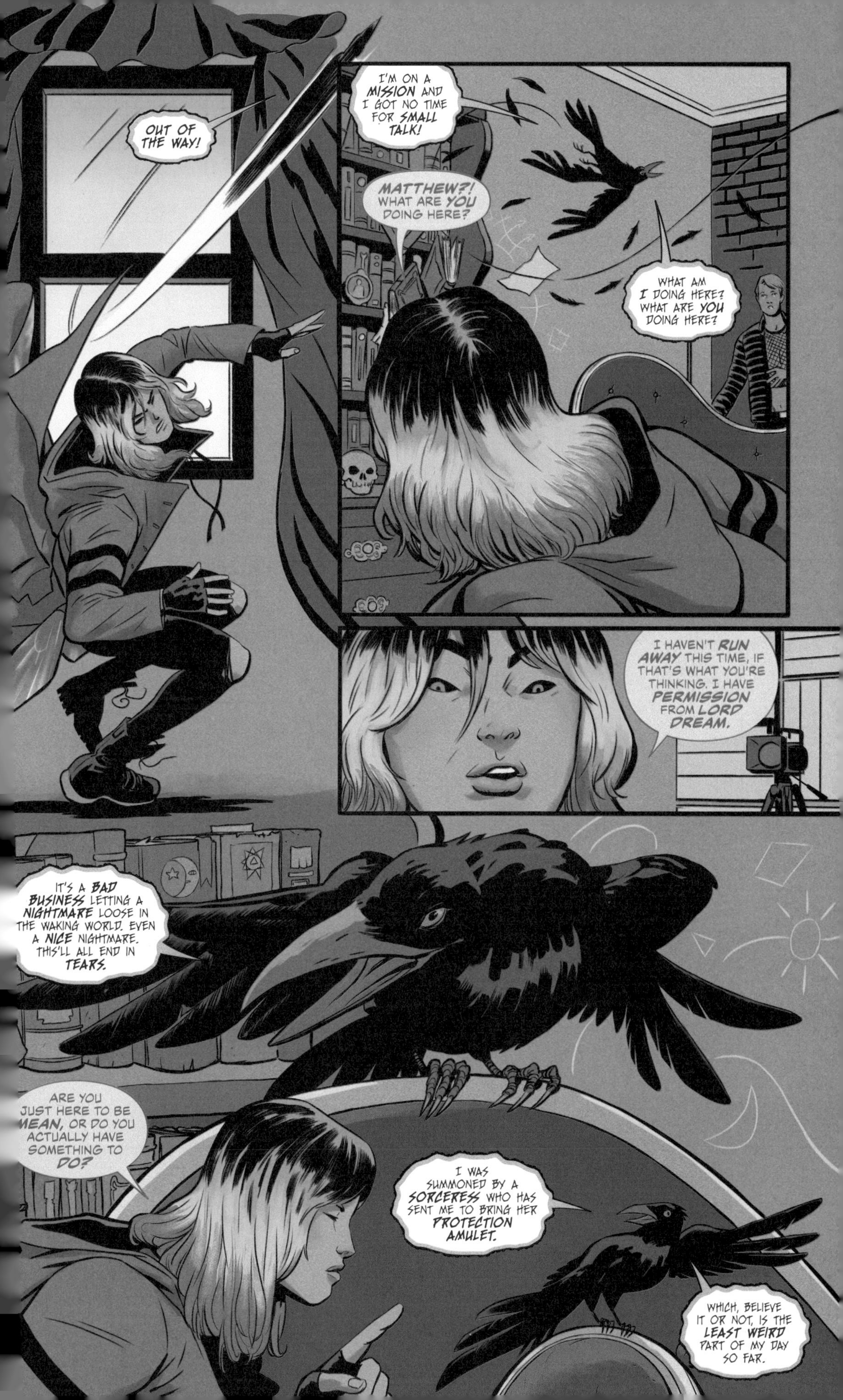
OUT OF THE WAY!
I'M ON A MISSION AND I GOT NO TIME FOR SMALL TALK!
MATTHEW?! WHAT ARE YOU DOING HERE?
WHAT AM I DOING HERE? WHAT ARE YOU DOING HERE?
I HAVEN'T RUN AWAY THIS TIME, IF THAT'S WHAT YOU'RE THINKING. I HAVE PERMISSION FROM LORD DREAM.
IT'S A BAD BUSINESS LETTING A NIGHTMARE LOOSE IN THE WAKING WORLD. EVEN A NICE NIGHTMARE. THIS'LL ALL END IN TEARS.
ARE YOU JUST HERE TO BE MEAN, OR DO YOU ACTUALLY HAVE SOMETHING TO DO?
I WAS SUMMONED BY A SORCERESS WHO HAS SENT ME TO BRING HER PROTECTION AMULET.
WHICH, BELIEVE IT OR NOT, IS THE LEAST WEIRD PART OF MY DAY SO FAR.

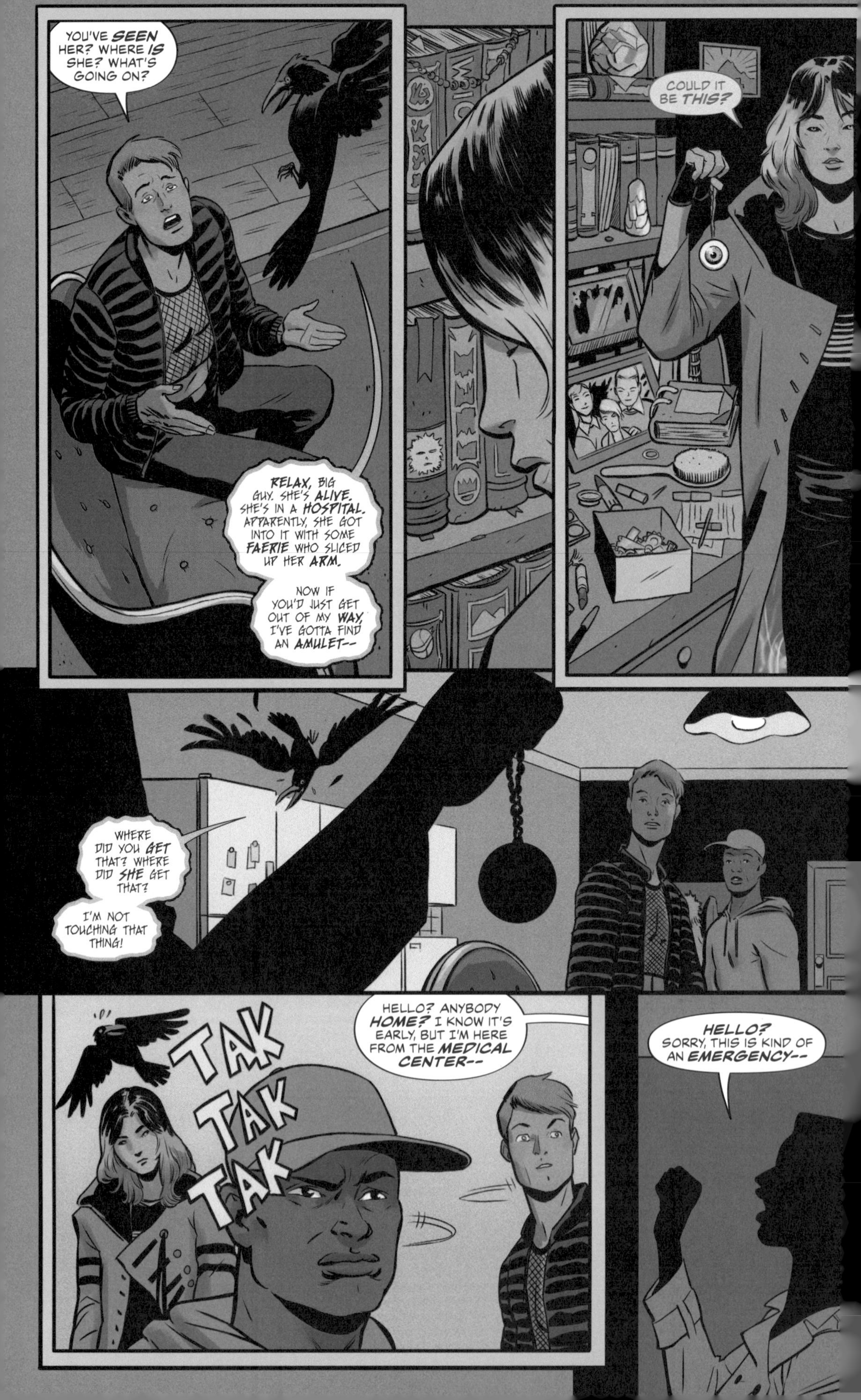
YOU'VE SEEN HER? WHERE IS SHE? WHAT'S GOING ON?
RELAX, BIG GUY. SHE'S ALIVE. SHE'S IN A HOSPITAL. APPARENTLY, SHE GOT INTO IT WITH SOME FAERIE WHO SLICED UP HER ARM.
NOW IF YOU'D JUST GET OUT OF MY WAY, I'VE GOTTA FIND AN AMULET--
COULD IT BE THIS?
WHERE DID YOU GET THAT? WHERE DID SHE GET THAT?
I'M NOT TOUCHING THAT THING!
TAK TAK TAK
HELLO? ANYBODY HOME? I KNOW IT'S EARLY, BUT I'M HERE FROM THE MEDICAL CENTER--
HELLO? SORRY, THIS IS KIND OF AN EMERGENCY--

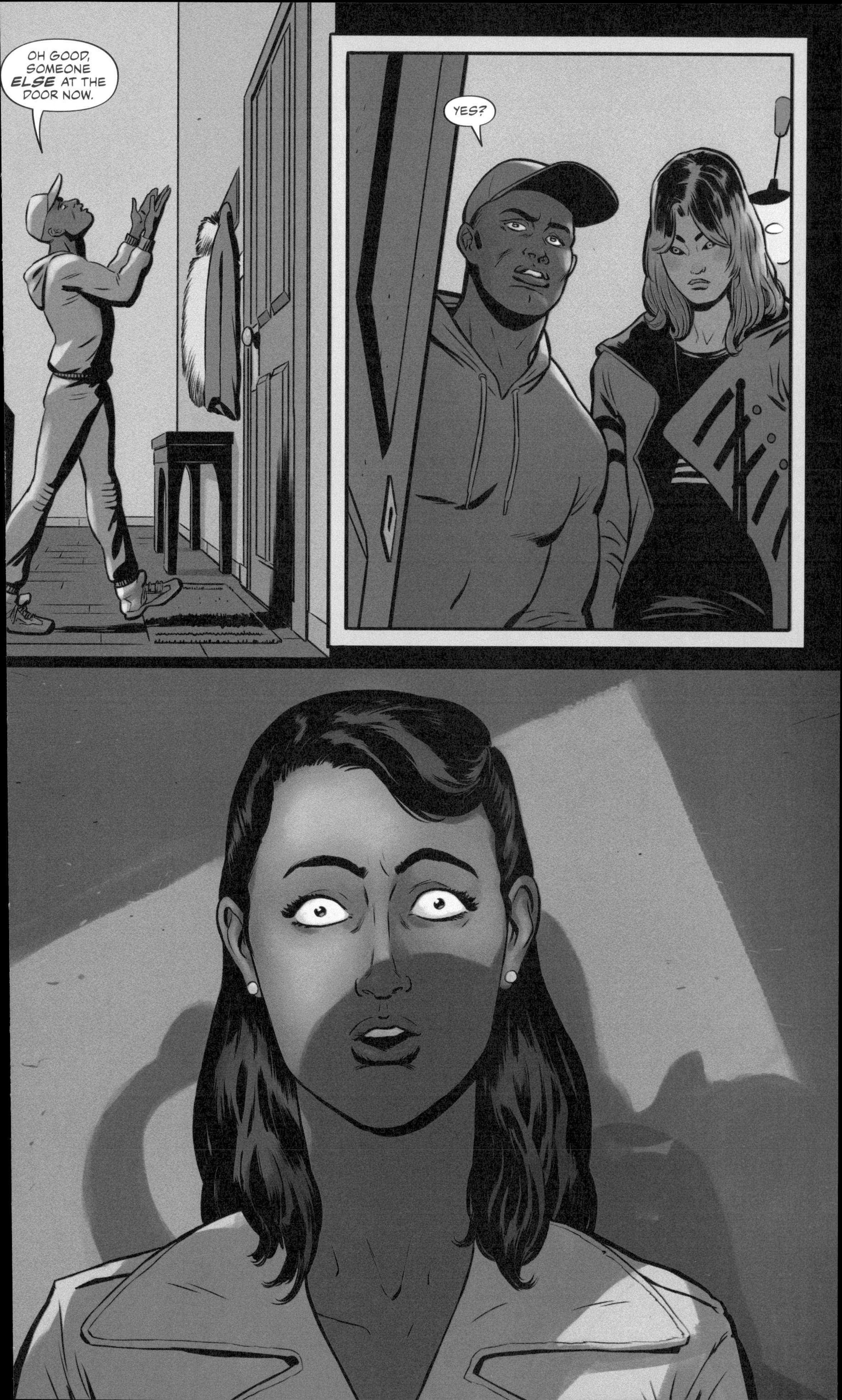
OH GOOD, SOMEONE ELSE AT THE DOOR NOW.
YES?

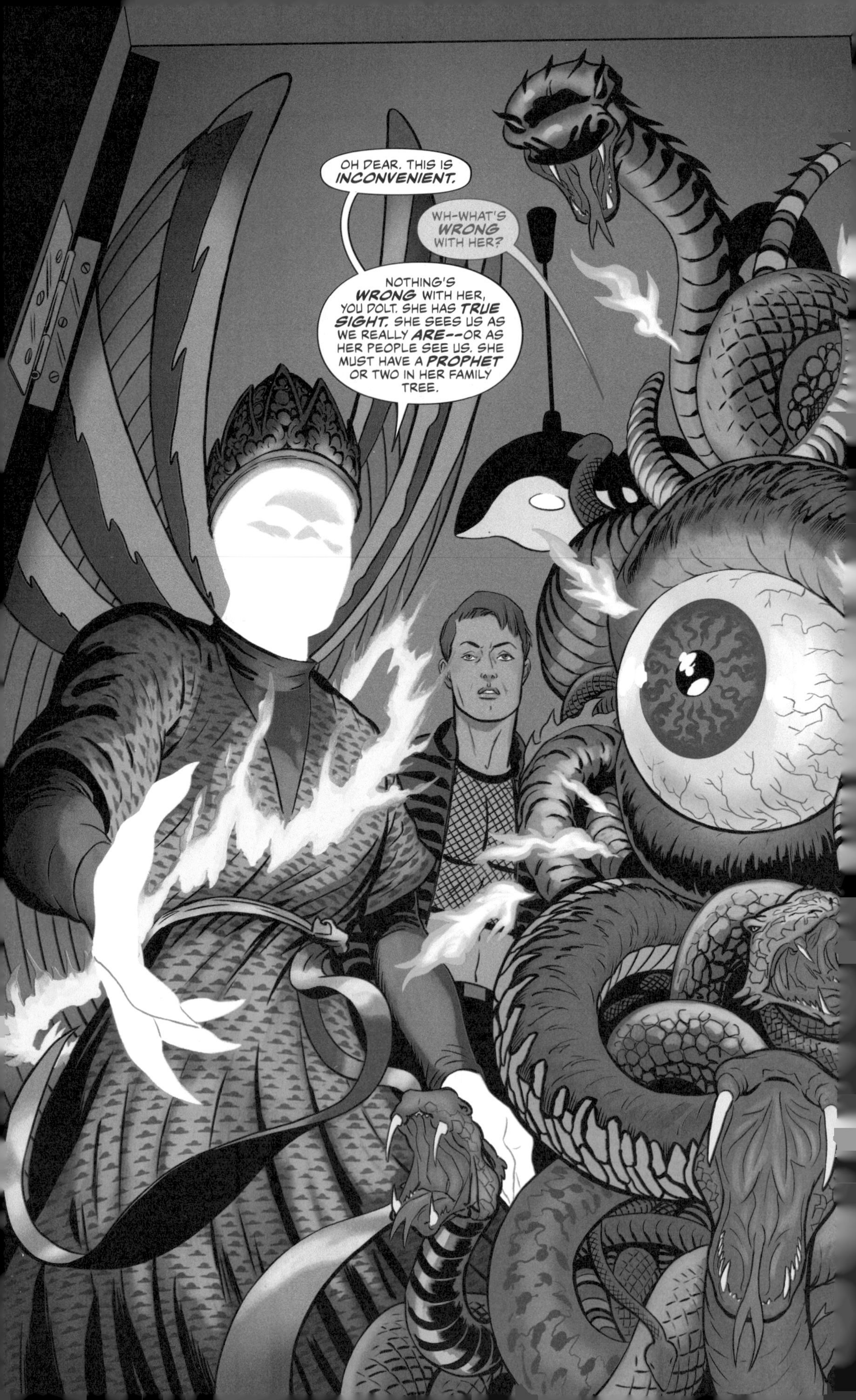
OH DEAR. THIS IS INCONVENIENT.
WH-WHAT'S WRONG WITH HER?
NOTHING'S WRONG WITH HER, YOU DOLT. SHE HAS TRUE SIGHT. SHE SEES US AS WE REALLY ARE--OR AS HER PEOPLE SEE US. SHE MUST HAVE A PROPHET OR TWO IN HER FAMILY TREE.

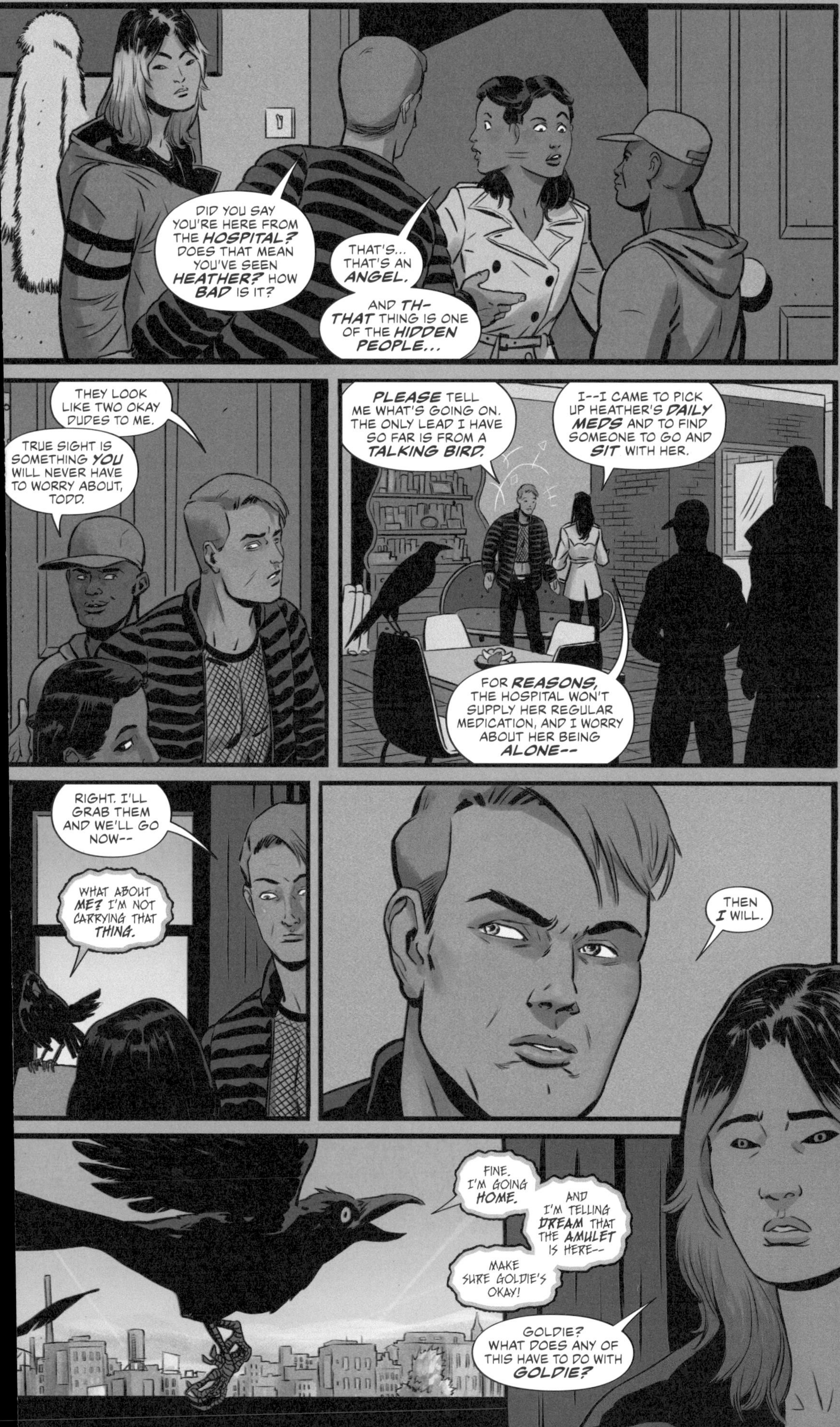
DID YOU SAY YOU'RE HERE FROM THE HOSPITAL? DOES THAT MEAN YOU'VE SEEN HEATHER? HOW BAD IS IT?
THAT'S... THAT'S AN ANGEL.
AND TH-THAT THING IS ONE OF THE HIDDEN PEOPLE...
THEY LOOK LIKE TWO OKAY DUDES TO ME.
TRUE SIGHT IS SOMETHING YOU WILL NEVER HAVE TO WORRY ABOUT, TODD.
PLEASE TELL ME WHAT'S GOING ON. THE ONLY LEAD I HAVE SO FAR IS FROM A TALKING BIRD.
I--I CAME TO PICK UP HEATHER'S DAILY MEDS AND TO FIND SOMEONE TO GO AND SIT WITH HER.
FOR REASONS, THE HOSPITAL WON'T SUPPLY HER REGULAR MEDICATION, AND I WORRY ABOUT HER BEING ALONE--
RIGHT. I'LL GRAB THEM AND WE'LL GO NOW--
WHAT ABOUT ME? I'M NOT CARRYING THAT THING.
THEN I WILL.
FINE. I'M GOING HOME.
AND I'M TELLING DREAM THAT THE AMULET IS HERE--
MAKE SURE GOLDIE'S OKAY!
GOLDIE? WHAT DOES ANY OF THIS HAVE TO DO WITH GOLDIE?

THERE'S NOTHING I HATE MORE THAN FEELING *HELPLESS.*

I HAVE TO REMIND MYSELF THAT THE MAGIC DOESN'T COME FROM MY *TOOLS,* FROM SOME *CHALK SCRIBBLES* ON THE FLOOR.

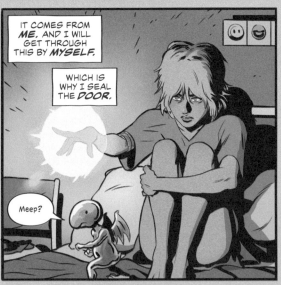

IT COMES FROM *ME,* AND I WILL GET THROUGH THIS BY *MYSELF.*

WHICH IS WHY I SEAL THE *DOOR.*

Meep?

YUP, JUST US *CHICKENS,* I'M AFRAID. THIS WAY NO *CIVILIANS* WILL WANDER IN HERE AND GET THE SHOCK OF THEIR *LIVES.*

AAH!

DAMN IT!

WE'RE RUNNING OUT OF *TIME.*

I NEED YOU TO *DO* SOMETHING FOR A SECOND.

Meep?

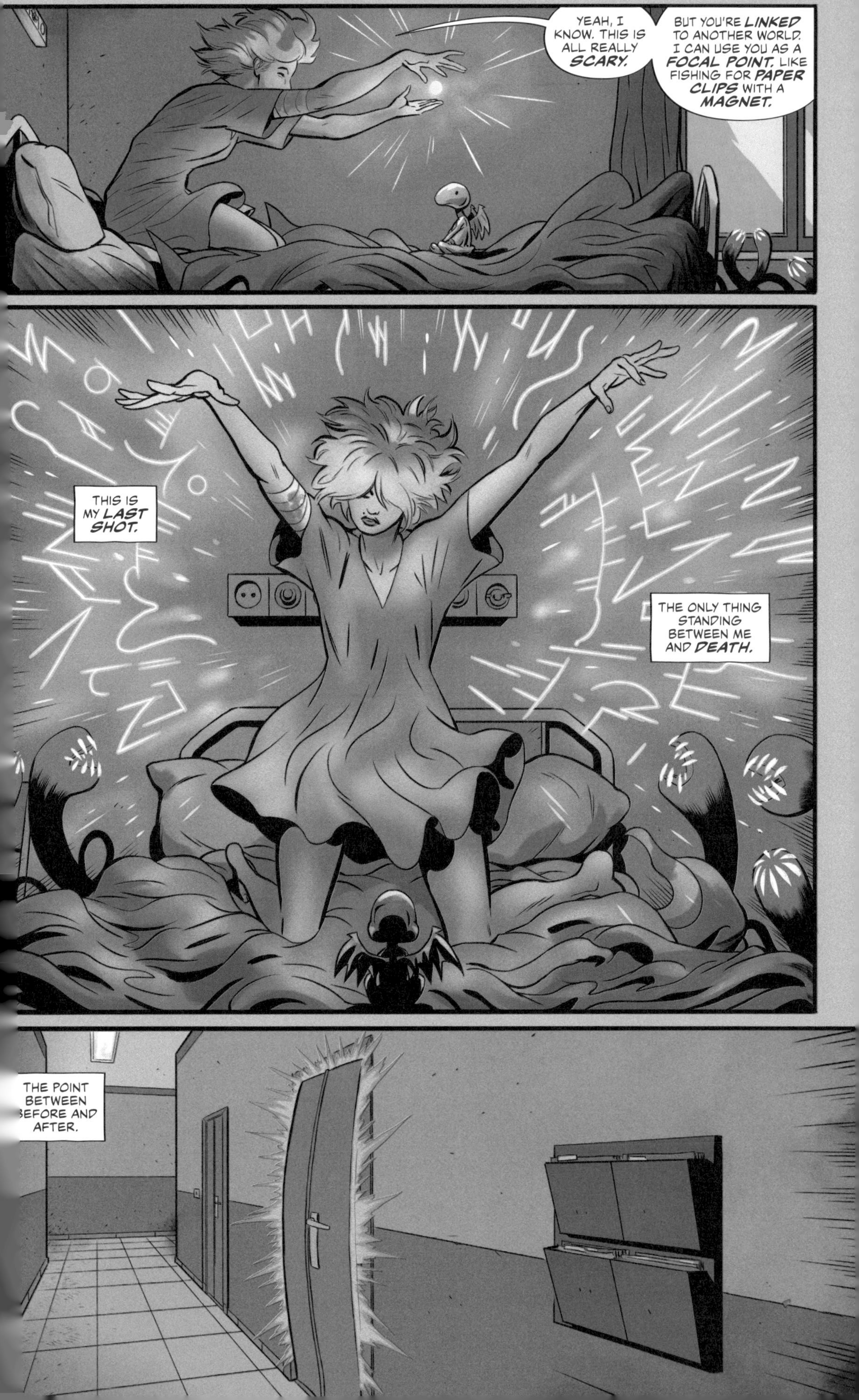
YEAH, I KNOW. THIS IS ALL REALLY SCARY.
BUT YOU'RE LINKED TO ANOTHER WORLD. I CAN USE YOU AS A FOCAL POINT, LIKE FISHING FOR PAPER CLIPS WITH A MAGNET.
THIS IS MY LAST SHOT.
THE ONLY THING STANDING BETWEEN ME AND DEATH.
THE POINT BETWEEN BEFORE AND AFTER.

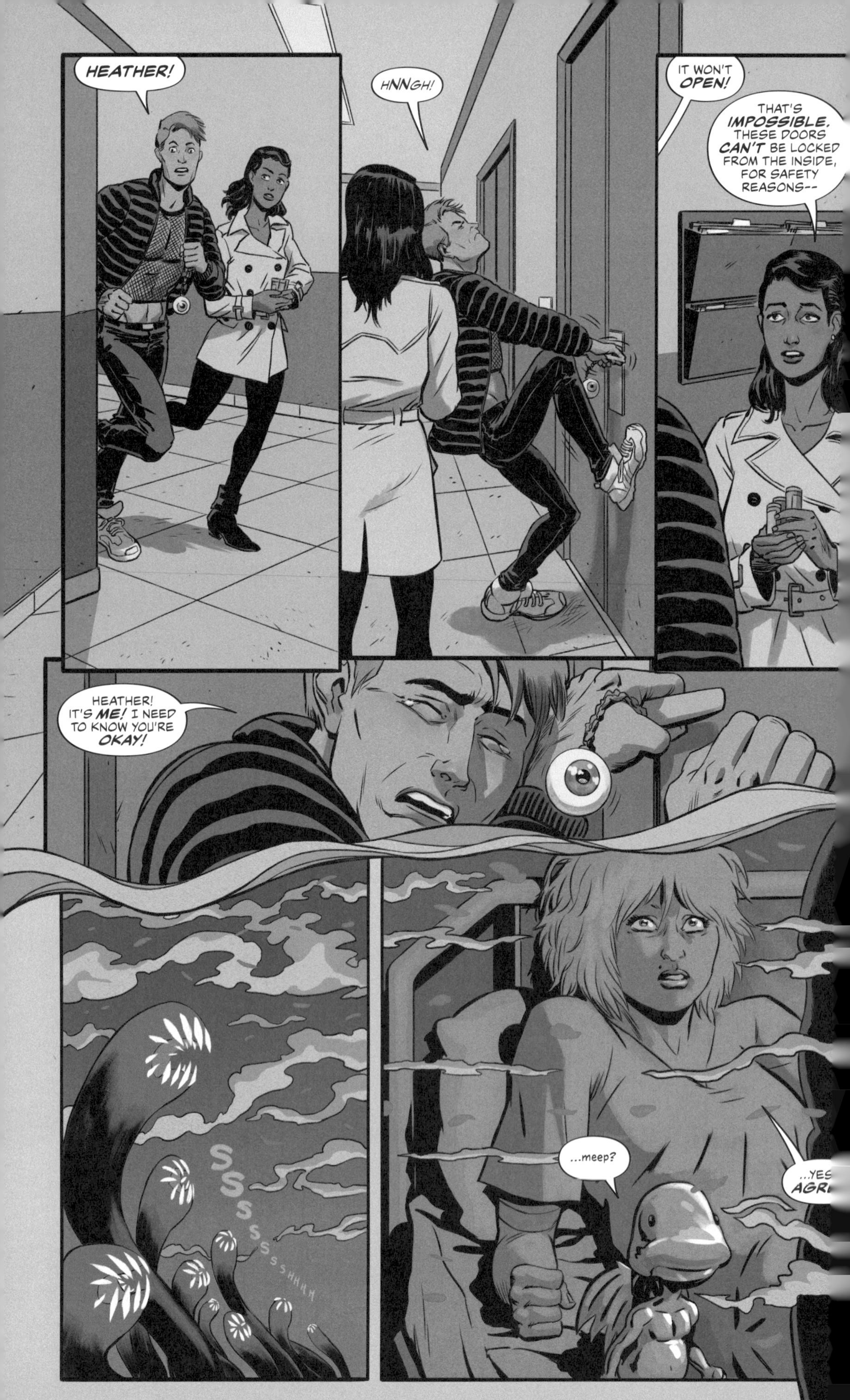
HEATHER!
HNNGH!
IT WON'T OPEN!
THAT'S IMPOSSIBLE. THESE DOORS CAN'T BE LOCKED FROM THE INSIDE, FOR SAFETY REASONS--
HEATHER! IT'S ME! I NEED TO KNOW YOU'RE OKAY!
SSSSSSHHHHH
...meep?
...YES

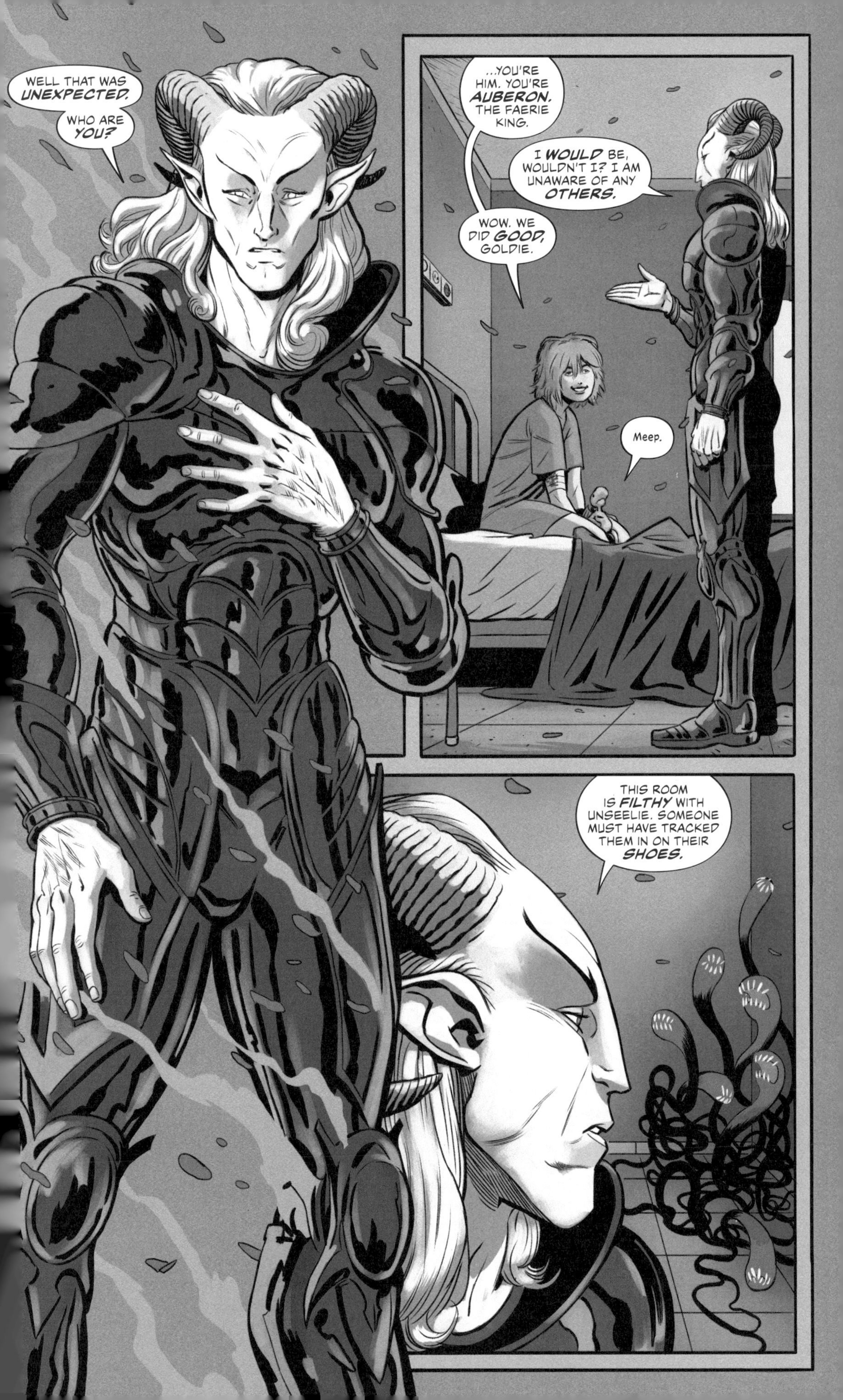
WELL THAT WAS UNEXPECTED.
WHO ARE YOU?
...YOU'RE HIM. YOU'RE AUBERON. THE FAERIE KING.
I WOULD BE, WOULDN'T I? I AM UNAWARE OF ANY OTHERS.
WOW. WE DID GOOD, GOLDIE.
Meep.
THIS ROOM IS FILTHY WITH UNSEELIE. SOMEONE MUST HAVE TRACKED THEM IN ON THEIR SHOES.

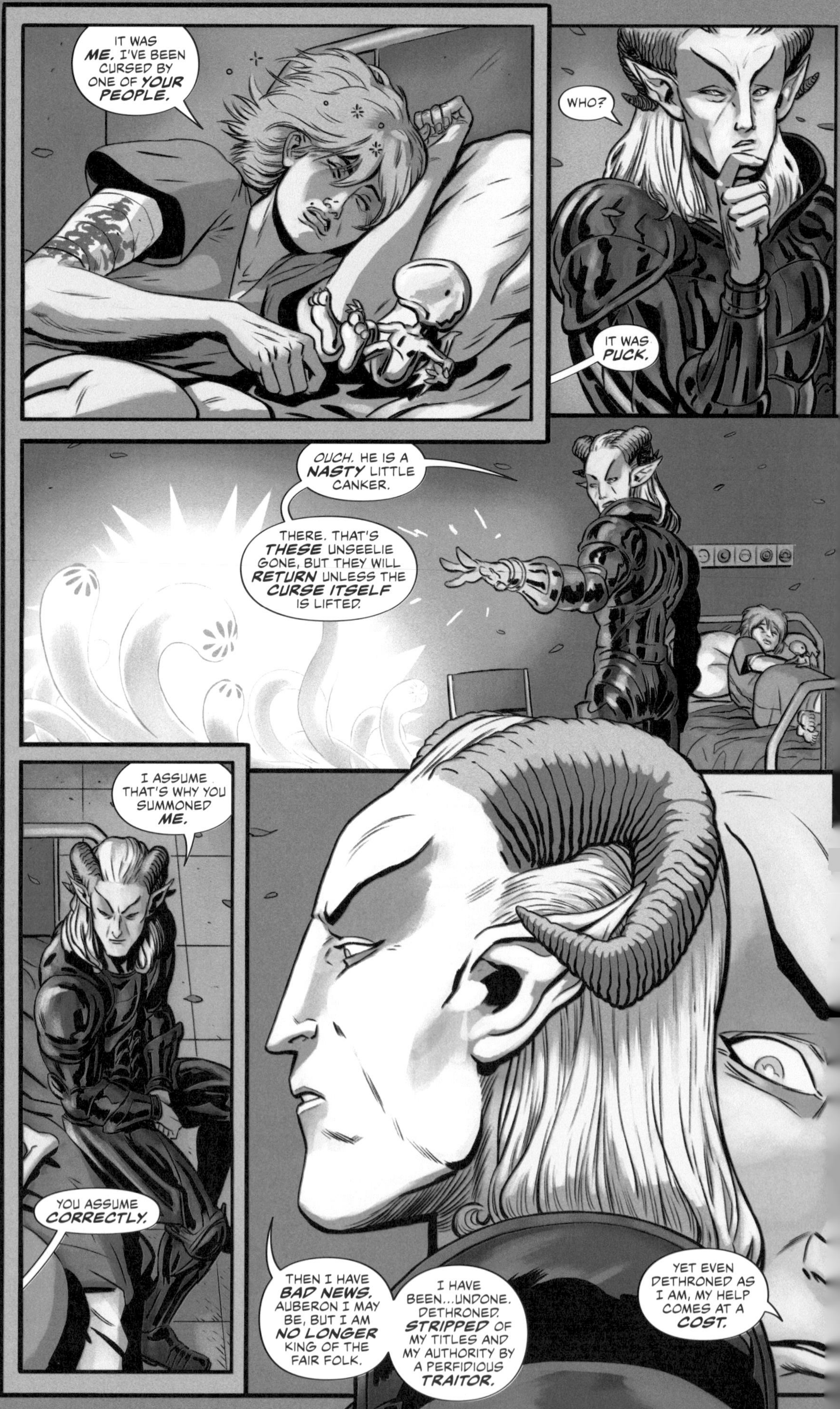

IT WAS ME. I'VE BEEN CURSED BY ONE OF YOUR PEOPLE.
WHO?
IT WAS PUCK.
OUCH. HE IS A NASTY LITTLE CANKER.
THERE. THAT'S THESE UNSEELIE GONE, BUT THEY WILL RETURN UNLESS THE CURSE ITSELF IS LIFTED.
I ASSUME THAT'S WHY YOU SUMMONED ME.
YOU ASSUME CORRECTLY.
THEN I HAVE BAD NEWS. AUBERON I MAY BE, BUT I AM NO LONGER KING OF THE FAIR FOLK.
I HAVE BEEN...UNDONE. DETHRONED. STRIPPED OF MY TITLES AND MY AUTHORITY BY A PERFIDIOUS TRAITOR.
YET EVEN DETHRONED AS I AM, MY HELP COMES AT A COST.

WE MET ON A *DATING APP.* I GUESS WE MUST'VE BOTH *SWIPED RIGHT.*

I DIDN'T THINK IT'D *GO* ANYWHERE. I THOUGHT WE WERE TOO *DIFFERENT.* LIKE I WAS TOO *BORING* FOR HER, AND SHE WAS...NOT LIKE *ANYBODY* I'VE EVER KNOWN BEFORE.

BUT SOON WE WERE TEXTING EACH OTHER *ALL DAY.*

WHEN WE FINALLY MET IN *PERSON,* SHE SEEMED REALLY *NERVOUS.* WE MET AT THIS SPORTS *BAR* I GO TO, AND SOME PEOPLE WERE *STARING.*

IT...NEVER EVEN *OCCURRED* TO ME THAT MAYBE *THIS* BAR WAS NOT THE *BEST* CHOICE.

SHE KEPT CHECKING HER *PHONE,* LIKE SHE WAS PLANNING HER ESCAPE.

I REALIZED SHE WAS *AFRAID.* OF *ME,* AFRAID I'D TAKEN HER SOMEWHERE *UNSAFE,* AFRAID I MIGHT *HURT* HER, OR GET UP AND *LEAVE.*

SO I ASKED HER IF SHE WANTED TO *GET OUT* OF THERE AND HAVE *DINNER* SOMEWHERE *NICE,* AND SHE SMILED THIS SMILE I WILL *NEVER FORGET.*

I THINK...I THINK *SHE* THINKS SHE'S *HARD* TO LOVE. BUT LOVING HER IS THE *EASIEST* THING I'VE EVER DONE.

AND NOW SHE WON'T LET ME IN...SHE WON'T LET ME *HELP...*

SHE'S *RESILIENT.* I COULD SEE THAT RIGHT AWAY. WE *HAVE* TO BELIEVE SHE'LL PULL THROUGH...

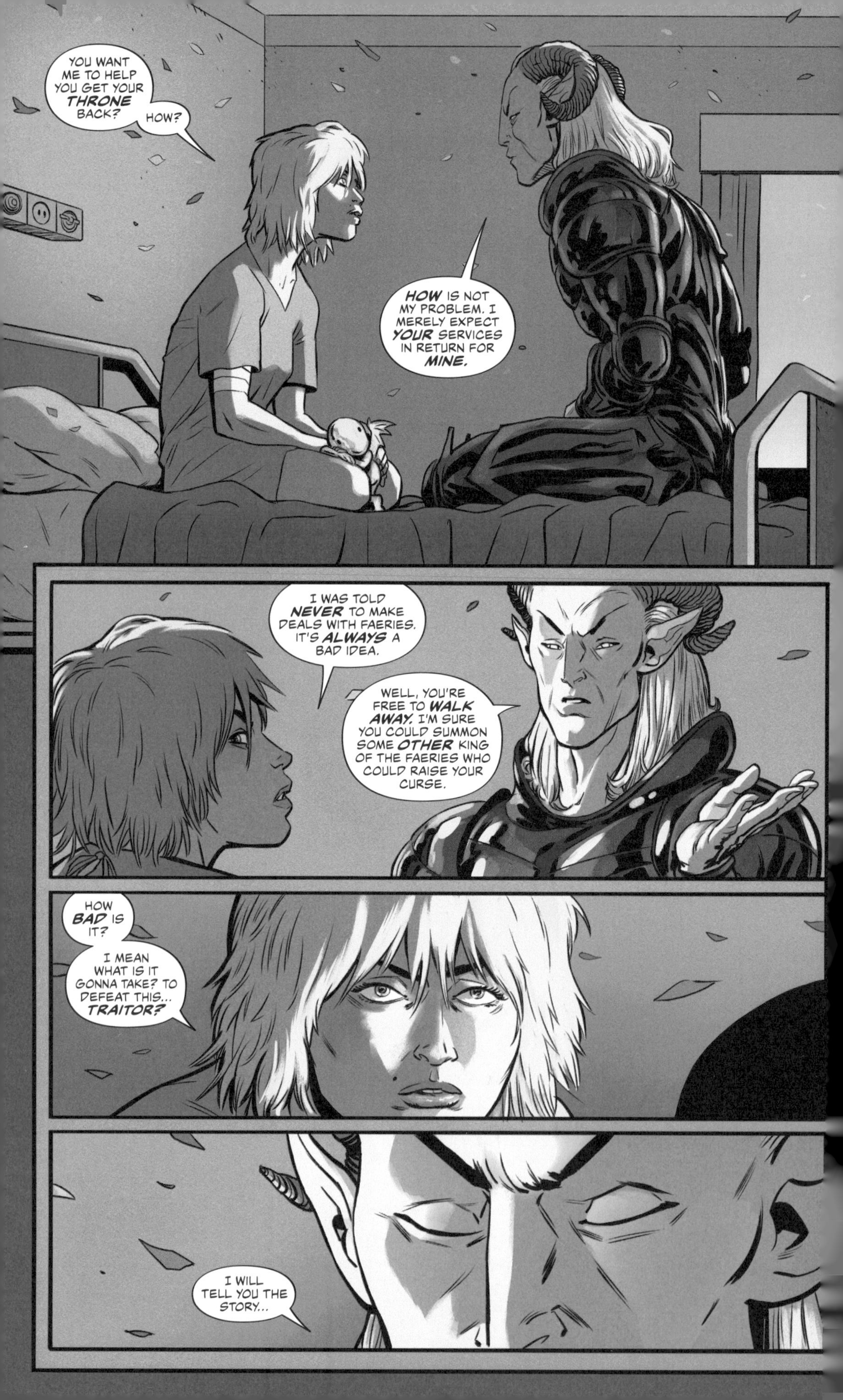

YOU WANT ME TO HELP YOU GET YOUR THRONE BACK?
HOW?
HOW IS NOT MY PROBLEM. I MERELY EXPECT YOUR SERVICES IN RETURN FOR MINE.
I WAS TOLD NEVER TO MAKE DEALS WITH FAERIES. IT'S ALWAYS A BAD IDEA.
WELL, YOU'RE FREE TO WALK AWAY. I'M SURE YOU COULD SUMMON SOME OTHER KING OF THE FAERIES WHO COULD RAISE YOUR CURSE.
HOW BAD IS IT?
I MEAN WHAT IS IT GONNA TAKE? TO DEFEAT THIS... TRAITOR?
I WILL TELL YOU THE STORY...

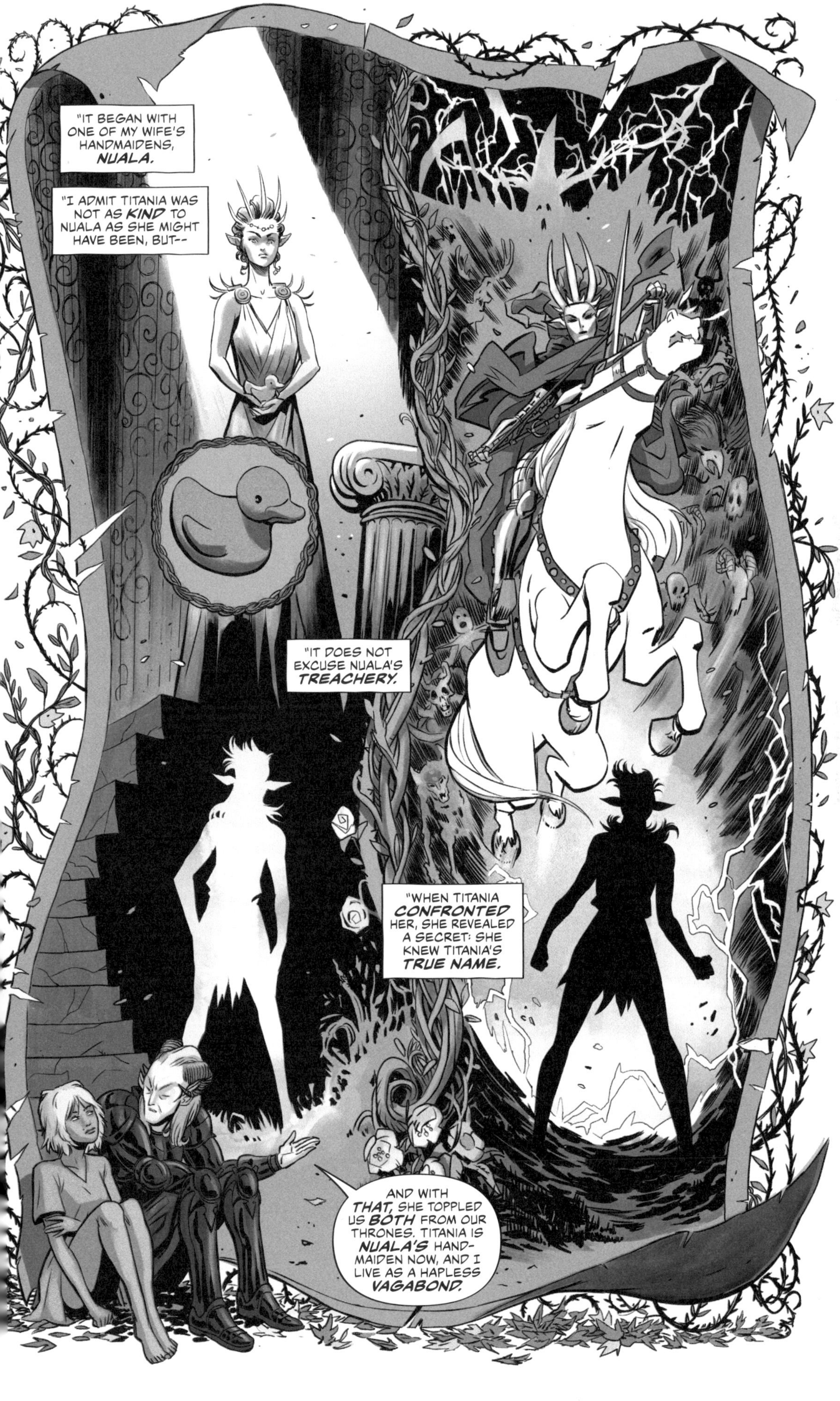
"IT BEGAN WITH ONE OF MY WIFE'S HANDMAIDENS, NUALA.
"I ADMIT TITANIA WAS NOT AS KIND TO NUALA AS SHE MIGHT HAVE BEEN, BUT--
"IT DOES NOT EXCUSE NUALA'S TREACHERY.
"WHEN TITANIA CONFRONTED HER, SHE REVEALED A SECRET: SHE KNEW TITANIA'S TRUE NAME.
AND WITH THAT, SHE TOPPLED US BOTH FROM OUR THRONES. TITANIA IS NUALA'S HAND-MAIDEN NOW, AND I LIVE AS A HAPLESS VAGABOND.

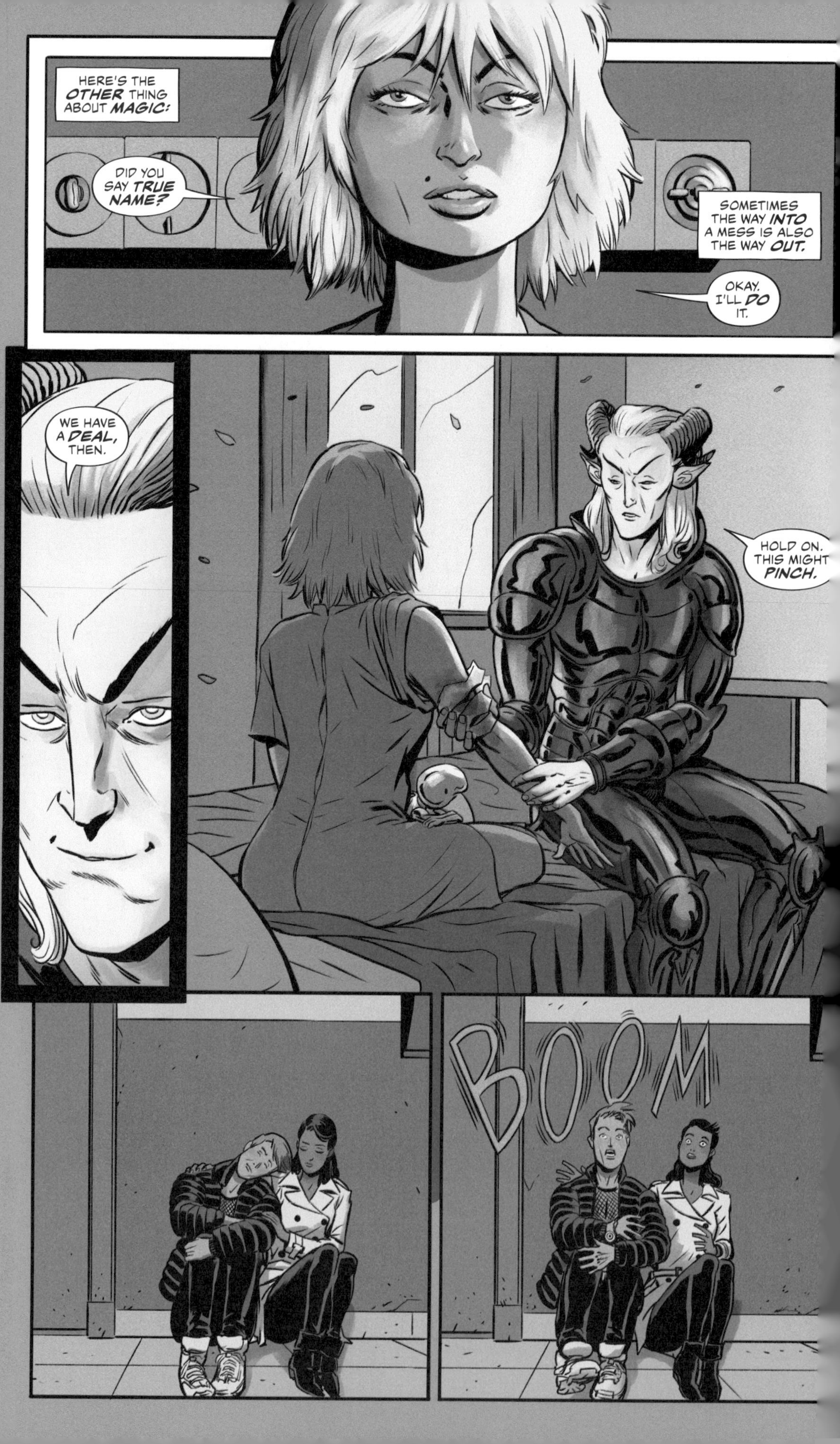
HERE'S THE OTHER THING ABOUT MAGIC:
DID YOU SAY TRUE NAME?
SOMETIMES THE WAY INTO A MESS IS ALSO THE WAY OUT.
OKAY. I'LL DO IT.
WE HAVE A DEAL, THEN.
HOLD ON. THIS MIGHT PINCH.
BOOOM

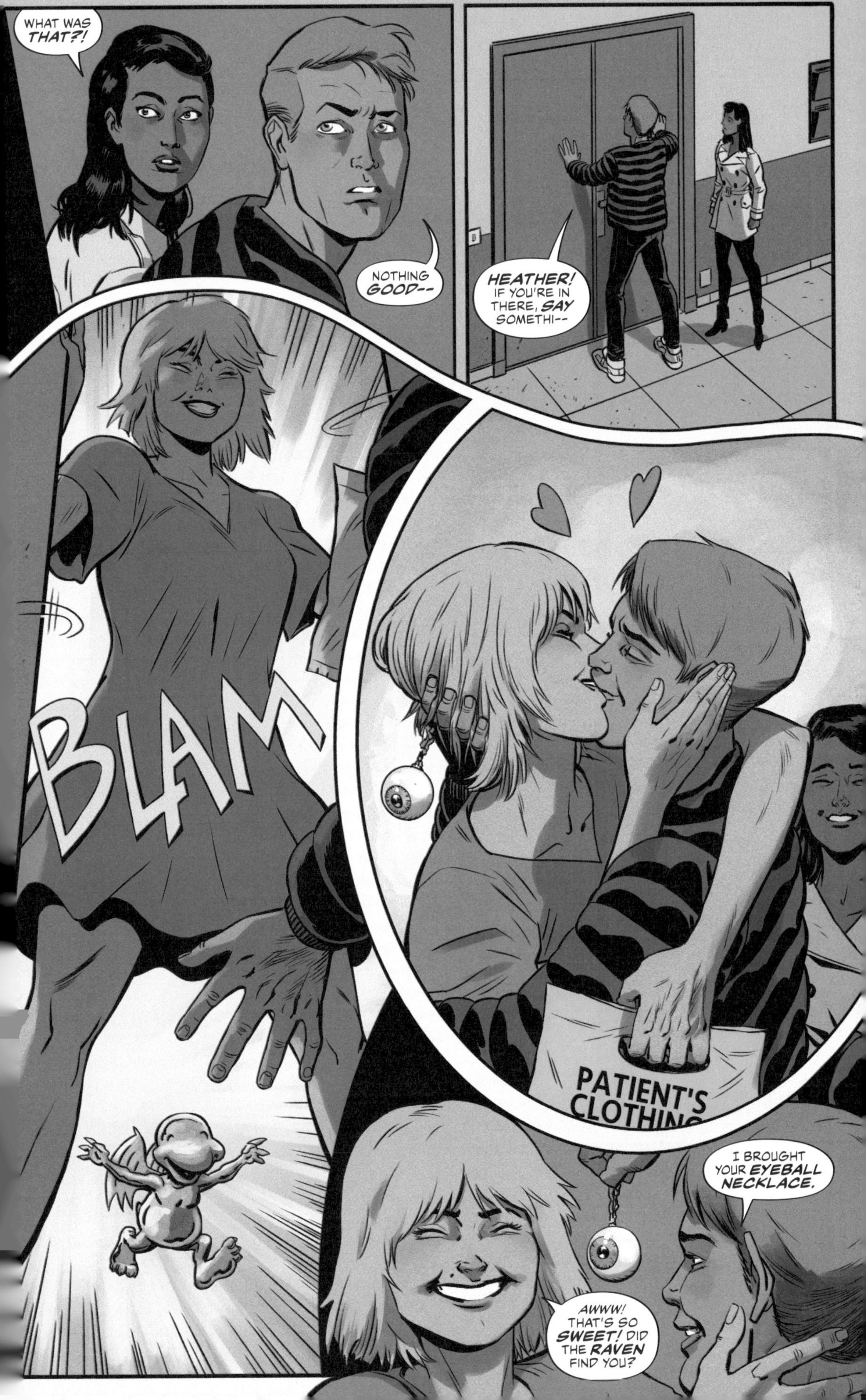
WHAT WAS THAT?!
NOTHING GOOD--
HEATHER! IF YOU'RE IN THERE, SAY SOMETHI--
BLAM
PATIENT'S CLOTHING
I BROUGHT YOUR EYEBALL NECKLACE.
AWWW! THAT'S SO SWEET! DID THE RAVEN FIND YOU?

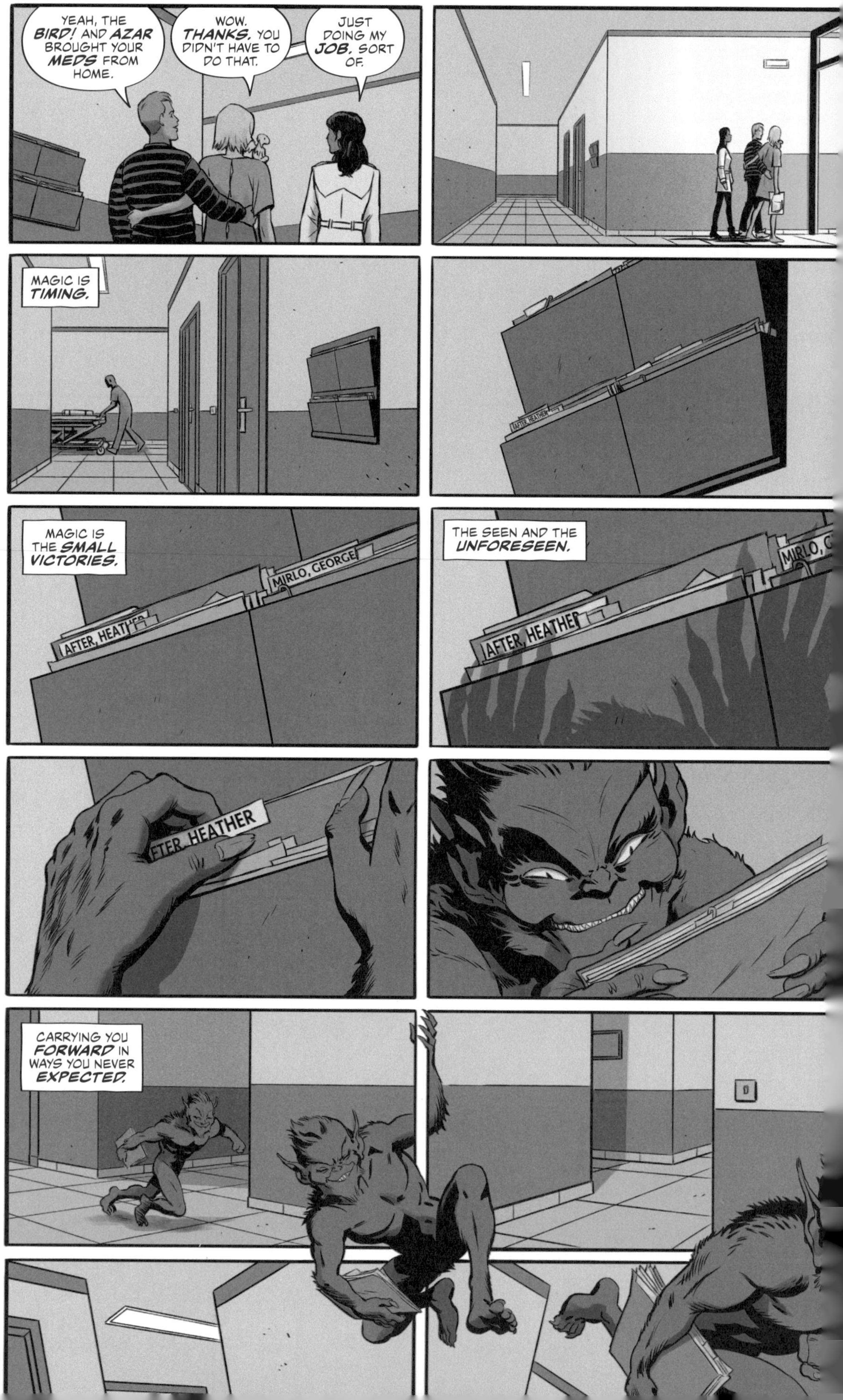
YEAH, THE BIRD! AND AZAR BROUGHT YOUR MEDS FROM HOME.
WOW. THANKS. YOU DIDN'T HAVE TO DO THAT.
JUST DOING MY JOB. SORT OF.
MAGIC IS TIMING.
AFTER, HEATHER
MAGIC IS THE SMALL VICTORIES.
MIRLO, GEORGE
AFTER, HEATHER
THE SEEN AND THE UNFORESEEN.
AFTER, HEATHER
AFTER, HEATHER
CARRYING YOU FORWARD IN WAYS YOU NEVER EXPECTED.

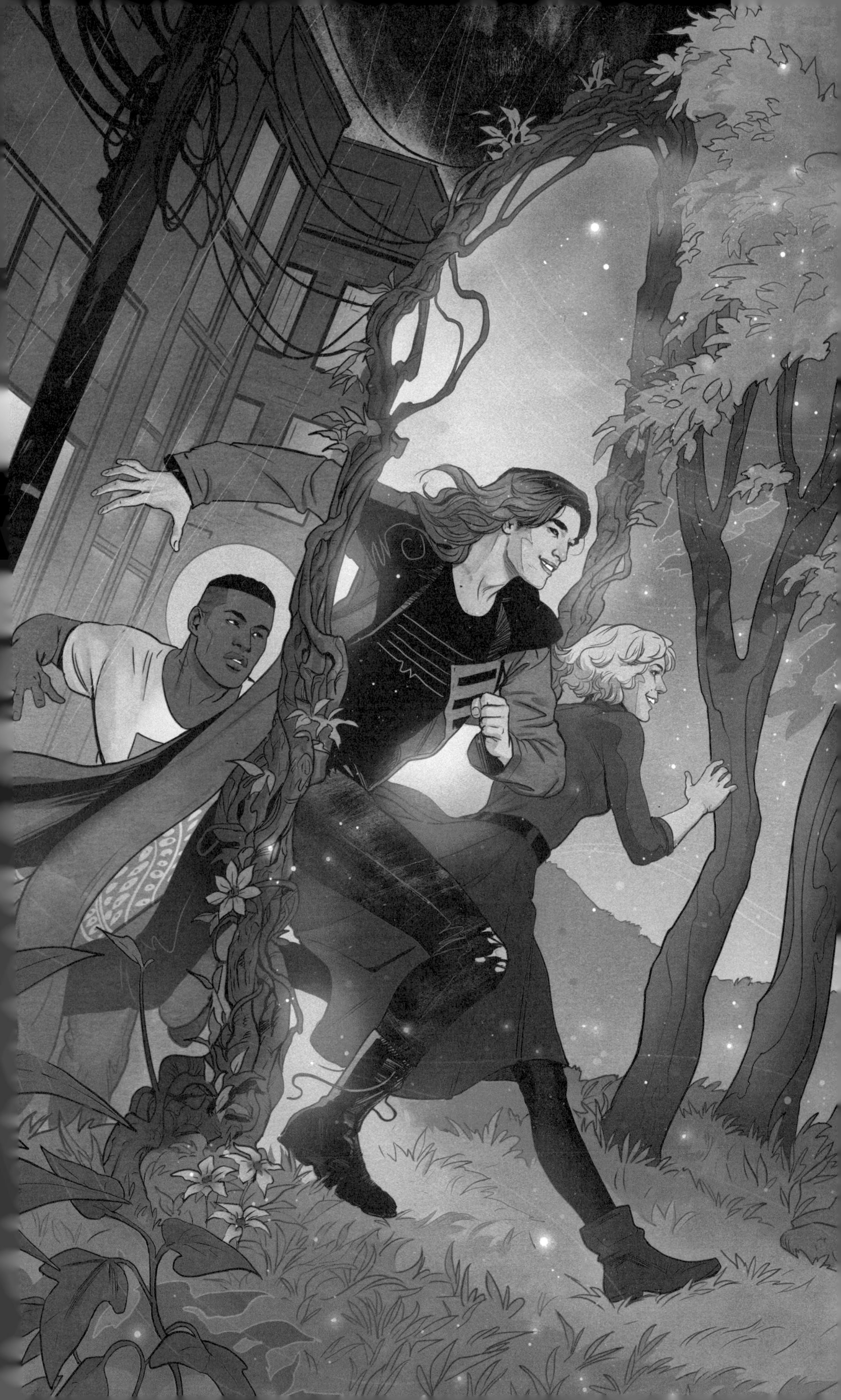

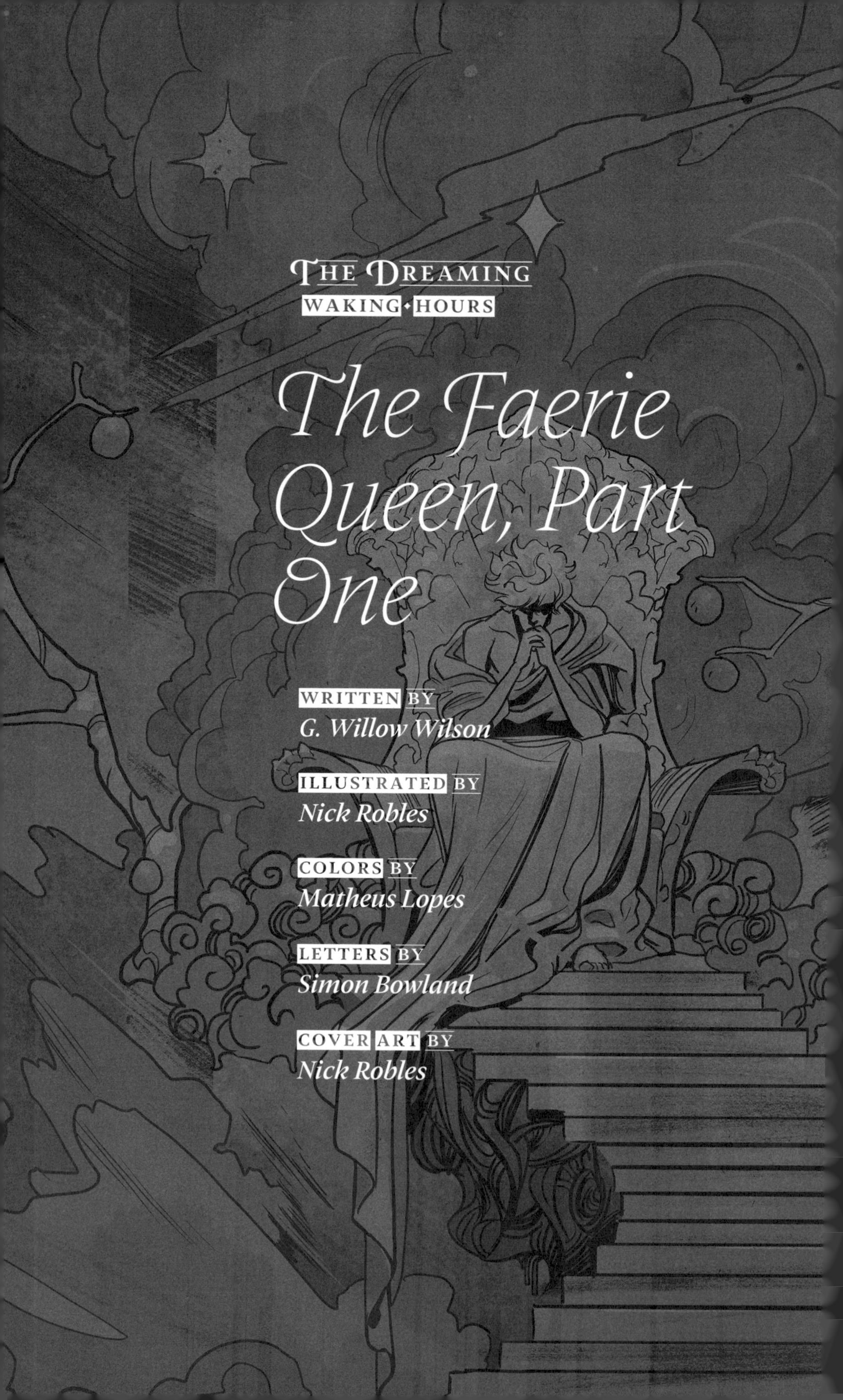

THE DREAMING

WAKING • HOURS

The Faerie Queen, Part One

WRITTEN BY
G. Willow Wilson

ILLUSTRATED BY
Nick Robles

COLORS BY
Matheus Lopes

LETTERS BY
Simon Bowland

COVER ART BY
Nick Robles

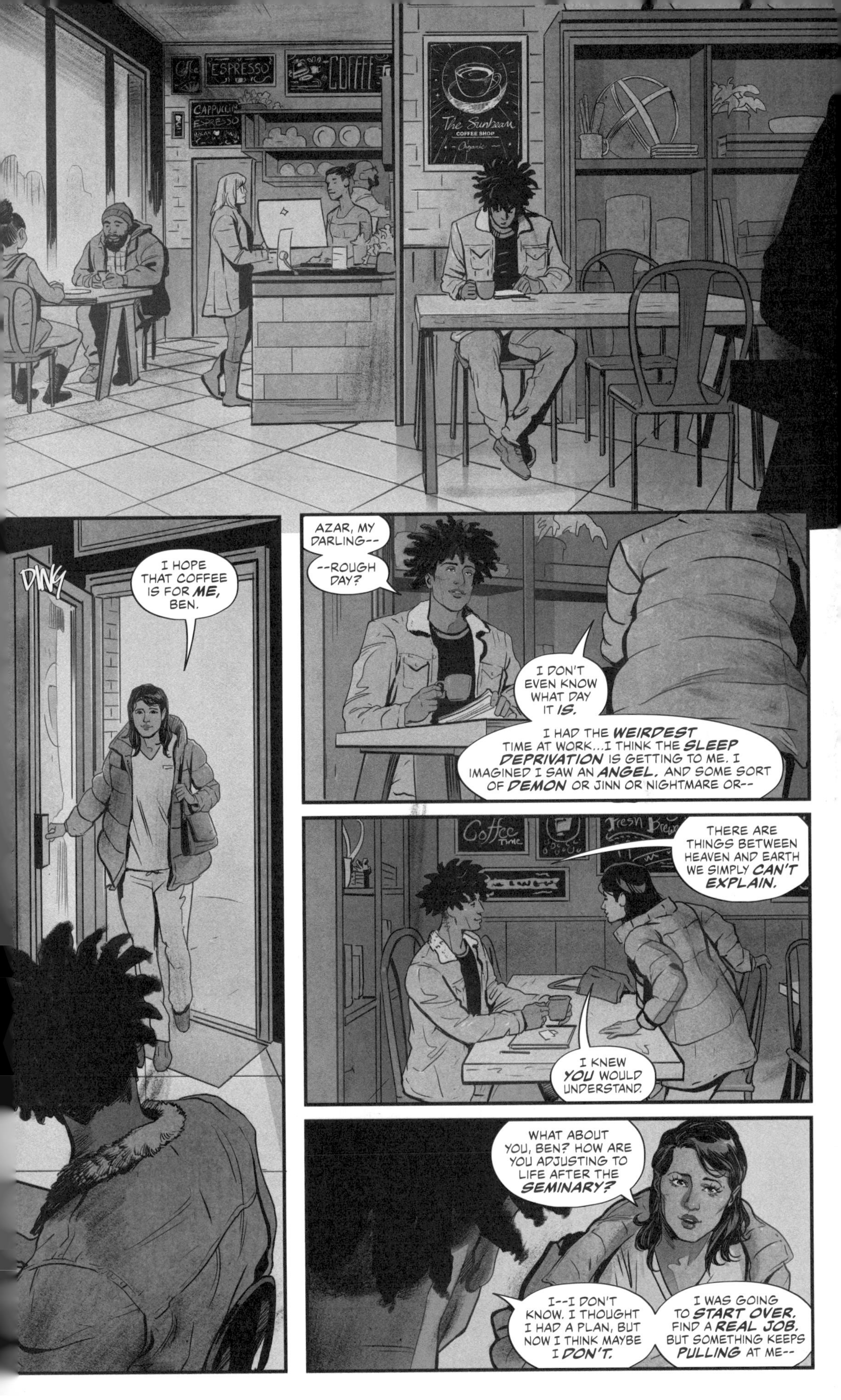

ESPRESSO
COFFEE
CAPPUCCINO
ESPRESSO
The Sunbean COFFEE SHOP Organic
DING
I HOPE THAT COFFEE IS FOR *ME,* BEN.
AZAR, MY DARLING--
--ROUGH DAY?
I DON'T EVEN KNOW WHAT DAY IT *IS.*
I HAD THE *WEIRDEST* TIME AT WORK...I THINK THE *SLEEP DEPRIVATION* IS GETTING TO ME. I IMAGINED I SAW AN *ANGEL,* AND SOME SORT OF *DEMON* OR JINN OR NIGHTMARE OR--
Coffee Time
THERE ARE THINGS BETWEEN HEAVEN AND EARTH WE SIMPLY *CAN'T EXPLAIN.*
I KNEW *YOU* WOULD UNDERSTAND.
WHAT ABOUT YOU, BEN? HOW ARE YOU ADJUSTING TO LIFE AFTER THE *SEMINARY?*
I--I DON'T KNOW. I THOUGHT I HAD A PLAN, BUT NOW I THINK MAYBE I *DON'T.*
I WAS GOING TO *START OVER.* FIND A *REAL JOB.* BUT SOMETHING KEEPS *PULLING* AT ME--

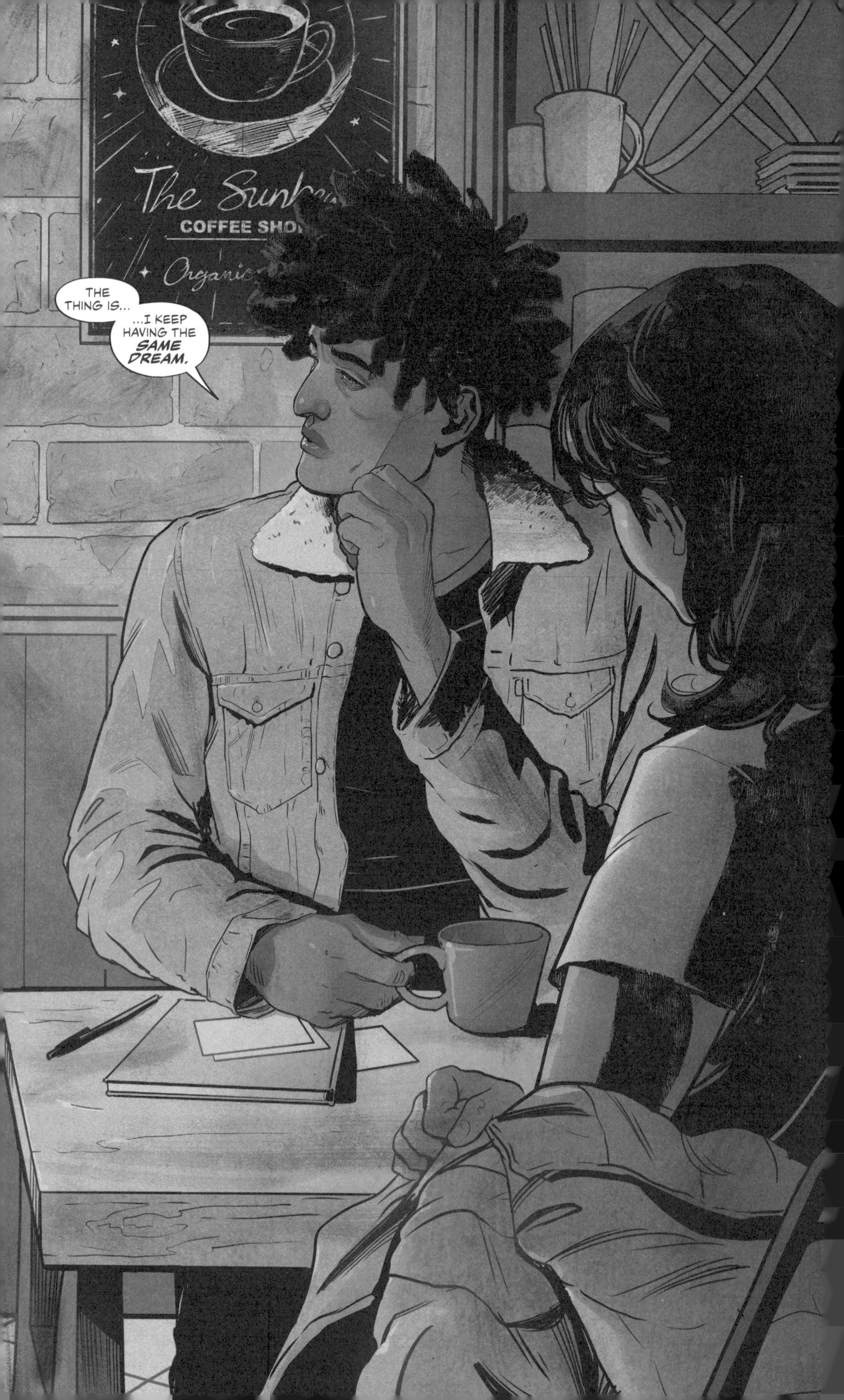
The Sunb
COFFEE SHO
Organic
THE THING IS...
...I KEEP HAVING THE SAME DREAM.

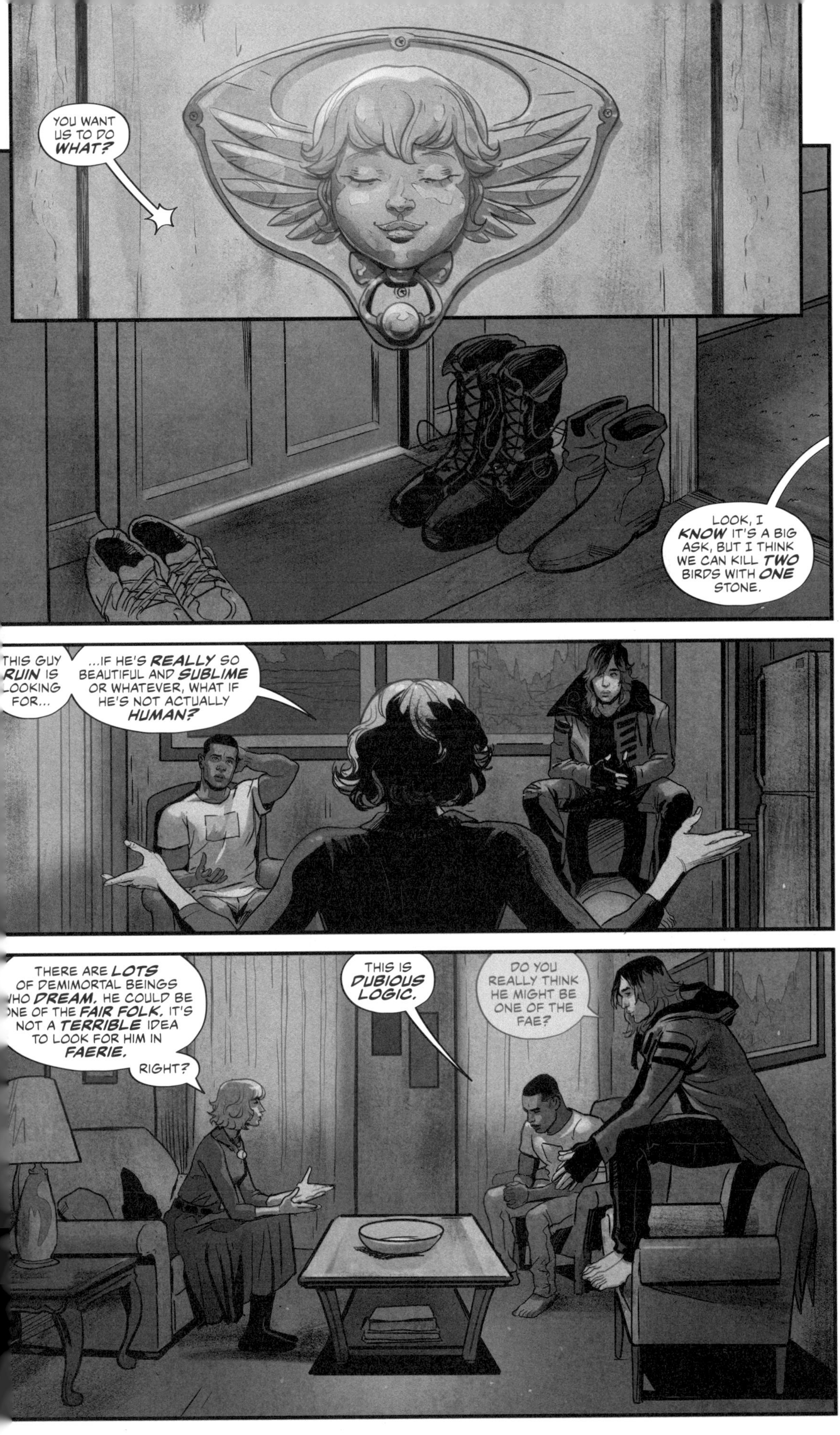
YOU WANT US TO DO WHAT?
LOOK, I KNOW IT'S A BIG ASK, BUT I THINK WE CAN KILL TWO BIRDS WITH ONE STONE.
THIS GUY RUIN IS LOOKING FOR...
...IF HE'S REALLY SO BEAUTIFUL AND SUBLIME OR WHATEVER, WHAT IF HE'S NOT ACTUALLY HUMAN?
THERE ARE LOTS OF DEMIMORTAL BEINGS WHO DREAM. HE COULD BE ONE OF THE FAIR FOLK. IT'S NOT A TERRIBLE IDEA TO LOOK FOR HIM IN FAERIE.
RIGHT?
THIS IS DUBIOUS LOGIC.
DO YOU REALLY THINK HE MIGHT BE ONE OF THE FAE?

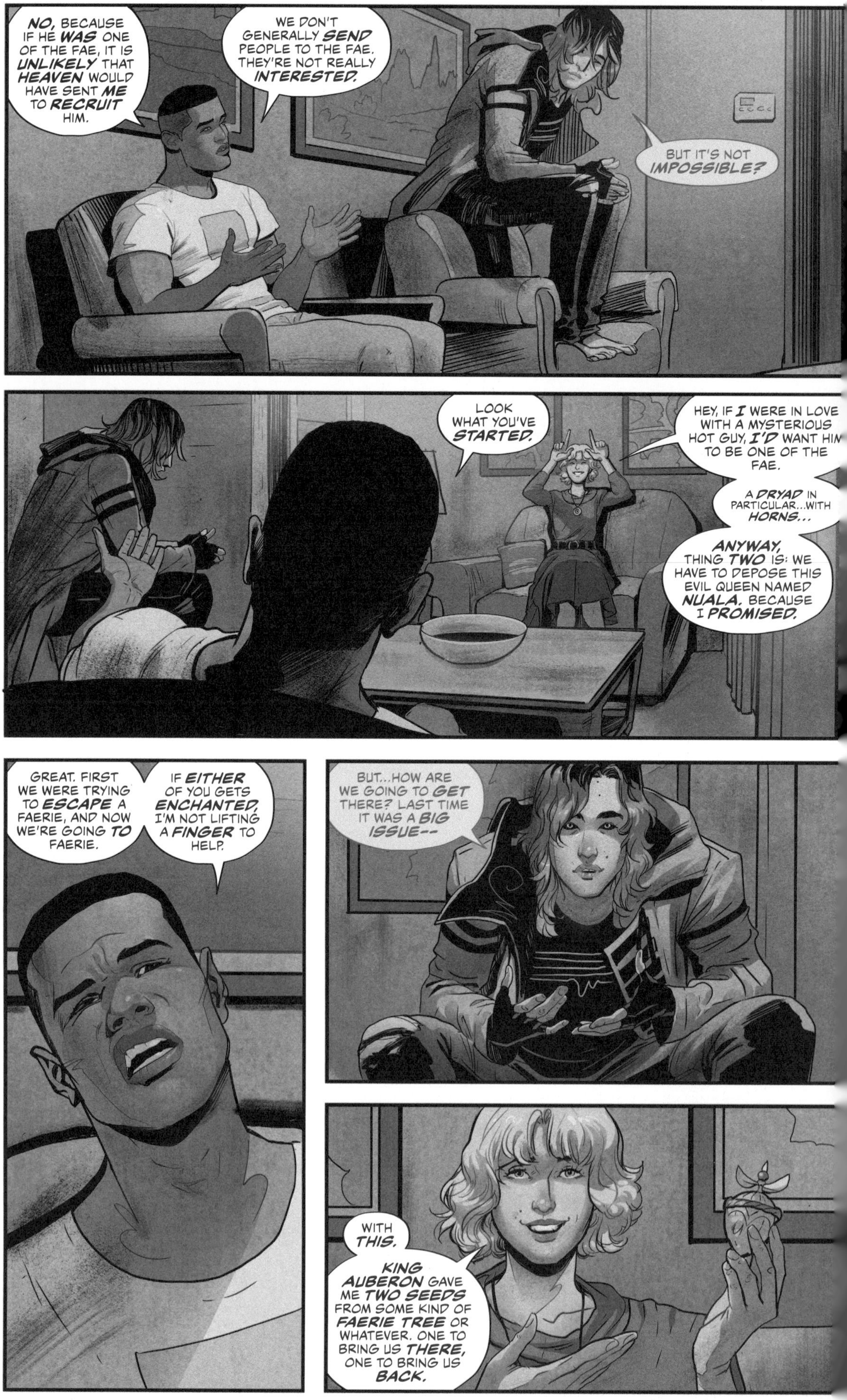
NO, BECAUSE IF HE WAS ONE OF THE FAE, IT IS UNLIKELY THAT HEAVEN WOULD HAVE SENT ME TO RECRUIT HIM.
WE DON'T GENERALLY SEND PEOPLE TO THE FAE. THEY'RE NOT REALLY INTERESTED.
BUT IT'S NOT IMPOSSIBLE?
LOOK WHAT YOU'VE STARTED.
HEY, IF I WERE IN LOVE WITH A MYSTERIOUS HOT GUY, I'D WANT HIM TO BE ONE OF THE FAE.
A DRYAD IN PARTICULAR...WITH HORNS...
ANYWAY, THING TWO IS: WE HAVE TO DEPOSE THIS EVIL QUEEN NAMED NUALA. BECAUSE I PROMISED.
GREAT. FIRST WE WERE TRYING TO ESCAPE A FAERIE, AND NOW WE'RE GOING TO FAERIE.
IF EITHER OF YOU GETS ENCHANTED, I'M NOT LIFTING A FINGER TO HELP.
BUT...HOW ARE WE GOING TO GET THERE? LAST TIME IT WAS A BIG ISSUE--
WITH THIS.
KING AUBERON GAVE ME TWO SEEDS FROM SOME KIND OF FAERIE TREE OR WHATEVER. ONE TO BRING US THERE, ONE TO BRING US BACK.

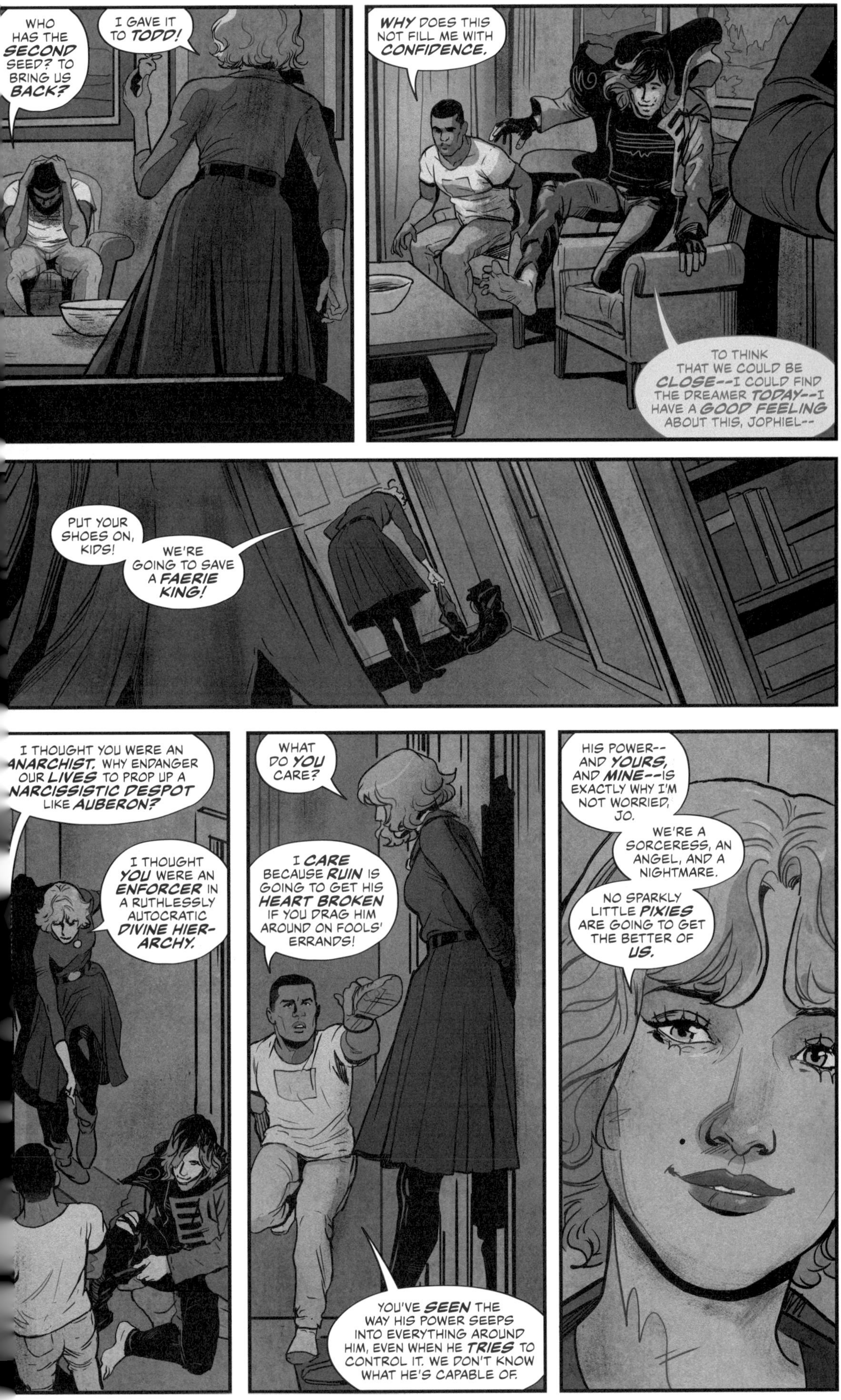
WHO HAS THE SECOND SEED? TO BRING US BACK?
I GAVE IT TO TODD!
WHY DOES THIS NOT FILL ME WITH CONFIDENCE.
TO THINK THAT WE COULD BE CLOSE--I COULD FIND THE DREAMER TODAY--I HAVE A GOOD FEELING ABOUT THIS, JOPHIEL--
PUT YOUR SHOES ON, KIDS!
WE'RE GOING TO SAVE A FAERIE KING!
I THOUGHT YOU WERE AN ANARCHIST. WHY ENDANGER OUR LIVES TO PROP UP A NARCISSISTIC DESPOT LIKE AUBERON?
I THOUGHT YOU WERE AN ENFORCER IN A RUTHLESSLY AUTOCRATIC DIVINE HIER-ARCHY.
WHAT DO YOU CARE?
I CARE BECAUSE RUIN IS GOING TO GET HIS HEART BROKEN IF YOU DRAG HIM AROUND ON FOOLS' ERRANDS!
YOU'VE SEEN THE WAY HIS POWER SEEPS INTO EVERYTHING AROUND HIM, EVEN WHEN HE TRIES TO CONTROL IT. WE DON'T KNOW WHAT HE'S CAPABLE OF.
HIS POWER--AND YOURS, AND MINE--IS EXACTLY WHY I'M NOT WORRIED, JO.
WE'RE A SORCERESS, AN ANGEL, AND A NIGHTMARE.
NO SPARKLY LITTLE PIXIES ARE GOING TO GET THE BETTER OF US.

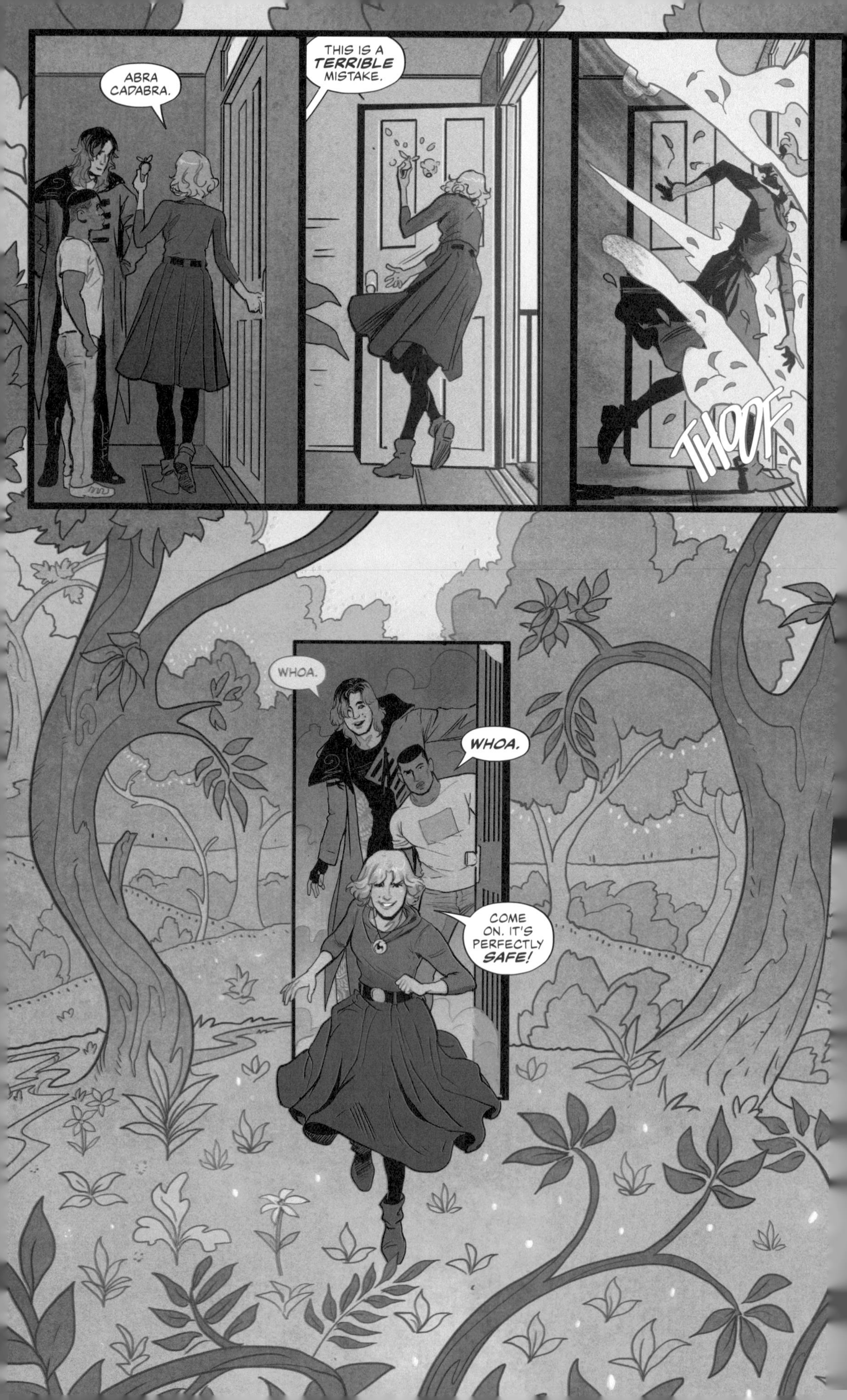
ABRA CADABRA.
THIS IS A TERRIBLE MISTAKE.
THOOF
WHOA.
WHOA.
COME ON. IT'S PERFECTLY SAFE!

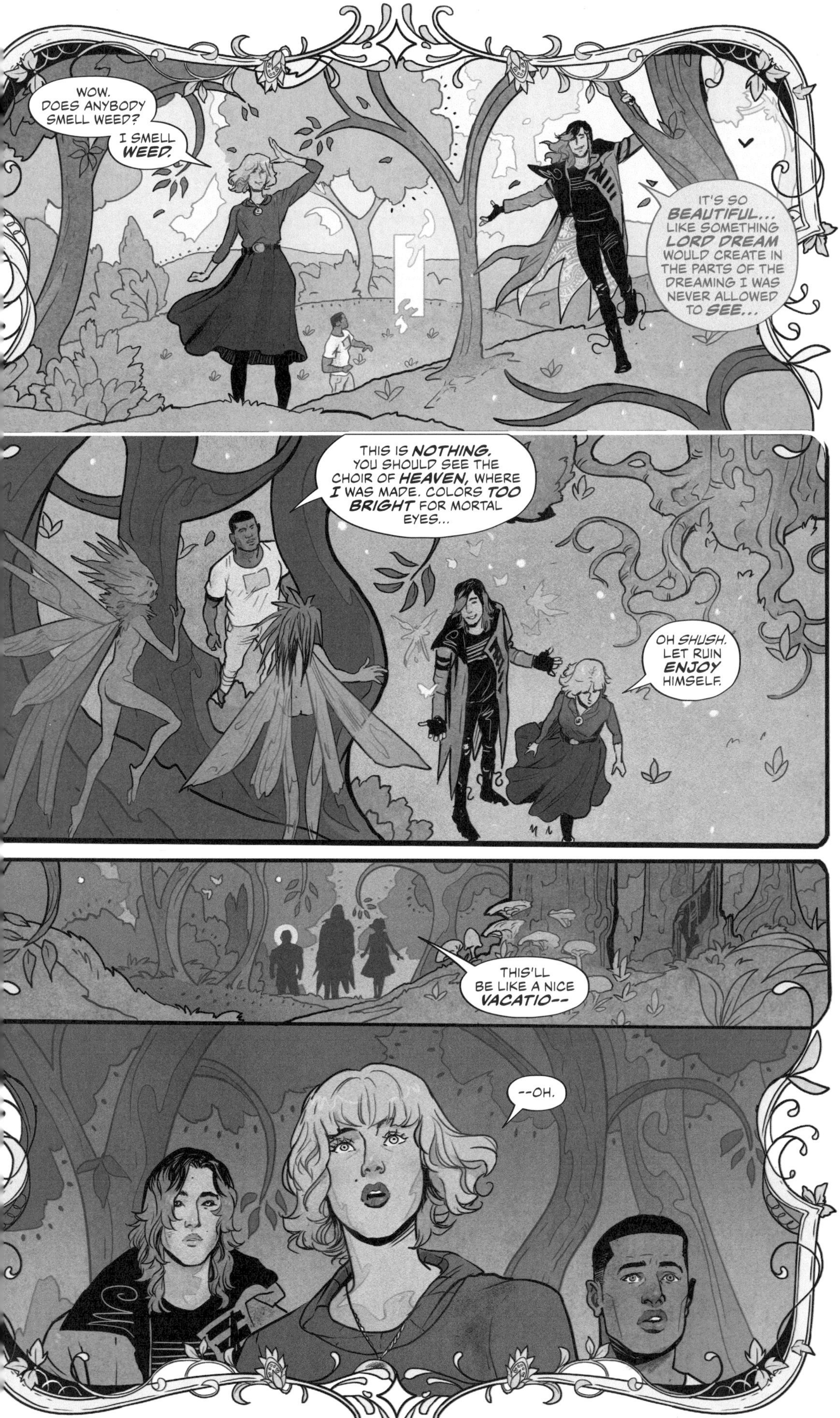

WOW. DOES ANYBODY SMELL WEED?
I SMELL WEED.
IT'S SO BEAUTIFUL... LIKE SOMETHING LORD DREAM WOULD CREATE IN THE PARTS OF THE DREAMING I WAS NEVER ALLOWED TO SEE...
THIS IS NOTHING. YOU SHOULD SEE THE CHOIR OF HEAVEN, WHERE I WAS MADE. COLORS TOO BRIGHT FOR MORTAL EYES...
OH SHUSH. LET RUIN ENJOY HIMSELF.
THIS'LL BE LIKE A NICE VACATIO--
--OH.

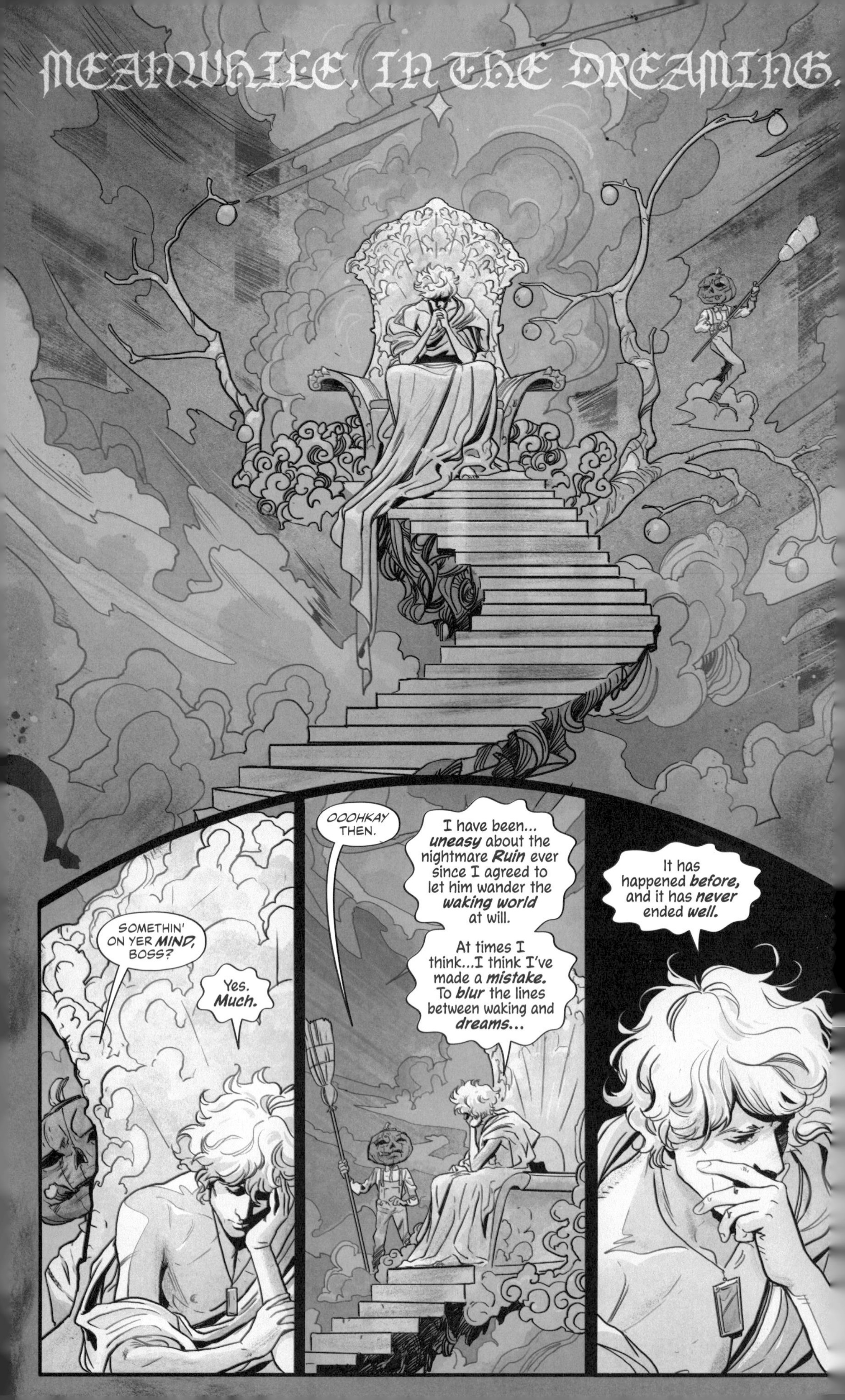
MEANWHILE, IN THE DREAMING.
SOMETHIN' ON YER MIND, BOSS?
Yes. Much.
OOOHKAY THEN.
I have been... uneasy about the nightmare Ruin ever since I agreed to let him wander the waking world at will.
At times I think...I think I've made a mistake. To blur the lines between waking and dreams...
It has happened before, and it has never ended well.

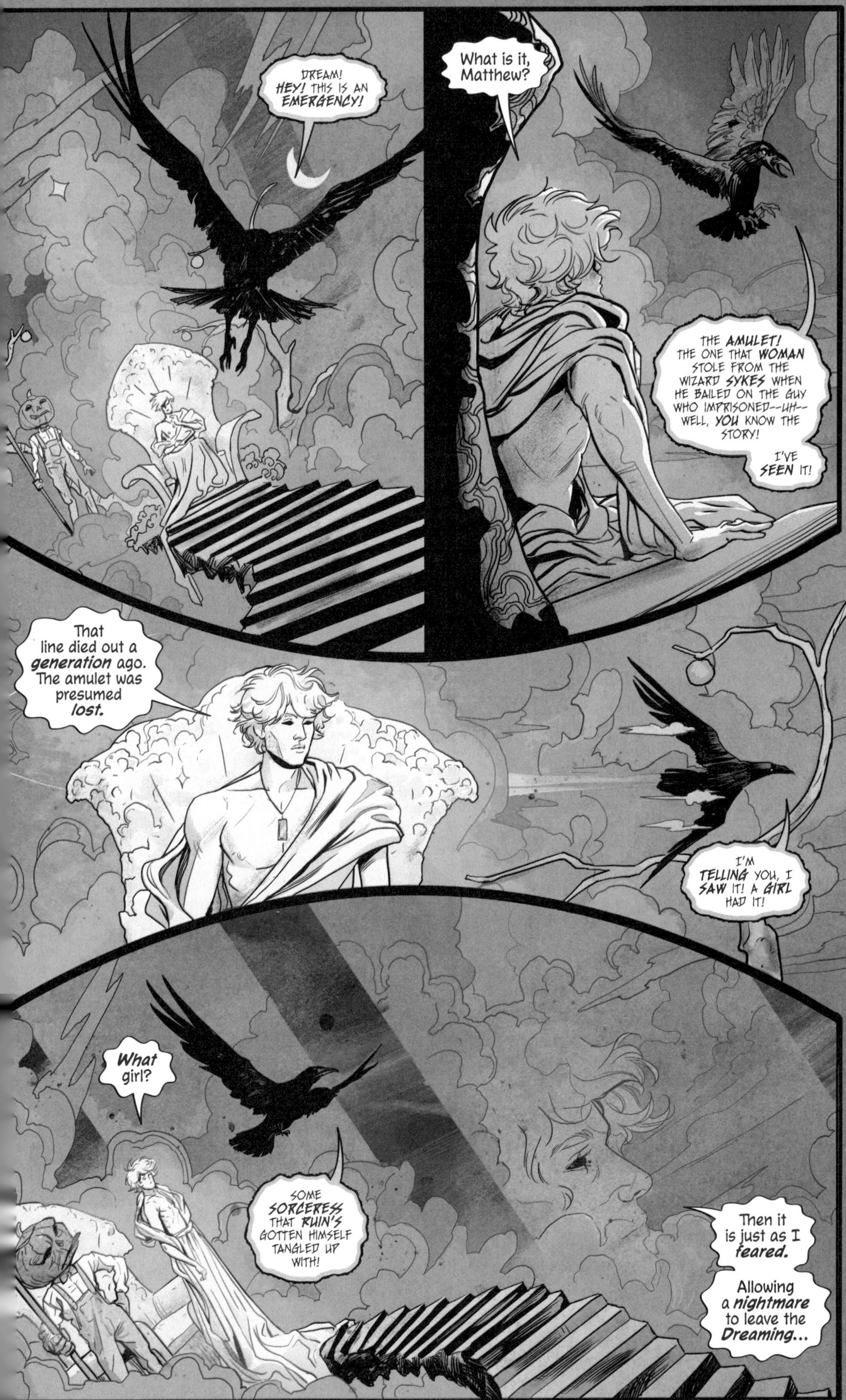
DREAM! HEY! THIS IS AN EMERGENCY!
What is it, Matthew?
THE AMULET! THE ONE THAT WOMAN STOLE FROM THE WIZARD SYKES WHEN HE BAILED ON THE GUY WHO IMPRISONED--UH-- WELL, YOU KNOW THE STORY!
I'VE SEEN IT!
That line died out a generation ago. The amulet was presumed lost.
I'M TELLING YOU, I SAW IT! A GIRL HAD IT!
What girl?
SOME SORCERESS THAT RUIN'S GOTTEN HIMSELF TANGLED UP WITH!
Then it is just as I feared.
Allowing a nightmare to leave the Dreaming...

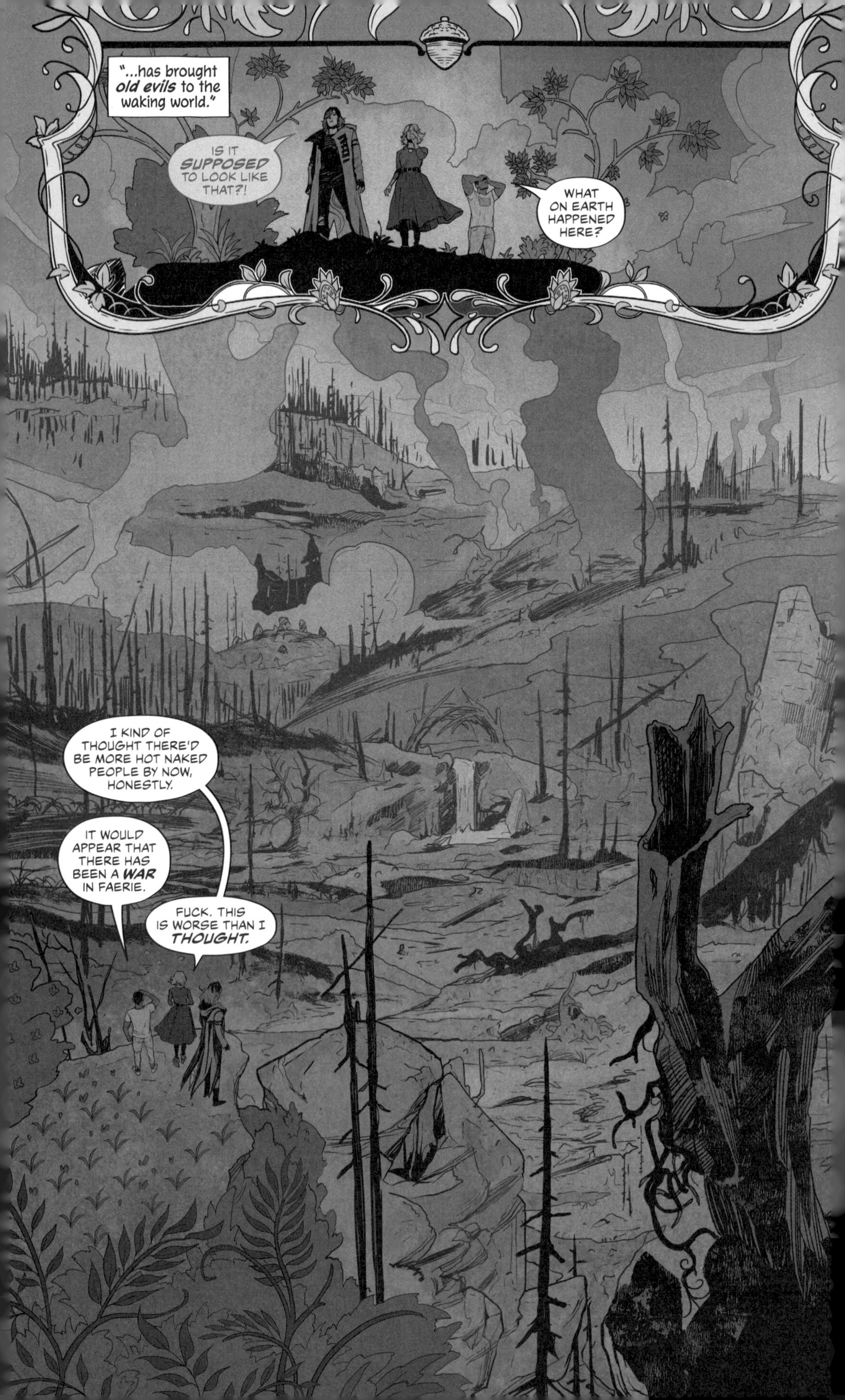
"...has brought *old evils* to the waking world."
IS IT *SUPPOSED* TO LOOK LIKE THAT?!
WHAT ON EARTH HAPPENED HERE?
I KIND OF THOUGHT THERE'D BE MORE HOT NAKED PEOPLE BY NOW, HONESTLY.
IT WOULD APPEAR THAT THERE HAS BEEN A *WAR* IN FAERIE.
FUCK. THIS IS WORSE THAN I *THOUGHT.*

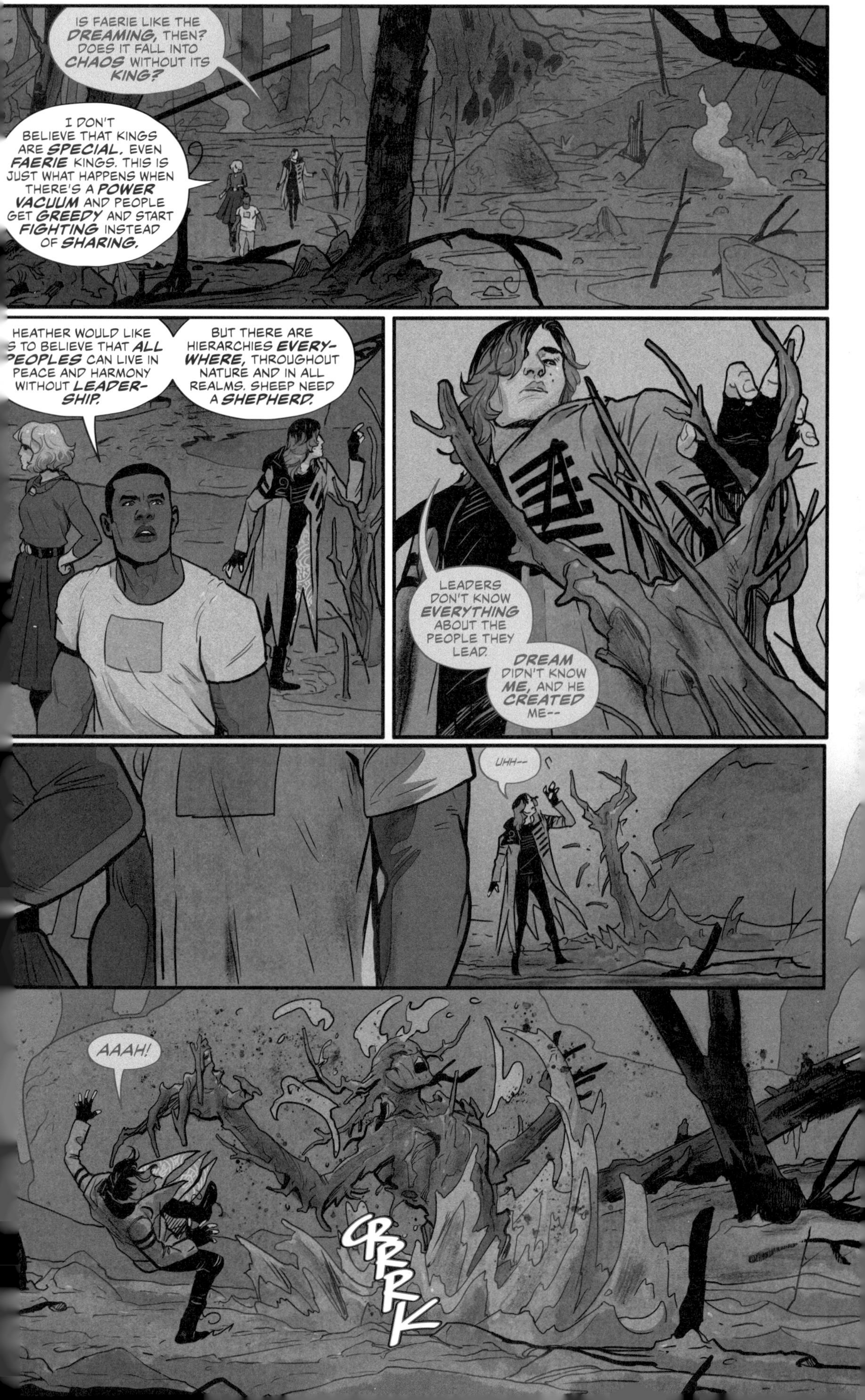
IS FAERIE LIKE THE DREAMING, THEN? DOES IT FALL INTO CHAOS WITHOUT ITS KING?
I DON'T BELIEVE THAT KINGS ARE SPECIAL. EVEN FAERIE KINGS. THIS IS JUST WHAT HAPPENS WHEN THERE'S A POWER VACUUM AND PEOPLE GET GREEDY AND START FIGHTING INSTEAD OF SHARING.
HEATHER WOULD LIKE US TO BELIEVE THAT ALL PEOPLES CAN LIVE IN PEACE AND HARMONY WITHOUT LEADERSHIP.
BUT THERE ARE HIERARCHIES EVERYWHERE, THROUGHOUT NATURE AND IN ALL REALMS. SHEEP NEED A SHEPHERD.
LEADERS DON'T KNOW EVERYTHING ABOUT THE PEOPLE THEY LEAD.
DREAM DIDN'T KNOW ME, AND HE CREATED ME--
UHH--
AAAH!
CRRRK

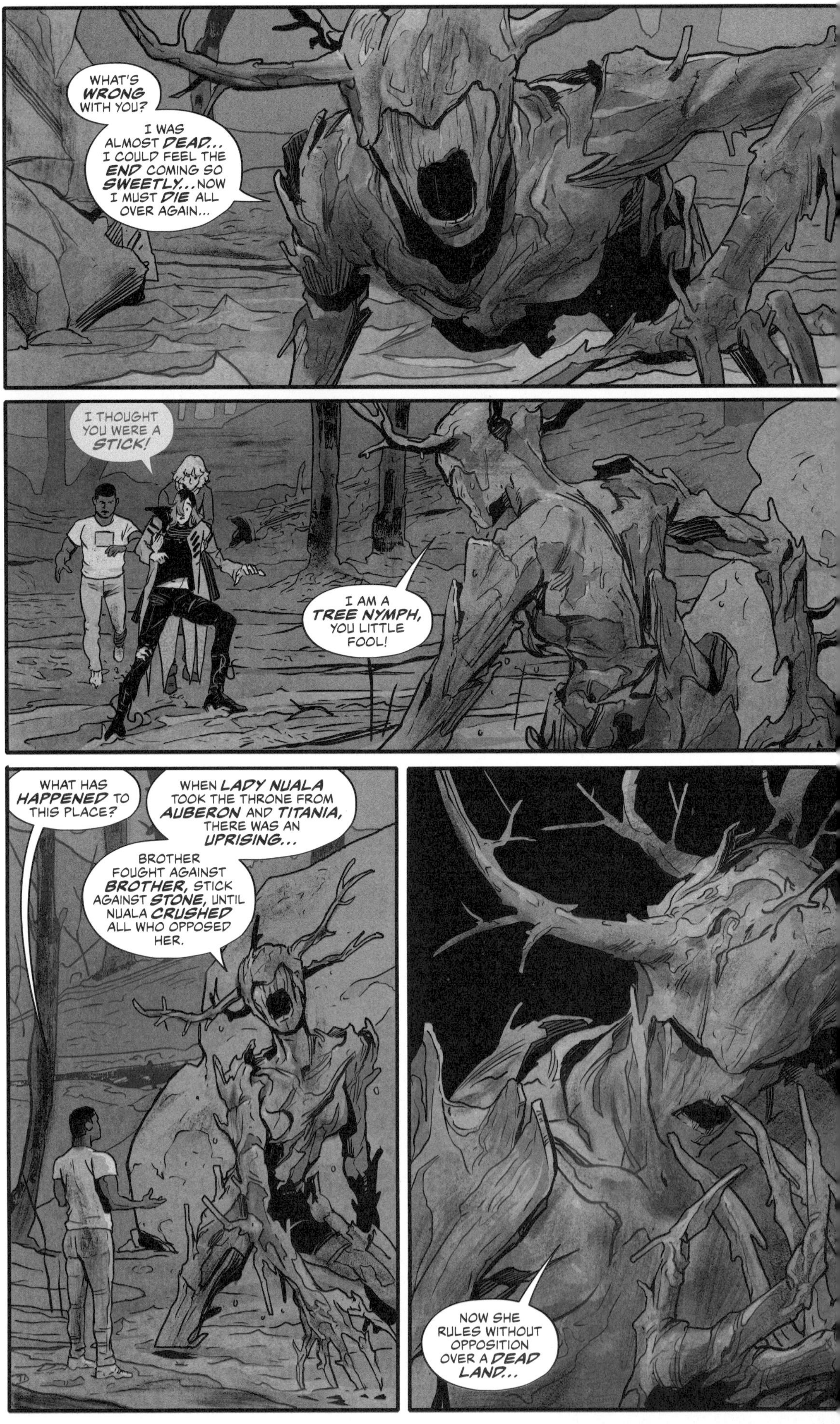

WHAT'S WRONG WITH YOU?
I WAS ALMOST DEAD... I COULD FEEL THE END COMING SO SWEETLY... NOW I MUST DIE ALL OVER AGAIN...
I THOUGHT YOU WERE A STICK!
I AM A TREE NYMPH, YOU LITTLE FOOL!
WHAT HAS HAPPENED TO THIS PLACE?
WHEN LADY NUALA TOOK THE THRONE FROM AUBERON AND TITANIA, THERE WAS AN UPRISING...
BROTHER FOUGHT AGAINST BROTHER, STICK AGAINST STONE, UNTIL NUALA CRUSHED ALL WHO OPPOSED HER.
NOW SHE RULES WITHOUT OPPOSITION OVER A DEAD LAND...

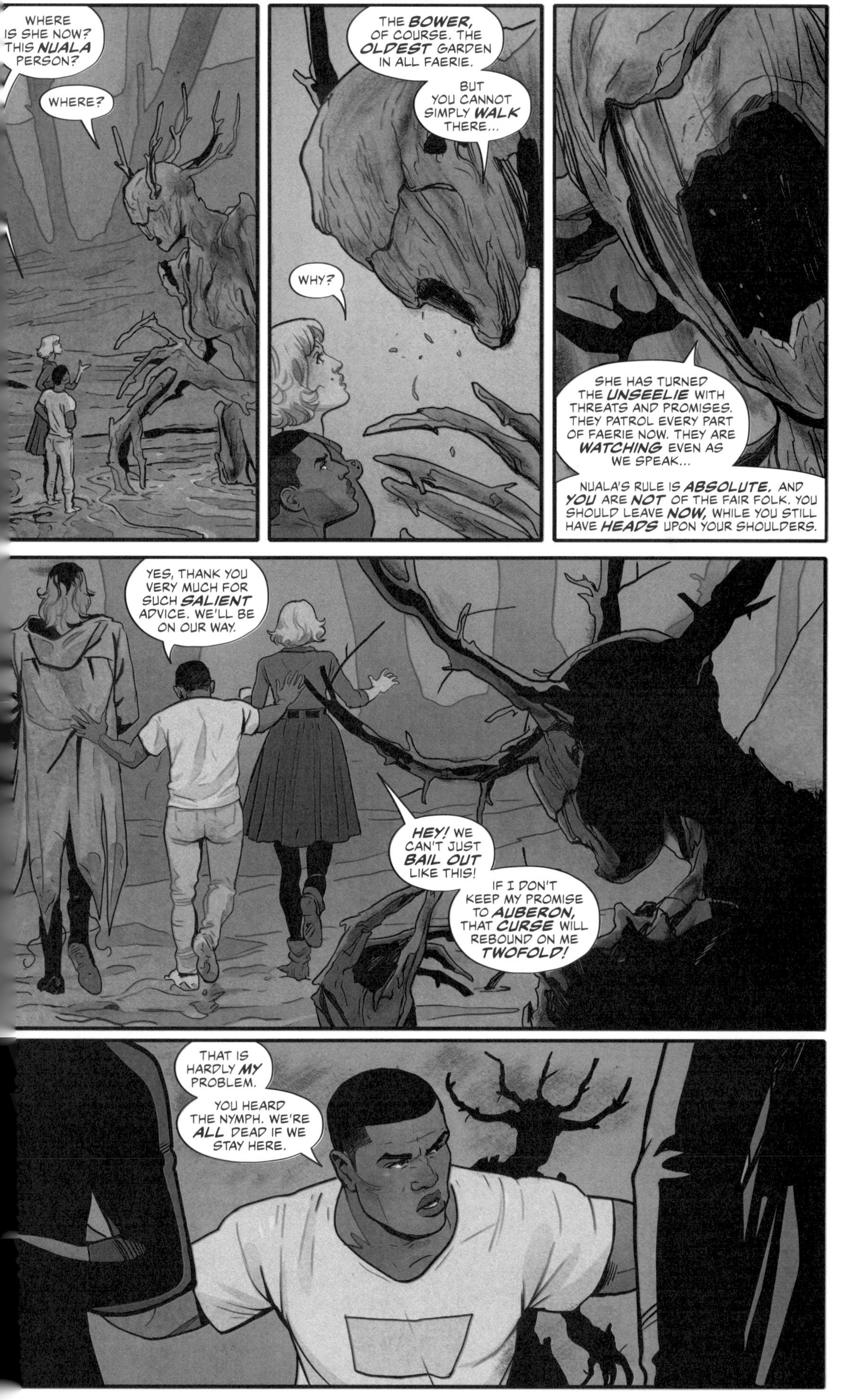
WHERE IS SHE NOW? THIS NUALA PERSON?
WHERE?
THE BOWER, OF COURSE. THE OLDEST GARDEN IN ALL FAERIE.
BUT YOU CANNOT SIMPLY WALK THERE...
WHY?
SHE HAS TURNED THE UNSEELIE WITH THREATS AND PROMISES. THEY PATROL EVERY PART OF FAERIE NOW. THEY ARE WATCHING EVEN AS WE SPEAK...
NUALA'S RULE IS ABSOLUTE, AND YOU ARE NOT OF THE FAIR FOLK. YOU SHOULD LEAVE NOW, WHILE YOU STILL HAVE HEADS UPON YOUR SHOULDERS.
YES, THANK YOU VERY MUCH FOR SUCH SALIENT ADVICE. WE'LL BE ON OUR WAY.
HEY! WE CAN'T JUST BAIL OUT LIKE THIS!
IF I DON'T KEEP MY PROMISE TO AUBERON, THAT CURSE WILL REBOUND ON ME TWOFOLD!
THAT IS HARDLY MY PROBLEM.
YOU HEARD THE NYMPH. WE'RE ALL DEAD IF WE STAY HERE.

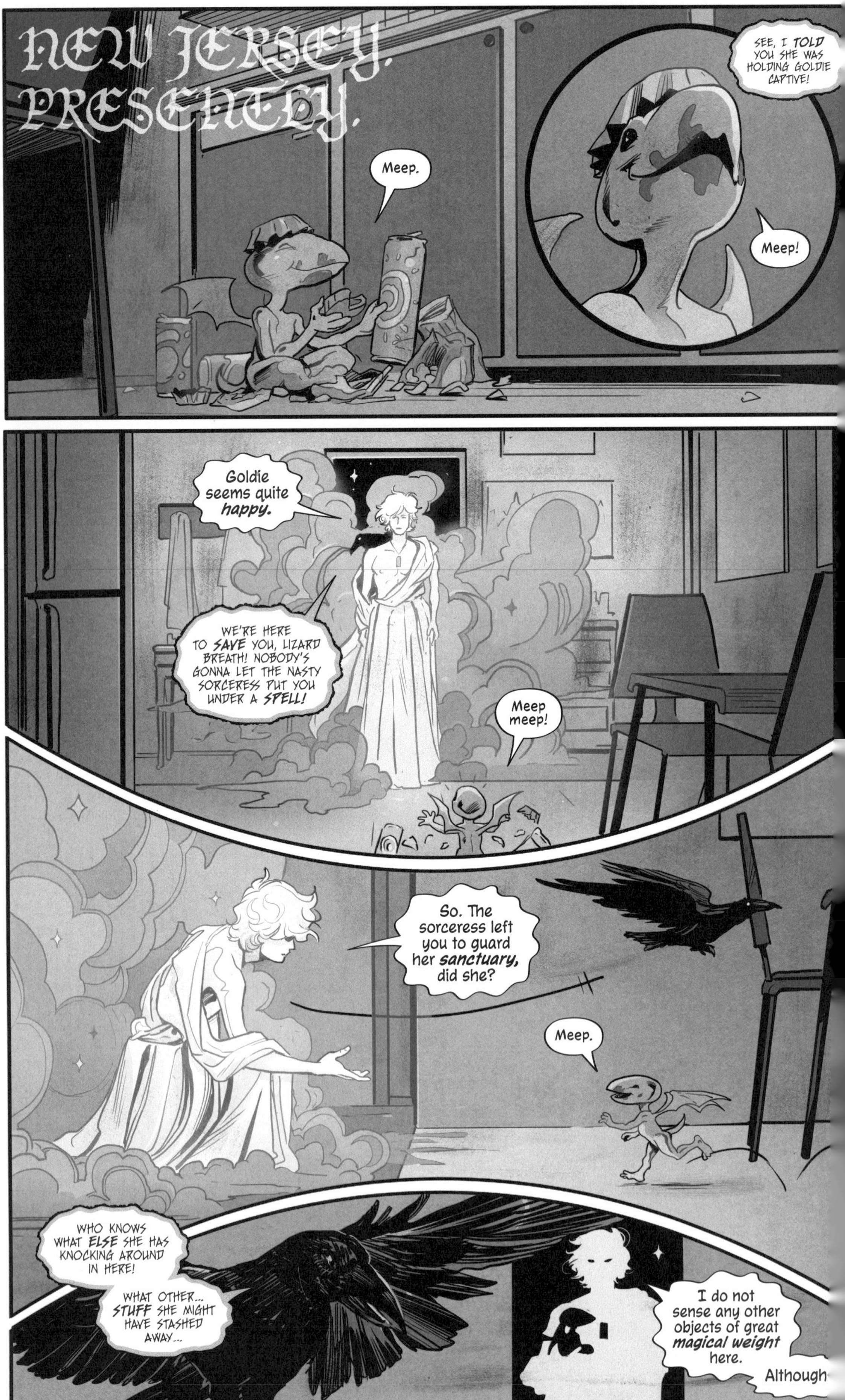
NEW JERSEY. PRESENTLY.
Meep.
SEE, I TOLD YOU SHE WAS HOLDING GOLDIE CAPTIVE!
Meep!
Goldie seems quite happy.
WE'RE HERE TO SAVE YOU, LIZARD BREATH! NOBODY'S GONNA LET THE NASTY SORCERESS PUT YOU UNDER A SPELL!
Meep meep!
So. The sorceress left you to guard her sanctuary, did she?
Meep.
WHO KNOWS WHAT ELSE SHE HAS KNOCKING AROUND IN HERE!
WHAT OTHER... STUFF SHE MIGHT HAVE STASHED AWAY...
I do not sense any other objects of great magical weight here.
Althoug

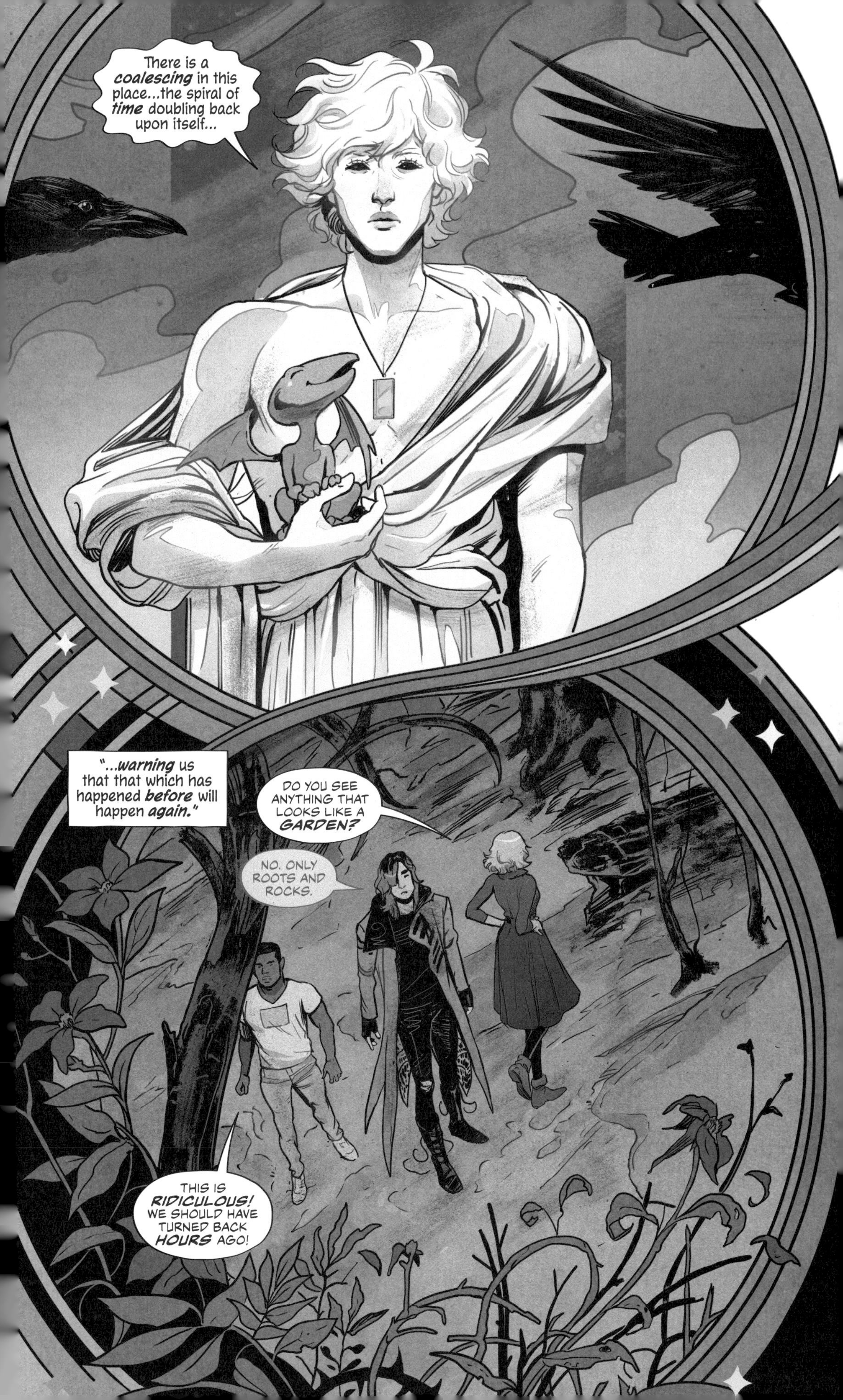
There is a *coalescing* in this place...the spiral of *time* doubling back upon itself...
"...*warning* us that that which has happened *before* will happen *again.*"
DO YOU SEE ANYTHING THAT LOOKS LIKE A *GARDEN?*
NO. ONLY ROOTS AND ROCKS.
THIS IS *RIDICULOUS!* WE SHOULD HAVE TURNED BACK *HOURS* AGO!

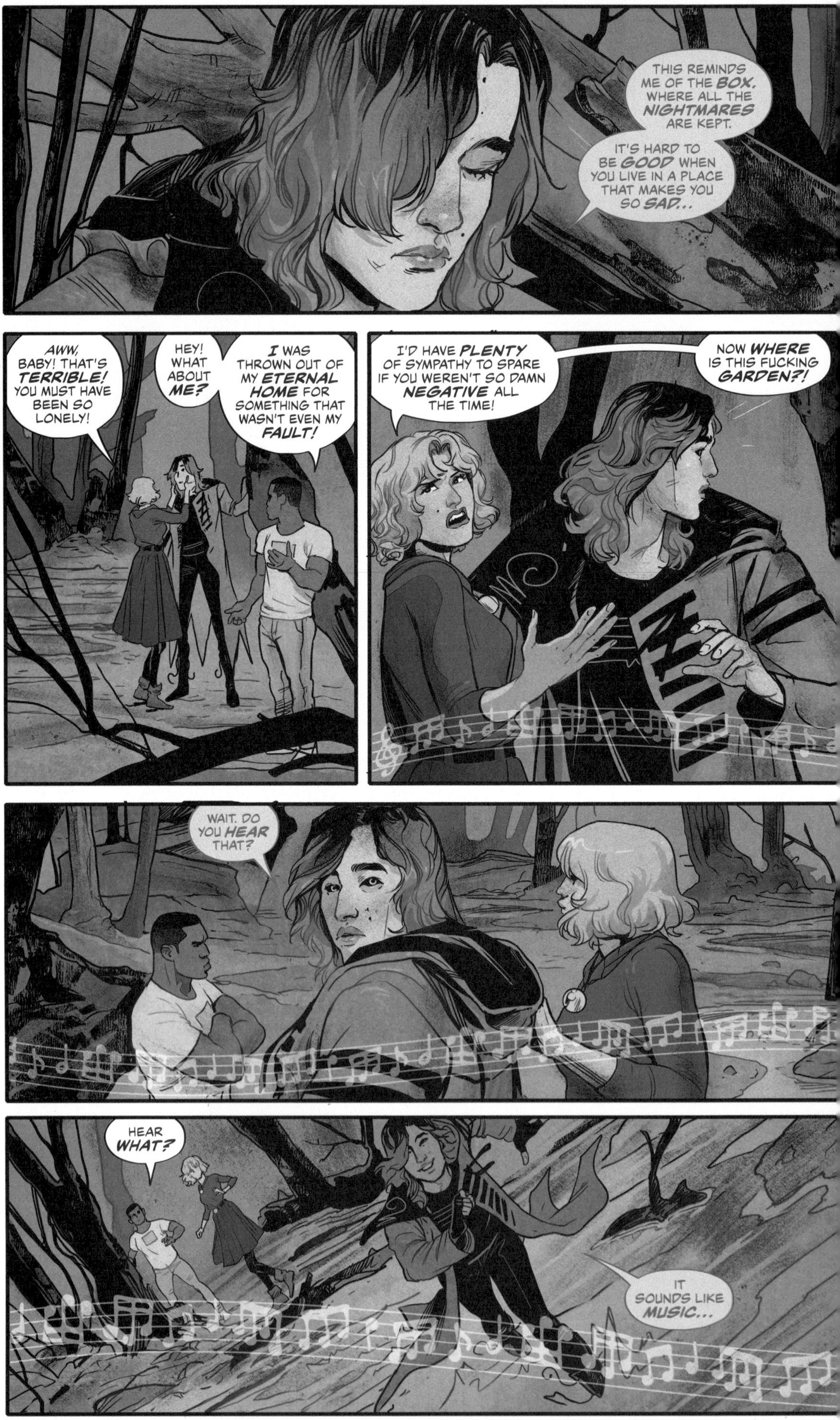
THIS REMINDS ME OF THE BOX. WHERE ALL THE NIGHTMARES ARE KEPT.
IT'S HARD TO BE GOOD WHEN YOU LIVE IN A PLACE THAT MAKES YOU SO SAD...
AWW, BABY! THAT'S TERRIBLE! YOU MUST HAVE BEEN SO LONELY!
HEY! WHAT ABOUT ME?
I WAS THROWN OUT OF MY ETERNAL HOME FOR SOMETHING THAT WASN'T EVEN MY FAULT!
I'D HAVE PLENTY OF SYMPATHY TO SPARE IF YOU WEREN'T SO DAMN NEGATIVE ALL THE TIME!
NOW WHERE IS THIS FUCKING GARDEN?!
WAIT. DO YOU HEAR THAT?
HEAR WHAT?
IT SOUNDS LIKE MUSIC...

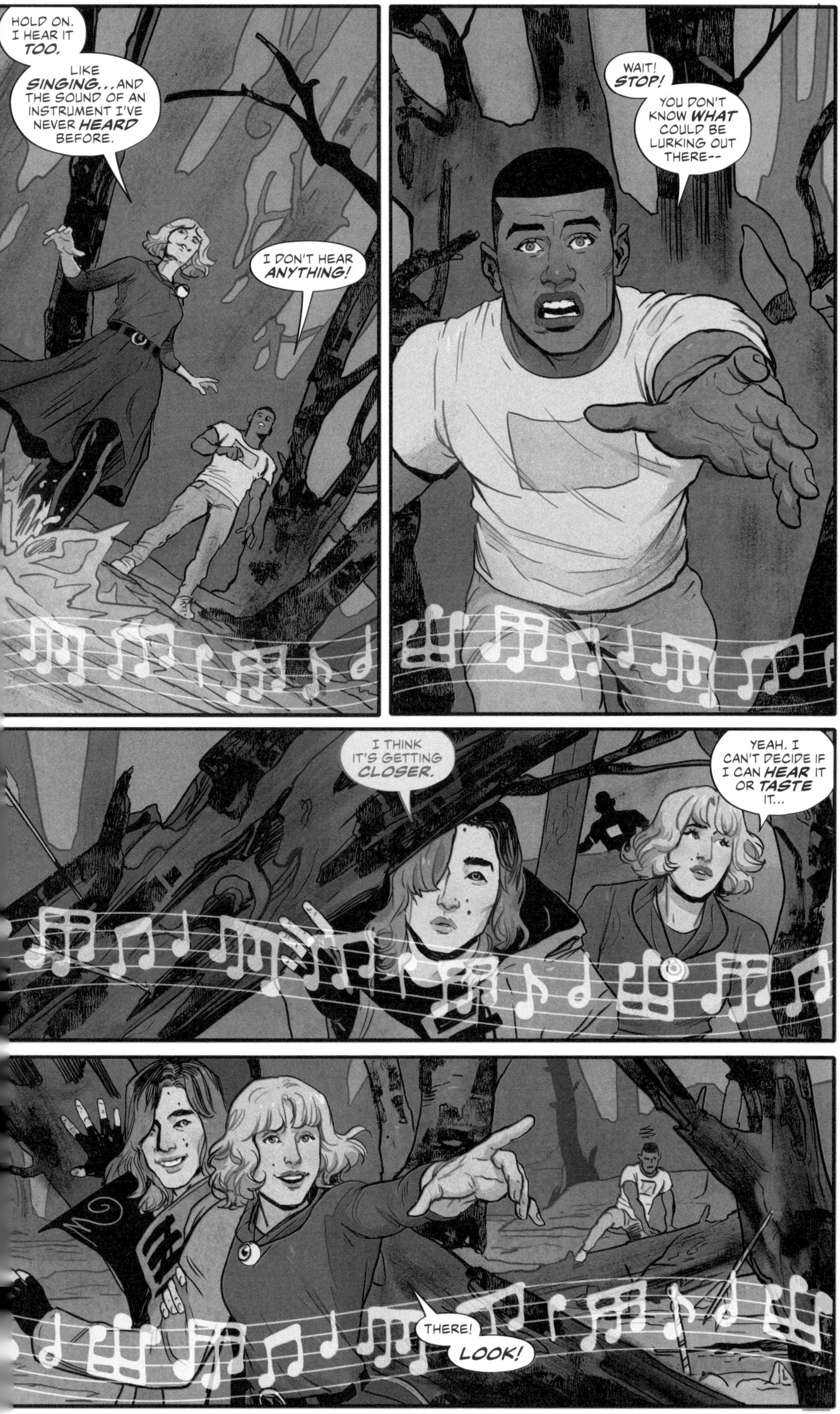
HOLD ON. I HEAR IT TOO.
LIKE SINGING...AND THE SOUND OF AN INSTRUMENT I'VE NEVER HEARD BEFORE.
I DON'T HEAR ANYTHING!
WAIT! STOP!
YOU DON'T KNOW WHAT COULD BE LURKING OUT THERE--
I THINK IT'S GETTING CLOSER.
YEAH. I CAN'T DECIDE IF I CAN HEAR IT OR TASTE IT...
THERE!
LOOK!

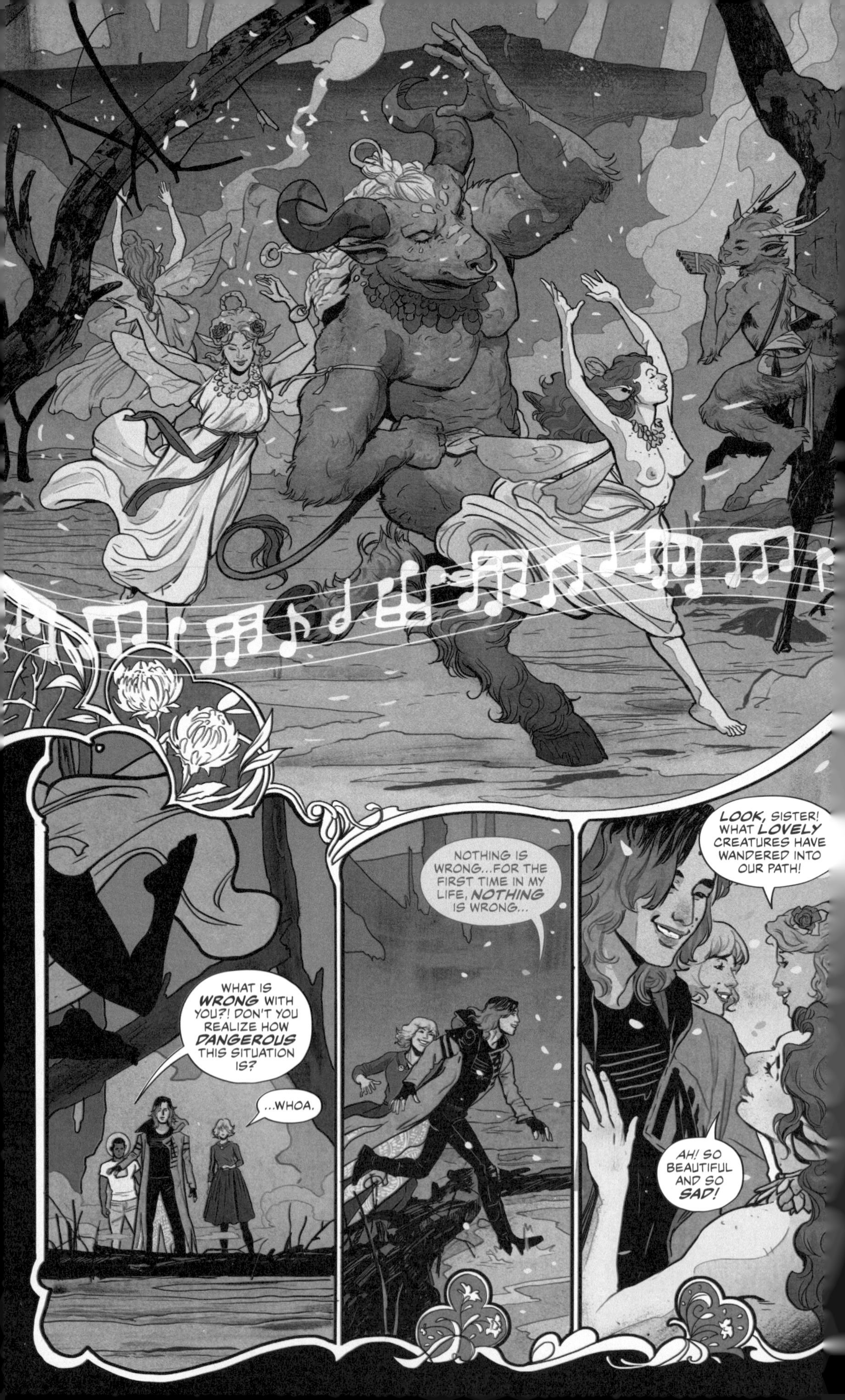
WHAT IS WRONG WITH YOU?! DON'T YOU REALIZE HOW DANGEROUS THIS SITUATION IS?
...WHOA.
NOTHING IS WRONG...FOR THE FIRST TIME IN MY LIFE, NOTHING IS WRONG...
LOOK, SISTER! WHAT LOVELY CREATURES HAVE WANDERED INTO OUR PATH!
AH! SO BEAUTIFUL AND SO SAD!

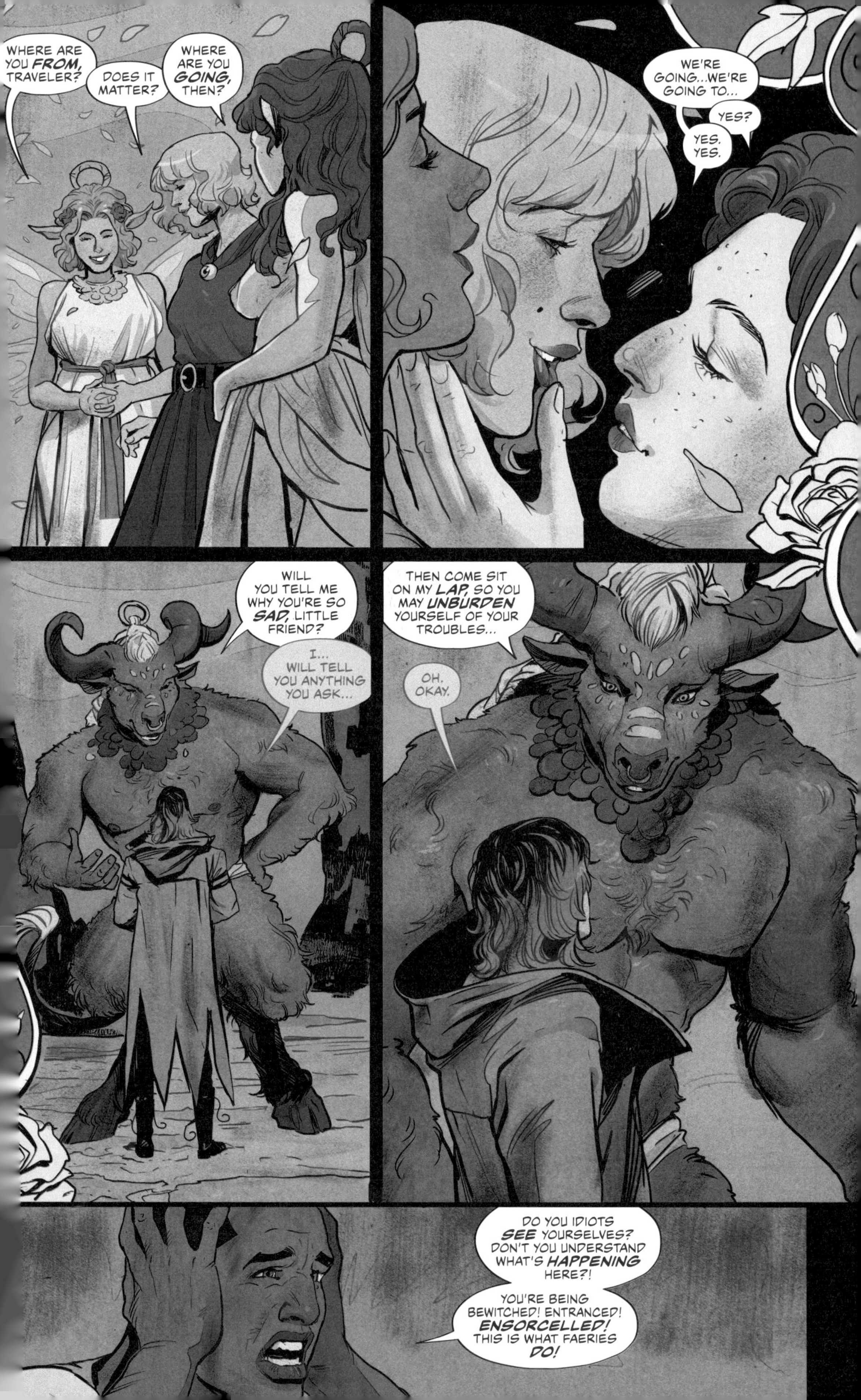
WHERE ARE YOU FROM, TRAVELER?
DOES IT MATTER?
WHERE ARE YOU GOING, THEN?
WE'RE GOING...WE'RE GOING TO...
YES?
YES. YES.
WILL YOU TELL ME WHY YOU'RE SO SAD, LITTLE FRIEND?
I... WILL TELL YOU ANYTHING YOU ASK...
THEN COME SIT ON MY LAP, SO YOU MAY UNBURDEN YOURSELF OF YOUR TROUBLES...
OH. OKAY.
DO YOU IDIOTS SEE YOURSELVES? DON'T YOU UNDERSTAND WHAT'S HAPPENING HERE?!
YOU'RE BEING BEWITCHED! ENTRANCED! ENSORCELLED! THIS IS WHAT FAERIES DO!

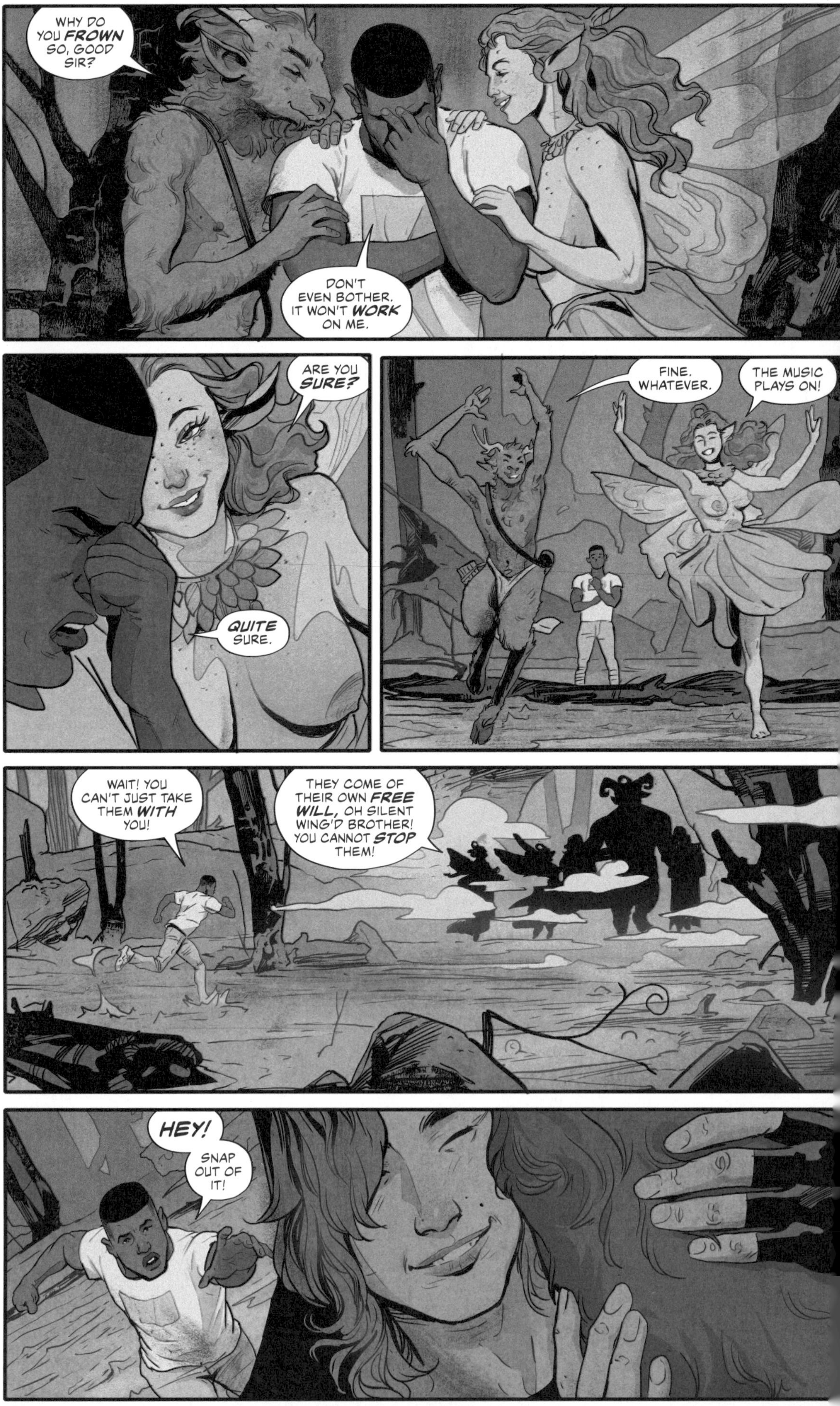
WHY DO YOU **FROWN** SO, GOOD SIR?
DON'T EVEN BOTHER. IT WON'T **WORK** ON ME.
ARE YOU **SURE?**
QUITE SURE.
FINE. WHATEVER.
THE MUSIC PLAYS ON!
WAIT! YOU CAN'T JUST TAKE THEM **WITH** YOU!
THEY COME OF THEIR OWN **FREE WILL,** OH SILENT WING'D BROTHER! YOU CANNOT **STOP** THEM!
HEY!
SNAP OUT OF IT!

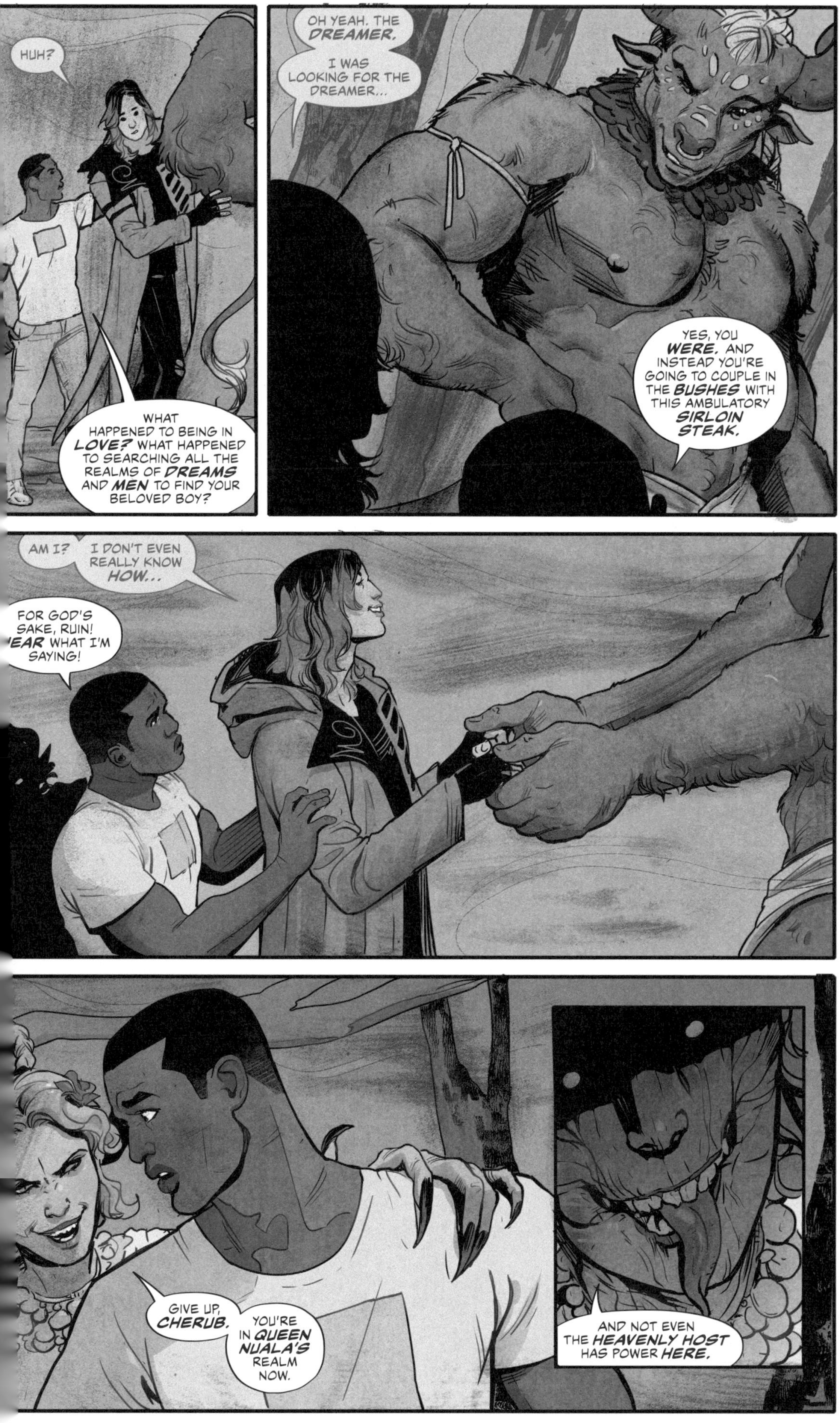
HUH?
WHAT HAPPENED TO BEING IN LOVE? WHAT HAPPENED TO SEARCHING ALL THE REALMS OF DREAMS AND MEN TO FIND YOUR BELOVED BOY?
OH YEAH. THE DREAMER.
I WAS LOOKING FOR THE DREAMER...
YES, YOU WERE. AND INSTEAD YOU'RE GOING TO COUPLE IN THE BUSHES WITH THIS AMBULATORY SIRLOIN STEAK.
AM I?
I DON'T EVEN REALLY KNOW HOW...
FOR GOD'S SAKE, RUIN! HEAR WHAT I'M SAYING!
GIVE UP, CHERUB.
YOU'RE IN QUEEN NUALA'S REALM NOW.
AND NOT EVEN THE HEAVENLY HOST HAS POWER HERE.

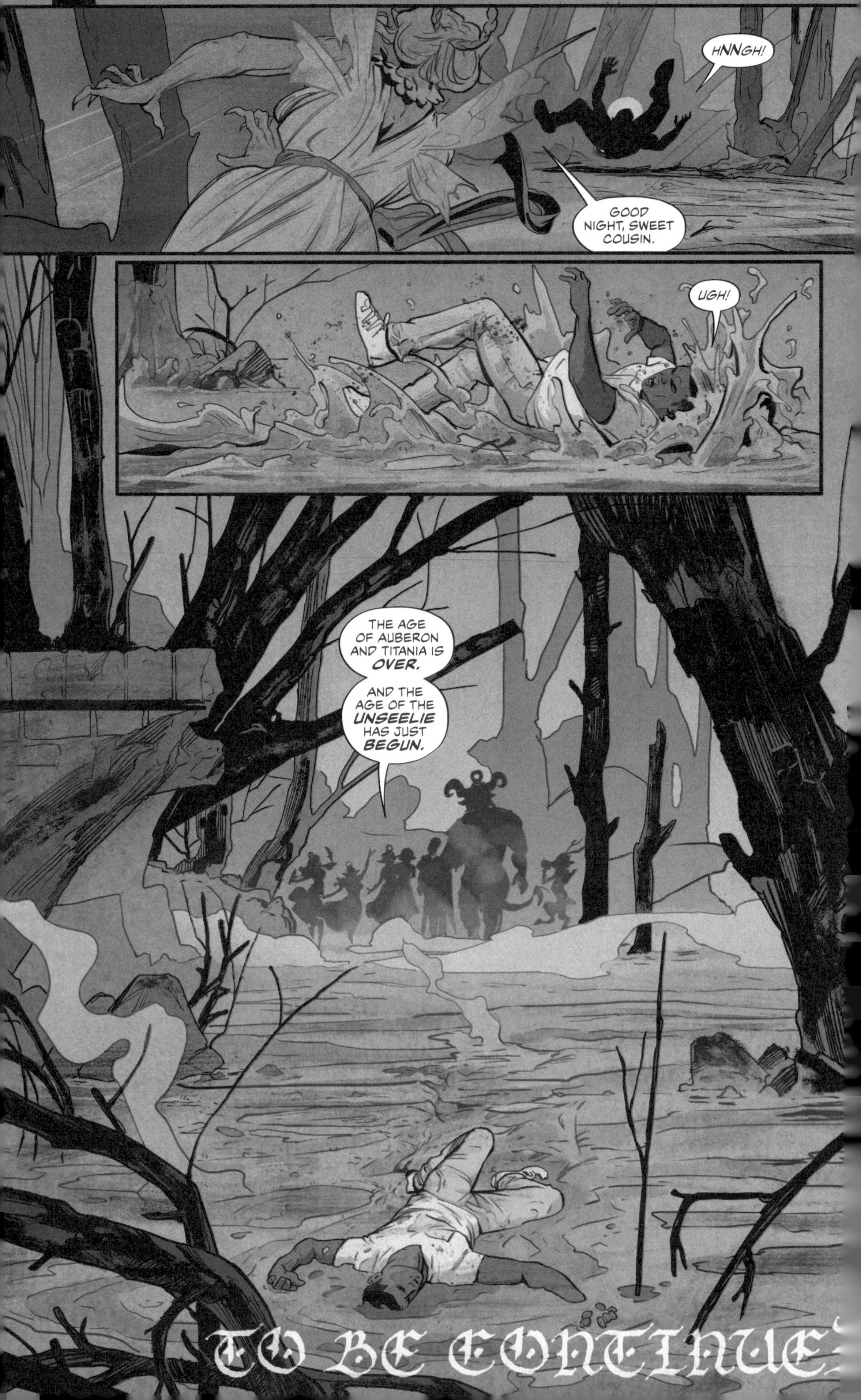
HNNGH!
GOOD NIGHT, SWEET COUSIN.
UGH!
THE AGE OF AUBERON AND TITANIA IS OVER.
AND THE AGE OF THE UNSEELIE HAS JUST BEGUN.
TO BE CONTINUE

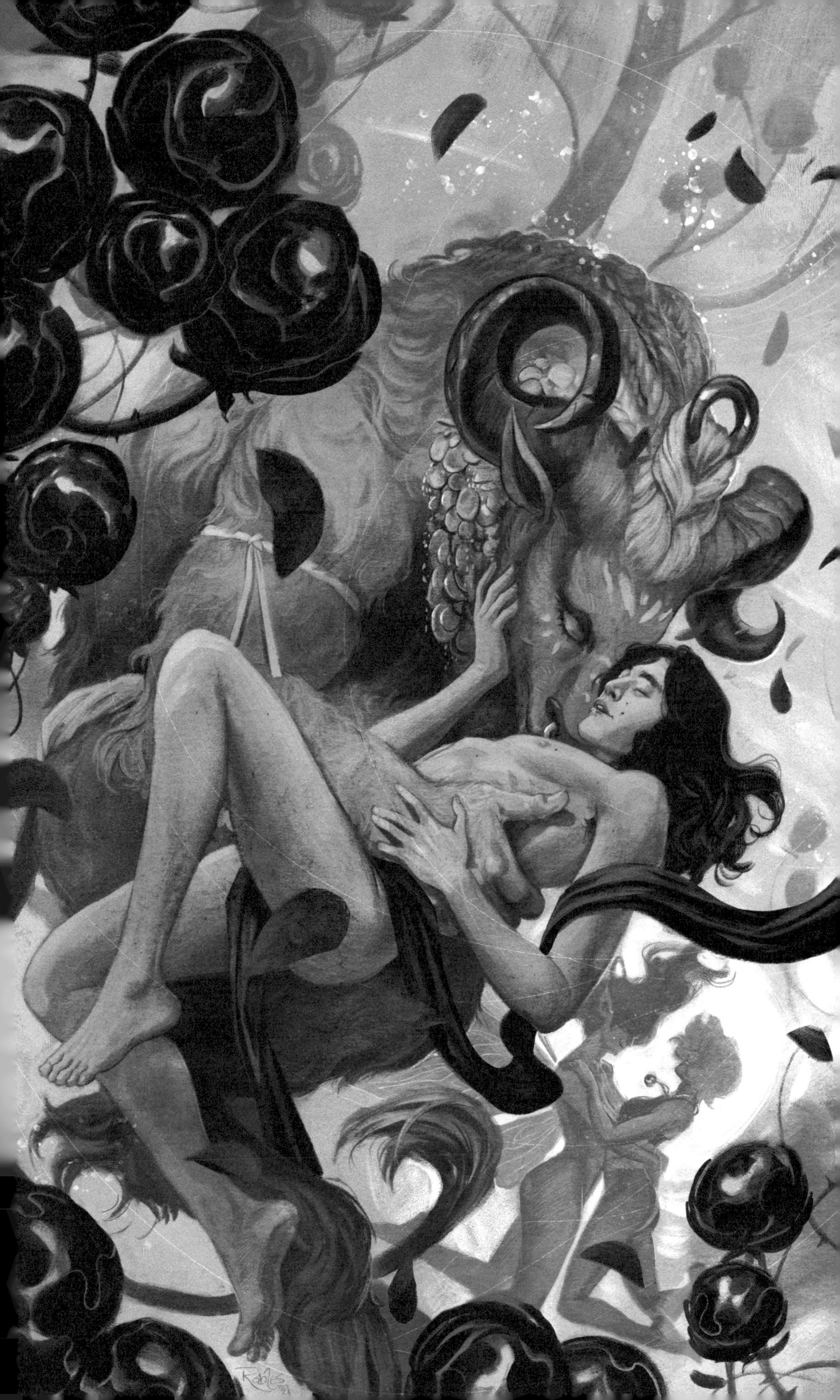

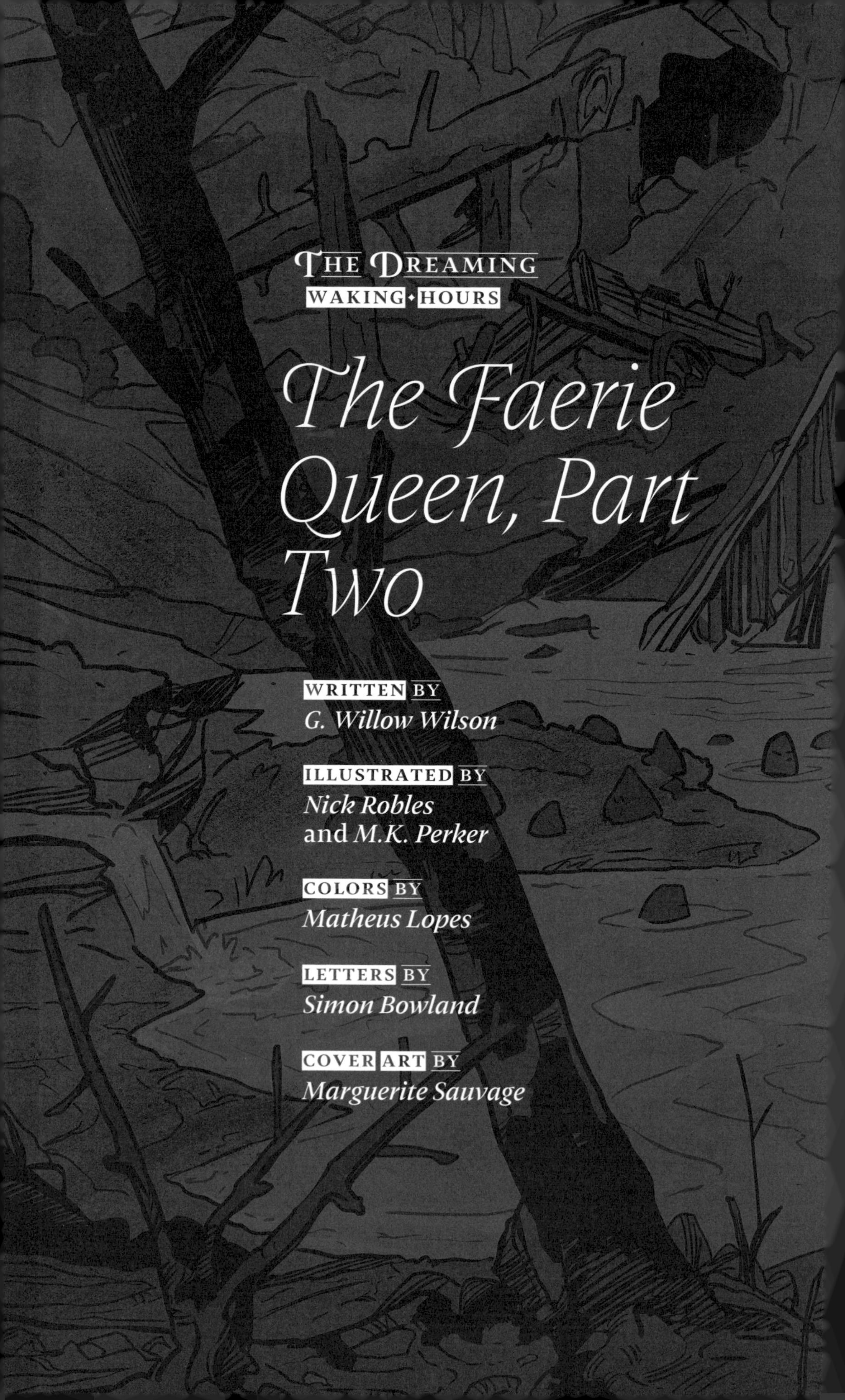

THE DREAMING
WAKING • HOURS

The Faerie Queen, Part Two

WRITTEN BY
G. Willow Wilson

ILLUSTRATED BY
Nick Robles
and *M.K. Perker*

COLORS BY
Matheus Lopes

LETTERS BY
Simon Bowland

COVER ART BY
Marguerite Sauvage

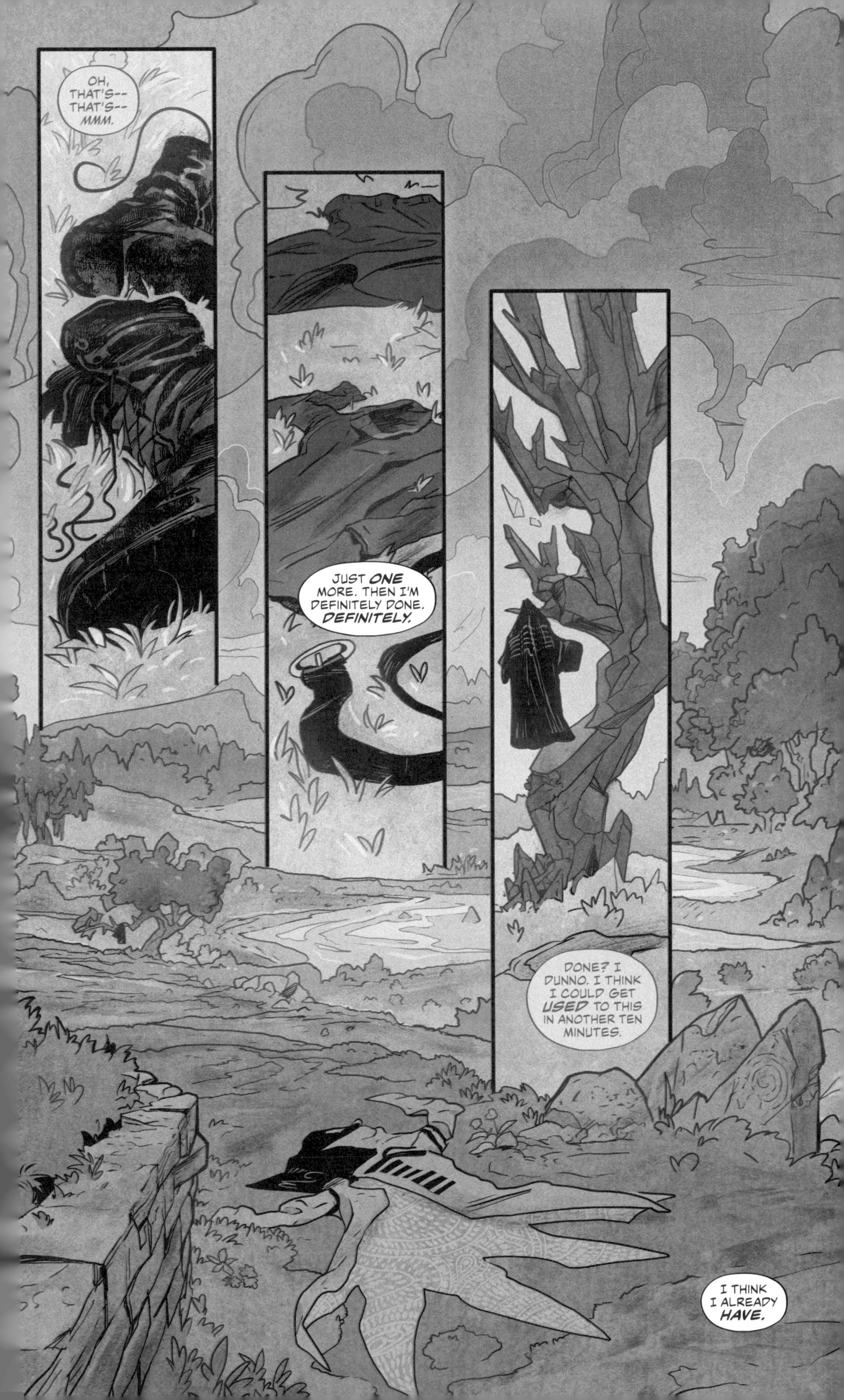
OH, THAT'S-- THAT'S-- MMM.
JUST ONE MORE. THEN I'M DEFINITELY DONE. DEFINITELY.
DONE? I DUNNO. I THINK I COULD GET USED TO THIS IN ANOTHER TEN MINUTES.
I THINK I ALREADY HAVE.

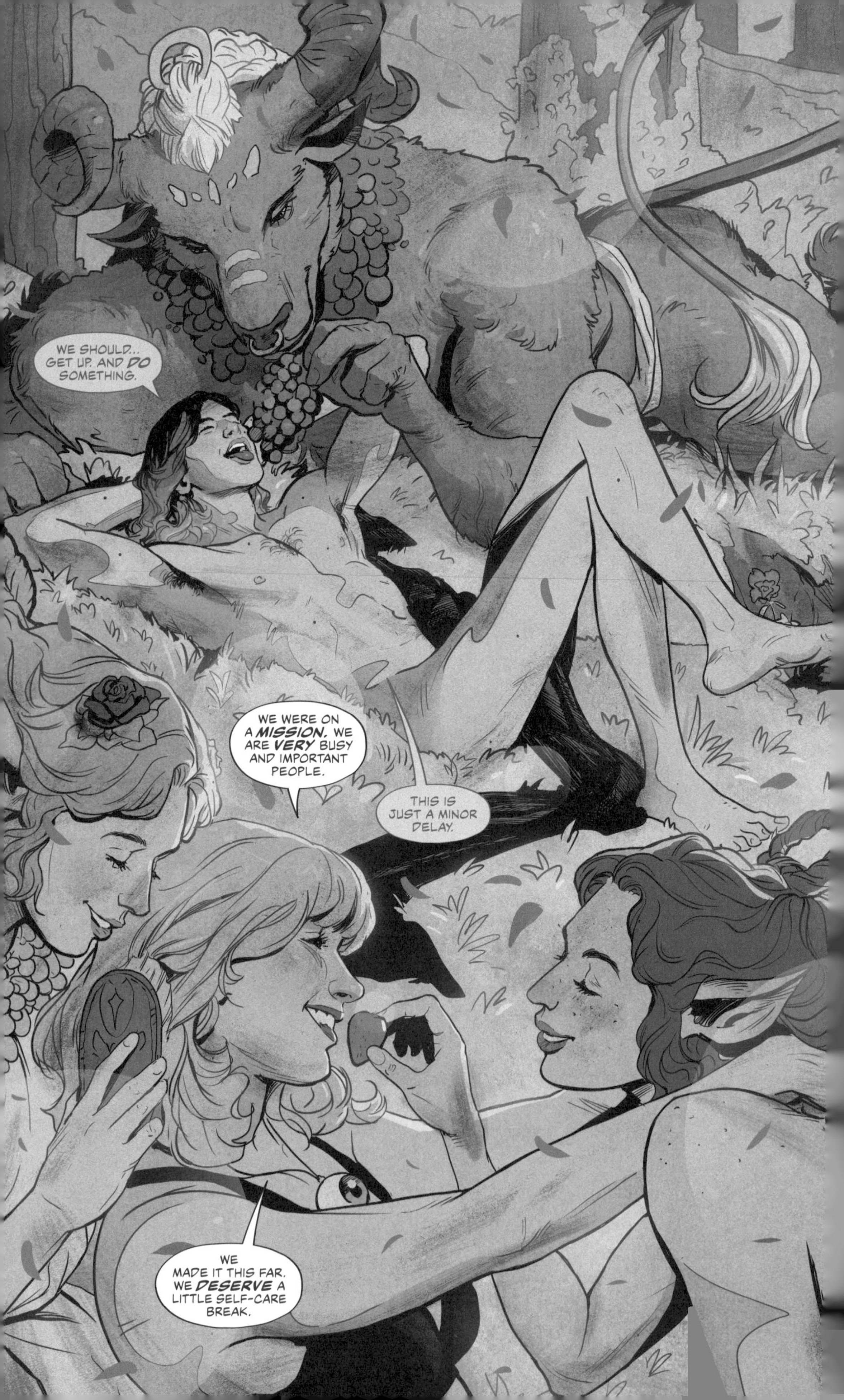

WE SHOULD... GET UP. AND DO SOMETHING.
WE WERE ON A MISSION. WE ARE VERY BUSY AND IMPORTANT PEOPLE.
THIS IS JUST A MINOR DELAY.
WE MADE IT THIS FAR. WE DESERVE A LITTLE SELF-CARE BREAK.

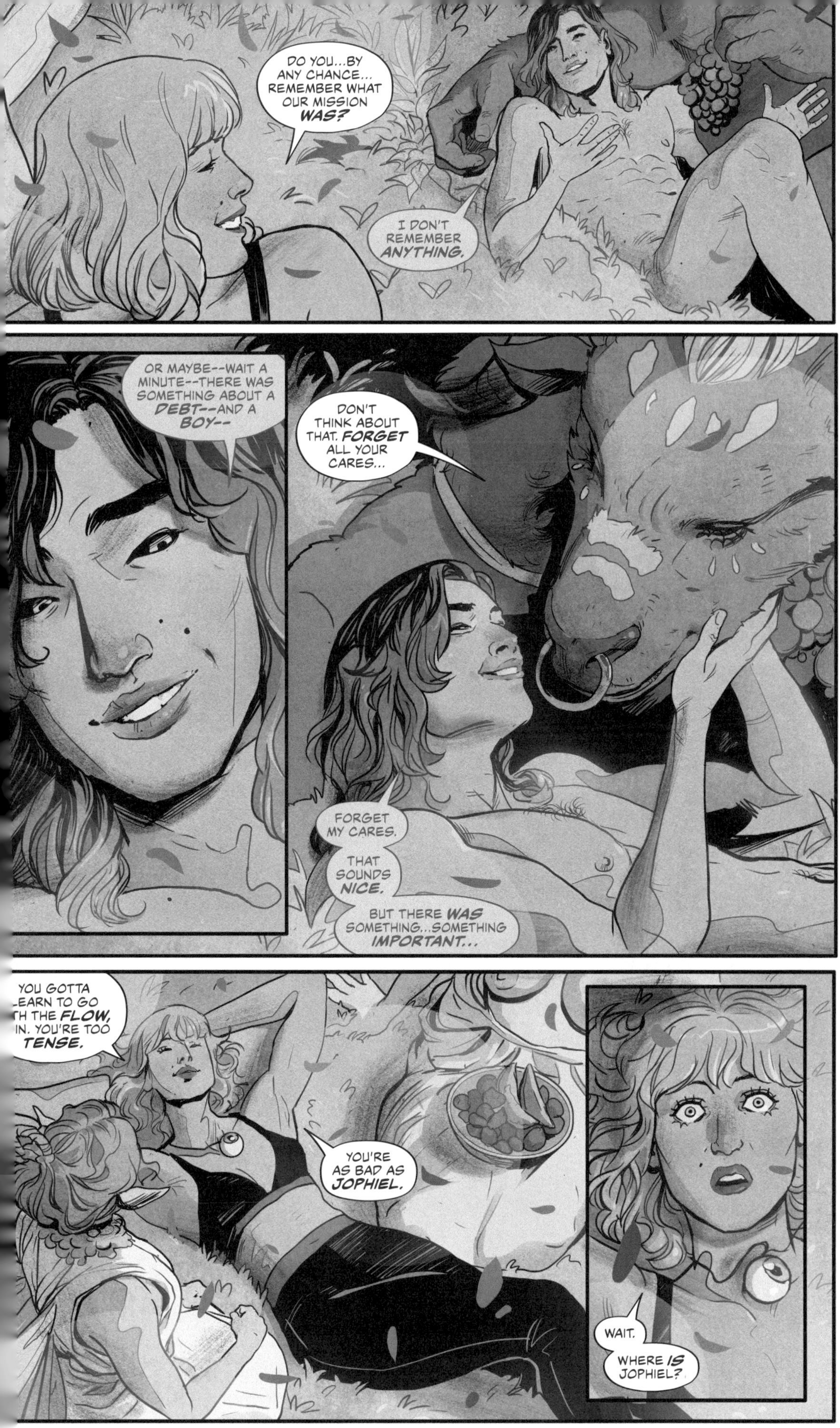
DO YOU...BY ANY CHANCE... REMEMBER WHAT OUR MISSION WAS?
I DON'T REMEMBER ANYTHING.
OR MAYBE--WAIT A MINUTE--THERE WAS SOMETHING ABOUT A DEBT--AND A BOY--
DON'T THINK ABOUT THAT. FORGET ALL YOUR CARES...
FORGET MY CARES.
THAT SOUNDS NICE.
BUT THERE WAS SOMETHING...SOMETHING IMPORTANT...
YOU GOTTA LEARN TO GO WITH THE FLOW, IN. YOU'RE TOO TENSE.
YOU'RE AS BAD AS JOPHIEL.
WAIT.
WHERE IS JOPHIEL?

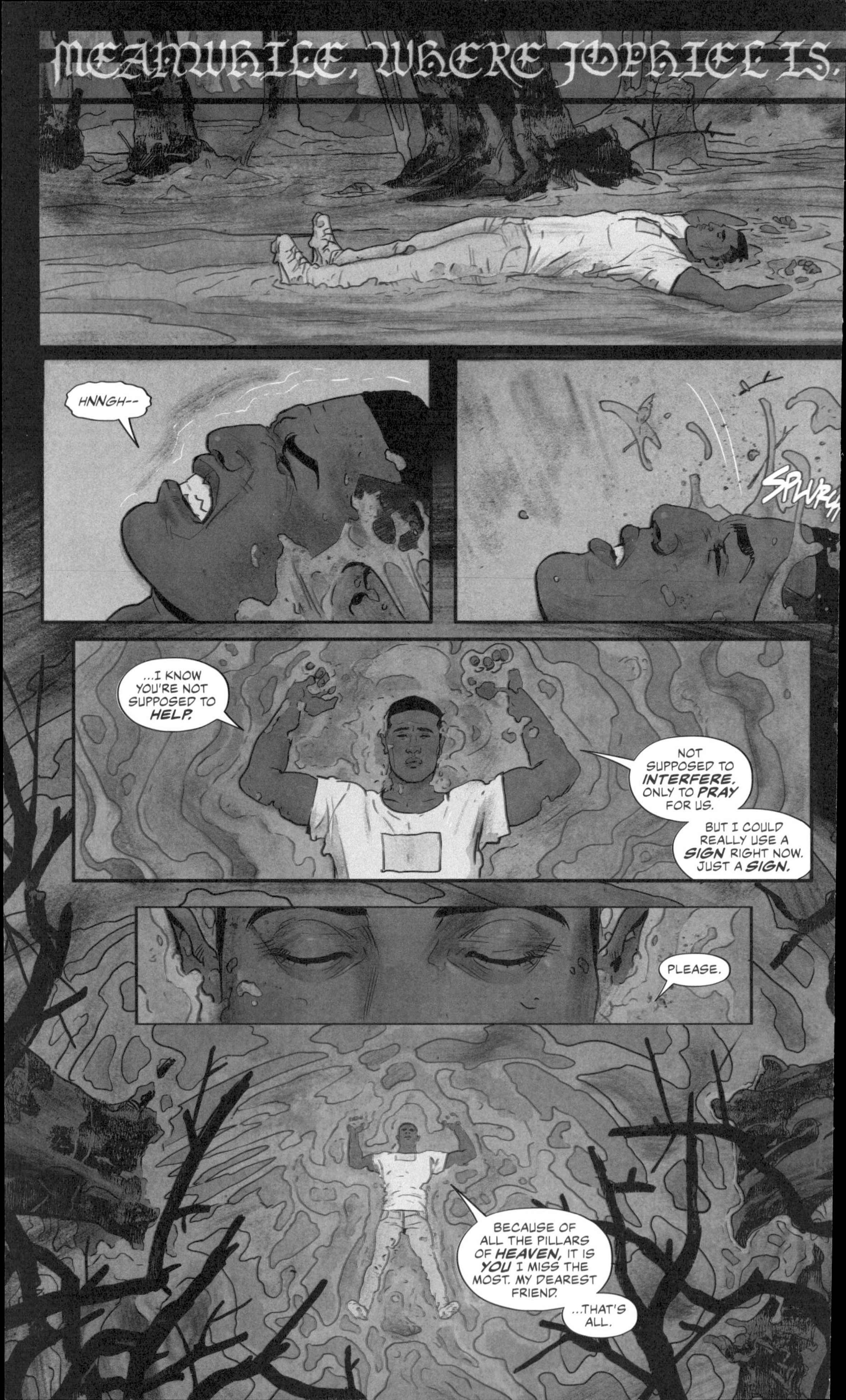
MEANWHILE, WHERE JOPHIEL IS.
HNNGH--
SPLURCH
...I KNOW YOU'RE NOT SUPPOSED TO HELP.
NOT SUPPOSED TO INTERFERE. ONLY TO PRAY FOR US.
BUT I COULD REALLY USE A SIGN RIGHT NOW. JUST A SIGN.
PLEASE.
BECAUSE OF ALL THE PILLARS OF HEAVEN, IT IS YOU I MISS THE MOST. MY DEAREST FRIEND.
...THAT'S ALL.

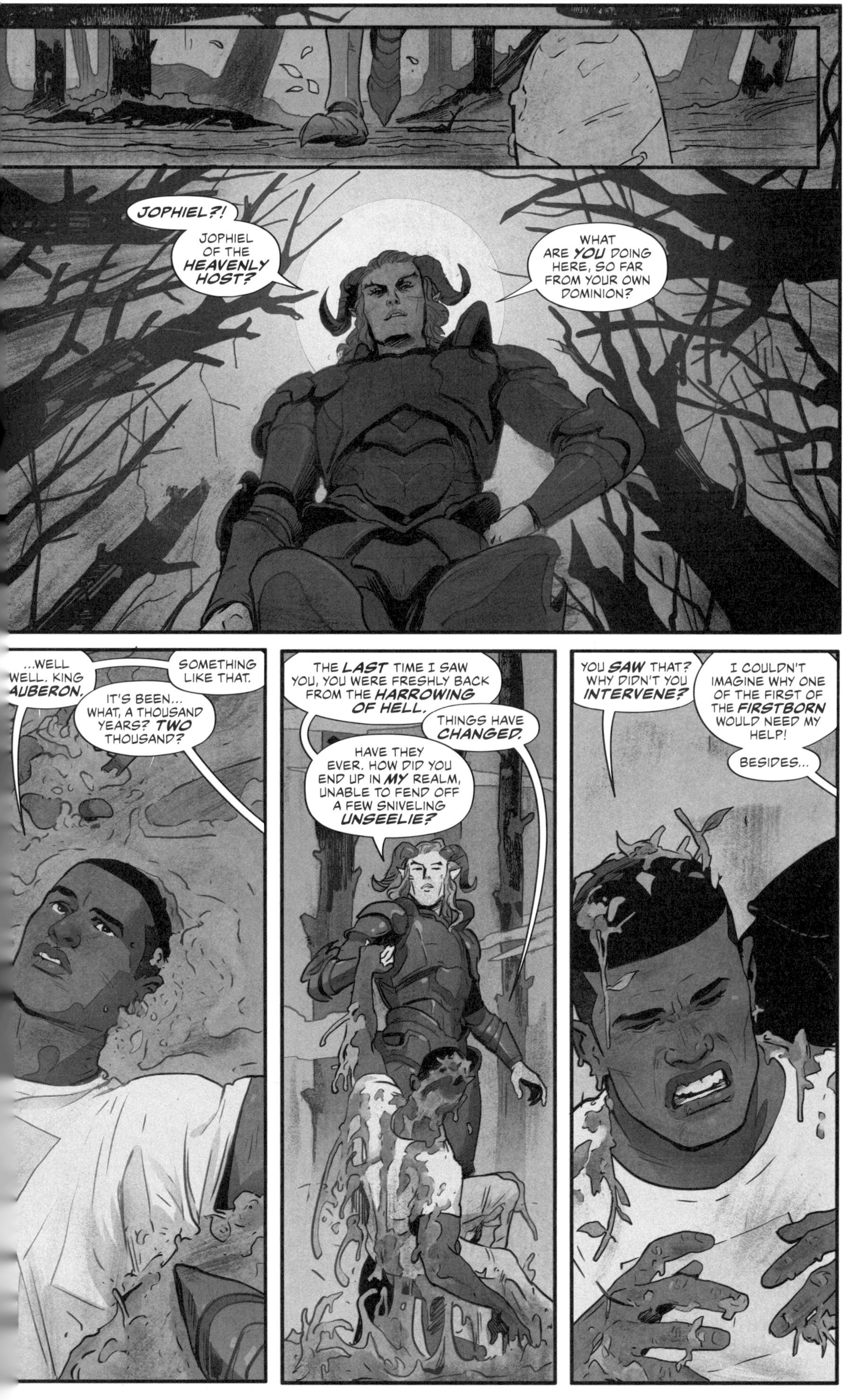
JOPHIEL?!
JOPHIEL OF THE HEAVENLY HOST?
WHAT ARE YOU DOING HERE, SO FAR FROM YOUR OWN DOMINION?
...WELL WELL. KING AUBERON.
SOMETHING LIKE THAT.
IT'S BEEN... WHAT, A THOUSAND YEARS? TWO THOUSAND?
THE LAST TIME I SAW YOU, YOU WERE FRESHLY BACK FROM THE HARROWING OF HELL.
THINGS HAVE CHANGED.
HAVE THEY EVER. HOW DID YOU END UP IN MY REALM, UNABLE TO FEND OFF A FEW SNIVELING UNSEELIE?
YOU SAW THAT? WHY DIDN'T YOU INTERVENE?
I COULDN'T IMAGINE WHY ONE OF THE FIRST OF THE FIRSTBORN WOULD NEED MY HELP!
BESIDES...

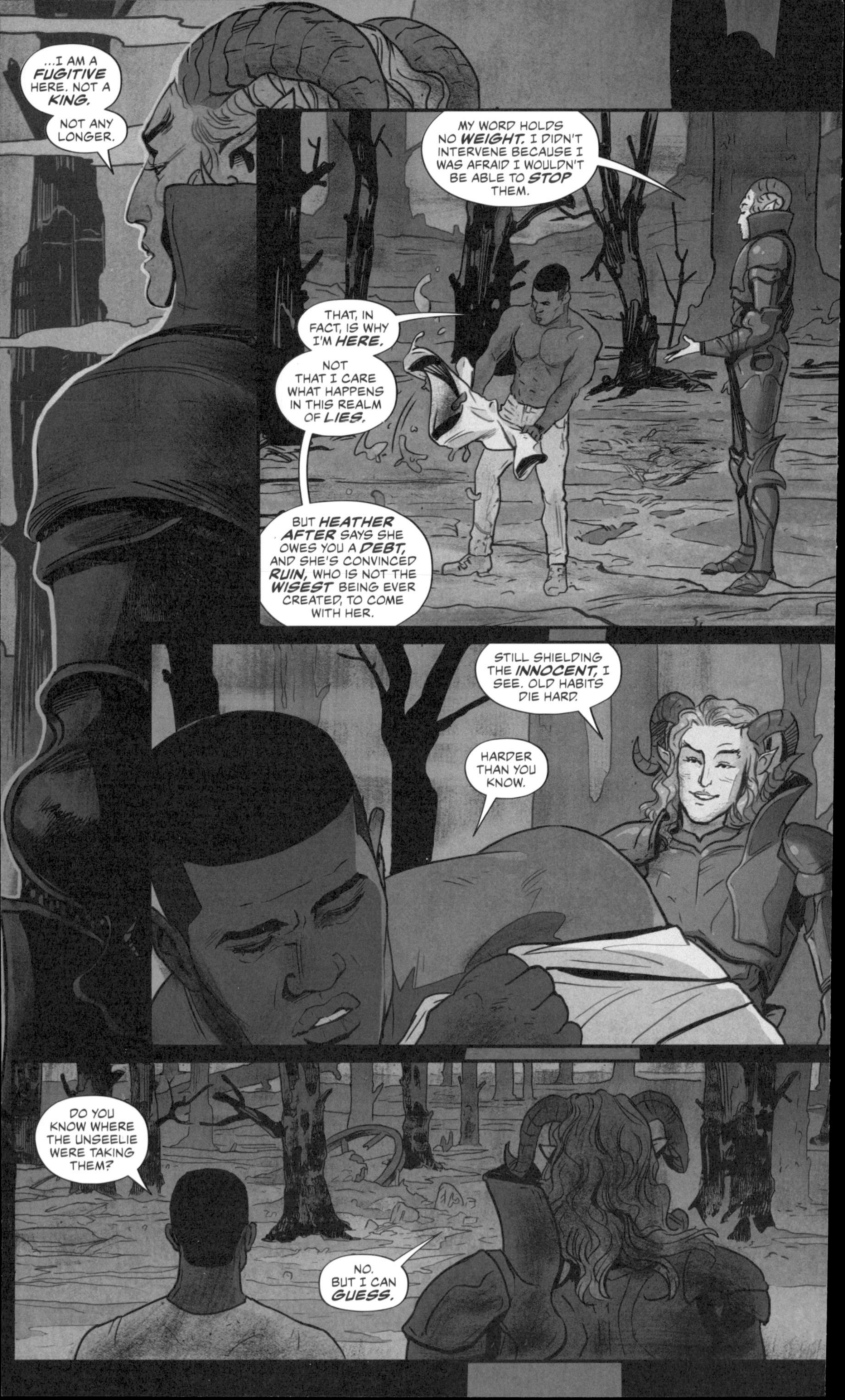
...I AM A *FUGITIVE* HERE. NOT A *KING.*
NOT ANY LONGER.
MY WORD HOLDS NO *WEIGHT.* I DIDN'T INTERVENE BECAUSE I WAS AFRAID I WOULDN'T BE ABLE TO *STOP* THEM.
THAT, IN FACT, IS WHY I'M *HERE.*
NOT THAT I CARE WHAT HAPPENS IN THIS REALM OF *LIES.*
BUT *HEATHER AFTER* SAYS SHE OWES YOU A *DEBT,* AND SHE'S CONVINCED *RUIN,* WHO IS NOT THE *WISEST* BEING EVER CREATED, TO COME WITH HER.
STILL SHIELDING THE *INNOCENT,* I SEE. OLD HABITS DIE HARD.
HARDER THAN YOU KNOW.
DO YOU KNOW WHERE THE UNSEELIE WERE TAKING THEM?
NO. BUT I CAN *GUESS.*

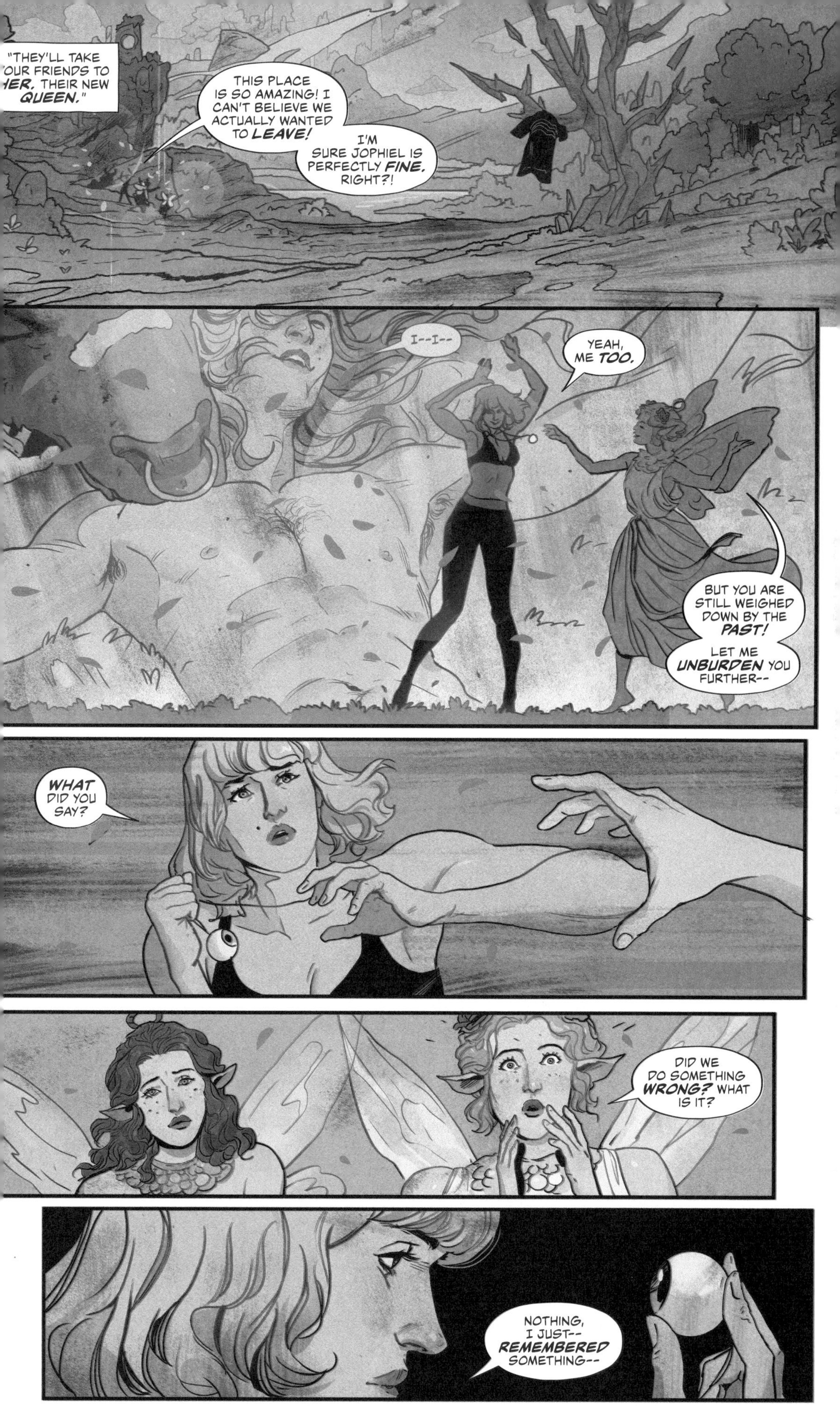
"THEY'LL TAKE OUR FRIENDS TO HER, THEIR NEW QUEEN."
THIS PLACE IS SO AMAZING! I CAN'T BELIEVE WE ACTUALLY WANTED TO LEAVE!
I'M SURE JOPHIEL IS PERFECTLY FINE. RIGHT?!
I--I--
YEAH, ME TOO.
BUT YOU ARE STILL WEIGHED DOWN BY THE PAST!
LET ME UNBURDEN YOU FURTHER--
WHAT DID YOU SAY?
DID WE DO SOMETHING WRONG? WHAT IS IT?
NOTHING, I JUST-- REMEMBERED SOMETHING--

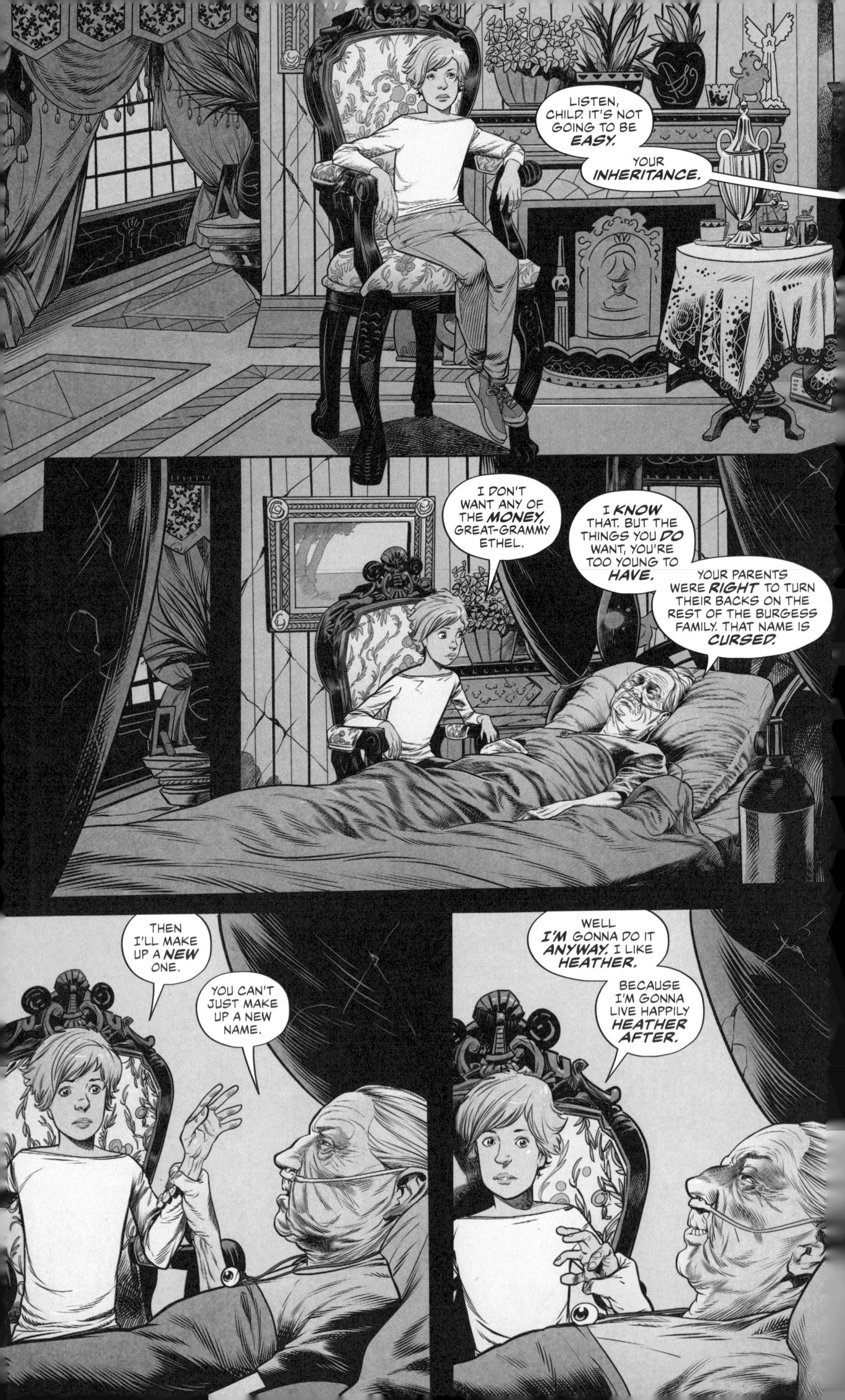
LISTEN, CHILD. IT'S NOT GOING TO BE EASY.
YOUR INHERITANCE.
I DON'T WANT ANY OF THE MONEY, GREAT-GRAMMY ETHEL.
I KNOW THAT. BUT THE THINGS YOU DO WANT, YOU'RE TOO YOUNG TO HAVE.
YOUR PARENTS WERE RIGHT TO TURN THEIR BACKS ON THE REST OF THE BURGESS FAMILY. THAT NAME IS CURSED.
THEN I'LL MAKE UP A NEW ONE.
YOU CAN'T JUST MAKE UP A NEW NAME.
WELL I'M GONNA DO IT ANYWAY. I LIKE HEATHER.
BECAUSE I'M GONNA LIVE HAPPILY HEATHER AFTER.

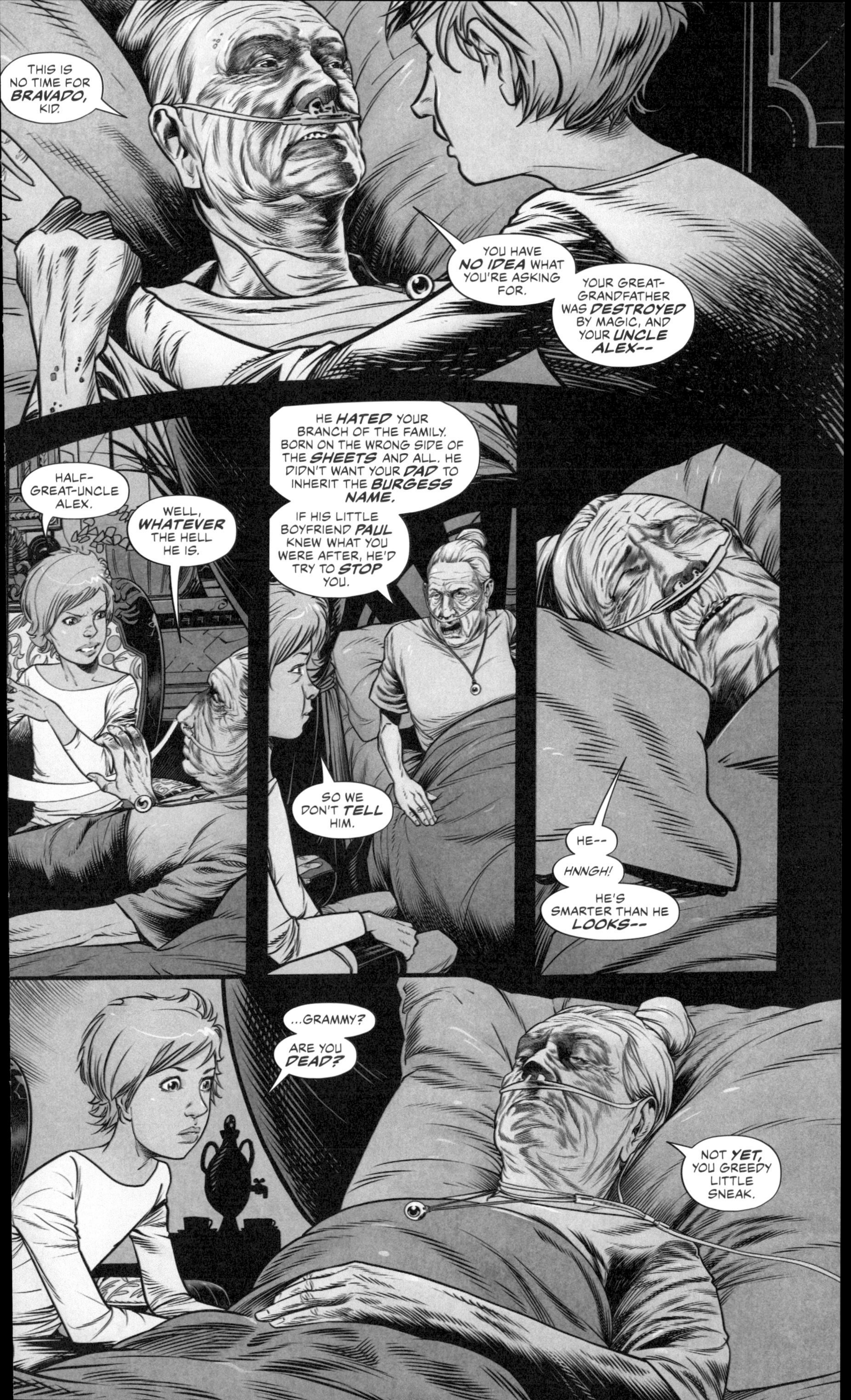
THIS IS NO TIME FOR BRAVADO, KID.
YOU HAVE NO IDEA WHAT YOU'RE ASKING FOR.
YOUR GREAT-GRANDFATHER WAS DESTROYED BY MAGIC, AND YOUR UNCLE ALEX--
HALF-GREAT-UNCLE ALEX.
WELL, WHATEVER THE HELL HE IS.
HE HATED YOUR BRANCH OF THE FAMILY. BORN ON THE WRONG SIDE OF THE SHEETS AND ALL. HE DIDN'T WANT YOUR DAD TO INHERIT THE BURGESS NAME.
IF HIS LITTLE BOYFRIEND PAUL KNEW WHAT YOU WERE AFTER, HE'D TRY TO STOP YOU.
SO WE DON'T TELL HIM.
HE--
HNNGH!
HE'S SMARTER THAN HE LOOKS--
...GRAMMY?
ARE YOU DEAD?
NOT YET, YOU GREEDY LITTLE SNEAK.

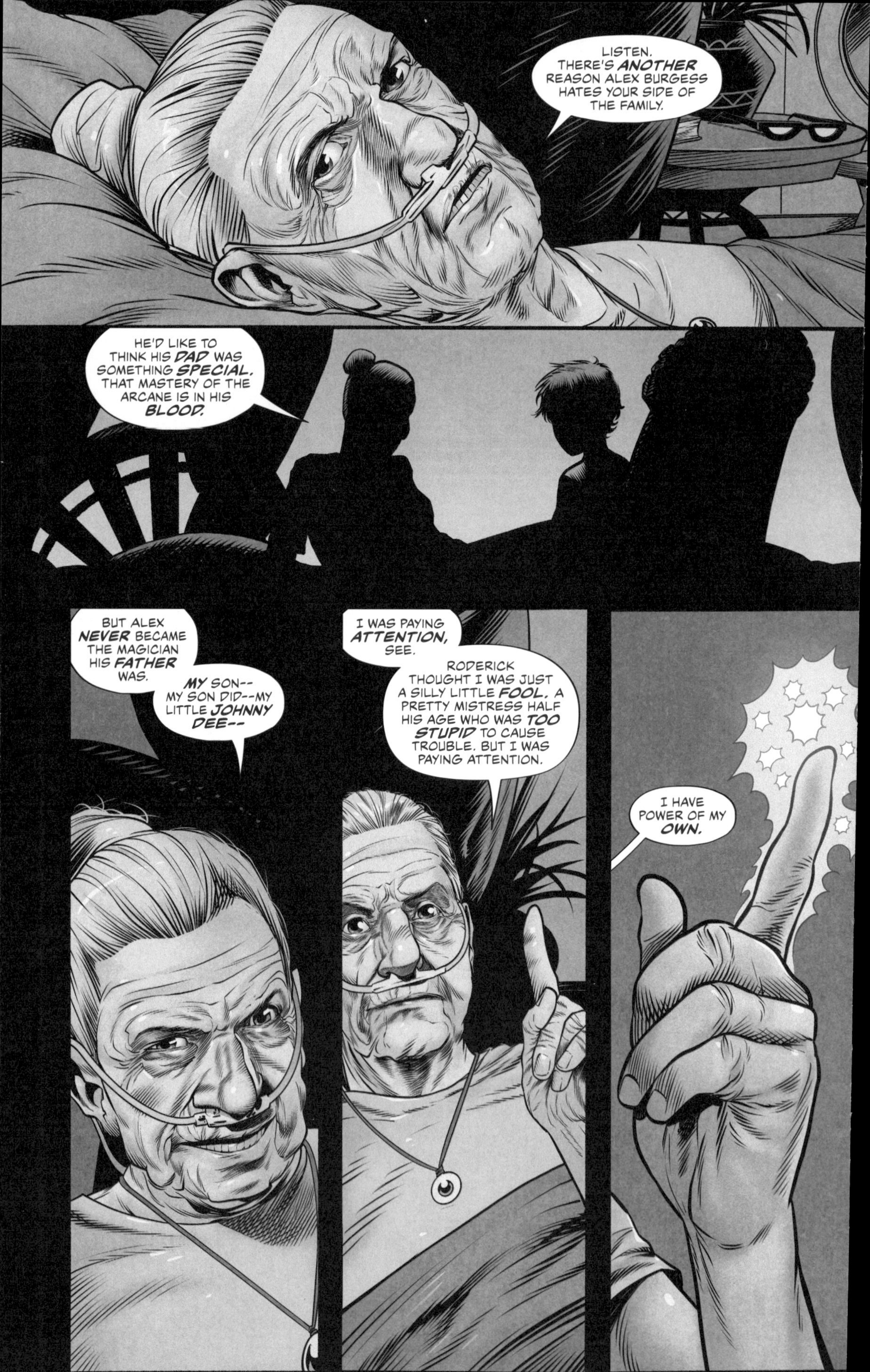
LISTEN. THERE'S ANOTHER REASON ALEX BURGESS HATES YOUR SIDE OF THE FAMILY.
HE'D LIKE TO THINK HIS DAD WAS SOMETHING SPECIAL, THAT MASTERY OF THE ARCANE IS IN HIS BLOOD.
BUT ALEX NEVER BECAME THE MAGICIAN HIS FATHER WAS.
MY SON-- MY SON DID--MY LITTLE JOHNNY DEE--
I WAS PAYING ATTENTION, SEE.
RODERICK THOUGHT I WAS JUST A SILLY LITTLE FOOL, A PRETTY MISTRESS HALF HIS AGE WHO WAS TOO STUPID TO CAUSE TROUBLE. BUT I WAS PAYING ATTENTION.
I HAVE POWER OF MY OWN.

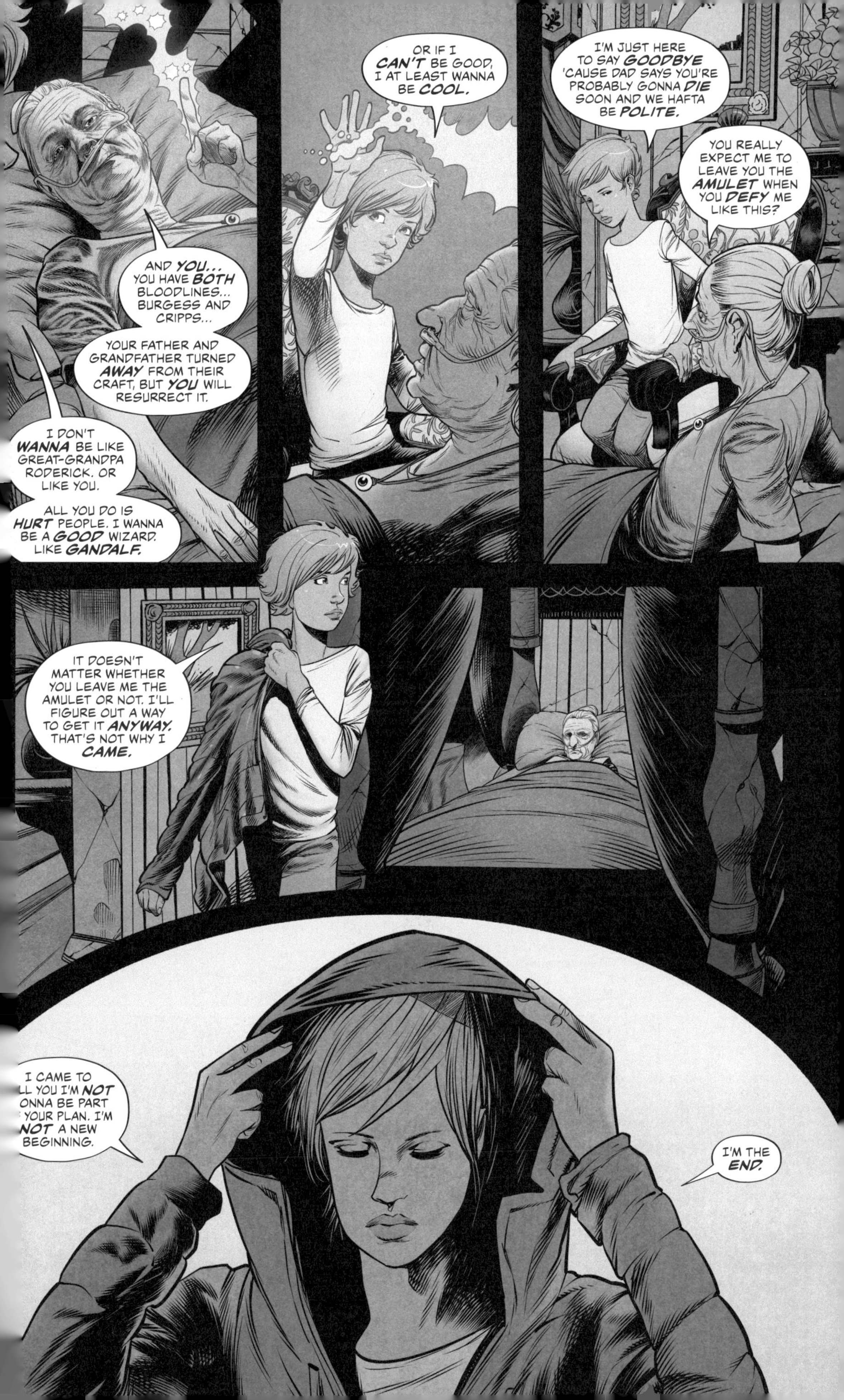
AND YOU... YOU HAVE BOTH BLOODLINES... BURGESS AND CRIPPS...
YOUR FATHER AND GRANDFATHER TURNED AWAY FROM THEIR CRAFT, BUT YOU WILL RESURRECT IT.
I DON'T WANNA BE LIKE GREAT-GRANDPA RODERICK. OR LIKE YOU.
ALL YOU DO IS HURT PEOPLE. I WANNA BE A GOOD WIZARD. LIKE GANDALF.
OR IF I CAN'T BE GOOD, I AT LEAST WANNA BE COOL.
I'M JUST HERE TO SAY GOODBYE 'CAUSE DAD SAYS YOU'RE PROBABLY GONNA DIE SOON AND WE HAFTA BE POLITE.
YOU REALLY EXPECT ME TO LEAVE YOU THE AMULET WHEN YOU DEFY ME LIKE THIS?
IT DOESN'T MATTER WHETHER YOU LEAVE ME THE AMULET OR NOT. I'LL FIGURE OUT A WAY TO GET IT ANYWAY. THAT'S NOT WHY I CAME.
I CAME TO LL YOU I'M NOT ONNA BE PART YOUR PLAN. I'M NOT A NEW BEGINNING.
I'M THE END.

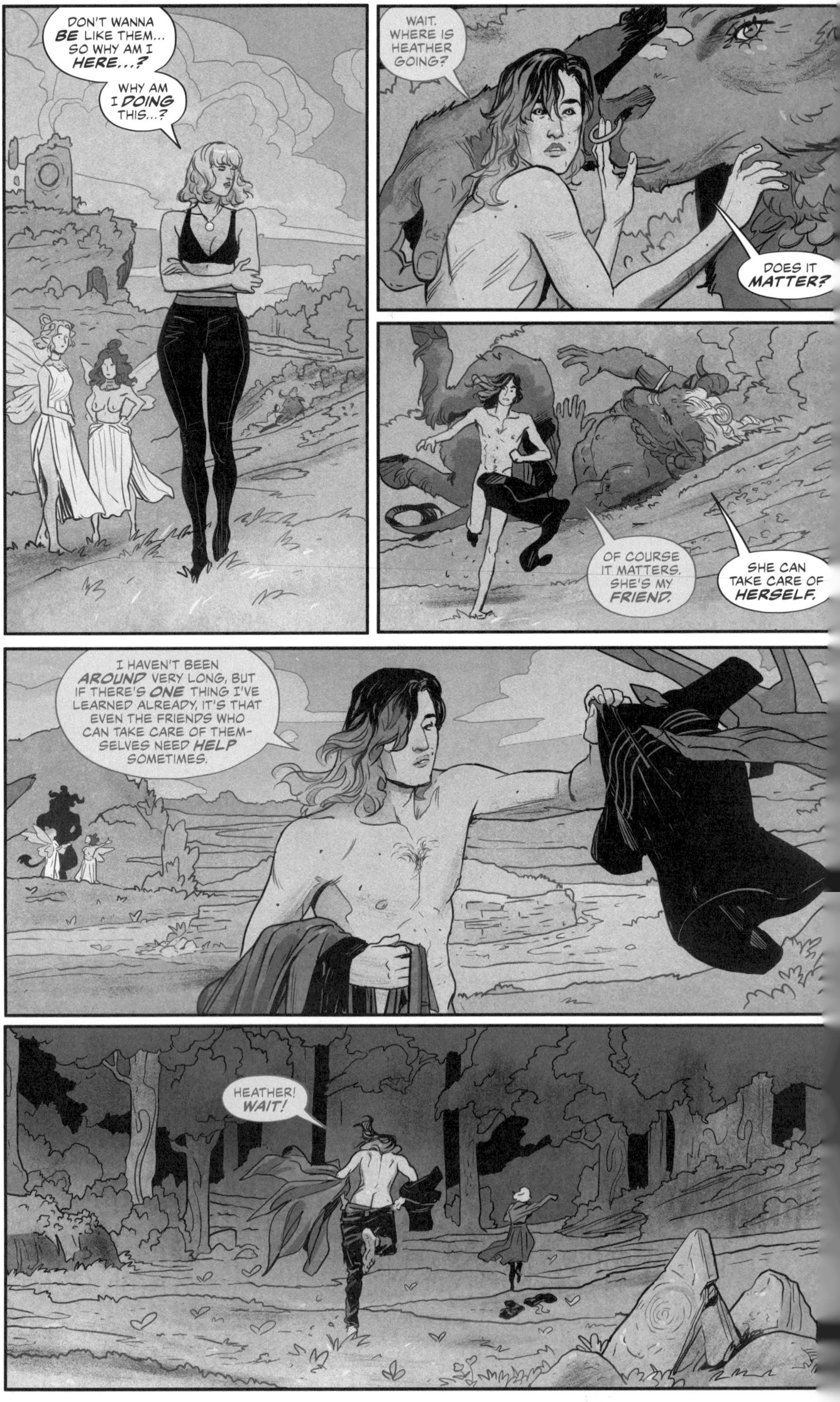

DON'T WANNA BE LIKE THEM... SO WHY AM I HERE...?
WHY AM I DOING THIS...?
WAIT. WHERE IS HEATHER GOING?
DOES IT MATTER?
OF COURSE IT MATTERS. SHE'S MY FRIEND.
SHE CAN TAKE CARE OF HERSELF.
I HAVEN'T BEEN AROUND VERY LONG, BUT IF THERE'S ONE THING I'VE LEARNED ALREADY, IT'S THAT EVEN THE FRIENDS WHO CAN TAKE CARE OF THEM-SELVES NEED HELP SOMETIMES.
HEATHER! WAIT!

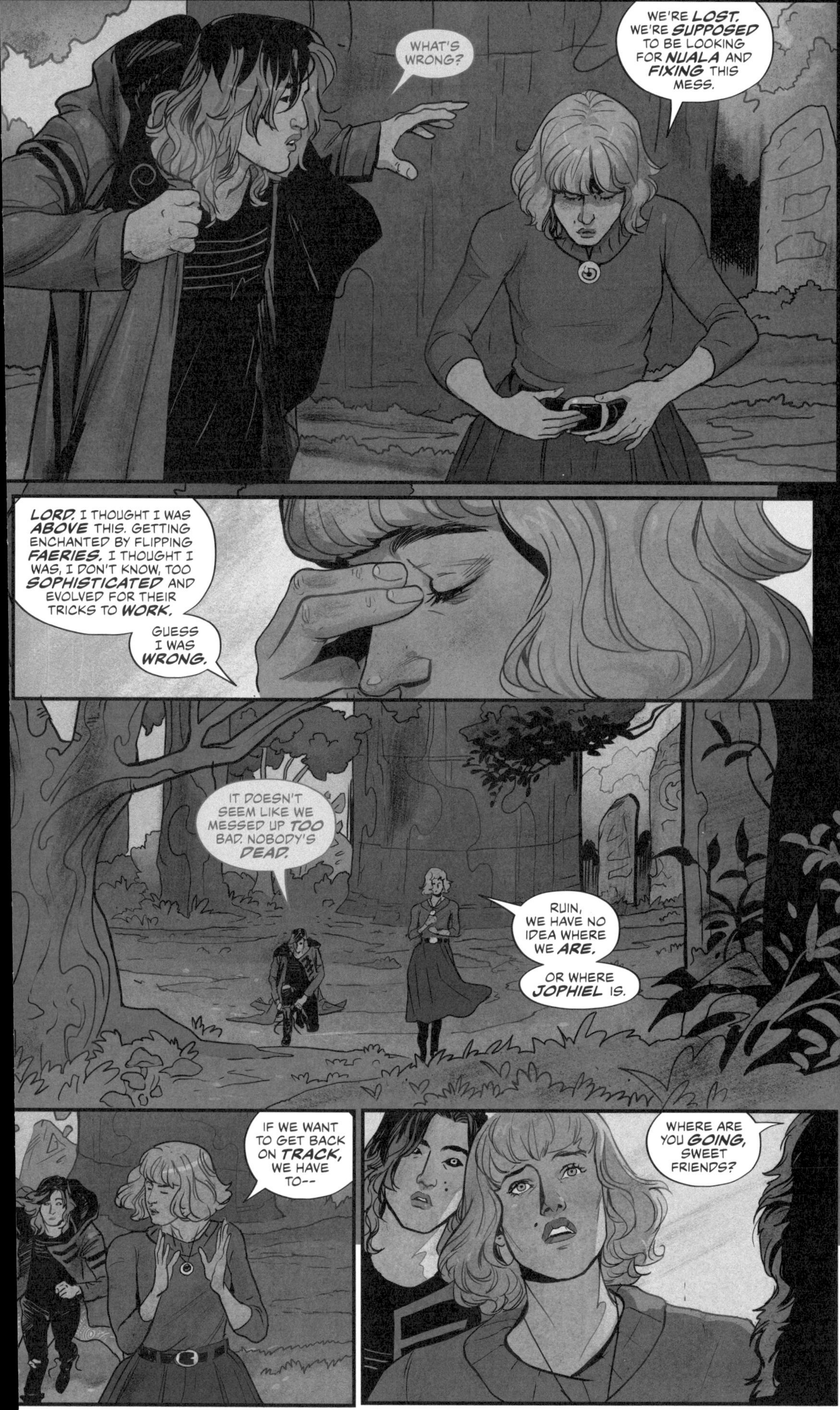
WHAT'S WRONG?
WE'RE LOST. WE'RE SUPPOSED TO BE LOOKING FOR NUALA AND FIXING THIS MESS.
LORD. I THOUGHT I WAS ABOVE THIS. GETTING ENCHANTED BY FLIPPING FAERIES. I THOUGHT I WAS, I DON'T KNOW, TOO SOPHISTICATED AND EVOLVED FOR THEIR TRICKS TO WORK.
GUESS I WAS WRONG.
IT DOESN'T SEEM LIKE WE MESSED UP TOO BAD. NOBODY'S DEAD.
RUIN, WE HAVE NO IDEA WHERE WE ARE.
OR WHERE JOPHIEL IS.
IF WE WANT TO GET BACK ON TRACK, WE HAVE TO--
WHERE ARE YOU GOING, SWEET FRIENDS?

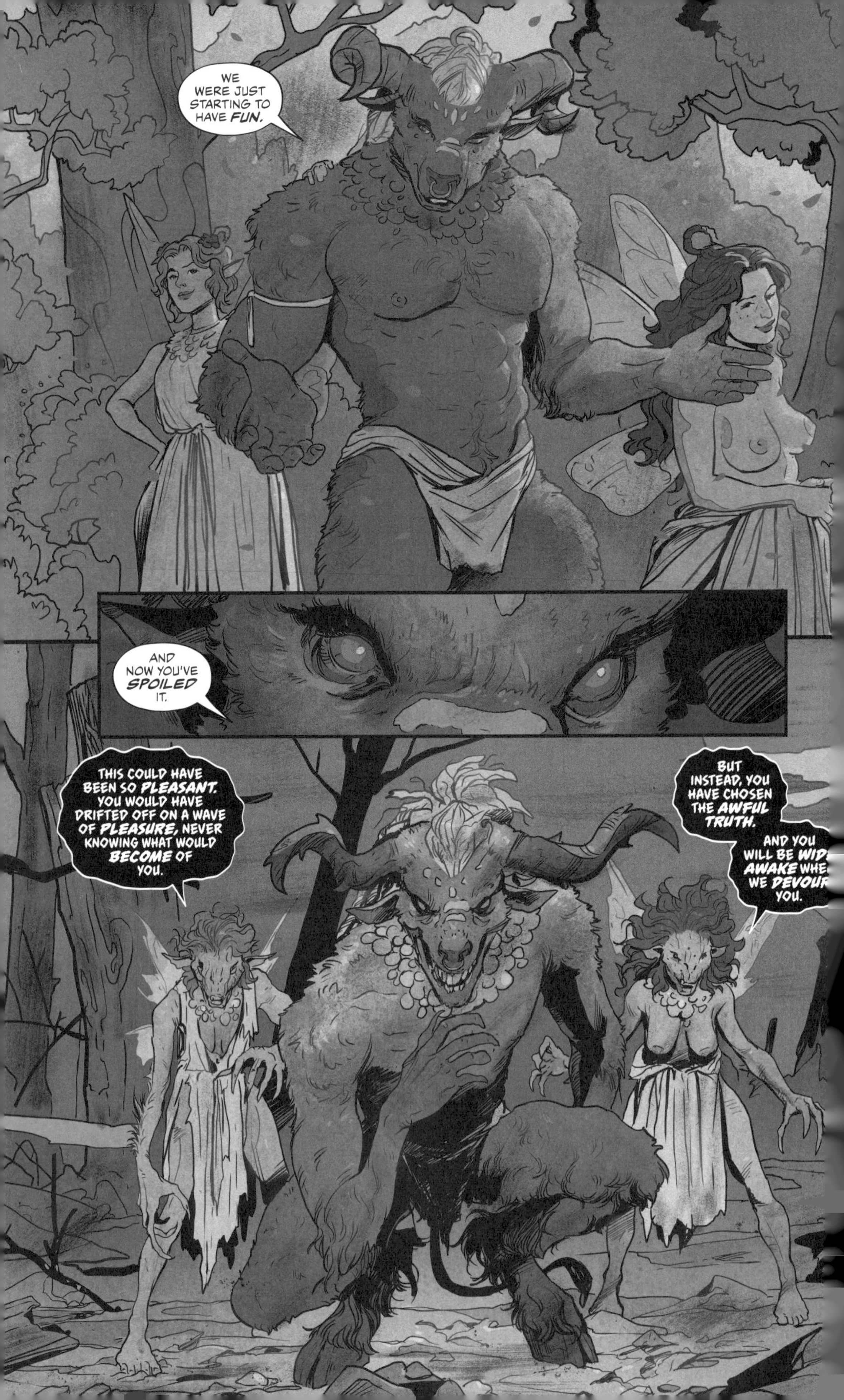
WE WERE JUST STARTING TO HAVE FUN.
AND NOW YOU'VE SPOILED IT.
THIS COULD HAVE BEEN SO PLEASANT. YOU WOULD HAVE DRIFTED OFF ON A WAVE OF PLEASURE, NEVER KNOWING WHAT WOULD BECOME OF YOU.
BUT INSTEAD, YOU HAVE CHOSEN THE AWFUL TRUTH.
AND YOU WILL BE WID AWAKE WHE WE DEVOUR YOU.

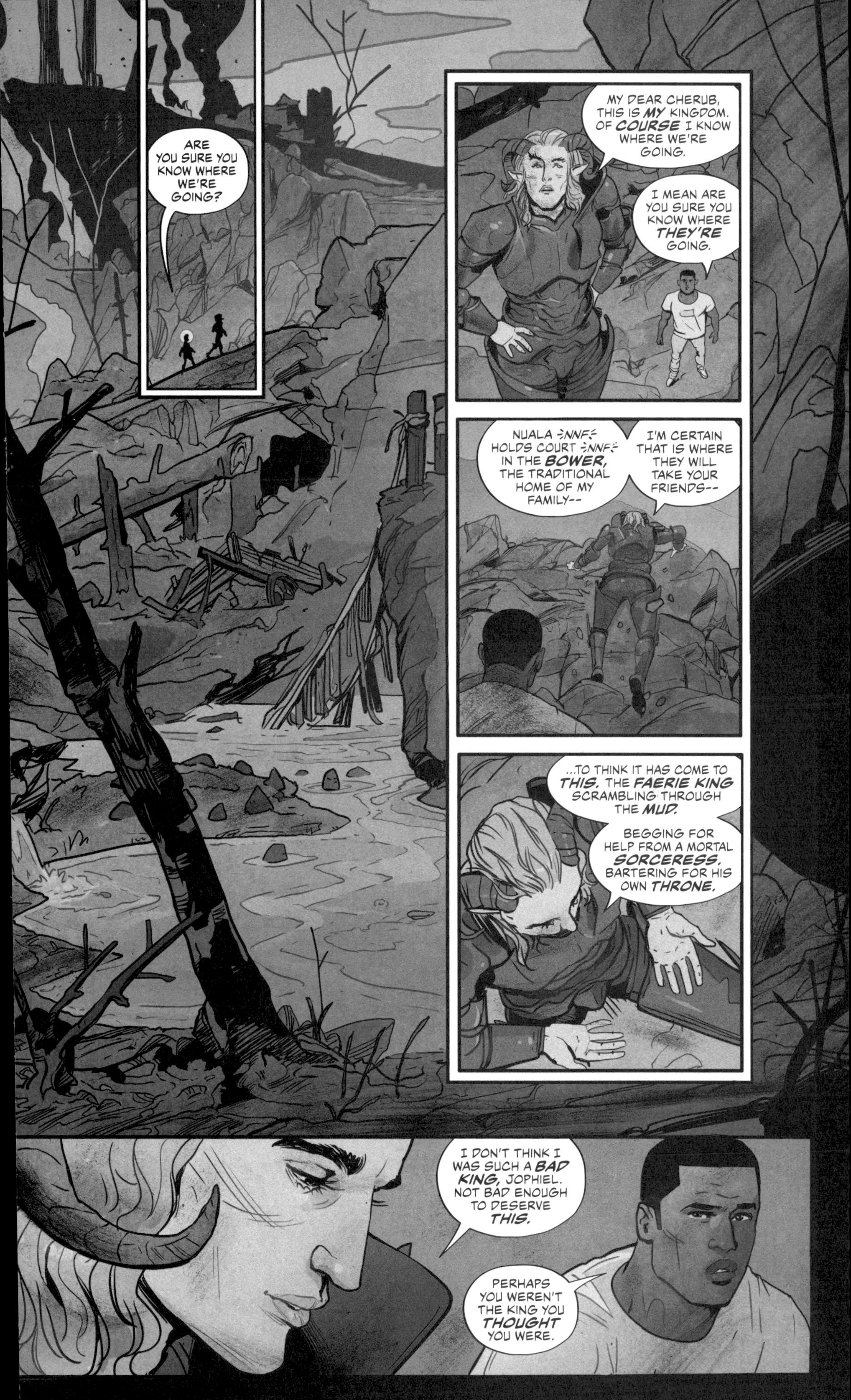
ARE YOU SURE YOU KNOW WHERE WE'RE GOING?
MY DEAR CHERUB, THIS IS MY KINGDOM. OF COURSE I KNOW WHERE WE'RE GOING.
I MEAN ARE YOU SURE YOU KNOW WHERE THEY'RE GOING.
NUALA -NNF- HOLDS COURT -NNF- IN THE BOWER, THE TRADITIONAL HOME OF MY FAMILY--
I'M CERTAIN THAT IS WHERE THEY WILL TAKE YOUR FRIENDS--
...TO THINK IT HAS COME TO THIS. THE FAERIE KING SCRAMBLING THROUGH THE MUD.
BEGGING FOR HELP FROM A MORTAL SORCERESS. BARTERING FOR HIS OWN THRONE.
I DON'T THINK I WAS SUCH A BAD KING, JOPHIEL. NOT BAD ENOUGH TO DESERVE THIS.
PERHAPS YOU WEREN'T THE KING YOU THOUGHT YOU WERE.

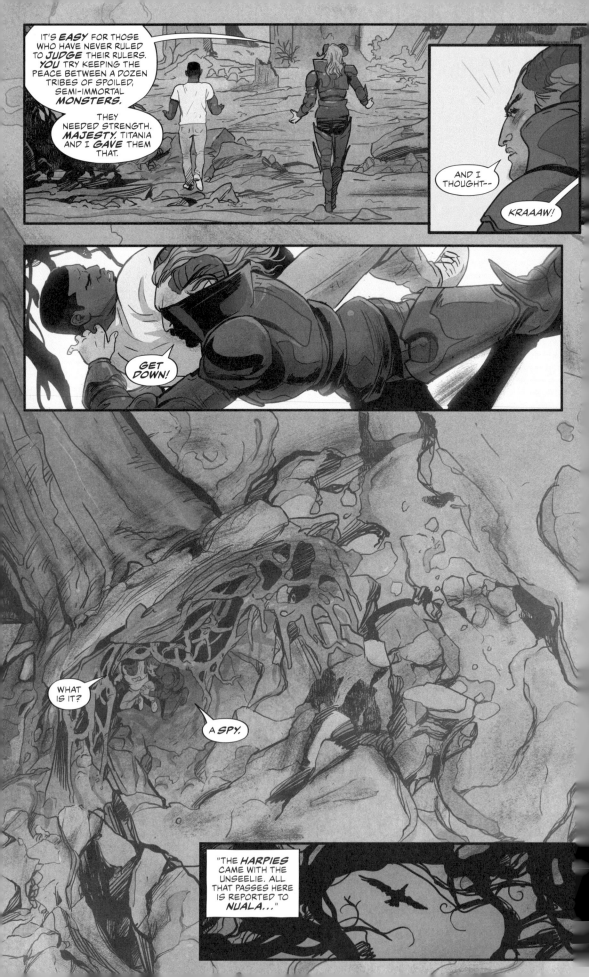

IT'S *EASY* FOR THOSE WHO HAVE NEVER RULED TO *JUDGE* THEIR RULERS. *YOU* TRY KEEPING THE PEACE BETWEEN A DOZEN TRIBES OF SPOILED, SEMI-IMMORTAL *MONSTERS.*

THEY NEEDED STRENGTH. *MAJESTY.* TITANIA AND I *GAVE* THEM THAT.

AND I THOUGHT--

KRAAAW!

GET DOWN!

WHAT IS IT?

A *SPY.*

"THE *HARPIES* CAME WITH THE UNSEELIE. ALL THAT PASSES HERE IS REPORTED TO *NUALA...*"

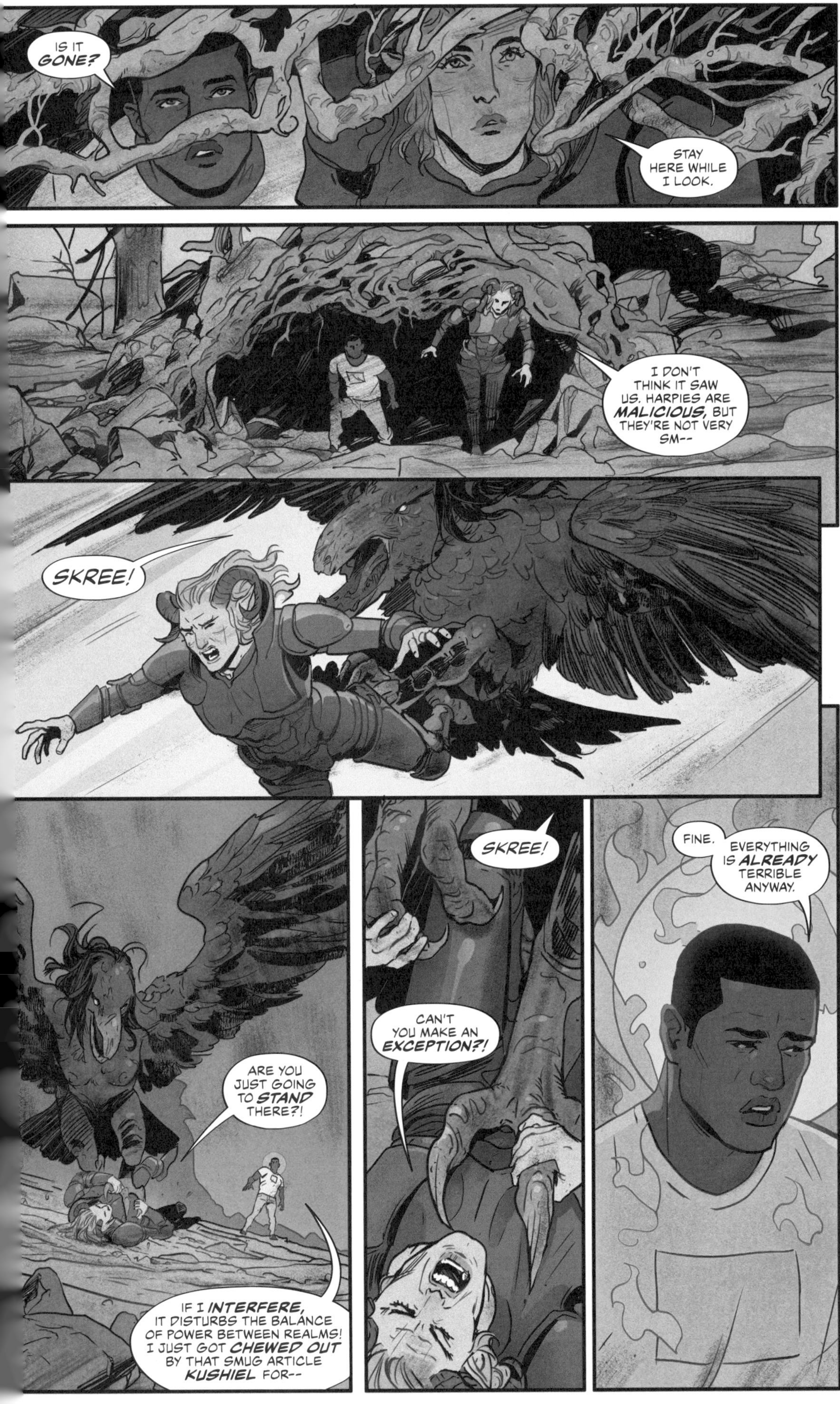
IS IT GONE?
STAY HERE WHILE I LOOK.
I DON'T THINK IT SAW US. HARPIES ARE MALICIOUS, BUT THEY'RE NOT VERY SM--
SKREE!
ARE YOU JUST GOING TO STAND THERE?!
IF I INTERFERE, IT DISTURBS THE BALANCE OF POWER BETWEEN REALMS! I JUST GOT CHEWED OUT BY THAT SMUG ARTICLE KUSHIEL FOR--
SKREE!
CAN'T YOU MAKE AN EXCEPTION?!
FINE.
EVERYTHING IS ALREADY TERRIBLE ANYWAY.

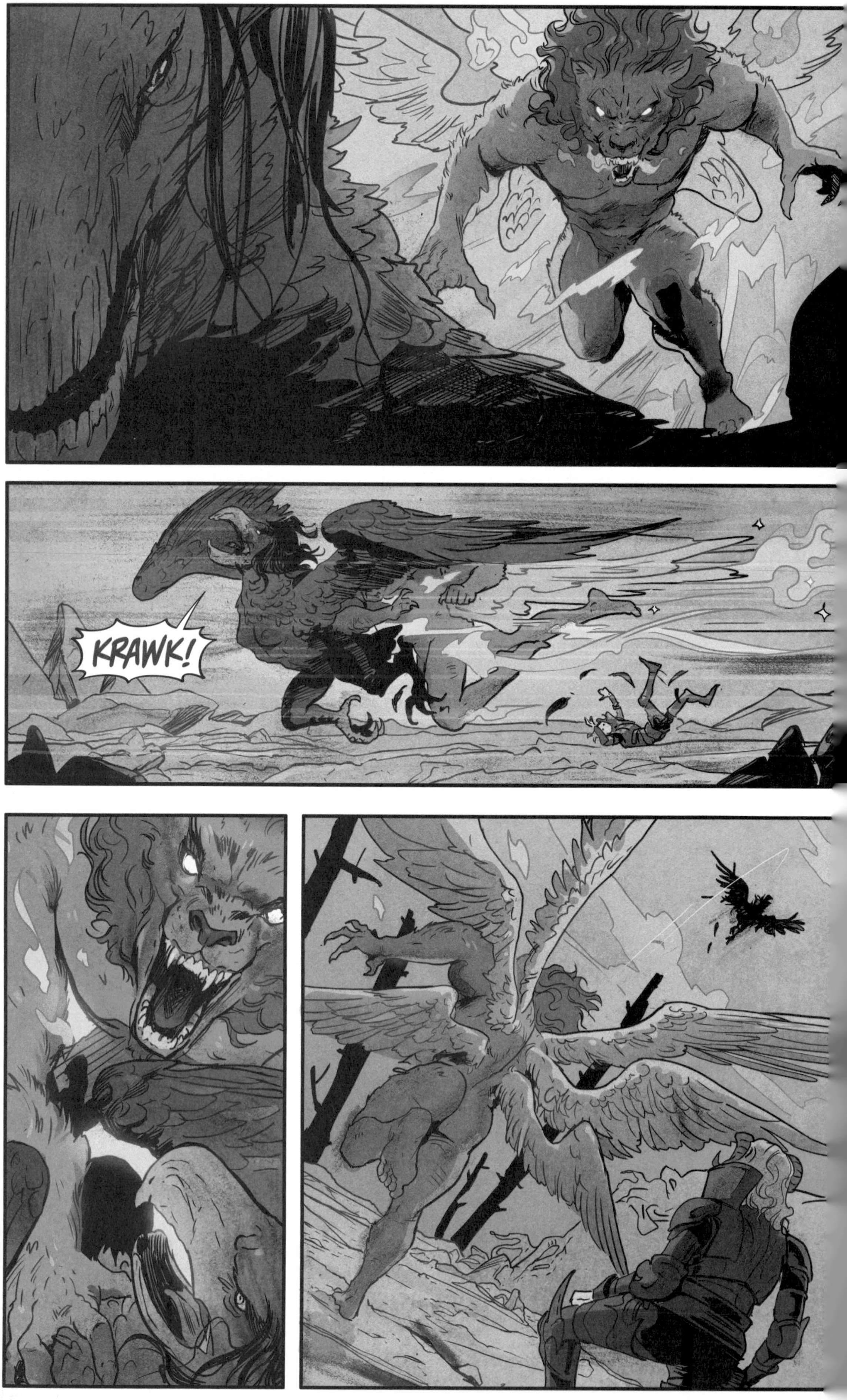
KRAWK!

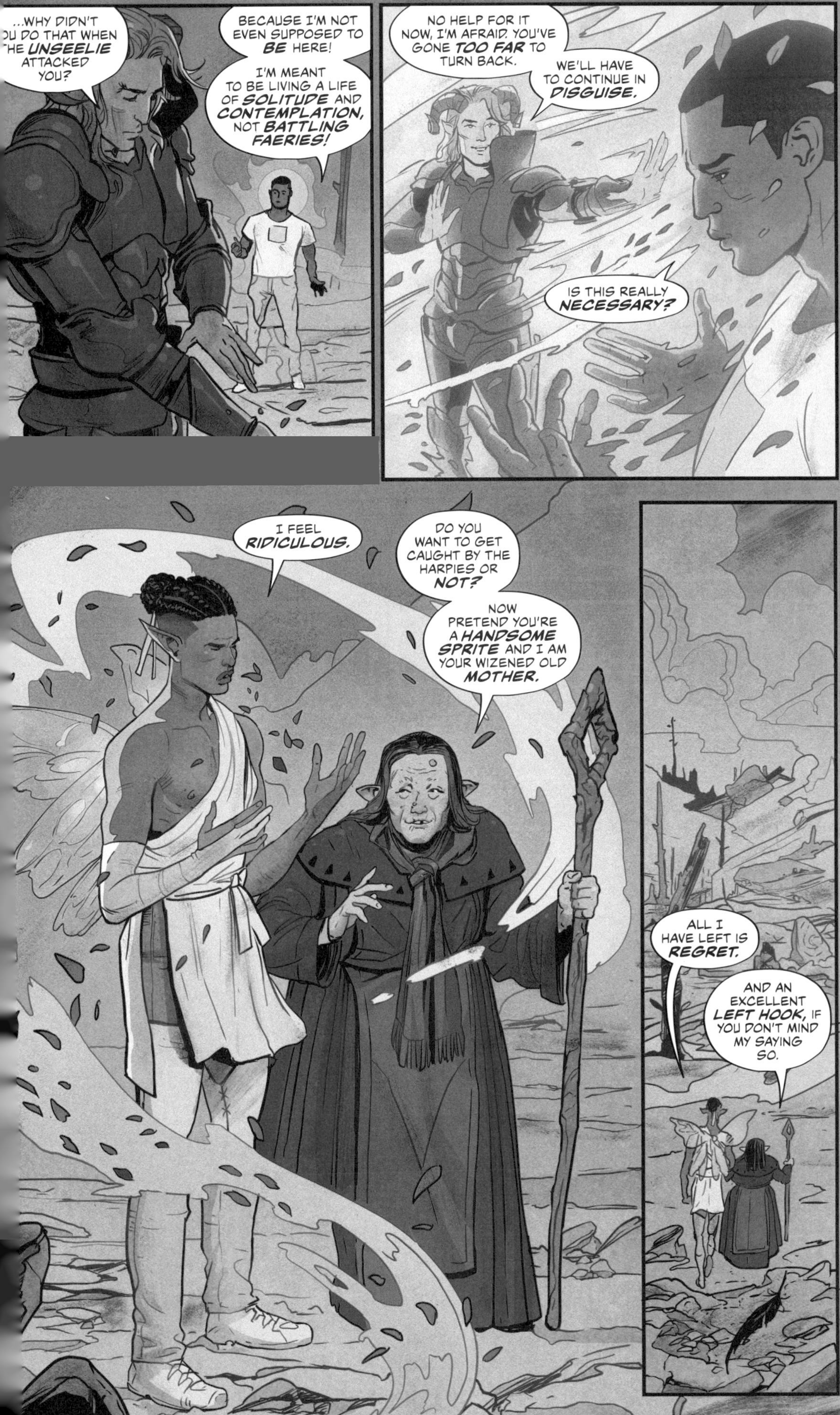
...WHY DIDN'T
OU DO THAT WHEN
HE UNSEELIE
ATTACKED
YOU?
BECAUSE I'M NOT EVEN SUPPOSED TO BE HERE!
I'M MEANT TO BE LIVING A LIFE OF SOLITUDE AND CONTEMPLATION, NOT BATTLING FAERIES!
NO HELP FOR IT NOW, I'M AFRAID. YOU'VE GONE TOO FAR TO TURN BACK.
WE'LL HAVE TO CONTINUE IN DISGUISE.
IS THIS REALLY NECESSARY?
I FEEL RIDICULOUS.
DO YOU WANT TO GET CAUGHT BY THE HARPIES OR NOT?
NOW PRETEND YOU'RE A HANDSOME SPRITE AND I AM YOUR WIZENED OLD MOTHER.
ALL I HAVE LEFT IS REGRET.
AND AN EXCELLENT LEFT HOOK, IF YOU DON'T MIND MY SAYING SO.

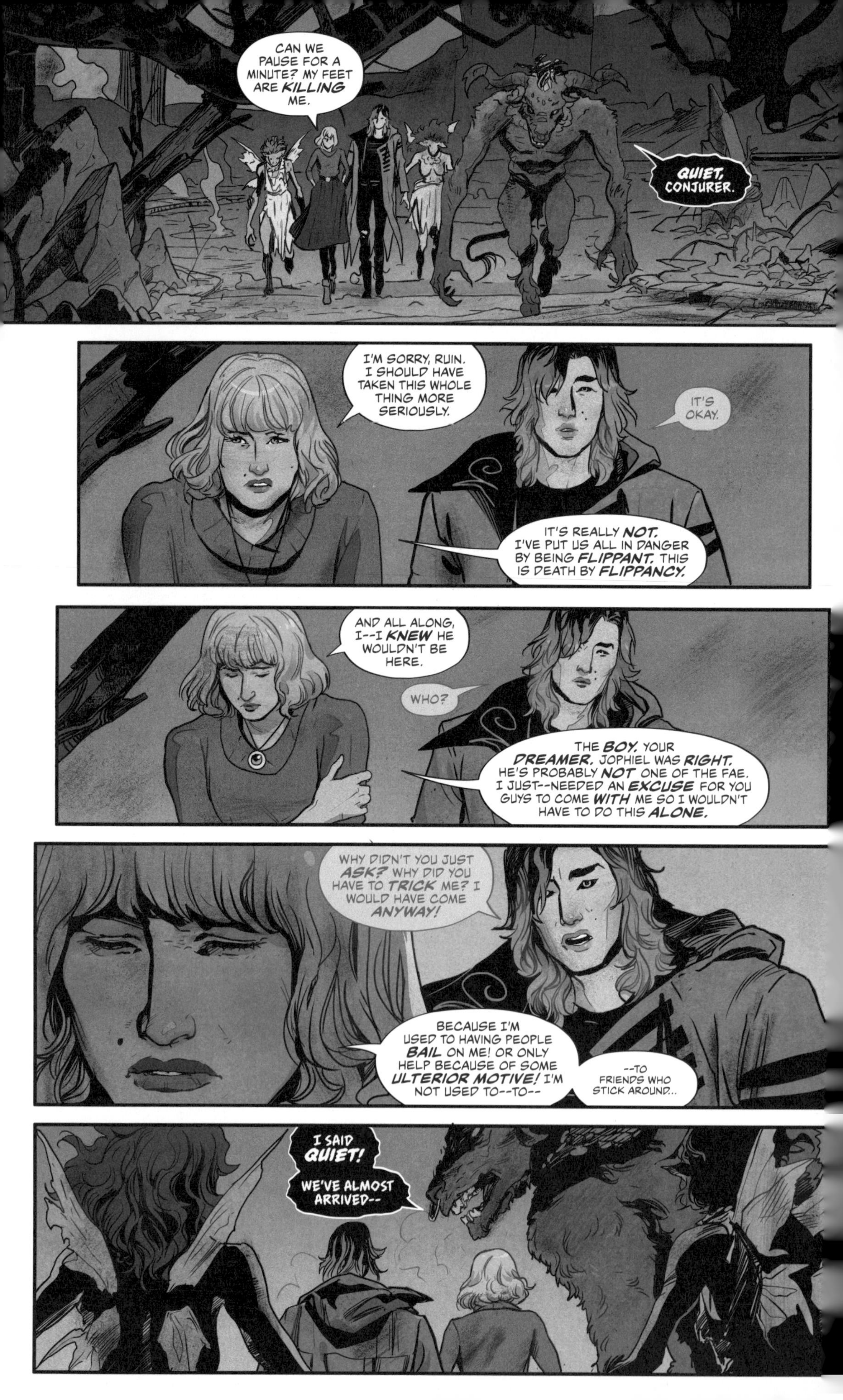
CAN WE PAUSE FOR A MINUTE? MY FEET ARE KILLING ME.
QUIET, CONJURER.
I'M SORRY, RUIN. I SHOULD HAVE TAKEN THIS WHOLE THING MORE SERIOUSLY.
IT'S OKAY.
IT'S REALLY NOT. I'VE PUT US ALL IN DANGER BY BEING FLIPPANT. THIS IS DEATH BY FLIPPANCY.
AND ALL ALONG, I--I KNEW HE WOULDN'T BE HERE.
WHO?
THE BOY. YOUR DREAMER. JOPHIEL WAS RIGHT. HE'S PROBABLY NOT ONE OF THE FAE. I JUST--NEEDED AN EXCUSE FOR YOU GUYS TO COME WITH ME SO I WOULDN'T HAVE TO DO THIS ALONE.
WHY DIDN'T YOU JUST ASK? WHY DID YOU HAVE TO TRICK ME? I WOULD HAVE COME ANYWAY!
BECAUSE I'M USED TO HAVING PEOPLE BAIL ON ME! OR ONLY HELP BECAUSE OF SOME ULTERIOR MOTIVE! I'M NOT USED TO--TO--
--TO FRIENDS WHO STICK AROUND...
I SAID QUIET!
WE'VE ALMOST ARRIVED--

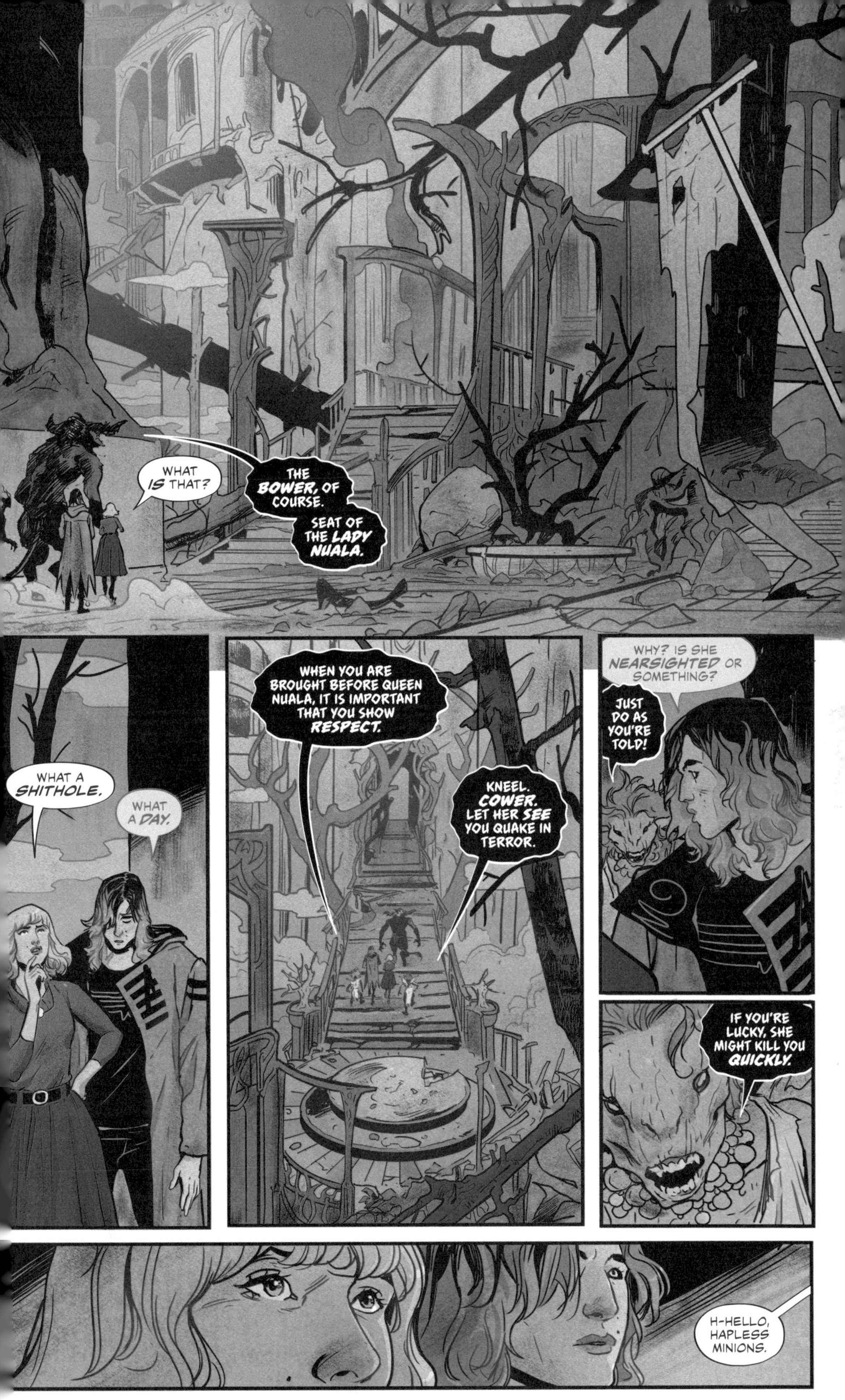
WHAT IS THAT?
THE BOWER, OF COURSE.
SEAT OF THE LADY NUALA.
WHAT A SHITHOLE.
WHAT A DAY.
WHEN YOU ARE BROUGHT BEFORE QUEEN NUALA, IT IS IMPORTANT THAT YOU SHOW RESPECT.
KNEEL. COWER. LET HER SEE YOU QUAKE IN TERROR.
WHY? IS SHE NEARSIGHTED OR SOMETHING?
JUST DO AS YOU'RE TOLD!
IF YOU'RE LUCKY, SHE MIGHT KILL YOU QUICKLY.
H-HELLO, HAPLESS MINIONS.

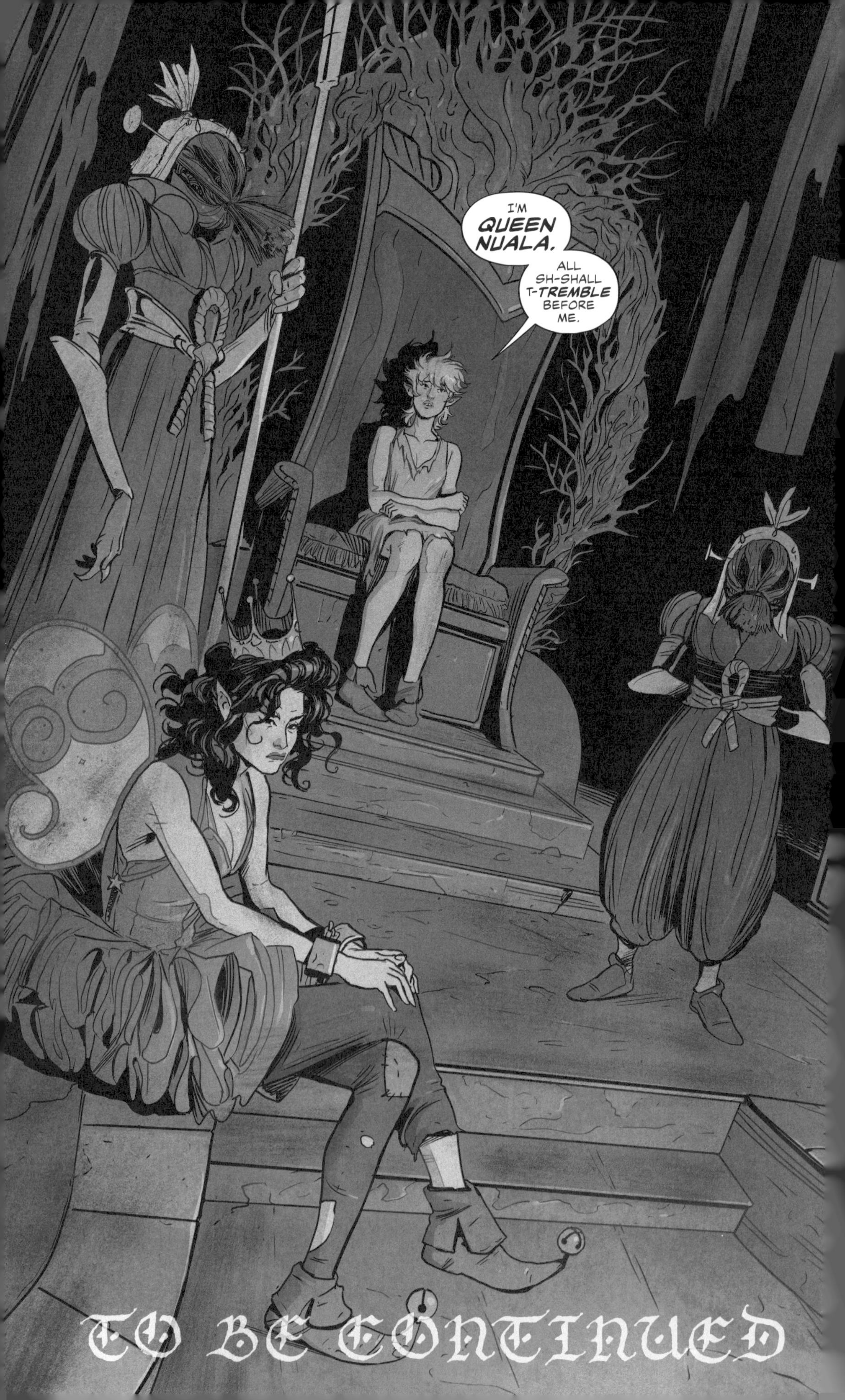
I'M QUEEN NUALA.
ALL SH-SHALL T-TREMBLE BEFORE ME.
TO BE CONTINUED

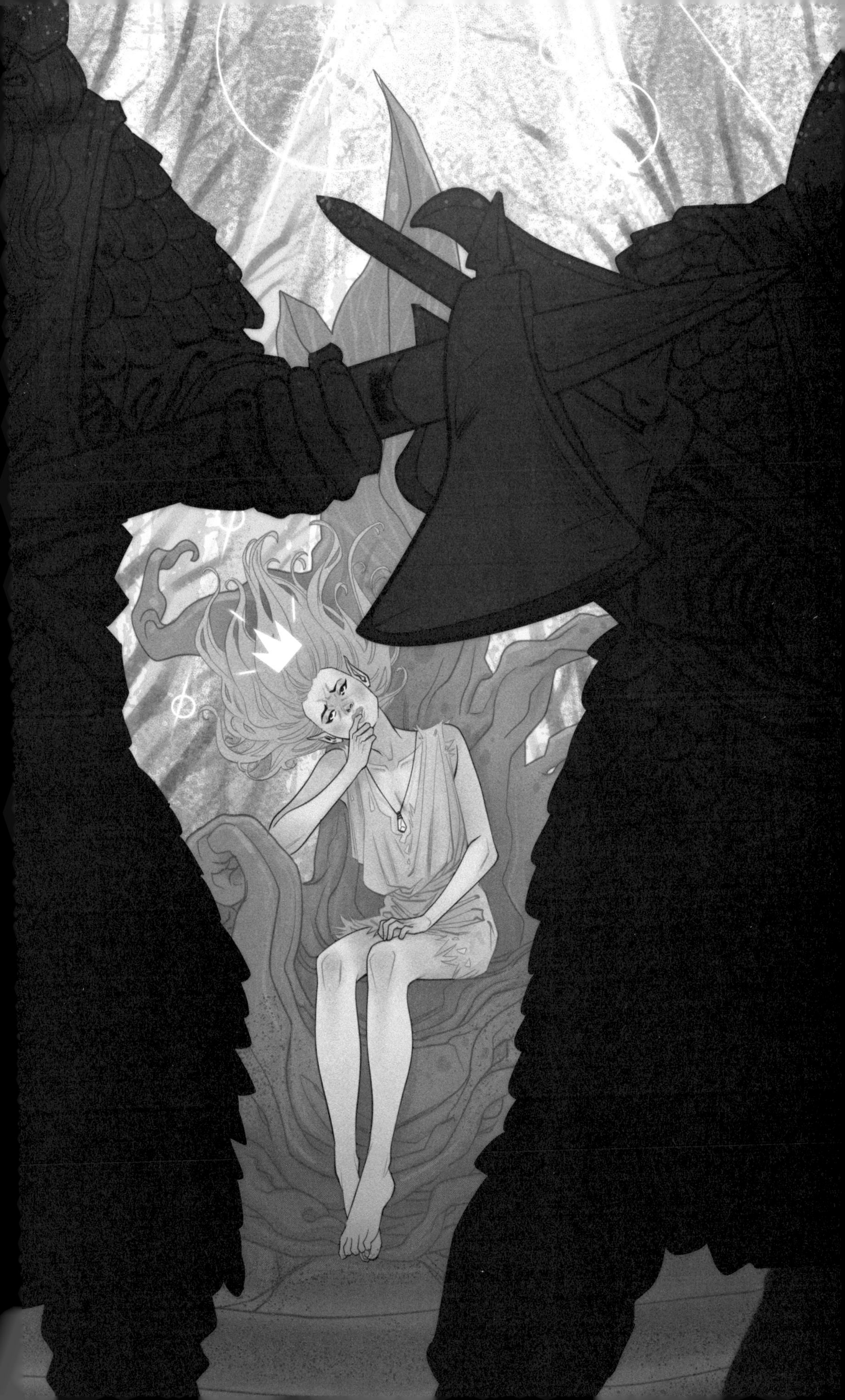

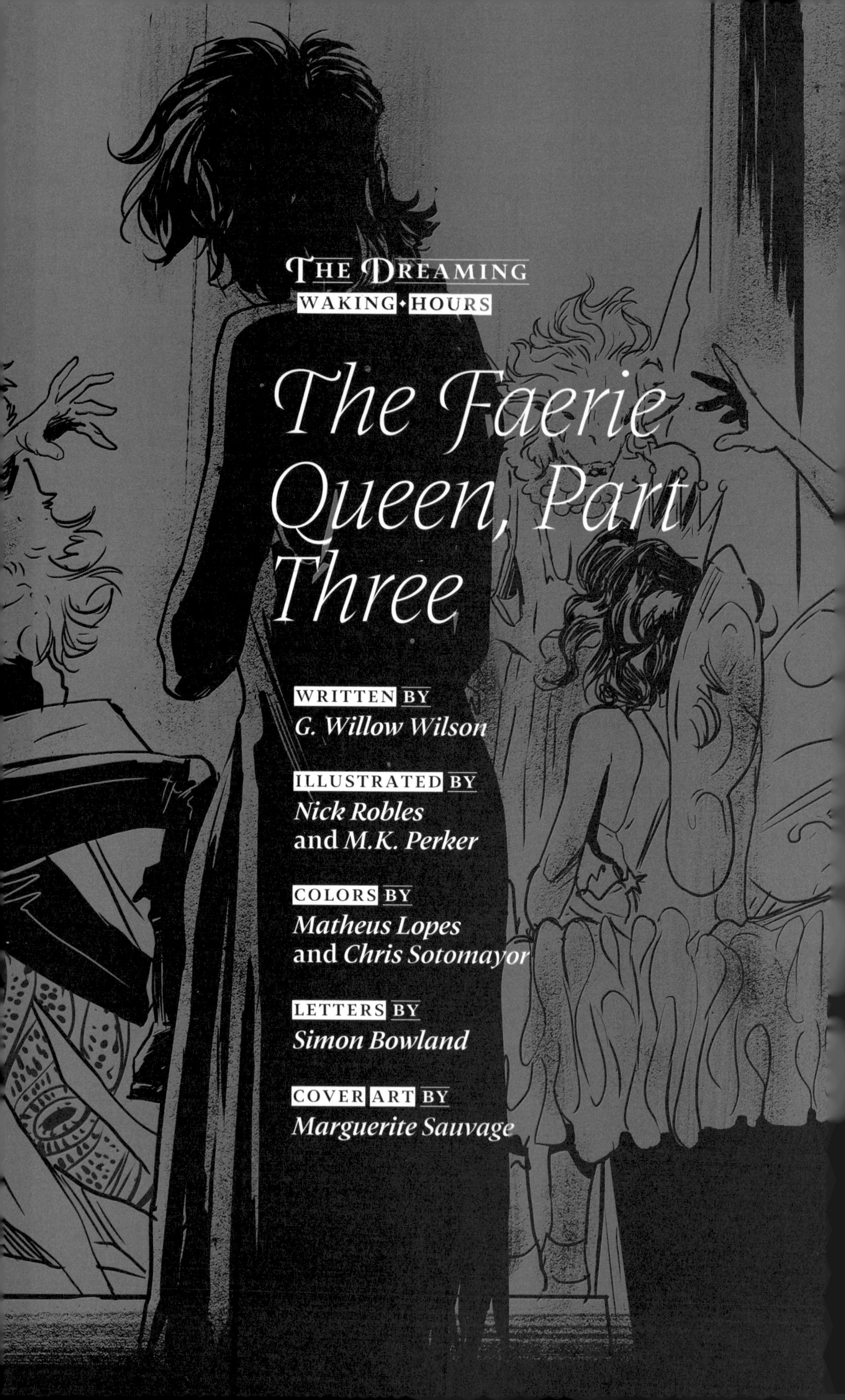

THE DREAMING

WAKING • HOURS

The Faerie Queen, Part Three

WRITTEN BY
G. Willow Wilson

ILLUSTRATED BY
Nick Robles
and *M.K. Perker*

COLORS BY
Matheus Lopes
and *Chris Sotomayor*

LETTERS BY
Simon Bowland

COVER ART BY
Marguerite Sauvage

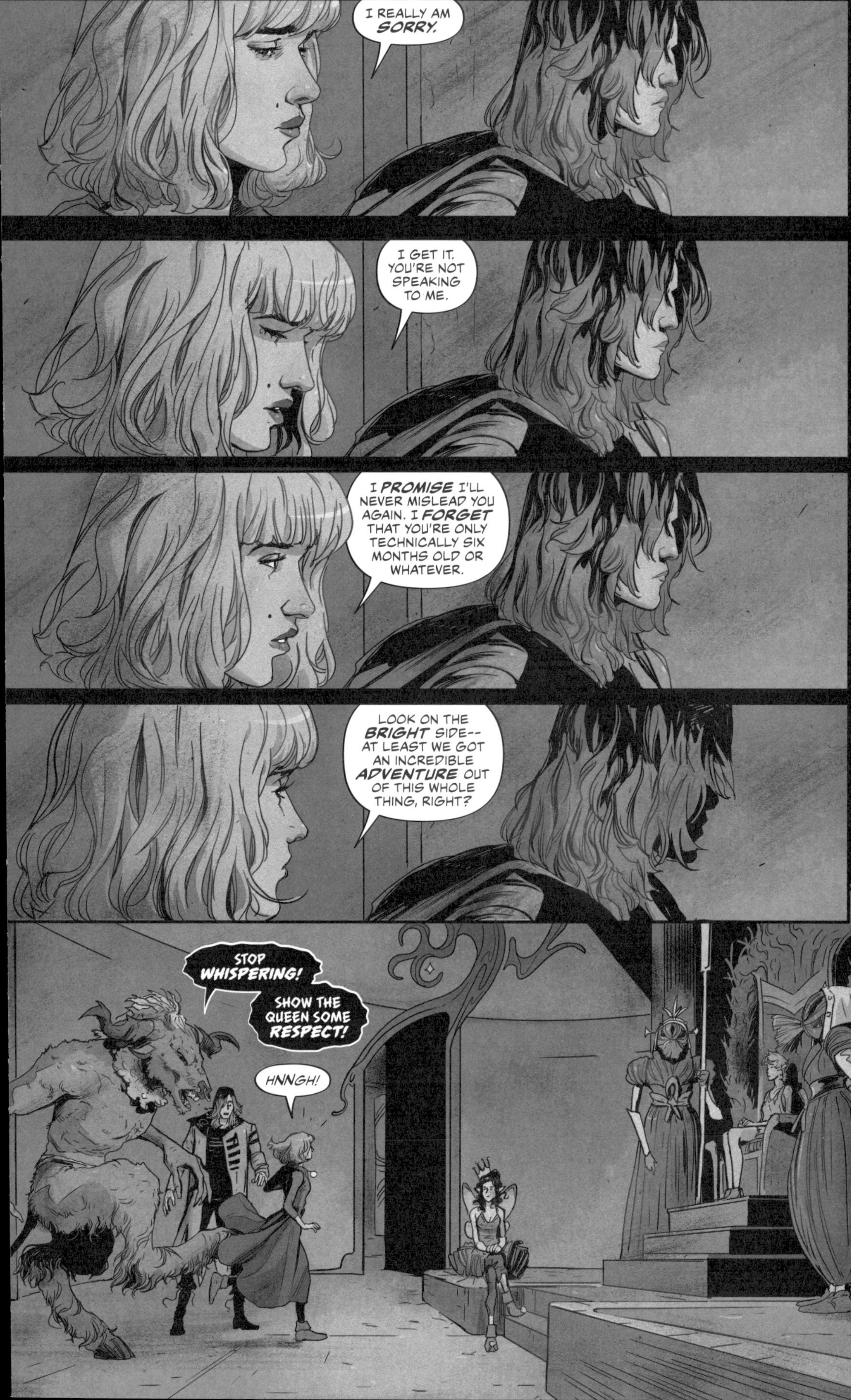
I REALLY AM SORRY.
I GET IT. YOU'RE NOT SPEAKING TO ME.
I PROMISE I'LL NEVER MISLEAD YOU AGAIN. I FORGET THAT YOU'RE ONLY TECHNICALLY SIX MONTHS OLD OR WHATEVER.
LOOK ON THE BRIGHT SIDE-- AT LEAST WE GOT AN INCREDIBLE ADVENTURE OUT OF THIS WHOLE THING, RIGHT?
STOP WHISPERING!
SHOW THE QUEEN SOME RESPECT!
HNNGH!

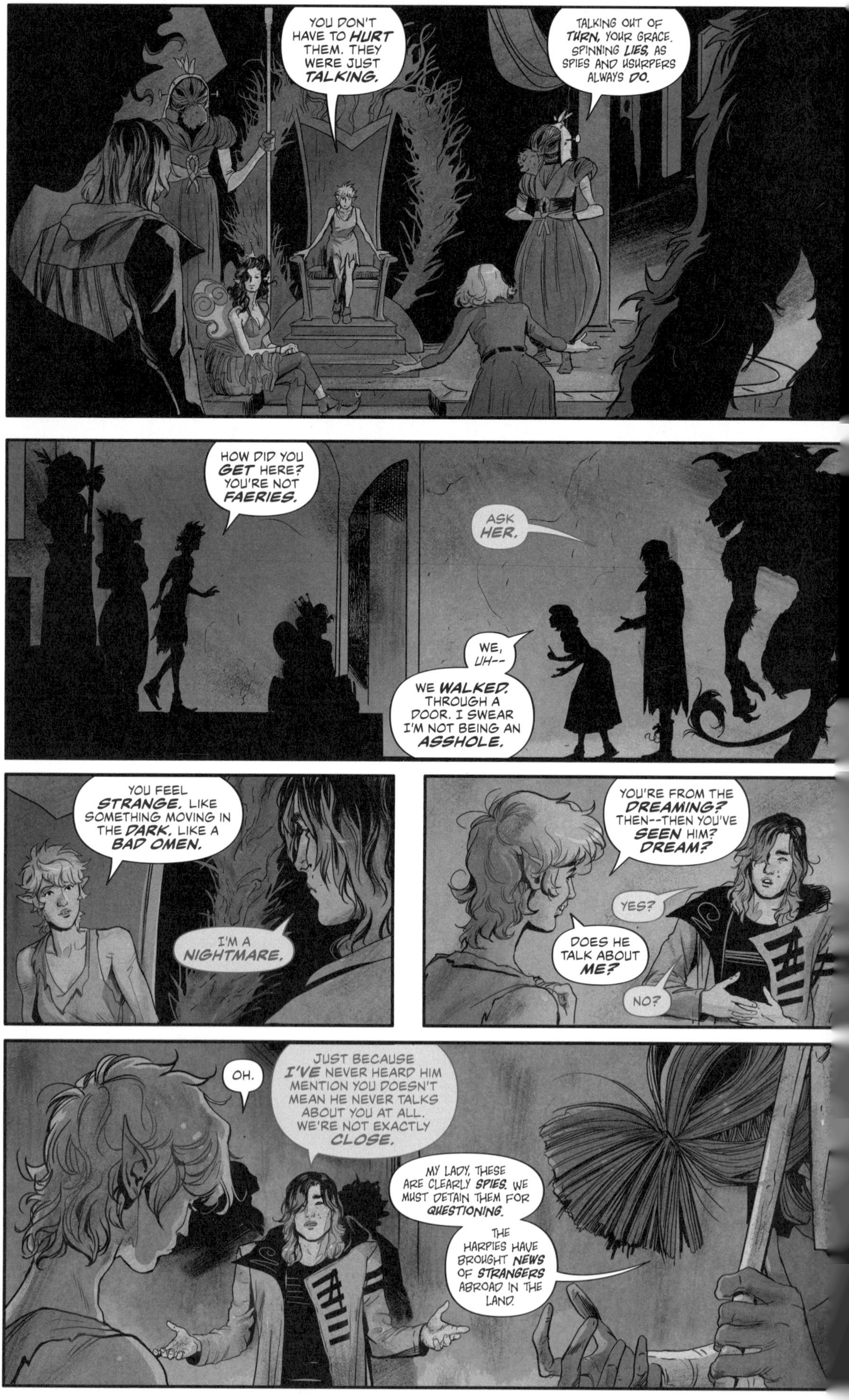
YOU DON'T HAVE TO HURT THEM. THEY WERE JUST TALKING.
TALKING OUT OF TURN, YOUR GRACE. SPINNING LIES, AS SPIES AND USURPERS ALWAYS DO.
HOW DID YOU GET HERE? YOU'RE NOT FAERIES.
ASK HER.
WE, UH--
WE WALKED. THROUGH A DOOR. I SWEAR I'M NOT BEING AN ASSHOLE.
YOU FEEL STRANGE. LIKE SOMETHING MOVING IN THE DARK. LIKE A BAD OMEN.
I'M A NIGHTMARE.
YOU'RE FROM THE DREAMING? THEN--THEN YOU'VE SEEN HIM? DREAM?
YES?
DOES HE TALK ABOUT ME?
NO?
OH.
JUST BECAUSE I'VE NEVER HEARD HIM MENTION YOU DOESN'T MEAN HE NEVER TALKS ABOUT YOU AT ALL. WE'RE NOT EXACTLY CLOSE.
MY LADY, THESE ARE CLEARLY SPIES. WE MUST DETAIN THEM FOR QUESTIONING.
THE HARPIES HAVE BROUGHT NEWS OF STRANGERS ABROAD IN THE LAND.

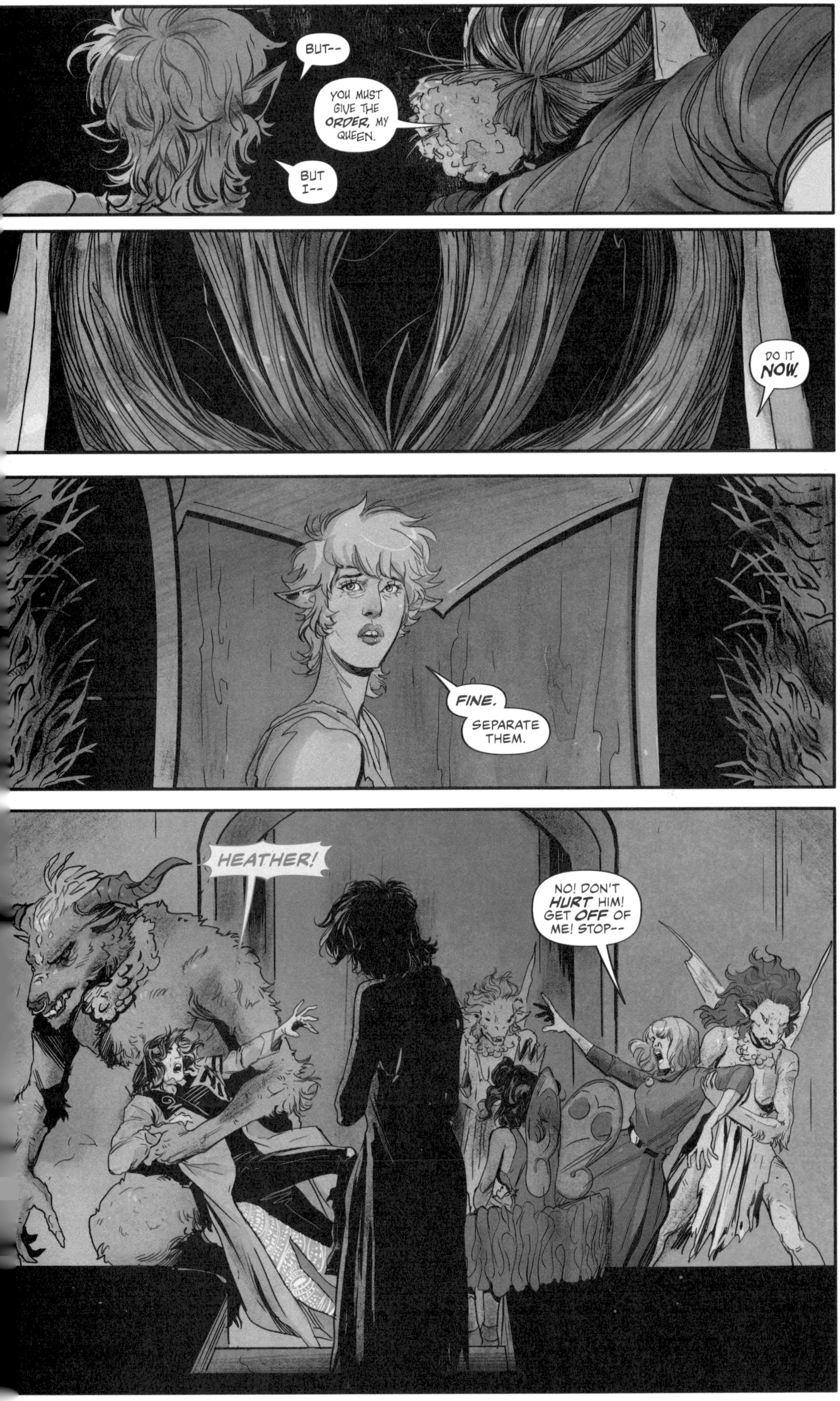
BUT--
YOU MUST GIVE THE ORDER, MY QUEEN.
BUT I--
DO IT NOW.
FINE.
SEPARATE THEM.
HEATHER!
NO! DON'T HURT HIM! GET OFF OF ME! STOP--

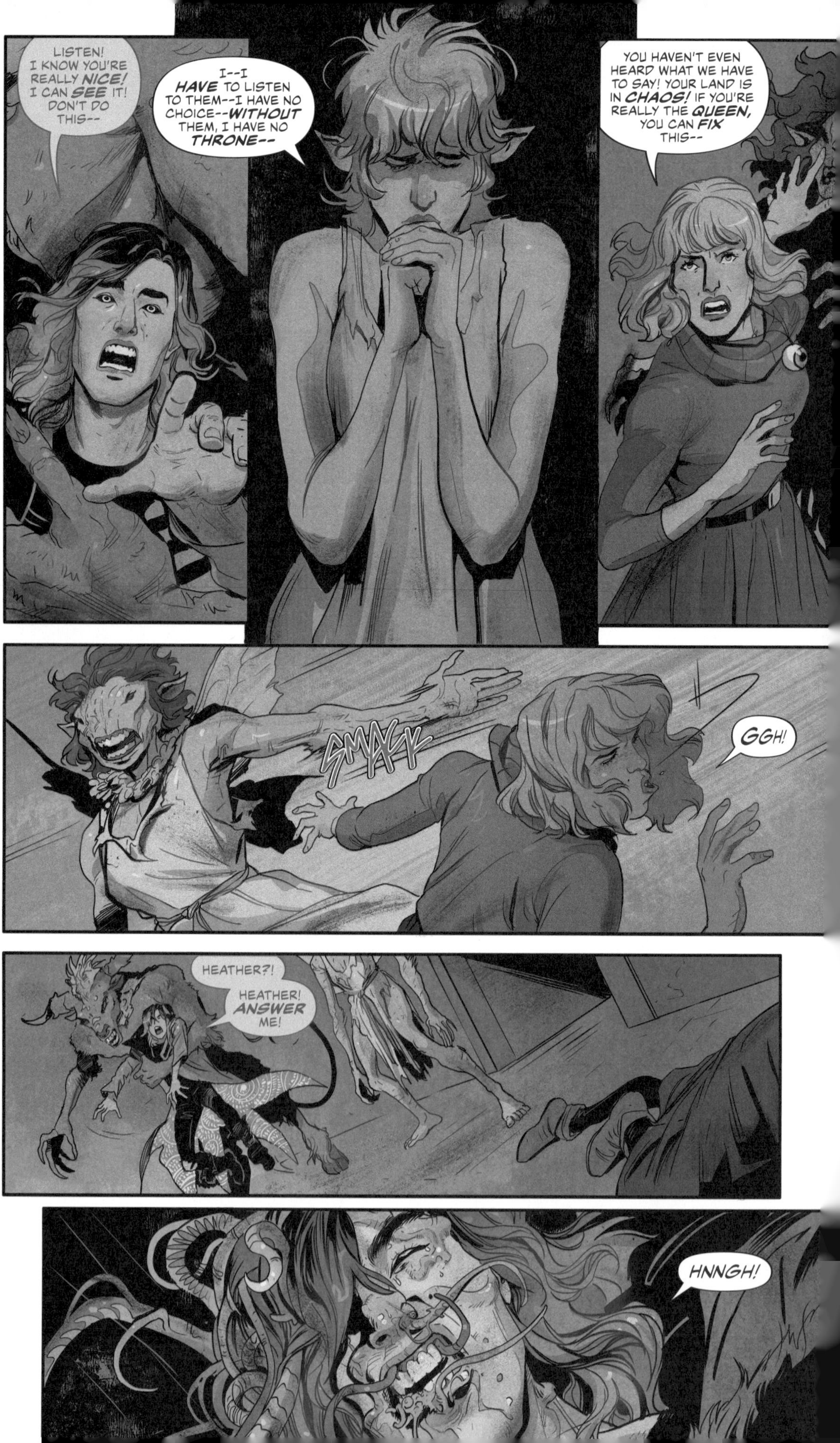
LISTEN! I KNOW YOU'RE REALLY NICE! I CAN SEE IT! DON'T DO THIS--
I--I HAVE TO LISTEN TO THEM--I HAVE NO CHOICE--WITHOUT THEM, I HAVE NO THRONE--
YOU HAVEN'T EVEN HEARD WHAT WE HAVE TO SAY! YOUR LAND IS IN CHAOS! IF YOU'RE REALLY THE QUEEN, YOU CAN FIX THIS--
SMACK
GGH!
HEATHER?!
HEATHER! ANSWER ME!
HNNGH!

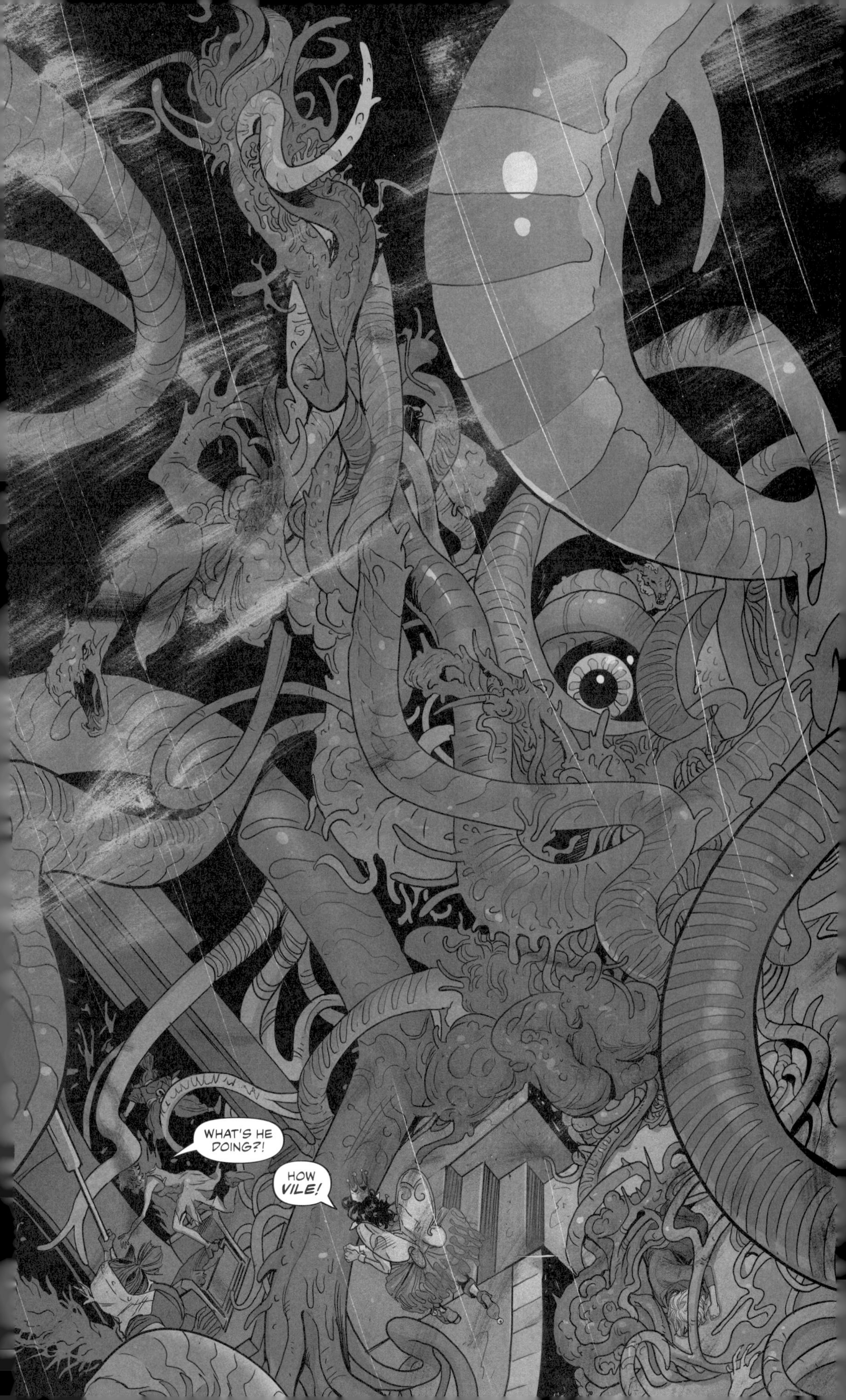
WHAT'S HE DOING?!
HOW VILE!

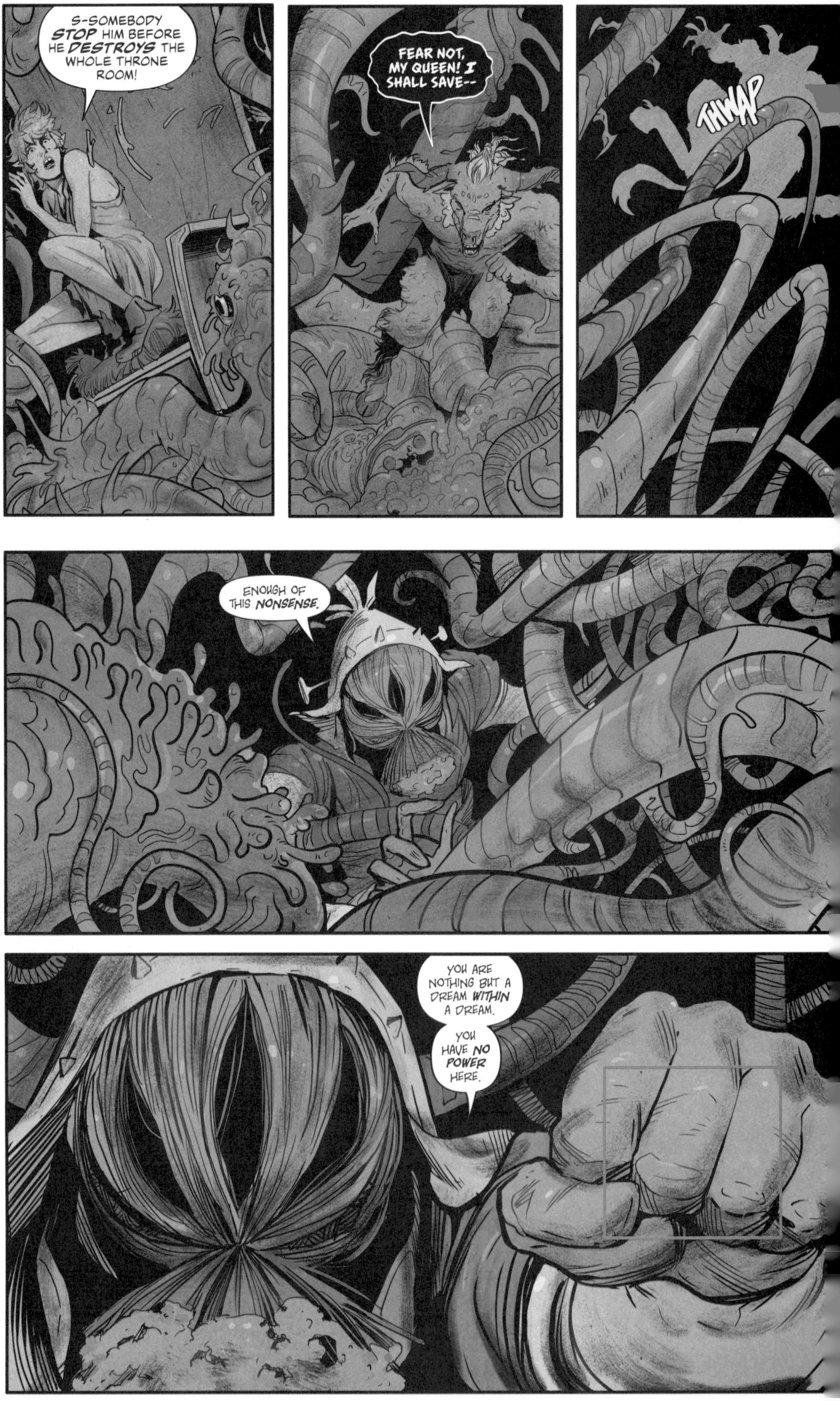
S-SOMEBODY STOP HIM BEFORE HE DESTROYS THE WHOLE THRONE ROOM!
FEAR NOT, MY QUEEN! I SHALL SAVE--
THWAP
ENOUGH OF THIS NONSENSE.
YOU ARE NOTHING BUT A DREAM WITHIN A DREAM.
YOU HAVE NO POWER HERE.

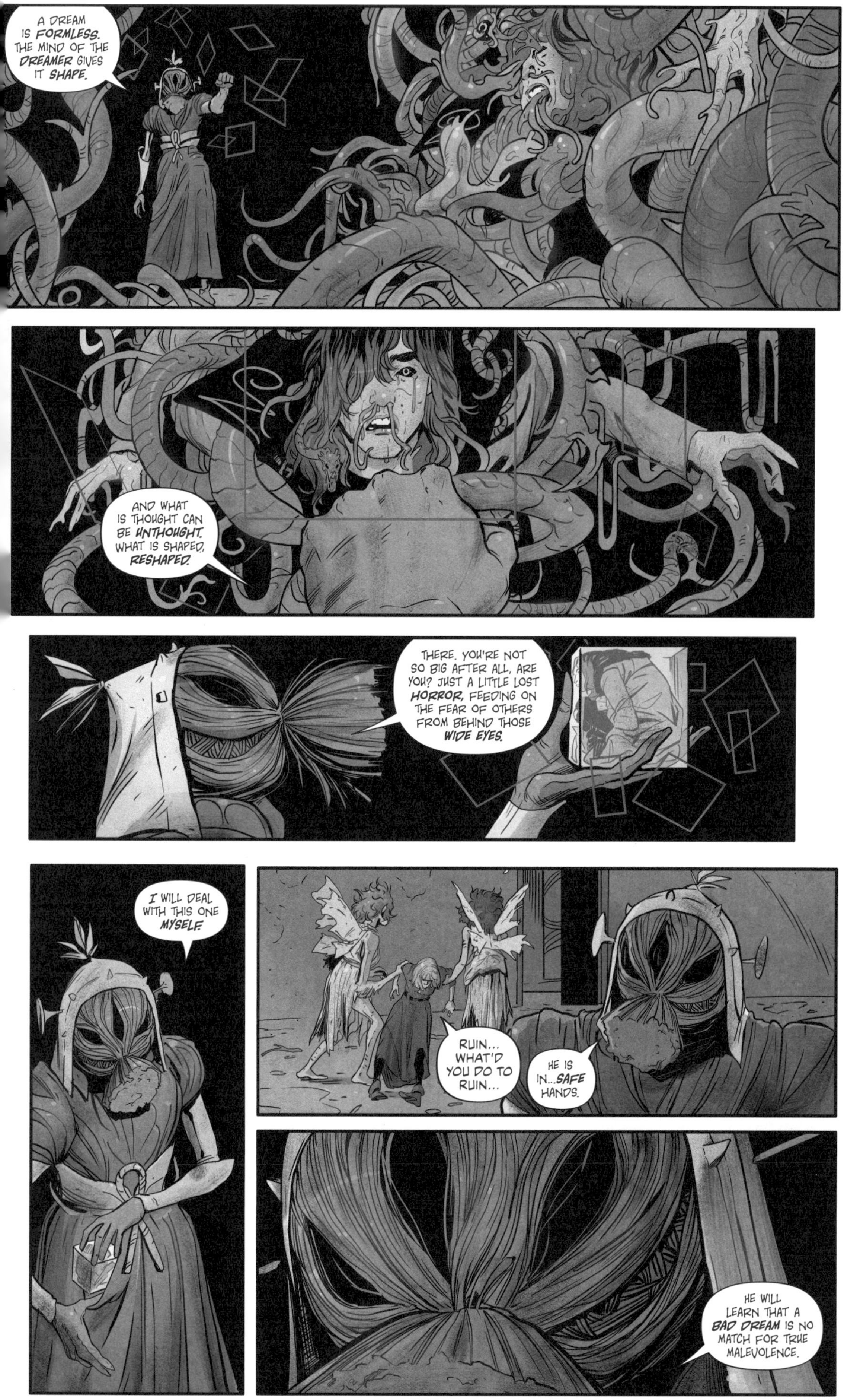
A DREAM IS FORMLESS. THE MIND OF THE DREAMER GIVES IT SHAPE.
AND WHAT IS THOUGHT CAN BE UNTHOUGHT. WHAT IS SHAPED, RESHAPED.
THERE. YOU'RE NOT SO BIG AFTER ALL, ARE YOU? JUST A LITTLE LOST HORROR, FEEDING ON THE FEAR OF OTHERS FROM BEHIND THOSE WIDE EYES.
I WILL DEAL WITH THIS ONE MYSELF.
RUIN... WHAT'D YOU DO TO RUIN...
HE IS IN...SAFE HANDS.
HE WILL LEARN THAT A BAD DREAM IS NO MATCH FOR TRUE MALEVOLENCE.

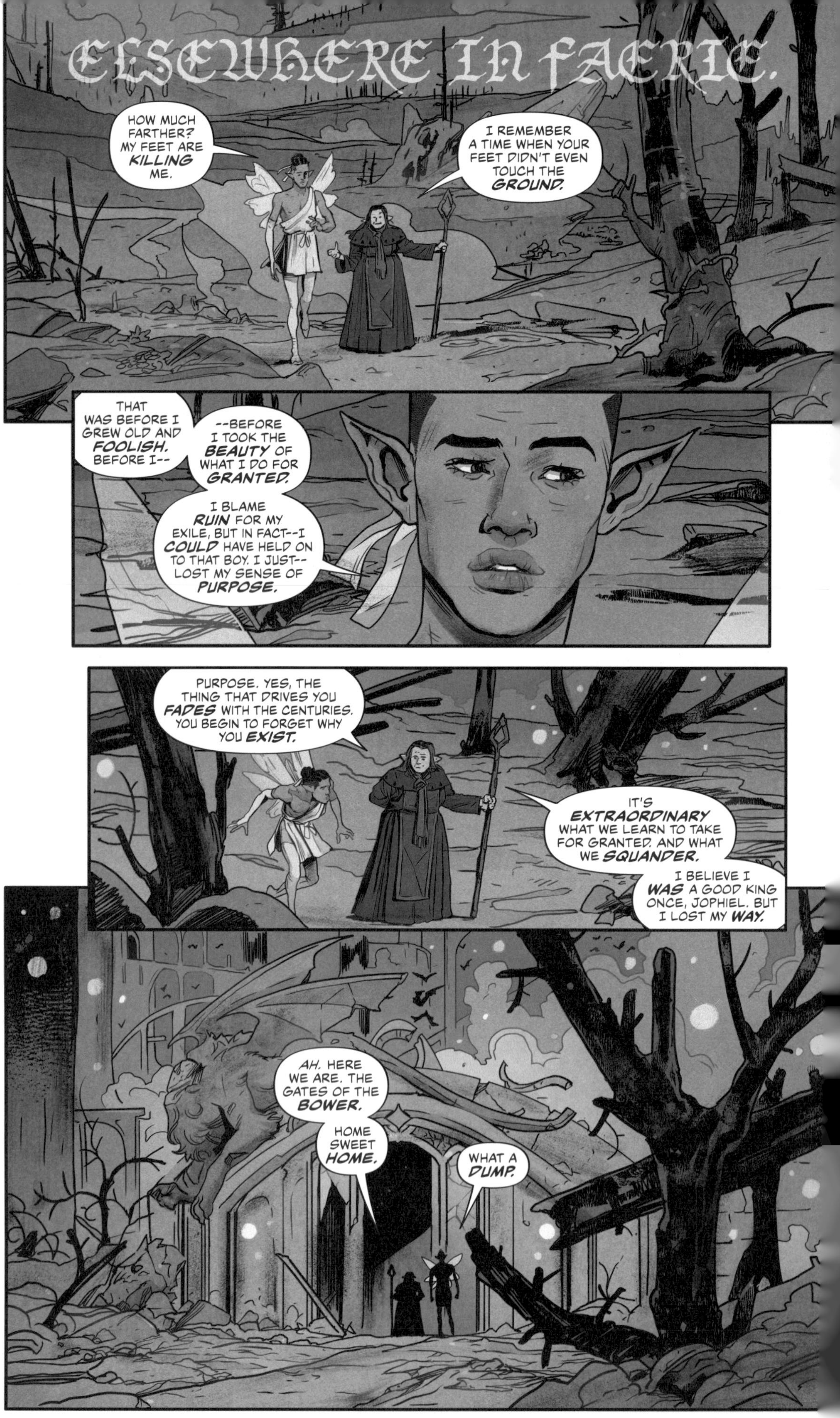
ELSEWHERE IN FAERIE.
HOW MUCH FARTHER? MY FEET ARE KILLING ME.
I REMEMBER A TIME WHEN YOUR FEET DIDN'T EVEN TOUCH THE GROUND.
THAT WAS BEFORE I GREW OLD AND FOOLISH. BEFORE I--
--BEFORE I TOOK THE BEAUTY OF WHAT I DO FOR GRANTED.
I BLAME RUIN FOR MY EXILE, BUT IN FACT--I COULD HAVE HELD ON TO THAT BOY. I JUST--LOST MY SENSE OF PURPOSE.
PURPOSE. YES, THE THING THAT DRIVES YOU FADES WITH THE CENTURIES. YOU BEGIN TO FORGET WHY YOU EXIST.
IT'S EXTRAORDINARY WHAT WE LEARN TO TAKE FOR GRANTED. AND WHAT WE SQUANDER.
I BELIEVE I WAS A GOOD KING ONCE, JOPHIEL. BUT I LOST MY WAY.
AH. HERE WE ARE. THE GATES OF THE BOWER.
HOME SWEET HOME.
WHAT A DUMP.

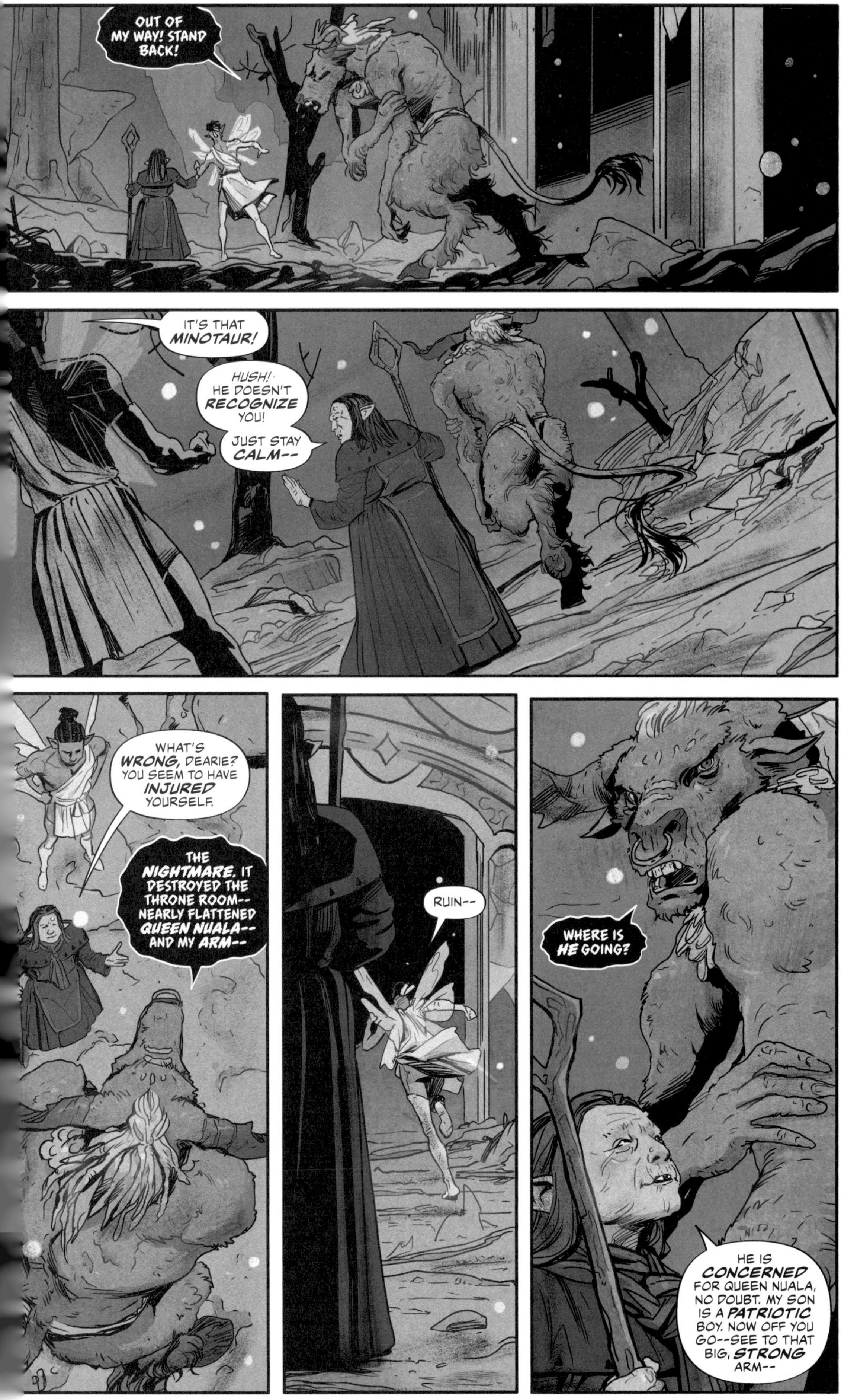
OUT OF MY WAY! STAND BACK!
IT'S THAT MINOTAUR!
HUSH! HE DOESN'T RECOGNIZE YOU!
JUST STAY CALM--
WHAT'S WRONG, DEARIE? YOU SEEM TO HAVE INJURED YOURSELF.
THE NIGHTMARE. IT DESTROYED THE THRONE ROOM-- NEARLY FLATTENED QUEEN NUALA-- AND MY ARM--
RUIN--
WHERE IS HE GOING?
HE IS CONCERNED FOR QUEEN NUALA, NO DOUBT. MY SON IS A PATRIOTIC BOY. NOW OFF YOU GO--SEE TO THAT BIG, STRONG ARM--

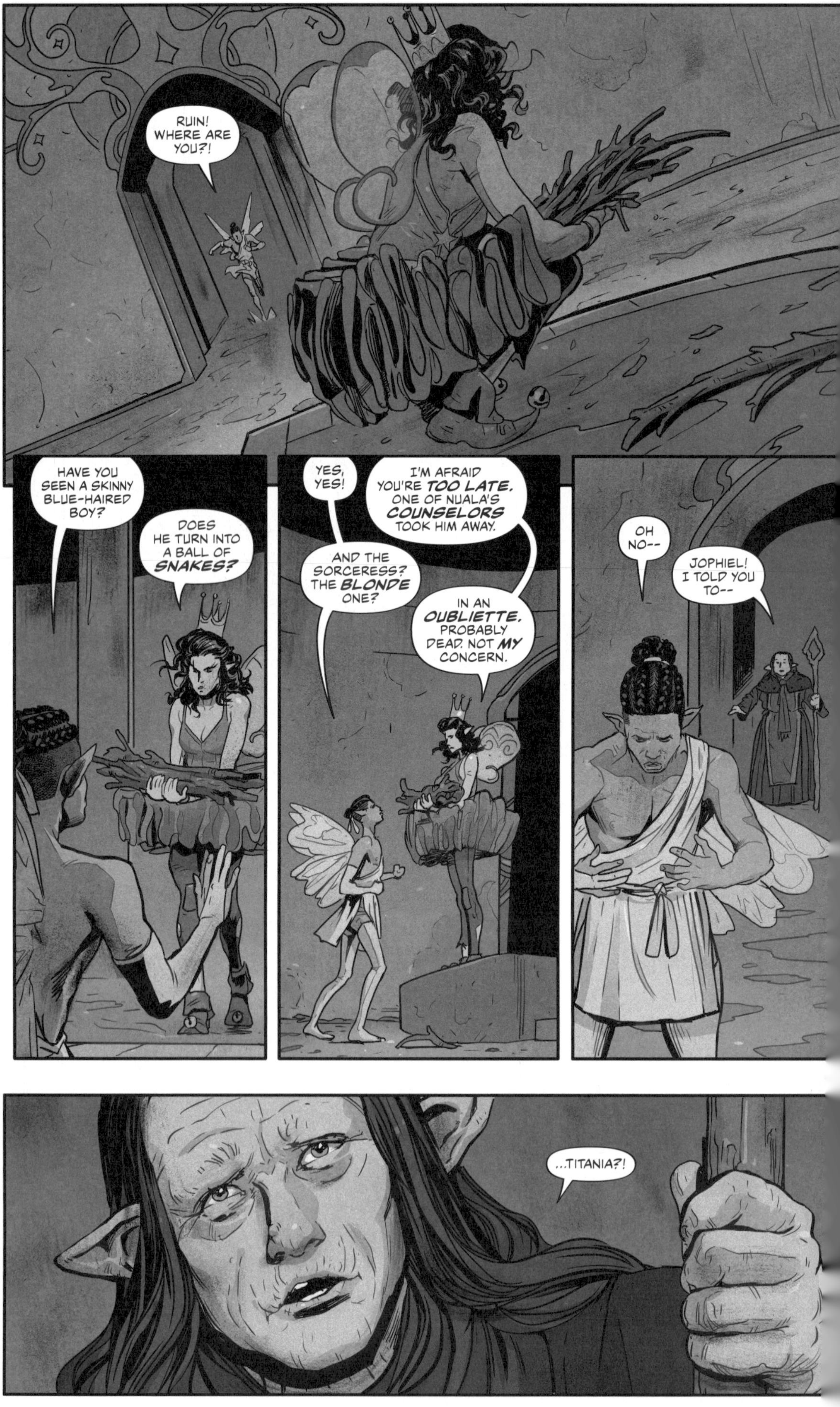
RUIN! WHERE ARE YOU?!
HAVE YOU SEEN A SKINNY BLUE-HAIRED BOY?
DOES HE TURN INTO A BALL OF SNAKES?
YES, YES!
I'M AFRAID YOU'RE TOO LATE. ONE OF NUALA'S COUNSELORS TOOK HIM AWAY.
AND THE SORCERESS? THE BLONDE ONE?
IN AN OUBLIETTE. PROBABLY DEAD. NOT MY CONCERN.
OH NO--
JOPHIEL! I TOLD YOU TO--
...TITANIA?!

HAVE YOU COME TO *GAWP* AT HOW FAR YOUR *QUEEN* HAS FALLEN?

AT HOW *LOW* OUR BEAUTIFUL KINGDOM HAS BEEN LAID?

YOU MAY AS WELL STARE.

LOOK AT WHAT THE *NEW* QUEEN HAS BROUGHT UPON US IN HER QUEST TO RIGHT THE WRONGS OF THE *PAST.*

EVEN MY OWN *HUSBAND* HAS ABANDONED ME...

PERHAPS HE ONLY LEFT TO SEEK *AID* FROM OTHER QUARTERS.

MY HUSBAND? THE WASTREL KING AUBERON? THAT WILL BE THE DAY. ARE *YOU* MARRIED, CRONE?

YES, IN FACT.

THEN YOU *KNOW* WHAT A *LONG MARRIAGE* IS LIKE. ON YOUR WEDDING DAY YOU SEE ONLY THE *PERFECT,* GOLDEN CREATURE WITH WHOM YOU FELL IN *LOVE,* THEN THE *YEARS* PASS.

YOU *REALIZE* YOU ARE NO LONGER MARRIED TO THAT PERSON. THEY HAVE BECOME SOMEONE *ELSE.*

AND YOU'RE NOT SURE *HOW* TO FALL IN LOVE WITH THAT NEW SOMEONE.

PERHAPS... PERHAPS THAT *NEW* SOMEONE STILL REMEMBERS HOW TO LOVE *YOU,* MY LADY.

YOU'RE VERY KIND.

I...I *SHOULD* HAVE BEEN *KINDER,* INSTEAD OF *SILENT* ALL THESE YEARS...

WHAT ON EARTH DO YOU *MEAN?*

NOTHING. NEVER MIND.

IF ONLY THAT *SUMMONER* WOULD UPHOLD *HER* END OF THE BARGAIN...

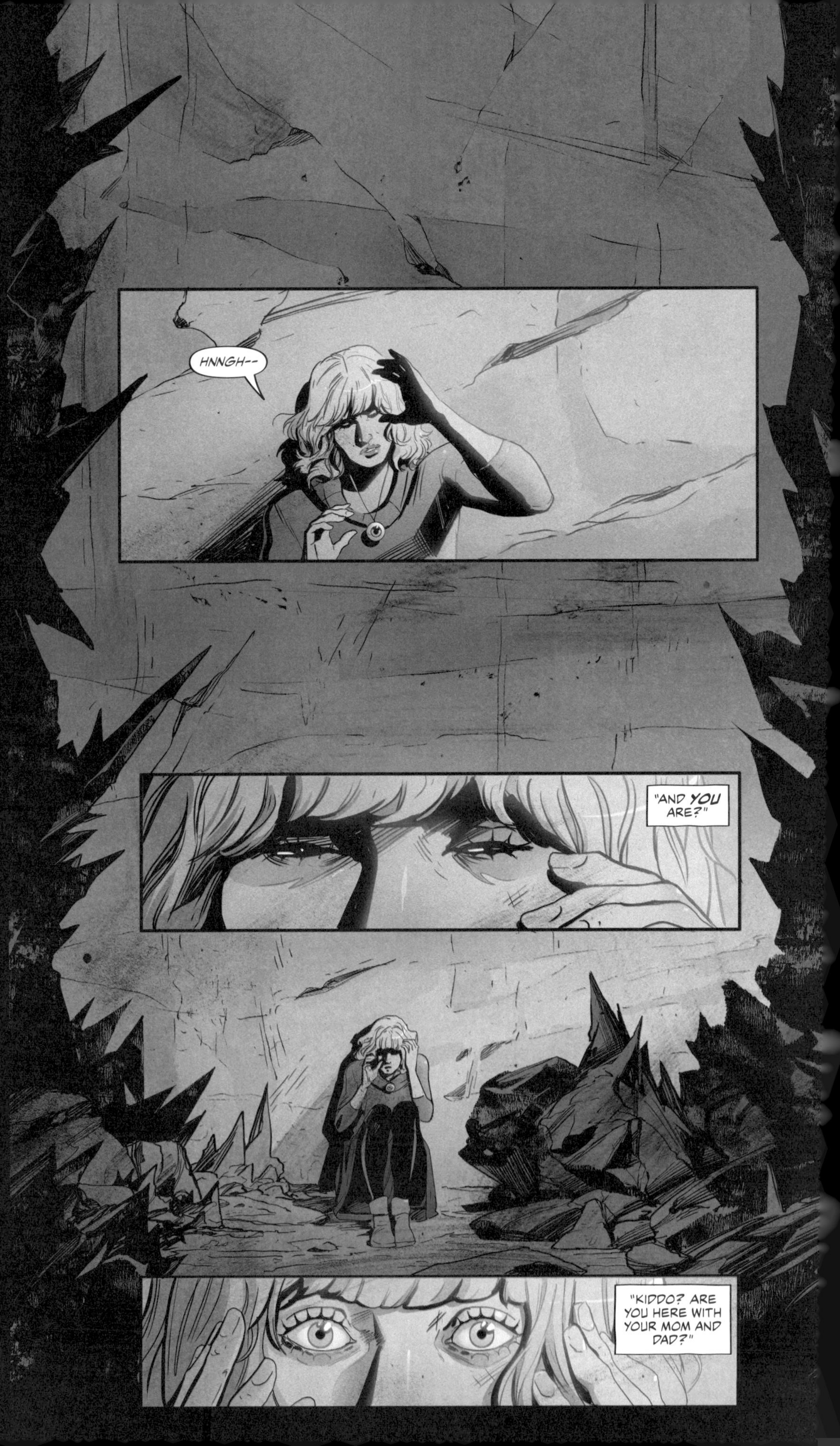
HNNGH--
"AND YOU ARE?"
"KIDDO? ARE YOU HERE WITH YOUR MOM AND DAD?"

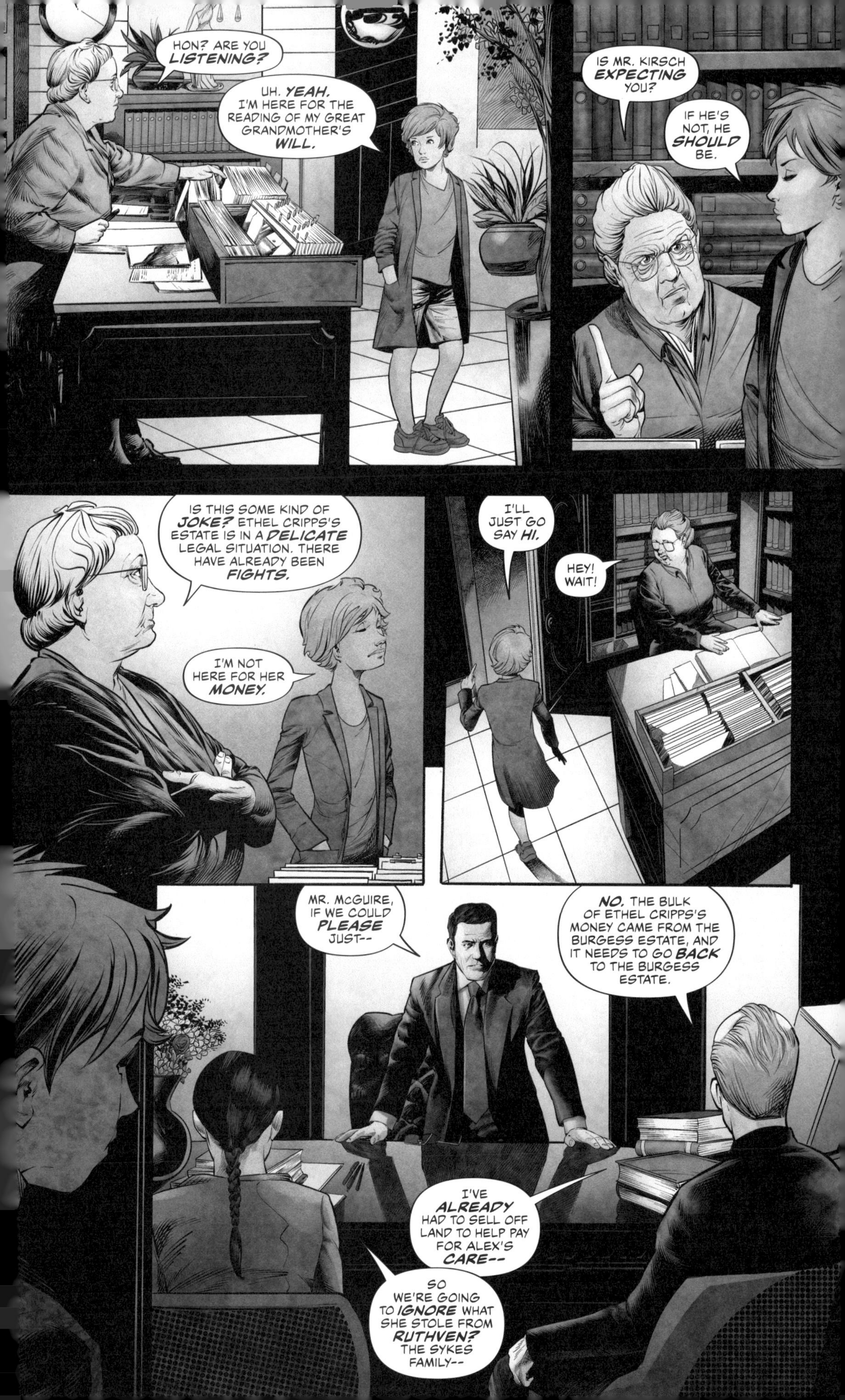
HON? ARE YOU LISTENING?
UH. YEAH. I'M HERE FOR THE READING OF MY GREAT GRANDMOTHER'S WILL.
IS MR. KIRSCH EXPECTING YOU?
IF HE'S NOT, HE SHOULD BE.
IS THIS SOME KIND OF JOKE? ETHEL CRIPPS'S ESTATE IS IN A DELICATE LEGAL SITUATION. THERE HAVE ALREADY BEEN FIGHTS.
I'M NOT HERE FOR HER MONEY.
I'LL JUST GO SAY HI.
HEY! WAIT!
MR. McGUIRE, IF WE COULD PLEASE JUST--
NO. THE BULK OF ETHEL CRIPPS'S MONEY CAME FROM THE BURGESS ESTATE, AND IT NEEDS TO GO BACK TO THE BURGESS ESTATE.
I'VE ALREADY HAD TO SELL OFF LAND TO HELP PAY FOR ALEX'S CARE--
SO WE'RE GOING TO IGNORE WHAT SHE STOLE FROM RUTHVEN? THE SYKES FAMILY--

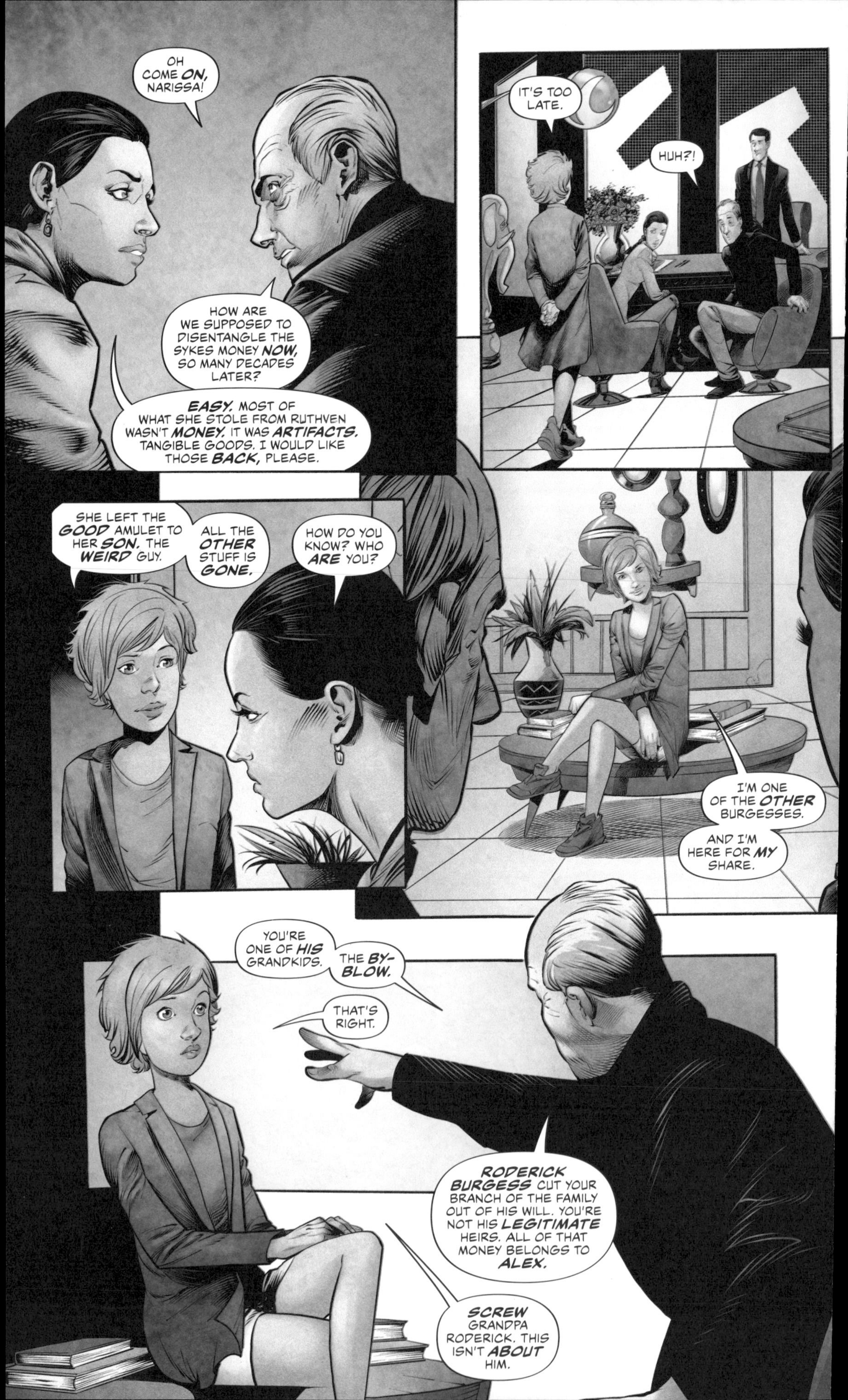

OH COME ON, NARISSA!
HOW ARE WE SUPPOSED TO DISENTANGLE THE SYKES MONEY NOW, SO MANY DECADES LATER?
EASY. MOST OF WHAT SHE STOLE FROM RUTHVEN WASN'T MONEY. IT WAS ARTIFACTS. TANGIBLE GOODS. I WOULD LIKE THOSE BACK, PLEASE.
IT'S TOO LATE.
HUH?!
SHE LEFT THE GOOD AMULET TO HER SON. THE WEIRD GUY.
ALL THE OTHER STUFF IS GONE.
HOW DO YOU KNOW? WHO ARE YOU?
I'M ONE OF THE OTHER BURGESSES.
AND I'M HERE FOR MY SHARE.
YOU'RE ONE OF HIS GRANDKIDS.
THE BY-BLOW.
THAT'S RIGHT.
RODERICK BURGESS CUT YOUR BRANCH OF THE FAMILY OUT OF HIS WILL. YOU'RE NOT HIS LEGITIMATE HEIRS. ALL OF THAT MONEY BELONGS TO ALEX.
SCREW GRANDPA RODERICK. THIS ISN'T ABOUT HIM.

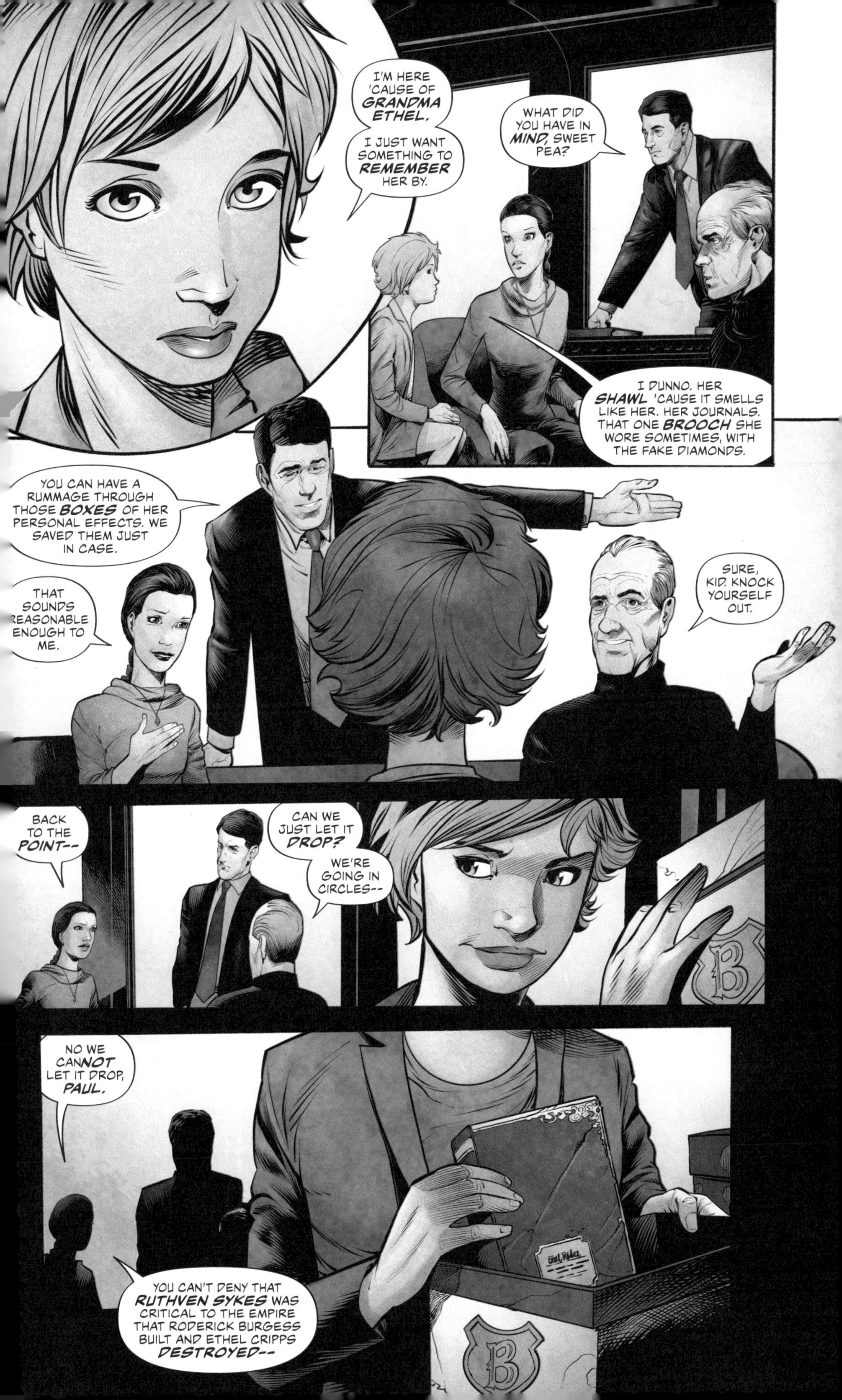
I'M HERE 'CAUSE OF GRANDMA ETHEL.
I JUST WANT SOMETHING TO REMEMBER HER BY.
WHAT DID YOU HAVE IN MIND, SWEET PEA?
I DUNNO. HER SHAWL 'CAUSE IT SMELLS LIKE HER. HER JOURNALS. THAT ONE BROOCH SHE WORE SOMETIMES, WITH THE FAKE DIAMONDS.
YOU CAN HAVE A RUMMAGE THROUGH THOSE BOXES OF HER PERSONAL EFFECTS. WE SAVED THEM JUST IN CASE.
THAT SOUNDS REASONABLE ENOUGH TO ME.
SURE, KID. KNOCK YOURSELF OUT.
BACK TO THE POINT--
CAN WE JUST LET IT DROP?
WE'RE GOING IN CIRCLES--
NO WE CANNOT LET IT DROP, PAUL.
YOU CAN'T DENY THAT RUTHVEN SYKES WAS CRITICAL TO THE EMPIRE THAT RODERICK BURGESS BUILT AND ETHEL CRIPPS DESTROYED--

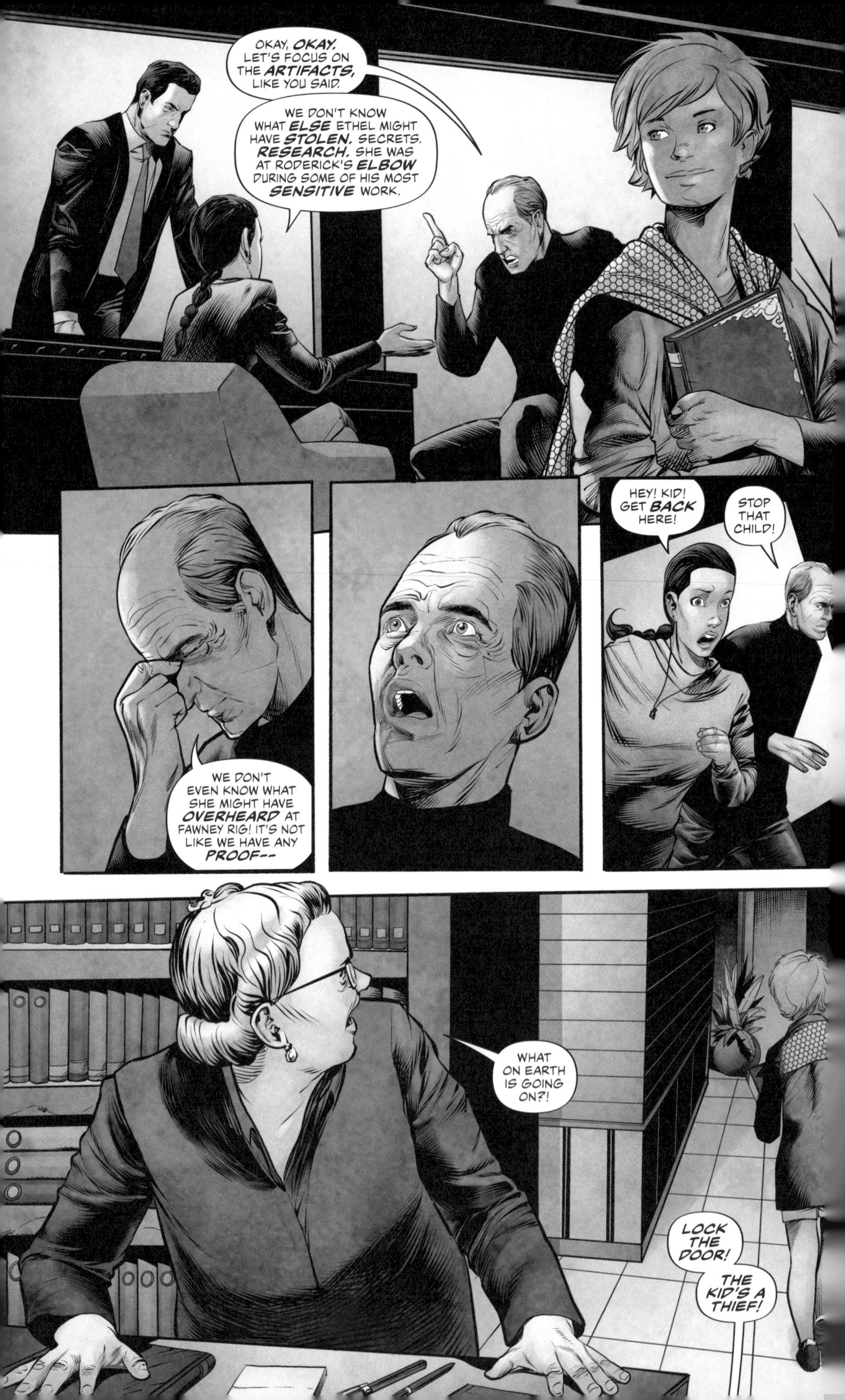
OKAY, OKAY. LET'S FOCUS ON THE ARTIFACTS, LIKE YOU SAID.
WE DON'T KNOW WHAT ELSE ETHEL MIGHT HAVE STOLEN. SECRETS. RESEARCH. SHE WAS AT RODERICK'S ELBOW DURING SOME OF HIS MOST SENSITIVE WORK.
WE DON'T EVEN KNOW WHAT SHE MIGHT HAVE OVERHEARD AT FAWNEY RIG! IT'S NOT LIKE WE HAVE ANY PROOF--
HEY! KID! GET BACK HERE!
STOP THAT CHILD!
WHAT ON EARTH IS GOING ON?!
LOCK THE DOOR!
THE KID'S A THIEF!

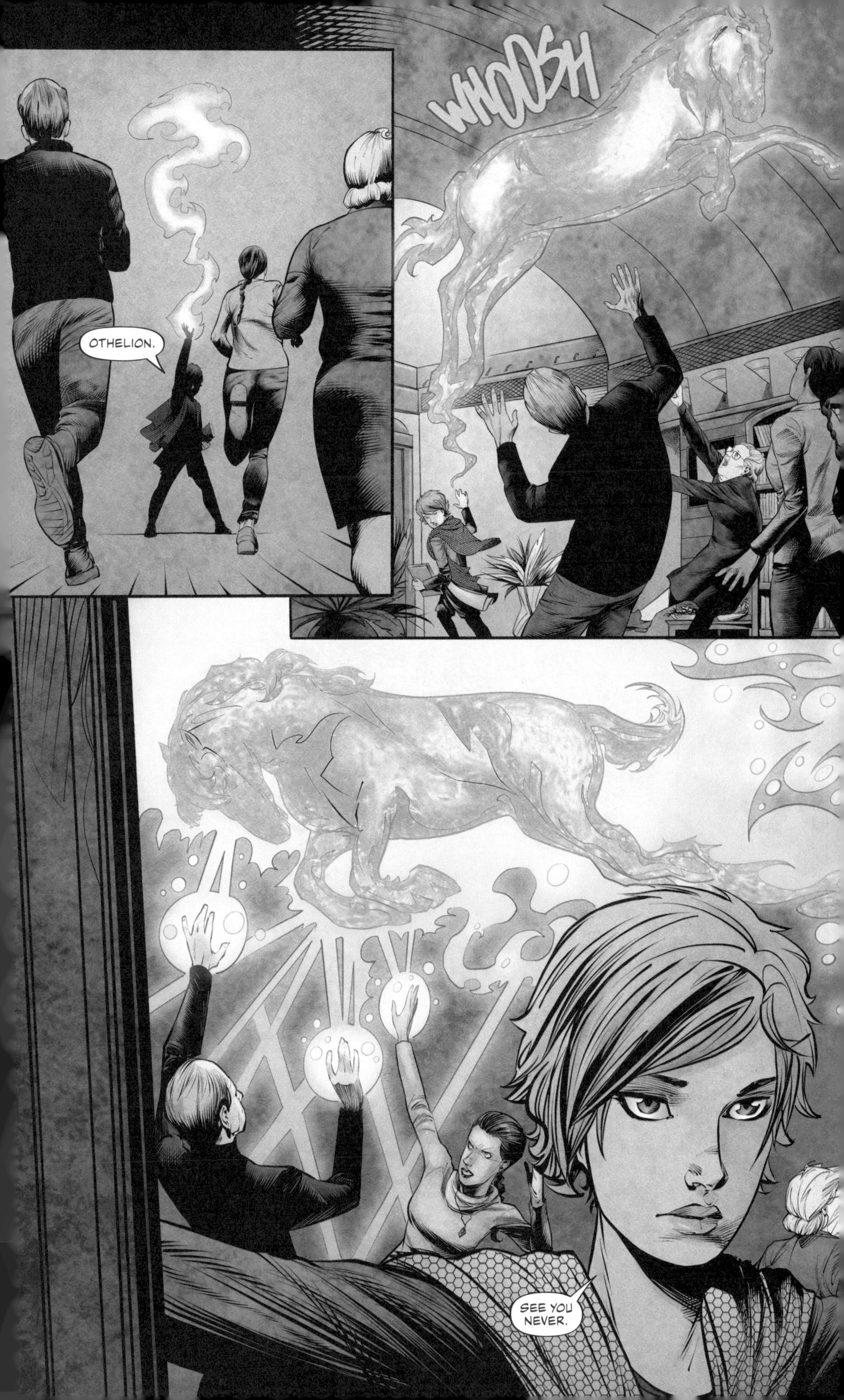
OTHELION.
WHOOSH
SEE YOU NEVER.

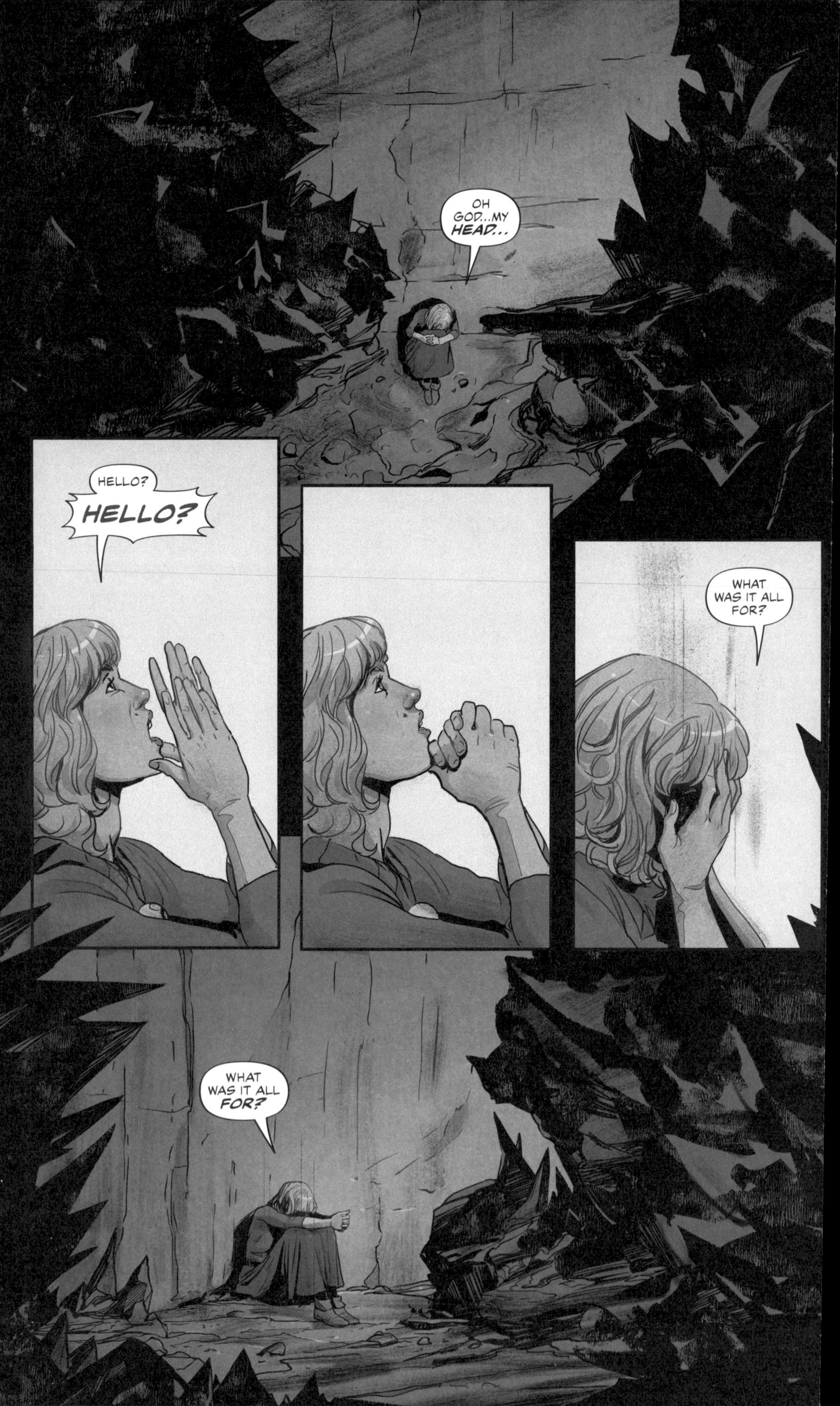
OH GOD...MY HEAD...
HELLO?
HELLO?
WHAT WAS IT ALL FOR?
WHAT WAS IT ALL FOR?

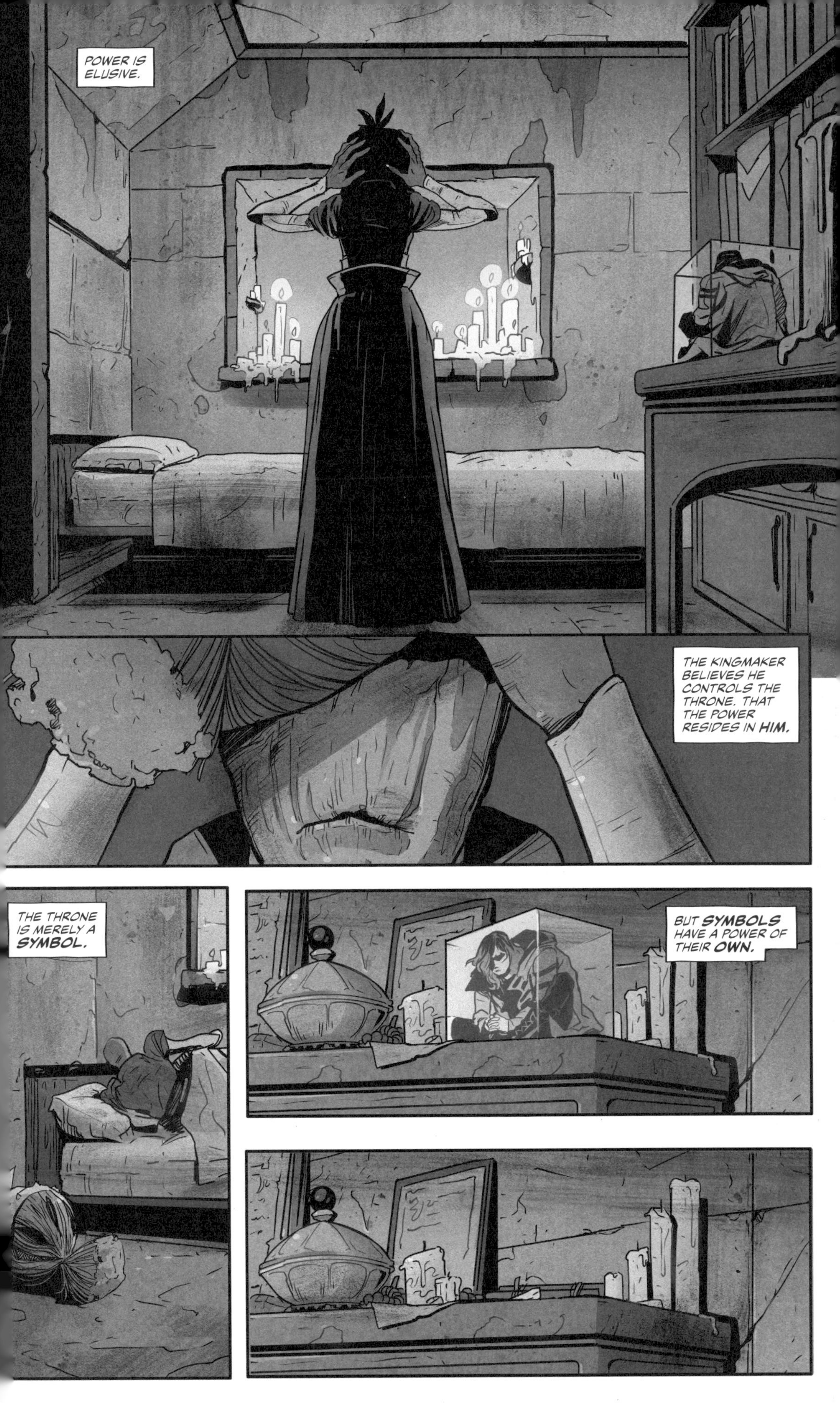
POWER IS ELUSIVE.
THE KINGMAKER BELIEVES HE CONTROLS THE THRONE. THAT THE POWER RESIDES IN HIM.
THE THRONE IS MERELY A SYMBOL.
BUT SYMBOLS HAVE A POWER OF THEIR OWN.

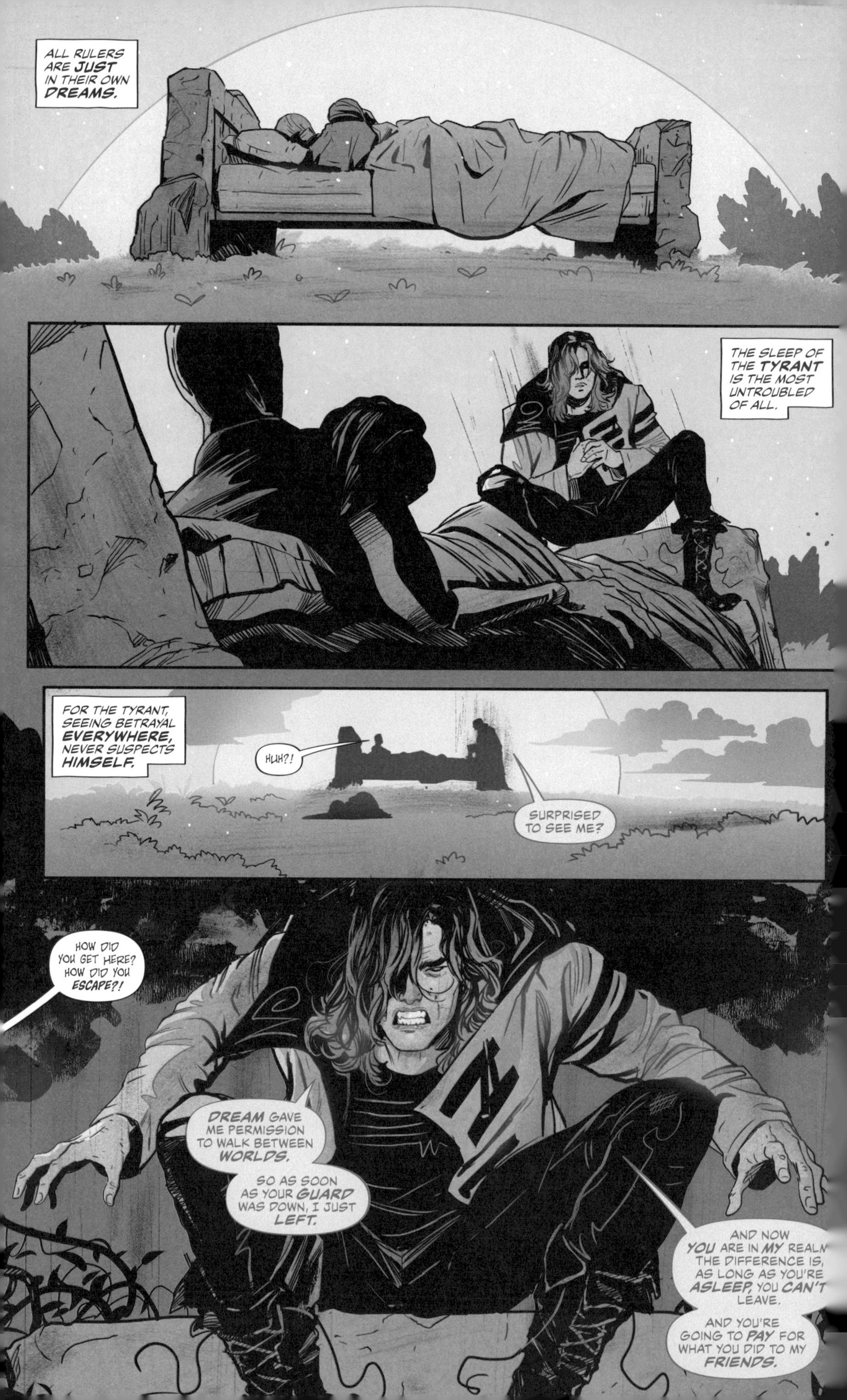
ALL RULERS ARE JUST IN THEIR OWN DREAMS.
THE SLEEP OF THE TYRANT IS THE MOST UNTROUBLED OF ALL.
FOR THE TYRANT, SEEING BETRAYAL EVERYWHERE, NEVER SUSPECTS HIMSELF.
HUH?!
SURPRISED TO SEE ME?
HOW DID YOU GET HERE? HOW DID YOU ESCAPE?!
DREAM GAVE ME PERMISSION TO WALK BETWEEN WORLDS.
SO AS SOON AS YOUR GUARD WAS DOWN, I JUST LEFT.
AND NOW YOU ARE IN MY REALM. THE DIFFERENCE IS, AS LONG AS YOU'RE ASLEEP, YOU CAN'T LEAVE.
AND YOU'RE GOING TO PAY FOR WHAT YOU DID TO MY FRIENDS.

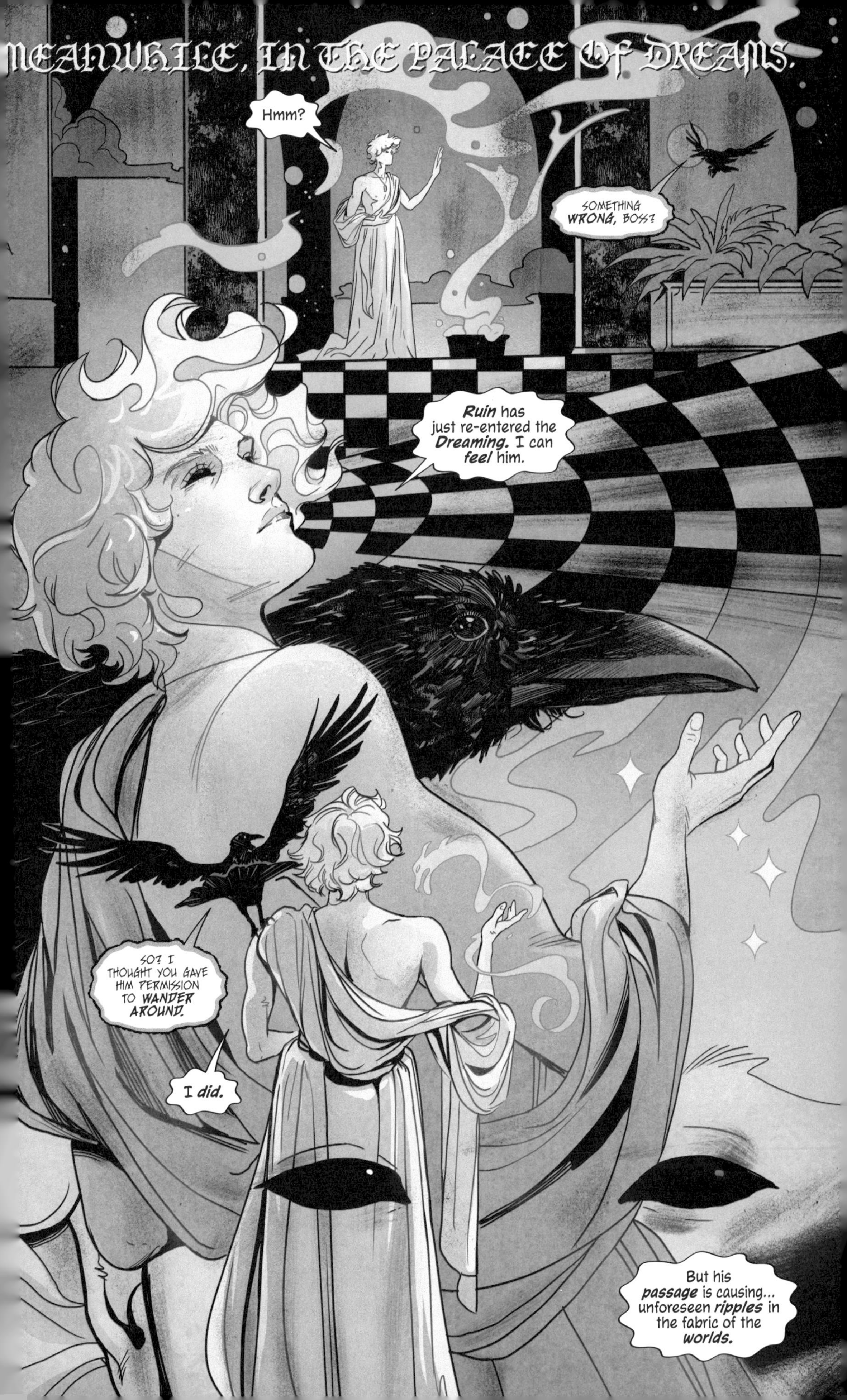
MEANWHILE, IN THE PALACE OF DREAMS.
Hmm?
SOMETHING WRONG, BOSS?
Ruin has just re-entered the Dreaming. I can feel him.
SO? I THOUGHT YOU GAVE HIM PERMISSION TO WANDER AROUND.
I did.
But his passage is causing... unforeseen ripples in the fabric of the worlds.

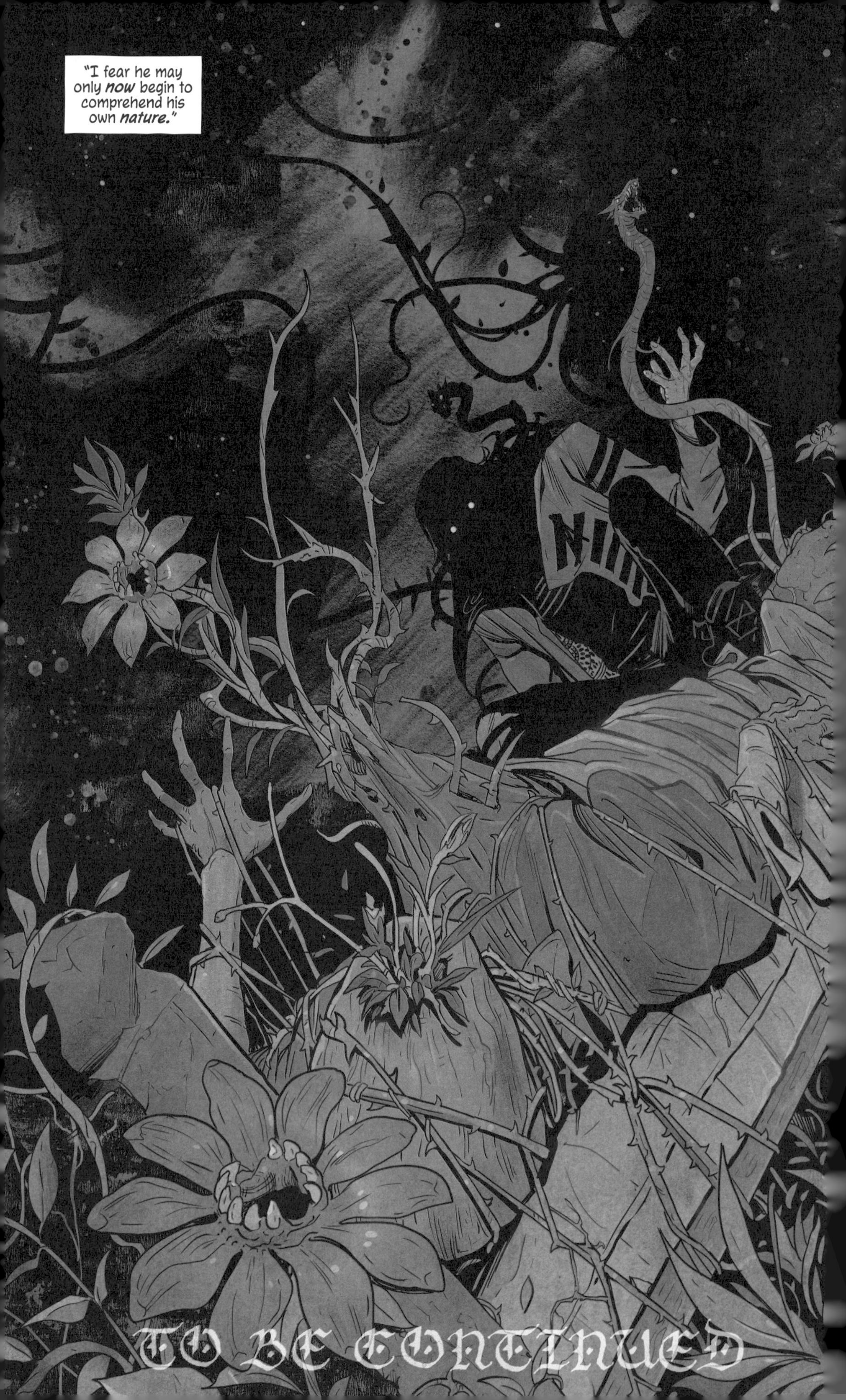
"I fear he may only *now* begin to comprehend his own *nature.*"
TO BE CONTINUED

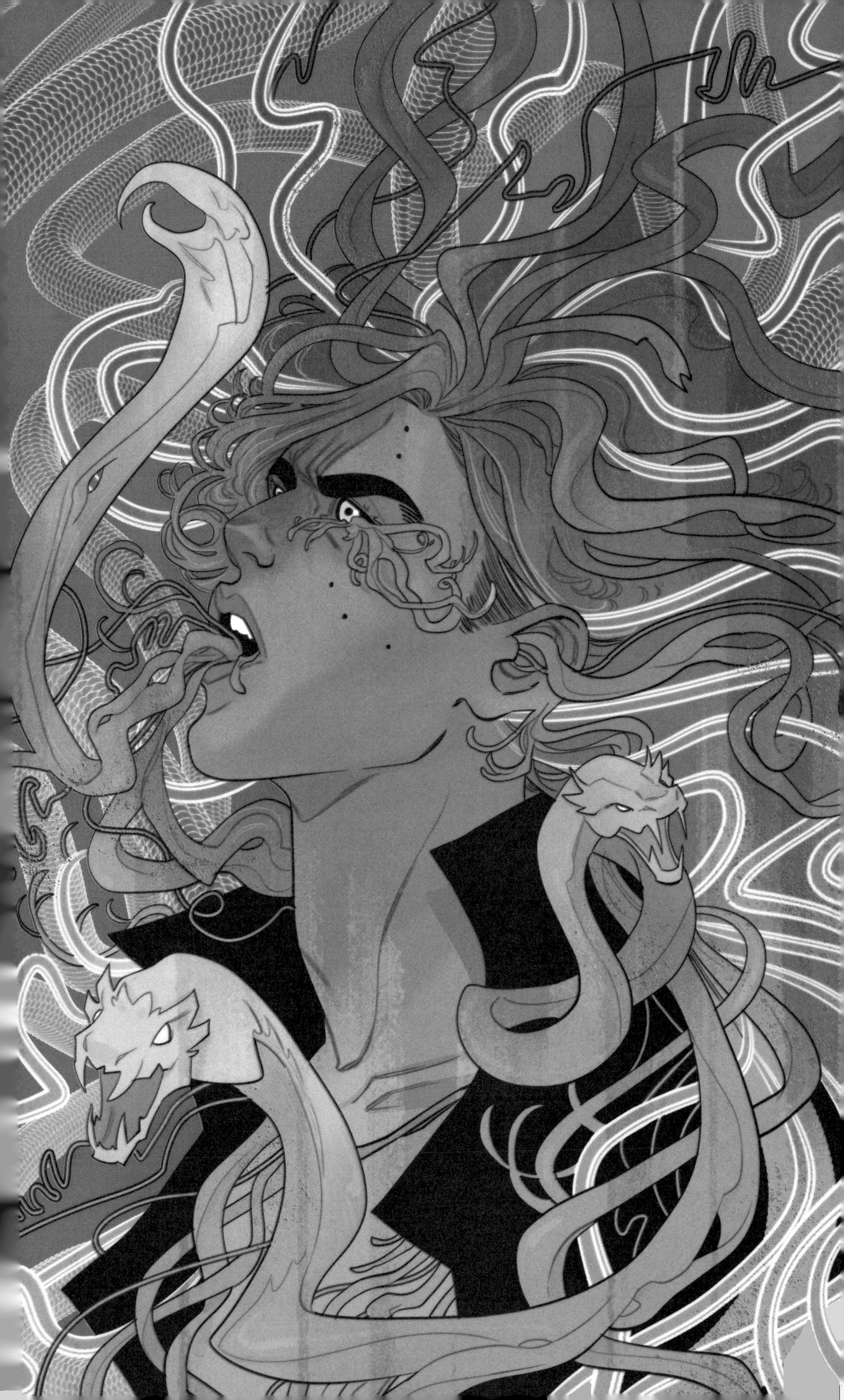

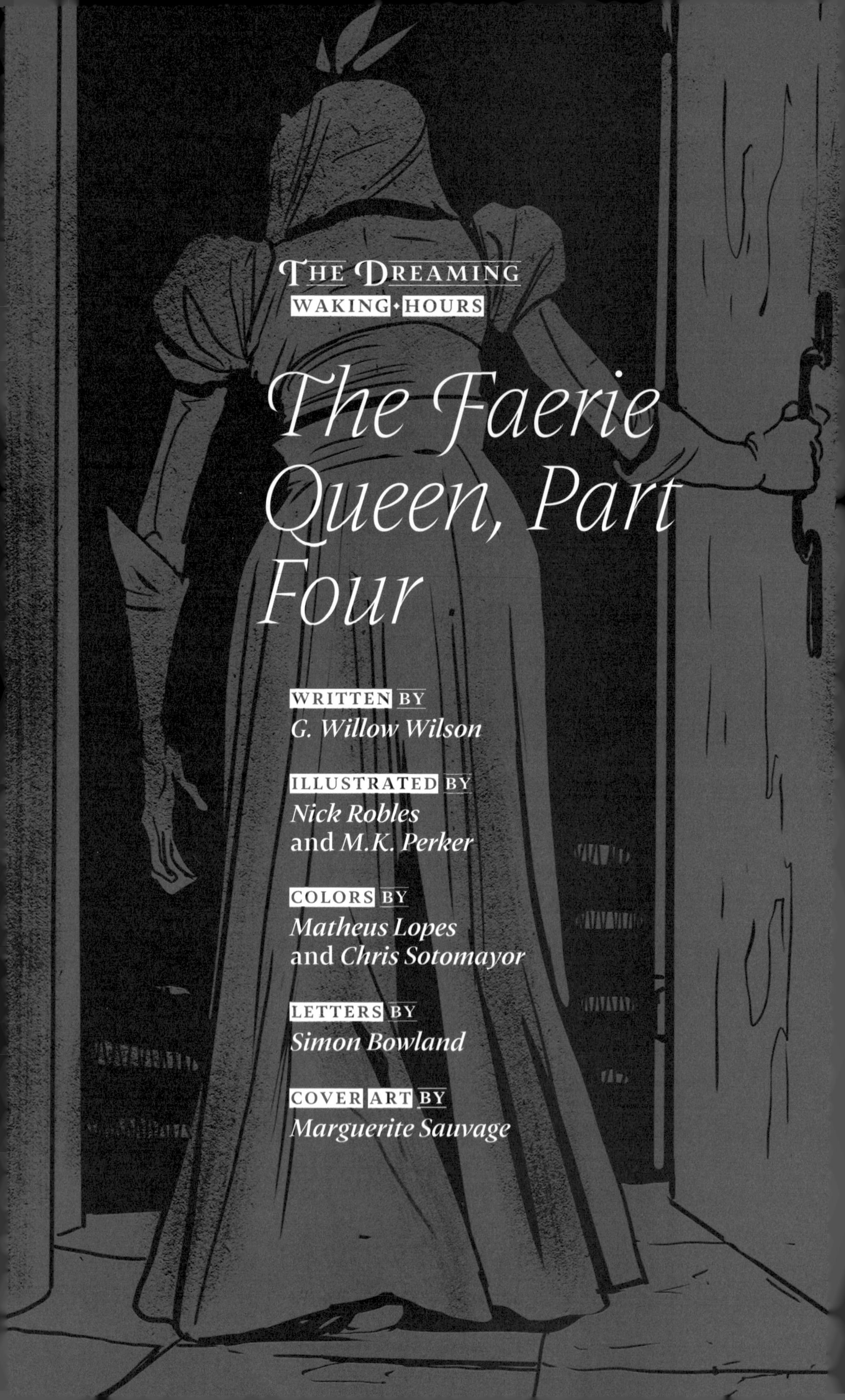

THE DREAMING
WAKING ✦ HOURS

The Faerie Queen, Part Four

WRITTEN BY
G. Willow Wilson

ILLUSTRATED BY
Nick Robles
and *M.K. Perker*

COLORS BY
Matheus Lopes
and *Chris Sotomayor*

LETTERS BY
Simon Bowland

COVER ART BY
Marguerite Sauvage

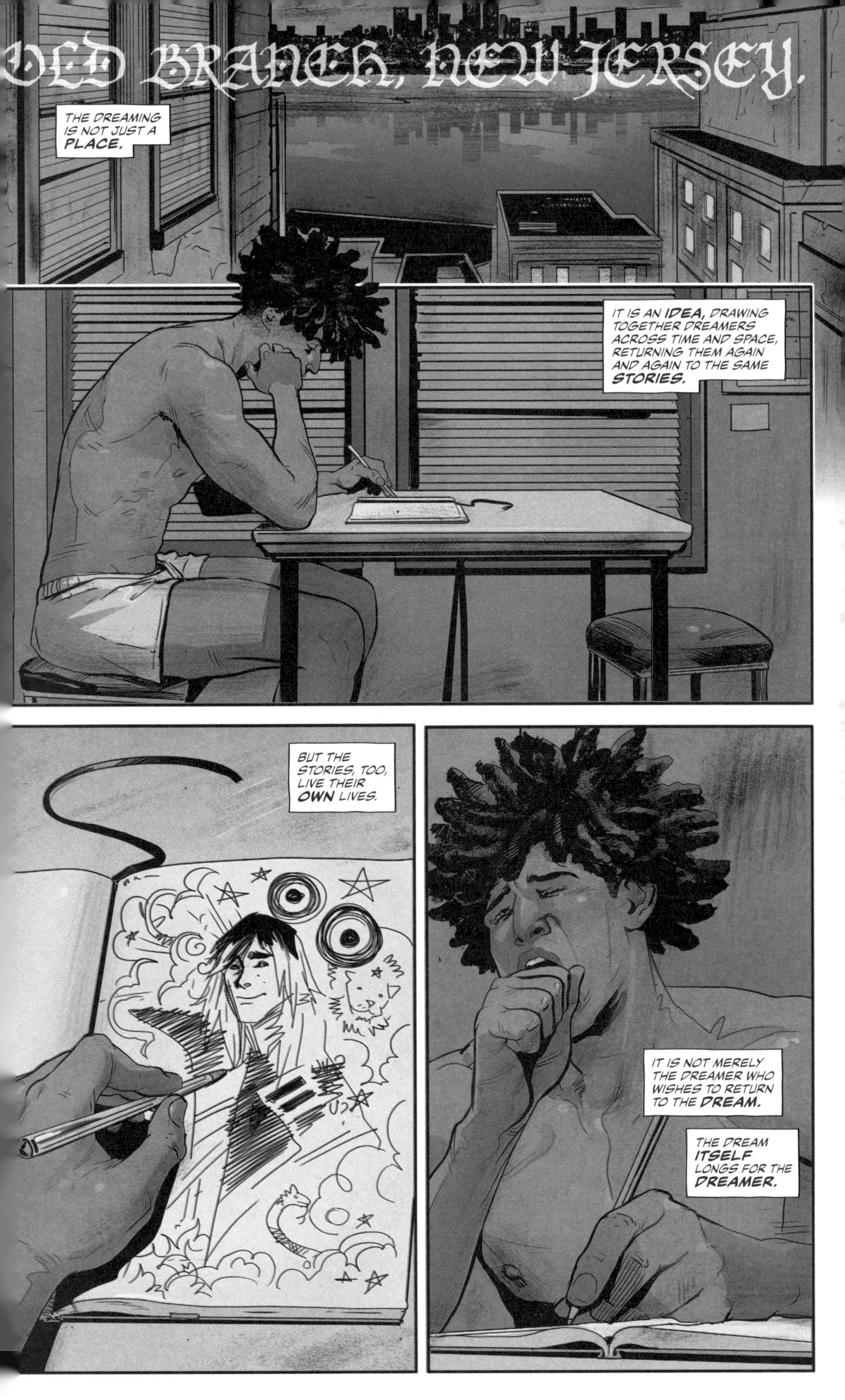
OLD BRANCH, NEW JERSEY.
THE DREAMING IS NOT JUST A PLACE.
IT IS AN IDEA, DRAWING TOGETHER DREAMERS ACROSS TIME AND SPACE, RETURNING THEM AGAIN AND AGAIN TO THE SAME STORIES.
BUT THE STORIES, TOO, LIVE THEIR OWN LIVES.
IT IS NOT MERELY THE DREAMER WHO WISHES TO RETURN TO THE DREAM.
THE DREAM ITSELF LONGS FOR THE DREAMER.

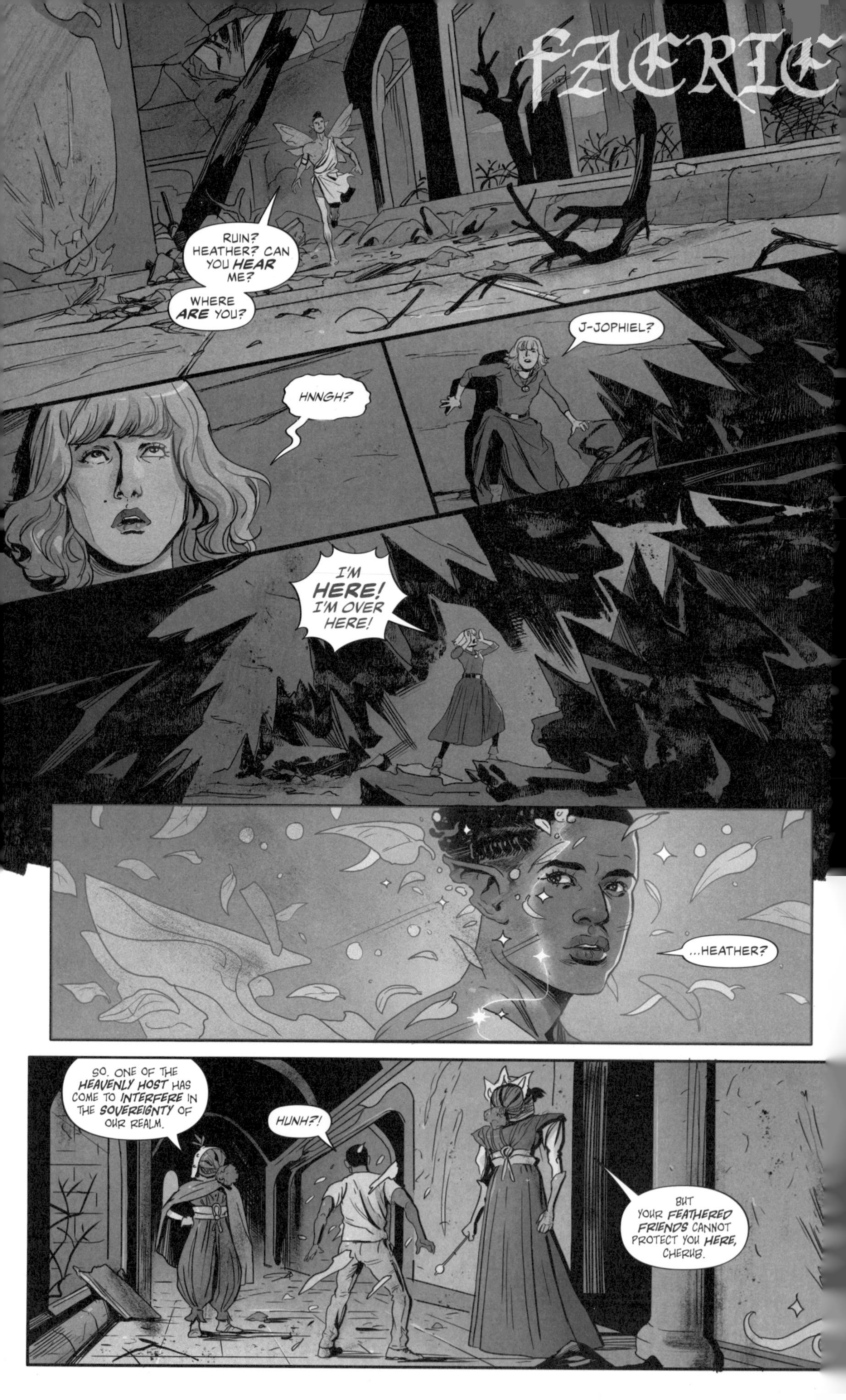
FAERIE
RUIN? HEATHER? CAN YOU HEAR ME?
WHERE ARE YOU?
J-JOPHIEL?
HNNGH?
I'M HERE! I'M OVER HERE!
...HEATHER?
SO. ONE OF THE HEAVENLY HOST HAS COME TO INTERFERE IN THE SOVEREIGNTY OF OUR REALM.
HUNH?!
BUT YOUR FEATHERED FRIENDS CANNOT PROTECT YOU HERE, CHERUB.

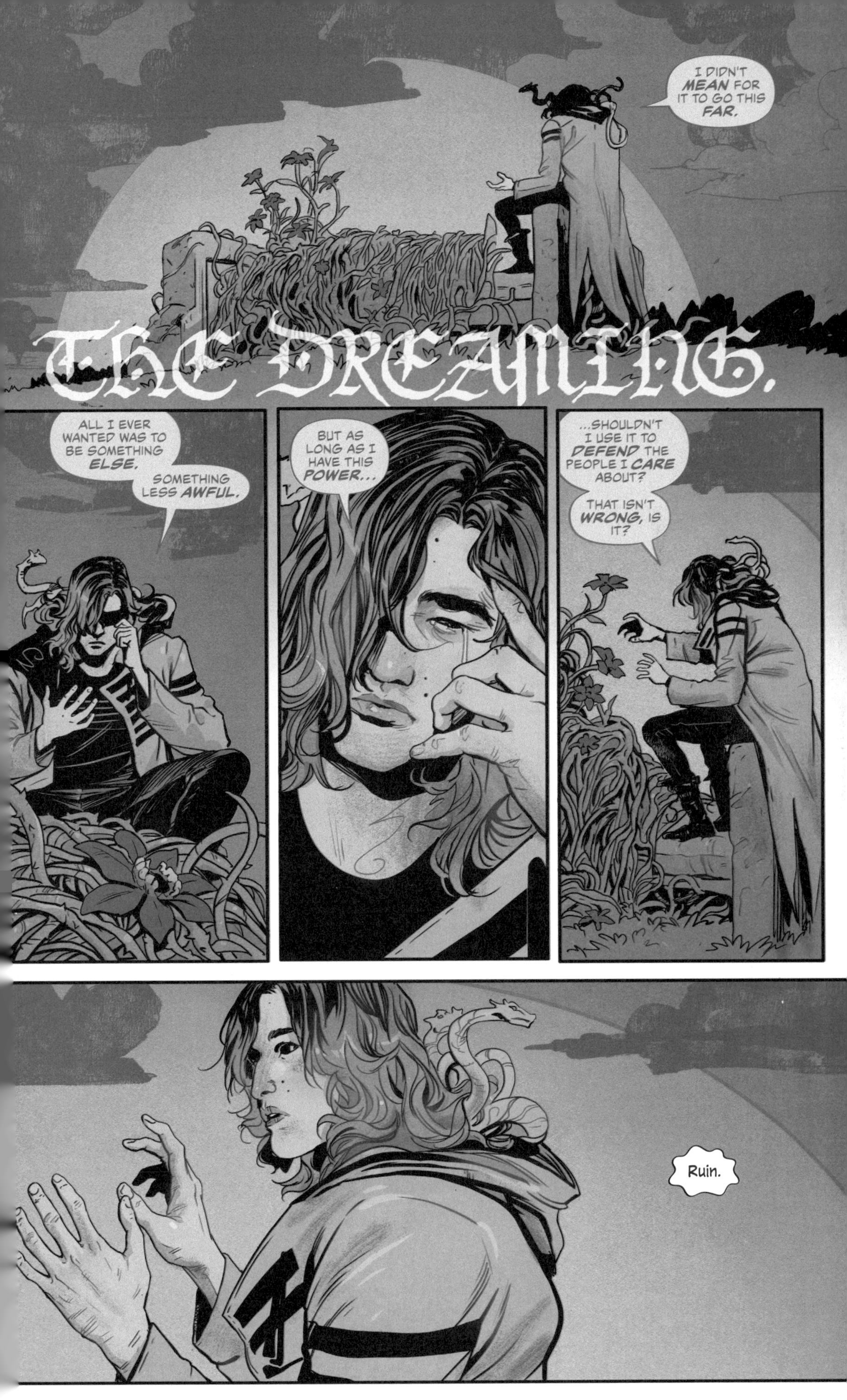
I DIDN'T MEAN FOR IT TO GO THIS FAR.
THE DREAMING.
ALL I EVER WANTED WAS TO BE SOMETHING ELSE.
SOMETHING LESS AWFUL.
BUT AS LONG AS I HAVE THIS POWER...
...SHOULDN'T I USE IT TO DEFEND THE PEOPLE I CARE ABOUT?
THAT ISN'T WRONG, IS IT?
Ruin.

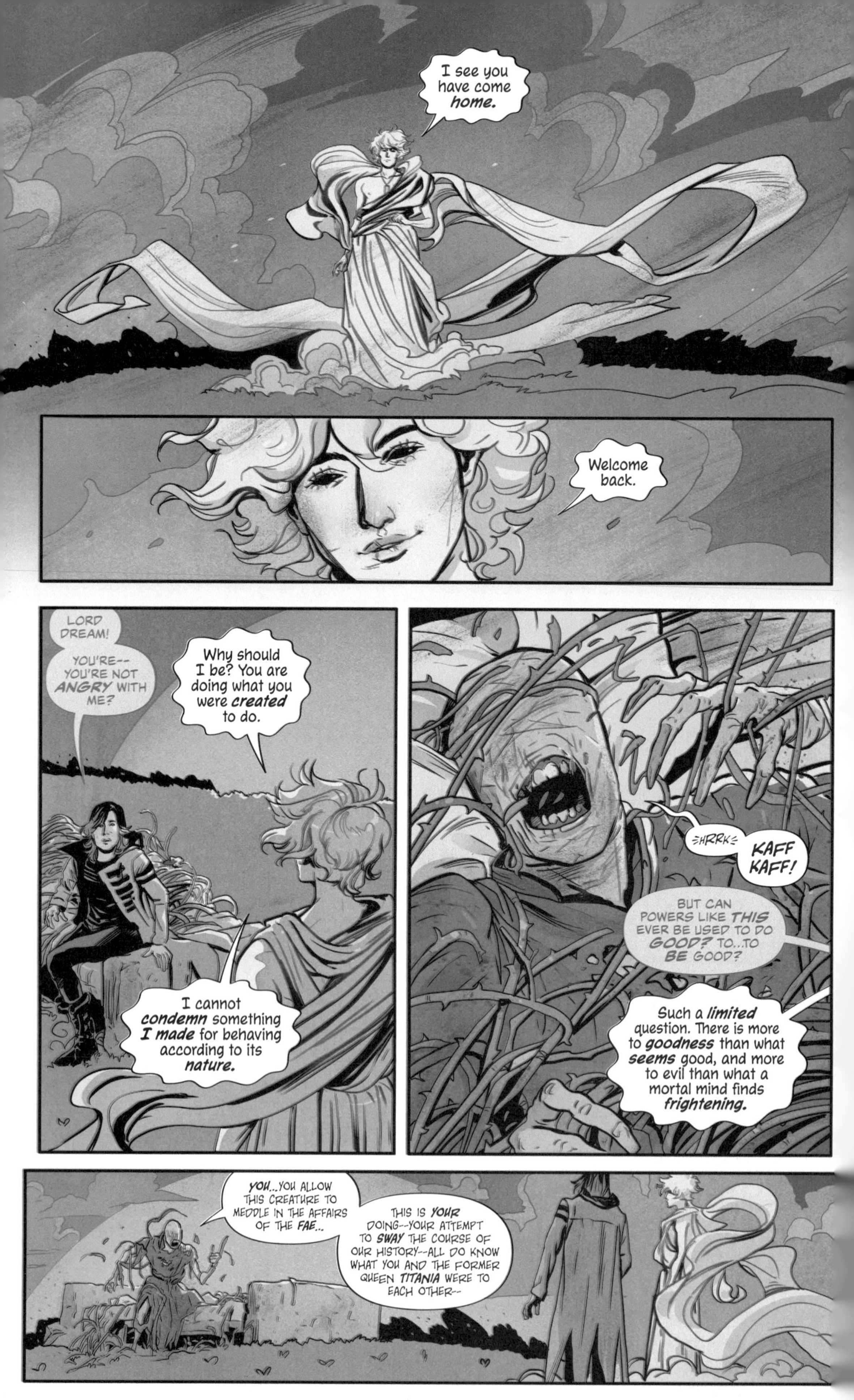
I see you have come home.
Welcome back.
LORD DREAM!
YOU'RE-- YOU'RE NOT ANGRY WITH ME?
Why should I be? You are doing what you were created to do.
I cannot condemn something I made for behaving according to its nature.
HRRK
KAFF KAFF!
BUT CAN POWERS LIKE THIS EVER BE USED TO DO GOOD? TO...TO BE GOOD?
Such a limited question. There is more to goodness than what seems good, and more to evil than what a mortal mind finds frightening.
YOU...YOU ALLOW THIS CREATURE TO MEDDLE IN THE AFFAIRS OF THE FAE...
THIS IS YOUR DOING--YOUR ATTEMPT TO SWAY THE COURSE OF OUR HISTORY--ALL DO KNOW WHAT YOU AND THE FORMER QUEEN TITANIA WERE TO EACH OTHER--

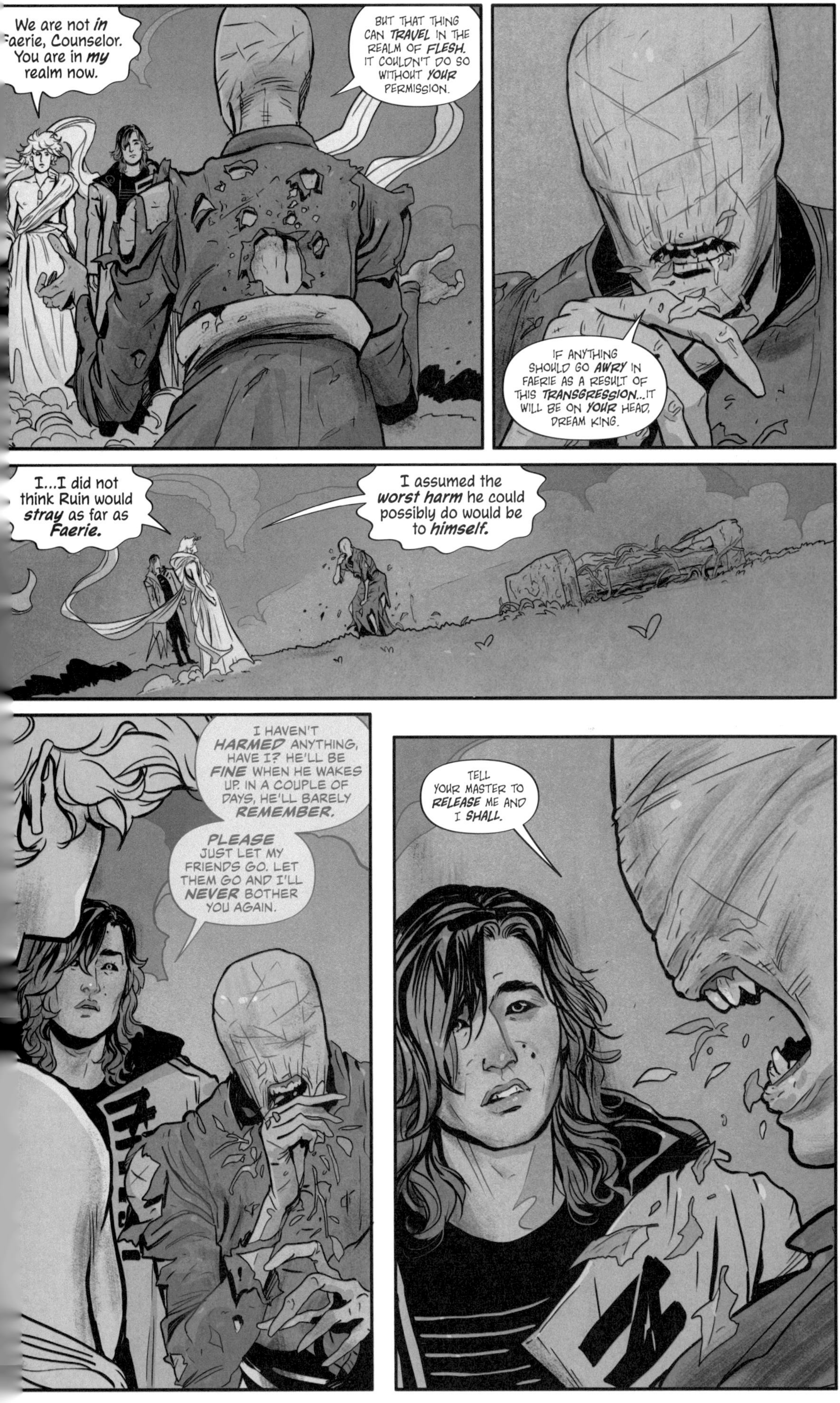
We are not in Faerie, Counselor. You are in my realm now.
BUT THAT THING CAN TRAVEL IN THE REALM OF FLESH. IT COULDN'T DO SO WITHOUT YOUR PERMISSION.
IF ANYTHING SHOULD GO AWRY IN FAERIE AS A RESULT OF THIS TRANSGRESSION...IT WILL BE ON YOUR HEAD, DREAM KING.
I...I did not think Ruin would stray as far as Faerie.
I assumed the worst harm he could possibly do would be to himself.
I HAVEN'T HARMED ANYTHING, HAVE I? HE'LL BE FINE WHEN HE WAKES UP. IN A COUPLE OF DAYS, HE'LL BARELY REMEMBER.
PLEASE JUST LET MY FRIENDS GO. LET THEM GO AND I'LL NEVER BOTHER YOU AGAIN.
TELL YOUR MASTER TO RELEASE ME AND I SHALL.

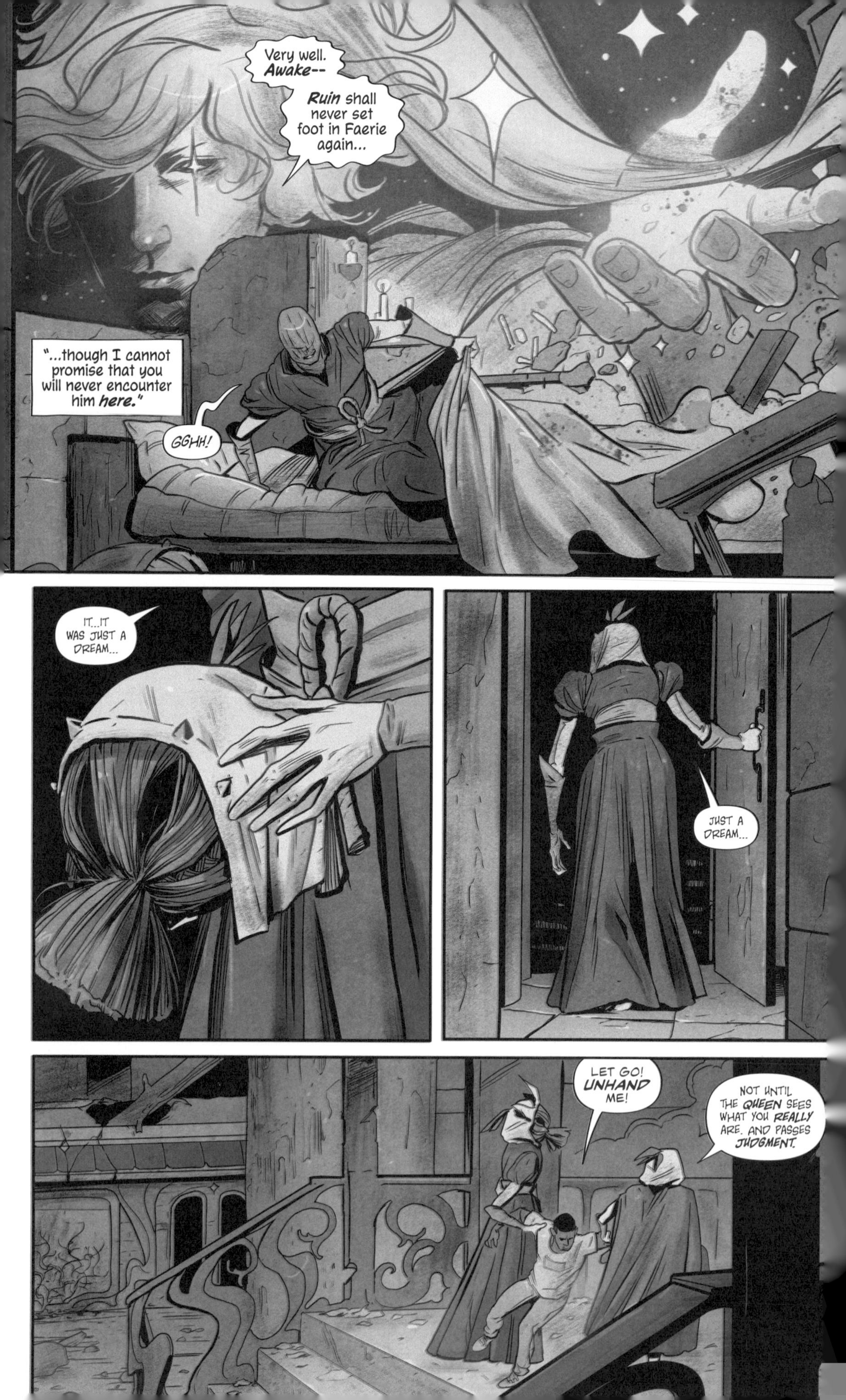
Very well. Awake--
Ruin shall never set foot in Faerie again...
"...though I cannot promise that you will never encounter him here."
GGHH!
IT...IT WAS JUST A DREAM...
JUST A DREAM...
LET GO! UNHAND ME!
NOT UNTIL THE QUEEN SEES WHAT YOU REALLY ARE. AND PASSES JUDGMENT.

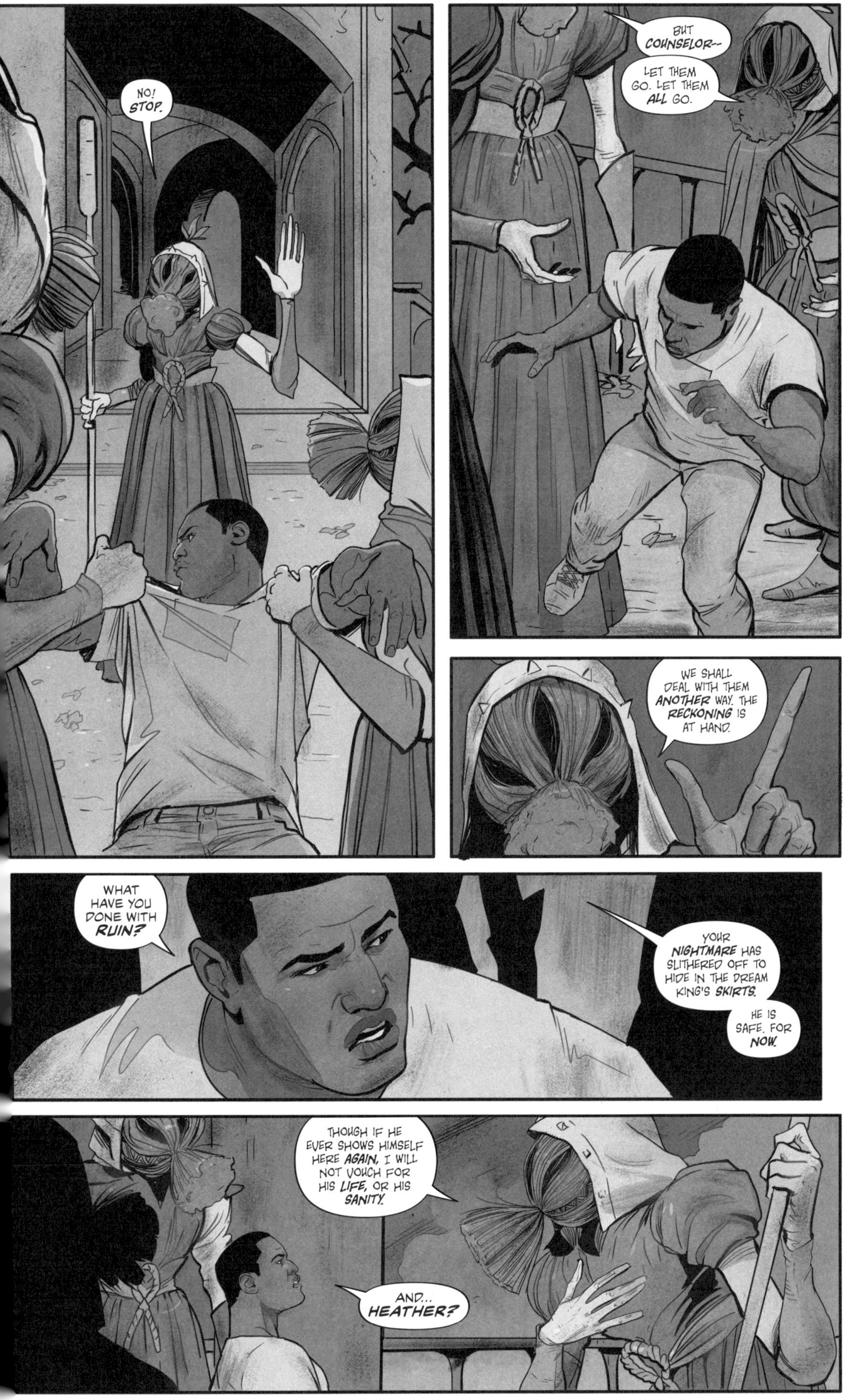
NO! STOP.
BUT COUNSELOR--
LET THEM GO. LET THEM ALL GO.
WE SHALL DEAL WITH THEM ANOTHER WAY. THE RECKONING IS AT HAND.
WHAT HAVE YOU DONE WITH RUIN?
YOUR NIGHTMARE HAS SLITHERED OFF TO HIDE IN THE DREAM KING'S SKIRTS.
HE IS SAFE. FOR NOW.
THOUGH IF HE EVER SHOWS HIMSELF HERE AGAIN, I WILL NOT VOUCH FOR HIS LIFE, OR HIS SANITY.
AND... HEATHER?

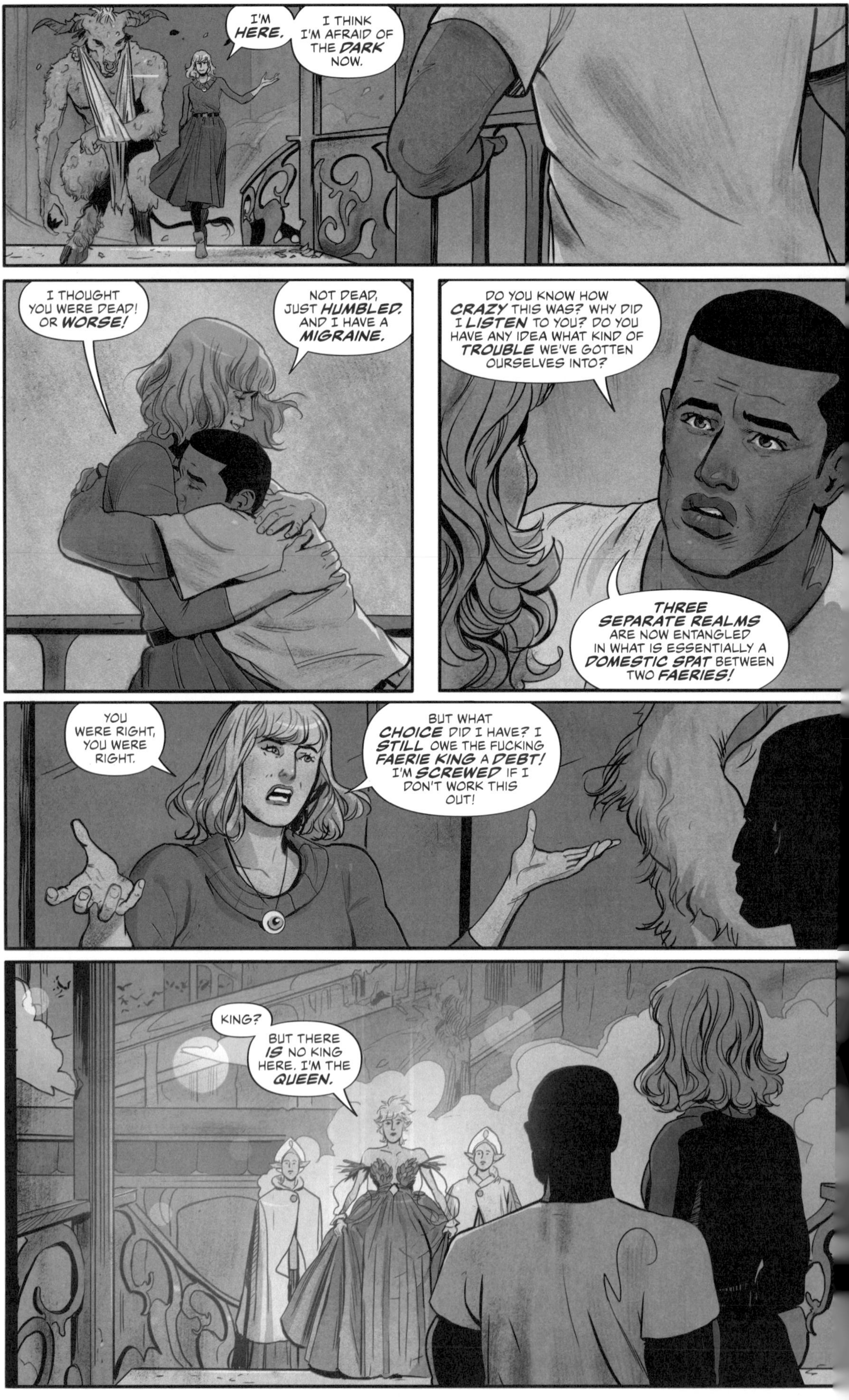

I'M HERE.
I THINK I'M AFRAID OF THE DARK NOW.
I THOUGHT YOU WERE DEAD! OR WORSE!
NOT DEAD, JUST HUMBLED. AND I HAVE A MIGRAINE.
DO YOU KNOW HOW CRAZY THIS WAS? WHY DID I LISTEN TO YOU? DO YOU HAVE ANY IDEA WHAT KIND OF TROUBLE WE'VE GOTTEN OURSELVES INTO?
THREE SEPARATE REALMS ARE NOW ENTANGLED IN WHAT IS ESSENTIALLY A DOMESTIC SPAT BETWEEN TWO FAERIES!
YOU WERE RIGHT, YOU WERE RIGHT.
BUT WHAT CHOICE DID I HAVE? I STILL OWE THE FUCKING FAERIE KING A DEBT! I'M SCREWED IF I DON'T WORK THIS OUT!
KING?
BUT THERE IS NO KING HERE. I'M THE QUEEN.

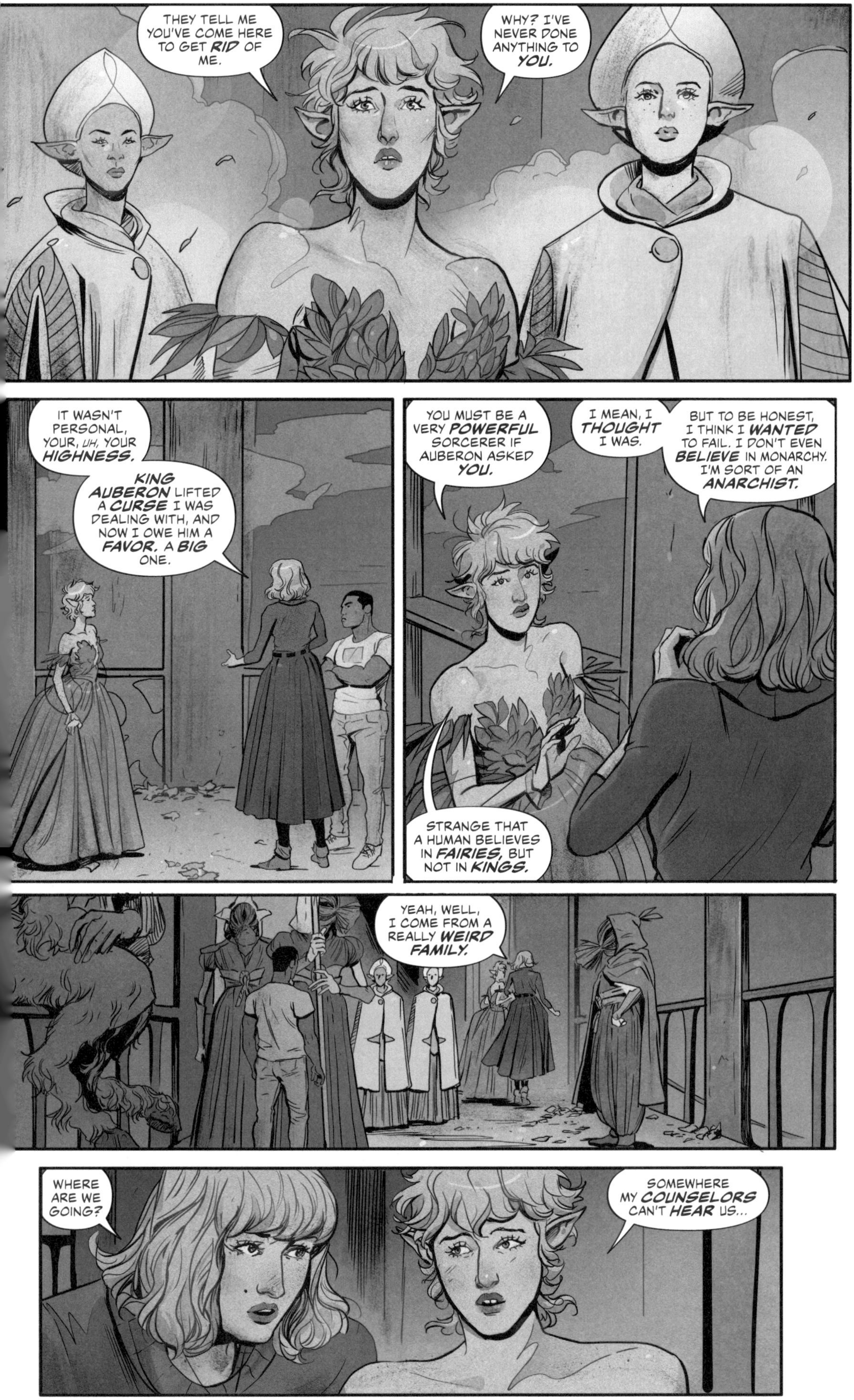
THEY TELL ME YOU'VE COME HERE TO GET RID OF ME.
WHY? I'VE NEVER DONE ANYTHING TO YOU.
IT WASN'T PERSONAL, YOUR, UH, YOUR HIGHNESS.
KING AUBERON LIFTED A CURSE I WAS DEALING WITH, AND NOW I OWE HIM A FAVOR. A BIG ONE.
YOU MUST BE A VERY POWERFUL SORCERER IF AUBERON ASKED YOU.
I MEAN, I THOUGHT I WAS.
BUT TO BE HONEST, I THINK I WANTED TO FAIL. I DON'T EVEN BELIEVE IN MONARCHY. I'M SORT OF AN ANARCHIST.
STRANGE THAT A HUMAN BELIEVES IN FAIRIES, BUT NOT IN KINGS.
YEAH, WELL, I COME FROM A REALLY WEIRD FAMILY.
WHERE ARE WE GOING?
SOMEWHERE MY COUNSELORS CAN'T HEAR US...

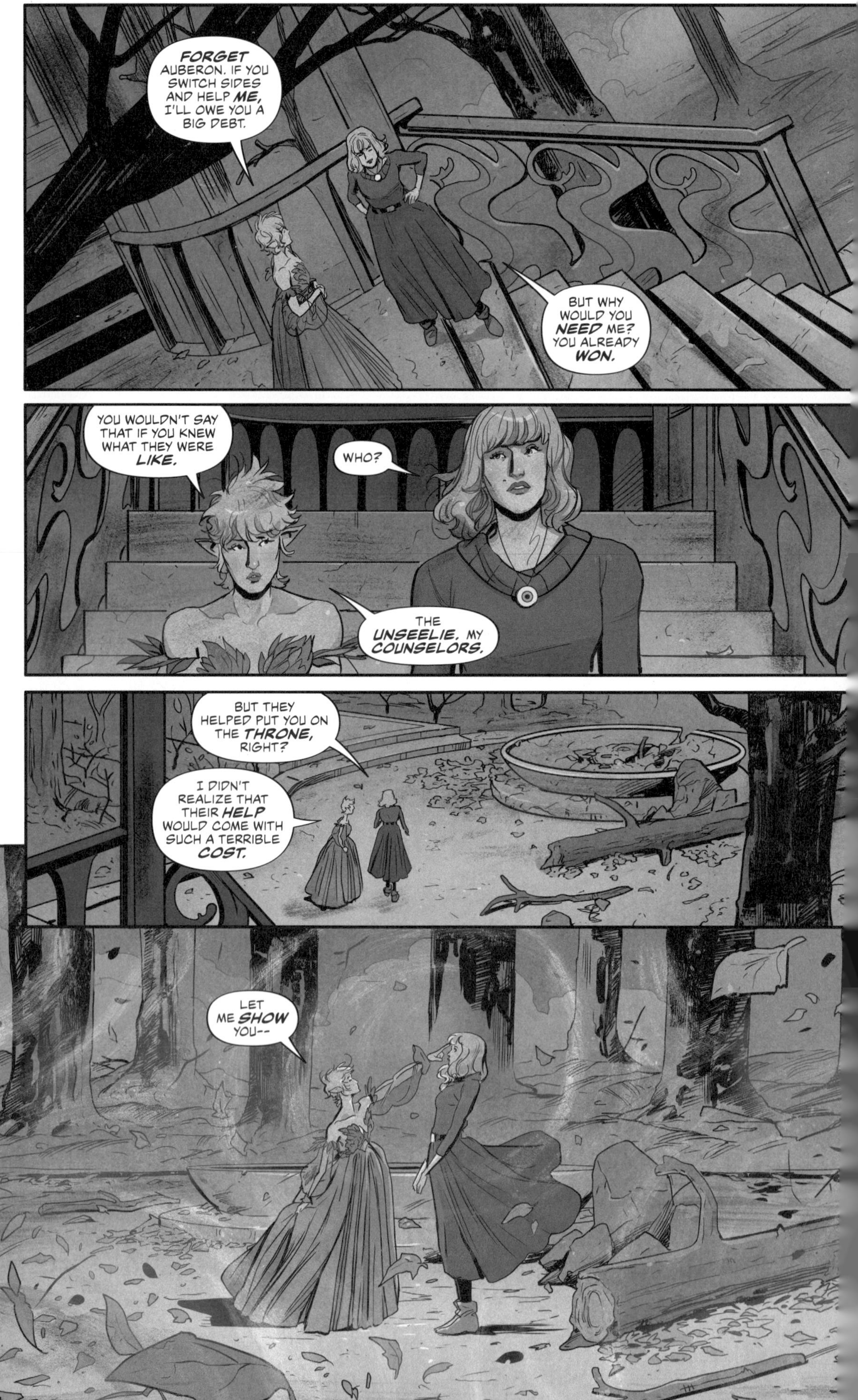
FORGET AUBERON. IF YOU SWITCH SIDES AND HELP ME, I'LL OWE YOU A BIG DEBT.
BUT WHY WOULD YOU NEED ME? YOU ALREADY WON.
YOU WOULDN'T SAY THAT IF YOU KNEW WHAT THEY WERE LIKE.
WHO?
THE UNSEELIE. MY COUNSELORS.
BUT THEY HELPED PUT YOU ON THE THRONE, RIGHT?
I DIDN'T REALIZE THAT THEIR HELP WOULD COME WITH SUCH A TERRIBLE COST.
LET ME SHOW YOU--

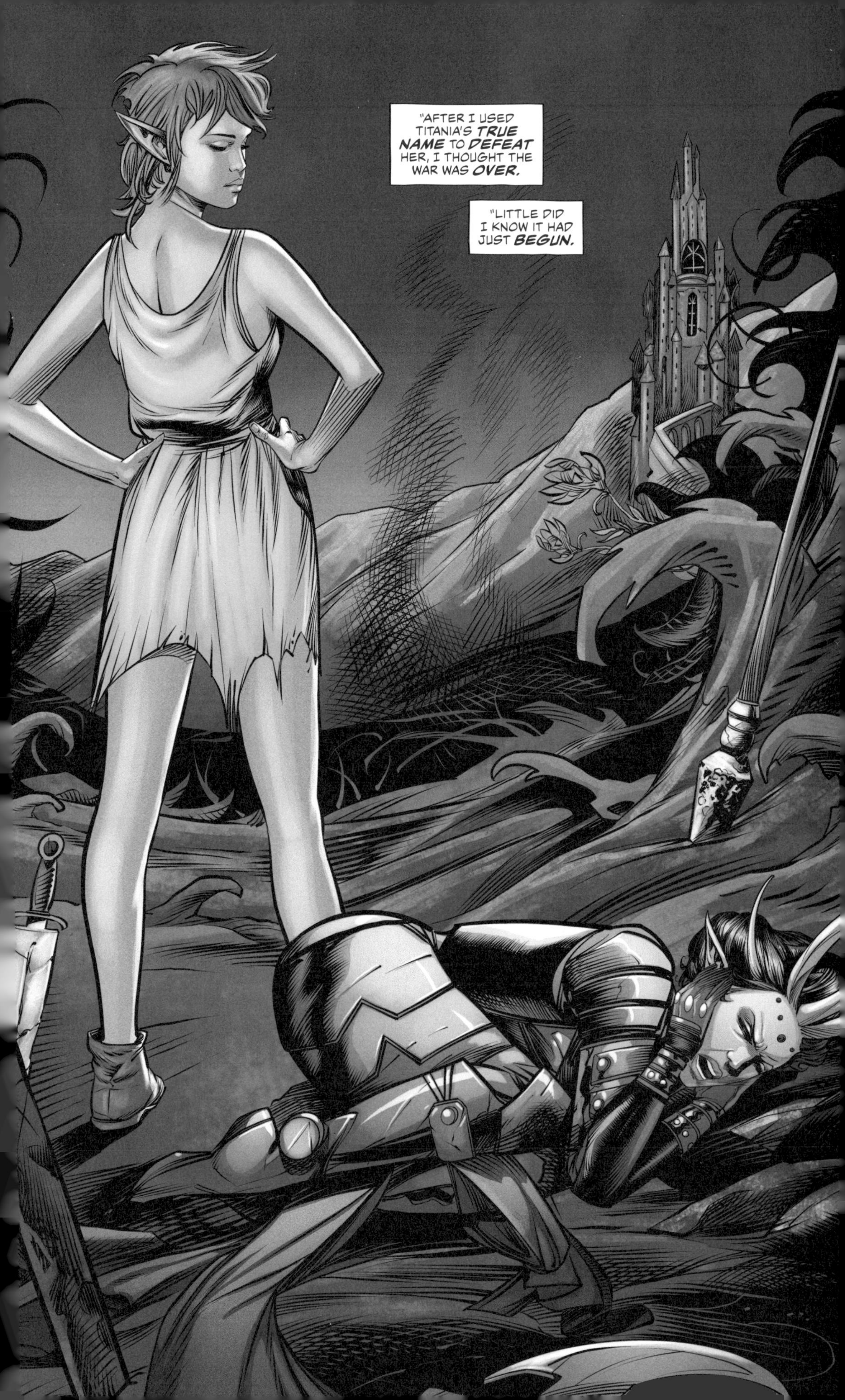
"AFTER I USED TITANIA'S TRUE NAME TO DEFEAT HER, I THOUGHT THE WAR WAS OVER.
"LITTLE DID I KNOW IT HAD JUST BEGUN.

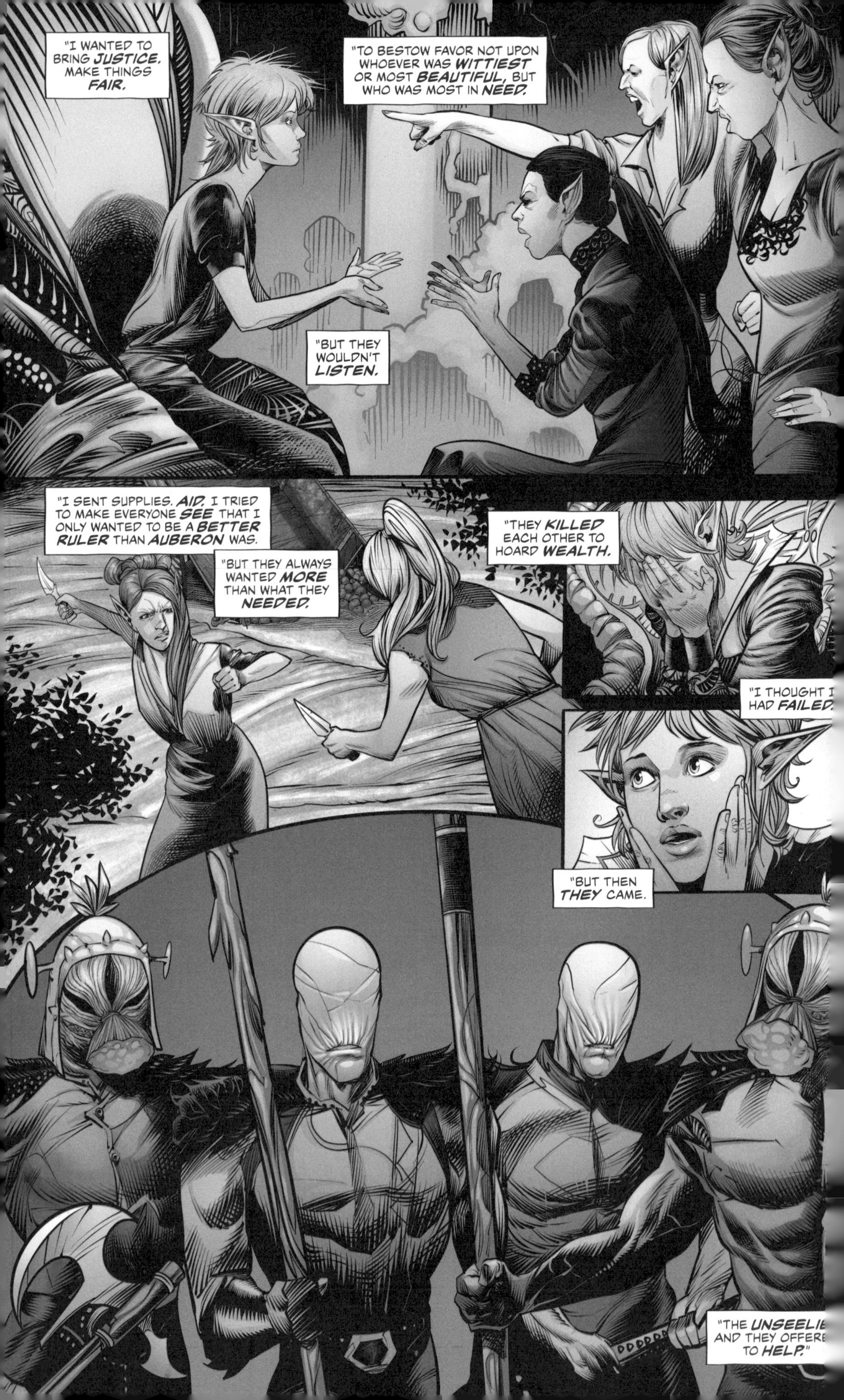
"I WANTED TO BRING JUSTICE, MAKE THINGS FAIR.
"TO BESTOW FAVOR NOT UPON WHOEVER WAS WITTIEST OR MOST BEAUTIFUL, BUT WHO WAS MOST IN NEED.
"BUT THEY WOULDN'T LISTEN.
"I SENT SUPPLIES. AID. I TRIED TO MAKE EVERYONE SEE THAT I ONLY WANTED TO BE A BETTER RULER THAN AUBERON WAS.
"BUT THEY ALWAYS WANTED MORE THAN WHAT THEY NEEDED.
"THEY KILLED EACH OTHER TO HOARD WEALTH.
"I THOUGHT I HAD FAILED.
"BUT THEN THEY CAME.
"THE UNSEELIE AND THEY OFFERE TO HELP."

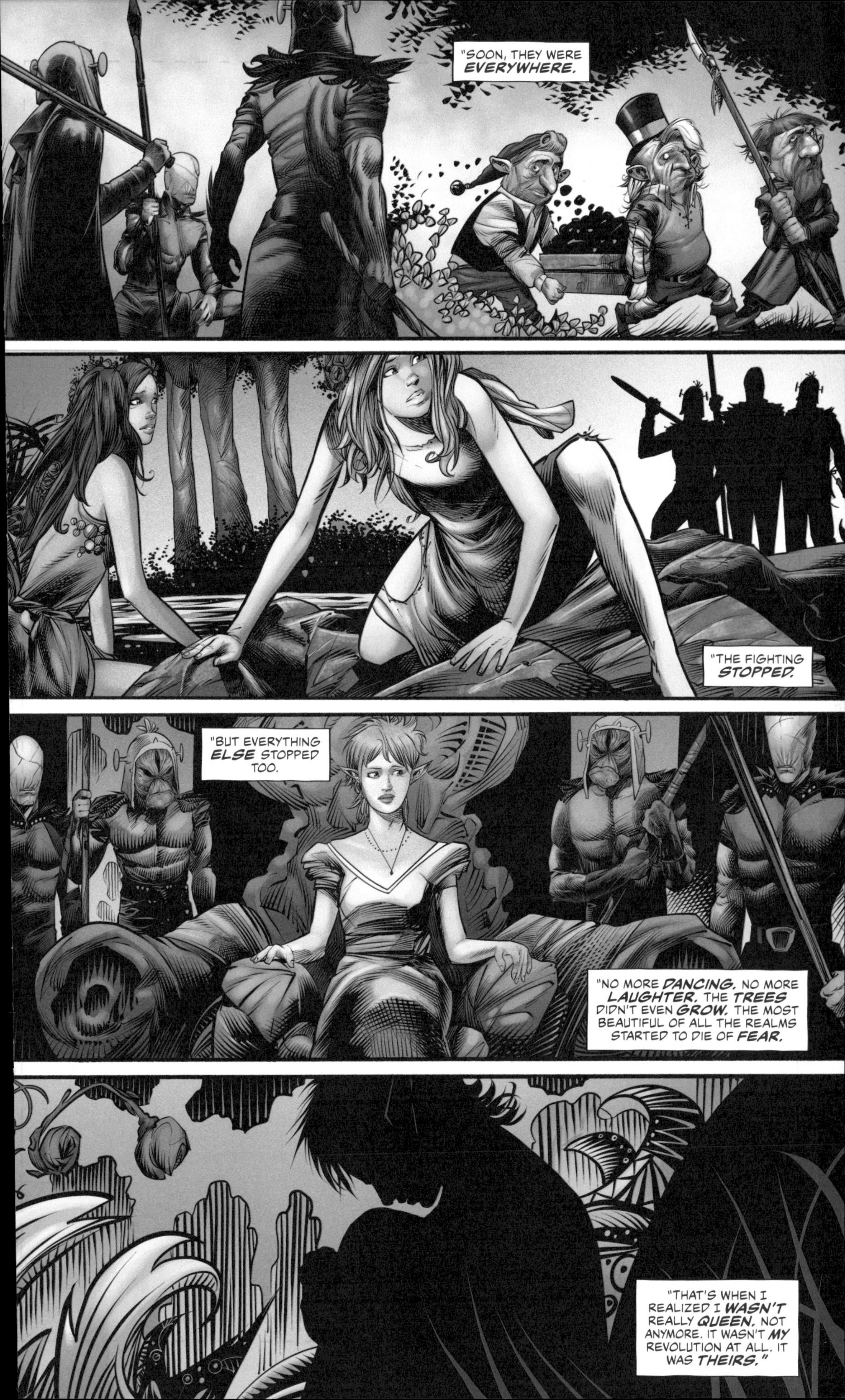
"SOON, THEY WERE EVERYWHERE.
"THE FIGHTING STOPPED.
"BUT EVERYTHING ELSE STOPPED TOO.
"NO MORE DANCING. NO MORE LAUGHTER. THE TREES DIDN'T EVEN GROW. THE MOST BEAUTIFUL OF ALL THE REALMS STARTED TO DIE OF FEAR.
"THAT'S WHEN I REALIZED I WASN'T REALLY QUEEN. NOT ANYMORE. IT WASN'T MY REVOLUTION AT ALL. IT WAS THEIRS."

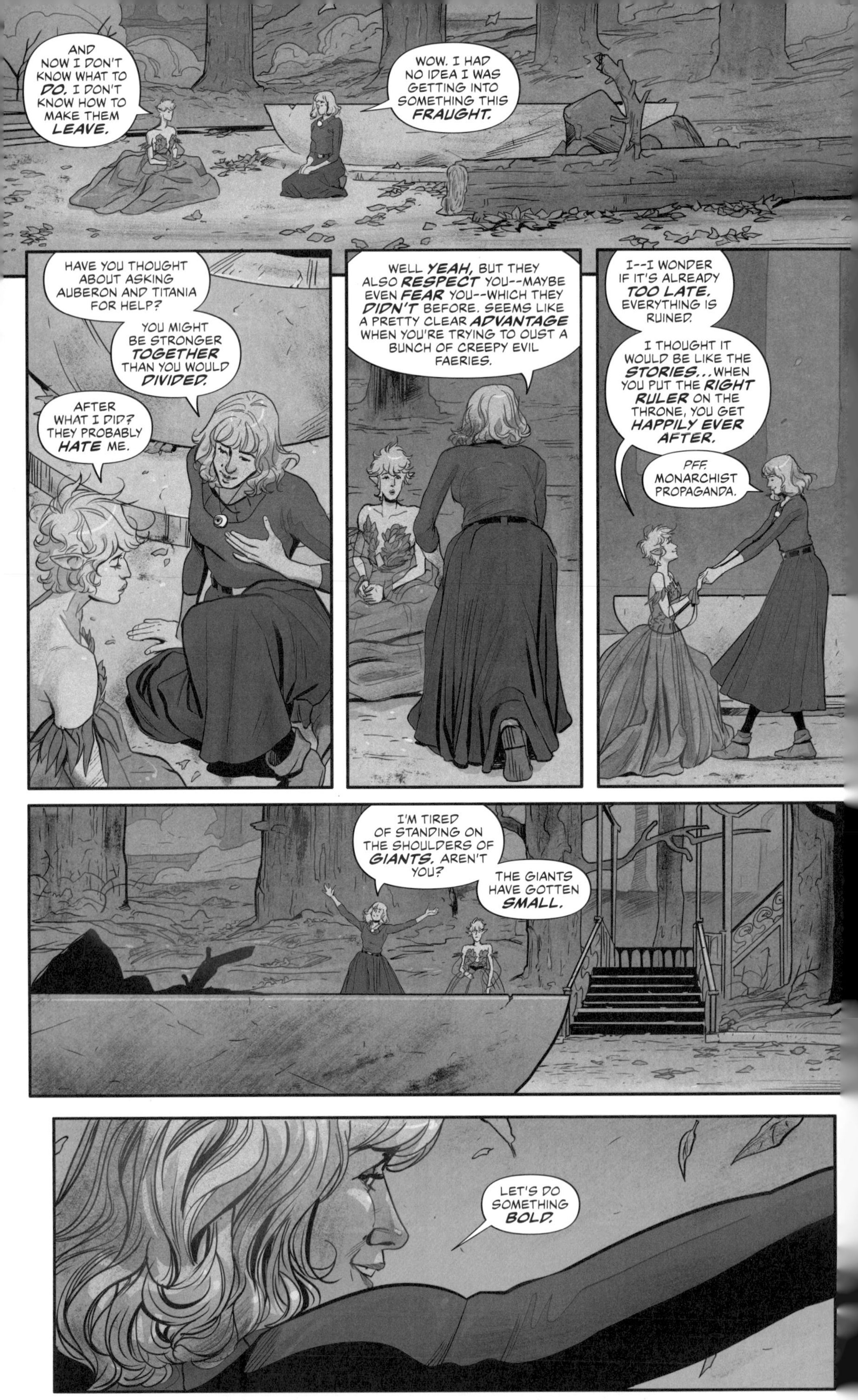

AND NOW I DON'T KNOW WHAT TO DO. I DON'T KNOW HOW TO MAKE THEM LEAVE.
WOW. I HAD NO IDEA I WAS GETTING INTO SOMETHING THIS FRAUGHT.
HAVE YOU THOUGHT ABOUT ASKING AUBERON AND TITANIA FOR HELP?
YOU MIGHT BE STRONGER TOGETHER THAN YOU WOULD DIVIDED.
AFTER WHAT I DID? THEY PROBABLY HATE ME.
WELL YEAH, BUT THEY ALSO RESPECT YOU--MAYBE EVEN FEAR YOU--WHICH THEY DIDN'T BEFORE. SEEMS LIKE A PRETTY CLEAR ADVANTAGE WHEN YOU'RE TRYING TO OUST A BUNCH OF CREEPY EVIL FAERIES.
I--I WONDER IF IT'S ALREADY TOO LATE. EVERYTHING IS RUINED.
I THOUGHT IT WOULD BE LIKE THE STORIES... WHEN YOU PUT THE RIGHT RULER ON THE THRONE, YOU GET HAPPILY EVER AFTER.
PFF. MONARCHIST PROPAGANDA.
I'M TIRED OF STANDING ON THE SHOULDERS OF GIANTS. AREN'T YOU?
THE GIANTS HAVE GOTTEN SMALL.
LET'S DO SOMETHING BOLD.

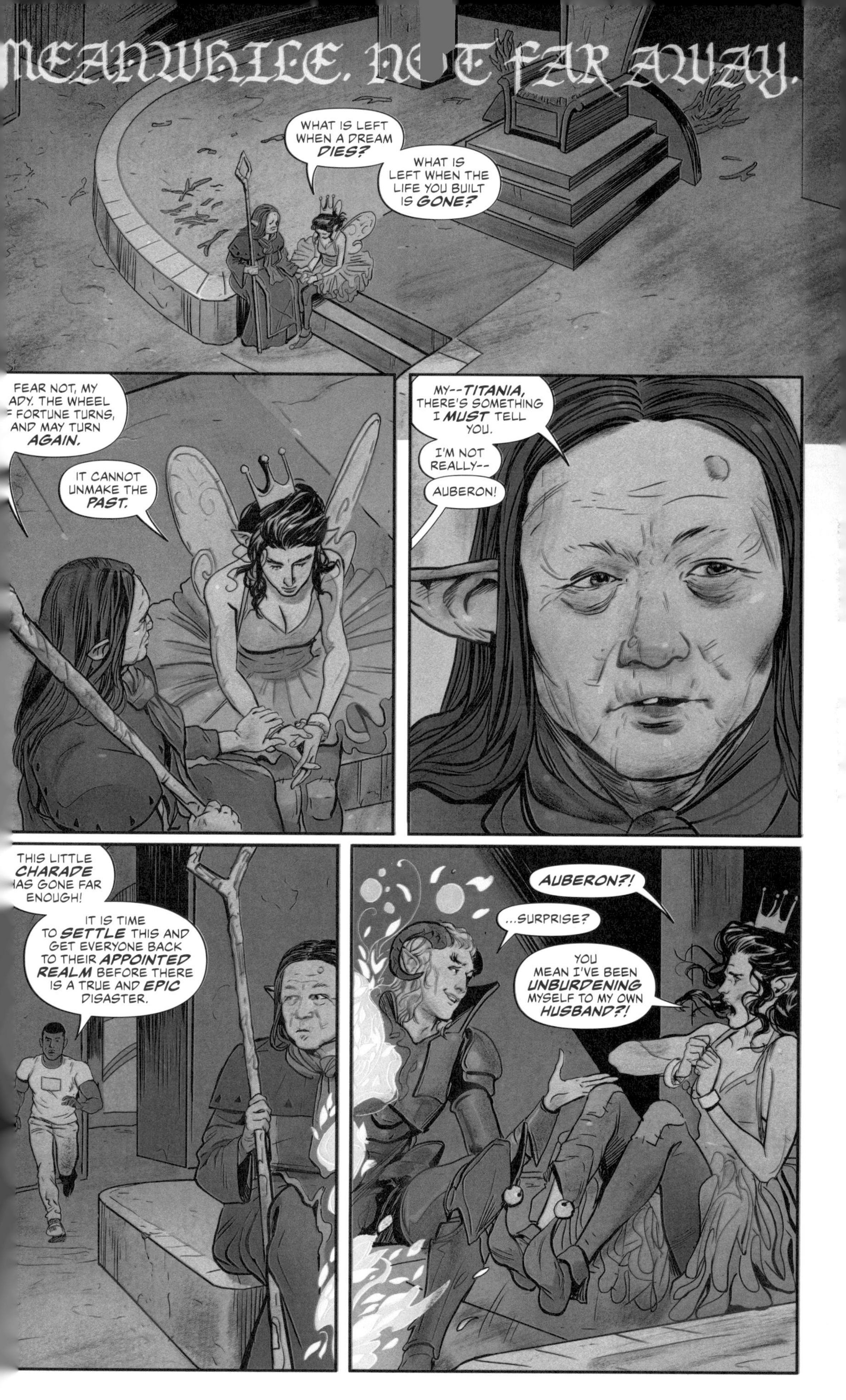
MEANWHILE. NOT FAR AWAY.
WHAT IS LEFT WHEN A DREAM DIES?
WHAT IS LEFT WHEN THE LIFE YOU BUILT IS GONE?
FEAR NOT, MY ADY. THE WHEEL F FORTUNE TURNS, AND MAY TURN AGAIN.
IT CANNOT UNMAKE THE PAST.
MY--TITANIA, THERE'S SOMETHING I MUST TELL YOU.
I'M NOT REALLY--
AUBERON!
THIS LITTLE CHARADE HAS GONE FAR ENOUGH!
IT IS TIME TO SETTLE THIS AND GET EVERYONE BACK TO THEIR APPOINTED REALM BEFORE THERE IS A TRUE AND EPIC DISASTER.
AUBERON?!
...SURPRISE?
YOU MEAN I'VE BEEN UNBURDENING MYSELF TO MY OWN HUSBAND?!

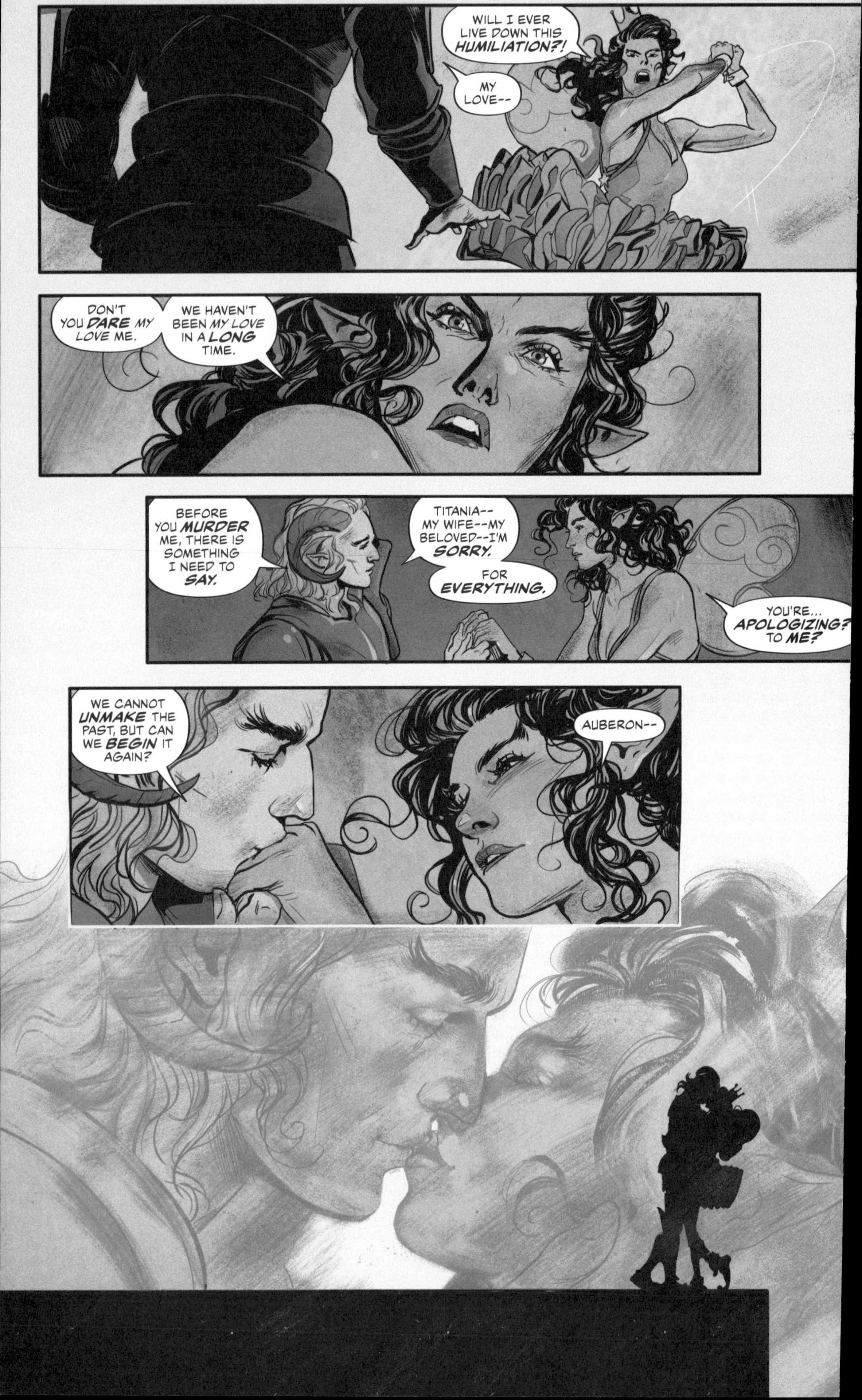

WILL I EVER LIVE DOWN THIS HUMILIATION?!
MY LOVE--
DON'T YOU DARE MY LOVE ME.
WE HAVEN'T BEEN MY LOVE IN A LONG TIME.
BEFORE YOU MURDER ME, THERE IS SOMETHING I NEED TO SAY.
TITANIA--MY WIFE--MY BELOVED--I'M SORRY.
FOR EVERYTHING.
YOU'RE... APOLOGIZING? TO ME?
WE CANNOT UNMAKE THE PAST, BUT CAN WE BEGIN IT AGAIN?
AUBERON--

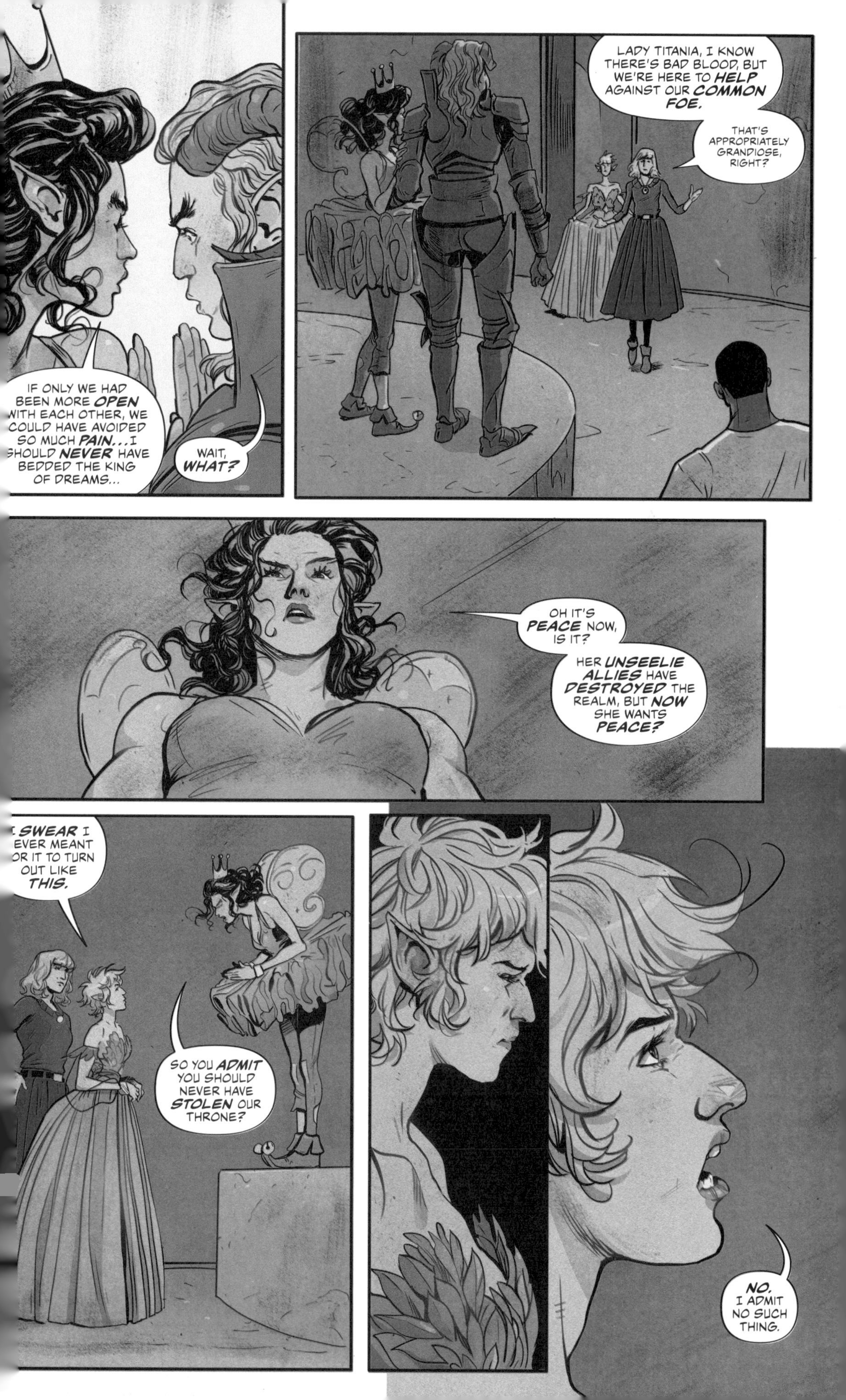
IF ONLY WE HAD BEEN MORE OPEN WITH EACH OTHER, WE COULD HAVE AVOIDED SO MUCH PAIN...I SHOULD NEVER HAVE BEDDED THE KING OF DREAMS...
WAIT, WHAT?
LADY TITANIA, I KNOW THERE'S BAD BLOOD, BUT WE'RE HERE TO HELP AGAINST OUR COMMON FOE.
THAT'S APPROPRIATELY GRANDIOSE, RIGHT?
OH IT'S PEACE NOW, IS IT?
HER UNSEELIE ALLIES HAVE DESTROYED THE REALM, BUT NOW SHE WANTS PEACE?
SWEAR I EVER MEANT OR IT TO TURN OUT LIKE THIS.
SO YOU ADMIT YOU SHOULD NEVER HAVE STOLEN OUR THRONE?
NO. I ADMIT NO SUCH THING.

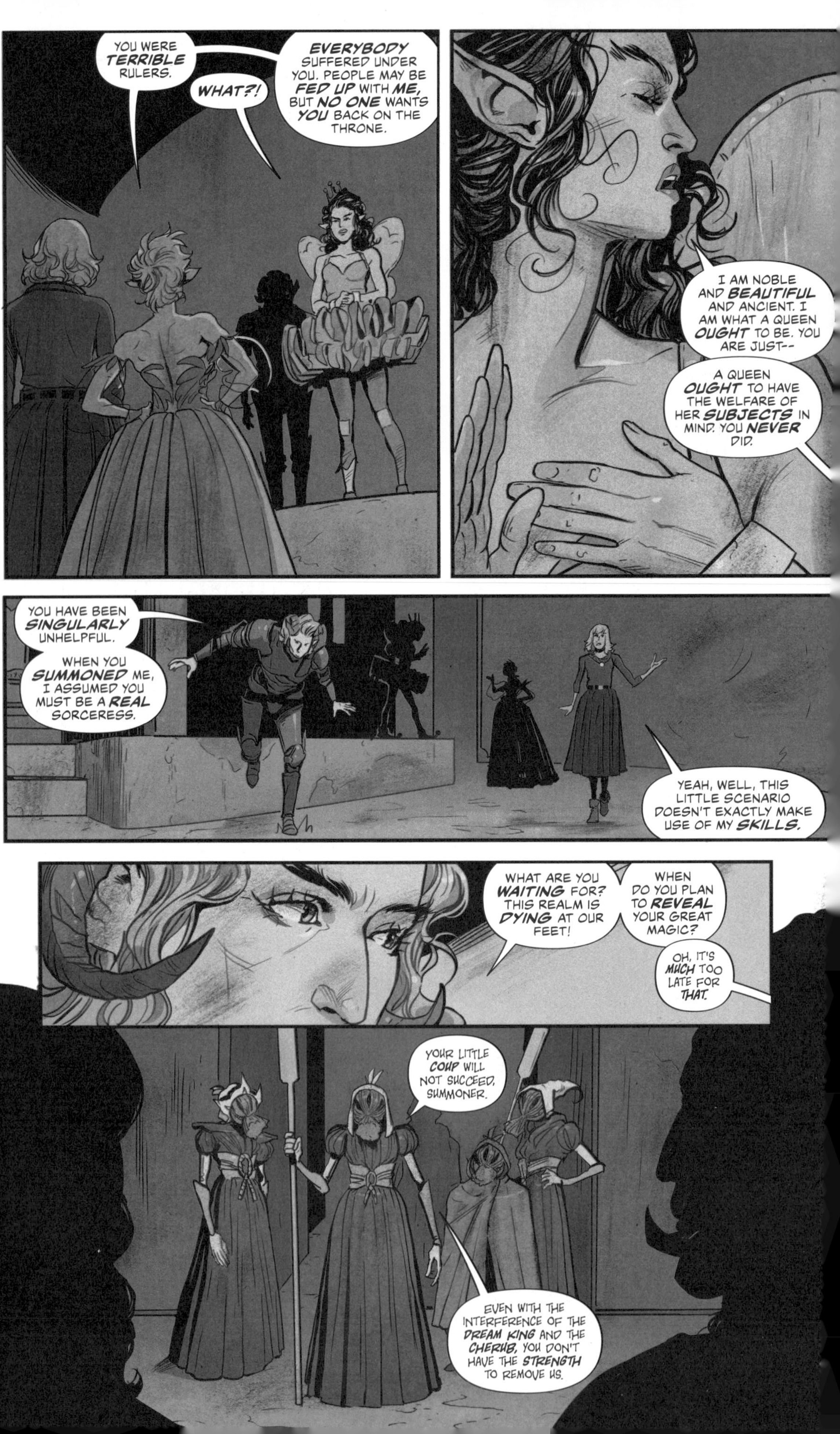
YOU WERE TERRIBLE RULERS.
WHAT?!
EVERYBODY SUFFERED UNDER YOU. PEOPLE MAY BE FED UP WITH ME, BUT NO ONE WANTS YOU BACK ON THE THRONE.
I AM NOBLE AND BEAUTIFUL AND ANCIENT. I AM WHAT A QUEEN OUGHT TO BE. YOU ARE JUST--
A QUEEN OUGHT TO HAVE THE WELFARE OF HER SUBJECTS IN MIND. YOU NEVER DID.
YOU HAVE BEEN SINGULARLY UNHELPFUL.
WHEN YOU SUMMONED ME, I ASSUMED YOU MUST BE A REAL SORCERESS.
YEAH, WELL, THIS LITTLE SCENARIO DOESN'T EXACTLY MAKE USE OF MY SKILLS.
WHAT ARE YOU WAITING FOR? THIS REALM IS DYING AT OUR FEET!
WHEN DO YOU PLAN TO REVEAL YOUR GREAT MAGIC?
OH, IT'S MUCH TOO LATE FOR THAT.
YOUR LITTLE COUP WILL NOT SUCCEED, SUMMONER.
EVEN WITH THE INTERFERENCE OF THE DREAM KING AND THE CHERUB, YOU DON'T HAVE THE STRENGTH TO REMOVE US.

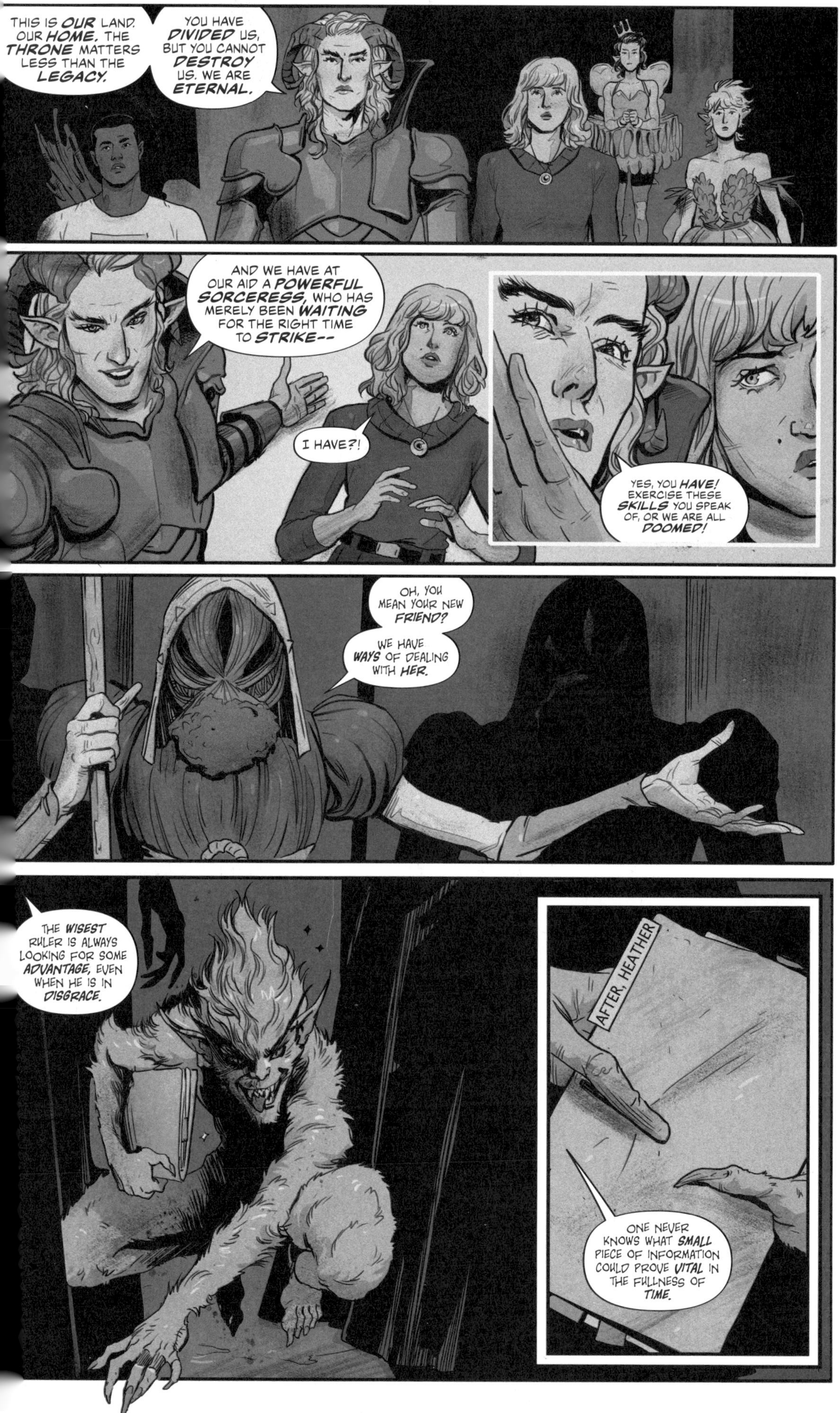
THIS IS OUR LAND. OUR HOME. THE THRONE MATTERS LESS THAN THE LEGACY.
YOU HAVE DIVIDED US, BUT YOU CANNOT DESTROY US. WE ARE ETERNAL.
AND WE HAVE AT OUR AID A POWERFUL SORCERESS, WHO HAS MERELY BEEN WAITING FOR THE RIGHT TIME TO STRIKE--
I HAVE?!
YES, YOU HAVE! EXERCISE THESE SKILLS YOU SPEAK OF, OR WE ARE ALL DOOMED!
OH, YOU MEAN YOUR NEW FRIEND?
WE HAVE WAYS OF DEALING WITH HER.
THE WISEST RULER IS ALWAYS LOOKING FOR SOME ADVANTAGE, EVEN WHEN HE IS IN DISGRACE.
AFTER, HEATHER
ONE NEVER KNOWS WHAT SMALL PIECE OF INFORMATION COULD PROVE VITAL IN THE FULLNESS OF TIME.

PUCK. YOU *TURNCOAT.* I MIGHT HAVE *KNOWN.*

I SERVE ONLY THE *VICTORS,* SIRE. AND, IN DOING SO, I SERVE *MYSELF.*

YOU DIDN'T THINK WE WOULD *PREPARE?* THAT WE ARE WITHOUT *RESOURCES* IN YOUR WORLD?

FAIRIES ARE *PATIENT.* OUR GRUDGES LAST CENTURIES.

AND YOU MADE THE *WRONG ENEMIES.*

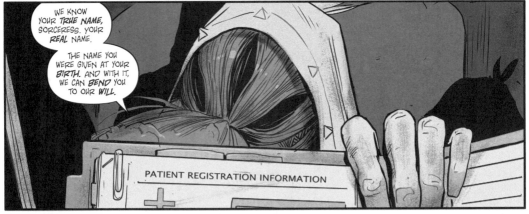

WE KNOW YOUR *TRUE NAME,* SORCERESS. YOUR *REAL* NAME.

THE NAME YOU WERE GIVEN AT YOUR *BIRTH.* AND WITH IT, WE CAN *BEND* YOU TO OUR *WILL.*

PATIENT REGISTRATION INFORMATION

YOUR *TRUE NAME* IS ELL--

--IS ELLIO--

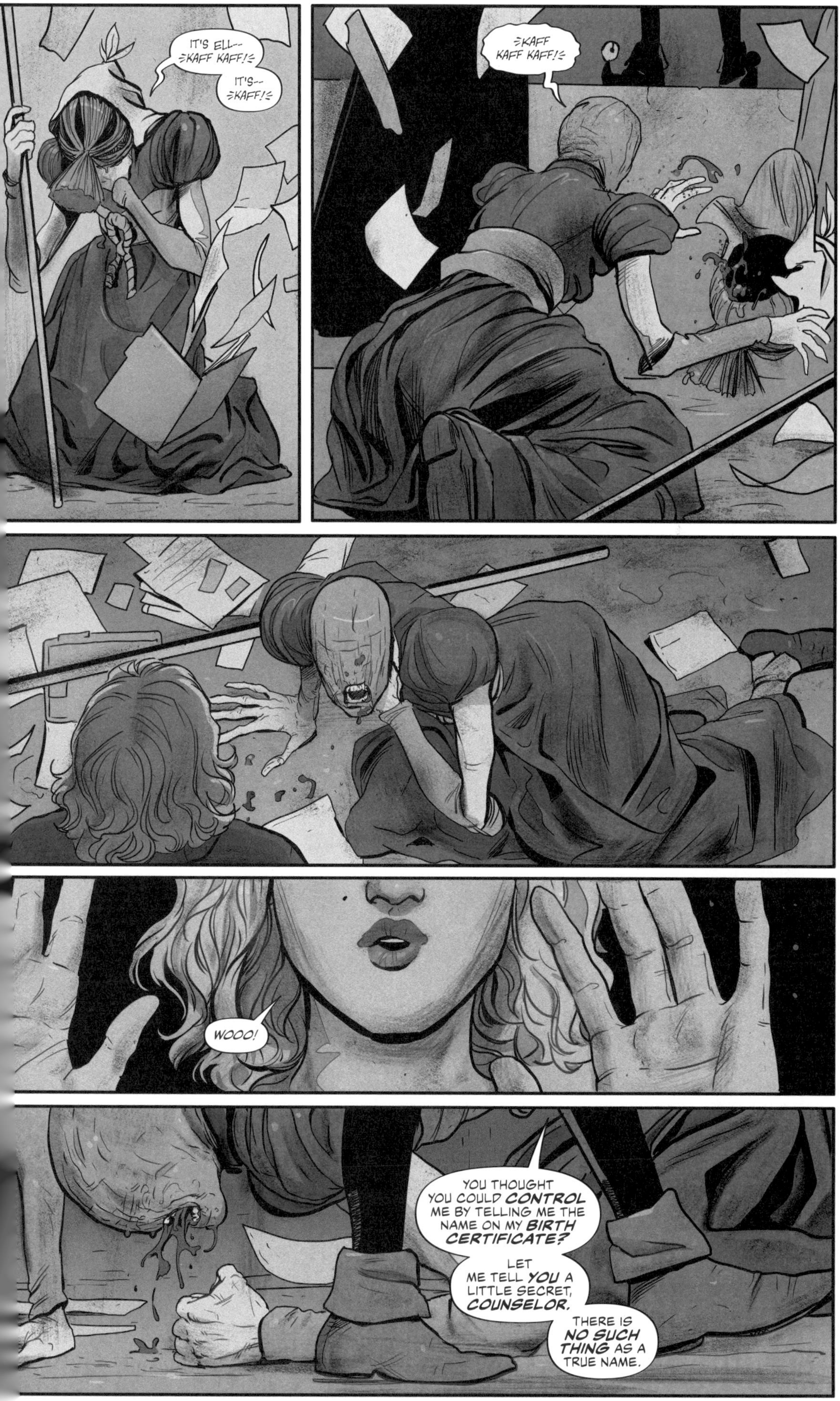

IT'S ELL-- ≠KAFF KAFF!≠
IT'S-- ≠KAFF!≠
≠KAFF KAFF KAFF!≠
WOOO!
YOU THOUGHT YOU COULD CONTROL ME BY TELLING ME THE NAME ON MY BIRTH CERTIFICATE?
LET ME TELL YOU A LITTLE SECRET, COUNSELOR.
THERE IS NO SUCH THING AS A TRUE NAME.

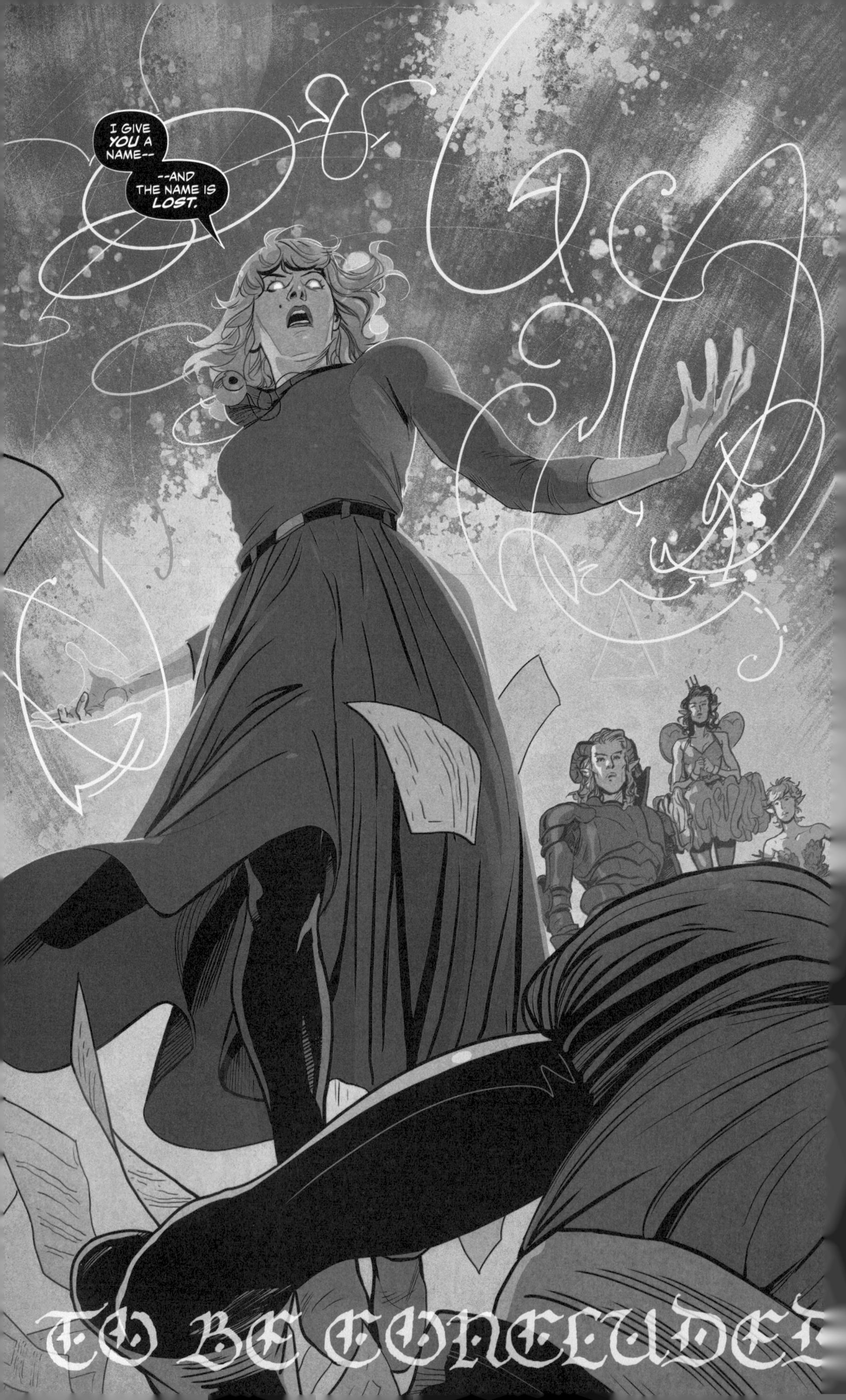
I GIVE YOU A NAME--
--AND THE NAME IS LOST.
TO BE CONCLUDED

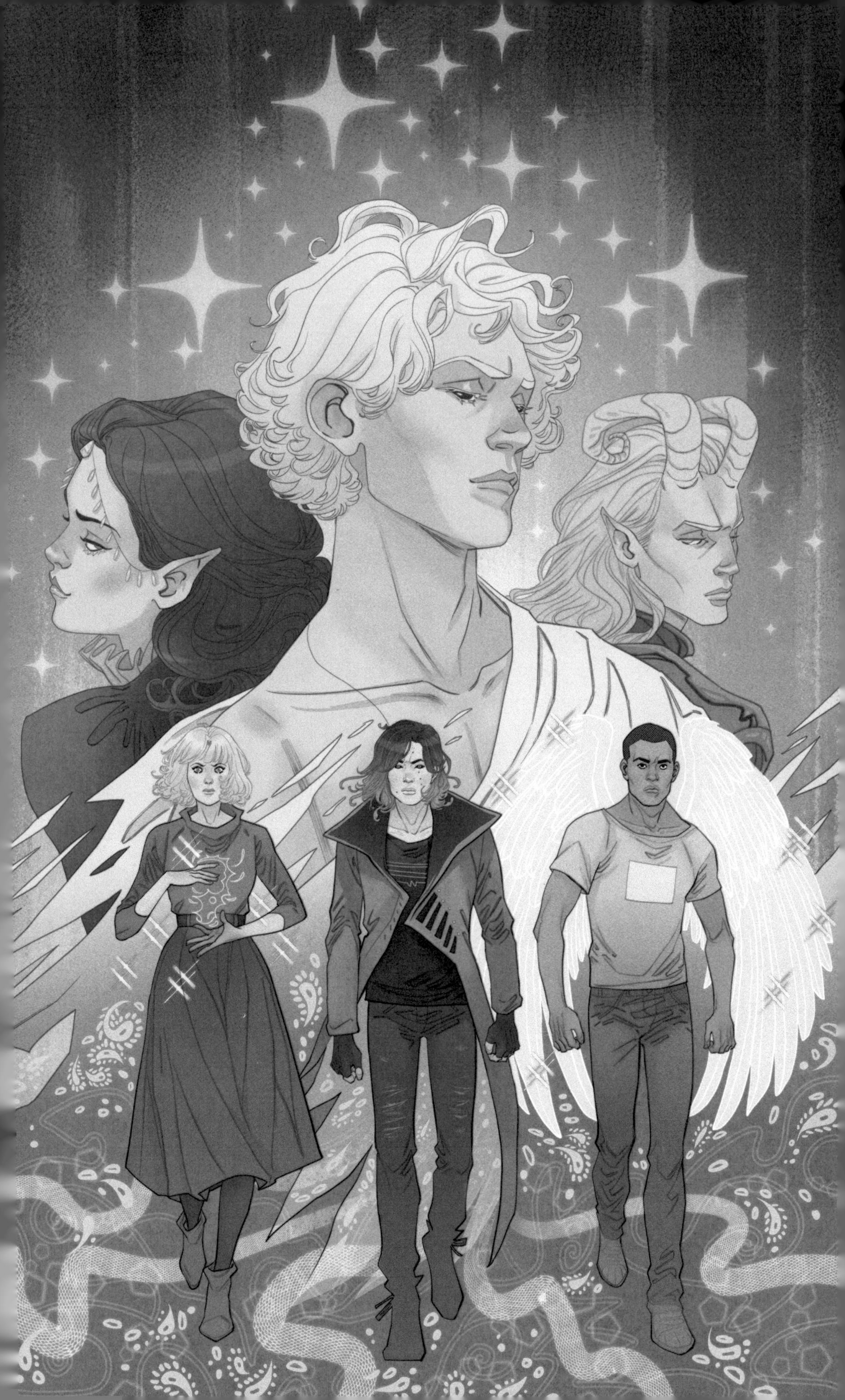

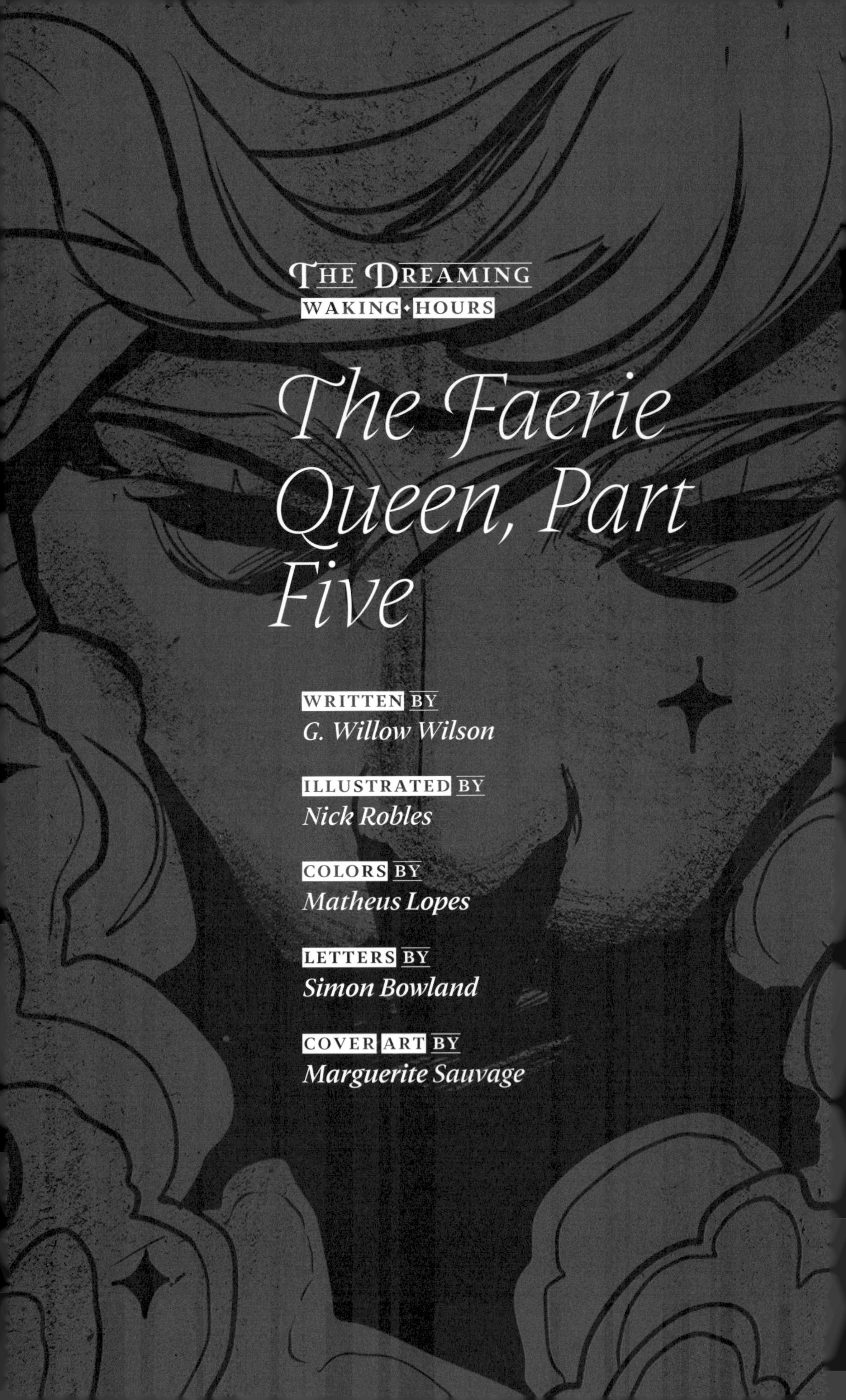

THE DREAMING
WAKING HOURS

The Faerie Queen, Part Five

WRITTEN BY
G. Willow Wilson

ILLUSTRATED BY
Nick Robles

COLORS BY
Matheus Lopes

LETTERS BY
Simon Bowland

COVER ART BY
Marguerite Sauvage

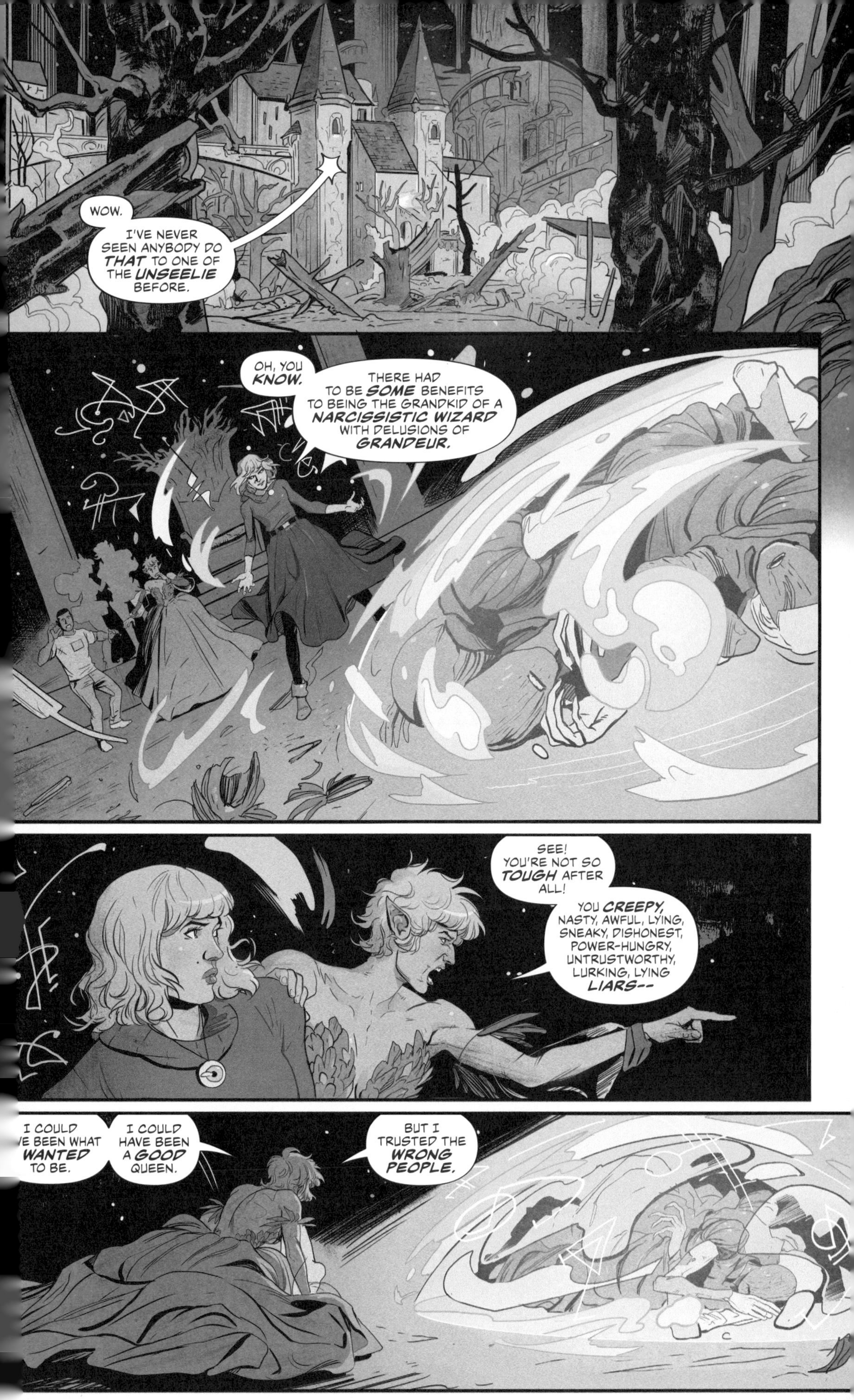
WOW.
I'VE NEVER SEEN ANYBODY DO THAT TO ONE OF THE UNSEELIE BEFORE.
OH, YOU KNOW.
THERE HAD TO BE SOME BENEFITS TO BEING THE GRANDKID OF A NARCISSISTIC WIZARD WITH DELUSIONS OF GRANDEUR.
SEE! YOU'RE NOT SO TOUGH AFTER ALL!
YOU CREEPY, NASTY, AWFUL, LYING, SNEAKY, DISHONEST, POWER-HUNGRY, UNTRUSTWORTHY, LURKING, LYING LIARS--
I COULD HAVE BEEN WHAT I WANTED TO BE.
I COULD HAVE BEEN A GOOD QUEEN.
BUT I TRUSTED THE WRONG PEOPLE.

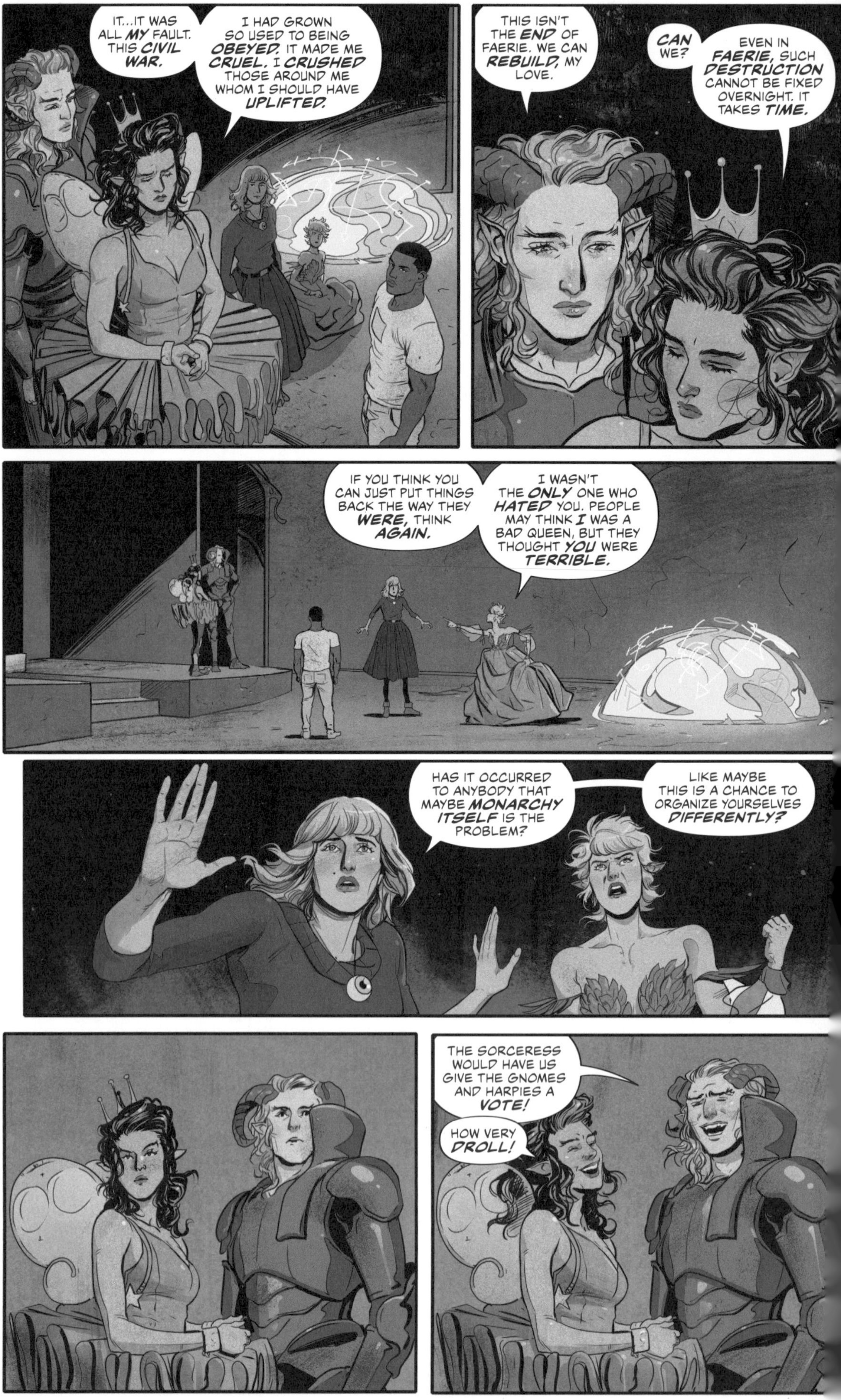
IT...IT WAS ALL MY FAULT. THIS CIVIL WAR.
I HAD GROWN SO USED TO BEING OBEYED. IT MADE ME CRUEL. I CRUSHED THOSE AROUND ME WHOM I SHOULD HAVE UPLIFTED.
THIS ISN'T THE END OF FAERIE. WE CAN REBUILD, MY LOVE.
CAN WE?
EVEN IN FAERIE, SUCH DESTRUCTION CANNOT BE FIXED OVERNIGHT. IT TAKES TIME.
IF YOU THINK YOU CAN JUST PUT THINGS BACK THE WAY THEY WERE, THINK AGAIN.
I WASN'T THE ONLY ONE WHO HATED YOU. PEOPLE MAY THINK I WAS A BAD QUEEN, BUT THEY THOUGHT YOU WERE TERRIBLE.
HAS IT OCCURRED TO ANYBODY THAT MAYBE MONARCHY ITSELF IS THE PROBLEM?
LIKE MAYBE THIS IS A CHANCE TO ORGANIZE YOURSELVES DIFFERENTLY?
THE SORCERESS WOULD HAVE US GIVE THE GNOMES AND HARPIES A VOTE!
HOW VERY DROLL!

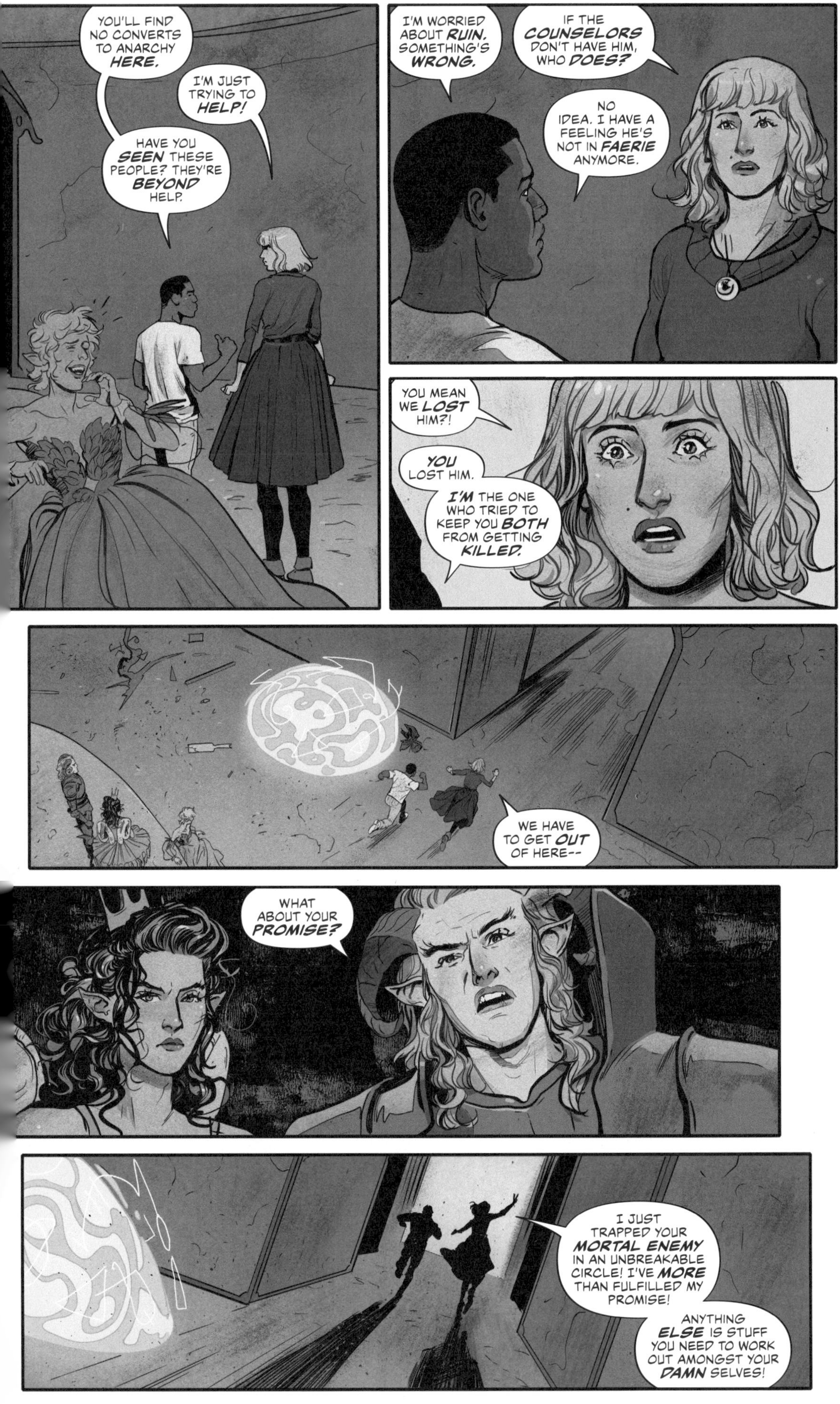
YOU'LL FIND NO CONVERTS TO ANARCHY HERE.
I'M JUST TRYING TO HELP!
HAVE YOU SEEN THESE PEOPLE? THEY'RE BEYOND HELP.
I'M WORRIED ABOUT RUIN. SOMETHING'S WRONG.
IF THE COUNSELORS DON'T HAVE HIM, WHO DOES?
NO IDEA. I HAVE A FEELING HE'S NOT IN FAERIE ANYMORE.
YOU MEAN WE LOST HIM?!
YOU LOST HIM.
I'M THE ONE WHO TRIED TO KEEP YOU BOTH FROM GETTING KILLED.
WE HAVE TO GET OUT OF HERE--
WHAT ABOUT YOUR PROMISE?
I JUST TRAPPED YOUR MORTAL ENEMY IN AN UNBREAKABLE CIRCLE! I'VE MORE THAN FULFILLED MY PROMISE!
ANYTHING ELSE IS STUFF YOU NEED TO WORK OUT AMONGST YOUR DAMN SELVES!

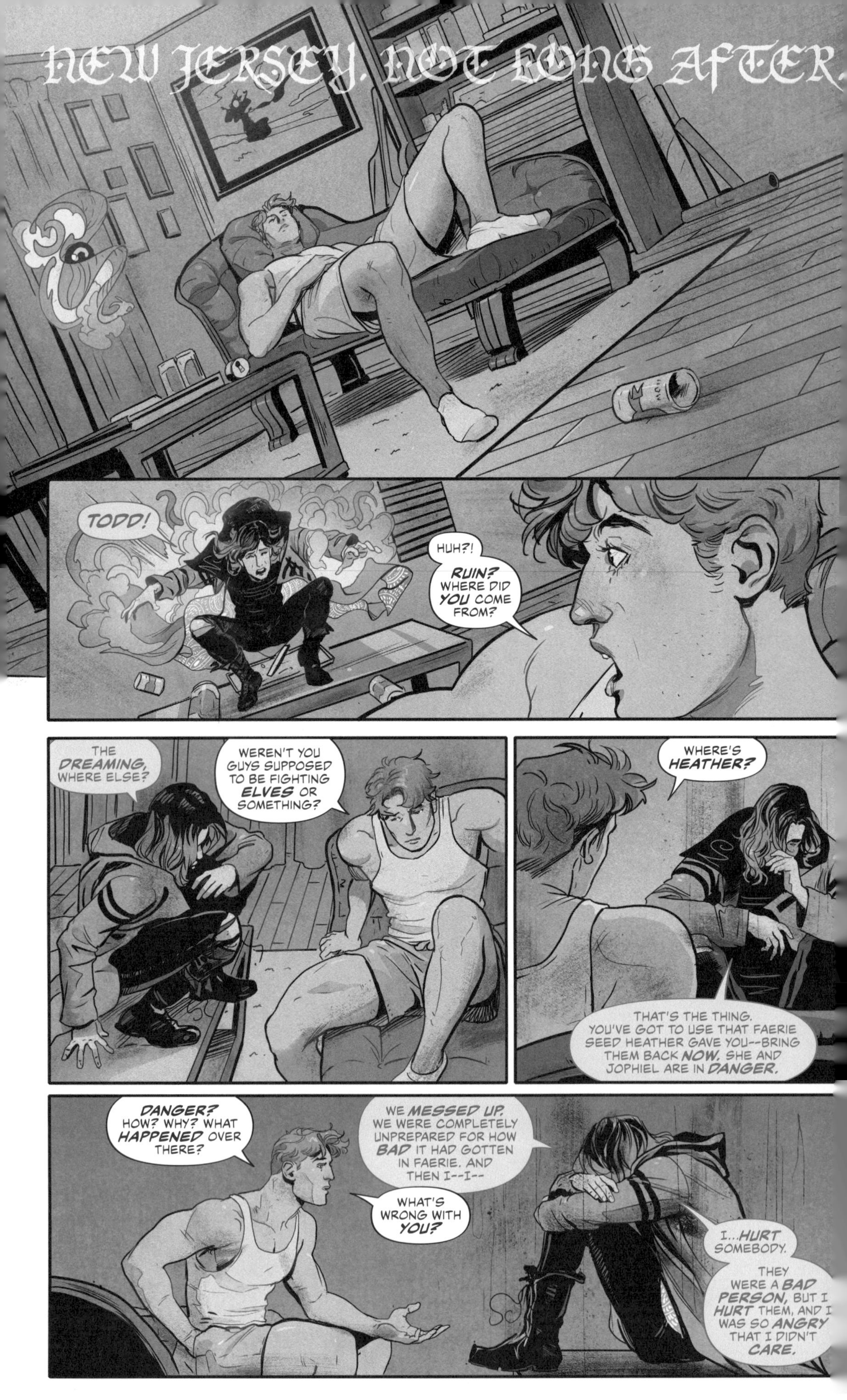
NEW JERSEY. NOT LONG AFTER.
TODD!
HUH?! RUIN? WHERE DID YOU COME FROM?
THE DREAMING, WHERE ELSE?
WEREN'T YOU GUYS SUPPOSED TO BE FIGHTING ELVES OR SOMETHING?
WHERE'S HEATHER?
THAT'S THE THING. YOU'VE GOT TO USE THAT FAERIE SEED HEATHER GAVE YOU--BRING THEM BACK NOW. SHE AND JOPHIEL ARE IN DANGER.
DANGER? HOW? WHY? WHAT HAPPENED OVER THERE?
WE MESSED UP. WE WERE COMPLETELY UNPREPARED FOR HOW BAD IT HAD GOTTEN IN FAERIE. AND THEN I--I--
WHAT'S WRONG WITH YOU?
I...HURT SOMEBODY.
THEY WERE A BAD PERSON, BUT I HURT THEM, AND I WAS SO ANGRY THAT I DIDN'T CARE.

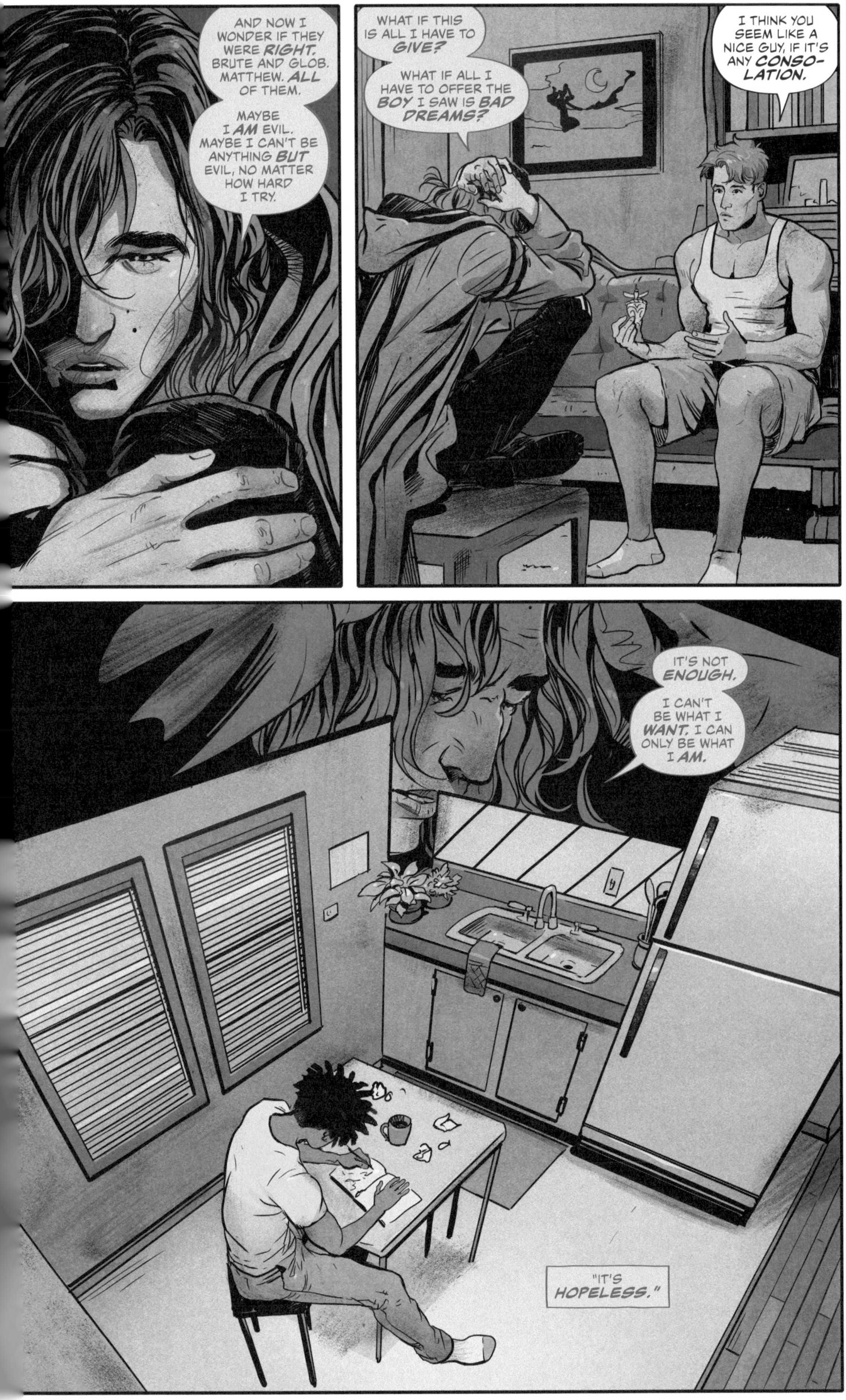
AND NOW I WONDER IF THEY WERE RIGHT. BRUTE AND GLOB. MATTHEW. ALL OF THEM.
MAYBE I AM EVIL. MAYBE I CAN'T BE ANYTHING BUT EVIL, NO MATTER HOW HARD I TRY.
WHAT IF THIS IS ALL I HAVE TO GIVE?
WHAT IF ALL I HAVE TO OFFER THE BOY I SAW IS BAD DREAMS?
I THINK YOU SEEM LIKE A NICE GUY, IF IT'S ANY CONSO-LATION.
IT'S NOT ENOUGH.
I CAN'T BE WHAT I WANT. I CAN ONLY BE WHAT I AM.
"IT'S HOPELESS."

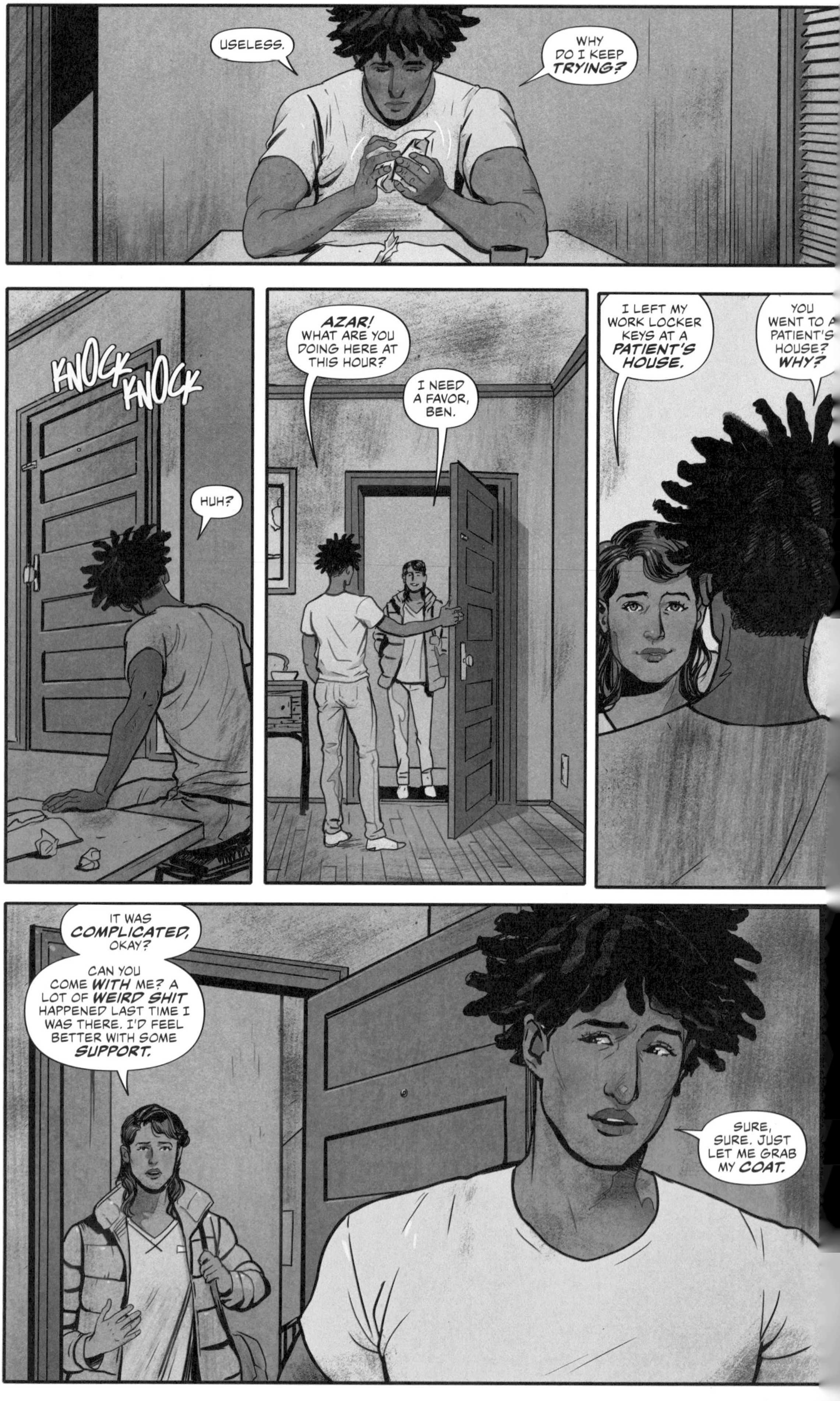
USELESS.
WHY DO I KEEP TRYING?
KNOCK KNOCK
HUH?
AZAR! WHAT ARE YOU DOING HERE AT THIS HOUR?
I NEED A FAVOR, BEN.
I LEFT MY WORK LOCKER KEYS AT A PATIENT'S HOUSE.
YOU WENT TO A PATIENT'S HOUSE? WHY?
IT WAS COMPLICATED, OKAY?
CAN YOU COME WITH ME? A LOT OF WEIRD SHIT HAPPENED LAST TIME I WAS THERE. I'D FEEL BETTER WITH SOME SUPPORT.
SURE, SURE. JUST LET ME GRAB MY COAT.

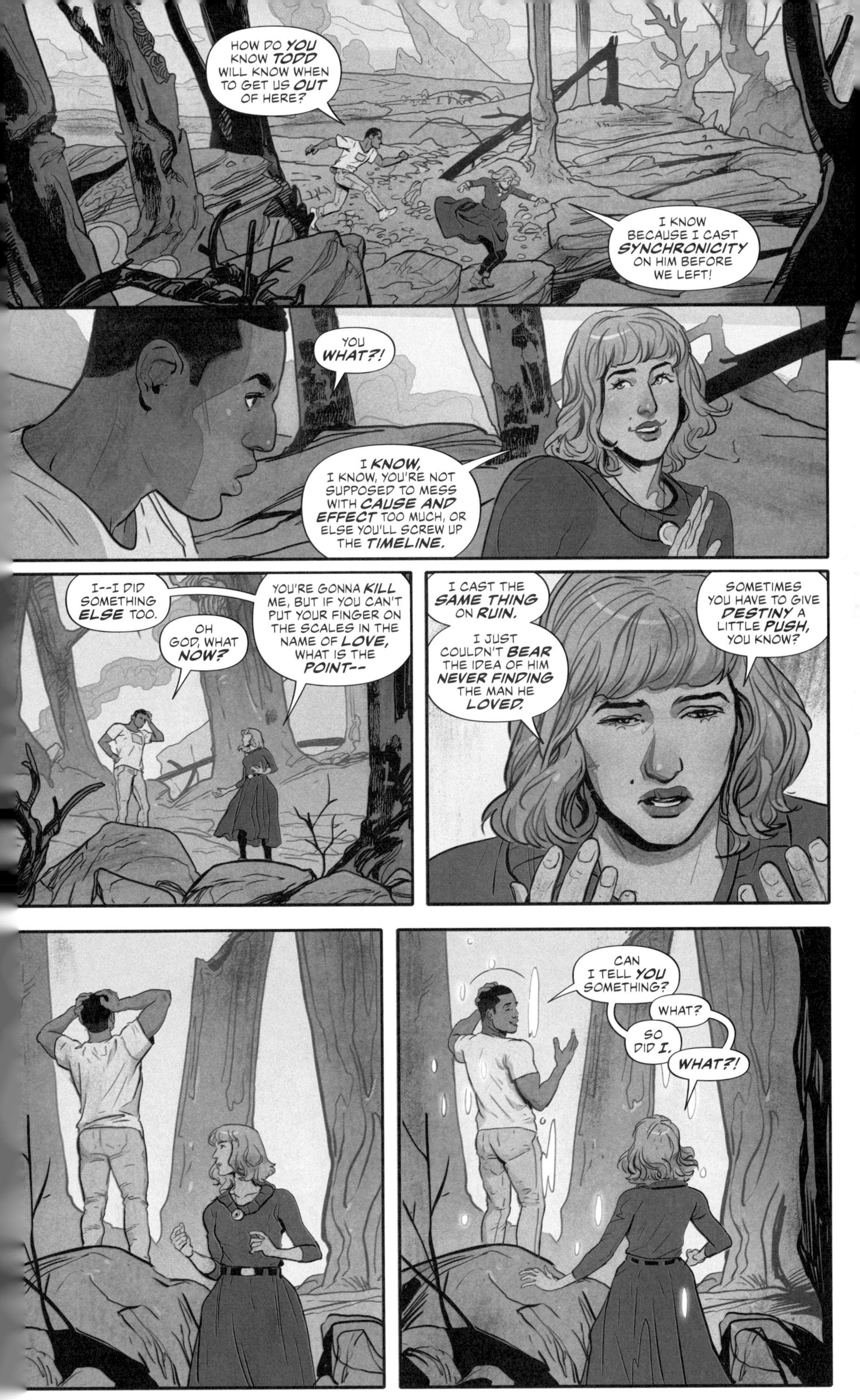
HOW DO YOU KNOW TODD WILL KNOW WHEN TO GET US OUT OF HERE?
I KNOW BECAUSE I CAST SYNCHRONICITY ON HIM BEFORE WE LEFT!
YOU WHAT?!
I KNOW, I KNOW, YOU'RE NOT SUPPOSED TO MESS WITH CAUSE AND EFFECT TOO MUCH, OR ELSE YOU'LL SCREW UP THE TIMELINE.
YOU'RE GONNA KILL ME, BUT IF YOU CAN'T PUT YOUR FINGER ON THE SCALES IN THE NAME OF LOVE, WHAT IS THE POINT--
I--I DID SOMETHING ELSE TOO.
OH GOD, WHAT NOW?
I CAST THE SAME THING ON RUIN.
I JUST COULDN'T BEAR THE IDEA OF HIM NEVER FINDING THE MAN HE LOVED.
SOMETIMES YOU HAVE TO GIVE DESTINY A LITTLE PUSH, YOU KNOW?
CAN I TELL YOU SOMETHING?
WHAT?
SO DID I.
WHAT?!

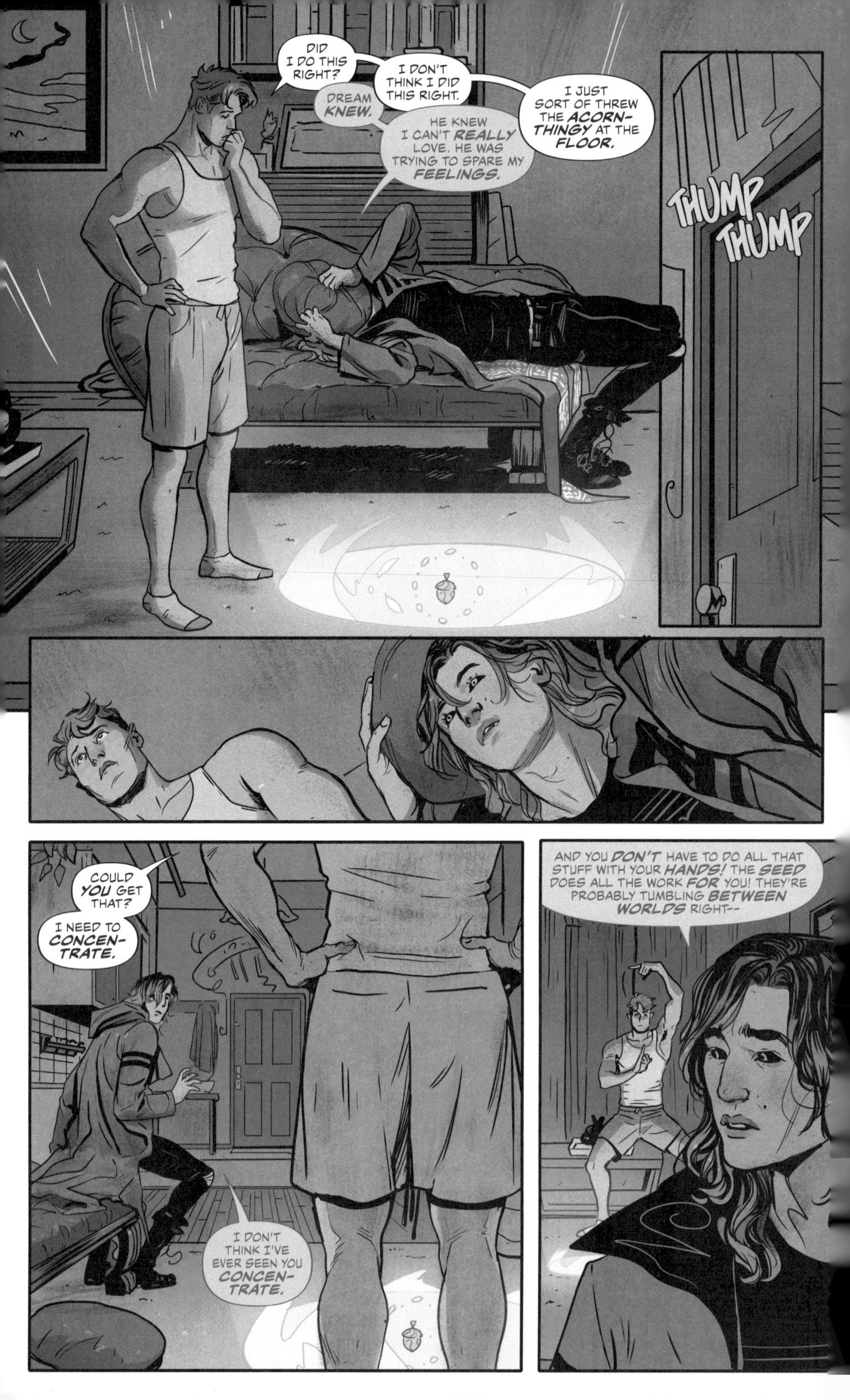

DID I DO THIS RIGHT?
I DON'T THINK I DID THIS RIGHT.
I JUST SORT OF THREW THE ACORN-THINGY AT THE FLOOR.
DREAM KNEW.
HE KNEW I CAN'T REALLY LOVE. HE WAS TRYING TO SPARE MY FEELINGS.
THUMP THUMP
COULD YOU GET THAT?
I NEED TO CONCEN-TRATE.
I DON'T THINK I'VE EVER SEEN YOU CONCEN-TRATE.
AND YOU DON'T HAVE TO DO ALL THAT STUFF WITH YOUR HANDS! THE SEED DOES ALL THE WORK FOR YOU! THEY'RE PROBABLY TUMBLING BETWEEN WORLDS RIGHT--

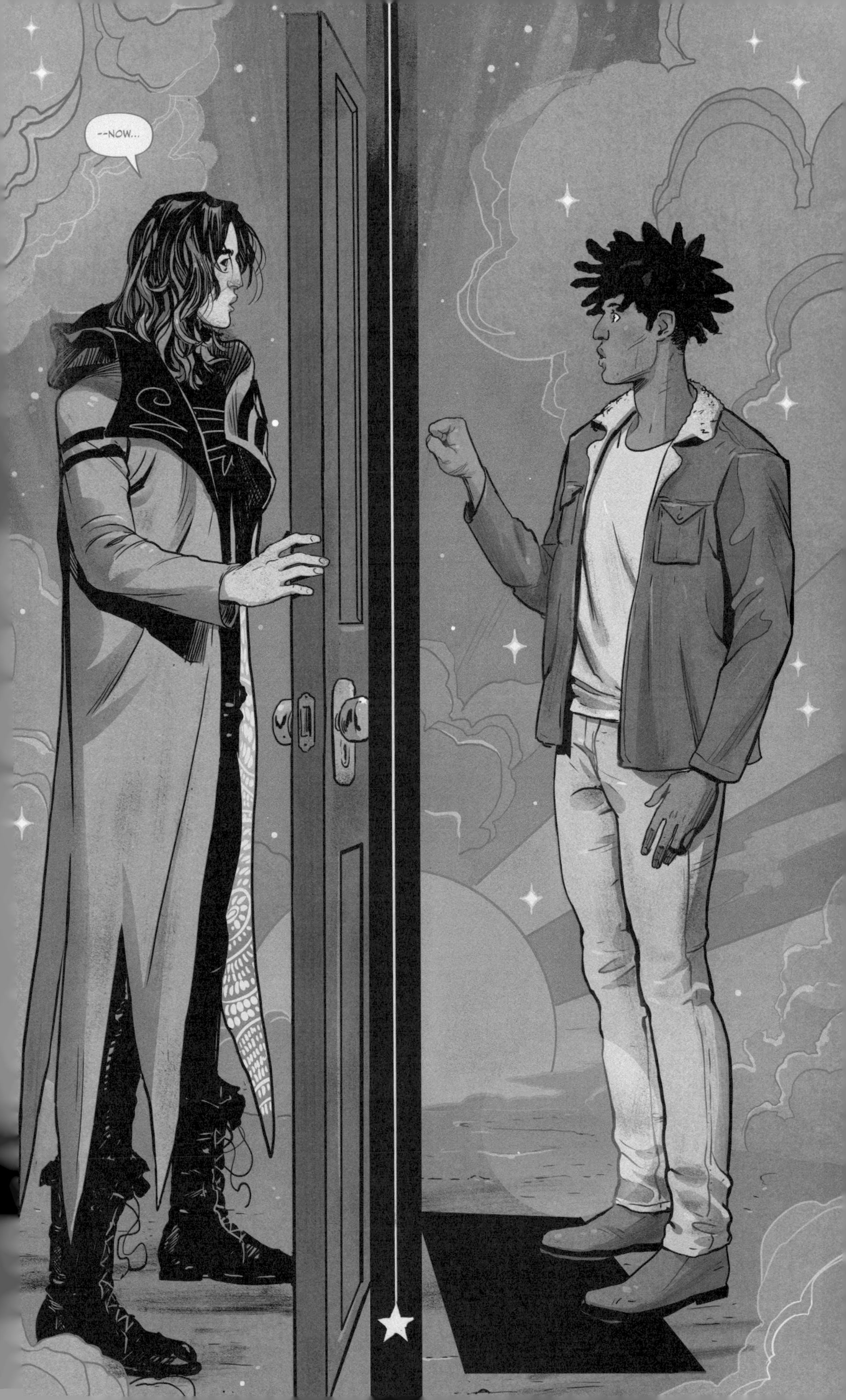
--NOW...

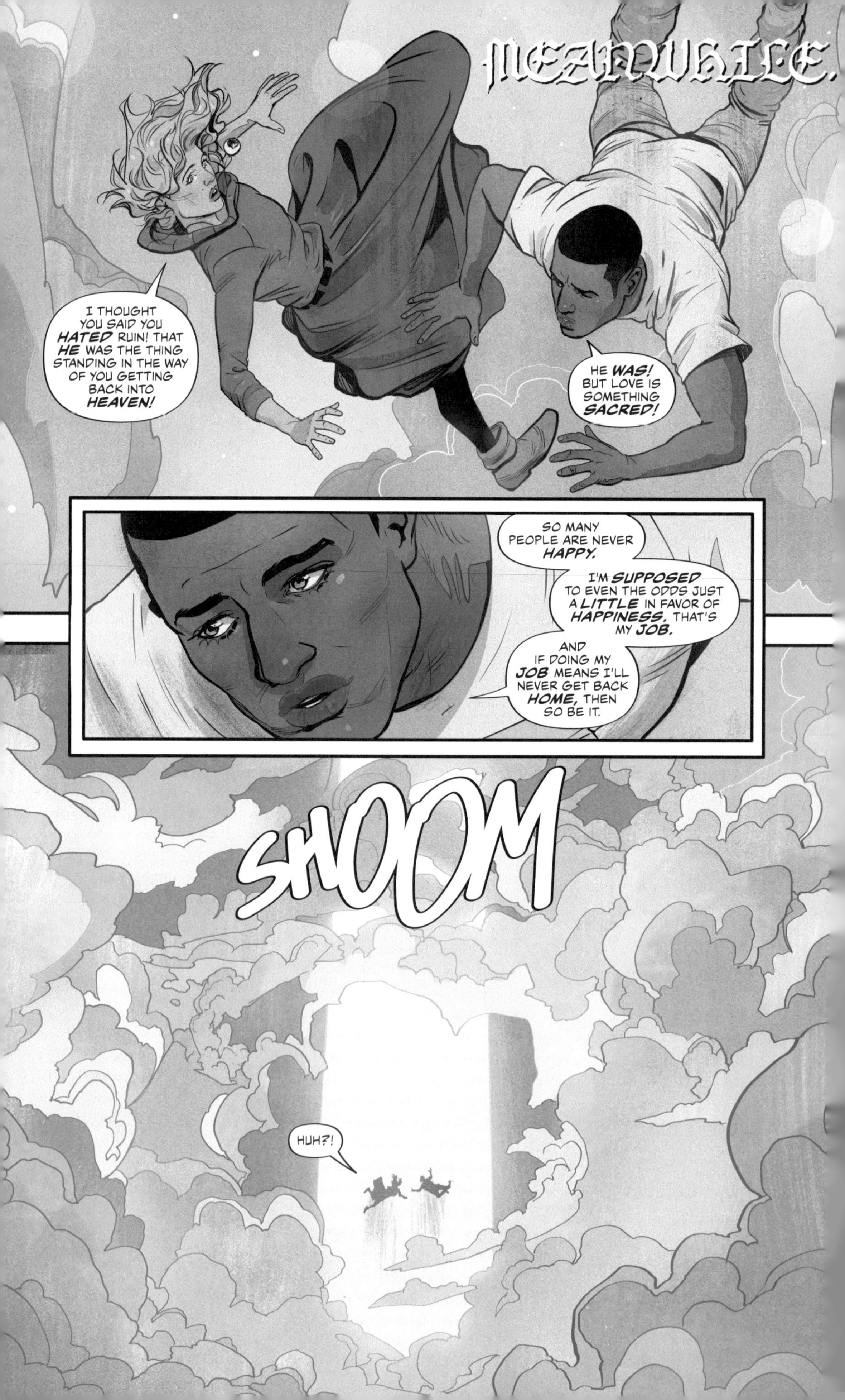
MEANWHILE.
I THOUGHT YOU SAID YOU HATED RUIN! THAT HE WAS THE THING STANDING IN THE WAY OF YOU GETTING BACK INTO HEAVEN!
HE WAS! BUT LOVE IS SOMETHING SACRED!
SO MANY PEOPLE ARE NEVER HAPPY.
I'M SUPPOSED TO EVEN THE ODDS JUST A LITTLE IN FAVOR OF HAPPINESS. THAT'S MY JOB.
AND IF DOING MY JOB MEANS I'LL NEVER GET BACK HOME, THEN SO BE IT.
SHOOM
HUH?!

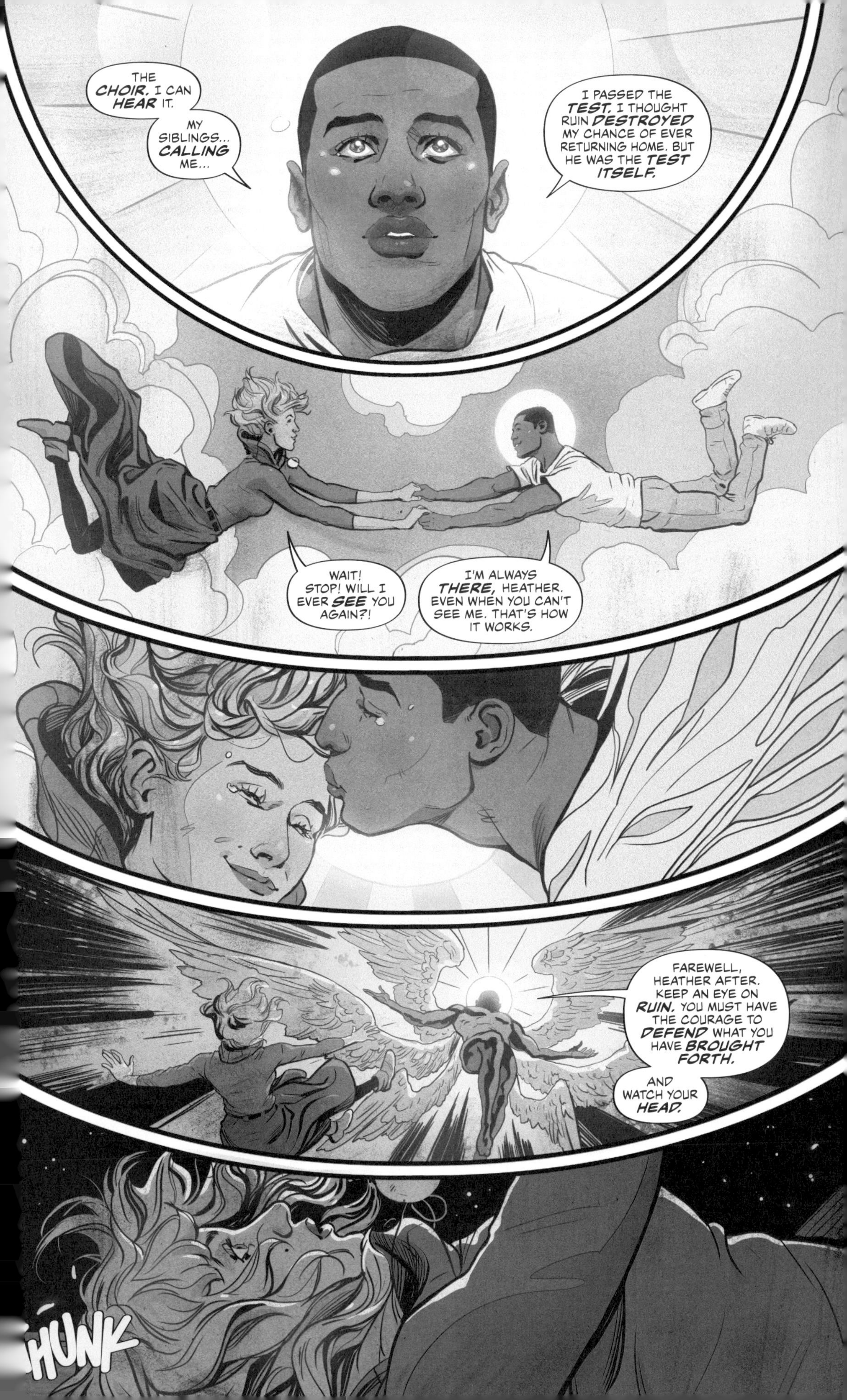
THE CHOIR. I CAN HEAR IT.
MY SIBLINGS... CALLING ME...
I PASSED THE TEST. I THOUGHT RUIN DESTROYED MY CHANCE OF EVER RETURNING HOME. BUT HE WAS THE TEST ITSELF.
WAIT! STOP! WILL I EVER SEE YOU AGAIN?!
I'M ALWAYS THERE, HEATHER. EVEN WHEN YOU CAN'T SEE ME. THAT'S HOW IT WORKS.
FAREWELL, HEATHER AFTER. KEEP AN EYE ON RUIN. YOU MUST HAVE THE COURAGE TO DEFEND WHAT YOU HAVE BROUGHT FORTH.
AND WATCH YOUR HEAD.
HUNK

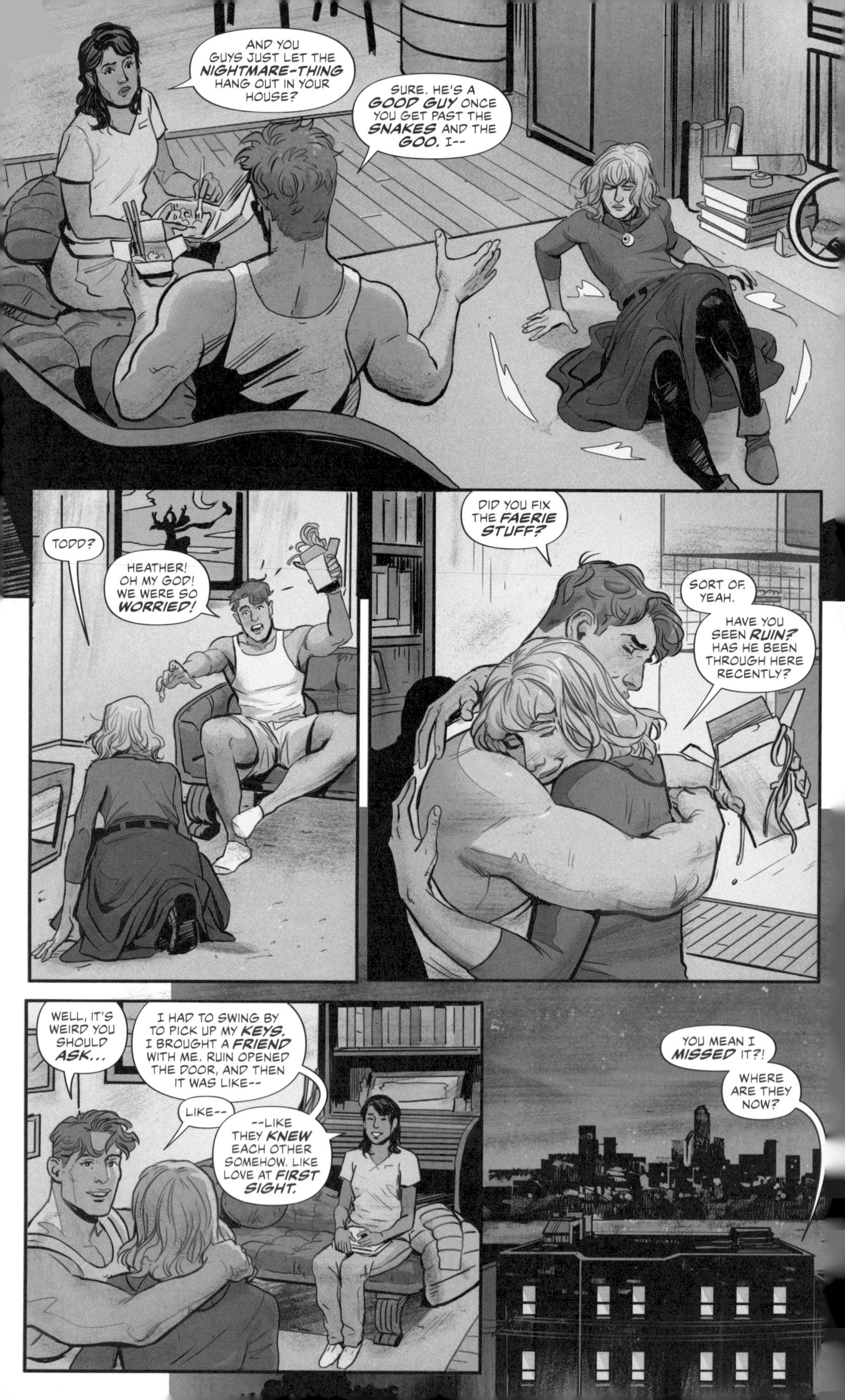
AND YOU GUYS JUST LET THE NIGHTMARE-THING HANG OUT IN YOUR HOUSE?
SURE. HE'S A GOOD GUY ONCE YOU GET PAST THE SNAKES AND THE GOO. I--
TODD?
HEATHER! OH MY GOD! WE WERE SO WORRIED!
DID YOU FIX THE FAERIE STUFF?
SORT OF. YEAH.
HAVE YOU SEEN RUIN? HAS HE BEEN THROUGH HERE RECENTLY?
WELL, IT'S WEIRD YOU SHOULD ASK...
I HAD TO SWING BY TO PICK UP MY KEYS. I BROUGHT A FRIEND WITH ME. RUIN OPENED THE DOOR, AND THEN IT WAS LIKE--
LIKE--
--LIKE THEY KNEW EACH OTHER SOMEHOW. LIKE LOVE AT FIRST SIGHT.
YOU MEAN I MISSED IT?!
WHERE ARE THEY NOW?

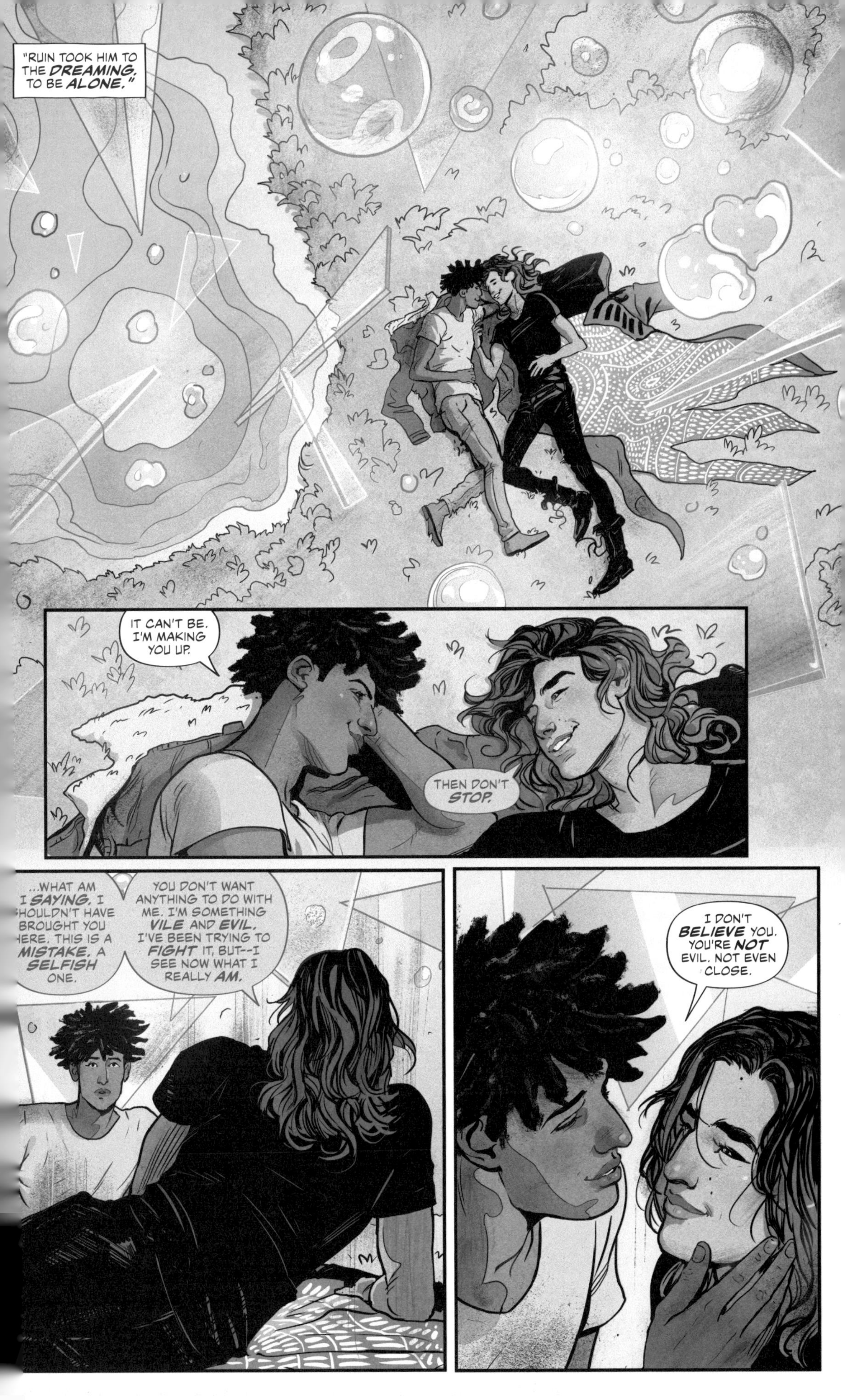
"RUIN TOOK HIM TO THE DREAMING, TO BE ALONE."
IT CAN'T BE. I'M MAKING YOU UP.
THEN DON'T STOP.
...WHAT AM I SAYING. I HOULDN'T HAVE BROUGHT YOU HERE. THIS IS A MISTAKE. A SELFISH ONE.
YOU DON'T WANT ANYTHING TO DO WITH ME. I'M SOMETHING VILE AND EVIL. I'VE BEEN TRYING TO FIGHT IT, BUT--I SEE NOW WHAT I REALLY AM.
I DON'T BELIEVE YOU. YOU'RE NOT EVIL. NOT EVEN CLOSE.

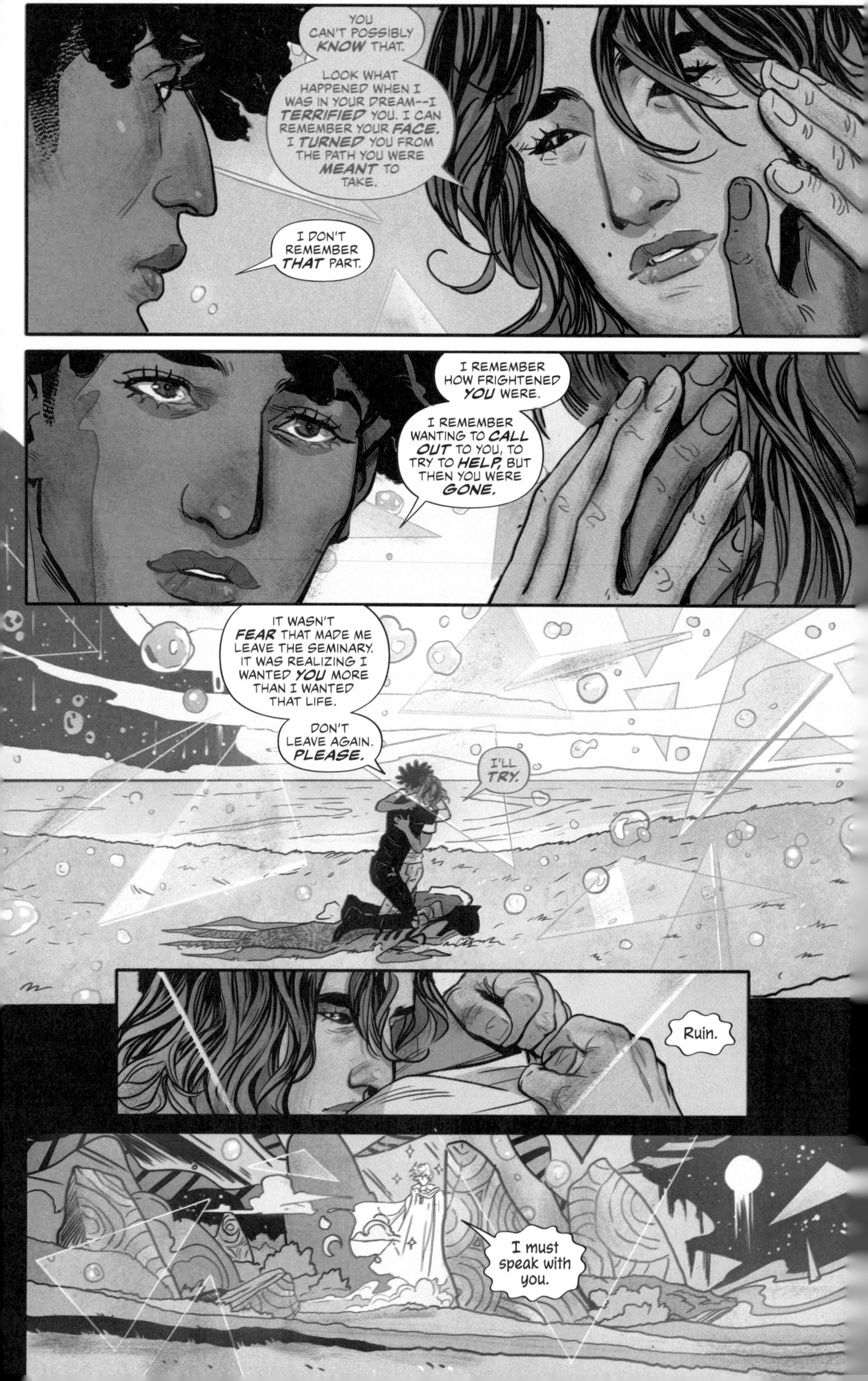
YOU CAN'T POSSIBLY KNOW THAT.
LOOK WHAT HAPPENED WHEN I WAS IN YOUR DREAM--I TERRIFIED YOU. I CAN REMEMBER YOUR FACE. I TURNED YOU FROM THE PATH YOU WERE MEANT TO TAKE.
I DON'T REMEMBER THAT PART.
I REMEMBER HOW FRIGHTENED YOU WERE.
I REMEMBER WANTING TO CALL OUT TO YOU, TO TRY TO HELP, BUT THEN YOU WERE GONE.
IT WASN'T FEAR THAT MADE ME LEAVE THE SEMINARY. IT WAS REALIZING I WANTED YOU MORE THAN I WANTED THAT LIFE.
DON'T LEAVE AGAIN. PLEASE.
I'LL TRY.
Ruin.
I must speak with you.

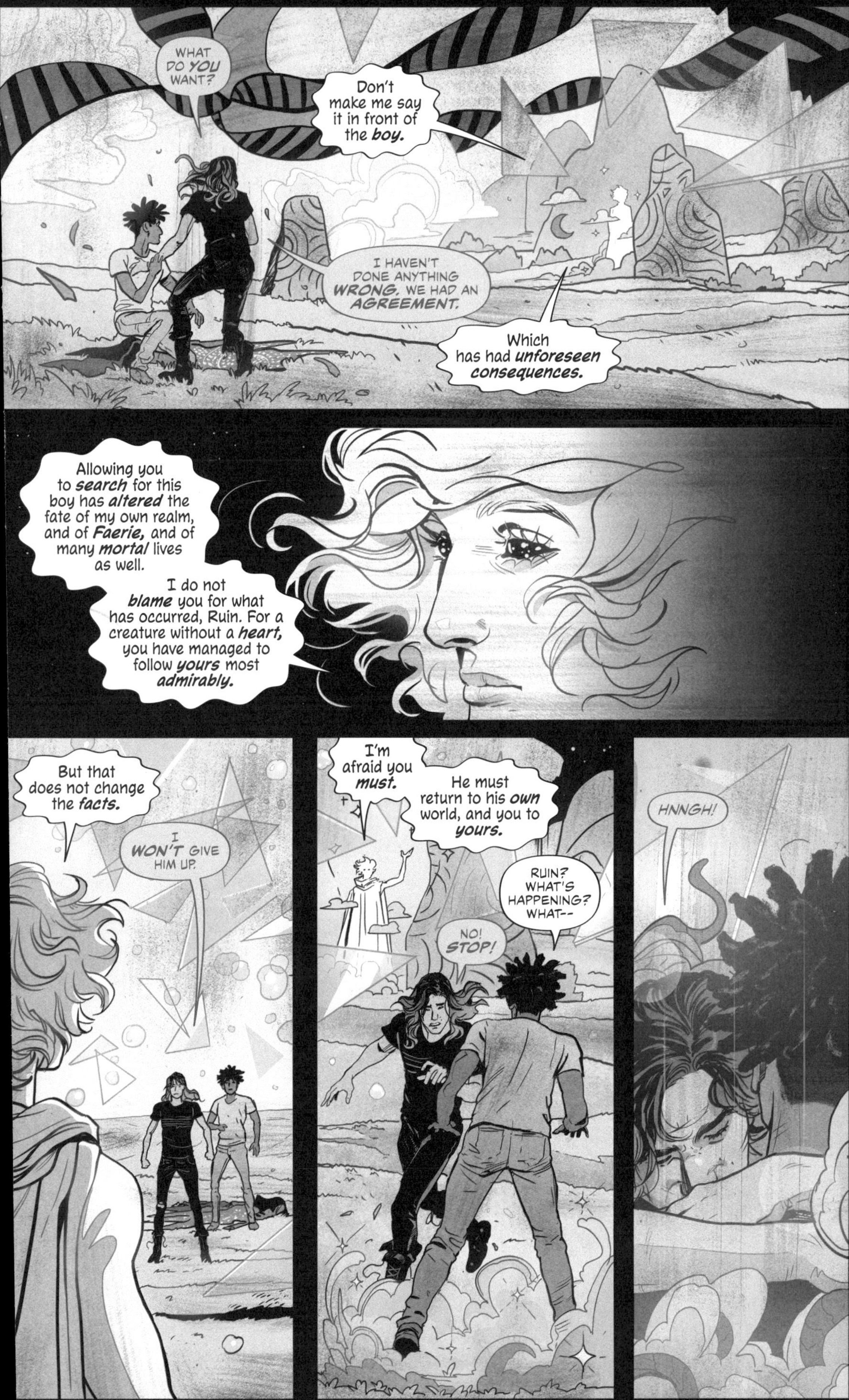

WHAT DO YOU WANT?
Don't make me say it in front of the boy.
I HAVEN'T DONE ANYTHING WRONG. WE HAD AN AGREEMENT.
Which has had unforeseen consequences.
Allowing you to search for this boy has altered the fate of my own realm, and of Faerie, and of many mortal lives as well.
I do not blame you for what has occurred, Ruin. For a creature without a heart, you have managed to follow yours most admirably.
But that does not change the facts.
I WON'T GIVE HIM UP.
I'm afraid you must.
He must return to his own world, and you to yours.
RUIN? WHAT'S HAPPENING? WHAT--
NO! STOP!
HNNGH!

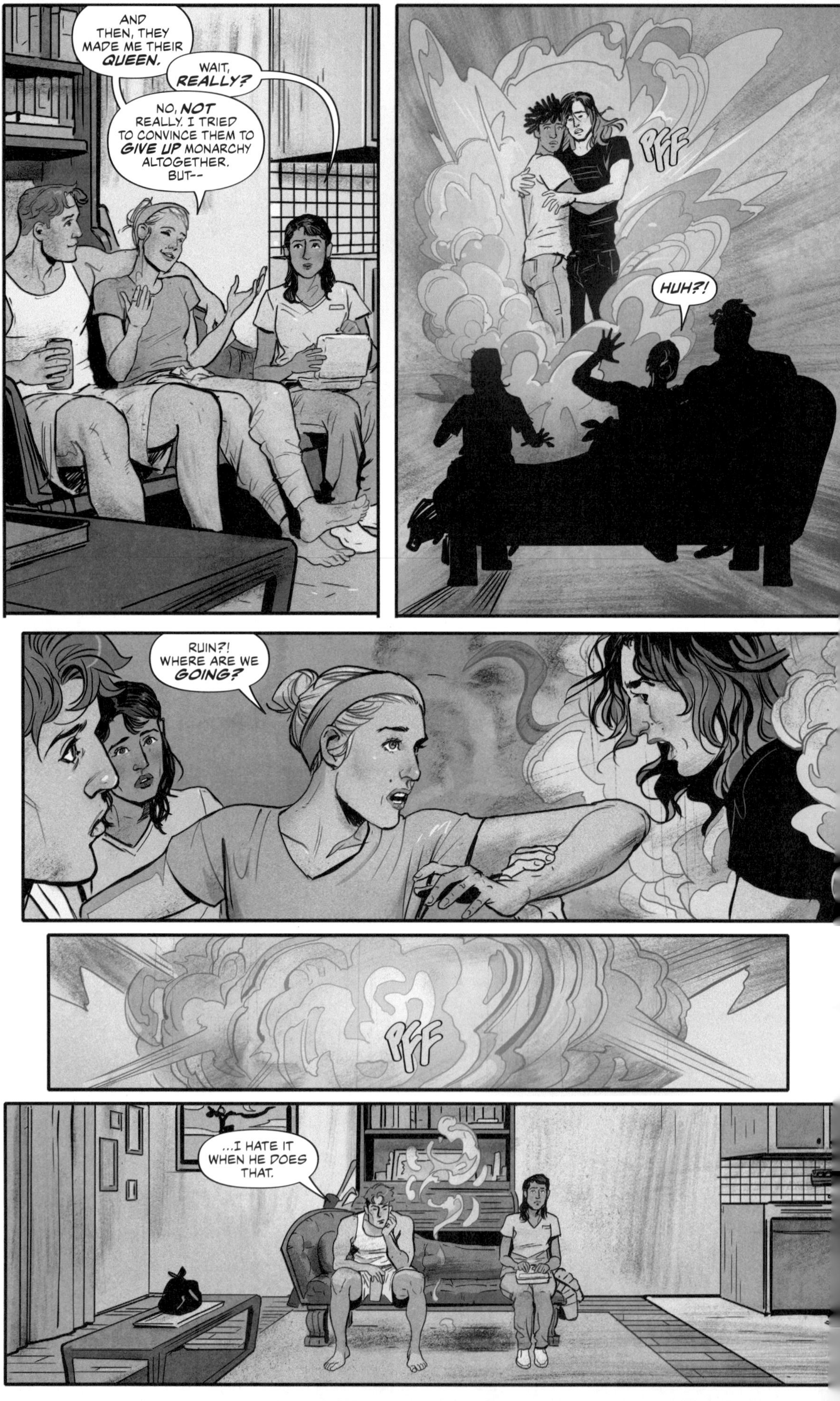
AND THEN, THEY MADE ME THEIR QUEEN.
WAIT, REALLY?
NO, NOT REALLY. I TRIED TO CONVINCE THEM TO GIVE UP MONARCHY ALTOGETHER. BUT--
PFF
HUH?!
RUIN?! WHERE ARE WE GOING?
PFF
...I HATE IT WHEN HE DOES THAT.

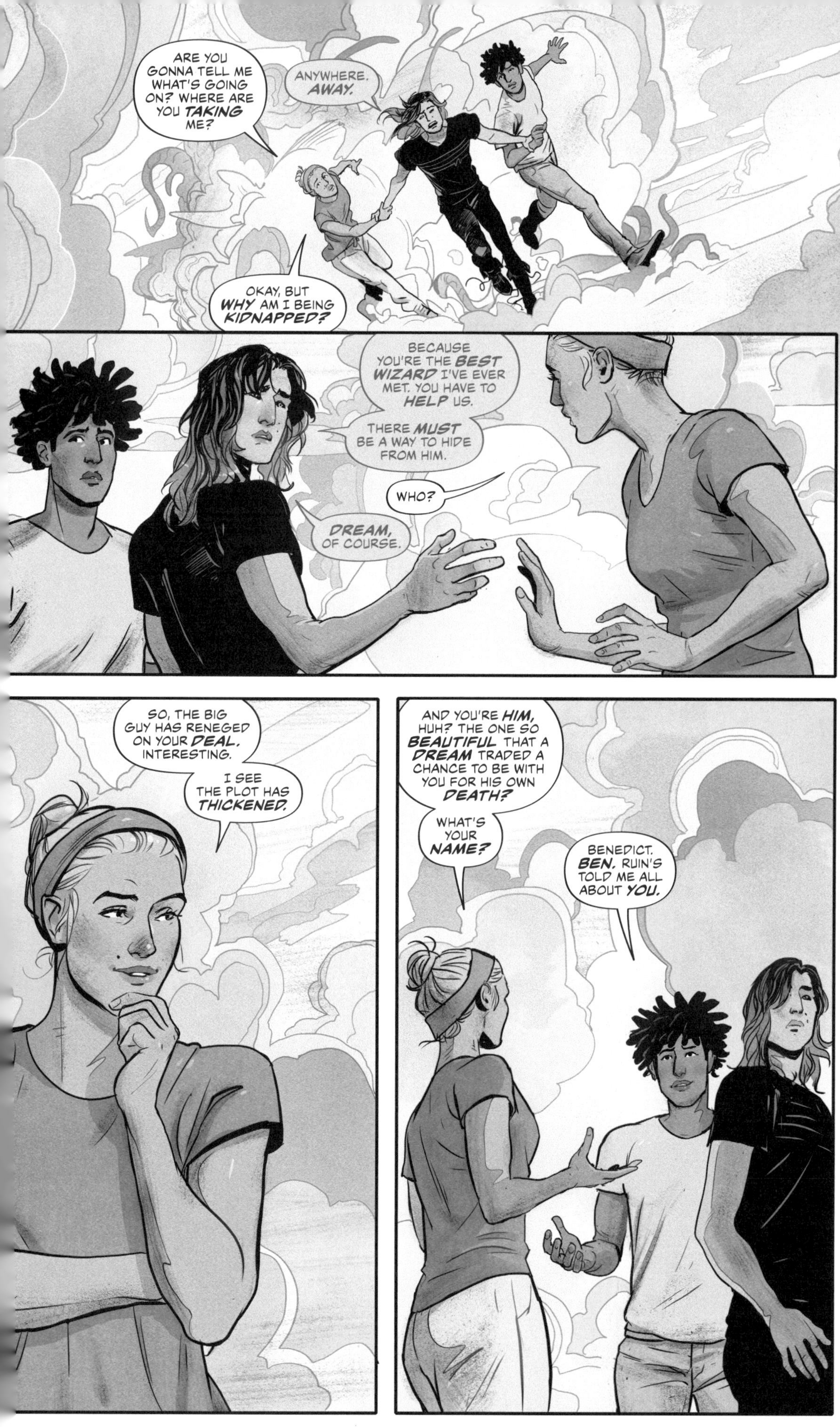
ARE YOU GONNA TELL ME WHAT'S GOING ON? WHERE ARE YOU TAKING ME?
ANYWHERE. AWAY.
OKAY, BUT WHY AM I BEING KIDNAPPED?
BECAUSE YOU'RE THE BEST WIZARD I'VE EVER MET. YOU HAVE TO HELP US.
THERE MUST BE A WAY TO HIDE FROM HIM.
WHO?
DREAM, OF COURSE.
SO, THE BIG GUY HAS RENEGED ON YOUR DEAL. INTERESTING.
I SEE THE PLOT HAS THICKENED.
AND YOU'RE HIM, HUH? THE ONE SO BEAUTIFUL THAT A DREAM TRADED A CHANCE TO BE WITH YOU FOR HIS OWN DEATH?
WHAT'S YOUR NAME?
BENEDICT. BEN. RUIN'S TOLD ME ALL ABOUT YOU.

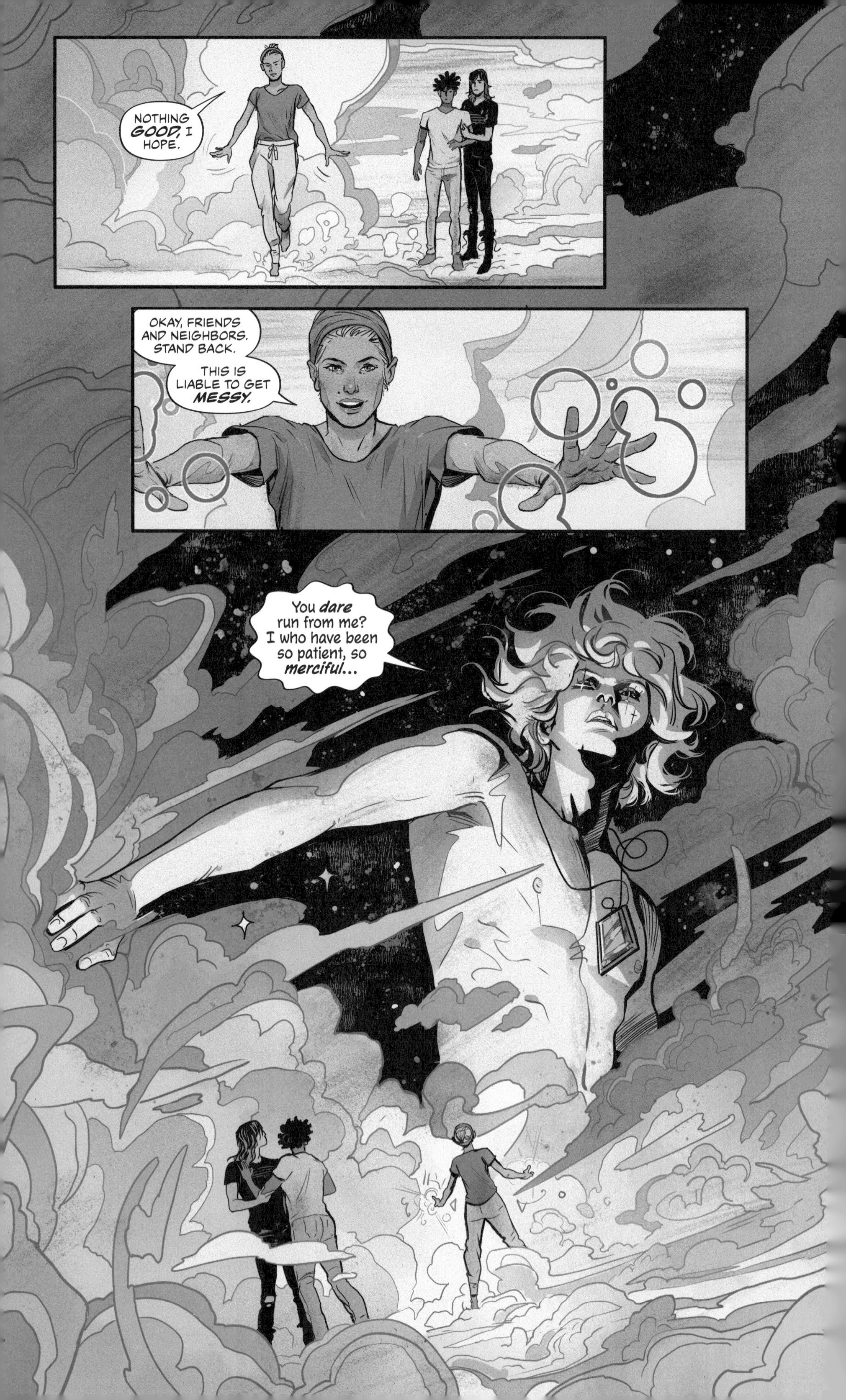
NOTHING GOOD, I HOPE.
OKAY, FRIENDS AND NEIGHBORS. STAND BACK.
THIS IS LIABLE TO GET MESSY.
You dare run from me? I who have been so patient, so merciful...

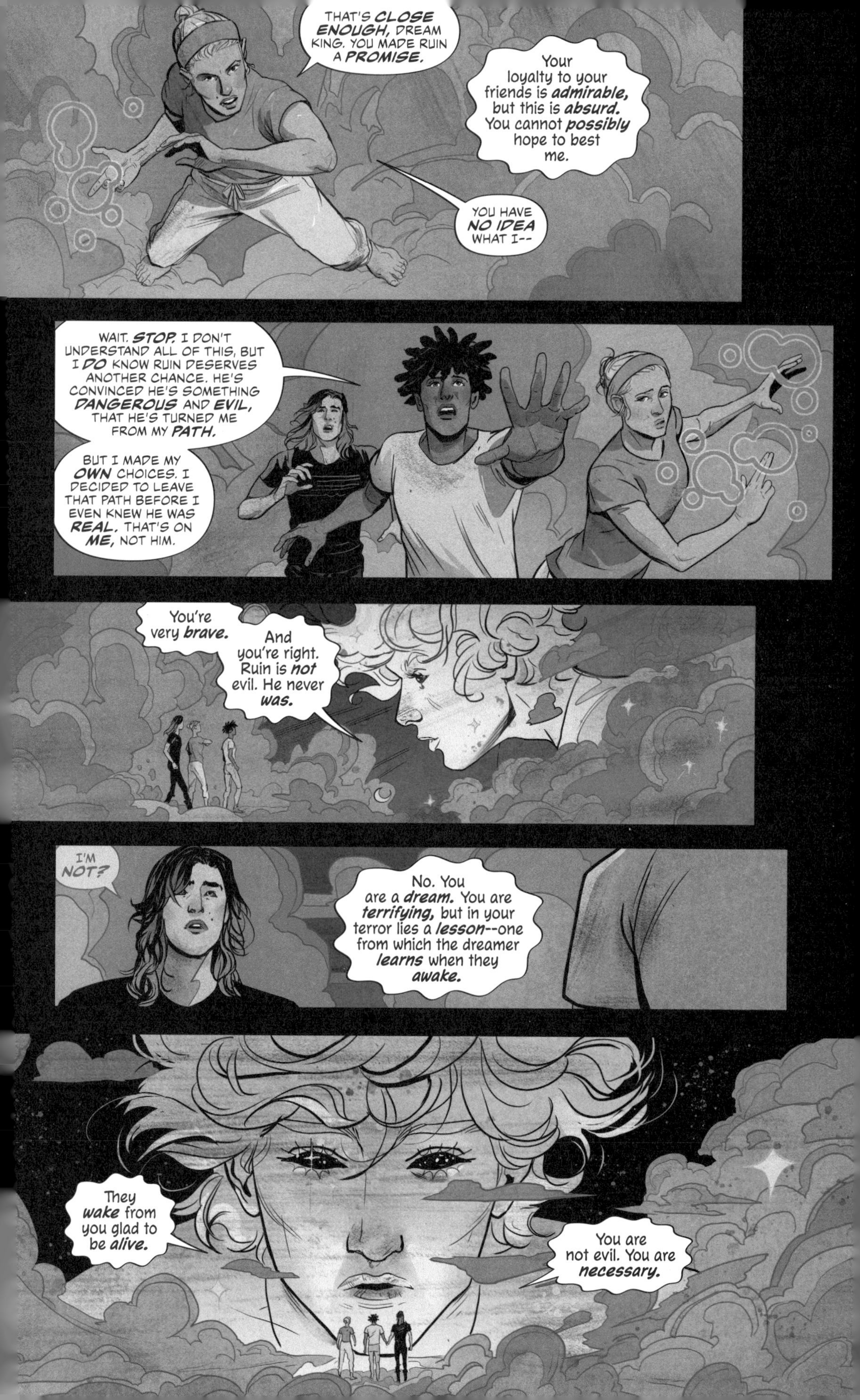
THAT'S CLOSE ENOUGH, DREAM KING. YOU MADE RUIN A PROMISE.
Your loyalty to your friends is admirable, but this is absurd. You cannot possibly hope to best me.
YOU HAVE NO IDEA WHAT I--
WAIT. STOP. I DON'T UNDERSTAND ALL OF THIS, BUT I DO KNOW RUIN DESERVES ANOTHER CHANCE. HE'S CONVINCED HE'S SOMETHING DANGEROUS AND EVIL, THAT HE'S TURNED ME FROM MY PATH.
BUT I MADE MY OWN CHOICES. I DECIDED TO LEAVE THAT PATH BEFORE I EVEN KNEW HE WAS REAL. THAT'S ON ME, NOT HIM.
You're very brave.
And you're right. Ruin is not evil. He never was.
I'M NOT?
No. You are a dream. You are terrifying, but in your terror lies a lesson--one from which the dreamer learns when they awake.
They wake from you glad to be alive.
You are not evil. You are necessary.

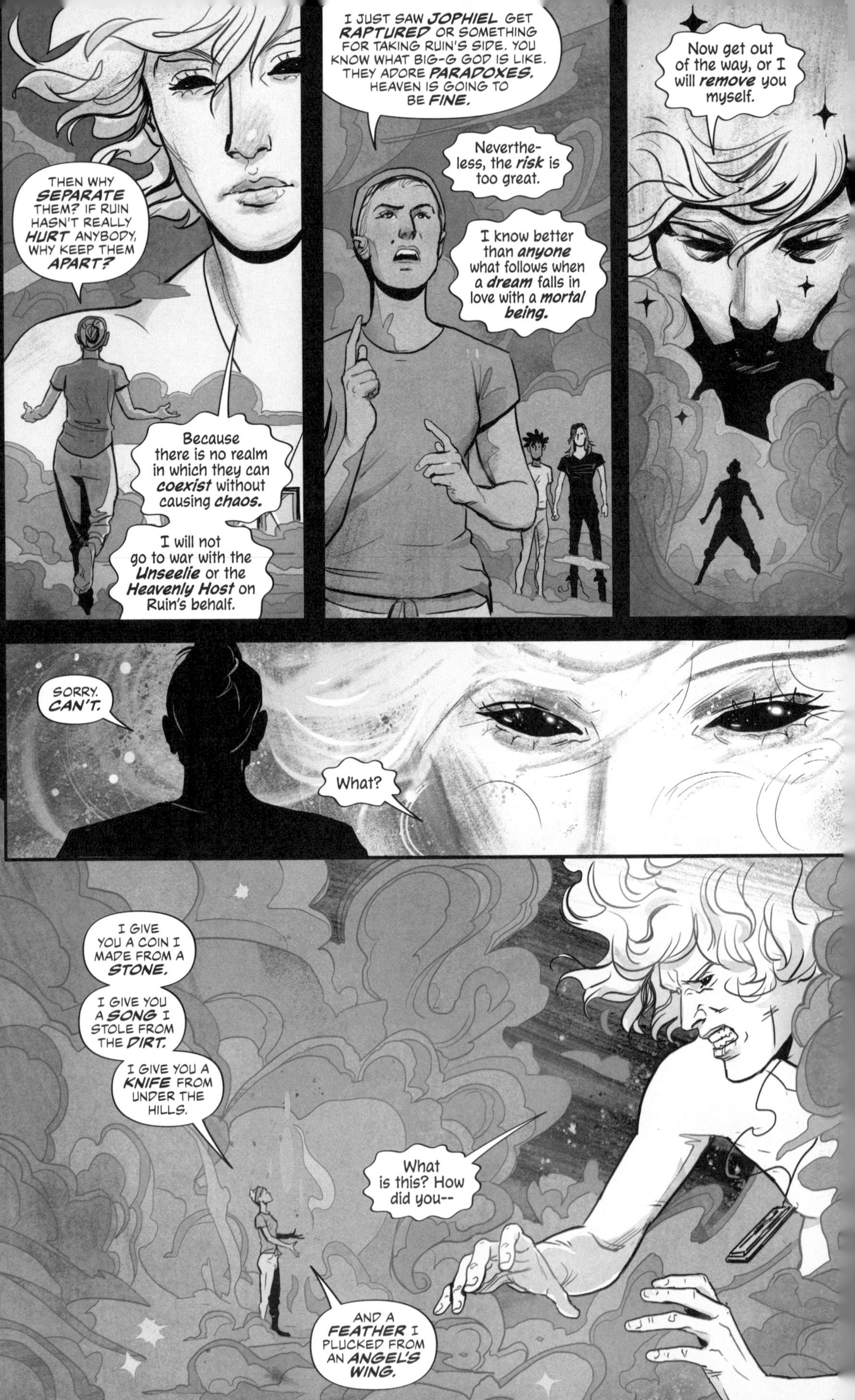
THEN WHY SEPARATE THEM? IF RUIN HASN'T REALLY HURT ANYBODY, WHY KEEP THEM APART?
Because there is no realm in which they can coexist without causing chaos.
I will not go to war with the Unseelie or the Heavenly Host on Ruin's behalf.
I JUST SAW JOPHIEL GET RAPTURED OR SOMETHING FOR TAKING RUIN'S SIDE. YOU KNOW WHAT BIG-G GOD IS LIKE. THEY ADORE PARADOXES. HEAVEN IS GOING TO BE FINE.
Neverthe-less, the risk is too great.
I know better than anyone what follows when a dream falls in love with a mortal being.
Now get out of the way, or I will remove you myself.
SORRY. CAN'T.
What?
I GIVE YOU A COIN I MADE FROM A STONE.
I GIVE YOU A SONG I STOLE FROM THE DIRT.
I GIVE YOU A KNIFE FROM UNDER THE HILLS.
What is this? How did you--
AND A FEATHER I PLUCKED FROM AN ANGEL'S WING.

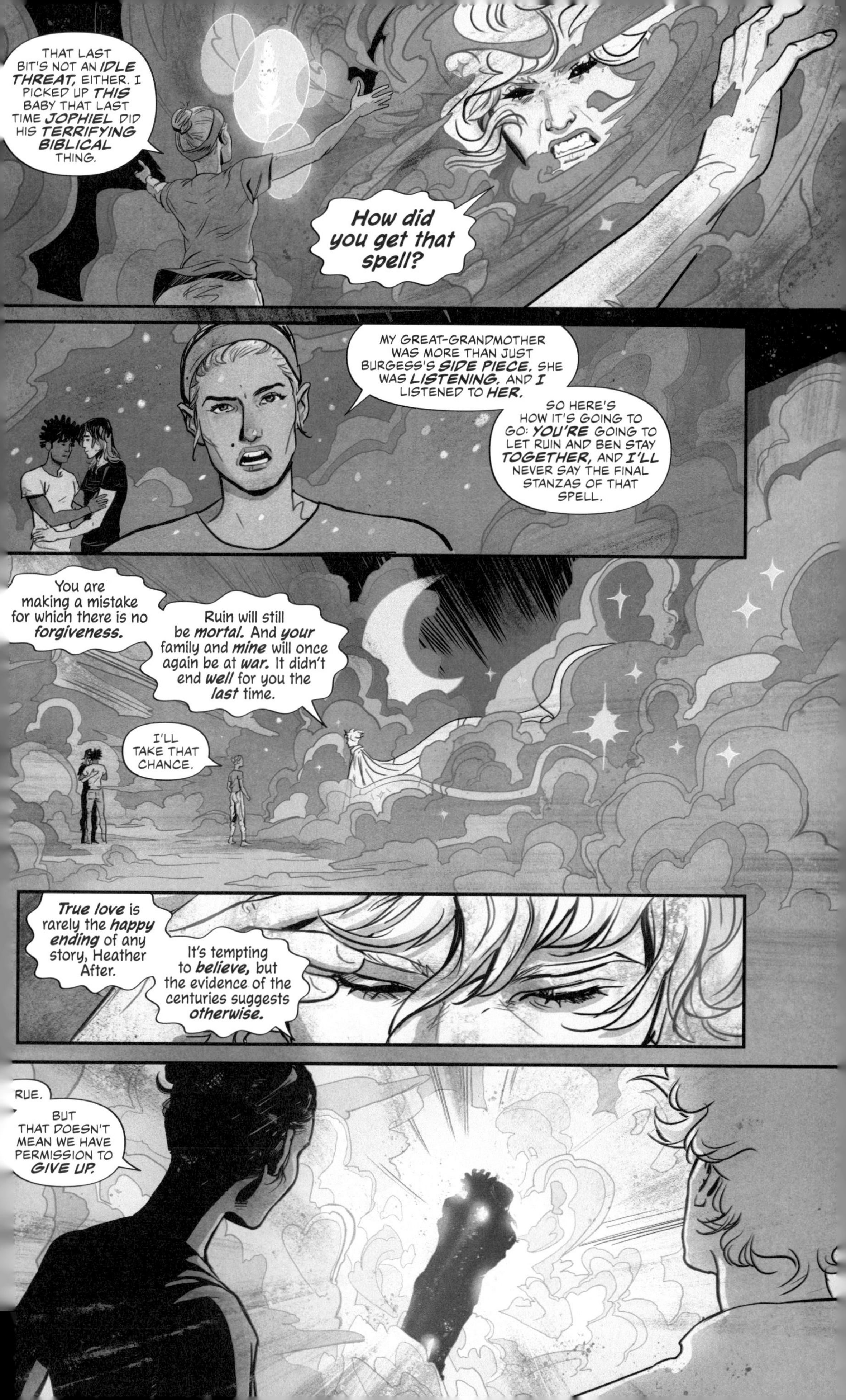
THAT LAST BIT'S NOT AN IDLE THREAT, EITHER. I PICKED UP THIS BABY THAT LAST TIME JOPHIEL DID HIS TERRIFYING BIBLICAL THING.
How did you get that spell?
MY GREAT-GRANDMOTHER WAS MORE THAN JUST BURGESS'S SIDE PIECE. SHE WAS LISTENING. AND I LISTENED TO HER.
SO HERE'S HOW IT'S GOING TO GO: YOU'RE GOING TO LET RUIN AND BEN STAY TOGETHER, AND I'LL NEVER SAY THE FINAL STANZAS OF THAT SPELL.
You are making a mistake for which there is no forgiveness.
Ruin will still be mortal. And your family and mine will once again be at war. It didn't end well for you the last time.
I'LL TAKE THAT CHANCE.
True love is rarely the happy ending of any story, Heather After.
It's tempting to believe, but the evidence of the centuries suggests otherwise.
RUE.
BUT THAT DOESN'T MEAN WE HAVE PERMISSION TO GIVE UP.

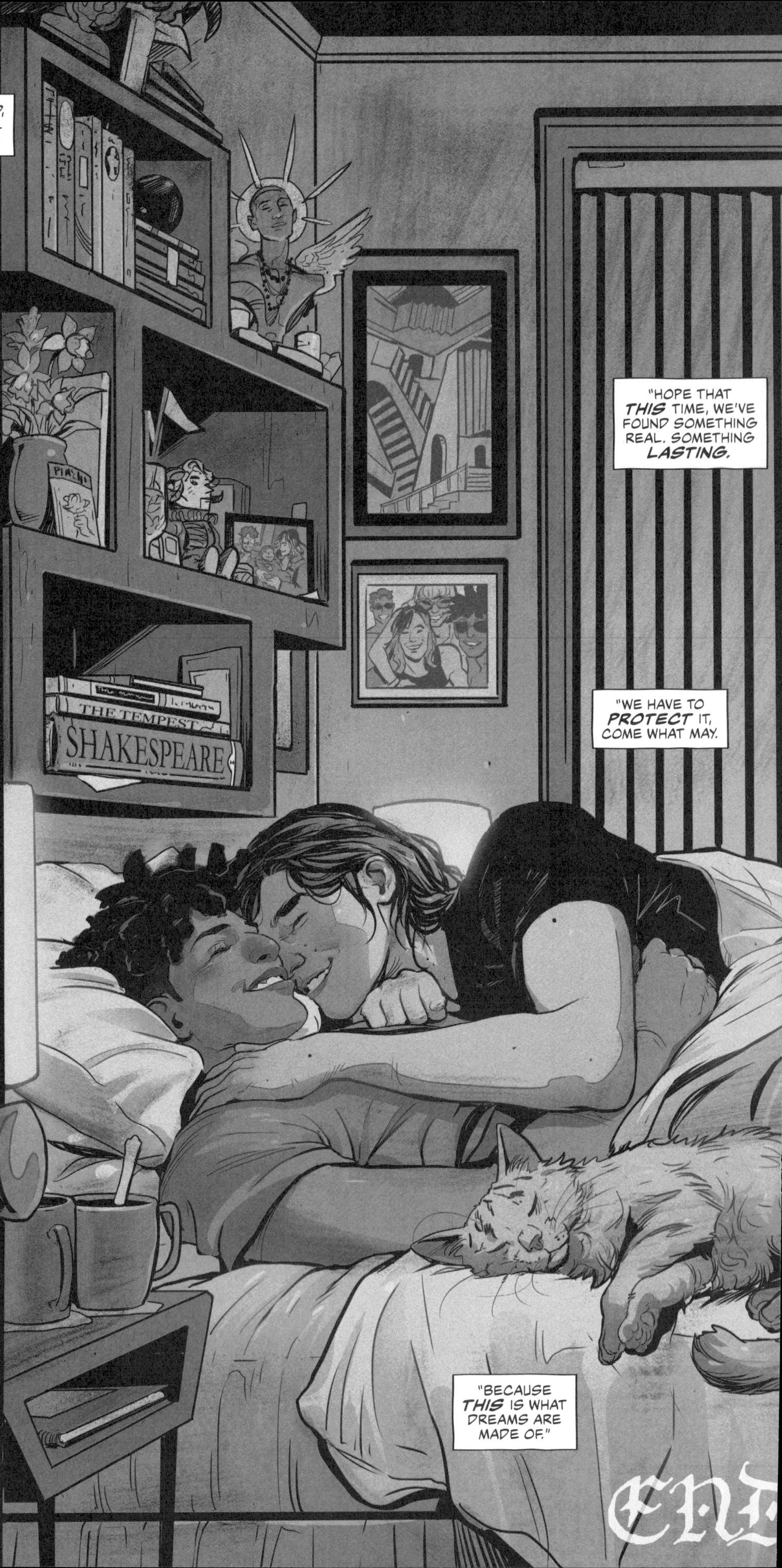
"IN THE END, THIS IS ALL WE HAVE.
"HOPE THAT THIS TIME, WE'VE FOUND SOMETHING REAL. SOMETHING LASTING.
"WE HAVE TO PROTECT IT, COME WHAT MAY.
"BECAUSE THIS IS WHAT DREAMS ARE MADE OF."
THE TEMPEST
SHAKESPEARE
END

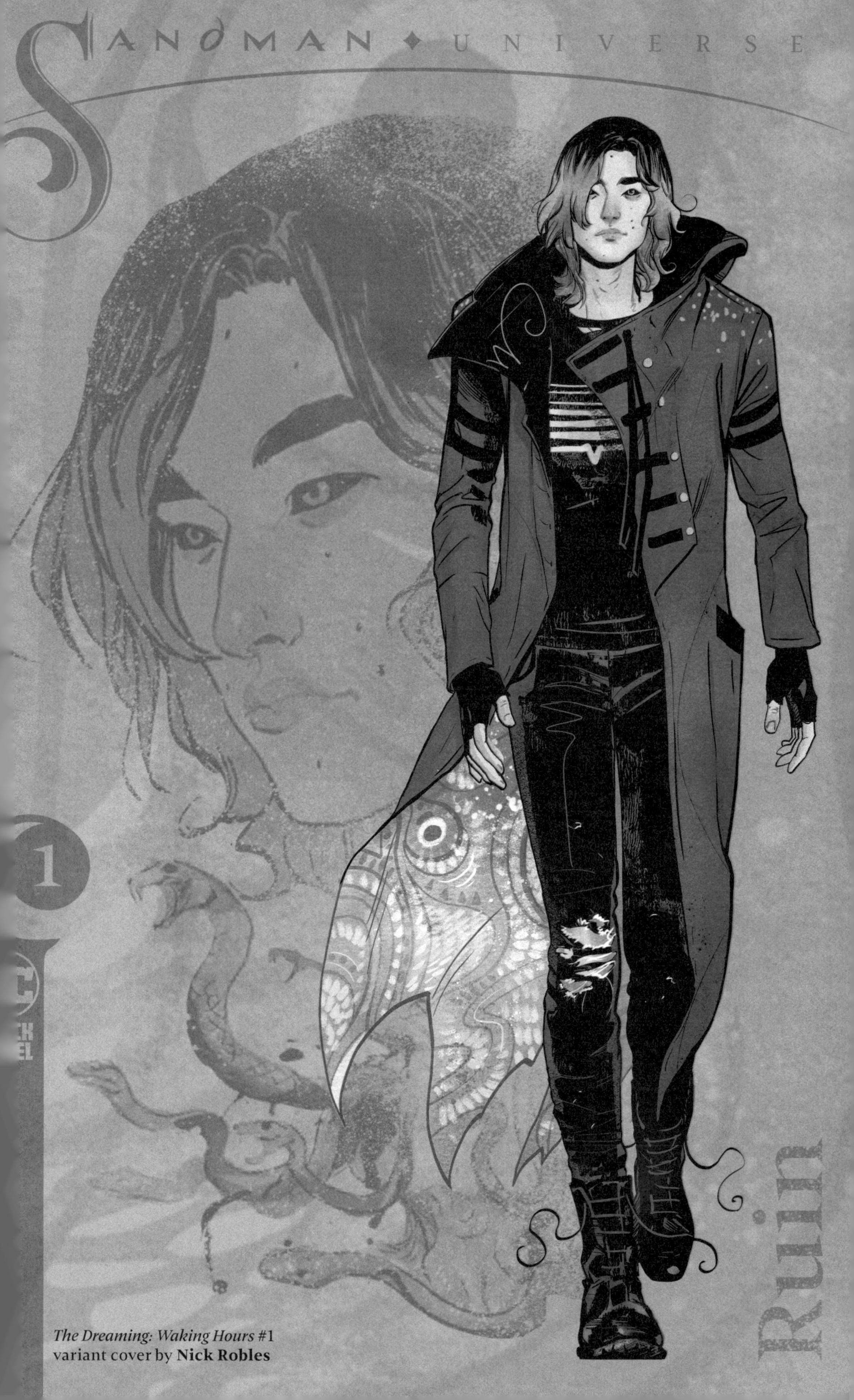
SANDMAN • UNIVERSE
1
Ruin

The Dreaming: Waking Hours #1
variant cover by **Nick Robles**

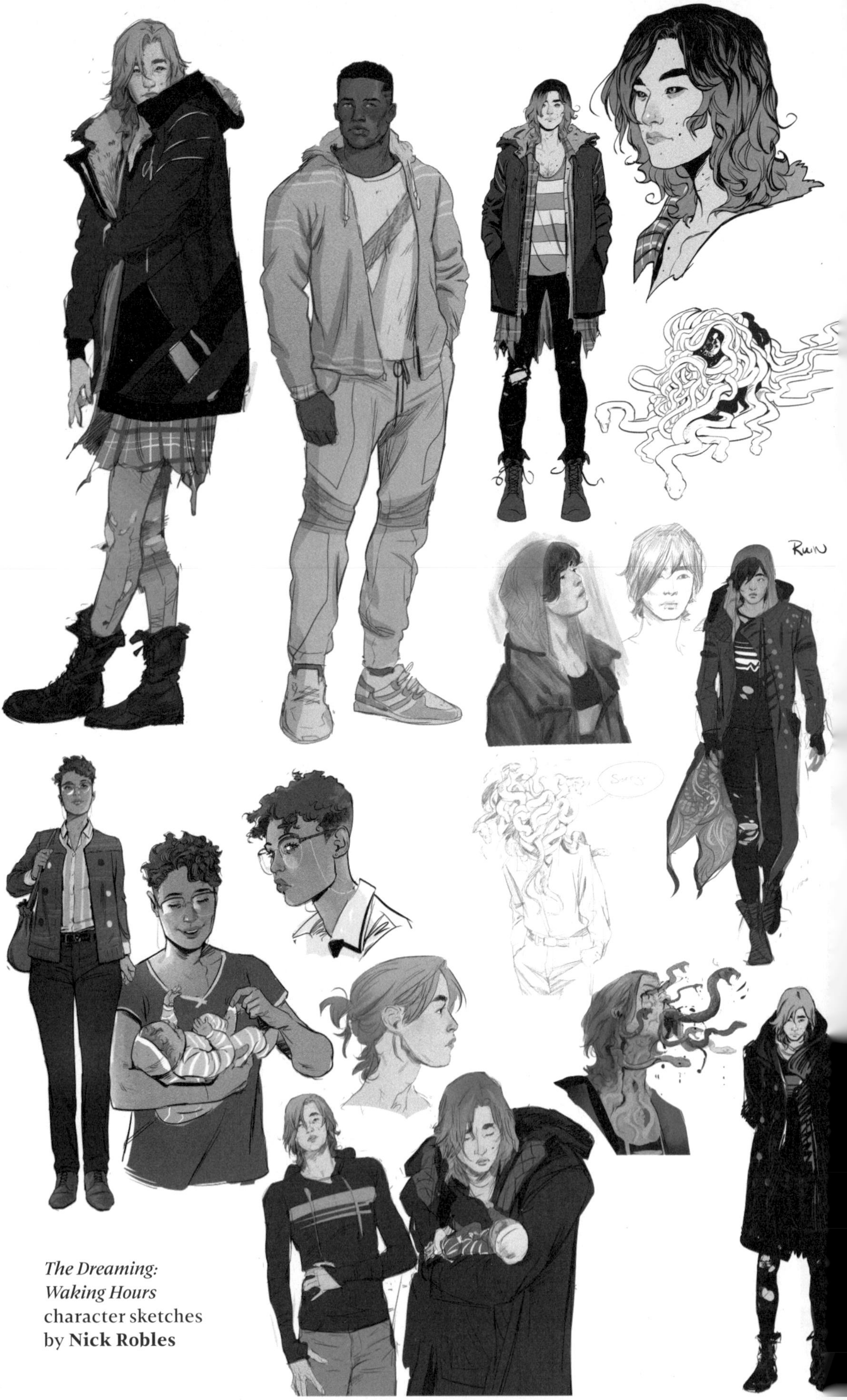
RUIN

The Dreaming: Waking Hours character sketches by **Nick Robles**

THE SANDMAN UNIVERSE

THE DREAMING
VOL. 1: PATHWAYS AND EMANATIONS

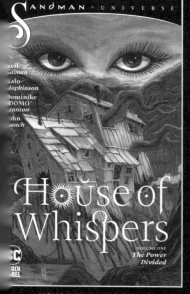

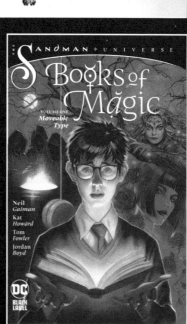

**HOUSE OF WHISPERS
VOL. 1: THE POWER DIVIDED**

**LUCIFER
VOL. 1: THE INFERNAL COMEDY**

**BOOKS OF MAGIC
VOL. 1: MOVEABLE TYPE**